The R

D0626248

Yorkshire

4

written and researched by

Jos Simon

Contents

Yorkshire's art and literature colour section following p.112

The great outdoors colour section following p.240

◀◀ York Minster ◀ Staithes Beck, North Yorkshire

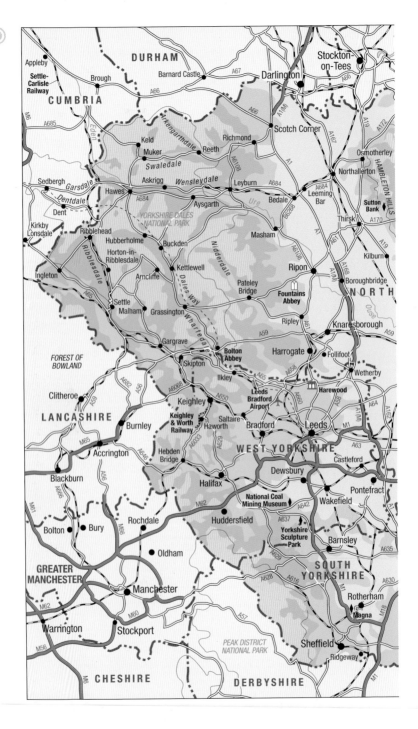

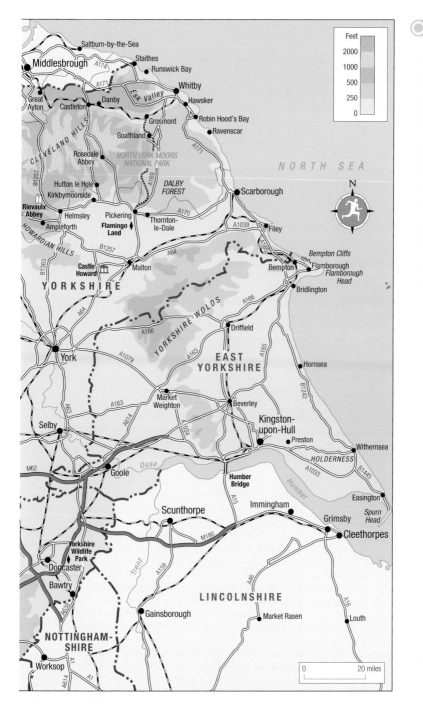

Feet
2000
1000
500
250
0

Saltburn-by-the-Sea
Staithes
Runswick Bay
Middlesbrough
A174
A171
Whitby
Esk Valley
Hawsker
Great
Ayton
Danby
Castleton
Grosmont
Robin Hood's Bay
Goathland
Ravenscar
CLEVELAND HILLS
Rosedale
Abbey
NORTH YORK MOORS
NATIONAL PARK
B1257
Hutton le Hole
A169
DALBY
FOREST
N O R T H   S E A
Kirkbymoorside
Rievaulx
Abbey
Helmsley
Pickering
Scarborough
N
HOWARDIAN HILLS
Ampleforth
Thornton-
le-Dale
A170
Filey
B1257
Flamingo
Land
A1039
B1363
A64
Bempton Cliffs
A165
Bempton
Flamborough
Flamborough
Head
Castle
Howard
Malton
Bridlington
YORKSHIRE
A166
A64
YORKSHIRE WOLDS
A166
Driffield
A165
A1079
EAST
YORKSHIRE
Hornsea
York
A163
B1242
A63
Market
Weighton
A1034
Beverley
Kingston-
upon-Hull
Selby
M614
A163
A1079
Preston
Withernsea
M62
Goole
Ouse
HOLDERNESS
A1033
B1445
Humber
Bridge
A15
Humber
Easington
Spurn
Head
Scunthorpe
Immingham
M180
Grimsby
Cleethorpes
Yorkshire
Wildlife
Park
A159
Doncaster
Trent
A46
Bawtry
A16
LINCOLNSHIRE
A638
NOTTINGHAM-
SHIRE
Gainsborough
Market Rasen
Louth
Worksop
A1
A614
A1

0   20 miles

Introduction to
Yorkshire

The very name Yorkshire – let it roll around your tongue – is redolent of dales and moors; of headlands, cliffs and enormous beaches; of city walls, churches and monasteries; of great estates and swathes of farmland; of steelworks, coal mines and woollen mills. This rich mixture is the secret of Yorkshire's appeal as a holiday destination – its countryside and coast can compete with anywhere in Britain for beauty, its cities with any in the UK for shopping, dining and clubbing. Its hotels and racecourses, its museums and art galleries and its writers and artists need bend the knee for quality to no other region. And as for pubs and breweries, Yorkshire is world famous for them.

Yorkshire, it has been said, is "a country in a county". In area it's by far England's largest. Its **geology** and **topography** boast such variety as to yield virtually every type of British landscape and habitat. And different stages of its human **history** are written on its landscape, layer upon layer – prehistoric long boats, Roman walls and roads, later castles, mansions, monasteries and minsters and the iron and steel bones of heavy industry. It has been a hotbed of capitalism, ferocious trade unionism and municipal urban development. Parts are traditionally high Tory, parts are red-hot socialist, parts are dyed-in-the-wool liberal.

As for present-day **Yorkshire folk**, their distinctive identity is recognized not only by themselves, but by the rest of the UK as well – while few celebrities are defined by their birthplace, who can doubt that Michael Parkinson, Alan Bennett, Dickie Bird or Brian Blessed are Tykes? Yorkshire people have the reputation of being dour and tight-fisted, with deep pockets and short arms. Some think Yorkshire men and women humourless, and it's true, they're no Scousers – they haven't got the attitude, the quick wit. But don't for a

minute think that they can't see the funny side of things. They'll quote the old saying "Yorkshire born, Yorkshire bred. Strong in't arm and thick in't 'ead", but it'll be said with a twinkle in the eye. Look at the county's track record – the plays of Alan Bennett and John Godber, the poetry of Simon Armitage and Ian MacMillan, the novels of Laurence Sterne and Kate Atkinson, the lyrics of Jarvis Cocker and Alex Turner, almost anything said by Fred Truman. Yorkshire humour is understated, subtle even. You might come across it in a pub and not notice it at all. But pay attention – it's there. Yorkshire folk, too, have an intriguing combination of optimism and pessimism – ask their football or cricket supporters. But they're down to earth, friendly, forthright or rude depending on your point of view, and really very welcoming.

Any visitor to Yorkshire will notice its succession of startling physical and human contrasts – between bucolic valleys and wild uplands in the Dales and Moors, lofty headlands and gentle beaches along the coast, urban chaos and pockets of striking countryside in West and South Yorkshire. Moody medieval Roche Abbey sits in a beautiful eighteenth-century Capability Brown-designed landscape on the edge of a typical pit village, while Beverley and Hull, not ten miles apart, couldn't be more different in ambience and political colouring.

Wherever you are in Yorkshire, then, you'll find a wide range of things to see and do. Choose your base carefully and, whether you're a history buff, a sports fanatic, a nature lover, a shop-till-you-dropper, a clubber, a fine-diner, a family with kids, or all these things, whether you need to count the pennies or are able to flash the cash, you're sure to find plenty to make your stay in Yorkshire memorable.

Where to go

Where you should go in Yorkshire depends entirely on what you hope to get out of your stay. If you just want to hike or cycle, then base yourself in the **Dales** or the **North York Moors** and get stuck in. If flora and fauna do it for you, seek out some of the nature reserves run by the Yorkshire Wildlife Trust or the RSPB (see p.323). And if you want big city attractions, head for Leeds or Sheffield. The golfer, the race goer, the water-sports enthusiast, the rock-climber and potholer are all well catered for (see p.32).

For those who just want to relax, enjoy good food and do enough sight-seeing to keep themselves occupied, or for families who have to cater to a range of ages and tastes, Yorkshire's variety makes it particularly suited. **South** and **West Yorkshire** (chapters 1 and 2) offer a range of spectacular museums – check out Magna in **Rotherham**, Kelham Island in **Sheffield**, Eureka! in **Halifax**, the National Coal Mining Museum and Yorkshire Sculpture Park in **Wakefield**, the Royal Armouries in **Leeds** and the National Media Museum in **Bradford**, together with a host of smaller museums and art galleries often staffed by knowledgeable enthusiasts. There are, too, lots of good parks and plenty of shops, cafés and restaurants – Leeds in particular would be difficult to match anywhere outside London. And the cities' public transport systems are efficient and relatively cheap – one of the best views of Sheffield is on the tram as it descends into the city.

The Vale of York (Chapter 3) boasts Yorkshire's single biggest tourist attraction – the **City of York** itself. Having played such a large part in the history

▲ Betty's in Harrogate

of Britain from the Celts onwards, York boasts a huge concentration of attractions. Not least are York Minster and the wonderful National Transport Museum, the Yorkshire Museum and Castle Museum, together with ghost walks, trips on the river, picturesque narrow lanes, good restaurants and shops and some fine hotels – all you need for a city break. But don't confine yourself to York – get out into the surrounding countryside and pleasant

towns like **Wetherby, Knaresborough, Harrogate** and **Ripon**, and try not to miss **Fountains Abbey**.

Yorkshire's lungs are its two national parks – the **Yorkshire Dales** (Chapter 4) and the **North York Moors** (Chapter 5). Both are areas of rugged upland scenery, with fertile valleys and bare heather-covered hills. The Dales also features waterfalls and caves, stone villages, dry-stone walls and field barns and some really imposing castles, of which **Richmond**'s is the best. The North York Moors have a famous steam railway (**The North York Moors Railway**), its own share of castles (Pickering, Helmsley, Scarborough), the impressive, medieval **Rievaulx Abbey** overlooked by the eighteenth-century **Rievaulx Terrace**, the working monastery of **Ampleforth** and, across the north, the pastoral **Esk Valley**. These are the places to go for the outdoors and fresh air, but don't stick too closely to national park boundaries – they reflect the history of the area, and don't include all that's worthwhile. So although **Nidderdale** is one of the Yorkshire Dales, and the **Howardian Hills** are a continuation of the North York Moors, neither is included in their respective national parks, but are designated Areas of Outstanding Natural Beauty. If the unique selling point of the Dales is **caves** and **waterfalls**, that of the North York Moors is the **coast**, with its lovely seaside towns and the beautiful coastal scenery, which continues into East Yorkshire (chapter 6). The big resorts are **Bridlington** and **Scarborough**, but you could go for one of the smaller, more sedate towns – **Filey** or **Whitby, Hornsea** or **Withernsea** – or for a picturesque coastal village such as **Robin Hood's Bay**, perhaps.

Chapter 6 covers an area of Yorkshire that is easy to miss yet has some of fascinating places to visit. **Kingston–upon–Hull** (or just **Hull**) is a large seaport with a past reputation for being on the rough side. However, now you'll find a vivacious, breezy city centre clustered around an attractive

9

▲ Victoria Quarter, Leeds

waterside. It also boasts **The Deep**, a terrific aquarium, and the hugely successful **Hull Truck Theatre**, both among the best in the country. **Beverley**, on Hull's doorstep, has its impressive Minster and beautiful St Mary's church and a good range of shops and restaurants. Just north, the **Yorkshire Wolds** undulate prettily and are dotted with numerous survivals from past ages, from Rudston's monolith to the abandoned medieval village at Wharram Percy. East of the Wolds, the East Yorkshire coast begins at **Flamborough Head**, with its colonies of seabirds, then plunges south through **Bridlington** as far as the weird and wonderful **Spurn Head**, haunted by migrating birds, Humber pilots and lifeboat-men.

When to go

Yorkshire's climate is much like all of the north of England, so although generally warm in **summer** (average August maximum 21°C) and cold in winter the weather really can change from day to day. If anything, its weather is more changeable because of the North Sea coast and the hills on its western and northern fringes. In **winter** the county also gets a fair amount of snow in the Pennines, Dales and North York Moors. **Spring** and summer are even more changeable, and it can **rain** at any time, though Yorkshire's recorded rainfall is lower than many parts of the UK. The advice to visitors is, then, hope for the best, prepare for the worst, and bring lots of layers and waterproofs. And if you're going walking in the hills, dress properly and take all the usual precautions. Holiday areas will be most crowded and expensive in **late July** and **August**, and to a lesser extent over **Easter** and half-term holidays. Cities —York in particular – get busy up to **Christmas** and during the January sales (often from Boxing Day). Other festivals take place all over Yorkshire throughout the year (see p.30) and can draw in the crowds.

20

things not to miss

It's not possible to see everything that Yorkshire has to offer in one trip – and we don't suggest you try. What follows, in no particular order, is a selective taste of the highlights of the region. They're arranged in four colour-coded categories to help you find the very best things to see, do and experience. All entries have a page reference to take you straight into the Guide, where you can find out more.

I ACTIVITIES I CONSUME I EVENTS I NATURE I SIGHTS I

01 Hutton-le-Hole Page **243** • North York Moors village with an undulating sheep-dotted green and the wonderful Ryedale Folk Museum.

02 Conisbrough Castle Page **83** • Built just after the Norman Conquest to keep stroppy Yorkshire folk in check, Conisbrough Castle appeared in Sir Walter Scott's romance *Ivanhoe*.

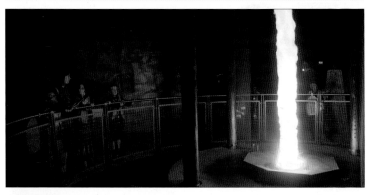

03 Magna Page **68** • Imaginative reconstruction of life in a Rotherham steelworks, centred on the spectacular "Big Melt".

04 Saturday Market, Beverley Page **288** • The name both of the street and what goes on there, in East Yorkshire's most vibrant town.

05 **The City of York** Page 141 •
See the city from its walls, then explore
its famous medieval streets.The Shambles, for
example, just below the Minster, are narrow
and cobbled, with overhanging upper storeys.

06 **Bradford curry houses**
Page 111 • A city famed for its curry
houses, there are hundreds in Bradford to
choose from.

07 **Rievaulx Abbey** Page 235 •
Ruins of one of Yorkshire's greatest
Cistercian monasteries, set in a beautiful
valley overlooked by formal eighteenth-
century Rievaulx Terrace.

08 **Flamborough Head** Page 298 • One of the best places in Britain to see, and hear,
nesting seabirds is Flamborough Head, at the two reserves run by the RSPB and YWT.

09 Tilting at the Royal Armouries

Page **98** • The clash of steel and the whinnying of horses at the Royal Armouries in Leeds as knights test their mettle in the joust.

10 Leeds Corn Exchange

Pages **98** & **102** • Iconic Leeds building with unique elliptical roof, now a top-end food emporium and restaurant.

12 Betty's

Pages **160** & **170** • A select group of wonderful tea-shops, Betty's have defied all attempts to get them to open branches outside Yorkshire.

11 Gliding

Page **228** • Experience the serenity of soaring above the lovely North Yorkshire countryside from the Yorkshire Gliding Club at Sutton Bank.

13 **Whitby** Page **247** • Yorkshire's prettiest seaside town, chock-full of history – the abbey, fishing, whaling, Captain Cook and, of course, Bram Stoker's *Dracula*.

14 **Breweries** Page **213** • Lashings of beer and the heady smell of hops in Masham, one of the prettiest towns in the Dales.

15 **Jorvik** Page **154** • Time capsules wend their way along the noisy, smoke-filled streets of tenth-century York.

16 **Hiking in the Dales** Page **186** • The Dales boast some of the very best hiking in Britain, from a gentle stroll around Malham to the rugged Three Peaks challenge.

17 **York Minster** Page **148** • Impressively massive Gothic church housing a thousand years of human history and a hundred fascinating stories.

18 **National Coal Mining Museum** Page **136** • Investigate all aspects of coal extraction, including the chance to go underground in a mine that was still working in the 1980s.

19 **Saltaire** Page **113** • Sir Titus Salt's colossal Victorian woollen mill set in his barely changed Victorian model village. It is now home to a huge collection of David Hockney's work.

20 **The Deep** Page **280** • One of the newest and best aquariums in the world, the Deep in Hull includes a viewing tunnel and an underwater lift.

Basics

Basics

Getting there

Approximately half way up the island of Great Britain and stretching from the North Sea almost to the Irish Sea, Yorkshire is one of the easier places to get to. Major road and rail links between the south of England and Scotland pass through it, as do the principal northern cross-country routes from east to west. On a good day it can take around three hours to get to Sheffield or Leeds from London by car (between four and five hours by coach) and little more than two hours by train. Manchester, the north of England's biggest airport, is an hour and a half away by train or car, and Yorkshire has its own regional airports – Leeds-Bradford and Doncaster-Sheffield – which are steadily building up links with the rest of the world. Furthermore, Yorkshire has its own major deep-sea port – around a million passengers a year travel back and forth to the continent through the Port of Hull.

By car

England's main north–south motorway, the **M1**, intersects with its main northern east–west motorway, the **M62**, just south of Leeds. This means that Yorkshire is very close in travel time to London and all points south, and with Liverpool and Manchester. Via the M6, the whole of the northwest, the Lake District and western Scotland is accessible. The other principal north–south route – the **A1** – also passes through Yorkshire, and is a very useful alternative to the M1; it is now dual carriageway, with no roundabouts, from the outskirts of London to Yorkshire and beyond – indeed, many parts of it have been upgraded to motorway status and are designated **A1(M)**. The A1 merges with the M1 to the east of Leeds, and continues north all the way to Tyneside and Edinburgh.

By coach

Because of its excellent motorway system, **coach travel** to Yorkshire is faster and more comfortable than to many other places in the UK. National Express (Ⓦwww.national express.com) routes link London with Leeds, Bradford, Huddersfield, Sheffield and York, at prices which are unbeatable.

By train

As with the roads, Yorkshire benefits from being at the intersection of major rail routes – the **East Coast Line** from London to Scotland, and the **TransPennine** line from the northwest to Yorkshire and the northeast. There are numerous high-speed trains from London to York, Leeds, Sheffield, Doncaster and Hull. Journey times are from 1 hour 40 minutes upwards. Fares vary widely – book as early as you can and be as flexible regarding travel times as possible. For all train times, check National Rail Enquires (Ⓣ08457 48 49 50, Ⓦwww.nationalrail.co .uk). Many of Yorkshire's towns and cities offer PlusBus whereby you can add discounted bus travel to your train ticket.

Rail link providers include:

CrossCountry Ⓦwww.crosscountrytrains.co.uk. From southwest England and the Midlands.
East Coast Ⓦwww.eastcoast.co.uk. From London, Edinburgh, Glasgow and Newcastle.
East Midlands Trains Ⓦwww.eastmidlands trains.co.uk. From London to Sheffield.
First Hull Trains Ⓦwww.hulltrains.co.uk. From London to Howden, the Wolds and Hull.
First TransPennine Express Ⓦwww.tpexpress .co.uk. From Liverpool, Manchester Airport, Newcastle and Middlesbrough into Yorkshire.
Grand Central Ⓦwww.grandcentralrail.co.uk. From London to Thirsk, Northallerton and York.

By plane

With the growth of Yorkshire's two regional airports – **Leeds-Bradford** (Ⓦwww .leedsbradfordairport.co.uk) and **Doncaster-Sheffield** (Ⓦwww.robinhoodairport.com) – plus nearby **Humberside** (Ⓦwww .humbersideairport.com), which is in Lincoln

shire, and **Manchester airport** (ⓦwww
.manchesterairport.co.uk), there are now
many routes into Yorkshire – from within the
UK, a few cities in North America, and, in
particular from other European destinations.

Flights from other parts of the UK and Ireland

Internal air travel is never likely to be as
popular in the UK as it is in big countries like
the US or Australia, and for most mainland
routes when travel to and from the airports is
taken into account it is often more convenient,
quicker and cheaper by train, coach or car. It's
certainly less harmful to the environment.
However, there are internal routes between
Yorkshire and other parts of the British Isles,
which include:
To Leeds-Bradford from: Aberdeen, Belfast,
Bristol, Dublin, Edinburgh, Exeter, London Gatwick,
Glasgow, Isle of Man, Knock, Newquay, Plymouth,
Southampton.
To Doncaster-Sheffield from: Belfast and Jersey.

Flights from the US and Canada

By far the largest number of direct services
linking the USA and Canada with the north
of England fly into **Manchester airport**,
which is close enough to Yorkshire, and

with good enough motorway and rail links,
to be convenient. However, Yorkshire's
own two regional airports do have links
as well:
To Manchester from the USA from: Atlanta,
Chicago, Las Vegas, New York, Orlando, Philadelphia.
To Manchester from Canada from: Calgary,
Toronto, Vancouver.
To Leeds-Bradford from: New York.
To Doncaster-Sheffield from: Boston, New York.

Flights from South Africa, Australia and New Zealand

There are no direct flights from South Africa,
Australia and New Zealand to Manchester
or to Yorkshire's regional airports. The
journey will therefore be **via London** with
internal flights to or from Manchester or
Leeds, or via European hubs.

By ferry

Car ferries run to **Hull** from **Rotterdam**
(11hr) and **Zeebrugge** (12hr 45min).
Voyages are overnight, so it is necessary to
book a cabin, but this is a very civilized route
– the ferries are like floating hotels, so you
get a good night's sleep, and drive off the
ferry in the morning with Yorkshire at your
feet. See ⓦwww.poferries.com.

Six steps to a better kind of travel

At Rough Guides we are passionately committed to travel. We feel strongly that only
through travelling do we truly come to understand the world we live in and the
people we share it with. But the extraordinary growth in tourism has also damaged
some places irreparably, and of course **climate change** is exacerbated by most
forms of transport, especially flying. This means that now more than ever it's
important to **travel thoughtfully** and **responsibly**. At Rough Guides we feel there
are six main areas in which you can make a difference:

• Consider what you're contributing to the **local economy**, and how much the
  services you use do the same.

• Consider the **environment** on holiday as well as at home. Try to patronize
  businesses that take account of this.

• Travel with a purpose, not just to tick off experiences. Consider **spending longer**
  in a place, and getting to know it.

• Give thought to how often you **fly**. Try to avoid short hops by air and more harmful
  night flights.

• Consider **alternatives to flying**, travelling instead by bus, train, boat and even by
  bike or on foot where possible.

• Make your trips "**climate neutral**" via a reputable carbon offset scheme. All
  Rough Guide flights are offset, and every year we donate money to a variety of
  charities devoted to combating the effects of climate change.

Get even closer to the wildlife

There's so much to see and do at the Yorkshire Wildlife Park:

- Explore Lion Country
- Walk with the Lemurs
- Wallaby Walkabout
- African Plains
- Mischievous Meerkats
- Zebras and Camels
- Wild Café
- Shows and Talks
- Jungle Play Barn
  and so much more

**Open daily
Check website for
times and prices**

Tel: 01302 535057
www.yorkshirewildlifepark.co.uk
Yorkshire Wildlife Park, off Warning Tongue Lane,
Branton, Doncaster DN4 6TB

YORKSHIRE
Wildlife Park

**The UK's No1 Walkthrough
Wildlife Adventure**

Getting around

For Yorkshire in general, the best way of getting around to see and do the most in the least time is by car. In the most isolated parts of rural Yorkshire it's the only really convenient option. But in urban areas, particularly in South and West Yorkshire, integrated public transport consisting of buses, trains and in some areas trams is highly developed and very efficient (for further details, see individual chapters). Even in some rural areas – particularly in the Yorkshire Dales and North York Moors National Parks – extra routes and buses are run during the holiday season, and heritage railway lines run regular trains. In these areas, too, many visitors enjoy the countryside from the saddle of a bike or on foot. For help in route planning, go to Ⓦwww.yorkshiretravel.net.

By car

Driving around Yorkshire is relatively easy, especially in South and West Yorkshire, where the national motorways double as interurban and suburban freeways – the main towns and cities of both hang from the M1, M62 and other motorways (eg M621, M606, M18, M180) like fruit from the branches of a tree. There being no toll, the local population use them continuously for short journeys – it's often quicker to use the motorway than to battle through traffic lights, roundabouts and one-way systems, even when it involves a considerably greater mileage. If you're using sat-nav, go for the fastest, not the shortest, route. Away from the big cities, dual carriageways are rare and journey times are unpredictable – you might well end up stuck behind tractors pulling farm machinery, or in a convoy behind a slow driver. In the heart of the two National Parks you might even be on single-lane roads with passing places.

Parking is plentiful and inexpensive in all but the biggest cities, and in these – especially Sheffield, Leeds and York – it might be as well to use the **park and ride** facilities. For visitors staying in city-centre hotels where parking isn't provided hotels usually have discount deals with nearby private car parks, though it can still be very expensive over an extended period.

By bus and train

Bus and rail services in Yorkshire are run by a plethora of private companies – for example,

no fewer than twelve companies operate buses in the **York** area alone (see Ⓦwww.york.gov.uk). **West Yorkshire** has an excellent integrated bus and train system (see Ⓦwww.wymetro.com). **South Yorkshire** has a similar system (Ⓦwww.travelsouth yorkshire.com), with the addition of **Sheffield**'s super Supertram network (Ⓦwww.supertram.com). **East Yorkshire** is served by East Yorkshire Motor Services (Ⓦwww.eyms.co.uk), which runs numerous bus routes, though rail travel in East Yorkshire is more limited.

Train services are provided by **First TransPennine Express** and **Northern Rail**, including the service on the Yorkshire Wolds Coast Line from Hull to Scarborough. First TransPennine Express also connects Leeds, Sheffield, Hull, York and Scarborough with Manchester. Northern Rail runs trains across the north, including direct access to the North York Moors, Yorkshire Dales, the Peak District and the coast. In addition, North Yorkshire is blessed with the wonderful heritage line the **North Yorkshire Moors Railway** from Pickering to Grosmont, where it connects with the beautiful **Esk Valley Railway** from Middlesbrough to Whitby, and with the **Settle-to-Carlisle** line. For North Yorkshire it's essential to pick up either the Dales Explorer or Moors Explorer timetable booklets from a local tourist office. For details of the Moorsbus in the North York Moors National Park, consult Ⓦwww.northyorkmoors.org.uk/moorsbus.

For information on local public transport, consult Ⓦwww.yorkshiretravel.net.

The following is an overview of journey times and frequencies for regional buses and trains from main destinations:

Buses

Harrogate to: Knaresborough (every 10min; 15–25min); Leeds (every 20min–1hr; 40min); Pateley Bridge (hourly; 50min); Ripon (every 20min; 30min).
Helmsley to: Pickering (hourly; 40min); Scarborough (hourly; 1hr 30min); York (Mon–Sat 3 daily; 1hr 30min).
Pickering to: Helmsley (hourly; 40min); Scarborough (hourly; 1hr); Whitby (4 daily; 55min); York (hourly; 1hr 15min).
Richmond to: Masham (Mon–Sat 2 hourly; 55min); Ripon (Mon–Sat 2 hourly; 1hr 15min).
Scarborough to: Bridlington (every 30min; 1hr 15min); Filey (every 30min; 30min); Helmsley (hourly; 1hr 30min); Hull (hourly; 2hr 50min); Leeds (hourly; 2hr 40min); Pickering (hourly; 1hr); Robin Hood's Bay (every 30min; 45min); Whitby (every 30min; 1hr); York (hourly; 1hr 35min).
Skipton to: Grassington (Mon–Sat hourly; 30min); Malham (Mon, Wed & Fri 4 daily, otherwise 2 daily; 40min); Settle (Mon–Sat hourly; 40min).
Whitby to: Robin Hood's Bay (every 30min; 25min); Staithes (hourly; 30min); York (4 daily; 2hr).
York to: Beverley (Mon–Sat hourly, Sun 7 daily; 30min); Hull (Mon–Sat hourly; Sun 7 daily; 1hr 45min); Leeds (every 30min; 55min); Pickering (hourly; 1hr 15min); Scarborough (hourly; 1hr 35min); Whitby (4 daily; 2hr).

Trains

Harrogate to: Knaresborough (every 30min; 10min); Leeds (every 30min; 35min); York (hourly; 40min).
Hull to: Beverley (Mon–Sat every 30min, Sun 6 daily; 13min); Leeds (hourly; 56min); London (6 daily; 2hr 45min); Scarborough (every 2hr; 1hr 30min); York (9 daily; 1hr).
Knaresborough to: Harrogate (every 30min; 10min); Leeds (every 30min–1hr; 45min); York (hourly; 30min).
Leeds to: Bradford (every 15min; 20min); Carlisle (3–7 daily; 2hr 40min); Harrogate (every 30min; 35min); Hull (hourly; 1hr); Knaresborough (every 30min; 45min); Lancaster (4 daily; 2hr); Liverpool (hourly; 1hr 50min); London (every 30min; 2hr 20min); Manchester (every 15min; 1hr); Scarborough (every 30min–1hr; 1hr 20min); Settle (3–8 daily; 1hr); Sheffield (every 30min; 40min–1hr); Skipton (hourly; 45min); York (every 10–15min; 25min).

Pickering to: Grosmont (April–Oct 5–8 daily, plus limited winter service; 1hr 10min).
Scarborough to: Bridlington (5–9 daily; 30min); Filey (5–9 daily; 15min); Hull (every 2hr; 1hr 30min); Leeds (hourly; 1hr 20min); York (hourly; 50min).
Sheffield to: Leeds (every 30min; 40min–1hr); London (hourly; 2hr 20min); York (every 30min–1hr; 1hr).
Whitby to: Danby (4–5 daily; 40min); Egton (4–5 daily; 20min); Great Ayton (4–5 daily; 1hr 5min); Grosmont (4–5 daily; 15min); Middlesbrough (4–5 daily; 1hr 30min).
York to: Bradford (hourly; 1hr); Durham (every 30min; 50min); Harrogate (hourly; 30min); Hull (9 daily; 1hr); Leeds (every 5–15min; 25min); London (every 30min; 2hr); Manchester (hourly; 1hr 30min); Newcastle (every 10min; 1hr); Scarborough (hourly; 50min); Sheffield (every 30min–1hr; 1hr).

By canal

Yorkshire has numerous **canals**, courtesy of the part it played in the Industrial Revolution. Waterways that were built to carry heavy industrial raw materials and finished goods now offer a peaceful, often picturesque, way of getting around the county. Numerous companies offer anything from short trips to

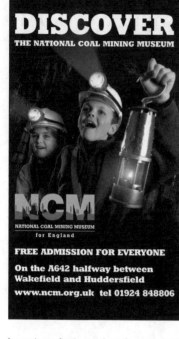

longer-term boat rental and canal boat holidays – for example Pennine Boat Trips (www.canaltrips.co.uk), Pennine Cruisers (01756/795 478, www.penninecruisers.com) and Snaygill Boats (www.snaygillboats.com) in Skipton, Shire Cruisers (www.shirecruisers.co.uk) in Sowerby Bridge or Bronte Boats Hire (www.bronteboathire.co.uk) in Hebden Bridge. If you are staying near a canal, the chances are that there will be a boat rental company not far away.

By bike

Cycling is popular in Yorkshire; in main cities or on busy main roads there are cycle lanes and paths in some areas, but coverage is patchy. For more detail see p.34.

On foot

None of Yorkshire's cities is so large that their city centres cannot be explored thoroughly on foot. There are numerous marked **public footpaths** across towns and cities, and for short trips it's often far quicker to walk than bother with buses or cabs. For more detail on hiking in Yorkshire, see p.33.

Accommodation

Accommodation for visitors in Yorkshire is plentiful though, as you'd expect, range and capacity are far greater in the main holiday areas – York, the Dales, the North York Moors and the coast – than in industrial South and West Yorkshire, or more remote East Yorkshire.

The popular tourist areas offer the whole accommodation gamut – country house establishments with all the luxury bells and whistles; ubiquitous huge international chains and more select groups of a few choice hotels; quality medium-sized family-owned and-run hotels; comfortable guesthouses and B&Bs; hostels (both YHA and other), bunkhouses and campsites. Look out too for pub accommodation – there has been a marked improvement, especially in the more rural areas, with many inns offering really well-appointed rooms at competitive rates.

In the industrial areas of South and West Yorkshire, the range of accommodation available is much narrower. Large chain hotels predominate, and these are usually located outside the town centres near motorway exits, since they depend on business clients and passing trade. This is not usually too inconvenient, since bus and taxi transport into the centres is relatively easy. Sheffield and Leeds boast a lot of city-centre accommodation, again mostly in big chain hotels.

Choosing accommodation can be difficult, given the bewildering array of types on offer, at wildly varying costs. This guide points you in the right direction, with a selection of good-quality accommodation to suit all pockets, but you can also consult the local tourist information centre (ask for the excellent Yorkshire Accommodation Guide, and also local accommodation sheets), and hotel review websites. Look out for the **England Quality Rose** emblem, awarded after inspection either by Visit Britain or the AA, which gives from one to five stars in a variety of categories – hotels, guesthouses, self-catering, campus, hostels and campsites. Hotels and guest-houses are further subdivided (for a full account of the scheme, go to @www.enjoyengland.com). Look out too for the symbols of the National Accessibility Scheme, which rates accommodation regarding suitability for people with disabilities (@www.tourismforall.org.uk).

Hotels, guesthouses and B&Bs

Yorkshire has some of the most luxurious **top-end hotels** in the UK, and although they tend to be set out in the countryside, a number are dotted around in heavily populated areas. They are usually housed in beautiful historical buildings, often listed, with attractive grounds, plush public rooms and impressive restaurants, and have all the spas, pools, gyms and so on that you'd expect. Although their publicly quoted rates can be eye-watering, their numerous discounts and special deals, which change from day to day, put them within reach of most of us – a rate of around £60 for a double room is quite common if you choose

---

Accommodation price codes

Throughout this guide, the accommodation is listed on a scale of ❶ to ❽, according to the cheapest room for two people in high season:

❶ £50 and under
❷ £51–70
❸ £71–90
❹ £91–120
❺ £121–150
❻ £151–200
❼ £201–250
❽ £251 and over

your night carefully. A word of warning – many of the big hotels now make a lot of their income by hosting weddings and corporate events, and when these are in progress the service to ordinary guests can seem to suffer. It is worth asking if anything is going on when you book.

All the big **international chains** are well represented in Yorkshire, from the cheap and cheerful to the staid and the stately. You'd expect a pretty uniform experience – but in fact they can vary a lot, presumably depending on the staff.

There are, also, numerous privately owned and run **hotels**, **guesthouses** and **B&Bs** throughout Yorkshire. Many smaller establishments have taken a leaf out of the big hotels' books and now offer similar services – en-suite bathrooms and tea- and coffee-making facilities, wi-fi, complimentary newspaper. Guesthouses and B&Bs in popular holiday areas often build up a loyal following of guests who return again and again, where hosts and guests come to think of themselves as friends.

And whatever accommodation you're considering, carefully check the availability of **parking**, especially in the city centres – it can be a real pain, and very expensive for all but the shortest stay.

Pubs

Always remember that, across Yorkshire but especially in the rural areas, there are lots of **pubs** that offer very acceptable accommodation. Two problems to look out for, though: they may be full – most have only a handful of rooms – and they may be noisy. So always reserve a room, check what time the bar closes and whether there's any live music or karaoke, and ask for a room as far from the public bar as possible.

Hostels

A variety of **hostels** and **bunkhouses** are available in Yorkshire, from the estimable establishments run by the **Youth Hostels Association** (ⓦ www.yha.org.uk), which may be in interestingly historical accommodation or superb locations (take a look at the one in Whitby, right next to the Abbey), to the rough barns converted into bunkhouse and camping barn accommodation you find largely in the

Yorkshire's finest

Restaurants

There are several chefs in Yorkshire who are widely respected and are operating at the top of their game:

Anthony's Anthony Flinn has three highly regarded establishments in Leeds. See p.102

Burlington Restaurant at *The Devonshire Arms*. Steve Smith is the acclaimed chef here, at the luxury hotel in Bolton Abbey. See p.199

The Clocktower Restaurant Stephanie Moon's restaurant at *Rudding Park* in Harrogate. See p.167

Harvey Nichols Leeds. The fourth-floor restaurant of this famous department store has chef Richard Walter-Allen at the helm. See p.102

The Pipe and Glass Just outside Beverley. Chef James Mackenzie has transformed this traditional pub into a Michelin-starred restaurant. See p.291

Star Inn Harome. Andrew and Jacquie Pern run this classy restaurant in a beautiful thatched inn. See p.233.

The Yorke Arms Nidderdale. Frances Atkins' Michelin-starred restaurant. See p.204

Hotels

Yorkshire has some of the finest luxury hotels in the country, and though they're expensive, it pays to look out for special deals which can be surprisingly affordable. Here are five of the best:

The Devonshire Arms Country house hotel in Bolton Abbey. Stay in Wharfedale as the guests of the Duke and Duchess of Devonshire. See p.199

Feversham Arms Helmsley. A Tardis of a hotel: country inn on the outside, luxury accommodation, swimming pool, hot tubs, spa and efficient, unobtrusive service within. See p.233

Middlethorpe Hall York. National Trust property, built in 1699, standing in a 20-acre garden five minutes from the centre of York. See p.146

Rudding Park Harrogate. Fusion of the traditional and the contemporary, with 300 acres of parkland and an 18-hole golf course. See p.167

Swinton Park Masham. A luxury castle hotel with 200 acres of parkland and an innovative approach to activities for guests. See p.214

Dales – for lists, take a look at Ⓦwww .yorkshirenet.co.uk or Ⓦwww.findabunkhouse .co.uk. Relative newcomers in this category are what are often called boutique hostels, establishments in city centres, nicely turned out but still containing multi-bunk dormitories, thus keeping the tariff low. Two of the best are in York (see p.147).

Camping

Rural areas of Yorkshire (especially North Yorkshire) have long been dotted with **campsites**, from the farmer's field and pub back yard to the full-on site with comprehensive facilities. But look out too for sites attached to great houses, like Castle Howard and Burton Constable Hall – half close your eyes and you can imagine yourself lord of the manor. Industrial areas, too, have more sites than you'd perhaps expect, though to visit cities like Leeds and Sheffield you'll need to look outside the city centre – Leeds has several sites north of the centre in Bardsey, whilst for Sheffield your best bet is to stay in the neighbouring Derbyshire Peak District and commute. York is blessed with a fine site within ten minutes of the centre, and others from which you can get into the centre by boat.

Self-catering

For extended stays **self-catering cottages** are an eminently viable proposition, and they're a brilliant way of getting to know the real life of an area. Many farms in lovely locations supplement their income by converting no longer needed barns and workmen's cottages into self-catering accommodation. Leaf through magazines like *Holiday Villas and Cottages* to get some idea of what's available, or take a look at the many websites devoted to this section of the market. Many are general sites that cover the whole of the UK and even abroad, but some are regional specialists:

Country Hideaways ⓦ www.countryhideaways .co.uk. Specialist in the Yorkshire Dales area.
Dales Holiday Cottages ⓦ www.dales-holiday -cottages.com.

Holiday Homes in Yorkshire ⓦ www .holidayhomesgroup.co.uk. Big choice of top-end properties.
Yorkshire Cottages ⓦ www.yorkshire-cottages .info. Covers the Dales, North York Moors, Vale of York and the Wolds.

A type of self-catering accommodation that is becoming increasingly popular is the **apartment hotel**, with bedroom(s), bathroom, kitchen and lounge but minimal services. These are often very luxurious, available on a nightly basis and can be surprisingly economical.

Food and drink

Yorkshire has always been known for its high-quality, locally produced food – its lamb, beef, pork, hams, baked goods, cheese, pies, fish, chocolate, even extra virgin rapeseed oil. Yorkshire ham, Yorkshire pudding and Yorkshire ales are world famous, and everybody knows that the moon is made of Wensleydale cheese. Increasingly, these wonderful ingredients get directly from producer to consumer, through farm shops and farmers' markets, and one of the joys of self-catering accommodation is searching out sources of good local produce. No wonder, then, that there has been a marked trend in the county for shops to sell locally produced food, and for restaurants to benefit from this cornucopia by increasingly using locally sourced ingredients.

In terms of cuisine, too, Yorkshire offers a huge range of dining experiences, catering for every taste and pocket. From internationally recognized top-end establishments to small local restaurants offering cuisine from all over the world to fish-and-chip shops, it is possible to eat well wherever you are in the county.

Deliciously Yorkshire

Look out for the **Deliciously Yorkshire** logo when shopping for food or choosing a hotel or restaurant. An initiative of the Yorkshire Regional Food Group, Deliciously Yorkshire (ⓦ www.deliciouslyyorkshire.co.uk) seeks to promote the county's food producers, retailers and places to eat, and the logo is displayed by establishments that supply, sell or use local Yorkshire produce. In addition, Deliciously Yorkshire awards – the county's food Oscars – are conferred annually in ten categories: prepared meat; fresh meat, poultry and game; confectionery; fish and seafood; prepared foods; drinks; fresh produce; dairy (including cheese); herbs, spices, preserves; and bakery.

Farmers' markets

South Yorkshire

Doncaster	Goose Hill	1st and 3rd Wed
Sheffield	The Moor	4th Sun
Wentworth	Hague Lane	2nd Sun

West Yorkshire

Halifax	Russell Street	3rd Sat
Holmfirth		3rd Sun
Leeds	Kirkgate Market	1st and 3rd Sun
Otley	Market Square	Last Sun

North Yorkshire

Harrogate	Market Place	2nd Thurs
Malton	Market Place	2nd Sun
Pateley Bridge	Nidderdale Showground	4th Sat/Sun
Richmond	Town Square	3rd Sat
York	York Auction Centre	1st and 3rd Sat
	Parliament Street	Last Fri

East Yorkshire

Driffield	Showground	1st Sat
Humber Bridge	Viewing area	1st Sun
South Cave		2nd Sat

Food

The restaurant scene in Yorkshire has been on the up for many years. Fine dining has proliferated across the county – there are six one-Michelin-star restaurants (three in North Yorkshire and one each in South, West and East Yorkshire) and many more establishments that offer similarly high quality. Indeed, cuisine is the new rock and roll, with named chefs being celebrated across the county (see box, p.27).

Small independent restaurants and gastropubs can be found in virtually every city, town and village, and top-end chains like *Loch Fyne*, *Ask* pizzerias, *Café Rouge*, *Café Nero* and *Pizza Express* are well represented. In **Betty's tearooms** – in York, Harrogate, Ilkley and Northallerton – Yorkshire has a mini-chain of uniquely stylish establishments selling the most delicious cakes and puddings in what might be called a Swiss/English fusion style. **Whitby** boasts some of the most highly reckoned fish restaurants in the country, **Bradford** and **Leeds** some of the best offering food from the Indian subcontinent. And look out for little regional clusters of restaurants in particular places – Eccleshall Road in

Sheffield, for example, much loved by the city's student population, or **Bawtry** near Doncaster, a small town with no fewer than fourteen establishments offering good food, including English, Chinese, Italian and Japanese cuisine, which draws in diners from Doncaster, Rotherham and beyond.

Drink

Yorkshire ale and Yorkshire pubs have a nationwide reputation. Yorkshire has over a hundred breweries, from the big boys like Samuel Smith's and John Smith's in Tadcaster to the small independent operators like Copper Dragon in Skipton or the Cropton Brewery in the North York Moors. Beer-loving visitors to Yorkshire should try to make a pilgrimage to **Masham**, a pretty Dales town that supports two superb breweries, both of which have excellent visitor centres and brewery tours.

Similarly Yorkshire has a wealth of public houses. It's no coincidence that the Yorkshire section of the Campaign for Real Ale's *Good Beer Guide* is the longest in the book – longer than the whole of London, longer than Scotland and Wales, much longer than

Lancashire. Leeds and Sheffield have some terrific bars and pubs with wonderful selections of beer (look out for *North*, *Whitelocks* or *Mr Foley's Cask Ale House* in Leeds, or the *Devonshire Cat* in Sheffield), towns like Harrogate, Wetherby, Ripon and Beverley have good old-fashioned town pubs (entering *Nellies* in Beverley is like stepping into the past), the coast has its share of smugglers' inns, and across the county almost every village has at least one country pub.

Less well known is the fact that Yorkshire has some of the most northerly **vineyards** in Europe – Leventhorpe Vineyard in Leeds, for example, and the Holmfirth Vineyard (appropriately located in the village where *Last of the Summer Wine* was filmed), who produce mainly white wines.

Festivals

Yorkshire cities, towns and villages host numerous festivals. Some have origins that are hidden in the mists of time; others owe more to local businesses trying to attract visitors during traditionally slow periods. Local tourist information centres will have detailed lists for each area, but here are some of the more noteworthy annual festivals.

General

Yorkshire Pudding Day 1st Sun in Feb. A light-hearted innovation started in 2008, inspired by various food days in the USA, probably started by an online cookery magazine.

Yorkshire Day Aug 1. Instigated in 1975 as a slightly tongue-in-cheek protest against the 1974 local government reorganization, and hosted in a different Yorkshire town every year. Includes civic ceremonies, charity fund-raising events and such all over the county.

South Yorkshire

Doncaster Hothouse Festival March ⓦwww .doncasterhothouse.co.uk. Comedy, drama, music and dance held in theatres, working men's clubs, churches across the borough.

Wath Festival of Music and Dance Late April/ early May ⓦwww.wathfestival.viviti.com. Largely folk music and dance, held in the Montgomery Hall and elsewhere.

English Mystery Plays June/July ⓦwww .monkbrettonpriory.org.uk. Recently established plays set in the ruins of Monk Bretton Priory, Barnsley.

Bradfield Traditional Festival of Music June ⓦwww.bradfieldfestivalofmusic.co.uk. Classical and some jazz music at St Nicholas Church, High Bradfield, Sheffield.

Doncaster Cultural Festival July. One-day free festival of all sorts of oddities – fire-eating to swordfighting, puppets to painting. Held in the Arts Park next to Doncaster Museum.

St Leger Festival Doncaster, Sept ⓦwww .doncaster-racecourse.co.uk. More than just the last classic race of the season – there are markets, street entertainers, live music and more throughout the week.

Art in the Gardens Sheffield, Sept ⓦwww .sheffield.gov.uk. Sheffield's superb Botanical Gardens become an art gallery.

Off the Shelf Literary Festival Oct ⓦwww .offtheshelf.org.uk. Sheffield's constantly improving literary festival in various venues.

Fright Night Sheffield, Oct ⓦwww .yellowbusevents.co.uk. One of Britain's biggest Halloween parties, held in the city centre.

Galvanize Sheffield, Nov–Dec ⓦwww .galvanizefestival.com. Exhibitions, tours and events related to silversmithing. Various venues in and around the city.

West Yorkshire

Wakefield Festival of Food, Drink and Rhubarb Feb ⓦwww.wakefield.gov.uk. Street entertainment, cookery demonstrations, walks, tours, market and visits to the rhubarb growers.

Huddersfield Literature Festival March ⓦwww .litfest.org.uk. The main emphasis is on poetry.

Bradford International Film Festival March. ⓦwww.bradfordfilmfestival.org.uk. Held at the National Media Museum.

Holmfirth Festival of Folk May ⓦwww .holmfirthfestivaloffolk.co.uk. Folk music in pubs and on the streets.

Haworth 1940s Weekend May ⓦwww .haworth1940s.co.uk. Forties clothing, music and events.

Hebden Bridge Arts Festival June/July ⓦwww .hebdenbridge.co.uk/festival. Comedy, music, dance, drama, literature and visual arts.

Bradford Mela June ⓦwww.bradfordmela .org.uk. Celebration of world cultures, with outdoor entertainment, food, street theatre, market stalls, children's activities and funfair rides.

Bradford Classic July ⓦwww.thebradfordclassic .com. Classic car show.

Ilkley Summer Festival Aug ⓦwww .summerfestival.ilkley.org. Music, drama and dance.

Leeds Festival Aug bank holiday weekend ⓦwww.leedsfestival.com. Around 70,000 music fans descend on Bramham Park outside Leeds – the sister festival to Reading Festival.

Sowerby Bridge Rushbearing Festival Sept. Craft market, Morris dancing and a decorated 16ft-high cart pulled by men in clogs.

Bite the Mango Bradford, Sept ⓦwww .nationalmediamuseum.org.uk. Weekend of world cinema at the National Media Museum.

Ilkley Literature Festival Oct ⓦwww .ilkleyliteraturefestival.org.uk. Authors' events, discussions, performances, workshops, poetry, with lots of big names.

Marsden Jazz Festival Oct ⓦwww .marsdenjazzfestival.com. Various venues.

Ted Hughes Festival Mytholmroyd, Oct ⓦwww .theelmettrust.co.uk. Poetry readings, talks, walks and a poetry competition in honour of the great man.

Light Night Leeds Oct ⓦwww.lightnightleeds .co.uk. Avant-garde goings-on in theatres, galleries, shopping arcades, museums, prison cells and city streets.

Christkindelmarkt Leeds, Nov ⓦwww .christmasmarkets.com. Traditional German Christmas market, including fairground rides, held in Millennium Square.

Bradford Animation Festival Nov ⓦwww.baf .org.uk. Held in the National Media Museum.

The Vale of York

Jorvik Viking Festival Feb ⓦwww.jorvik-viking -centre.co.uk. Viking simulations and events.

York Literature Festival March ⓦwww .yorkliteraturefestival.co.uk. Festival of fiction and poetry – readings, signings, performances, workshops.

York Festival of Science and Technology March ⓦwww.scy.org.uk. Special events and activities at the University of York.

Harrogate Spring Flower Show April ⓦwww .flowershow.org.uk. Competitions, displays, cookery.

York Roman Festival May ⓦwww .yorkromanfestival.org.uk. Roman themed events and activities across the city.

Late Music Festival York, June ⓦwww .latemusicfestival.org.uk.

Bramham Horse Trials Wetherby, June ⓦwww .bramhamhorse.co.uk.

Harrogate International Festival July ⓦwww .harrogate-festival.org.uk. Music, drama and film (the Summer Festival) and the Old Peculiar Crime Writing Festival.

York Mystery Plays July (every four years) ⓦwww.yorkmysteryplays.co.uk. Medieval drama performed on wagons rolling through the streets.

York Early Music Festival July ⓦwww.ncem .co.uk. Various venues in the city.

Great Yorkshire Show Harrogate, July ⓦwww .greatyorkshireshow.com. One of the country's premier agricultural shows.

York Festival of Food and Drink Sept ⓦwww .yorkfestival.com.

Harrogate Autumn Flower Show Sept ⓦwww .flowershow.org.uk.

National Book Fair York, Sept ⓦwww .yorkbookfair.com. Held at the racecourse.

York Lesbian Arts Festival Oct ⓦwww.ylaf.org .uk. Books, performing arts and music with a lesbian theme.

Wetherby Festival Oct–Nov ⓦwww .wetherbyfestival.co.uk. Music, performing arts, comedy and cabaret.

York Ghost Festival Oct–Nov ⓦwww .yorkghostfestival.co.uk. A variety of ghost-related activities in various venues.

St Nicholas Fayre York, Nov ⓦwww.yuletideyork .com. Christmas events at the Opera House, the York Castle Museum, National Railway Museum and others.

York Early Music Christmas Festival Dec ⓦwww.ncem.co.uk.

Festival of Angels York, Dec ⓦwww.yorkfestivals .com. Live ice-sculpting, stalls, outdoor food and drink, street entertainment and guaranteed snow.

The Yorkshire Dales

Dales Festival of Food and Drink Leyburn, May ⓦwww.dalesfestivaloffood.org. Food hall, cookery and farming demonstrations, plus beer festival.

Swaledale Festival June ⓦwww.swaledale -festival.org.uk. Music, talks and art throughout the dale.

Grassington Festival June–July ⓦwww .grassington-festival.org.uk. Mixed festival of art, music and performance with walks and workshops on subjects as varied as beekeeping and dry-stone walling.

Grassington Dickensian Festival Dec ⓦwww .grassington.uk.com. Usual festival activities, but in Victorian dress.

North York Moors and coast

Ryedale Folk Weekend May ⓦwww .efestivals.co.uk/festivals/ryedale. Folk music and workshops in the Ryedale Folk Museum in Hutton-le-Hole.

Morris Dance Festival Robin Hood's Bay, July ⓦwww.yorkshirecoastmorris.org.uk. A weekend of dancing in the village hall and on the streets and beach.

Seafest Festival Scarborough, July ⓦwww .scarborough.gov.uk. Boats, food, music.

Whitby Regatta Aug ⓦwww.whitbyregatta.co.uk.

Proms Spectacular Castle Howard, Aug ⓦwww .castlehoward.co.uk. Classical music in the park, with picnic and fireworks.

Pickering Folk Festival Aug ☎ 01751/473 780.

Scarborough Jazz Festival Sept ⓦwww .scarboroughjazzfestival.co.uk. Held in the Spa Complex.

East Riding of Yorkshire

Hull International Short Film Festival April ⓦwww.hullfilm.co.uk.

Spring Kite Festival Driffield, May ⓦwww.kite -festival.co.uk.

Early Music Festival Beverley, May ⓦwww .ncem.co.uk. Music, talks and lectures.

Whitby Moor and Coast Festival May ⓦwww .moorandcoast.co.uk. Music, song and dance, food and drink at Whitby Rugby Club.

Beverley Folk Festival June ⓦwww .beverleyfestival.com. Held in a marquee and in pubs throughout the town.

Hull Jazz Festival Aug ⓦwww.hullcc.gov.uk. Performances and workshops in venues across the city.

Maritime Festival Hull, Sept ⓦwww.hullcc.gov .uk. Songs and shanties around Hull Marina.

Hull Fair Oct ⓦwww.realyorkshire.co.uk. Huge funfair off Walton St.

Sport and outdoor activities

The big four spectator sports in Yorkshire are football, cricket, Rugby League and horseracing, while the county also offers an unrivalled range of outdoor sports and activities in which to participate.

Spectator sports

Yorkshire's connection with **association football** (**soccer**) goes back to the game's very beginnings – Sheffield FC is recognized by the European and World administrators of the beautiful game as its birthplace. Despite near fanatical support in parts of the county, Yorkshire's many teams have in recent times been very disappointing in terms of their achievements – at the time of writing not a single Yorkshire team graced the game's top level, the Premiership (compared to arch rival's Lancashire's seven), with so many in the Championship (despite the name, football's second tier) that some call it the Yorkshire League. Thus once-mighty Sheffield

United and Leeds now play in the Championship, and Sheffield Wednesday have slipped even further, into the third-tier First Division.

Until very recently it was the same story in **cricket**. Yorkshire Cricket Club, the most successful in the sport's history with over thirty Championships, and one that famously refused to use any players not born in the county, hit the doldrums from the late 1970s onwards, and mixed fortunes continued into the new millennium, with a County Championship in 2001 closely followed by relegation into the second division in 2002. Since then they have fought their way back into the top level. Great Yorkshire cricketing names abound: Len Hutton, Fred Truman, Geoff

Boycott, Ray Illingworth, Brian Close are discussed, argued about and revered throughout the county. In Yorkshire, even an umpire – Dickie Bird – can become a star. Cricket is widely played across Yorkshire, with many local leagues and teams, and the fortunes of the national teams of England, India, Pakistan, Sri Lanka and Bangladesh are keenly followed.

The third of Yorkshire's great sporting quartet is **Rugby League**, invented in the county when breakaway Rugby Union clubs, fed up with the sport's strictly enforced amateurism, formed their own league in which players could be paid expenses. This took place in the *George Hotel* in Huddersfield. From then on, the rules of Rugby League and Rugby Union diverged – for example the lineout was abolished and the number of players reduced from 15 to 13. More recently, with the advent of the Super League, the season was moved from the winter to the summer, and clubs started to adopt American-style names like the Leeds Rhinos.

The final spectator sport in Yorkshire's big four is **horseracing** – the county has nine of the UK's most famous racetracks which hold more than 170 meetings each year. Six of the nine hold only flat race meetings (York, Beverley, Pontefract, Redcar, Ripon and Thirsk), two are mixed (Catterick and Doncaster) and one specializes in National Hunt meetings (Wetherby).

Golf

Some of the finest golf courses in the UK are in Yorkshire. Nine of the best eighteen-hole courses are:

Alwoodley Golf Club ☎0113/268 1680, ⓦwww .alwoodley.co.uk. Just north of Leeds, regularly hosts county and national tournaments.

Bradford Golf Club ☎01943/875 570, ⓦwww .bradfordgolfclub.co.uk. One of Yorkshire's best-kept courses. Near the village of Hawksworth.

Fulford Golf Club ☎01904/413 579, ⓦwww .fulfordgolfclub.co.uk. A mile from York city centre, Fulford has been played by, amongst others, Jacklin, Lyle, Torrance, Norman, Weiskopf and Trevino.

Ganton Golf Club ☎01944/710 329, ⓦwww .gantongolfclub.com. In the Vale of Pickering between York and Scarborough. Gary Player called it "the only inland course worthy of hosting the Open Championship".

Fixby Golf Club ☎01484/426 203, ⓦwww .huddersfield-golf.co.uk. "The Home of Yorkshire Golf" (the Yorkshire Union of Golf Courses is based here) Huddersfield's golf course is just a mile from J24 on the M62.

Ilkley Golf Club ☎01943/600 214, ⓦwww .ilkleygolfclub.co.uk. Deceptively difficult course – with a par 69. The course record, held by Colin Montgomery, is only five shots below this.

Moor Allerton Golf Club ☎0113/266 1154, ⓦwww.magc.co.uk. Many world-class players have played the course during national and international events, including Seve Ballesteros, Tom Weiskopf, Tony Jacklin, Gary Player and Greg Norman. Just outside Leeds.

Moortown Golf Club ☎0113/268 6521, ⓦwww .moortown-gc.co.uk. Another Leeds course, this one was created by top course designer Dr Alister MacKenzie.

Pannal Golf Club ☎01423/872 628, ⓦwww .pannalgolfclub.co.uk. On what was once part of the Harewood Estate near Harrogate.

Walking

Yorkshire is renowned for its walking. Most of the best-known routes are in the **Dales** and the **North York Moors**, and the National Park Authorities for these two areas offer lots of advice, maps and other information at their visitor centres. But elsewhere too, even in the most heavily urbanized areas, there are walks galore. Every town and city, even in the most urban, industrialized areas, has its way-marked paths (ask for maps at the local tourist information centre, and for Leeds and Sheffield take a look at ⓦwww.walkit.com). There are numerous walks around Yorkshire Water's reservoirs and along canals, and circular walks around most Dales and North York Moors villages. Themed walks, too, are popular: Yorkwalk, Leeds Owl Trail, the Seven Seas Fish Trail in Hull, Beverley Sculpture Trail, Ghost walks around York or Whitby, the Passionate Brontës in Haworth, all add interest to urban strolls. In rural areas too there are organized walks – Ingleton Waterfalls Trail, Hardcastle Crags near Hebden Bridge, Ramsden Reservoir Walk in Holmfirth, and many more. Check at tourist offices or consult ⓦwww.yorkshire.com.

Finally, several **long-distance national trails** cross parts of Yorkshire – the Pennine Way/Pennine Bridleway, the Cleveland Way and the Yorkshire Wolds Way, together with others like the Transpennine Trail, the Minster Way, the Wolds Way and many more. For details check ⓦwww.nationaltrail.co.uk and ⓦwww.yorkshire.com. You might also want to test yourself on an annual event like the Yorkshire Three Peaks Challenge (see p.192).

Cycling

Cycling is a popular pastime in Yorkshire, especially in the industrial areas – there are no fewer than sixty clubs in West Yorkshire alone. You'll often see twenty or thirty cyclists bowling along in their full cycling gear, a study in ferocious dedication. However, for the weekend cyclist the least challenging cycling is in the Vale of York and East Yorkshire – it's far less hilly. Elsewhere, routes along canals and reservoirs can also be relatively gentle, or forest rides such as the ones in Dalby Forest.

The city of York lies at the intersection of two routes on the National Cycle Network – from Middlesbrough to Selby and Doncaster (National Route 65) and from Beverley and Pocklington to the east (National Route 66). At the time of writing the western section of this route (to Harrogate and Leeds) had not been completed. Other routes with sections in Yorkshire include National Routes 1, 6, 62, 67, 68 and 69, and regional routes 10 and 52. Check out the Sustrans websites (ⓦwww.sustrans.org.uk) – new routes and sections are being added all the time.

Rock-climbing

Yorkshire offers a wide range of **rock-climbing** opportunities on both gritstone and limestone routes. Consult the Rockfax databases for both types of climbing (ⓦwww.rockfax.com) – number and type of routes, range of grades, length and difficulty of approach and how sunny/shaded they are – and also the UK Climbing website (ⓦwww.ukclimbing.com). If the weather's bad, you can climb indoors at Foundry Indoor Climbing Centre or Climbing Works in Sheffield (see p.61). Or if you just want to sit in comfort and watch other people doing all the work, get along to the Sheffield Adventure Film Festival (ShAFF) at the Showroom Cinema, Sheffield, in March.

In addition, there are several activity centres in Yorkshire that involve **climbing wires** and swinging from poles. Try: Go Ape at Dalby (see p.244); Aerial Extreme at Bedale (see p.215) or How Steen Gorge Via Ferata (see p.205).

Potholing and caving

Yorkshire's great **potholing** and **caving** region is the Yorkshire Dales. Incomprehensible to claustrophobes, unaccompanied clambering about under ground is not recommended for the untrained. But there are numerous show caves (many are mentioned in the text) where you can enjoy the beauties of stalagmites and stalactites, travertine formations and so on. And you can arrange potholing and caving instruction from experts and accompanied expeditions through private companies like ⓦwww.yorkshiredalesguides.co.uk.

Fishing

Yorkshire is famous for its **fishing**, and enthusiasts of every type of angling will find places in which to indulge their sport. ⓦwww.yorkshirefishing.net lists over 200 day-ticket fishing venues – rivers, reservoirs, lakes, canals and gravel pits – across the whole of South, West, North and East Yorkshire. For sea fishing, again there are lots of opportunities to get stuck into beach, boat and kayak fishing – check out ⓦwww.whitbyseaanglers.co.uk, ⓦwww.whitby-sea-fishing.co.uk and ⓦwww.discoverywhitbycoast.com, as well as numerous sites for boat charter companies. Or just stroll along the quays at any of Yorkshire's harbours and ports – fishing trips are advertised at them all.

Water sports

You can indulge in **water sports** in many parts of Yorkshire – not only on the coast, but at lakes and reservoirs throughout the region.

Sailing, windsurfing and sea kayaking

Allerthorpe Lakeland Park ⓦwww.allerthorpelakelandpark.co.uk. Near York.
Craven Sailing Club ⓦwww.cravensailingclub.org.uk. Embsay reservoir.
East Barnby Outdoor Education Centre ⓦwww.outdoored.co.uk. Activity centre near Whitby which includes canoeing and sea kayaking.

Filey Sailing Club @ www.fileysc.co.uk.
Hornsea Mere @ www.hornseameremarine.com.
Thornton Steward Sailing Club @ www
.thornton-steward-sailingclub.co.uk. Near Bedale.
The Watersports Centre Pugneys Country Park
Wakefield ☎ 01924/302 360.
Yorkshire Dales Sailing Club @ www
.yorkshiredales.sc. Grimwith reservoir near
Grassington.

Surfing

Yorkshire's broad beaches, while not able to compete with those in the premier surfing areas like the West Country, can still allow dedicated surfers to chase the wave. Best bet for surfers is **Scarborough** – try Cayton Bay Surf Shop and Surf School (☎ 01723/585 585).

Jet skiing

Fosse Hill Jet Ski Centre (☎ 01964/542 608) in East Yorkshire, between Beverley and Hornsea.

In the air

Some places to check out if you want to get up there into the wide blue yonder – for parachuting, gliding, hang-gliding, paragliding or ballooning – are:

Active edge @ www.activeedge.co.uk. Near Harrogate, school for paragliding and paramotoring training.

Airborne Adventures @ www.airborne.co.uk. Balloon flights over the Yorkshire Dales.

Airsports @ www.airsportstraining.co.uk. Training for microlight instruction in Rufforth.

British Skysports Centre Parachuting centre just outside Bridlington (see p.294).

Dales Hang-gliding and Paragliding Club @ www.dhpc.org.uk. For experienced hang-gliders – lists 21 flying sites.

Sunsoar Paragliding @ www.sunsoar-paragliding .com. For those who want to learn, paragliding courses just over the Cumbria border west of Swaledale in Kirkby Stephen.

York Gliding Centre @ www.yorkglidingcentre .co.uk. On Rufforth Aerodrome, Vale of York.

Yorkshire Gliding Club @ www.ygc.co.uk. On Sutton Bank, North York Moors (see p.228).

Travel essentials

Costs

If you can afford it, Yorkshire's as fine a place to live the good life as anywhere in the UK. You can stay at top-end hotels, eat at Michelin-starred restaurants and buy designer clothes and gifts to your heart's content. Cost-wise, the sky's the limit. However, if you want to make a determined effort to keep costs down, then again Yorkshire's a good place – here are a few suggestions on how to spend wisely.

Phone around when looking for a **hotel**. Smaller hotels, guesthouses and B&Bs can be very reasonable, and even the big luxurious places, who have rates which change from day to day, can be surprisingly so if you catch them at the right time. **Hostels**, those of the YHA and others, often

pan out at around £20 a night or less, and campsites are even cheaper.

Use **public transport**, especially in the cities – it is fast, efficient and reasonably priced.

Eat cheaply. For picnics or those in self-catering accommodation, buy food in the local market. For eating out, pub food is usually very good value, especially as publicans are aware that Yorkshire folk have a reputation for demanding value for money.

There are several ways of keeping the bill for **attractions** down:

Join the **National Trust** (☎ 0870 458 4000, @ www.nationaltrust.org.uk) and **English Heritage** (☎ 0870 333 1181, @ www.english -heritage.org.uk), which will give you free entry to all their properties – between them they have nearly 70 properties in the county.

Ten of the best free museums in Yorkshire

Henry Moore Institute Leeds, p.97

Museum Quarter Hull, p.276

National Coal Mining Museum Wakefield, p.136

National Media Museum Bradford, p.108

National Railways Museum York, p.157

Royal Armouries Museum Leeds, p.98

Weston Park Museum Sheffield, p.57

Winter Garden and Millennium Galleries Sheffield, p.54

York Art Gallery York, p.151

Yorkshire Sculpture Park Wakefield, p.137

They are indicated in the guide by NT and EH respectively.

Buy a **Yorkshire Pass** (1–6 days, £30–70; Ⓦwww.yorkshirepass.com), which not only gets you into over 70 of Yorkshire's biggest attractions free, but gives you discount vouchers for lots of other attractions, entertainment, restaurants and shops.

In addition, some of the top-notch Yorkshire museums are free (see box above), and of course, many of Yorkshire's most popular pastimes don't cost you anything, such as walking, cycling (if you've got your own bike), spending a day at the beach or at a local park – a number of Yorkshire towns and cities such as Rotherham and Hull have remodelled their public parks and now offer excellent children's play areas.

Crime and personal safety

Crime in Yorkshire follows similar patterns to the rest of the country. Rural areas are relatively crime free, but in the big cities caution should be exercised as to which areas you visit. In the main tourist areas you should take the same precautions as you would anywhere else in the world – avoid the overt display of expensive cameras, watches and jewellery, don't flash wads of money,

keep an eye out for pickpockets. It's not necessarily in the city centres that difficulties might be encountered – they are well policed, covered by CCTV and patrolled by community support officers. Away from the immediate centres, though, you should keep your guard up. In common with the cities, even relatively small towns can become raucous on Friday and Saturday nights, with local youth indulging in the binge-drinking that has become a national pastime.

If you are robbed, you'll need to report it to the police in order to get a Crime Reference Number for your insurers.

The **emergency numbers** for the police, fire brigade, ambulance, mountain rescue and coastguard are ☎999 or ☎112.

Customs

Travellers coming into Britain directly from most other EU countries can bring almost as many cigarettes and as much wine or beer into the country as they can carry. The guidance levels are 10 litres of spirits, 90 litres of wine and 110 litres of beer – any more than this and you'll have to provide proof that it's for personal use only. The general guidelines for tobacco are 3200 cigarettes, 400 cigarillos, 200 cigars or 3kg of loose tobacco – note that the limits from some new EU member countries are lower than this. If you're travelling to or from a non-EU country, you can still buy a limited amount of duty-free goods, but within the EU, this perk no longer exists. If you need any clarification on British import regulations, contact **HM Revenue and Customs** (☎0845 010 9000 or +44 292/050 1261 for international callers; Ⓦcustoms.hmrc.gov.uk).

Electricity

The **electricity supply** in Yorkshire, in common with the rest of the UK, is 240 volts AC, delivered through sockets that accept plugs with three square pins. American appliances will need a transformer to step up the voltage, European, Australian and New Zealand only a plug adapter.

Entry requirements

Citizens of the European Union have the right to move freely throughout the UK armed only with a passport or ID card. Those from the

Buy a **Yorkshire Pass** for Great Value Sightseeing

the **Yorkshire** Pass

6 DAY ADULT   03 027870 3   Exp:03/11

Gives entry to Yorkshire's Top Attractions including Castle Howard, Jorvik Viking Centre, The Deep and many more.

Free Guidebook and exclusive offers booklet with every pass.

Buy online at yorkshirepass.com **enter promotional code** ROUGH2010 **and receive** 20% discount.

Telephone 01904 550099 **or email** info@yorkshirepass.com

Welcome to Yorkshire
yorkshire.com   **yorkshirepass.com**

USA, Canada, South Africa, Australia and New Zealand need only a valid passport to stay for up to six months without a visa. Citizens from the European Economic Union and Switzerland do not need visas, though there are regulations concerning permission to work. All other nationalities require a visa, which can be obtained for the British Consul's office in the country of origin. For detailed requirements, see Ⓦwww.ukvisas .gov.uk.

Health

Citizens of EU and EEA countries are entitled to free medical treatment within the National Health Service (which covers most doctors and hospitals) on production of a **European Health Insurance Card** (Ⓦwww.ehic.org.uk) obtainable before leaving home. Similarly, a number of countries have reciprocal agreements with the UK (Australia and New Zealand, for example), and their citizens too are entitled to free treatment. All others must pay for treatment, so holiday health insurance is strongly recommended.

Pharmacists (known as **chemists** in Britain) can dispense only a limited range of drugs without a doctor's prescription. Most chemists are open standard shop hours, though in large towns some stay open until 10pm – information will be posted on pharmacy doors. For generic, off-the-shelf pain-relief tablets, cold cures and the like, the local supermarket is usually the cheapest option.

Minor complaints and injuries can be dealt with at a **doctor's (GP's) surgery** – any tourist office or hotel should be able to point you in the right direction. For complaints that require immediate attention, you can turn up at the 24-hour casualty (A&E) department of the local **hospital** (detailed in our main city and town accounts). In an **emergency,** call an ambulance on ☎999 or 112. **NHS Direct** (☎0845/4647, Ⓦwww .nhsdirect.nhs.uk) provides 24-hour medical advice by phone, and also runs an increasing number of walk-in centres (usually daily 7.30am–9pm) in the bigger towns and cities.

Insurance

Standard holiday insurance is perfectly adequate for most holiday visits to Yorkshire. However, more extreme sorts of activity and sport may need to be covered separately. So, if you're intent on gliding, parachuting, rock-climbing or any other activity that you're not sure of, consult your insurer.

Internet access

Most towns and cities in Yorkshire have **internet cafés** whose rates (£1–3/hr, with lower half- and full-day rates) and machine speeds vary enormously. Many **public libraries** and **tourist information centres** offer free internet access, and the availability of **wi-fi** is spreading rapidly, with lots of hotels, guesthouses, B&Bs, hostels, pubs, cafés and even campsites now offering this facility. Chains such as *Starbucks*, *McDonald's* and *Wetherspoon's* increasingly offer wi-fi as a matter of course.

Laundry

Larger hotels provide **laundry services**, but they're usually expensive. Most towns of any size have a launderette which is open well into the evening, and many offer service washes where you can drop your washing off, go for a drink or a meal, then pick it up (usually £5–7). Self-catering accommodation – cottages, apartments, apartment-hotels – invariably have washing machines, as do many campsites.

Mail

As in the rest of the UK, the postal system in Yorkshire is operated by Royal Mail (☎0845 774 0740, ⓦwww.royalmail.com), whose customer service line and website details postal services and current postage costs, and can help you find individual post offices. Virtually all post offices are open Monday to Friday from 9am to 5.30pm, and on Saturdays from 9am to 12.30 or 1pm, with smaller branches closing on Wednesday afternoons too. In the big cities main offices stay open all day Saturday, while in small and rural communities you'll find sub-post offices operating out of general stores, though post office facilities are only available during the hours above even if the shop itself is open for longer. Rural post offices are under threat, so if you can, use them or lose them. As well as in post offices, stamps are on sale at newsagents and other stores advertising them. Postage rates depend on the size and weight of the envelope or package, and when you want it to arrive – first-class should arrive next day, second-class within three working days. Airmail to European destinations, too, should arrive within three working days, and to countries outside Europe within five. Slower "surface mail" and express delivery services are also available.

Maps

Yorkshire is a relatively coherent area, though many of the **maps** which cover it are either too general (and include the rest of the North of England, for example) or concentrate on one particular part of Yorkshire: there are many tourist maps of the Dales and the North York Moors, including some very useful guides produced by the two National Park authorities. One of the most useful general maps to cover the whole county, and which includes a mass of information about attractions in the area, is the Philips Red Books

Leisure and Tourist Map of Yorkshire (ⓦwww .octopusbooks.co.uk), a snip at £4.25.

The principal producer of maps on a large enough scale for walkers and cyclists is the Ordnance Survey – their Landranger (pink, 1:50,000) and Explorer (orange 1:25,000) are the most useful. Landranger maps 98–101, 104–107 and 110–111 cover Yorkshire, the Explorer series are too numerous to mention, but look out for the ones (prefixed OL) that cover particularly popular holiday areas, like OL2 Yorkshire Dales Southern and Western Areas or OL26 North York Moors Western Area. The National Cycle Network produces excellent waterproof maps of their routes (ⓦwww .sustrans.org.uk) and also lists other local sources of cycling route maps – 21 for Yorkshire.

Otherwise, for general route-finding there are numerous road atlases: those published by the AA, RAC, Geographers A–Z and Collins for example, with scales of around 1:250,000. And there's always sat-nav.

Most of these maps are available from large bookshops or specialist map and travel stores, either in the flesh or online. In the UK main bookshops usually stock a good range of local/regional maps, while those passing through London should call in at Stanfords (ⓦwww.stanfords.co.uk), England's premier map and travel specialist. Yorkshire's tourist information centres also stock a wide range of maps and guides, including some excellent locally produced ones to walks and bike rides in their areas.

Money

Britain's currency is the **pound** sterling (£), divided into 100 pence (p). Coins come in denominations of 1p, 2p, 5p, 10p, 20p, 50p and £1 and £2. Notes are in denominations of £5, £10, £20 and £50. Scottish and Northern Irish banknotes are legal tender throughout Britain, though some traders may be unwilling to accept them. If you're having difficulty getting rid of them, change them at a bank. Every sizeable town and village has a branch of at least one of the main high-street banks: Barclays, Halifax, HSBC, Lloyds-TSB and NatWest. The easiest way to get hold of cash is to use your debit card in an **ATM**; there's usually a daily withdrawal limit of £250. You'll find ATMs outside banks, at all major points of arrival and motorway service areas, at most large supermarkets, some petrol stations and even in some pubs, rural post offices and village shops (though a charge may be levied on cash withdrawals at small, stand-alone ATMs). Depending on your bank and your debit card, you may also be able to ask for "cash back" when you shop at supermarkets. Some overseas travellers still prefer sterling **travellers' cheques**, at least as a back-up. The most commonly accepted are issued by American Express, followed by Visa. American Express will not charge commission if you exchange cheques at their own offices, nor will some banks (such as NatWest) – otherwise you will be charged 2–3 percent commission. Outside banking hours, you can change cheques or cash at post offices and bureaux de change – the latter tend to be open longer hours and are found in most city centres, and at major airports and train stations. Avoid changing cash or cheques in hotels, where the rates are normally poor. Finally, **credit cards** can be used widely either in ATMs or over the counter. MasterCard and Visa are accepted in most hotels, shops and restaurants in Britain, American Express and Diners Club less so. Plastic is less useful in rural areas, and smaller establishments, such as B&Bs, will often accept cash only. Remember that cash advances from ATMs using your credit card are treated as loans, with interest accruing daily from the date of withdrawal.

Opening hours and public holidays

General **business hours** for most businesses, shops and offices are Monday to Saturday 9am to 5.30 or 6pm, although the supermarket chains tend to stay open until 8 or 9pm from Monday to Saturday, with larger ones staying open round the clock. Many major stores and supermarkets now open on Sundays, too, usually from 11am or noon to 4pm, though some provincial towns still retain an early-closing day (usually Wed) when most shops close at 1pm. Banks are usually open Monday to Friday from 9am to 4pm, with some branches also open on Saturday mornings.

Public holidays

Britain's public holidays (sometimes referred to as Bank Holidays) are:

January 1
Good Friday
Easter Monday
First Monday in May
Last Monday in May
Last Monday in August
December 25
December 26
Note that if January 1, December 25 or December 26 falls on a Saturday or Sunday, the next weekday becomes a public holiday.

You can usually get fuel any time of the day or night in larger towns and cities (though note that not all motorway service stations are open 24hr). Full opening hours for specific museums, galleries and other tourist attractions are given in the Guide. Banks, businesses and most shops close on public holidays, though large supermarkets, small corner shops and many tourist attractions don't. However, nearly all museums, galleries and other attractions are closed on Christmas Day and New Year's Day, with many also closed on Boxing Day (Dec 26).

Phones

The flimsy **BT phone kiosk** is still to be found throughout Yorkshire, though they're not as ubiquitous as once they were. Most will allow you to pay by coin, credit card or phone card. There are, too, quite a few surviving red phone boxes in rural areas (the iconic design by Sir Giles Gilbert Scott), and in Hull and Beverley you'll see the same ones but cream in colour, and minus the crown over the door. For **mobile phones** (cell phones), which are as common in Yorkshire than everywhere else, coverage is good in Yorkshire's cities but can be patchy in the Dales and the North York Moors.

Shopping

Although "shop till you drop" has become a British motto, and the cliché "retail therapy" is a fair reflection of shopping's place in the mentality of many, it can be tricky to find anywhere individual and inspiring – high streets throughout Yorkshire feature the same chain stores. Out-of-town shopping centres and supermarkets have been accused of sucking the life out of town centres, though it could just as well be argued that they have invigorated town and city life by taking workaday shopping out of the centres, releasing space for a vibrant mix of cafés, bars, bistros, restaurants, pubs and specialist shops. And across Yorkshire, there are alternatives. Every major town in South and West Yorkshire has its own **covered market**, some of which have become bywords for cheap, good-quality fresh meat and vegetables, and for bargains in a range of clothes, electronic equipment and more. Weekly **street markets** are often the best places to pick up craft items, though you may have to wade among a proliferation of twee bric-a-brac to find anything truly original. Markets are also the only places (apart from antique shops and some secondhand shops) where haggling is acceptable, even expected. Yorkshire towns host numerous **farmers' markets** (see p.29) where good Yorkshire food products are on offer. You'll also find similarly authentic local items in **rural farmshops**, usually signposted by the side of the road.

Retail villages and outlets are popular in Yorkshire, where designer brands are available at a fraction of the original cost – **Hornsea's Freeport Outlet** (see p.299) claims to have been the first in the UK. And for top-end, up-to-the-minute designer shopping, you could hardly do better than the **Victoria Quarter** in Leeds, which boasts the first Harvey Nichols to be opened outside London.

Yorkshire is probably no cheaper to shop in than anywhere else, though Yorkshire folks' reluctance to part with their cash has been much remarked on. Most goods in the UK, with the chief exceptions of books and food, are subject to 20 percent **Value Added Tax** (VAT), which is included in the marked price. Visitors from non-EU countries can save a lot of money through the Retail Export Scheme (tax-free shopping), which allows a refund of VAT on goods to be taken out of the country.

(Savings will usually be minimal for EU nationals because of the rates at which the goods will be taxed upon import to the home country.) Note that not all shops participate in this scheme (those doing so will display a sign to this effect), and that you cannot reclaim VAT charged on hotel bills or other services.

Time

Greenwich Mean Time (GMT) is used from late October to late March, when the clocks go forward an hour for **British Summer Time** (BST). GMT is five hours ahead of US Eastern Standard Time and ten hours behind Australian Eastern Standard Time.

Tourist information

Yorkshire's tourist industry is promoted by an umbrella tourist organization, **Welcome to Yorkshire**, made up of the relevant individual tourist authorities for the county, which cover everything from local accommodation to festival dates, attractions to food. It has a well-organized website (Ⓦ www.yorkshire .com), which offers sophisticated book marking and itinerary-planning facilities, a mobile site for people using handhelds, and a twitter feed. Tourist offices (also called **Tourist Information Centres**, or "TICs" for short) exist in virtually every Yorkshire town, though they can vary from large, well-stocked, enthusiastically staffed offices in the principal tourist areas (York say) to a bank of tourist leaflets and booklets in an unstaffed corner of the local council offices or the local library (Barnsley for example, or Huddersfield). Even some places that you wouldn't think of as tourist magnets have excellent tourist offices – Halifax, Wakefield and Rotherham spring to mind. Their locations and opening hours are listed throughout this guide. Opening hours vary, with no real pattern, though hours tend to be longer the more popular the area, and usually get shorter out of season. Staff at tourist offices will nearly always be able to book accommodation, reserve space on guided tours, and sell guidebooks, maps and walk leaflets. They can also provide lists of local cafés, restaurants and pubs, though they aren't supposed to recommend particular places. An increasing number of offices have internet access for visitors, but rarely have the space to look after baggage while you sally forth.

Yorkshire's two great **National Parks** have their own dedicated information centres, which offer similar services to TICs but can also provide expert guidance on local walks and outdoor pursuits. They sometimes double up as TICs.

Useful tourist websites

The official visitor site for Yorkshire is Ⓦwww.yorkshire.com. Also try:

Visit Hull and East Yorkshire Ⓦwww.realyorkshire.co.uk

Visit York Ⓦwww.visityork.org

Yorkshire Dales and Harrogate Ⓦwww.yorkshiredalesandharrogate.com

Yorkshire Moors and Coast Ⓦwww.yorkshiremoorsandcoast.com

Yorkshire South Ⓦwww.yorkshiresouth.com

Travellers with disabilities

In many ways, the UK is ahead of the field in terms of facilities for travellers with disabilities. All new public buildings – including museums, galleries and cinemas – are obliged to provide **wheelchair access**, though historic sights can be more problematic. Train stations and airports are generally fully accessible, many buses have easy-access boarding ramps, and dropped kerbs and signalled crossings are the rule in every city and town. The number of accessible hotels and restaurants is also growing, and Blue Badge parking bays are available almost everywhere, from shopping malls to museums. If you have specific requirements, it's always best to talk first to your travel agent, chosen hotel or tour operator, or individual restaurants, attractions and venues you hope to use.

Travelling with children

Yorkshire is a wonderful area for family holidays, with lots to do: beaches, theme parks, child-friendly museums and castles, petting farms and, for the older ones, adventure activities. Lots of **places to stay** are child-friendly, such as campsites, some with all sorts of activities and kids' clubs, self-catering accommodation and child-friendly hotels; the old seaside boarding house dragon-landlady is a dying breed. Attitudes to travellers with children in Yorkshire are similar to those in other areas of the UK – compared with countries like Greece or Spain, parents with young children can sometimes feel a little unwelcome, though this varies with an increasing number of places – pubs and restaurants, even churches and cathedrals – providing boxes of toys, colouring books and crayons to keep the youngsters happy. **Baby-changing apparatus** is usually available in shopping centres and train stations, while pharmacies and supermarkets stock a useful range of products (shops in rural areas will have less choice). As a rule children are not allowed in **pubs**, though this can vary – children are permitted where food is being served (and that includes at least one room in most pubs these days), there are often family rooms or beer gardens (though since the total smoking ban the latter sometimes sit under a cloud of cigarette smoke). It all rather depends on the attitude of the landlord/landlady – some are vigilant in enforcing the letter of the law and see children as an enemy to be kept at bay, others are as welcoming as anyone could hope. Some hotels, B&Bs and campsites won't accept children under a certain age (usually 12), though in the big family holiday areas like Scarborough or Bridlington children are widely accepted – it would be a bad business decision not to be. Under-5s generally travel free on **public transport** and get in free to attractions; 5- to 16-year-olds are usually entitled to **concessionary rates** of up to half the adult rate/fare. Don't expect huge discounts for children in the main commercial tourist attractions, though – it rarely amounts to more than a pound or two. For further advice and services, try Ⓦwww.travellingwithchildren.co.uk and Ⓦwww.babygoes2.com.

Guide

Guide

1

South Yorkshire

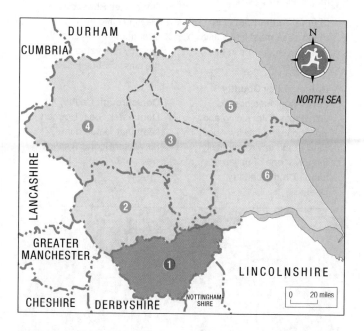

CHAPTER 1 # Highlights

✳ **Peace Gardens, Sheffield**
Along with neighbouring
Winter Garden, this is the
heart of South Yorkshire's
greatest city, vibrant on a
summer afternoon. See p.54

✳ **The Fat Cat, Sheffield** Time-
capsule pub, with real ale,
good food, and no gaming
machines. See p.59

✳ **Magna, Rotherham** One
of the best, most innovative
industrial museums in the
world. See p.68

✳ **Rother Valley Country
Park** Wide open spaces
with cable water skiing and
wakeboarding facility – both
family- and environmentally
friendly – one of only a
handful in the country.
See p.69

✳ **Barnsley Market** A rabbit-
warren of bargain-offering
market stalls that have
colonized the town centre.
See p.72

✳ **Cannon Hall, Barnsley** A
country house museum with
a top-notch farm attraction in
the grounds. See p.77

✳ **Doncaster Racecourse**
Meetings and events
throughout the year at the
recently renovated home of
the classic St Leger.
See p.81

✳ **Conisbrough Castle,
Doncaster** Great Norman
keep that featured in
Sir Walter Scott's *Ivanhoe*.
See p.83

▲ Peace Gardens, Sheffield

1

South Yorkshire

S OUTH YORKSHIRE's heart, sinews and blood were the traditional British heavy industries, and its contribution to one of the county's great claims to fame – the Industrial Revolution – was through iron and steel (mainly in Sheffield and Rotherham), coal (everywhere but especially in Barnsley and Doncaster), and engineering. Consequently, these industries' decline from the late twentieth century onwards has hit the region hard, leaving behind much economic and social deprivation. However, South Yorkshire's four metropolitan boroughs – Sheffield, Rotherham, Barnsley and Doncaster – have made sterling efforts to adapt to twenty-first-century realities, and with the help of national and European funding are making great strides in redeveloping the region's infrastructure.

Though South Yorkshire is unlikely to spring to mind as your main holiday destination, it does have a surprising amount to offer. The quality of local provisions is high, with excellent public transport, numerous swimming pools and sports centres, first-rate children's playgrounds and municipal parks, flourishing covered and street markets, and lively libraries and arts centres. Furthermore, and perhaps unexpectedly, South Yorkshire is well endowed with medieval abbeys, castles and churches, and, more predictably, with a full spectrum of industrial museums, from the small, enthusiast-run to the internationally renowned. There's even, in amongst the post-industrial grunge, some pockets of lovely countryside.

The place you're most likely to visit in South Yorkshire is **Sheffield** – it is metropolitan in ways that Rotherham, Doncaster and Barnsley are not. Though it lacks any killer attractions, its big city atmosphere is unmistakeable. **Rotherham**, though much more a traditional industrial town, boasts a fine church and in the magnificent **Magna** science centre it has a world-class tourist attraction. **Doncaster**, another largely industrial town, is given a certain air by the fact that it has one of Yorkshire's most famous **racetracks**. And **Barnsley** is known for its **market**, as well as for the relatively large number of celebrities that hail from it.

The organization of this chapter keeps to the county's division into four metropolitan boroughs. Do remember, however, that this is a densely populated but remarkably small geographical area – if you're planning a day out, you need to check across the whole chapter (and indeed the next one, on West Yorkshire) before you draw up your itinerary.

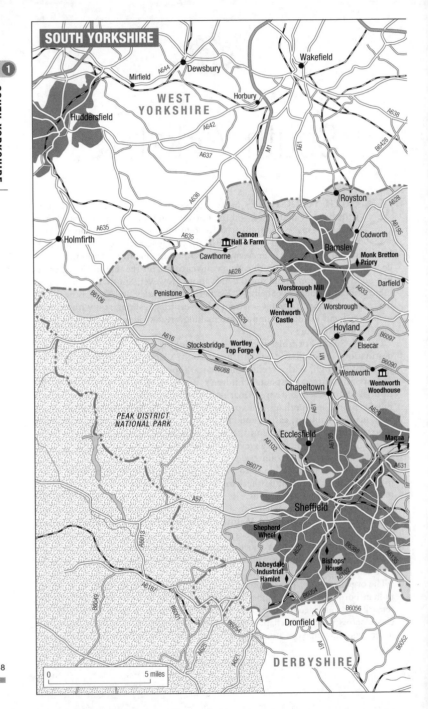

SOUTH YORKSHIRE

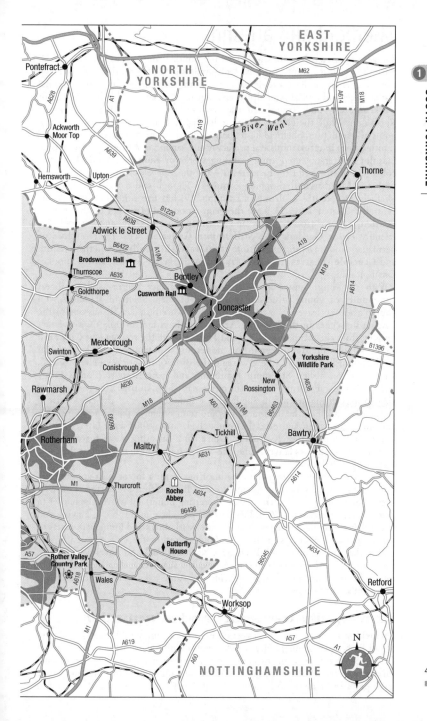

Sheffield and around

Spreading westwards from the M1 to the South Pennine hills, **SHEFFIELD**, once the greatest manufacturer of high-grade steel in the world, is reinventing itself as a vital, modern, provincial city. South Yorkshire's undoubted regional leader, Sheffield's vitality, culture and heritage make it a likely day-trip or weekend break, and certainly an essential stopover on any visit to this part of Yorkshire. While the ebbing of the industrial tide has left behind its brackish pools of dereliction, Sheffield hasn't been slow to recognize the resulting opportunities, both in terms industrial preservation – such as at **Abbeydale Industrial Hamlet**'s water-powered knife-grinding works or **Kelham Island Museum**'s collection of steel industry behemoths – and the redevelopment of derelict land with the **Meadowhall** shopping complex. Though still a work in progress, Sheffield city centre is already a triumph. Within five minutes' walk of the centrally situated Town Hall are the giant wood-and-glass tent of the **Winter Garden**, full of tropical trees and flowers; the sparkling and oh-so-child-friendly **Peace Gardens**; the **Millennium Galleries**, with their mixture of permanent and travelling exhibitions; the **Graves Art Gallery**, and the **Lyceum** and **Crucible theatres** (the latter famous as the venue for the World Snooker Championships).

With two huge universities slap-bang in the city centre, and a vibrant community of young professionals – many of them Sheffield graduates who couldn't bear to leave – the city is a bustling, youthful place. It has one of the best music scenes in the UK (the **Arctic Monkeys** are no fluke) with venues ranging from the intimate *Leadmill* and *Plug*, through the resplendent **City Hall** to the colossal **Sheffield Arena**. And more sport than you could shake a stick at – Championship football (the Owls and the Blades), ice-hockey (The Steelers), athletics (Don Valley Stadium), swimming and general sport (Pond's Forge Sports Centre), and, using one of the city's many hills, Europe's biggest artificial **ski-slope**. Getting around in Sheffield is a doddle – most of the city centre is eminently walkable, the integrated bus and tram system make longer hops easy, and, for journeys in and out, the remodelled railway/bus/tram interchange is butted right up to the city centre. Don't bank on using a car for exploring Sheffield, though – its labyrinthine one-way system will defeat all but the most knowledgeable local.

The surrounding area isn't quite so inspiring, with a lot of post-apocalyptic-looking industrial wasteland. Being located in Yorkshire's extreme southwest corner, most of the city's attractive or interesting hinterland is over the border in Derbyshire, or in parts of Yorkshire covered elsewhere in this book. Having said that, Sheffield is one of the few English cities with direct and immediate access to picture-postcard countryside. Indeed, about a third of the city, apparently, lies within the borders of the **Peak District National Park**. So travel west by bus, train or car out of the city (you can even walk it if you're feeling fit), and within minutes you're surrounded by green fields, dry-stone walls, limestone caves, lakes, pretty villages and country pubs.

Arrival, city transport and information

Sheffield must be one of the easiest cities in the country to get to. The Robin Hood Doncaster-Sheffield airport (ⓦ www.robinhoodairport.com) is 25 miles from the city centre, while by car the city is approached along six miles of dual carriageway from the M1's junction 33; there's ample **parking** including four large **park and ride** stations around the city's perimeter linking with the trams.

The city's excellent **bus**, **coach** and **train interchange** is right in the city centre on either side of Sheaf Street. It also has one of the best urban transport systems, with an efficient **tram** and **bus** system (combined tickets start with a one-day Explorer at £5 and a week-long tram/bus Megarider for £12), a free city-centre bus service (the FreeBee), and a considerable network of marked and unmarked cycle routes within the city and reaching far out into the surrounding countryside. Excellent guides to all these services are available at the transport interchange, at the **tourist information centre**, 14 Norfolk Row (Mon–Fri 10am–5pm, Sat 10am–4pm; ☎0114/221 1900), and in the **central library** in Surrey Street. Pick up, too, the monthly *Definitive Guide to What's On in Sheffield* (35p).

Accommodation

Sheffield has a good assortment of hotels, the best in South Yorkshire. The tourist office offers accommodation booking.

Hilton Victoria Quays ☎0114/252 5500, ⓦwww .hilton.co.uk/sheffield. Recently built, yet with a solid, old-fashioned feel inside, the Sheffield *Hilton* is in a perfect location – quayside tranquillity in redeveloped Victoria Quays within 5min walk of city-centre pubs, shops and restaurants. It has its own *Quays* restaurant, pool, sauna and gym. ④

Houseboat Hotels ☎01909/569 393, ⓦwww.houseboathotels.com. An interesting alternative to ordinary hotels, *Houseboat Hotels* offer quality accommodation with all mod-cons in three houseboats – *Ruby*, *Lilly-May* and *Mallard* – moored near the *Hilton*, 5min walk from the city centre. You get exclusive use of your own boat, from £59 to £150 per night in any combination of one to four people. Guests can use the facilities of the *Hilton* (pool, sauna and gym) for around £5, and continental breakfasts are available at £8, full English at £10 (but you have to cook it yourself!). ②

Leopold Hotel 2 Leopold St ☎0114/252 4000, ⓦwww.leopoldhotel.co.uk. Billed as Sheffield's first boutique hotel, the *Leopold* occupies a Grade II listed building, once a boys' grammar school. The keynote is solid luxury but with a quirky edge – many original features have been kept and whimsical touches added. Centrally located, the hotel backs onto tiny but beautifully

remodelled Leopold Square, which boasts no fewer than eight places to eat; the hotel also has a highly rated restaurant. Complimentary wi-fi is available in the bar. Limited parking. ④

Mercure St Paul's Hotel 119 Norfolk St ☎0114/278 2000, ⓦwww.mercure.com. Sandwiched between the Peace Gardens and Tudor Square, this modern hotel couldn't be more central. Indeed, the bar opens directly into the palm-thronged Winter Garden, giving it a distinctly tropical feel. Comfortable rather than innovative, with understated (if a little anodyne) decor and all the usual pool, fitness centre, sauna, and wi-fi bells and whistles. Its 163 rooms are supremely well appointed, and the higher you go the better the view. Not cheap, but look out for deals, especially at weekends. Parking service. ④

Park Inn Blonk St ☎0114/220 4000, ⓦwww .parkinn.co.uk. Breezy, informal business hotel near the river, quays and markets, with a good bar and restaurant. All rooms are stylishly furnished, some with futons – handy for families. Parking. ③

Sheffield University ☎0114/222 8822, ⓦwww .shef.ac.uk/accommodation/summervacation. Student rooms are available in various parts of the city during the long summer vacation, starting at £26 per night (not including VAT).

The city centre

Sheffield's immediate **centre**, bounded by The Moor to the south, Devonshire Green to the west, the Cathedral and Paradise Square to the north, and Arundel Gate and the transport interchange to the east, is as busy and vital as any in the country. A good starting point for its exploration is the Peace Gardens/Winter Garden/Millennium Galleries complex.

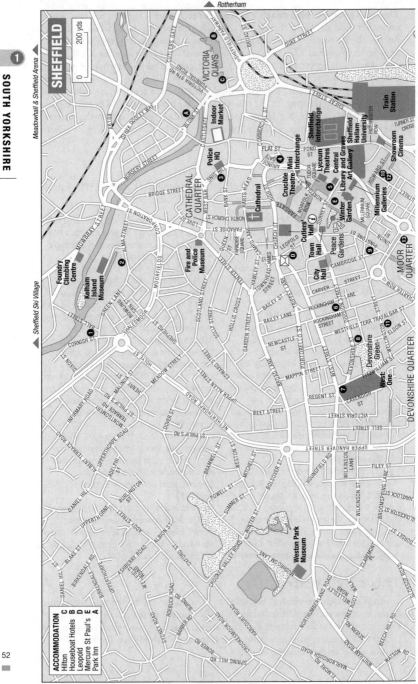

SOUTH YORKSHIRE

1

52

SHEFFIELD

0   200 yds

▲ Rotherham

◀ Meadowhall & Sheffield Arena

◀ Sheffield Ski Village

ACCOMMODATION
Hilton   C
Houseboat Hotels   B
Leopold   D
Mercure St Paul's   E
Park Inn   A

Foundry Climbing Centre
Kelham Island Museum
Fire and Police Museum
Police HQ
Indoor Market
CATHEDRAL QUARTER
Cathedral
VICTORIA QUAYS
Crucible Theatre
Mini Interchange
Sheffield Interchange
Police HQ
Lyceum Theatres
Central Library and Graves Art Gallery
Sheffield Hallam University
Train Station
Showroom Cinema
Millennium Galleries
Cutlers' Hall
Winter Garden
Town Hall
Peace Gardens
City Hall
Leopold
MOOR QUARTER
Devonshire Green
West One
DEVONSHIRE QUARTER
Weston Park Museum

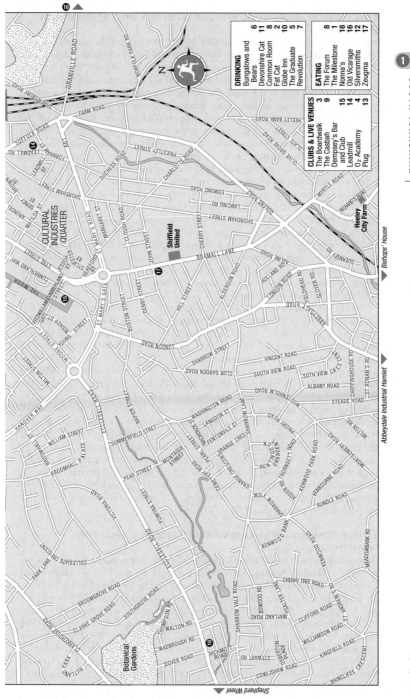

DRINKING
Bungalows and Bears	6
Devonshire Cat	11
Common Room	8
Fat Cat	2
Globe Inn	10
The Graduate	5
Revolution	7

EATING
The Forum	8
The Milestone	1
Nonna's	18
Old Vicarage	16
Silversmiths	12
Zeugma	17

CLUBS & LIVE VENUES
The Boardwalk	3
The Casbah	9
Dempsey's Bar and Club	15
Leadmill	14
O₂ Academy	4
Plug	13

Bishops' House ▼

Abbeydale Industrial Hamlet ▼

Shepherd Wheel ▲

The Peace Gardens, Winter Garden and Millennium Galleries

Since the wrong turnings and dead ends of the 1960s, Sheffield has had a stylish heart transplant, provided appropriately by the Heart of the City Project from 1994 onwards. The Peace Gardens and Winter Garden between them form an all-weather oasis of calm, an eye in the centre of the city storm, and are thronged with people throughout the year. On sunny days the **Peace Gardens** (open all year; free), with huge bronze water features inspired by Bessemer converters pouring out molten steel, are crowded with people sitting on benches or on the grass. Kids strip off and run in and out of the pulsing jets of the pavement-level fountain, or float paper boats down the converging ceramic-lined rills (they represent the rivers that gave Sheffield steel mills their power), or giggle at their reflections in the surrounding steel balls that dribble water from their crowns. There's no nonsense about "Keep off the grass" or "Stay out of the fountains" – the Peace Gardens are there for the people of Sheffield to use and to enjoy.

Right next to them, the **Winter Garden** (daily 8am–6pm; free), a twenty-first-century version of a Victorian conservatory on a huge scale – all unvarnished, slowly weathering wood and polished glass – offers a different kind of experience. At 230ft long, 73ft wide and high, with over 2000 square yards of glass, it shelters fully grown eucalyptus trees and Norfolk pines, paths that wind through verdant jungle and benches beneath soaring trees. A delightfully warm place even in the depths of winter, it is kept cool in summer by a complex arrangement of automatically controlled fans and vents.

Next to the Winter Garden, and opening into it, are the *Mercure St Paul's Hotel* on one side (see p.51), and the **Millennium Galleries** (Mon–Sat 8am–5pm, exhibitions open 10am, Sun 11am–5pm; free; ℡0114/278 2600, ⓦwww.museums-sheffield.org.uk) on the other. Although a separate building fronting onto Arundel Gate, the Millennium Galleries' link with the Winter Garden is seamless, with a long corridor flanked by a series of display rooms. The **Ruskin Gallery** contains a collection of books, art and other artefacts assembled by the great nineteenth-century critic John Ruskin as part of his drive to alleviate the suffering of the industrial poor through art and education. The **Metalwork Gallery** features not only the city's collection of priceless silver and stainless steel, but also hands-on displays explaining the processes and development of the steel industry. The final two galleries provide a flexible space for visiting exhibitions. In the corridor is an extensive shop, and an amusing interactive statue of a multi-headed monster, made entirely of cutlery, operated by three push-buttons, guaranteed to fascinate kids. At the end of the corridor an escalator drops down to Arundel Gate and the pleasantly Mediterranean-feeling **Café Azure** (Mon–Sat 8am–5pm, Sun 11am–5pm; ℡0114/278 2633).

Tudor Square, the Graves Art Gallery and the theatres

As you come out of the Winter Garden into Surrey Street, ahead lies the recently remodelled **Tudor Square**, flanked on the right by the Central Library and Graves Art Gallery and the Lyceum Theatre, ahead by the Crucible Theatre, and on the left by several bars. The Central Library and Graves Art Gallery is the only part of a proposed 1920s redevelopment of the square that was ever actually built. It has an imposing Beaux Arts facade and many understated Art Deco details. The **Graves Art Gallery** (Mon–Sat 10am–5pm; free; ℡0114/278 2600, ⓦwww.museums-sheffield.org.uk) is on the top floor of the library building, and is based on the collection of local mail-order magnate and philanthropist **J.G. Graves**. The collection includes paintings by Turner, Cézanne, and Burne-Jones, more contemporary works such as Marc Quinn's *Kiss* and Sam Taylor-Wood's *Self Portrait Suspended VII*, and some really excellent visiting exhibitions. The two **theatres** are each interesting in their own way – the **Crucible** for its modern and the **Lyceum** for its traditional architecture (see p.54).

Fargate and Orchard Square
Left across Norfolk Street, a walk up pleasantly pedestrianized Norfolk Row past the well-stocked **tourist information centre** (see p.51) brings you to the city's main shopping street **Fargate**. Wide, busy, traffic-free, it hosts all sorts of temporary structures such as amusement park rides (at the time of writing it was the 197ft-high **Sheffield Wheel**) and usually echoes to the sound of buskers, *Big Issue* sellers, political rallies and so on. At its southern end stands the imposing **Town Hall** (appropriately topped with the figure of the god Vulcan), which backs onto the Peace Gardens. Opening off Fargate is **Orchard Square**, a highly successful 1987 development that manages to blend old and new buildings into an agreeable public space, which includes a pub and shops around a modern clock tower out of which, when the clock strikes the hour, working figures of male and female knife-grinders rotate – a modern spin on a medieval tradition.

The Cathedral and Cutlers' Hall
Across the top of Fargate cuts another main shopping drag, Church Street/High Street, this one loud with trams and buses, with Sheffield Cathedral standing over it. The **Cathedral Church of St Peter and St Paul** (Ⓦwww .sheffield-cathedral.co.uk for details of recitals and tours), to give it its full title, was a simple parish church before 1914, and subsequent attempts to give it a more dignified bearing have frankly failed. It's a mish-mash of styles and changes of direction, and you'd need a PhD in ecclesiastical architecture to make any sense of it. However, the magnificent **Shrewsbury Chapel**, at the east end of the south isle, is definitely worth a look. Built around 1520, it contains the tombs of the fourth and sixth earls of Shrewsbury, whose detailed alabaster effigies adorn their tombs. The fourth earl's likeness lies between effigies of his two wives, Anne and Elizabeth, all dressed in sumptuous Elizabethan costume. The sixth earl, in full armour, lies alone – he became estranged from his second wife Bess of Hardwick, partly perhaps because of the strains of the task he was charged with by Elizabeth I – looking after Mary Queen of Scots during her long captivity. The area in front of the cathedral is paved with gravestones, many, it will be noted, dating from the 1830s when Sheffield suffered a major cholera epidemic.

Across Church Street from the cathedral stands the imposing, not to say pompous, **Cutlers' Hall** (Ⓣ0114/276 8149, Ⓦwww.cutlers-hall-sheffield.co.uk), built to celebrate the Company of Cutlers, a craft guild started in the seventeenth century to regulate the city's leading industry. This is the third and last of Sheffield's cutlers' halls, built in 1832, and it contains a series of luxurious reception rooms, lobbies, banqueting halls and the Master Cutler's room, furnished with, among other things, the panelling and chandeliers from the White Star liner *Olympic*. The hall is still used for great civic and business events, including the annual Cutlers' Feast, and is not open to the casual visitor.

Paradise Square
Behind the cathedral, sloping downward off Campo Lane, is **Paradise Square**, as beautiful an ensemble of Georgian houses as can be found anywhere. Despite its coherence and harmony, it is actually the result of two separate building periods and much renovation, though none the worse for that. The square has housed at

Sheffield iron and steel

Sheffield was known for its production of **steel** as early as the Middle Ages – it is mentioned in Chaucer's *Canterbury Tales*. Two types of expensive, high-quality steel – **blister steel** from the seventeenth and **crucible steel** from the eighteenth centuries – were made in Sheffield, with manufacture tending to congregate along the fast-flowing streams coming down from the Peak District into the west of the city. Cutlery and weapons that were "Made in Sheffield" were renowned for their quality throughout the world. Then, in the nineteenth century, the development of the Bessemer and Open Hearth processes of producing cheap steel in large quantities by burning all the impurities out of the pig iron, then adding the correct amount of carbon, moved the industry to the east of the city, where steel for buildings, railways, shipping and so on was manufactured. Such steelworks as remain are still to be found on the eastern side of the city.

various times the doctor who delivered Queen Victoria, a Freemasons' Lodge and a home for fallen women, and various public speakers have used the slope of the square to address large crowds – John Wesley preached from the balcony of no.18, and Chartist orators inspired large crowds here during the 1830s and 1840s.

Fire and Police Museum

North of Paradise Square, on the roundabout between West Bar and West Bar Green, is the **Fire and Police Museum** (Sun 11am–5pm; ☎0114/249 1999, ⓦwww.firepolicemuseum.org.uk) housed in an old (1900) fire station – the doors through which the fire-engines once thundered are still there. Though niche, and with limited opening hours, the enthusiasm with which it's run is appealing. There's a café and shop, and lots of fire and police vehicles, equipment, uniforms and other artefacts.

Kelham Island Museum

To appreciate the world importance and vast scale of Sheffield's historic steel industry a visit to the **Kelham Island Museum** (Mon–Thurs 10am–4pm, Sun 11am–4.45pm; £4; ☎0114/272 2106, ⓦwww.simt.co.uk) is a must. Sitting on an artificial river island just north of the city centre, off Alma Street, and housed in what was, until the 1930s, the generating station that supplied power to the city's trams, you get an immediate taste of what's in store as you pass the colossal Bessemer converter that stands guard over the entrance. Inside, displays explain the development of steel production, from blister and crucible steel through the Bessemer and open-hearth processes to the modern electric arc furnace. Additional displays cover every aspect of steel production and the vast array of things that were "Made in Sheffield". Exhibits vary from a tiny exhibition "Year Knife" (it has 365 blades) to one of Barnes Wallis's gigantic "Grand Slam" World War II earthquake bombs which, with its tail fin, was over 22ft long and weighed ten tonnes. Other highlights include an early flush toilet invented by Joseph Bramah (1748–1814), a hydraulic press also developed by him for Royal Ordnance map-making, and the magnificent Sheffield Simplex roadster, built in 1920 to challenge Rolls Royce's stranglehold on the luxury motor car market. The star of the collection, though, is undoubtedly the **River Don engine**, the most powerful surviving steam engine in Britain. As high as a three-storey house, it was built in 1905 and has been used at different times in the production of armour plate, nuclear reactor shields and North Sea oil rigs. You can see it in steam at noon and 2pm (and Sun 4pm), a magnificent combination of power, economy and elegance, a symphony in hissing stream and ringing metal. There's also an audio-visual presentation which outlines the development of Sheffield (every hour 10.30am–2.30pm), a museum shop, and (across the way from the main entrance) a **café** which offers a range of hot meals and snacks.

Outside the centre

There are a few interesting attractions away from the city centre, but easily accessible by car or bus. Several are connected to the city's industrial heritage, while others make a good escape from the bustle of the city.

Abbeydale Industrial Hamlet

On the A621 southwest of the city centre, **Abbeydale Industrial Hamlet** (buses #97, #98 & #218; Mon–Thurs 10am–4pm, Sun 11am–4.45pm; free; ℗0114/236 7731, ⓦwww.simt.co.uk) is an industrial museum which is the equal of, but very different from, Kelham Island. An early steel-making community, preserved more or less complete (and donated to the city by J.G. Graves, of Graves Art Gallery fame), it sits on the banks of the river Sheaf. Powered by four water wheels (though there was a secondary steam engine from 1855), it was a sort of one-stop-shop for scythe blades and other edged tools. All the processes needed for making steel and then using it to make edged blades took place on this one site. There's a crucible steel furnace where the steel was made. Beyond it, a tilt forge built in 1785 consists of two huge tilt hammers, driven by the main waterwheel, used to make blades, sandwiching the expensive steel edge between two layers of (much cheaper) wrought iron. A grinding hull of 6ft-high stones and two glazing stones, hung in water to keep them wet, sharpened the new blades, while a boring shop drilled holes in them for the rivets and a blacking shop painted them to prevent rust. Together with the manager's house, the counting house and workmen's cottages, the whole cluster of buildings form what the Pevsner guide calls a "harmonious and picturesque group". Next to the works is the dam used as a reservoir to power the wheels, whose shores are now usually dotted with colourful anglers' umbrellas. The contrast between the dam and the works when it was in furious operation must have been startling. There's a café, a shop and ample car parking. Take care on wet days – the bricks underfoot can get very slippery.

Shepherd Wheel

In many ways more typical of Sheffield's early steel industry, the **Shepherd Wheel**, in Whiteley Woods just off Hangingwater Road (℗0114/236 7731, ⓦwww.simt.co.uk), was used to power just one process – sharpening cutlery. An 18ft-high wheel powered twenty grindstones and several glazing stones, which are all now contained in two restored workshops, together with all the tools of the trade. The wheel isn't easy to visit, there are no facilities and no parking, and it was shut for renovation at the time of writing. One for aficionados, then.

Weston Park Museum

North of the Shepherd Wheel, on the A57 out of the city, the **Weston Park Museum** (buses #51 & #52; Mon–Sat 10am–5pm, Sun 11am–5pm; free; ℗0114/278 2600) was a finalist in the Gulbenkian museum awards in 2007 and the *Guardian* newspaper's Family Friendly museum of the year in 2008. You can see why. A hugely varied collection of objects and interactive displays arising from Sheffield's history offer insights into all sorts of natural, scientific and artistic aspects of the city's life and times, and there are five "trails" for kids aged 4 to 11 to follow. There's a café, picnic area and toilets, and several activity areas.

Bishops' House

A rare survival from pre-Industrial Revolution Sheffield, and the city's best-preserved Tudor building (stone on the ground floor, half-timbered above), the **Bishops' House** (buses #44 & #53; April–Dec Sat 10am–4.30pm, Sun 11am–4.30pm; free; ☏0114/278 2600) occupies a corner of Meersbrook Park, just off the main A61 to Chesterfield about two miles from the city centre. Although some of the house dates from around 1500, its interiors owe more to the early seventeenth century, with oak panelling, wooden floors and ornate plasterwork. There's no evidence that bishops ever lived in the house – indeed, for many years before it became a museum in 1976, park keepers lived in it. Situated on a substantial hill above the city centre, the views from it of modern tower blocks contrast happily with the off-centre character of this lovely old building.

Heeley City Farm

Barely a mile north of the Bishops' House, **Heeley City Farm** (buses #32, #48 & #53 or walkable from the centre; daily 9.30am–5pm, 4.30pm in winter; free; ☏0114/258 0482, ⊛www.heeleyfarm.org.uk) is something of a surprise. You don't expect to find livestock and piles of manure in a pleasant suburb so close to a modern city centre – very *The Good Life*. A registered charity, the farm allows children (and adults) to get close to a variety of domestic animals, including poultry, large black pigs, Soay sheep, goats, an Exmoor pony and a cow. But it's not just a petting farm: it takes its responsibility to the environment very seriously. There's a peat-free **garden centre**, a **café** selling a range of delicious organic food, herb gardens and vegetable plots, renewable energy displays, a **children's playground**, and information about recycling and composting. It lacks the slickness of some commercial farm attractions, but is none the worst for that. And again, as with the Bishops' House, there are extensive views across the city centre which contrast intriguingly with the farm's animals, wellies and smellies.

Botanical Gardens

Opened in 1836 by the Sheffield Botanic and Horticultural Society, the nineteen acres of the **Botanical Gardens** (buses #22, #82 & #83; summer Mon–Sat 8am–7.45pm, Sat & Sun 10am–7.45pm; winter Mon–Fri 8am–4pm, Sat & Sun 10am–4pm; free; ☏0114/268 601, ⊛www.sbg.org.uk) were designed along Gardenesque principles – with an informal layout – on a site that slopes down from the main entrance on Clarkehouse Road to other entrances on Thompson and Botanical roads. Following a £7million restoration, the gardens and their associated buildings are now in mint condition, and they're a delight. A series of themed plots, including Rose, Woodland, Prairie and Asia gardens, intersperse lawns and meandering paths, and interest is added by a bear pit, a statue of Pan, and a fossilized tree. Like a diamond tiara across the top of the gardens stand the superb **pavilion glasshouses**, consisting of a central seven-bay pavilion flanked by two of three bays. Within the classically columned main entrance to the gardens is a gift shop, and next to it, in the Curator's House, a café with an attractive terrace. There is, however, no parking, so you'll have to hunt for on-street parking near one of the three entrances, or get there by bus.

Eating and drinking

Sheffield has become a regional centre for eating and drinking, with lots of choice; **Ecclesall Road** in particular has a cluster of places that attracts the city's students. As is true elsewhere in the country, the division between places to eat and places to drink is becoming blurred – with most of the pubs listed, for example, serving food as well.

Cafés and restaurants

Forum 127–29 Devonshire St ☎0114/272 0569, ☺www.forumsheffield.co.uk. A vibrant mixture of bar, café, music venue and boutique mall, the *Forum* has a lively clientele of students, office workers and shoppers who use it as a breakfast bar, lunch spot, after-work drinks bar and evening eatery, comedy club and disco. Daily 10am–1am, Fri & Sat till 2am, with snacks and main meals till 10pm (8pm Sat & Sun), most priced between £5 and £10. Choice of three areas – main bar, sunny conservatory, and multi-hued terrace overlooking Devonshire Green – with deck chairs during the summer. Check out the website for specialist evenings, music nights, comedy club and barbecues.

Milestone 84 Green Lane ☎0845 201 3179 or 0114/272 8327, ☺www.the-milestone.co.uk. Close to Kelham Island, and in an attractive listed building, the award-winning *Milestone* offers gastropub and upmarket restaurant menus at reasonable prices, with pub starters around £5 and main courses £10, or a taster menu for £34.95; the upstairs restaurant is £25 for two courses, £30 for three. All meat is locally sourced, all vegetables fresh and seasonal, all food home-made, and the whole place has a lovely atmosphere. You can also attend cocktail and cookery classes.

Nonna's 535–541 Ecclesall Rd ☎0114/268 6166 (ext 1), ☺www.nonnas.co.uk. Since it opened in 1996, *Nonna's* has become a Sheffield institution. With a long bar, café, two restaurant rooms and a delicatessen, on the lively, student-dominated Ecclesall Rd, *Nonna's* is the place to be seen throughout the day. Prices are moderate – antipasti at around £5–6, secondi from £12 to £18 – and the atmosphere noisy, informal and congenial.

Old Vicarage Ridgeway Village ☎0114/247 5814, ☺www.theoldvicarage.co.uk. As the only Michelin-starred restaurant in the region, the *Old Vicarage*, out in Sheffield's southeast suburbs, is not cheap, though set menus – two courses for £30, three for £40 at lunchtime, four-course dinner menu for £60, or a seven-course tasting menu for £65 – makes it less daunting. Beautifully housed in (yes) an old vicarage, the atmosphere, food and wine are all spot on, making it a wonderful venue for a special occasion.

Silversmiths 111 Arundel St ☎0114/270 6160, ☺www.silversmiths-restaurant.com. A "kitchen nightmare" turned around in 2008 by Gordon Ramsay, city-centre *Silversmiths* supplies top-notch Yorkshire food from locally sourced ingredients in a 200-year-old ex-silversmith's workshop. Menu changes weekly or fortnightly, depending on season – look out for venison sausages and pies or spinach tart with Yorkshire

Blue cheese. Tuesday is pie night (£8.50) and there's a three-course set menu from Wednesday to Saturday (£15). Tues–Thurs 5.30–11.30pm, Fri & Sat 5.30pm–midnight. Reservations recommended.

Zeugma 146 London Rd ☎0114/258 2223, ☺www.zeugmaiki.com. Cracking Turkish restaurant within a stone's throw of Sheffield United's football ground. Known for big portions, lively atmosphere and a good selection of grilled meats done on open grills, the restaurant's success has been such that there are now two restaurants (the other is *Zeugma Iki*, ☎0114/275 6666), both on London Road. Prices are reasonable – main courses from £8 to £12, wine at £10.95 to £13.50, or you can take your own bottle for £2.95 corkage.

Pubs and bars

Bungalows and Bears Old Fire Station, 50 Division St ☎0114/279 2901, ☺www.bungalows andbears.com. A bar situated in an old fire station, populated by comfy sofas and floor-to-ceiling mirrors. An ideal venue for a daytime drink and bite to eat, or an off-the-wall retro start to a night. DJ nights are a regular feature, along with jumble sales and even knitting lessons.

Common Room *The Forum*, 127–29 Devonshire St ☎0114/280 8221, ☺www.common-room.co.uk. Thirteen full-sized American pool tables, and a quiz and nine-ball knockout competition every Monday. Wednesday is student night and there's a pool competition on Sunday nights.

Devonshire Cat Wellingtons St, off Devonshire Green ☎01142/796 700, ☺www .devonshirecat.co.uk. Big, busy and functional, the *Devonshire Cat* is all about beer. It offers a dizzying range of draft and bottled beers, ciders and barley wines from all over the world, together with robust food – burgers, steaks, sandwiches and pub favourites like fish and chips, with prices ranging from £6.50 to £13. Strategically placed between Sheffield's two universities but not confined to a student clientele, it can be chaos at weekends and on weekday nights, but pleasant and good value for the rest of its 11.30am–1am opening hours.

Fat Cat Alma St ☎0114/249 4801, ☺www .thefatcat.co.uk. Stepping into the *Fat Cat*, just around the corner from the Kelham Island Museum, is like travelling back in time. Bought by real ale enthusiasts in 1981 after a brewery sell-off, it is now a Sheffield institution which offers a wide range of bottled and draft beers, ciders and country wines, and a hearty pub-grub menu (meals around £4.50). With its open fires, polished mahogany bar and etched mirrors, and its total absence of flashing gaming machines and piped music, this is pub-going as it used to be.

1

The Globe Inn 54 Howard St ☎0114/276 3124. Situated directly opposite Sheffield Hallam University, this is inevitably an archetypal student pub. Rock music and cheap, basic solid offerings of food and drink – even cheaper if you can obtain one of their yellow student cards. Daily noon–12.30am.
The Graduate 94 Surrey St ☎0114/275 3767. With the chosen name, you can guess the target market.

Pool, cheap drinks and a good Sunday lunch – if you can handle the simultaneous pub quiz.
Revolution 1 Fitzwilliam St ☎ 0114/273 9469, ⊛www.revolution-bars.co.uk. Lots of leather, polished wood and vodka, just as you would expect from this higher-quality chain vodka bar. Quite pricey, unless you're a member of their loyalty scheme.

Nightlife and entertainment

Sheffield is by far the best place in South Yorkshire to seek out nightlife. Not only do the students of its two huge universities ensure a good range of **pubs** and of top **live music venues** – as you'd expect from the city that produced the Arctic Monkeys, Pulp, Richard Hawley (plus of course Def Leppard) to name just a few – but the city's healthy social and intellectual mix supports a fine regional theatre in the **Crucible** and a flourishing independent cinema in the **Showcase**. For what's on at **Sheffield Arena**, see ⊛www.motorpointarena.co.uk.

Theatre and cinema

The Crucible Tudor Square ☎0114/249 6000, ⊛www.sheffieldtheatres.co.uk. Next to the Lwyceum, opened in 1971 and was granted Grade II status in 2008. It offers not only theatrical productions, but is also the home of the annual World Snooker Championships. Despite a £15million refurbishment followed by a 2010 reopening, the essential nature of its auditorium – a thrust stage surrounded by seating on three sides – remains.

The Lyceum Theatre Tudor Square, same phone number and website as the Crucible. Built in the 1890s, this late Victorian gem, is the only work of theatre and music hall designer W.G.R. Sprague to survive outside London (his most famous theatre is the Aldwych), and is all gilded rococo plasterwork and plush boxes inside, and decorated stucco on the outside. The Lyceum hosts touring West End and Opera North productions, as well as plays put on by local companies.

Showroom Cinema 7 Paternoster Row ☎0114/276 3534, ⊛www.showroomworkstation.org.uk. Independent cinema and creative hotbed located near Sheffield train station in a beautifully renovated 1930s structure. Shows a range of offerings from current film releases to classic cinema, family films and the best cinema from around the world. Festivals and special screenings provide a regular and welcome trip off the beaten track of the mainstream film. Box office opens from 10am, Sat & Sun 10.30am. Café/bar Mon–Thurs 10am–11pm, Fri 10am–midnight, Sat 11am–midnight, Sun noon–10.30pm. Food served Mon–Sat until 9pm, Sun noon–4pm.

Live music and clubs

The Boardwalk 39 Snig Hill ☎0114/279 9090, ⊛www.theboardwalklive.co.uk. Popular venue for indie bands, rock, folk and blues.
The Casbah 1 Wellington St ☎0114/275 6077. As in "Rock the…", which tells you what to expect – a stroll down punk/rock memory lane, with current indie and alternative nights as well.
Dempsey's Bar and Club 1 Hereford St ☎0114/275 4616, ⊛www.dempseys-sheffield .com. The best established gay venue in the city, licensed until the small hours.
The Leadmill 7 Leadmill Rd ☎0114/221 2828, ⊛www.leadmill.co.uk. Larger venue offering live music, as well as specific club nights on Fridays. Music spans funk to reggae, industrial to forged beats/krautrock on rotation through the month. Mondays and Thursdays are "Shag" – student night – featuring r'n'b and the pop chart in the main room, with indie, rock and punk in room two. Cheap drinks and free glow sticks.
O2 Academy 37–43 Arundel Gate ☎0114/253 7777, ⊛www.o2academysheffield.co.uk. Large live music venue catering to a wide audience from fans of Mika to The Pogues. As well as live music, the *Academy* hosts "Propaganda", a huge indie night running every Friday from 10.30pm till 3am.
Plug 14 Matilda St ☎0114/241 3040, ⊛www .the-plug.com. Mid-sized music venue featuring everything from live acoustic folk to diverse club nights, including the award-winning "Jump Around" every Thursday from 10.30pm. Watch out for the sloping tiles in the loo – they can make you feel drunk, even when you've not touched a drop.

Shopping

Sheffield has all the national chain stores and other shops you'd expect in the city centre, with top-end shops concentrated particularly along **Fargate** and **High Street** on one side of the Peace Gardens and budget alternatives along **The Moor** on the other, with large department stores dotted around on both sides. **Sheffield City Market**, suffering by being slightly outside the centre, has the air of having been left behind by the city's development, and, with two hundred stalls, is not in the same league as the markets in Rotherham, Doncaster and Barnsley. On the western side of city, around **Devonshire Green** and along **Ecclesall Road** as far as Hunter's Bar there are lots of boutiques and specialist shops.

Since it opened in 1990 on the site of a derelict steelworks, the **Meadowhall Centre**, three miles and an easy tram ride east of the centre, has dominated Sheffield shopping like a colossus, pulling in 30 million shoppers a year from all over the north of England. Blamed from the start for urban decay as far away as Scunthorpe, it was expected to decimate city centre shopping in the rest of South Yorkshire. Twenty years later, the jury's still out. With hundreds of shops under one roof, it's either Meadowheaven or Meadowhell, depending on your point of view. But even those who hate it find its weatherproof nature and free parking hard to resist. Meadowhall and the horribly named Valley Centertainment less than a mile away, between them have big stores, a multiplex cinema, a bowling alley and lots of fast food outlets.

Sport

Sheffield has, with reason, come to see itself as a sporting city. It boasts the oldest football club in the world (Sheffield FC), and two Championship clubs who have both seen better days.

Don Valley Stadium Worksop Rd ☎0114/223 3600, ⓦwww.donvalleystadium.co.uk. Not only the country's largest outdoor athletics venue, but also home to the Sheffield Eagles Rugby League club and, currently, Rotherham United FC.

Ice Sheffield Coleridge Rd ⓦwww.icesheffield.com. Has hosted many national ice-skating championships including British Ice Dance Championships and the British Ice Figure and Dance Championships. Open to the public for variety of different sessions for £3–5, family tickets £20.

Ponds Forge International Sports Centre Sheaf St ☎0114/223 3400, ⓦwww.ponds-forge.co.uk. Olympic-standard swimming and diving pools and sports hall within the city centre. Membership from £5.

Sheffield United (The Blades) Bramall Lane ☎0871 995 1889, ⓦwww.sufc.co.uk. Tickets cost £10–£34 at the gate, £1 extra if bought by phone or online.

Sheffield Wednesday (The Owls) Hillsborough ☎0871 900 1867, ⓦwww.swfc.co.uk. Tickets cost £18–£25; £2 extra if ordered by phone.

Mountain pursuits

As befits a city which lies partly inside the Peak District National Park, Sheffield has a number of centres at which you can hone your bouldering, rock-climbing, snowboarding or skiing skills.

Climbing Works Off Abbeydale Rd ☎0114/250 9990, ⓦwww.climbingworks.com. In a cluster of commercial buildings just off Abbeydale Rd, Climbing Works claims the biggest bouldering wall in the world, where your fee gives you a full day's access to the wall. There's a small café and a shop.

Foundry Indoor Climbing Centre ☎0114/279 6331, ⓦwww.foundryclimbing.com. A 10min walk from the city centre, just off junction 9 of the new inner ring road. Offers full climbs as well as bouldering – over 200 routes on 1000 square metres of climbing walls. There's a substantial café and a well-stocked climbing shop (Crag X). You must be experienced and will have to sign a form to that effect, or you can book ahead to receive instruction.

Sheffield Ski Village ☎0114/276 0044, ⊛www .sheffieldskivillage.co.uk. Up the hill beyond the Foundry and visible for miles around, Sheffield's Ski Village caters for everybody, from serious skiers and snowboarders wanting to sharpen their skills to complete novices wanting to learn. One of the largest artificial ski centres in Europe, it offers a range of slopes (two nursery slopes, a mogul field, half pipe and quarter pipe), snowtubing and tobogganing, together with non-snow-based activities like ten-pin bowling (eight lanes) and quad biking. There's also a terrific adventure playground, and a bar and restaurant. Parts of the complex look distinctly run down, but the combination of a variety of activities and wonderful views across the city make it a pretty good bet for families trying to please everybody.

Listings

Buses Traveline ☎01709/515 151.
Car rental Avis ☎0844 581 0014; Hertz ☎0114/276 0121.
Hospital Royal Hallamshire, with NHS Walk-In centre, Glossop Rd ☎0114/271 1900; Northern General, Herries Rd ☎0114/243 4343
Internet At Central Library, Surrey St ☎0114/273 4712 (Mon 10am–8pm, Tues & Thurs–Sat 9.30am–5.30pm, Wed 9.30am–8pm), and Mail Boxes Etc, Devonshire Green ☎0114/272 0777 (Mon–Fri 9am–5.30pm), behind *The Forum*.
Pharmacy Boots Market St ☎0114/256 9122.
Police West Bar ☎0114/220 2020.
Post office 234 Shoreham St or 248–50 West St.

Rotherham and around

ROTHERHAM developed in Saxon times as a market town at a ford across the River Don. During the Industrial Revolution it flourished as a coal and steel town. Today Rotherham looks like a typical victim of post-industrial decline – a quarter of a million people stranded by the ebbing economic tide, overshadowed by nearby (and resurgent) Sheffield, with high unemployment, social deprivation and manifest poverty. Being identified as somewhere that needs to be told how to eat by Jamie Oliver, how to read by Dolly Parton and how to dress by Gok Wan can't have helped the image either. Look deeper, though, and you'll see the great strengths of this indomitable community, with pride in its heritage, and an imaginative addressing of its problems.

Rotherham is certainly a mixed bag of a town. On the positive side the city has an impressive Gothic **Minster**, a couple of museums and the markets. Throughout the day the town centre is flooded with students from Rotherham College, and there's a lively outdoor pub-and-café society, even in the depths of winter, courtesy of the smoking ban. Furthermore, there's a huge and busy refurbishment going on – Rotherham Renaissance (⊛www.rotherhamrenaissance.co.uk) isn't just a grandiloquent title, it's a fact. On the downside, though, the architecture of much of the town centre can only be described as brutal yawn-to-horrible early postwar. And there's apparently no excuse – Rotherham largely escaped Sheffield's pounding by the Luftwaffe. Similarly, much of the town's hinterland has been scarred by heavy industry. Even potentially attractive features, like the views of multiple weirs as you cross the walkway over the Don to Tesco or the riverside walk, are tainted by litter and graffiti. But keep your wits about you – embedded in the mid-twentieth-century architectural tat you'll find gems like the **Imperial Buildings** (now being developed as a small café/bar/shop complex), next to the Minster, and the **Old Town Hall**.

And within the municipal borough boundaries and easily accessible from the town centre are England's largest country house, **Wentworth-Woodhouse**, the

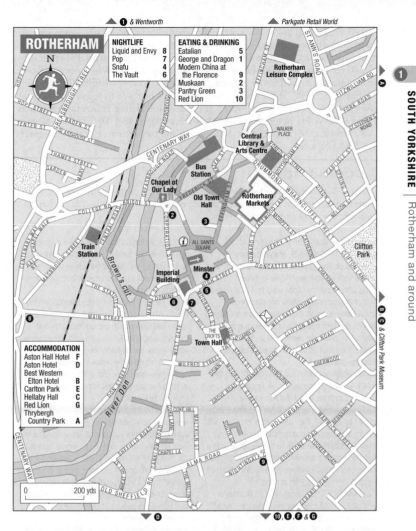

ROTHERHAM

NIGHTLIFE
Liquid and Envy	8
Pop	7
Snafu	4
The Vault	6

EATING & DRINKING
Eatalian	5
George and Dragon	1
Modern China at the Florence	9
Muskaan	2
Pantry Green	3
Red Lion	10

ACCOMMODATION
Aston Hall Hotel	F
Aston Hotel	D
Best Western Elton Hotel	B
Carlton Park	E
Hellaby Hall	C
Red Lion	G
Thrybergh Country Park	A

SOUTH YORKSHIRE | Rotherham and around

superb, multi-award winning science adventure centre, **Magna**, **Rother Valley Country Park** with its delightful cable waterskiing, the excellent **Tropical Butterfly House**, **Wildlife and Falconry Centre** and the atmospheric **Roche Abbey**. You're not going to visit Rotherham for its town centre, or for the beauty of much of its surroundings, but if you're in the area, or just passing through, there's a lot of other good stuff to see and do.

Arrival and information

Rotherham town centre lies in the angle between the M1 and the M18, and can be accessed from junctions 33 and 34 on the M1, or junction 1 on the M18. There is ample well-signposted **public parking** in the town centre, and visitors are strongly recommended to use it – one-way streets and pedestrianization make town-centre driving a nightmare. A well-organized **bus station** (Traveline

63

⊕01709/515 151) lies on the northern edge of the centre, with frequent services to surrounding towns and villages, and to Doncaster and Sheffield. Rotherham **train station** lies on the western edge of the town centre, separated from it by the River Don and accessible across the Chantry Bridge. While not itself on a main line, there are regular services from Rotherham to Sheffield (15min) and Doncaster (20min), from which connections can be made to towns and cities all over the UK. There's a well-stocked and helpful **visitor information centre** (Mon–Wed & Fri 9am–5pm, Thurs & Sat 9am–1pm; ⊕01709/835 904, ⊛www .visitrotherham.org) facing the Minster, on the corner where Bridgegate enters All Saints Square.

Accommodation

There is little **accommodation** in Rotherham town centre – most of the bigger hotels, which rely on corporate and private events and the passing trade rather than tourism, are close to motorway exits.

Aston Hall Hotel Worksop Rd, Aston ⊕0114/287 2309, ⊛www.tomahawk hotels.co.uk. An eighteenth-century country house a mile from M1 junction 31. Set in its own 55-acre park, with a recently added wing and total renovation of the rest, the facilities and decor in the individually designed and named rooms are superb. Much used for weddings (the parish church is right next door), corporate events and so on – some guests have found that during these staff can become stretched. ❸

Aston Hotel Britannia Way, Catcliffe ⊕0845 058 4745, ⊛www.astonhotels.co.uk. Not to be confused with the *Aston Hall Hotel*, the well-reckoned and recently built *Aston Hotel* is virtually on M1 junction 33. The hotel itself is excellent, with spacious rooms, relaxing bar and restaurant and clean uncluttered decor. More of a business than a holiday hotel, it is rather isolated in the middle of an industrial estate – if you don't have a car, you'll need to rely on taxis. Free parking. ❸

Best Western Elton Hotel Main St, Bramley ⊕01709/545 681, ⊛www.bw-eltonhotel.co.uk. A mile or so west of, and well signposted from, junction 1 on the M18. A popular, cosy, medium-sized family-run hotel in the old part of Bramley. Small bar and pleasant restaurant. Quiet (especially in the rear annexe), and within walking distance of local shops. Ample free parking and bus stop immediately outside. ❸

Carlton Park 102/104 Moorgate Rd ⊕01709/849 955, ⊛www.carltonparkhotel.com. Between M1 junction 33 and Rotherham town centre, just past

the General Hospital, the *Carlton Park* is clean, modern and comfortable, with bar and restaurant and small but comprehensive leisure facilities. Frequent buses (or a 15min walk) into town centre, and free parking. ❸

Hellaby Hall Old Hellaby Lane ⊕01709/702 701, ⊛www.hellabyhallhotel.co.uk Four-star luxury and seventeenth-century character two minutes east of the M18's junction 1. Smart understated decor and all the in-room, hotel-wide and health club bells and whistles you'd expect, at a surprisingly reasonable cost. Although next to an industrial estate, screened from it by attractive grounds. Free parking. ❹

Red Lion Sheffield Rd, Todwick ⊕01909/771 654, ⊛www.redlion-todwick.com. Early nineteenth-century farmhouse (oak beams, stone floors) a mile from M1 junction 31. Easy to get to and from by car, and there are regular buses to Rotherham and Sheffield. Comfortable and cosy, though Ye Olde Worlde decor a bit over done for some tastes. Negotiate tariffs, especially at weekends. Restaurant tables can be booked (recommended), or take pot luck. Free parking. ❸

Thrybergh Country Park Camping and Caravan Site Doncaster Rd ⊕01709/850 353. Off the main Rotherham–Doncaster road and attached to Thrybergh Country Park, the site has 24 caravan pitches (with electricity) and twelve tent pitches, and a shower and toilet block. Small visitor centre and café next to the site. Regular buses into Rotherham and Doncaster town centres from immediately outside the site.

The Town

Rotherham's magnificent **Minster** stands imperiously above **All Saints Square** and, indeed, the rest of the town centre. Other highlights include the **Crofts**,

Clifton Park, with its truly superb children's playgrounds and odd-but-attractive **Clifton Museum**, a welcoming **Arts Centre**, a rare bridge-chapel and the locally renowned and lively **Rotherham Markets** – indoor, outdoor and, on certain days, on the streets.

Rotherham Minster – the Church of All Saints

"The best work in the county" according to Simon Jenkins, **Rotherham Minster** (daily 9am–4pm, Wed & Sat closes at 1pm; refreshments 10.30am–noon) dominates the centre of the town – its 180ft-high spire, topped by a 7ft-high gilded weather vane, is a useful navigational aid. Though churches have occupied the site for at least a thousand years, in its current Perpendicular Gothic form it dates from the early fifteenth century. The Minster is welcoming to visitors, with a coffee bar to the right, a clear, easily absorbed history of the church to the left as you enter through the porch, and a useful single-sheet guide. Look out for Green Men hidden among the stone foliage at the top of the pillars in the nave, the attractive "wine glass" pulpit dating from 1604, and in the chancel the poppyhead (bench end) carvings of nativity figures (Archangel Gabriel, Mary and Joseph, the Three Wise Men) dating from 1480. Look too at the 77 individually carved oak roof bosses in the nave, the great 1420 fan-vault under the tower, and the organ, installed in 1777 by star organ builder Johann Snetzler, with an impressive black and gold case and – a Snetzler signature – a keyboard with the black and white keys reversed.

The Crofts

Behind the Minster, at the top of Moorgate Street and easily missed, lies **the Crofts**, an open area that was once Rotherham's main cattle market. Now a pleasant paved square with two reasonable pubs, the *High House* and *Cross Keys*, it was one of the region's biggest animal marts until the mid-nineteenth century, when it was first closed by an outbreak of rindpest (don't you hate it when that happens?), then eclipsed by the new market in Sheffield. The handsome building taking up its east side was built in the 1920s as the West Riding Courthouse and converted in the 1990s into Rotherham's **Town Hall**, outside of which is a reminder both of one of the town's great industries and of one of its greatest families. The **Walker Cannon**, an 8ft long muzzle loader weighing a tonne and a quarter, dates from between 1790 and 1820, and was made in the local factory of Samuel Walker and Company, one of Britain's premier gun manufacturers – at the time of the American Wars of Independence and the wars against France they produced a quarter of all the guns used by the Royal Navy, including 79 of the 105 guns aboard HMS *Victory*.

All Saints Square

Your first impression of **All Saints Square** is that it is an opportunity missed. Separated from the stately minster by low sandstone public toilets, the square certainly doesn't enhance the dignity of the church. Yet somehow it works. The discreet entrance to the toilets is flanked on one side by the vegetable racks of a greengrocer's shop, the other by the pavement customers of *Churchill's Café*. The rest of the square is thronged with people, all more in keeping with medieval town squares, perhaps, than the frozen perfection of more famous examples elsewhere.

Rotherham markets

At the other end of Effingham Street from All Saints Square lie **Rotherham markets** with **indoor** and **covered outdoor** sections housed in a bleak brick and concrete building (indoor: Mon–Sat 8.30am–5pm; outdoor: Mon, Fri & Sat 8.30am–4.30pm, though some stalls close earlier). There's also a weekly **street market** (Tues) and a monthly **farmers' market** (last Wed of the month) in

Effingham Street. Here again, the setting might be dowdy, yet the spirit is in keeping with Rotherham's nine-hundred-year history as a market town. Prices are incredibly low – dresses for a fiver, phones unlocked for £10, huge Desperate Dan breakfasts (at *Robert's* café) at £2.20. And get a look at the Smoking Joint ("Roll your own specialists") offering a bewildering choice of pipes, papers, tips, matches and lighters – for the smoking of unfashionable tobacco.

The Central Library and Arts Centre

Beyond the markets, the **Central Library and Arts Centre**, Walker Place (Mon & Thurs 9am–7pm, Tues, Wed & Fri 9am–5.30pm, Sat 9am–4pm) lies in yet another modern building the warmth of whose internal welcome seems to be at odds with its severe external functionality. Turn left in the main lobby and you come to the **art gallery** and beyond that the well-displayed collection of the **York and Lancaster Regiment**. Upstairs in the Central Library, while only residents can borrow books, all other services, including reference books, newspapers and magazines and internet access – are for everyone. It's a nice place to rest up, or take refreshment in the **café** on the same floor (Mon–Fri 9am–5pm, Sat 9am–3.45pm).

The Chapel of Our Lady

Along Frederick Street, past the bus station, it's worth a quick visit to the fourteenth-century **Chapel of Our Lady**, one of only three or four surviving medieval bridge chapels in the country. Said to have briefly housed Mary Queen of Scots (she did get about), it is now open only on Tuesdays (for communion at 11am) or by arrangement for weddings. It's an interesting building, though looking a little sad and neglected.

Clifton Park Museum

The history of **Clifton Park Museum** (Mon–Thurs & Sat 10am–5pm, Sun 1.30–4.30pm; free; ☎01709/336 633) is typical of many such municipal museums. Built in the 1780s for Joshua Walker (1749–1815), son of Samuel, founder of the Rotherham ironworks, and designed by John Carr of York, the house is Palladian in style and originally commanded fine views across the town. Rotherham Corporation bought it in the second half of the nineteenth century, turning the grounds into characteristically Victorian Clifton Park (see below) in 1891 and the house into a characteristically Victorian **Clifton Park Museum** in 1893. Today, courtesy of a 2005 make-over, it is a stimulating and child-friendly museum. Just to the left of the entrance is a small play room for young children (the Lion's Den), with, among other things, a stuffed lion called Nelson and a Victorian rocking horse. Throughout, good use is made of the inevitable miscellany of artefacts that it has inherited – a stuffed bear and pheasant, a canoe paddle from Papua New Guinea, odd shells, a piece of wrapping for a mummy. There's a wealth of information about Rotherham's history – the Walker ironworks and family, Ebenezer Elliot the Corn Law Rhymer, roads and canals and so on – and, a really nice touch, a series of "House Detective" boards explaining the function of each of the rooms, together with information about servants (name, title, duties) drawn directly on the walls. Facilities include a café, gift shop and toilets.

Clifton Park

An £8million 2009 refurbishment of **Clifton Park** funded from a variety of sources has turned what was a rather tired Victorian-style public space into a twenty-first-century gem. Within easy walking distance of the town centre, the park has been transformed as paths have been relaid, flower beds refreshed, the rock garden, bandstand and cenotaph renovated. Above all, a magnificent new **play area** has been built, with a series of interconnected zones for different ages – a modern playground for very young children, an impressive adventure playground area with high towers, a zip wire, tubular slides, suspension bridges and climbing frames, an exciting water play area for all ages (much of it interactive), and an amusement park. A number of woodland settings offer a variety of foresty activities – Enchanted Wood, Forest Fun, Wild Wood. There's also the opportunity to practise skateboarding and cycling skills at the Skate Plaza, and a pleasant place to just sit around, read or chat in the Chill Out Lounge. There's even a limited simulation of a beach holiday (A Day at the Dunes) – Rotherham's a long way from the coast. If you've got kids, it's the place to be.

Eating and drinking

Much of the **eating and drinking** in Rotherham town centre takes place in cafés and pubs, with a scattering of small restaurants as well.

Eatalian 29a High St ☎01709/820 150. Good Italian food, largely Neapolitan, in intimate surroundings (so it can feel a little crowded). Expect to pay around £15 for the meal, and wine starts at around £10 a bottle. No parking, as it's in the town centre. Evenings only, booking advisable on Fridays and Saturdays. Closed Sunday.

George and Dragon 85 Main St, Wentworth ☎01226/742 440. A lovely old pub in a lovely old village, the food at the *George and Dragon* is superior pub grub – Jamie Oliver uses it when filming in the area, apparently. Snug and cosy two-level bar downstairs, restaurant upstairs. Allow £13–15 per person for food, and wine starts at just under £12 a bottle. Children welcome, large garden. Some parking on yard at front.

Modern China at the Florence Moorgate Rd ☎01709/360 606. A short distance out from the Croft, *Modern China at the Florence* is well reckoned by locals, and provides the usual range of Chinese food in comfortable surroundings and with friendly service. Set menus start at £18.

Muskaan 3–5 Corporation St ☎01709/839 955. Specializing in Bangladeshi meat curries,

especially chicken and lamb tikka, and fish dishes – look out for begun fishwala and tandoori king prawn – in a smart modern interior, at reasonable prices. Starter and main course with drinks is likely to come to around £20. Evenings only (from 5.30pm onwards).

Pantry Green Red Lion Yard ☎01709/364 077. Tucked away behind the *Red Lion* (the entrance to the yard is on Effingham St), *Pantry Green* provides comfortable seating at which you can eat your sandwiches or baguettes, cooked meals or salads away from the bustle of the main thoroughfares. Closed evenings and Sundays.

Red Lion Sheffield Rd, Todwick ☎01909/771 654, ⓦwww.redlion-todwick.com. One of the northernmost of a chain of taverns run by Suffolk's Green King brewery, the *Red Lion* provides pub meals that are hearty in both size and quality but reasonable in price. Starters cost around £4, main courses £10, with frequent special offers – two meals for £9.95 for example. There's a pleasant, friendly atmosphere, with open fires, flagged floors and wooden panelling. Booking's recommended – it's a very popular restaurant.

Nightlife and entertainment

Though overshadowed by the big city nightlife and entertainment offered in nearby Sheffield, Rotherham still manages its own mix of sporting facilities and entertainment venues. As for theatre and the arts, check out what's on at the **Arts Centre and Studio Theatre** (see p.66) and the **Civic Theatre** (☎01709/823 640, ⓦwww .visitrotherham.org). Clubs, mostly clustered right in the town centre, include:

Liquid and Envy Main St ☎01709/558 344. Live music and resident and visiting DJs specializing in chart and dance music and r'n'b – Mondays are electro, bassline and bump'n'grind r'n'b. "Envy" is for over-25s on Saturdays. Good for cheap drinks.

Pop (formerly *Synergy*) Ship Hill ☎01709/720 124. A mix of nights throughout the week: "Elektrik Prom" every Monday provides r'n'b, commercial/ funky house and electro; Thursdays are home to "Urban Junkyard", with the indie/rock "High Voltage" in room two. "Disko Pop" every Friday gives you indie to pop in the main room, with upfront house in room two. Saturday nights feature dance, r'n'b and pop.

Snafu 22–30 High St ☎01709/836 991, ⓦwww .fubar-snafu.co.uk. A live rock venue which has an annual battle of the bands. Goth night is every second Thursday of the month, every Tuesday is

jam night. Live music every Friday and Saturday, with happy hour Monday to Friday 5–8pm.

The Vault 2–3 Domine Lane (formerly *Underground*) ☎01709/378 314. Resident DJs providing speed garage, house, and old-school anthems. Thursday is "Rock the Vault", featuring live bands and a diet of grunge, metal, emo and indie.

Shopping

Although Rotherham no doubt suffers from the proximity of Sheffield and of the huge Meadowhall shopping complex, it still manages a fair range of town centre shops. In addition, there's the flourishing **Rotherham Markets**, where prices of food, clothing and so on are rock bottom (see p.65), and **Parkgate Retail World** (Stadium Way, Parkgate) a mile from the town centre, a retail park at which all the big chains are represented.

Listings

Buses Traveline ☎01709/515 151.

Car rental Enterprise Rent-A-Car ☎0800 230 0218; Budget ☎01709/377 773; Hire Power ☎01709/522 227.

Hospital Rotherham General Hospital, Moorgate (☎01709/820 000).

Internet access Available in the Public Library in Walker Place (☎01709/823 621).

Pharmacy Boots, 10–12 Howard St (☎01709/365 671).

Post office 53 Wellgate (☎08457 223 344).

Sport and activities You can swim at Rotherham Leisure Complex (☎01709/722 555, ⓦwww .dcleisurecentres.co.uk), skate on an artificial ice rink at Virtual Ice (☎01709/830 011, ⓦwww .virtualice.co.uk), drive go-karts at Avago Karting (☎01709/578 707, ⓦwww.avagokarting.co.uk), waterski or water-board at Rother Valley Country Park (see opposite), walk or cycle on a variety of routes (maps available at the tourist centre) or play golf at one of eight courses within the borough.

Around Rotherham

Only thirty percent of Rotherham metropolitan borough actually counts as "urban", the rest being either semi-rural or rural. It is best defined by motorways, with the town and most of the attractions within the horseshoe bounded by the M1 and M18, but with an equal area, less liberally dotted with attractions, to the south and east.

Magna

Housed in an old steelworks on Sheffield Road, a couple of miles southwest of Rotherham town centre, a mile from the M1's complicated exit 34 and well sign-posted from both, **Magna** (bus #69 from Rotherham or Sheffield; daily 10am–5pm; adult £8.95, child £7.15, family tickets available; ☎01709/720 002, ⓦwww.visitmagna.co.uk) is far and away Rotherham's main tourist attraction, and its popularity is fully justified. A science adventure centre built in and around the giant decommissioned Templeborough steelworks, it combines imaginatively presented information about steel and the lives of the people involved in its production with hundreds of hands-on, interactive displays illustrating a whole range of scientific principles and effects.

Having entered through a cavernous, dark and echoing **Face of Steel**, designed to set the scene, you climb to a central walkway which travels the length of this colossal building. Along the walkway touch-screen computers fill you in on life among the steelworkers (in their own language, Yorkshire, with English subtitles), and "Steel Reveal" units explain the functions of the huge shadowy machines and equipment that you see around you – direct the beam of a powerful spotlight, and a concise illustrated explanation of what you're illuminating comes up on the attached screen.

From the walkway, a lift and stairs mounted in the **Transformer House** gives access, above and below, to four separate pavilions dealing with earth, air, fire and water. The highest of these, of course, is **air**, appropriately housed in an enormous blimp which floats up near the ceiling. Then comes **fire**, **water** and finally, in the basement, **earth**. There are hundreds of exciting interactive displays illustrating the principles of practical science – air cannons, speaking tubes, a hydrogen rocket, a hot air balloon, a fire tornado, blue whirlpool – and you can do hundreds of interesting things: have a steel-saver race using electromagnets to ferry cans, operate a JCB, blast rock in a quarry, fire water cannons, sit on a gyroscopic chair, and many many more. The *Fuel Restaurant* and *Energy Café* offer refreshment and there's a gift shop. Across the road from the entrance are a huge, modern children's playground (Sci-Tek) and water play area (Aqua-Tek). Plan for a whole day – you'll not only want to get full value for the stiffish entry fees, but you really will need it.

Rother Valley Country Park

Further south, and well signposted ten minutes west from the M1 (exit 31), **Rother Valley Country Park** (#29 bus, but it's a long walk from the bus stop; daily: summer [BST] 8.30am–8.30pm; winter [GMT] 8.30am–6pm; cars £3, disabled parking, minibuses and coaches free; ☎0114/247 1452, ⊛www.rothervalleycountrypark .co.uk) is another good bet for a full day out. Opened in 1983, the park was the result of the redevelopment of a large open-cast coal mine, and was designed not only to provide recreational facilities, but also to develop wildlife habitats and to control flooding. Extensive **footpaths** and **cycle tracks** encircle a series of lakes, a **watersports centre** offers bike, boat, canoe and windsurf rental (☎0114/247 1452), there's a grass skislope, a narrow-gauge railway, a play area for 2–14 year olds (Playdales: April–Sept daily 10am–6.30pm; Oct–March Sat, Sun & school holidays only, with earlier closing; £3.20, toddlers £2), **fishing** (day tickets: adults £3.50, concessions £2), a **golf centre** (☎0114/247 3000 for details), a **café** and an information point. The park also offers **cable waterskiing** (☎01142/511 717, ⊛www.sheffieldcable waterski.com) – it's one of the few places in the country that does. An electric cable (imagine a ski-lift that goes around a lake instead of up a mountain) pulls up to eight waterskiers or wakeboarders at intervals around a shallow lake, at speeds which can be varied from 16 miles/hr (beginners) to 36 miles/hr (experts). It's environmentally friendly, and costs a fraction of what you'd pay for speedboat-towed skiing. All equipment can be rented at the ski centre, and there are full facilities – toilets, changing rooms, showers, a café and even a campsite.

Tropical Butterfly House, Wildlife and Falconry Centre

Also off exit 31 of the M1 (the best bus from Rotherham is the #19A) but five minutes east instead of west, the **Tropical Butterfly House, Wildlife and Falconry Centre** (Easter–Sept Mon–Fri 10am–4.30pm, Sat, Sun & school holidays 10am–5.30pm; Oct–Easter daily 10am–dusk, school holidays 10am–5.30pm; adult £7.50, child £6.50; ☎01909/569 416, ⊛www.butterflyhouse.co.uk) may not exactly bear a snappy title, but it does exactly what it says on the tin. At its heart is the steamy **Tropical House**, warm and damp, with a bunch of snakes, birds, crocodiles, terrapins, frogs, insects, snails, crabs, bats, hedgehogs, and lush tropical greenery, as well as the huge variety of multicoloured butterflies that flap disconcertingly around your head. Look out in particular for the speckled caiman (it's a crocodile), the three iguanas that roam free, White's tree frog (it's brown, hardly moves, and looks surprised), the big, knobbly stick insects, giant African snails and hermit crabs, and the green tree python, pygmy hedgehogs and leathery fruit bats of the nocturnal room. Some of the insects are the stuff of nightmares – try the domino and death's head cockroaches, the scorpions, the assassin bugs – but it's altogether a riveting experience. When you arrive you're handed a list of events for the day – a parrot show, bird of prey display, ferret roulette, the chance to handle exotic species or even milk a goat.

Roche Abbey

From junction 1 on the M18 head for the pit village of Maltby. As you arrive, at the *White Swan*, bear right (signposted East Retford) and after a mile and a half, turn right down the cobbled lane to the car park. It's not that easy to find, but worth it. There are buses to Maltby (#2), but it's a half-hour walk from the village.

Established in 1147 by Cistercian monks from Northumberland, **Roche Abbey** (April–Sept Thurs–Sun 11am–4pm; adult £3, child £1.50; EH) is an unexpected delight – the medieval elegance of its Gothic remains, the intricate outline of its ground plan, bisected by a fast flowing stream, are set in parkland of ethereal loveliness.

It owes its beauty, oddly, to two acts of vandalism. First it was despoiled and looted in 1538, during the dissolution of the monasteries, when locals grabbed whatever was left after Henry VIII had taken first pick. Then, having been inherited by the Earl of Scarborough in the eighteenth century, it was developed by Capability Brown, who destroyed buildings, earthed and turfed over much of the site, and created the wonderful parkland that now surrounds it. Finally, excavation in the 1920s resurrected the remains of the abbey, revealing the winning combination of medieval ruins and elegant parkland.

After visiting the abbey, turn right and follow the fence onwards and to the right. This will take you on a delightful, fifteen-minute **walk** which includes a waterfall, stepping stones, a lake, and wonderful views of the abbey, bringing you back to the abbey entrance.

Wentworth

In the northwestern corner of greater **Rotherham** (bus #227), a couple of miles from the M1 (exit 35), the village of **WENTWORTH** seems a million miles away from Rotherham's urban sprawl. It makes for a visit that is both fascinating and frustrating. Fascinating not only for the obvious attraction of its stone-built houses and two lovely pubs – the **Rockingham Arms** and the **George and Dragon** (see p.67), both of which do excellent meals – its huge garden centre, craft workshops and Family Farm, but also because, just outside the village, stands what is thought to be England's largest stately home – **Wentworth Woodhouse**. Clear views of its 606ft-high frontage are possible from the footpath across its deer park, you can examine the renovated kitchen garden of the house (daily: April–Sept 10am–5pm; Oct–March 10am–4pm), now maintained by Wentworth Garden Centre, with its ornamental statues, maze and bear pit, and at various high points in the vicinity you can explore a number of the house's famous follies – **Hoober Stand**, the **Needle's Eye**, **Keppel's Column** and **Wentworth Mausoleum**.

What you can't do is visit the house itself – it's not open to the public. Why this is so is one of the twentieth century's most intriguing stories, involving the alleged mental illness of an elder son, a disputed birth in the wilds of Canada, and bitter squabbling between a host of family members, all of which led to the fall, after 1902, of one of England's richest and most august dynasties – the Fitzwilliams. You can get the lowdown on all this in *Black Diamonds* by Catherine Bailey – a terrific read.

Barnsley and around

Though old enough to have appeared in the Domesday Book, **BARNSLEY**'s rapid rise from small beginnings to regional prominence took place in the seventeenth century, and arose from its geographical position – it became an important meeting of the ways between the other South Yorkshire towns of Sheffield, Rotherham and Doncaster and those of what is now West Yorkshire, especially Leeds and Wakefield. Then, when the Industrial Revolution gathered impetus in the eighteenth and nineteenth centuries, it developed into a centre for the production of glass and more particularly for the extraction of coal – flanking the shield on the town's coat of arms are a glass worker and a coal miner. Despite the efforts of local firebrand Arthur Scargill, the coal industry has since disappeared, but Barnsley nevertheless retains one of the strongest senses of community in the region.

That Barnsley is somehow different from the rest of South Yorkshire seems to be widely accepted. Its speech is different, and is renowned for being impenetrable. If outsiders comment on the strength of a Barnsley resident's accent, they are likely to be told that, on the contrary, "it's posh for Barnsley". Barnsley's geographical location, up in the county's northern hills and away from the other three main conurbations, adds to this sense of separation.

The town itself expects few visitors, but it's well worth taking a look at this bustling and unpretentious place which caters well to its residents' needs. It's thronged most days with shoppers, families and students from its town-centre **Barnsley College**, a campus of the University of Huddersfield.

As with many towns hit by industrial decline and economic recession, regeneration and remodelling work is proceeding apace, with new office space and apartments springing up everywhere. Though the plans to become a sort of Tuscan hill town drawn up by architect Will Alsop in 2003 might have been the source of much mirth elsewhere in the country (or even in other Yorkshire towns), the Remaking Barnsley project is already underway. The thirty-year plan, some of which has already been completed, includes a glass palace housing the new council offices, the exciting **Civic building** to encourage the arts, a redeveloped transport interchange, planned development of the old (1933 and Grade II listed) **Town Hall** into a resource for the community (museum, archive, local history library and more), and above all, the rebuilding of **Barnsley Markets**, all hopefully transforming what was something of a dispirited post-industrial mess into a market town that works. Indeed, the Gateway Plaza development, which includes a hotel, bar and restaurant, is already complete. If the range of shopping on offer in Barnsley town centre comes as a surprise, so too does the beauty of the surrounding area, with a handful of worthwhile attractions (see p.75). As with other South Yorkshire towns you're unlikely to choose Barnsley for a main holiday, but honestly, you could do worse.

Arrival and information

Barnsley lies just east of the M1, about half way between Sheffield and Leeds. The town centre is only a mile from junction 37, but junction 36 can be used for the south of the borough, and 38 for the north. There's ample well-signposted **parking** throughout the town (free at weekends), and a new, efficient and architecturally interesting **transport interchange** on the northeast edge of the town centre which gives access to local and national travel by train, coach, bus and taxi. Although there's no staffed tourist information centre in the town, there's a room in the Civic Hall on Eldon Street that has a comprehensive selection of pamphlets about local attractions.

Accommodation

Apart from the *Barnsley Central Premier* located in the Gateway Plaza development, **accommodation** in the Barnsley area tends to be in chain hotels which rely on corporate and private events and the passing trade rather than tourism, and are close to motorway exits.

Barnsley Central Premier Gateway Plaza ☎0871 527 9204, ⓦwww.premierinn.com. Brand-new hundred-bed hotel, part of the town centre redevelopment; affordable cleanliness and comfort right in the heart of Barnsley town centre. Coffee shop and restaurant. ❷

The Bluebell Inn Elmhirst Lane, Dodworth ☎0871 200 2289, ⓦwww.newcountry inns.com. In Dodworth, the *Bluebell Inn* is an excellent budget option, especially if you've got children – there are family rooms with pull-out beds, the bar and restaurant are very child-friendly, and there's crazy golf in the car park. ❷

🏃 **Cubley Hall Inn** Mortimer Rd, Penistone ☎01226/766 086, ⓦwww.cubleyhall.co.uk. Just south of Penistone, *Cubley Hall* is a handsome, ivy-covered ex-moorland farm which has been converted into a delightful inn. Comfortable rooms with many Victorian features, popular pub, conservatory, bar food and carvery, with pleasant gardens, wrought-iron pavilion which is much featured in weddings, and lovely views. ❸

Greensprings Touring Park Just over a mile from M1 junction 36 ☎01226/288 298. *Greensprings Touring Park* has sixty pitches (22 caravan, 15 tent and 23 mixed) set in pleasant countryside. Pitches between £10 and £15. Open April–Oct.

Tankersley Manor Church Lane, Tankersley ☎01226/744 700, ⓦwww.qhotels.co.uk/hotels /tankersley-manor-barnsley.aspx. A seventeenth-century manor house, all mellow stone and oak beams, sitting in well-maintained grounds a couple of minutes off junctions 35A or 36 on the M1, with a high level of modern comfort, a choice of where to eat (*Manor* restaurant or *Onward Arms* bar), and a swimming pool and spa. Rooms are comfortable and tastefully done. ❹

The Town

There aren't many specific attractions in Barnsley's town centre – it's a practical, workaday kind of place – but everything is within walking distance. Dominating the town centre, and visible for miles around, is the impressive **Town Hall**, whose distinctive tower is a useful navigation aid. The new **Civic**, on the site of the old Civic theatre, offers a variety of performance art and creative display space, a venue for music and comedy and a very nice coffee bar/lounge, while the older and more traditional **Cooper Gallery** and **Lamproom Theatre** provide, respectively, art displays and drama productions. Surprisingly to an outsider, who might stereotypically think in terms of flat caps, mufflers and clogs, Barnsley is famous throughout the region for its high-end **clothes shops** – the **Arcade** has numerous boutiques, and at the heart of the town, taking up a considerable chunk of the centre, is the colossal **Barnsley Market**.

Barnsley Market

Barnsley has had a regular **market** (main and meat and fish Mon–Wed, Fri & Sat 8.30am–5pm; open market the same hours except closed Mon; Tues second-hand and collectibles, Sun car boot) ever since receiving royal approval in 1249, and the current one is, apart from the impressive list of celebrities who come from the area (most notably Michael Parkinson), the thing for which the town is most famous. A labyrinthine sprawl of 100 open, 119 semi-open and 110 indoor stalls sell meat, fish and vegetables, together with everything from books to bedding, fishing tackle to flowers, wigs to watches, home-brew equipment to homeopathic medicine, paste jewellery to picture frames to pet supplies, clothing to cooked foods to craft equipment. There's even a stall that just sells Barnsley memorabilia. There are numerous cafés and street food kiosks, and there's access to the **Alhambra** shopping mall next door (Mon–Sat 9am–5.30pm, Sun & bank holidays

10am–4pm), and also to a large multistorey car park. On Sundays stalls spill out onto nearby pedestrianized streets, parking is free throughout the town, and various street performers enliven the scene. The architecture may be modern, but the atmosphere is vibrantly medieval.

The Cooper Gallery

In a sympathetically modernized stone house on Church Street near the town hall, bearing a blue plaque with the name of the great railway engineer Joseph Locke, who attended the grammar school here, the **Cooper Gallery** (Mon–Fri 10.30am–4pm, Sat 10am–3pm; free; ☎01226/242 905) opened at the start of World War I to display the art collection of local philanthropist Samuel Joshua Cooper. While his collection of paintings by Corot, Ruskin and others still forms the heart of the gallery, works by Turner, Henry Moore, Vanessa Bell and Paul Nash are also now on view, and there are periodic exhibitions of contemporary works. There's also a café here.

The Civic

The Civic (Hanson St; ☎01226/237 000, ⓦwww.barnsleycivic.co.uk), built in 1877 but now completely remodelled, is a multi-use building designed to support creative activities within the town. It includes **The Assembly Room**, which hosts performances of all sorts, theatre, music, dance, comedy; the **Gallery@**, which puts on art exhibitions and has work-spaces for local artists; and the **Lounge at the Civic**, run by the Koffi Bean Company, which has built up a reputation for coffee (of course), cool surroundings and good food. The adjacent Mandela gardens, with water-wall fountain, open lawn and steel-rod benches, still looks a bit bleak, though it will be a pleasant congregating point when it has bedded in, and it's beautifully lit at night.

Eating and drinking

Arena Café/Bar The Arcade ☎01226/321 293. Choice of comfortable leather sofas or tables and chairs on two floors, and an all-weather outside seating area – you've still got the arcade roof over your head. Modern café decor, and a wide selection of food – sandwiches, light snacks, burgers, main courses and sizzlers, with a specials board that changes daily. Food comes in at £6–9.

Bistro Romano's Shambles St ☎01226/240 000. Traditional Italian restaurant, with starters at around £4, main courses between £11 and £16, and pizzas between £8 and £10. There's an early evening deal – starter and main course for £10.95. Takeaway service. Closed Sundays.

Chilli Indian Restaurant Market St ☎01226/290 333. Modern store-front restaurant at the end of traffic-free Market Street, the *Chilli* has clean, uncluttered lines, a good-value lunch menu (all meals under £5), and evening meals with starters at £5 to £8, main courses from £8 to £16, and six or seven vegetarian options for around £6.

The Corner Pin Wellington St. Particularly good, honest, solid pub, ideal for a pint and a hearty bite to eat. Food is a strong feature (served Mon–Sat 11am–3pm), as is the excellent service. Teeming, with a friendly regular feel on Saturdays, and steadily busy on Fridays and Sundays. The down-to-earth landlord and landlady make this pub a pleasure to visit any time.

Cubley Hall Cubley ☎01226/766 086, ⓦwww.cubleyhall.co.uk. On the edge of Penistone (see p.78), the *Cubley Hall* offers a wide range of sandwiches, snacks, pizzas and pasta dishes in the bar and conservatory at very reasonable prices – only the steaks exceed £10 – and carvery meals in the splendid setting (massive oak beams, slate floors, rustic furniture) of the restaurant (set price £9.75 a head).

Grille Steakhouse Market St ☎01226/294 333. Next door to the *Chilli*, and under the same management, the *Grille Steakhouse* has similar decor, though with slate instead of wood underfoot. Steaks cost from £18 to £25, other meats from £11.50 to £16.95, and there's a Sunday lunch menu – two courses for £8.50, three for £10.50.

The Lounge at the Civic Hansen St ☎01226/240 9250. Agreeable Koffi Bean Company lounge (there's another at the Cooper Gallery) providing good-quality coffee, friendly service (they ask how strong you want your coffee), and a small selection of delicious food at very reasonable prices – try one of their huge bacon baps, which, with a coffee, comes to £3. **Pinocchio's** New St ☎01226/770 121, ⓦwww .pinocchios-restaurant.co.uk. Highly reckoned locally for value, authenticity and friendly informal surroundings. *Pinocchio's* starters vary from an olive and asparagus dip at £3.50 to King Prawn Gamberoni a Zafferano at £7.25, and main courses from around £8–16.95. There's a children's menu from which children can eat free up to 7pm (one/ adult). Limited parking.

Rileys at the Rose and Crown Barnsley Rd, Hoylandswaine ☎01226/762 227. On the hill up through the village, the stone-built 1804 *Rose and Crown* is a gastropub with an excellent reputation. Imaginative sandwiches such as

sausage, black pudding and onion, with chips, and lunch menus (starters at around £5, main courses at around £10) are available during the day, and the evening à la carte menu has main courses that come in at around £10–17. Look out for two-for-one deals on most meals. All menus are stoutly English-with-a-twist made from largely locally sourced food. Some parking.

The Spencer Arms Cawthorne ☎01226/792 795, ⓦwww.spencerarms .co.uk. Beautiful, award-winning old (1720) pub in a pretty village. You can eat in the traditional beamed-and-panelled bar areas or in the linen-tablecloth luxury of the restaurant. Extensive lunch and à la carte menus, with pizzas, salads and desserts on the former (nothing's more than £10), and main courses on the latter starting at £12.50 (haddock and chips): top price, fillet of beef at £18.95. Extensive parking.

Nightlife and entertainment

As you'd expect in a town with university and further education colleges, both in the town centre, Barnsley has a lively pub and club scene, especially in the triangle defined by Shambles Street, Wellington Street and the relief road – *That 70s Bar*, the *Corner Pin* (see above) and *Soviet* are all cheek-by-jowl on Wellington Street, *The Jelly Bar* is on Shambles Street, and *Millstones* on Peel Street.

Two annual events dominate Barnsley's calendar – the **Summer Carnival and Mayor's Parade** in July, and the **All Barnsley Diversity Festival** in September and October (for details phone ☎01226/787 771).

Clubs

Escapades 27 Wellington St ☎01226/293 000, ⓦwww.clubescapade.co.uk. Two-room venue with a total capacity of two thousand, five bars and an open terrace, which puts on a mixture of dance club, r'n'b and party on Saturdays, Fridays and Wednesdays, and has a retro and revival night on Sundays.

Funny Gals Wellington St ☎01226/321 532. The place to go for drag acts, comedy and lively entertainment.

The Lucorum Hanson St ☎01226/299 921, ⓦwww.lucorum.com. Bar, cocktail bar and nightclub next to the Civic, which offers a mix of DJs, live music and special events, student nights on Wednesdays, live indie bands on Fridays, and baseline and funky house on Saturdays.

Theatre and cinema

Assembly Room Hanson St ☎01226/237 000, ⓦwww.barnsleycivic.co.uk. Venue at the Civic which hosts performances of all sorts including theatre, music, dance and comedy.

Lamproom Theatre At the top of Westgate ☎01226/200 075. In what was a Nonconformist chapel, a Grade II listed building dating from 1780. The side of the building fronting the road doesn't look like much, but the opposite side is a delight. The theatre hosts a variety of performances, from national professional tours to local amateur dramatics, "Evenings with…" and pantomimes. There's a theatre bar on performance nights, and parking in the car park across the road is free after 6pm.

Parkway Cinema 62–68 Eldon St ☎01226/248 218, ⓦwww.barnsley.parkwaycinemas.co.uk. Something of a rarity these days, Barnsley has a small (two-screen) town centre cinema.

Shopping

In addition to all the national chains represented in the town centre, and apart from the star in Barnsley's shopping firmament – the markets and the Mall next door – there are numerous independent designer clothes shops in the town centre (especially the two most famous clothing shops **Frank Bird Menswear** in The Arcade and **Pollyanna**, on Market Hill).

Listings

Buses Traveline ☎ 0871 200 2233.
Car rental Blue Line Taxis (Barnsley) Ltd ☎ 01226/244 444, Bob's Taxis ☎ 01226/240 222, AA Taxis ☎ 01226/245 555, A1 Taxis ☎ 01226/200 000, Elite Taxis ☎ 01226/298 888, Regency Taxis ☎ 01226/201 111.
Hospital Barnsley Hospital, Gawber Rd ☎ 01226/730 000.
Internet Free access available at Barnsley Central Library, Shambles St ☎ 01226/773 931.

Sports and activities Just outside the town centre, the Metrodome (Queens Ground, Queens Rd; ☎ 01226/730 060, ⊛ www.themetrodome.co.uk) offers a comprehensive range of sports, fitness equipment, a leisure pool with wave machine and white-knuckle rides.
Pharmacy Boots, 34–40 Cheapside ☎ 01226/282 616.
Post office Pitt St ☎ 0845 722 3344.

Around Barnsley

If you decide to visit any of the attractions in the countryside around Barnsley – **Monk Bretton Priory** just east of the town, the gorgeous gardens around **Wentworth Castle**, stately **Cannon Hall** with its museum, grounds and walled gardens, **Cannon Hall farm** next to it, the industrial museums at **Worsbrough Mill** and **Elsecar**, the attractive hill villages of **Cawthorne** and **Penistone** – you'll take country lanes across rolling landscapes with hill-top churches and great swathes of deciduous woodland, much taken advantage of, and added to, by the landscapers of the great estates.

Monk Bretton Priory

Just a mile east of the town centre (buses #31, #57, #59) **Monk Bretton Priory** (daily 10.00am–3pm; free; EH) is one of the few Cluniac monasteries in England. A tenth- to twelfth-century back-to-basics breakaway Benedictine group, the Cluniacs were pledged to clean up the order and rid it of corrupt practices such as the buying and selling of religious office (simony) and openly sexual relationships between monks and women (concubinage). Run by English Heritage, the site has a ground plan that is easy to follow, and the remains of a later, fifteenth-century gatehouse. There's an excellent single-sheet guide to the priory, available from the Civic Hall, which not only tells you what you're looking at, but also fills in a lot of detail about the daily routine of the monastery, how monks joined the order, and much else.

The Maurice Dobson Museum and Heritage Centre

About three miles further east on the main road to Doncaster (A635), the **Maurice Dobson Museum** (Wed 1–4pm, Sat 10am–2pm; Easter–Oct also Sun 2–5pm; Maurice Dobson room free, £1 for other two rooms; ☎ 01226/753 440, ⊛ www.darfield.co.uk) in **DARFIELD** is one of several village museums set up under an initiative by Barnsley Municipal Council. While not worth a special trip, it's an interesting half hour if you happen to be passing during the museum's very restricted visiting hours. And it's not just the miscellaneous memorabilia on show – of the mining industry, World War I, domestic and village life and so on – that attract, but the local interest and pride that fired its establishment.

Worsbrough Mill Museum and Country Park

Two and a half miles south of Barnsley, **Worsbrough Mill** at Worsbrough Bridge (April–Oct Mon–Wed, Sat & Sun 11am–4pm; Nov, Dec & March Sun only

11am–4pm; free, though charges for some events; ☎01226/774 527) is both a museum of flour milling and a country park. If you arrive by car, leave it in the off-road **car park** (pay and display) and take the pleasantly tree-shaded five-minute walk to the mill, a picturesque cluster of buildings sitting below the modern Worsbrough Reservoir. The first, and oldest, part of the mill you come to dates from the eighteenth century, when it ground corn for local farmers, with the miller taking his toll of the flour. All the original machinery, including cogs, drive shafts and the water wheel itself, would have been made of wood, though this was replaced with cast iron after a new steam mill was built next to the original one in the early 1840s – that's the three-storey building that now holds much of the museum. By the early twentieth century the traditional mill was being replaced by commercial roller mills nearer the ports and the population centres, and the steam engine was sold for scrap. The water mill, however, continued milling crops for local farmers right up to the 1960s. Tracing the structures and processes used to grind the corn is fascinating: from the millpond that sits above the mill, fed by a modern reservoir above it, to the 14ft-high water wheel which drives the internal machinery right through to the tail race that returns the water to the river. It's a model of environmental friendliness, all explained in the excellent booklet *Worsbrough Mill Museum* by Martin Watts, available in the museum shop. Also on sale are pamphlets outlining three graded **walks** in the country park, from just over a mile to just over three miles. Allow at least a couple of hours for this gem of a museum.

Wentworth Castle

A couple of miles west of Worsbrough, on the other side of the M1 (bus #23), lies a gem of a different sort. **Wentworth Castle** (daily: April–Sept 10am–5pm; Oct–March 10am–4pm, last admission 30min before closing; gardens £4.75, family tickets £11.50–16.00; parking £2 if you're just visiting the park, included with garden ticket; RHS members pay for car park only; ☎01226/776 040, ⓦwww.wentworthcastle.org), actually a country house, was built in the eighteenth century by a cousin of the family who owned Wentworth Woodhouse (see p.70), its opulence and scale a result of rivalry between the two. The house itself is now the home of Northern College Adult Education, and is not open to the public (though you can join guided tours on certain days during the summer – phone for details; £2.50). The gardens, however, are open, and are a delight. Two trails are available: the Garden Trail and the Parkland Trail, which is free. The **Garden Trail** includes Stainborough Castle, a folly with superb views, the Stumpery (full of, yes, stumps), the Fernery, the Wilderness, the Victorian Flower Garden, the Union Jack Gardens and the John Arnold Garden, together with the dilapidated but soon-to-be restored conservatory, which featured on Griff Rhys Jones's TV series *Restoration* (he called the grounds of Wentworth Castle "one of the nation's sublime parkland estates"). The two-mile-long **Parkland Trail** takes in the beautiful estate surrounding the house, a number of restored follies, including the Duke of Argyll Column, the Queen Anne Monument, the Rotunda, the Serpentine lakes, the Strafford Gate, the Palladian Bridge and the Home Farm, with striking views of the house itself.

Victoria Jubilee Museum

Four miles or so west of Barnsley (bus #85A), just off the A635, is the pretty stone village of **CAWTHORNE**, home to the **Victoria Jubilee Museum** (Sat, Sun & bank holidays 2–5pm; 50p), another volunteer-run village jewel. Interesting for its own history as well as for its collections, it was founded in 1884 by the formidable local vicar Charles Pratt to encourage the village's young people to take an interest in their surroundings. They gathered stuffed birds, birds' eggs, wild flowers, butterflies, moths, fossils and a wide range of domestic paraphernalia and memorabilia, and put them on display. After it outgrew its original premises, Pratt succeeded in persuading the local squire Sir Walter Spenser Stanhope of Cannon Hall and his artist brother Roddam and his Pre-Raphaelite Brotherhood friends (including John Ruskin) to use estate craftsmen to build the museum's current rather splendid home. Splendid too are the typically Victorian exhibits – the two-headed lamb, the stuffed mongoose fighting a stuffed snake, a 9.5lb stone removed from a horse's intestine, the figure of John Wesley carved out of whalebone and a man-trap.

Also in the village are a maze, the **Maize Maze** (℡01226/791 855, ⊛www .maizemaze.co.uk), which offers tractor and trailer rides as well as the chance to get lost, one of the best gastropubs in the area, the *Spencer Arms* (see p.74), together with an excellent museum and a huge petting zoo (see below).

Cannon Hall Museum

Just on the edge of the village of **CAWTHORNE** (bus #92, but with a fair walk) is the car park for **Cannon Hall** (April–Oct Mon–Wed, Sat & Sun 11am–5pm; Nov, Dec & March Sun 11am–4pm; garden and park open all year; free; ℡01226/790 270). Once home to local iron-magnates the Spencer-Stanhopes, and now maintained by Barnsley Metropolitan Council, it consists of a museum housed in the Hall itself, fine walled gardens and greenhouses, and acres of elegant parkland. The **Cannon Hall Museum** contains an extensive collection of ceramics, paintings and furniture. In particular, try to see the Victorian glass sculptures of ships, fruit and animals, a rare portrait by landscape painter John Constable, many original bookcases (one of which came from *The Times* newspaper offices in Printing House Square), a fascinating Victorian bedroom, with window-views that look like Constable landscapes, and, on the top floor, the Regimental museum of the 13th/18th Royal Hussars and the Light Dragoons, most famous for their part in the Charge of the Light Brigade, with creditably interesting displays on the Charge itself and on the Crimean War in general. In the grounds, well-served by information boards, the walled garden is next to the house and close to the stables, and includes glasshouses, some parts of which may date back to the eighteenth century, truly enormous espaliered pear trees, some nearly two hundred years old, and the remains of a hothouse used to grow exotic plants, including the much-prized pineapple. Half way up the drive is a deer shed, much finer than it sounds with stone walls and a slate roof held up by four enormous yew trunks, designed to offer shelter to the herds of ornamental deer, and a ha-ha (a hidden wall) to stop them wandering up to the house.

Cannon Hall Farm

Right next to the Hall is privately owned **Cannon Hall Farm** (April–Oct Mon–Wed, Sat & Sun 11am–5pm; Nov, Dec & March Sun 11am–5pm; ℡01226/790 270, ⊛www.cannonhallfarm.co.uk). Once Cannon Hall's home farm, it was developed by its current owner Roger Nicholson, after he inherited it at the age of 16, into one of the region's biggest attractions, drawing in visitors and school parties from miles around. It's still a working farm, but also now has an extensive collection of domesticated animals from around the world. There are numerous opportunities for children to handle the animals and to milk (artificial) cows, plus a huge adventure playground, with a separate section for the under-3s, delicatessen, tearooms and an ice-cream parlour. Look out in particular for the Hungarian mangalitza pigs, which, disconcertingly, have thick white fleeces like sheep, the huge metal Roundhouse that allows you to climb up onto a central gantry to view the cattle in the segmented enclosures below, and the panorama walk that lets you see the animals relaxing in large paddocks against the background of extensive views of the countryside. Most of the food on sale in the shop and tearooms is produced on the farm.

Penistone

Southwest of Cawthorne, just off the A628 (bus #21), the village of **PENISTONE**, though part of Barnsley local authority area, feels like a hill town miles from anywhere, and is worth a quick visit or a longer stay – it's a good centre for exploring the villages and moors around. As you approach the town from the east past the elegant 29-arch **viaduct** that carries the Sheffield-to-Huddersfield line, it nestles invitingly in the valley of the River Don. There's a weekly **market** (Thurs), a monthly **farmers' market** (second Sat), and the famously old-fashioned Paramount Cinema (℡01226/767 532, ⊛www.penistoneparamount.co.uk), which offers a mixture of films, live shows, comedy and music. In the surrounding area there's good **walking**, especially the Penistone and Thurgoland walks and the TransPenine Trail, which runs through the parish, and a recently constructed viewing point at Royd Moor, overlooking extensive vistas and a clutch of wind turbines.

Wortley Top Forge

Though of limited appeal to the non-specialist, anybody interested in the nuts and bolts of industrial history will find **Wortley Top Forge** (Easter–Nov 5 Sun & bank hols 11am–5pm; £3; ℡0114/288 7576, ⊛www.topforge.co.uk) a wonderful day out. The dam, races and sluices designed to control the water power, the wheels, drop hammers, cranes, bellows and furnaces associated with the forging of wrought iron, and the domestic buildings are all on show. It's run by volunteer enthusiasts, so opening hours are limited, and you might find some of the displays slightly obscure, but industrial archeologists will be in seventh heaven.

Elsecar Heritage Centre

Home to the only Newcomen atmospheric engine in the world to still be on its original site, and housed in the former ironworks and colliery of the Fitzwilliams of Wentworth Woodhouse, the **Elsecar Heritage Centre** (bus #66; daily 10am–5pm, though opening times of shops and businesses vary; ⊛www.elsecar-heritage-centre .co.uk) represents an interesting marriage of conservation and commerce in an historical setting. In addition to the engine, the listed buildings and the steam railway built to haul coal from the mine (℡01226/746 746, ⊛www.elsecarrailway.cjb.net) there are craft shops, an antique centre, artists' studios, a children's indoor play area and pleasant tearooms. Parking and entry are free, though you'll have to pay for railway trips, driver experience courses and special events.

Doncaster and around

DONCASTER has always made things – from mighty steam locomotives (both the world-record holding *Mallard* and the *Flying Scotsman* were built here) to sweets that became household names (Parkinson's butterscotch, Nuttall's Mintoes, Murray Mints). Under the Romans Doncaster was an important town known as Danum. It played a prestigious part in aviation history when the first air display in Britain was held here in 1909 and it became renowned for coal extraction. But perhaps above all the town is known for its racecourse, home since the eighteenth century to the classic race the St Leger, which gives the place a certain raffishness that is missing from other South Yorkshire towns.

Alas, the town itself shows little sign of this long history, but a number of town-centre sites are worth a visit – **Doncaster Racecourse**, **St George's Minster**, **Doncaster Market**, **Doncaster Museum**, together with the whole redeveloped area called **Lakeside**, which has a retail outlet, the town's new sports stadium, a cinema and bowling complex and lots of pleasant lakeside walks.

Outside Doncaster, however, the pickings are much better, with a handful of worthwhile sights, including two country houses, a castle, a wildlife park and the small town of **Bawtry**, with some excellent pubs and restaurants.

Arrival and information

Doncaster's connections with the rest of the country are excellent – it's no wonder that so many companies have distribution warehouses in and around the town. It lies in the angle between the M18 and A1(M), giving it access not only to those two motorways but also to the M1 and M62. Rail links too are first-rate, since Doncaster sits astride the main east-coast rail route between London and Scotland, and also the Trans-Pennine line to Manchester and the northwest. For local transport, **buses** and **trains** head off to Sheffield, Leeds, York, Hull, Grimsby, Worksop and Mansfield, from the new, very well-organized **transport interchange** – and if you have to wait, you can shop in the Frenchgate Centre which is upstairs. Finally, just outside the town is the UK's newest **airport**, Robin Hood Doncaster-Sheffield, to which there are frequent shuttle services from the interchange. The **tourist information centre** is at the Blue Building, 38–40 High St (Mon–Thurs 9am–5pm, Fri 10am–5pm, Sat 9am–4pm; ☎01302/734 309, ⓦwww.visitdoncaster.co.uk).

Accommodation

The Crown Market Place, High St, Bawtry ☎01302/710 341, ⓦwww.crownhotel-bawtry .com. Bawtry's only surviving coaching inn, this venerable posting house looks from the outside the same as it did in the late eighteenth century. Inside it's a different matter, with all the modern decor and facilities of a recent refit. It's now a good medium-to-top-end business and wedding hotel. With 76 rooms, you have a choice of standard, superior or executive rooms with nightly rates of £115, £135 and £155. And with a range of restaurants (Chinese, Italian, Indian, Japanese; see p.82) and food pubs on the doorstep, you needn't always eat in at the hotel. ❹

Danum Hotel High St ☎01302/342 261, ⓦwww .danumhotel.com. Slap-bang in the centre of Doncaster, the venerable Edwardian *Danum* has been a feature of the town for a century. Though some rooms are rather tired, the bar and restaurant have been refurbished, and the rather old-fashioned atmosphere is in keeping with its history. Wonderful location right in the thick of things, so it's perfectly placed for visiting the town's pubs, clubs and restaurants, but it can be

noisy, especially at weekends. Look out for deals – it can be remarkably cheap. ❸

Grand St Leger Racecourse Roundabout, Bennetthorpe ☎01302/364 111, ⓦwww.grandstleger .com. Directly across the road from Doncaster Racecourse, the *Grand St Leger* occupies a solid 1810 Grade II listed building which has housed, at different times, the *Turf Inn* and accommodation for stable rooms – the hotel offers understated luxury. Drinks and snacks available in the *Paddock* bar, and fine dining in *Carrington's* restaurant. ❷

Mount Pleasant Great North Rd ☎01302/868 696, ⓦwww.mountpleasant .co.uk. Winner of the White Rose tourism awards 2009, the *Mount Pleasant*, half way between Doncaster and Bawtry, is an attractive mix of traditional architecture and up-to-the-minute modern facilities. Public areas are sumptuous, rooms are luxurious, there are three bars, an excellent restaurant, a health and wellness centre, and extensive grounds. Ample parking, and you do need a car, though there are frequent buses from immediately outside to Doncaster, Robin Hood airport, and Bawtry. ❹

Regent Regent Square ℡01302/364 180, ⓦwww.theregenthotel.co.uk. In the town centre, the *Regent*, a boutique-style hotel, occupies a cluster of eighteenth-century buildings looking out onto a pleasant Georgian square. Its bars, restaurant, public areas and rooms can seem labyrinthine, but services are good, rooms contemporary and comfortable, and there's often live music – in the *Abbey Road* bar (yes, the Beatles stayed here in the 1960s). **④**

The Town

Doncaster's **town centre** is defined by the racecourse and Lakeside to the south, the transport interchange to the west, the river to the north, and the covered and open-air markets to the east. It's easy to explore on foot – everywhere is within walking distance of everywhere else.

Doncaster Minster

Though it can't compete in age with Rotherham's Minster, **Doncaster Minster Church of St George** (Mon–Sat 10.30am–3.30pm; free; ℡01302/323 748) is just as interesting in its own way. Considered to be one of the finest examples of Gothic Revival architecture in Britain – "Victorian Gothic at its very best", according to John Betjeman – it was designed by Sir George Gilbert Scott, the architect of, among many other edifices, St Pancras Station and the Albert Memorial in London. The original church having burnt down in 1853, Scott's hugely impressive cathedral-like parish church was completed five years later. Externally it is cruciform, with a massive 170ft-high Perpendicular tower and a nave and chancel in the early Decorated style. Inside, it boasts good Victorian stained-glass windows, a clock by Dent (who also designed Big Ben), and a huge five-manual organ by Edmund Schulze. Though at a distance it dominates its surroundings, it is unfortunately isolated from the rest of the town centre by the swirling traffic of an inner ring road and a new bridge across the Don.

Doncaster Market

Established in 1248, **Doncaster Market** is based in and around the Corn Exchange, just across from the Minster. One of the biggest markets in the north of England, with around four hundred indoor and two hundred outdoor stalls, it opens on Tuesdays, Fridays and Saturdays, selling fresh food, clothes, crafts and gifts. There's also a farmers' market on the first and third Wednesday of every month. Within the Corn Exchange building, above the stalls, the Forum offers a range of entertainments and exhibitions.

Mansion House

Worth a quick look in the town centre is the **Mansion House** (group visits can be arranged on ℡01302/734 032), an elegant civic building in the High Street which dates from 1749, one of only three such buildings in the country – the others being the mansion houses of London and York. Designed by James Paine, it is still used for civic functions by the mayor, but public access is limited to one open day a year, plus group tours.

Doncaster Museum and Art Gallery

In Chequer Road just south of the town centre, Doncaster's **Museum and Art Gallery** (Mon–Sat 10am–5pm, Sun 2–5pm; free; ℡01302/734 293) has some fascinating displays relating to the town's ecclesiastical, coal mining, engineering and sporting history, the geology and wildlife of the surrounding area and much else besides. Kids will enjoy the roaring bears as you go in, and the tunnels. Upstairs are displays of ceramics and art. Attached to the museum is the

Regimental Museum of the King's Own Yorkshire Light Infantry. There's a small shop, and coffee is available.

Doncaster Racecourse

One of the oldest and largest in Britain, **Doncaster Racecourse** (reception open Mon–Fri 9am–5pm; tickets generally £5–35; ℡01302/304 200, Ⓦwww .doncaster-racecourse.co.uk) has hosted horse racing since the sixteenth century. One of nine racecourses in Yorkshire, and the only one in South Yorkshire, the course was first marked out in 1614. Two famous races were established in the eighteenth century – the **Doncaster Cup** in 1766 and the **St Leger** in 1776. Both survive to this day, and are run during the St Leger meeting in the second week of September. Having recently undergone a £35 million refurbishment, Doncaster Racecourse is now state-of-the-art for both flat and jump racing. Look out in particular for the "Go Racing in Yorkshire" festival in July, family days in the summer, Championship days throughout the year, and in particular the St Leger, the last classic race of the flat season. Great fun too is Ladies Day during St Leger week, when women dress up to the nines, attend the races, then throng pubs throughout the area in their finery.

Lakeside

At the other side of the southbound Bawtry Road from Doncaster Racecourse is **Lakeside** (Mon–Fri 10am–10pm, Sat 9am–9pm, Sun 11am–5pm, bank holidays 10am–6pm; Ⓦwww.lakeside-village.co.uk), a mixed development built around a man-made lake. The lake itself is nicely laid out, with islands linked by wooden bridges, an artificial beach and miles of paths for walking. Water sports are also planned. Around the town end of the lake stand a **multiplex cinema** and a **bowling alley**, while at the far end is a retail outlet with nearly fifty shops offering up to sixty percent discounts on a range of famous brands, together with indoor and outdoor children's play areas, cafés, and plentiful parking. Beyond this lies the **Keepmoat Stadium**, home to the town's league football team Doncaster Rovers, and to the Doncaster Belles, one of the country's premier women's teams.

At the entrance to the development is the **Dome** (℡01302/370 777, Ⓦwww .the-dome.co.uk), a leisure complex that includes a two-level ice-skating rink, a large leisure pool with a wave machine, a variety of slides and an open tube that swings out into the fresh air, a health club and spa, a concert venue, and a number of food outlets. They often have special offers available so it's well worth checking their website.

Aeroventure

Further into the Lakeside development, and tucked behind the multiplex and bowling alley (follow the brown propeller signs), on what was once RAF Doncaster, **Aeroventure** aircraft museum (Wed–Sun plus bank hols & Tues during school hols: April–Oct 10am–5pm; Nov–March 10am–4pm; £5; ℡01302/761 616, Ⓦwww.aeroventure.org.uk) occupies – and spills out of – a group of hangars and huts. Run entirely by enthusiastic volunteers, it's a great hotchpotch of planes, aircraft parts, helicopters (a particular strength), engines, missiles, bombs and airfield vehicles and equipment. With aircraft of all sorts suspended from the hangar ceiling, it looks like an adolescent giant's bedroom. For enthusiasts it's well worth browsing in the excellent model and gift shop and chatting to the knowledgeable attendants.

Eating and drinking

The centre of Doncaster is a good place to eat and drink, though it can get very boisterous on Friday and Saturday nights. A good alternative is **Bawtry**, eight miles to the south (buses #25 & #99), which has developed into the restaurant capital of the region, with lots of choice and a pleasantly grown-up atmosphere, even at weekends.

Doncaster centre

Black Bull 12 Market Place ☎ 01302/361 661. A large, traditional pub that's packed with punters on market days (Tues, Fri & Sat). A good choice for Sunday lunch if you have a large appetite – portions are gigantic.

Carlos 5 Nether Hall Rd ☎ 01302/363 447, ⓦ www.carlosdoncaster.co.uk. This is a large family-run Italian restaurant in the town centre which has built up an excellent reputation over thirty years. Lots of room in main restaurant plus cellar extension, good service and excellent convivial atmosphere. Main courses £10.50–14.50, pizzas £6.50–8.50, fair wine list starting at £11.50 for the house wine.

Hare and Tortoise 329 Bawtry Rd ☎ 01302/867 329, ⓦ www.vintageinn.co.uk/thehareandtortoise-doncaster. A typical Vintage Inn – interesting building, in this case eighteenth-century, once an inn attached to a toll house, with mismatched furniture, open fires, exposed beams and pleasant garden giving it a welcoming country atmosphere, despite its position on a busy main road junction a few miles south of the town centre. Good variety of food and wine, with starters at around £3–5, main courses £6.50–15. Bookings accepted, though not compulsory, at weekends. Ample parking; on main Bawtry and Robin Hood bus routes, and with palatial smokers' shelter.

White Swan 34 Frenchgate ☎ 01302/366 573. A small, long-established inn that proves popular with the real ale drinkers due to the superior range of reasonably priced beer. Also does food.

Bawtry

China Rose 16 South Parade ☎ 01302/710 461, ⓦ www.chinarose.co.uk. This large, family-owned and-run Cantonese restaurant is well known throughout South Yorkshire for the quality of its food and service. Smart decor, plenty of room between tables and warm atmosphere. Booking essential at peak times, and if you arrive early there's a comfortable bar area in which to have a drink and order your food. Parking is limited, and you might have to leave the car in the centre of Bawtry – a two-minute walk from the restaurant. Starters £5 to £10, main courses £6 to £12, set menus for two to six people £18.50 to £26 per person.

The Crown Market Place, High St. Eighteenth-century coaching inn in contemporary clothes.

Dower House Market Place ☎ 01302/719 696, ⓦ www.dower-house.com. In a large building on the market place adjoining Bawtry Hall, the *Dower House* attracts diners from all over the area. Good varied Indian menu, bar often thronged with people waiting for their tables or take-away customers. Starters £3–4.50, main courses £7–14. Limited parking, so you may have to use the market place.

The Ship Gainsborough Rd ☎ 01302/710 275, ⓦ www.theship-bawtry.com. On the edge of Bawtry town centre, this is a typical local whose owners have, since taking over in 2007, re-invented it as a hugely popular food pub without alienating its long-term customers. The lounge bar largely caters for diners and the public bar for those just having a drink. Wide menu on chalkboard, generous portions of well-cooked food and choice of beautifully kept real ale. Child-friendly.

Turnpike Market Place ☎ 01302/711 960. Good atmosphere, real ale: this is the bar where people have a drink before moving on to their chosen restaurant.

Zinnis Market Place ☎ 01302/711 115. Tuscan cuisine in cool modern surroundings. Popular at lunchtime and in the evenings, but can get manic at weekends.

Nightlife and entertainment

Hogans Bar Silver St ☎ 07807 890 342. An excellent venue for watching the match, with plenty of DJ action. Karaoke on Mondays and football on Saturdays with cheap offers – running into the guest DJ spot on Saturday nights.

The Leopard 2 West St, near Doncaster train station ☎ 01302/363 054, ⓦ www .myspace.com/theleoparddoncaster The dowdy, brown-tiled exterior hides a treasure of a grungy music venue. Live bands every Friday and Saturday. A surprisingly diverse clientele drinking a good range of fine ale.

The Priory Club Lazarus Court, Bradford Row ☎ 01302/768 204, ⓦ www.theprioryclub.com. A compact nightclub with a strong focus on guest DJs/club nights. A wide range of genres are featured throughout the week, from house on Saturdays at "Vibe" to indie on Fridays when it's "Club NME", and metal (Wednesdays', Rock"n'Rolla").

Toast Bar Priory Walk ☎01302/369 138, ⓦwww
.toastbar.co.uk. Low-lit and chic, with DJs spinning
records for lovers of dance music old and new,
from up-to-the-minute house and garage to funk
and soul. Two rooms connected by a long terrace
enable two themes on some nights. Tuesdays are
home to "Soulblock" (7pm–2am), offering up soul,
funk, and hip-hop. On Fridays (6pm–3am) the two
separate rooms house "Electro" and "Hey Friday"!;
"Soultrain" and "Owen & Friends" fill Saturdays
(6pm–3am) with funk, house and garage including
live percussion accompaniment.

Trilogy Silver St ☎01302/556 555, ⓦwww
.trilogynightclub.co.uk. Doncaster's all-singing,
all-dancing weekend venue, boasting four rooms
decked out with different themes and the largest
laser in Yorkshire. Fridays (10pm–3am) provide a
solid offering of chart and r'n'b, while Saturdays
(10.30pm–3am) also throw house into the mix for
good measure. Not to mention "Rock City" on
Thursday nights (10pm–3am), which caters to
lovers of indie, rock and alternative.

Shopping

Doncaster offers all the big **chain stores** you'd expect in a moderately large town.
There are retail parks north and east of the centre (with the usual chain stores like
PC World, Currys, Staples and so on); Lakeside Village (see p.81) offers discounted
goods from such as Marks & Spencers, Clarks shoes and numerous clothing
retailers; and the Frenchgate Centre is a recently built mall which combines
shopping with an excellent transport hub. And there's always Doncaster Market.

Listings

Buses Traveline ☎01709/515 151.
Car rental Europcar, Balby Rd ☎01302/248 470;
Enterprise, First Ave ☎0870 350 3000; National,
Balby Rd ☎01302/245 705.
Hospital Doncaster Royal Infirmary, Armthorpe Rd
☎01302/366 666.

Internet access Zone Out Gamin Centre, Nether
Hall Rd ☎01302/810 285; Doncaster Central
Library, Waterdale ☎01302/734 314.
Pharmacy Boots, 47–48 Market Place
☎01302/342 107.
Post office 24 Priory Place ☎08457 223 344.

Around Doncaster

The area around Doncaster arguably has more going for it than the city itself, not
least two lordly country houses open to the public – **Brodsworth** and **Cusworth**
halls – the magnificent Norman castle at **Conisbrough** (it featured in Sir Walter
Scott's *Ivanhoe*), and a fine children's attraction at Brockholes Farm – the **Yorkshire
Wildlife Park**. Worth a visit too is the small town of **Bawtry** which has become
the pub, restaurant and car-buying capital of the area.

Conisbrough Castle

CONISBROUGH (buses #x78, #221 & #220), a picturesque and heavily
wooded village halfway between Doncaster and Rotherham on the A630, is
dominated by **Conisbrough Castle** (April–June & Sept Mon–Wed, Sat & Sun
10am–5pm; July & Aug daily 10am–5pm; Oct–March Mon–Wed, Sat & Sun
10am–4pm; ☎01709/863 329; EH), particularly the magnificent
Norman keep. Built in around 1180 on the site of an earlier motte-and-bailey
castle, it stands 90ft high, with walls 15ft thick at the base, and is universally
recognized as the finest of its type (circular, with buttresses) in England. The
castle featured (if somewhat unhistorically) in Sir Walter Scott's medieval tale
Ivanhoe, and is now jointly maintained by English Heritage and the Ivanhoe
Trust. The information available in the castle is spot on – informative, but not

too detailed. There's an excellent single-sheet colour guide (0.75p) on sale in the modern **visitor centre**, where there's also an informative display on the history of the castle, and individual parts of the castle are clearly posted with information boards. Views from the roof of the keep are extensive, and there's a free **car park** on the main road at the bottom of the hill – it's a five-minute climb up to the castle. Those with disabled badges can park next to the visitor centre. If you have the time, it's worth taking the short walk to **St Peter's Church** in the village – the oldest stone building in South Yorkshire, apparently, and one of the ten oldest in England.

By taking the short drive back towards Doncaster, then travelling north from junction 36 and coming off at junction 37 on the A1(M), you will, at the bottom of the slip road, come to signs for Doncaster's two great country houses, one to the west (Brodsworth Hall) and the other to the east (Cusworth Hall).

Brodsworth Hall

Brodsworth Hall (bus #203; house: mid-March to Sept Tues–Sun 1–5pm, plus bank holidays; Oct Sat & Sun noon–4pm; gardens and tearooms: mid-March to Oct daily 10am–5.30pm; Nov to mid-March 21 Sat & Sun 10am–4pm; gardens and house £8.50, garden only £5; T01302/724 969; EH) is a mid-Victorian house with a fascinating history. On the death of its creator Theophile Thellusson in 1797, the original estate became enmeshed in a complicated legal dispute which rumbled on for over half a century. Finally the matter was resolved in the 1850s, when local industrialist Charles Thellusson inherited it, knocked down the original house, and built the present one as a home fitting for one of the county's wealthiest landowners and father of six children. After his death in 1885, the estate, and its declining income, were inherited by each of his four sons in turn, and then, since they were all childless, by his daughter Constance. By the 1980s her granddaughter Pamela and her husband were camped out in a single room with an oil heater, unable to maintain the crumbling and increasingly leaky edifice. She finally gave the house to English Heritage in 1990, and the house and gardens were sympathetically and gently renovated to give an excellent impression not only of how the landed classes lived in the mid-nineteenth century, but also of how room-use could change over time. It is, in many ways, an interestingly untypical house. Rooms are more intimate, less grand than in many similar mansions. Instead of being stuck in the attics, the servants had their own wing – it's the lower one on the right as you face the main entrance and porte-cochère. The magnificent mainly grass and evergreen **gardens** are worth visiting at any time of year. Look out in particular for the fern dell, the archery range, the west lawns set up with croquet hoops, and features such as the eye-catcher, the summer house, the target house, and the long rose pergola. There's a café, toilets and a children's playground. The gardens are open all year, but the house shuts during the winter.

Cusworth Hall

Cusworth Hall and Park (bus #42; Mon–Fri 10.30am–5pm, Sat & Sun 1–5pm; tearooms daily 10am–4pm; free; T01302/782 342, Wwww.cusworth-hall.co.uk) stands on a hill surrounded by trees overlooking an ornamental lake and, in the distance, the sprawl of Doncaster. Its story is a familiar one – built in the eighteenth century for a local merchant family, it declined over time until, in the early 1960s, soaring maintenance costs and stiff death duties forced its owner to sell it to the local authority. Now a **museum** run by Doncaster Municipal Council, it has an interesting hotchpotch of displays on various aspects of the region's social and industrial history – costume, jewellery, toys, toilet articles, coal mining, transport – all with enlightening information boards. The building itself is of interest, with a kitchen, library and chapel and much Georgian plasterwork. There are **tearooms** (☏01302/390 959) and a shop. Entry to the museum is free, with pay-and-display parking (50p/hr).

Yorkshire Wildlife Park

Clearly signposted off the A638 Doncaster to Bawtry road, the **Yorkshire Wildlife Park** (Mon–Fri 10am–6pm, last entry 5pm; £10.50, family ticket £30; ☏01302/535 057, ⓦwww.yorkshirewildlifepark.com) is a fine day out for families with young children. A well-organized and up-to-date wildlife facility which makes full use of its rural setting, there's a clutch of buildings inside the entrance, including a large café/restaurant, a comprehensive play barn, an outdoor play area, a gift shop, aviary and area where children can have contact with the animals. Beyond it is a trail which loops out into open grass and woodland, with enclosures of well-kept animals and birds – both common domesticated animals such as dogs, chickens, ducks and geese, and more exotic racoons, meerkats, lamas, red river hogs and painted hunting dogs. There's a huge **African Plains** enclosure, with zebra, antelopes called lechwe (which can run and swim well, and can escape predators by submerging themselves in water, leaving only their nostrils above the surface), ankoli cattle, with hollow horns that can span up to 12ft, and ostriches. They are often, alas, a long way away, but there is a coin-in-the-slot talking telescope which helps you to see them while telling you all about them. Beyond the African Plains enclosure, two fenced areas allow the public to mingle with animals after passing through a double gate – the wallaby enclosure, and the lemur woods. And everywhere there are picnic spots and information boards detailing the sort of wildlife that might be encountered.

Bawtry and Tickhill

On the Yorkshire/Nottinghamshire border eight miles south of Doncaster, two satellite towns have become popular as destinations for local days out. **BAWTRY** (buses #25 & #99), which owes its existence to travel – as a port on the River Idle, as a staging post on the Great North Road, and as a base for bomber command (RAF Finningley) and England's newest airport – Robin Hood – has become the pub and restaurant capital of the region (for specific suggestions, and also attracts evangelicals to the Christian centre in Bawtry Hall, browsers to its numerous independent shops, and wheeler-dealer tyre-kickers to its thrice-weekly car auctions. **TICKHILL** (bus #22), clustered around its 1777 Buttercross, grew up around a motte-and-bailey castle, whose remains are still there, indistinct from the ground but clearly visible in aerial shots, and boasts a beautiful millpond, a superb church, and its own share of pubs and restaurants.

2

West Yorkshire

CHAPTER 2 # Highlights

✳ **Leeds Corn Exchange and Arcades** Top-end eating and shopping in elegant Victorian surroundings. See p.98

✳ **Royal Armouries Museum, Leeds** World-class collection related to war, peace and hunting, with hands-on displays. See p.98

✳ **Thackray Medical Museum, Leeds** The horrid history of disease shouldn't be this entertaining, but it is. See p.99

✳ **National Media Museum, Bradford** Interactive introduction to photography, television, film and animation. See p.108

✳ **Saltaire** Sir Titus Salt's Victorian factory town and mill that now contains a range of galleries, cafés and shops. See p.113

✳ **Hebden Bridge** Pretty mill town, now an artistic and new-age destination, sitting astride a canal. See p.125

✳ **Red House Museum and Oakwell Hall** Two museums with Brontë connections. See p.132

✳ **Yorkshire Sculpture Park** Art and nature come together in wide-open spaces dotted with fascinating sculptures. See p.136

✳ **National Coal Mining Museum** A working coal mine until the mid-1980s, now a museum. Visits can include a trip underground. See p.137

▲ Hebden Bridge

2

West Yorkshire

The five Metropolitan counties of **West Yorkshire** account for more than half the population of Yorkshire as a whole. The area's wealth and power traditionally arose from wool and coal – roughly, textiles to the west (Halifax, Huddersfield and Bradford) and coal to the east (Wakefield), while regional capital Leeds had a foot in both camps. With the decline of textiles and coal, many areas have struggled to develop alternatives. Without doubt, the most successful has been Leeds, now a major centre for financial services and a popular destination for recreational and business tourism. But the other four Metropolitan boroughs have also made great efforts to diversify and encourage inward investment, often with the help of national and European funding.

The whole region is doing its best to attract visitors, and has enthusiastically participated in attempts to sell the county as a holiday destination under the umbrella of Welcome to Yorkshire. Each Metropolitan borough has at least one world-class attraction, or a good range of smaller ones, or both. In addition to the preponderance of industrial artefacts, there are many other things to look out for – castles, monasteries, great houses, gardens, museums, villages, market towns and attractive countryside. So in **Leeds** some of the main draws are the Royal Armouries, the Thackray Medical Museum, the great house of Temple Newsam and a number of Victorian arcades. It does, of course, also take pride of place in the region for interesting places to stay, eat and go out. **Bradford** and the surrounding area is known for the excellent National Media Museum, Salt's Mill at **Saltaire** and the world-famous Brontë parsonage at **Haworth**. **Halifax** boasts Eureka!, the only museum in Britain to be aimed specifically at primary-age children, and also lovely **Calderdale**, centred on **Hebden Bridge**. In **Huddersfield** check out the Red House Museum and Oakwell Hall, and near **Wakefield** the National Coal Mining Museum and the Yorkshire Sculpture Park.

West and South Yorkshire are so crowded with towns that many of these attractions fall between them. For example, the National Coal Mining Museum, though in the Wakefield Metropolitan Borough, is just as close to Huddersfield in West Yorkshire and Barnsley in South Yorkshire, and is equally accessible from either. So it's worth checking across the whole chapter – and even glancing at places in contiguous chapters – when planning itineraries for good days out.

Leeds

LEEDS is Yorkshire's greatest city. The inhabitants of Sheffield, York and Hull, even Bradford, may deny it, but they know in their hearts that it's true. Just as Manchester owed its huge industrial expansion to the development and mechanization of the

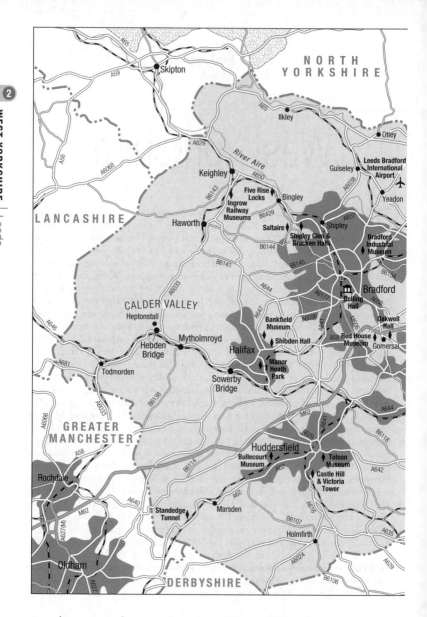

Lancashire cotton industry, Leeds grew up as the power behind the similar growth of the Yorkshire woollen industry – together Manchester and Leeds in the nineteenth century clothed the world.

As soon as you arrive in Leeds, you feel the metropolitan buzz of its burgeoning culture and commerce, its successful redevelopment and the in-your-face chutzpah of its magnificent Victorian architectural heritage. It's the home of the regional

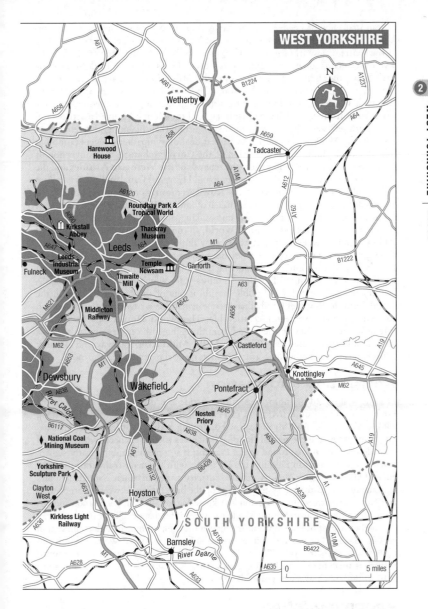

WEST YORKSHIRE

N

Harewood House

Roundhay Park & Tropical World

Kirkstall Abbey

Thackray Museum

Leeds

Leeds Industrial Museum

Fulneck

Temple Newsam

Thwaite Mill

Garforth

Middleton Railway

Castleford

Knottingley

Dewsbury

Wakefield

Pontefract

Nostell Priory

National Coal Mining Museum

Yorkshire Sculpture Park

Clayton West

Kirkless Light Railway

Hoyston

SOUTH YORKSHIRE

Barnsley
River Dearne

0   5 miles

Wetherby

Tadcaster

studios of the BBC and ITV, its Grand Theatre hosts Opera North and gets regular visits from Northern Ballet, and it has a range of top-end shops, fine restaurants, good pubs and museums and art galleries galore. Forget flat caps and whippets – Leeds is up there, if not with London, then certainly with Manchester and Birmingham as a bright and fast-moving modern city that has built on its august industrial past.

Your first view of Leeds if you arrive by train, **City Square**, seems to encapsulate what the city is all about – an island of Victorian municipal statuary standing at the centre of a swirl of heavy traffic, surrounded by modern tower blocks. The two other major squares also sum up aspects of Leeds history – **Park Square** the early days of eighteenth-century growth, **Millenium Square** a mixture of Victorian (City Museum), inter-war (Civic Hall) and twenty-first-century (Mandela Gardens). Just down the road there's a cracking fine arts complex made up of the **Library**, the **City Art Gallery**, and the **Henry Moore Institute** – all free. Though Leeds didn't avoid the excesses of urban planning and redevelopment in the 1960s, since the 1980s a great deal of sympathetic regeneration has taken place, including the renovation of the **Corn Exchange**, the conversion of older buildings such as **The Light**, the renewal of the **Victorian Arcades** and the development of the areas along the Leeds and Liverpool Canal and the River Aire – especially the dock upon which the **Royal Armouries Museum** is built.

Outside the city centre, too, there is much of interest. **Roundhay Park**, the largest municipal open space in Leeds, offers fine walking, an attractive café and shop in the mansion, and the excellent **Tropical World**, all run by the City Council. **Kirkstall Abbey**'s gaunt medieval remains, together with the museum across the road, offers an insight into the world of Cistercian monks whose medieval wool dealings laid the foundations of Yorkshire's all-conquering textile industry. The **Thackray Museum** on the massive St James's Hospital (Jimmy's) site, which deals with nineteenth-century medical practices and public health, is one of the best of its kind in the world. **Temple Newsam** Elizabethan/Jacobean mansion is a wonderful introduction to sixteenth-and seventeenth-century life; **Harewood House**, one of Britain's foremost stately homes, to the period from the eighteenth century onwards. And a trio of industrial museums – **Thwaite Mills**, **Middleton Railway** and **Armley Mills** – gets down to the nitty-gritty of what made the city of Leeds great.

Arrival and information

Leeds is well served by motorways, sitting astride as it does the intersection of the UK's main north–south (M1) and east–west (M62) routes, and with the A1(M), M621, A58(M) and A64(M) all nearby. For driving in the city, there's a complicated one-way system, but the central "loop" at least gives you the chance, if you've missed your destination, to go around again. **Parking** is at a premium, but clearly signed. Inter-city and suburban rail links too are good, with the main **train station** at the edge of the city centre on City Square. For **city transport** there's an efficient and reasonably easy-to-use bus system centred on the **bus station** between George Street and New York Street, directly behind Kirkgate Market, though Leeds' train and bus stations are too far apart to be a single transport interchange. There is, however, a comprehensive set of bus stops and an efficient cab rank right next to the train station on City Square. For bus and train information for the whole of West Yorkshire, go to ⓦwww.wymetro.com. The train station also houses a well-stocked **tourist information centre** (Mon 10am–5.30pm, Tues–Sat 9am–5.30pm, Sun 10am–4pm; ⓣ0113/242 5242, ⓦwww.visitleeds.co.uk).

Accommodation

Leeds has a growing number of city centre **chain hotels**, luxury and budget, most of them within a few minutes' walk of the train station. There are also some interesting **boutique hotels**, though small-scale guesthouses and privately owned hotels are few and far between. Parking can be a problem, and except for the rare hotel with its own (such as the *Hilton*), most have arrangements to use nearby commercial car parks at subsidized rates (around £12/24hr).

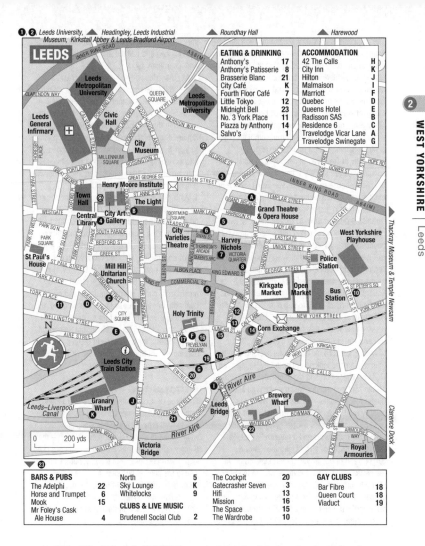

1, **2**, Leeds University, Headingley, Leeds Industrial Museum, Kirkstall Abbey & Leeds Bradford Airport · Roundhay Hall · Harewood

LEEDS

EATING & DRINKING		ACCOMMODATION	
Anthony's	17	42 The Calls	H
Anthony's Patisserie	8	City Inn	K
Brasserie Blanc	21	Hilton	J
City Café	K	Malmaison	I
Fourth Floor Café	7	Marriott	F
Little Tokyo	12	Quebec	D
Midnight Bell	23	Queens Hotel	E
No. 3 York Place	11	Radisson SAS	B
Piazza by Anthony	14	Residence 6	C
Salvo's	1	Travelodge Vicar Lane	A
		Travelodge Swinegate	G

Thackray Museum & Temple Newsam

Clarence Dock

BARS & PUBS		North	5	The Cockpit	20	GAY CLUBS	
The Adelphi	22	Sky Lounge	K	Gatecrasher Seven	3	Bar Fibre	18
Horse and Trumpet	6	Whitelocks	9	Hifi	13	Queen Court	18
Mook	15			Mission	16	Viaduct	19
Mr Foley's Cask		**CLUBS & LIVE MUSIC**		The Space	15		
Ale House	4	Brudenell Social Club	2	The Wardrobe	10		

42 The Calls 42 the Calls ☎0113/244 0099, ⓦwww.42thecalls.co.uk. *42 The Calls* is in an eighteenth-century corn mill, with many original features allied to top-quality modernist decor and fittings. It goes out of its way to be quirky – fishing rods in rooms overlooking the canal, twelve varieties of sausages for breakfast, a late-night trust-the-customer bar. Being next to the Centenary footbridge, it can sometimes suffer from noisy passers-by. ⑤

City Inn Granary Wharf ☎0113/241 1000, ⓦwww.cityinn.com/leeds. Beautifully located on Granary Wharf, 5min walk from the train station. Luxurious rooms, friendly, committed staff,

choice of ecstatically reviewed ground- and top-floor restaurants. Parking under railway arches, or at reduced rate in the nearby commercial car park. An impressive addition to Leeds city-centre hotels. ⑦

Hilton Neville St ☎0113/244 2000, ⓦhilton.co.uk. Right next to the train station, and with its own parking. Perfectly acceptable accommodation, though the building is beginning to look a bit tired, and staff seem distinctly under-trained. ⑤

Malmaison 1 Swinegate ☎0113/398 1000, ⓦwww.malmaison-leeds.com. One of a string of twelve city- and town-centre hotels which claim to be following in Napoleon's Josephine's footsteps.

The emphasis is on luxury accommodation in interesting old buildings – in this case, the Leeds tram and bus company office just east of the train station. Decorated in dark browns, creams and maroons. Gym, brasserie, bar and – a nice touch – local musicians performing on Sunday nights. **⑥**

Marriott 4 Trevelyan Square ☎0113/236 6366, ⓦwww.marriott.co.uk. Highly reckoned for all types of guests, the *Leeds Marriot* combines city-centre location (just off Boar Lane) with the tranquillity of Trevelyan Square. A large hotel with comprehensive facilities. If you want a change from the two in-house restaurants, you could try one of the city's top-rated restaurants, *Anthony's* (see p.102), which is just across the square. **④**

Quebec 9 Quebec St ☎0113/244 8989, ⓦwww.theetoncollection.com. Part of the same group of boutique hotels as *42 The Calls*. Ornate 1891 ex-Liberal Club boutique hotel with superb terracotta exterior, Victorian interior trappings and rooms of understated opulence, just off City Square. Very limited parking (six spaces) – phone just before arrival to try to bag one, though they're not cheap at £12/24hr. Otherwise commercial parking nearby at same rate. **③**

Queens Hotel City Square ☎0113/243 1323, ⓦwww.qhotels.co.uk. Huge hotel backing onto the train station and looking out onto City Square. The *Queens Hotel*'s Portland stone gravitas and refurbished Art Deco interior would make Fred and Ginger feel at home – 1930s style, twenty-first-century mod cons. With bar and restaurant much used by local business people, you feel at once a part of the metropolis and a favoured guest. **④**

Radisson SAS No. 1 The Light, the Headrow ☎0113/236 6000, ⓦwww.radissonblu.co.uk. At the western end of the Headrow, next to the Henry Moore Institute, the *Radisson* is spacious and well appointed, with a modern Art Deco-influenced style, and with immediate access to the pools, fitness suite, shops and cafés of The Light. Rooms vary in size, so check before accepting. Levels of both lighting and heating are low – take a torch and a cardigan. **⑤**

Residence 6 3 Infirmary St ☎0113/285 6250, ⓦwww.residencesix.com. "White Rose" Gold award-winner for best self-catering apartment in Yorkshire, *Residence 6* is centrally located in the old Post Office building just off City Square. Superb accommodation with complementary wi-fi, games console and fully equipped kitchen/dining rooms. If you don't want to cook you can order in. Very limited parking – otherwise reduced-rate parking nearby. **⑥**

Travelodge The two city centre, one on **Vicar Lane** (97, Vicar Lane; ☎0871 984 6337), the other off **Swinegate** (Blayd's Yard; ☎0871 984 6155) offer the usual budget accommodation, sometimes at ludicrously low tariffs – £9 a night is not uncommon. For your money you get a basic room right at the heart of the city. However, don't expect peace and quiet – street noise, music from clubs, slamming doors and so on is common, but in fairness there is a warning about this on the website. Great for somewhere to crash after drinking or clubbing, not so good if you're looking for a good night's sleep. No hotel parking – in both cases, there are NCP car parks nearby. **①**

Campsites

The three best campsites near Leeds are along the same road – Blackmoor Lane, in Bardsey, on the way to Wetherby. All are within walking distance of what claims to be the oldest pub in Britain – the *Bingley Arms* – which is delightful, and does good food. There are buses into the city, but it's about a mile to the nearest bus stop. All three sites – **Highfield** (☎01937/574 658), **Glenfield** (☎01937/574 657) and **Moor Lodge** (☎01937/572 424) – are equally good, and Moor Lodge is adults only.

The city centre

Leeds city centre is compact enough for extensive exploration on foot, from the trio of **squares** along its western border – City, Park and Millennium – the hospital and university complexes to the northwest, and the **shopping arcades** and **markets** along the eastern edge, with two great shopping streets – **the Headrow** and **Briggate** – which cross in the centre. The best place to start an exploration is on its southwestern edge at City Square.

City Square and around

At first sight **City Square** looks like a glorified traffic island. It's worth, though, a more careful look and half an hour's exploration. Built between 1893 and 1903 to mark the elevation of Leeds to city status, it features a large and impressive **equestrian**

statue of the Black Prince, whose connection with the city seems obscure, a semi-circle of eight rather sexy **nymphs** and four life-sized **statues** of great men from the city's past: James Watt (again, connection obscure, though his steam engines were important in the growth of the woollen industry), John Harrison, an early woollen cloth merchant and builder of St John's, Dr Hook (an ex-vicar of Leeds, not the band), and Joseph Priestley, who lived in the city from 1767 to 1773. Immediately behind the statues and a contemporary pavement fountain stands the former General Post Office, built in 1896, which now houses, among other things, two upmarket restaurants and a stylish hotel. Other buildings were added over time: the 1921 Majestic Cinema, now the *Majestyk* nightclub, and the 1937 **Queen's Hotel** facing the square with its back to the station and worth popping into for the Art Deco interior. The only building on the square to predate its late nineteenth-century remodelling is the **Mill Hill Unitarian Church**, which was built in 1847 to replace the one where Joseph Priestley was a minister. The whole square works despite the thundering traffic − it has the air of a Victorian dowager who has fallen asleep and woken to find herself surrounded by towering modern descendants.

Leaving City Square by Infirmary Street, to the right of the General Post Office, you'll come to a little square on the right called Bond Court − it's a short cut across the corner to East Parade. Here is the delightful, if little heralded, **Leeds Petanque Court** − a wedge of gravel overlooked by a noticeboard bearing the rules of petanque, or boules. There are tables and chairs around the court, and boules can be borrowed from *Centre Fillings*, a sandwich shop in the square − it's free, and you don't even have to pay a deposit. All they ask is that they get the boules back by closing time (3pm). The nicest touch of all, though, is the statue of a man squatting, boule in hand, considering his next shot, and of another man leaning on the square's central lamp post, with his wife and small child, watching the game.

Park Square

Beyond Infirmary and St Paul's streets you come to **Park Square**, something of a Georgian surprise in largely Victorian-and-later Leeds. The fact that it wasn't conceived and built as a unified whole adds to its charm, with slightly varying styles and roof-lines. An interesting exception to the largely eighteenth-century architecture is **St Paul's House**, built in 1878 as a factory and warehouse for John Barren, pioneer of ready-made clothes. Having seen circular saws being used to cut wood veneer, he adapted the idea to cloth-cutting, and never looked back. By the time of his death in 1905 he was employing three thousand people. The building, now an office block, is in what might be called Moorish style, and though heavily restored (the little minarets, apparently, are made of fibreglass) it's still rather impressive.

Millennium Square

The largely modern and sloping **Millennium Square**, a five-minute walk from Park Square, stands at the heart of a cluster of important buildings and attractions. On its northern edge is **Civic Hall**, looking like a bull with gold wing mirrors, and beyond it **Leeds Metropolitan University**, which, together with the **Colleges of Art and Technology**, ensure that the square seems permanently thronged with students.

The west of the square is dominated by the Victorian **Leeds General Hospital**, designed by Sir George Gilbert Scott. To the east stands the impressive **City Museum** (Tues, Wed & Fri 11am–6pm, Thurs 11am–8pm, Sat & Sun 11am–5pm; free; ☎0113/224 3732, ⊛www.leeds.gov.uk/citymuseum), which was the Mechanics Institute until 2005. Designed by Cuthbert Broderick its stern Victorian exterior belies its brightly modern hands-on content. Galleries on ancient civilizations, life on earth, costume, domestic life, fossils, military history and ethnography make good use of the city's typical Victorian collection. Look out particularly for the numerous stuffed animals, including the famous Leeds tiger. At the heart of the museum is the **Leeds Arena**, a huge interactive map of the city which you can walk on or observe from the circular balcony.

The square itself hosts a variety of events – fun fairs and musical events, for example, and an annual temporary ice rink. At the southern end of the square are the new **Mandela Gardens**, in honour of both the great man and of the city's partnership with Durban in South Africa.

The Town Hall

South of the Millennium Square along Westgate stand (from west to east) the Town Hall, the Library, the City Art Gallery and the Henry Moore Institute. The **Town Hall** is one of the most splendid municipal buildings in the UK. The Leeds Improvement Society, formed in 1851 by a group of prominent industrialists and businessmen, bought the site and drew up a specification for an architectural competition, to be judged by Sir Charles Barry. Of the sixteen submissions, one by a virtually unknown young architect – **Cuthbert Broderick** of Hull – was chosen. He would go on to design the Mechanics Institute (now the City Museum) and the Corn Exchange. A stroll around the outside of the Town Hall will reveal much of its grandeur – the ranks of stately columns, the 225ft-high clock tower – and many interesting details, such as the carved faces looking snootily down at the wheelie bins along the west (Oxford Place) side. The inside is equally magnificent, though is only open to the public for concerts and civic functions.

The City Art Gallery and Henry Moore Institute

East of the Town Hall stands the **Central Library** and City Art Gallery. Opened in 1884, the library is housed in what was once the Municipal Buildings, while the art gallery occupies an extension dating from 1888. The **City Art Gallery** (Mon, Tues & Thurs–Sat 10am–5pm, Wed noon–5pm, Sun 1–5pm; free; ☎0113/247 8256, ⓦwww.leeds.gov.uk/artgallery), where Alan Bennett used to potter around as a break from doing his homework in the library, has an important collection of largely nineteenth- and twentieth-century paintings, prints, drawings and sculptures, some on permanent display, others rotated. It also hosts a constant stream of visiting exhibitions, together with numerous talks, workshops and classes. As you would expect, there are works by Barbara Hepworth and Henry Moore, both Yorkshire born and bred, who studied at Leeds School of Art (now the College of Art) – Moore's *Reclining Woman* stands just to the right of the Art Gallery entrance. Look out, too, in the entrance lobby for Anthony Gormley's *Brick Man*, a scale model for a proposed 100ft-high statue to stand near Leeds train station. It was never built, its rejection by the then city council, due, according to Gormley, to a "lack of nerve". The Library and Art Gallery are joined by the tearoom and shop in the magnificent **Tiled Hall**, with granite pillars, tiled walls with relief portraits of Homer, Milton, Burns and others, a beautifully vaulted ceiling with hexagonal bricks of different colours forming a mosaic, and gold bosses that are part of the original ventilation system, still working today. You'll not find a more palatial place to have a cup of tea and a bun anywhere in the country. If all this art and beauty leave you wanting to own some, head to the downstairs **Craft Centre and Design Gallery** (Tues–Fri 10am–5pm, Sat 10am–4pm; free; ☎0113/247 8241, ⓦwww.craftcentreleeds.co.uk), with lots of modern jewellery, glass and metalwork for sale.

Next to the Library and Art Gallery, and joined to them by a walkway, is the **Henry Moore Institute** (daily 10am–5.30pm, Wed until 9pm; free; ☎0113/234 3158, ⓦ www.henry-moore.org/hmi), created in 1993 out of a disused warehouse – the facade, which on first sight might seem to be glass, is in fact highly polished igneous rock. Dedicated to the study of sculpture, it has galleries, a library and a sculpture archive and mounts extensive exhibitions. What it doesn't have, surprisingly, is Henry Moore sculptures. For those you'll need to travel to the Yorkshire Sculpture Park in Wakefield (see p.136), the artist's home, gardens and studios in Perry Green, Hertfordshire, or the Art Gallery of Ontario in Toronto.

The Headrow

East of Cookridge Street, Westgate becomes the **Headrow**, a development that spanned World War II and which now contains numerous large shops, most notably in the centre called **The Light** (core opening Mon–Fri 6am–12.30am, Sat & Sun 8am–12.30am; individual shops vary; ⓦ www.thelight.co.uk). Consisting of two blocks dating from 1930 joined together by overarching glass roofs and new structures, it is a modern shopping mall which is airy and light (hence the name), yet which has retained its original character. It includes shops, a health and fitness club, a multiscreen cinema and a luxury hotel. As the Headrow dips downwards, in the distance you'll see a building that looks like something out of *Flash Gordon*. Opened in 1993, this is known locally as the Kremlin, home of the Department of Health, but also several arts-related organizations, including the West Yorkshire Playhouse (see p.104).

Briggate and the Arcades

Crossing Headrow about half way down the hill is Briggate – **New Briggate** to the north, **Briggate** to the south. Though together they feature a trio of excellent theatres (see p.104), it is not primarily for the arts that the street is world famous, but for shopping. Pedestrianized, thronged with shoppers and buskers, Briggate is the trunk off which the city's famous arcades branch. The two oldest are on the right as you walk south – **Thornton's Arcade** (1877), and **Queen's Arcade** (1889). Both have impressive clocks, the former at the end of the arcade, the latter at the entrance. Most famous, though, is the **Victoria Quarter** (ⓦ www.v-q .co.uk) where between 1898 and 1904 the slums around the shambles, or meat market were cleared. The two cross streets between Briggate and Vicar Lane – Queen Victoria and King Edward streets – were entirely enclosed by high glass roofs, creating three blocks divided by two main east–west lanes and a number of cross lanes. The buildings themselves are riots of brick and terracotta, with arches, domes, urns, gables and turrets, and the shop-windows prosperous in shiny mahogany and glass. What a setting for the plethora of top-end names – Vivienne Westwood, Nicky Clarke, Mulberry, Louis Vuitton, *Anthony's Patisserie* (see p.102), Harvey Nichols and a host of others – who ply their trade here.

City Markets

Turning right out of the Victoria Quarter's lower exit into Vicar Lane brings you to a completely different shopping experience – the **City Markets** (Mon–Sat 9am–7pm; ⓦ www.leedsmarket.com), often known as **Kirkgate Market**. With entrances on Vicar Lane, Kirkgate and George Street, it is said to be the largest market in Europe, containing over eight hundred stalls inside and outside. The indoor market building dates from 1904, though with remnants of the 1857 building it replaced, and is a symphony of balustrades, steeples and domes on the outside and of cast-iron and steel columns and girders supporting glass clerestory windows, lantern roofs and a central octagon within. It has the whole gamut of stalls, together with a specialist Butchers' Row, Game Row and Fish Market. The outdoor market (closed Wed & Sun) stretches across to Leeds bus station, and is where Michael Marks set up his first stall ("Don't ask the price – it's a penny") which grew into ubiquitous Marks & Spencer.

The Corn Exchange

Just south of the City Markets, on Call Lane, one of Leeds' most iconic buildings rises above the surrounding roofs. **The Corn Exchange** (Mon–Sat 9am–6pm, Sun 11am–4pm; Ⓦ www.cornx.net), also by Cuthbert Brodrick, is one of the few oval domed buildings to be constructed. On the outside, note the diamond-pointed stone which gives the building an incredibly rich texture, especially when the sun is low in the morning and evening, the two rows of arch-topped windows separated by what looks like mini-millstones, and the rosettes above the second row of windows (a Broderick signature) which look very like Yorkshire roses. Inside, a flagstoned open basement (now *Piazza by Anthony*; see p.102) is reached down wood-and-iron steps, with similar steps leading up to a cast-iron balcony. Over the whole space arches a wonderful elliptical iron and wood dome with large glazed openings. At one end, where the ribs converge, is a clock flanked by sheaves of corn; at the other end the city's civic arms.

Nearby, it's worth taking a look at the extension of Crown Street due south of the Corn Exchange. The building on the left now occupied by an Italian restaurant and a bistro/club was, from 1777, the city's **Assembly Rooms**, a place to drink and dance the night away.

Royal Armouries Museum

A fifteen-minute walk, via the Centenary Footbridge just below the Calls, will bring you to the tower blocks and nascent office/apartment/shopping development Clarence Dock, of which the **Royal Armouries Museum** (daily 10am–5pm; free; Ⓣ 0113/220 1999, Ⓦ www.armouries.org.uk) is the centrepiece. Built in 1995–96 to house the relocated collection of the Tower of London, it's a modern take on a medieval fortress in grey brick, with an imposing entrance and a huge octagonal glazed tower. The core contains a comprehensive display of weapons and armour (the Hall of Steel) around which twists an octagonal spiral staircase that serves the museum's galleries. There are, thank heavens, lifts as well. The result is one of the best museums of its type in the world, with five enormous galleries containing beautifully displayed weapons for war, tournament and hunting, armour and other artefacts, dating from Roman times onwards. Particularly spectacular are the reconstruction of a tiger hunt; the Indian elephant armour consisting of 8500 iron plates (the heaviest armour in the world); fabulously decorated ceremonial suits of full plate armour; a Sikh "quoit turban" which carried a blood-curdling array of throwing quoits, garrotting wires and knives; Samurai, Mongol and Indian armour and weapons; and many ornate guns, from a reconstruction of an enormously long Essex punt gun to an exquisite Tiffany-decorated Smith and Wesson .44 Magnum. To make the most of your visit pick up a *What's On Today* leaflet from the admissions desk (free), which gives details of that day's events and live interpretations, or a *Royal Armouries Souvenir Guide* (£3, and worth every penny). There's also a shop, bistro and restaurant, and in the area outside is the tiltyard, which mounts jousting, military skills and falconry exhibitions, plus a menagerie where the birds and horses used in the tiltyard are kept, and a craft court where you can see a gun-maker and armourer at work. Some may think that the museum glorifies war; it doesn't – in its own words "Learn from the past, hope for the future". This museum is an absolute gem, and alone would justify a trip to Leeds.

Out of the centre

Venturing away from the immediate city centre gives access to many more attractions, most, but not all, of which are easily accessible by public transport.

Roundhay Park and Tropical World

Three miles northeast of the city centre lies **Roundhay Park** (buses #2 & #12 from city centre; ⓦwww.roundhaypark.org.uk), Leeds' largest public open space and one of the largest public parks in Europe. Owned by Leeds City Council it consists of an impressive mansion (dating from the early nineteenth century) and extensive landscaped parkland, with gardens, lawns, trees, woods, two lakes, a ravine, a gorge and a castle folly, together with a golf course, bowling green and tennis courts, renovated in 2008 and kept in perfect condition by an army of local authority gardeners. Much used by local people, yet big enough to offer peace and quiet (except when big names play here – Bruce Springsteen in 1985, Pulp in 1995 and Robbie Williams in 2006), it has two watering holes – a lakeside café and a restaurant in the mansion. There's a shop, plenty of parking and a good food pub – the *Roundhay Fox* (☎01132/693 352) on the main road.

On the eastern edge of the park is the well-worth-visiting **Tropical World** (daily: summer [BST] 10am–6pm; winter [GMT] 10am–4pm; £3.25; see the Roundhay Park website). Tropical World was developed from a set of conservatories built in 1911 for tropical plants, and consists of a beautifully thought-out series of tropical habitats – rainforest, desert, swamp, jungle – through which wooden walkways meander. There's a nocturnal section, the largest collection of tropical plants in the UK outside Kew Gardens, a wooden bridge, a substantial waterfall which you can view from inside as well as out, and a variety of birds, reptiles, fish and mammals, some of which roam freely within the enclosure. There's a shop, and, in a separate building, the *Explorer's Café*.

Thackray Museum

Next to the giant St James's Hospital (Jimmy's), two miles northeast of the city centre is the **Thackray Museum** (buses #4, #42, #49, #50, #50A & #61; daily 10am–5pm, last admission 3pm; £6.50; ⓦwww.thackraymuseum.org), which can't be over-praised. It's different, it's imaginative, it's interactive and it's vastly entertaining. Appropriately set in a Victorian workhouse building (which is how Jimmy's hospital began), the museum takes as its starting point the horrendous problems suffered by people in one particular place and time – Leeds in 1842 – and follows the processes by which these problems were solved. The account of public health issues, cholera, TB and so on are enough to turn the stomach. The pie-seller resting his tray on the edge of a midden (and you get not only the sights and sounds, but the smells), the horrendous butchers' shop, the little girl having her leg amputated (without anaesthetic) after a mill accident, will stay with you for the rest of your life. And the weird-and-wonderful cures that were used will make you want to laugh and cry. You can pick up a card with details of a real person (Alice Finch, a 7-year-old bookseller's daughter, Mary Holmes, 27-year-old dressmaker, and many more), follow their fortunes through the museum, then find out how they died. The most noteworthy exhibits include large and small iron lungs (for adults and children), prosthetic limbs, the "Iron Man" made entirely of metal plates used in surgery, a canvas "boobs and belly" suit to give dads an insight into the discomforts of pregnancy, and two large mannequins showing modern replacement joints and acupuncture points. The **Life Zone** gallery is specifically for young children but adults will enjoy it as well – it deals with everything from how long your intestines are (29ft), to how your muscles work and how your different teeth do different jobs. And where else could you experience being a pea travelling through the intestinal tract from mouth to, well, the other end? Remember the name Thackray Museum. Don't miss it.

Temple Newsam

Temple Newsam (Tues–Sun 10.30am–4/5pm; £3.50; ☎113/264 7321, Ⓦwww .leeds.gov.uk/templenewsam) lies five miles east of Leeds city centre (and is not easy to get to – there's a Sunday bus service, otherwise drive, or take a taxi). The manor of Newsam dates at least from the time of the Domesday Book, and a fine mansion was built on the present site in early Tudor times by Thomas Darcy, a chum of Cardinal Wolsey – it was in this house that Lord Darnley was born, second husband of Mary Queen of Scots and father of King James I of England. Both came to a sticky end – Darcy on the Tower Hill scaffold, Darnley when he was strangled in Scotland at the age of 21, many thought by his wife's lover (and in due course, third husband) Lord Bothwell. The house was bought and completely rebuilt in 1622 by Sir Arthur Ingram, a Yorkshire financial tycoon, and remains largely untouched since then, a fine example of a Jacobean mansion. Architecturally important, aesthetically beautiful, stuffed with priceless paintings, porcelain and furniture, set in wonderfully landscaped parkland, with a visitor centre, shop and tearooms in the stable block, it will engender wonder or envy, depending on your nature. Around the parapet of the house, in 2ft-tall letters, is the following invocation, given in full to save you from a stiff neck: "all glory and praise be given to god the father, the son and holy ghost on high, peace on earth good will towards men, honour and true allegiance to our gracious king, loving affection amongst his subjects, health and plenty be within this house".

In the grounds stands Europe's largest **rare-breeds farm** (Tues–Sun 10am–5pm, 4pm in winter; £3.25) which might give kids a rest from history and art.

Thwaite Mill

Though there have been water mills on the site since the seventeenth century, the present **Thwaite Mill** (bus #110; Sat & Sun 1–5pm, plus Tues–Fri during Leeds school holidays 10am–5pm; £3.10; Ⓦwww.leeds.gov.uk/thwaitemills) complex was built in 1823–25 on an island between the River Aire and the Aire and Calder Navigation, and consisted of the mill building, warehouse and workshop, stables, rather fine late Georgian house and (now demolished) workmen's cottages. Water wheels, of course, only provided the power – how it was used changed over time, from turning rape seed into oil, through grinding flint for glazes, to grinding chalk into putty. The mill closed in 1975 when the weir which directed the water along the mill races collapsed, but the machinery is in working order. At the heart of the mill are the two wheels, and what giants they are – 18ft in diameter, and over 14 feet wide and 8ft wide respectively, each revolving once every five seconds, driving all the other machines in the building. The whole site was a model of well-organized, sustainable industry and, surrounded by water, it's a wildlife haven just two miles from Leeds city centre.

Middleton Railway

Just down the road from Thwaite Mill, and just two miles south of the city centre, the **Middleton Railway** (Sat & Sun; Ⓦwww.middletonrailway.org.uk) claims to be the oldest working railway in the world, having started as horse-drawn colliery railway in 1758, with steam power being used from 1812. Never a passenger railway, and only just surviving after the pit closed by hauling for local industry, it was taken over by Leeds University students led by indomitable Fred Youell during Rag Week in 1960, after which it never looked back. The students and other volunteers, while preserving engines and rolling stock, increasingly tried to attract tourist passengers to fill the void as industry declined. Finally, with lottery funding, it celebrated a grand opening in its present form in 2007. As a tourist attraction, it isn't the slick final product you'll get at some other volunteer-run railways – opening hours are extremely restricted (check the website for details), though there is a small café and shop, and ample free parking – but for railway buffs, those interested in industrial history generally, or families with kids who want a day out, it's great fun – a one-and-a-quarter mile trip on standard gauge rails, steam or diesel hauled, with the option at the other end of coming straight back or having a wander around Middleton Park.

Leeds Industrial Museum

Leeds Industrial Museum (buses #5 & #72; Tues–Sat 10am–5pm, Sun 1–5pm; £3.10; ☏0113/263 7861, ⓦwww.leeds.gov.uk/armleymills) occupies the buildings of Armley Mills, a nineteenth-century woollen mill in the Kirkstall valley, two miles northwest of the city centre. Having started as an eighteenth-century fulling mill – basically a set of water-powered hammers bashing the finished to consolidate the fibres – Armley Mill became, following rebuilding after a fire in 1805, simply the biggest woollen mill in the world, introducing machine mass production and steam power. Although it includes displays on the cinema and on printing in Leeds, most of its collection reflects the dominance of the wool industry in the city, from the days of the huge spinning mules and power looms to the later production of off-the-peg clothing for famous names such as Hepworth and Burton. There's a shop and dressing-up clothes are available for kids. Access is easy and there's plenty of parking. You can also get to the museum from the Vue Cinema complex just across the river – there's a footbridge next to *Frankie and Benny's* (buses #733 to #736).

Kirkstall Abbey

Two miles further out from Leeds Industrial Museum (buses #33 & #33A) lie the remains of **Kirkstall Abbey** (dawn to dusk; free; ⓦwww.leeds.gov.uk /kirkstallabbey), a Cistercian monastery built in the twelfth century and destroyed during the sixteenth-century dissolution of the monasteries by Henry VIII. Access is free, and there's a map with a marked route around the ruins for you to follow. In each section of the abbey – the church, the cloister, the infirmary, refectory and kitchen – information boards give you all you need to understand what you're looking at. Directly across the main road from the abbey is the **Abbey House Museum** (Tues–Fri & Sun 10am–5pm, Sat noon–5pm; £3.60; ⓦwww.leeds.gov .uk/abbeyhouse), once the gatehouse to the abbey, then, after the dissolution, a private residence, and finally, from 1927, a museum. Particularly child-friendly (and there's a children's playground in the park on the other side of the car park as well), it concentrates on aspects of Victorian life in Leeds, with reconstructed shops and streets, pubs and homes, costume and toys. There's a shop and restaurant, and pleasant gardens.

Harewood House

Harewood House (bus #36 from Leeds or Harrogate; April–Oct staterooms noon–4pm, other parts of house/gardens 10/10.30am–4pm/5pm/5.30pm/6pm; £9–£13; ⓦwww.harewood.org), seven miles north of the city centre, is one of the UK's greatest country mansions, created in the mid-eighteenth century by an all-star cast: designed by John Carr of York, interiors by Robert Adam, furniture by Thomas Chippendale, with paintings by Turner, Reynolds, Titian and El Greco, all sitting in beautiful grounds landscaped by Capability Brown. It doesn't get any better than that. Tours of the house include the below-stairs kitchen and servants' quarters as well as the innumerable galleries, halls, reception rooms and staircases, dripping with antiques and priceless art treasures, in which the family lived. But it's not just its historical and artistic natural advantages that won it the large visitor attraction of the year award in 2009, so much has been added that it really is a wonderful family day out. There's an adventure playground, gardens – including the famous bird garden – special-interest tours and talks on things like bee-keeping, photography and food, and events such as craft fairs, concerts, car rallies and kite-flying festivals, plus refreshment areas, from the *Terrace Tearooms* to the *Courtyard Café*. Although this is the home of the Earl and Countess of Harewood, visitors are not made to feel part of the great unwashed allowed in out of economic necessity. On the contrary, the whole experience is warm and welcoming, an invitation to share in admiration and delight at the achievements of a past age. Incidentally, the village is pronounced "Harewood" as it is spelt, while the house is pronounced as if the spelling was "Harwood House".

Eating and drinking

Leeds has the greatest concentration of highly reckoned and popular **restaurants** in Yorkshire, together with a plentiful supply of chain restaurants and gastropubs.

Cafés and restaurants

Anthony's ☎0113/245 5922, ⊛www.anthonys restaurant.co.uk. Anthony Flinn has taken the Leeds restaurant scene by storm since opening his first establishment in 2004. You can now eat his multiple-award-winning food in three places, all within a couple of minutes' walk of each other: **Anthony's**, the original restaurant, on attractive little Trevelyan Square, just off Boar Lane (tasting menu £60 per head; lunch two courses £19.95, three for £23.95; à la carte two courses £34, three courses £42); **Anthony's Patisserie**, at the lower end of Queen Victoria St in the Victoria Quarter (around £2–8.50); and

Piazza by Anthony in the nearby Corn Exchange (brunch from £1.35, starters from £4.85, mains from £8.75, desserts from £4.50). This latest venture isn't just a restaurant – there's a bakery, patisserie, chocolatier, wine shop, cheese shop and charcuterie as well. Food is well cooked, mainly English, with a range of meat and fish dishes, unpretentiously described (though you do need to know your monkfish ceviche from your sous vide mackerel). Top-quality food in beautiful surroundings.

Brasserie Blanc Victoria Mill, Sovereign St ☎0113/220 6060, ⊛www.brasserieblanc.com. One of seven restaurants in England run by Raymond Blanc, housed in an old mill 5min walk from Leeds train station. Brick walls, cast-iron pillars and brick-vaulted ceiling and outdoor tables available in summer. French regional cooking in relaxed rather than haute cuisine mode. At lunch time mains are around £9.25–16.50; in the evening, starters are £6–7.50, mains £10.50–27.50; kids' menu and half adult portions available.

City Café Granary Wharf ☎0113/241 1039. The restaurant of the *City Inn* on the canal side at Granary Wharf, the *City Café* offers fast friendly service, interesting choice of dishes – set menus of around £9.95–17.95 for two or three courses – excellent food and an extensive wine list, half of which is available by the glass.

Fourth Floor Café, Harvey Nichols 107 Briggate ☎0113/204 8000, ⊛www.harvey nichols.com. As you'd expect from the famous top-end department store, the restaurant is something special. Traditional meat and fish dishes – lamb rack, pork shoulder, rib-eye steak – for around £11.50–18.50 served in light elegant surroundings with good views across the rooftops of Leeds. The restaurant shares the top floor with the wine shop, deli and sushi bar and is accessible through the shop or, for evenings from Thursday to Saturday, via an express lift. Set menus for £16.50–19.50; ten percent service charge added.

Little Tokyo 24 Central Rd ☎0113/243 9090. Popular Japanese restaurant in the city centre, with variety of noodle, sushi and sashimi courses and bento "four-course meals in a box". Lively atmosphere, good service, and no booking so you take your chances.

Midnight Bell 101 Water Lane ☎0113/244 5044, ⊛www.midnightbell.co.uk. A 10min walk south of the train station, the *Midnight Bell* in Water Lane is one of three pubs owned by the 2007-established Leeds Brewery. Cool contemporary decor in a converted Grade II listed foundry building, and locally sourced food during lunch times (£4.50–8.95) and evenings (mains around £14.95).

No. 3 York Place 3 York Place ☎0113/245 9922, Ⓦwww.no3yorkplace.co.uk. All polished wood, white walls and modern art, *No. 3 York Place* is restrained in decor and French brasserie in style of food (mains £16–20)

Salvo's 115 & 109 Otley Rd ☎0113/275 5017, Ⓦwww.salvos.co.uk. Probably the best-known Italian restaurant in Leeds, winner of "best local Italian restaurant" in Gordon Ramsay's *The F Word*, it's worth the drag out to Headingley, with quality favourites at prices which don't exclude students. Lovely atmosphere, friendly service with pizzas for around £7, pasta dishes around the £10 mark and most main courses £14–16.

Bars and pubs

The Adelphi 1–3 Hunslet Rd ☎0113/245 6377, Ⓦwww.theadelphi.co.uk. Joshua Tetley's first pub, just south of the river across the Leeds Bridge. The splendidly Victorian *Adelphi* is all things to all men (and women). With four contrasting bars, a wide range of draft beers, ciders, wine and food – snacks, pub grub and full meals. There's a comedy club on Mondays and music on Saturdays and the last Sunday of the month.

Horse and Trumpet 51–53 the Headrow ☎0113/245 5961. The *Horse and Trumpet* is a no-nonsense city drinking establishment, divided into small areas with wood panelling and unbeliev-ably cheap food – burgers, pies, fish and chips – for £3–5 all day, every day. No children under18. There is a dress code, but it isn't overly strict – no baseball caps or tracksuits. Grill nights, curry nights and Sunday roasts.

Mook Hirst's Yard ☎0113/245 9967. Situated down an alley just off Call Lane, *Mook* is hard to find but well worth the hunt. Cool, relaxed and friendly with a happy hour running every day from 4pm to 9pm, including their excellent range of cocktails. The back bar is generally quieter than the

front, and there is a sizeable dance floor for those looking to shake their tail feather to the cleanly mixed funk and electro. It's right next to *The Space* (see p.104), so makes an ideal start for a night out. Open till 2am.

Mr Foley's Cask Ale House 159 the Headrow. Super Victorian pub near the Town Hall, with several bars on different levels, draught beers listed on a blackboard with strengths and tasting notes, and refrigerated world bottled beers. Food at around a fiver.

North 24 New Briggate ☎0113/242 4540. Just north of the Headrow, *North* is a long, narrow bar with wooden floor, small tables and chairs (except for the much-prized Chesterfield at the back) and, on the wall opposite the bar, the names of hundreds of beers from all over the world – including "Arrogant Bastard" and "Kelpie Seaweed Ale". It serves a small range of food, such as a steak and ale pie for £3.30 (pie and a pint for £5) but a much wider beer menu.

Sky Lounge City Inn, Granary Wharf ☎0113/241 1000, Ⓦwww.cityinn.com. Situated on the thirteenth floor of the *City Inn* hotel, the *Sky Lounge* is very popular with Leeds' young profes-sional crowd. Often busy, and certainly expensive, but well worth a visit for the wide range of exquisitely prepared cocktails served with the best views of the city available from its wraparound terrace. Sun–Thurs open till midnight, Fri & Sat till 1am.

Whitelocks Turks Head Yard ☎0113/245 3950. *Whitelocks* is not easy to find (go down Briggate from the Headrow and it's the first alley on the right) but well worth tracking down. A pub probably dating from 1716, with an interior that is all polished brass and copper, tile-inlaid counters and engraved mirrors definitely dating from 1886. Good selection of real ales, and, further up the alley, another bar and a restaurant.

Nightlife and entertainment

Around the city are a number of drama, dance, music and comedy venues, at which you can experience anything from one-off performances to regular world-famous events such as the **Leeds International Piano Competition** (☎0113/244 6586, Ⓦwww.leedspiano.com), **Leeds International Concert Season** (☎0113/224 3801, Ⓦwww.leedsconcertseason.com), the biennial **FuseLeeds** (☎0113/213 7700, Ⓦwww.fuseleeds.org.uk), **Live at Leeds** (☎0113/244 3446, Ⓦwww.liveatleeds.com), and **Leeds Festival**, held over the August bank holiday weekend at Bramham Park, and attracting around 70,000 people for big-name bands (☎0115 /912 9000, Ⓦwww.leedsfestival.com).

The city is known, too, for its **dance**, hosting the Northern Ballet (☎ 0113/274 5355, Ⓦwww.northernballet.com), Phoenix Dance Theatre (☎0113/242 3486, Ⓦwww.phoenixdancetheatre.co.uk) and RJC Dance (☎0113/239 2040, Ⓦwww.rjcdance.org.uk) and is home to the Northern School of Contemporary Dance

(℡0113/219 3000, ⓦwww.nscd.ac.uk) and Yorkshire Dance (℡/0113 243 9867, ⓦwww.yorkshiredance.com), while a flourishing comedy scene uses venues from the largest hall to the smallest, most intimate pub. Finally, there are several popular **outdoor venues** in and just outside the city, including Millennium Square (see p.95), Kirkstall Abbey (see p.101) and Roundhay Park (see p.99). Check out ⓦwww.leedsguide.co.uk.

Theatres and venues

Carriageworks Theatre Millenium Square ℡0113/224 3801, ⓦwww.carriageworkstheatre .org.uk. Along the southern edge of the square, housed in a small development called the Electric Press, its home since it was kicked out of the Mechanics Institute by the City Museum, the Carriageworks Theatre puts on a variety of plays, shows and festivals, many of them for children.

City Varieties Music Hall Swan St ℡0113/391 7777, ⓦwww.cityvarieties.co.uk. Built in 1865. Harry Lauder, Charlie Chaplin and Harry Houdini all appeared here (older Brits will remember it as the venue for television's "Good Old Days" from 1953 onwards), and Dara O'Briain still reckons it to be "the best venue for stand-up in the nation". A £9million-plus renovation due to be completed by spring 2011 (though fundraising is still ongoing, so this may change) should return the theatre to its original pristine condition, when it will be run jointly with the Grand Theatre.

Grand Theatre and Opera House New Briggate ℡0844 848 2706, ⓦwww.leedsgrandtheatre.com. See below.

Howard Assembly Rooms New Briggate ℡0844 848 2727, ⓦwww.operanorth.co.uk /howard-assembly-room. Between them, the Grand Theatre and Opera House and the splendidly restored Howard Assembly Rooms offer an eclectic range of performances, from the high culture of Opera North and Northern Ballet productions to one-man/-woman shows, stand-up comedy, spectacular musicals and children's productions.

West Yorkshire Playhouse Playhouse Square, Quarry Hill ℡0113/213 7700, ⓦwww.wyp.org.uk. Based in the "Kremlin", the West Yorkshire Playhouse is one of the best regional theatres in the UK, putting on a variety of new and existing plays – many of its productions have transferred to the West End.

Clubs and live music

Brudenell Social Club 33 Queen's Rd ℡0113/275 2411, ⓦwww.brudenellsocialclub .co.uk. Most famous for hosting secret gigs for bands like Franz Ferdinand and the Kaiser Chiefs, the *Social Club* emphasizes live music and is a great supporter of up-and-coming bands. Originally a working men's club, it has been a primary cog in the Leeds music scene for a number of years. Cool

and inexpensive with great sound. Mon–Sat till 11pm, Sun 10.30pm.

The Cockpit Bridgend House, Swinegate ℡0113/244 1573, ⓦwww.thecockpit.co.uk. Leeds' premier independent live music and club venue, situated 5min by foot from the train station, under three railway arches. Gigs take place on their three stages most nights of the week showcasing local and international bands. Friday nights is "The Session" with guitar and electro tracks in the main room, backed up by retro indie in room 2, and everything else from Eighties pop to hip-hop in the last. Saturdays play host to "The Garage" – wall-to-wall rock in its various guises. Room 3 is reserved for a cycle of different nights throughout the month. Doors open 7pm.

Gatecrasher Seven 54 New Briggate ℡0113/245 4577, ⓦwww.gatecrasher.com. One of the well-presented Gatecrasher brand, offering mainstream dance music. A variety of nights run from Thursday to Saturday, centring largely on fresh house and club classics, with big-name DJs and club nights. There's the Main Room dance floor, Deco to retreat to for a relaxed, chic environment, and Bed, in the basement, providing a happy medium with its own sound system and dance floor in a more intimate setting.

Hifi 2 Central Rd ℡0113/242 7353, ⓦwww.thehifi club.co.uk. Three times winner of both "best nightclub" and "best live music venue" at the annual Leeds Bar & Club Awards, this little club plays everything from Motown to drum'n'bass, with live music on selected days. Regular nights through the month cater to lovers of jazz, funk, soul, rock and hip-hop. "The Sunday Joint" is also popular, with a live band with your Sunday roast, and more live music running on into the evening. Open till 3am.

Mission 8 Heaton's Court ℡0870 122 0114, ⓦwww.clubmission.com. Recently revamped, *Mission* is a large venue with enough space for 1500 clubbers. A great range of nights feature big-name DJs every weekend. The Thai beach party "Full Moon" runs on Thursday nights, with house/ electro and hip-hop/r'n'b in arenas 1 and 2 respectively. Thurs open till 3am, Fri 4am, Sat 5am.

The Space Hirst's Yard ℡0113/246 1030, ⓦwww.thespaceleeds.com. Literally an underground club, *The Space* is a well-established leader in the Leeds dance music scene. It focuses strongly on house and electro, shunning the mainstream in favour of darker sounds and richer beats. It's perhaps best known for the full-on Sunday club night "Funky Dory", which bangs out high-octane mixes until 5am on Monday morning. Tues open till 3am, Wed 4am, Thurs–Sun 5am.

The Wardrobe 6 St Peter's Square ℡0113/383 8800, ⓦ www.thewardrobe.co.uk. Stylish and cool, *The Wardrobe* is well worth the trip – it's east of the centre. Excellent food upstairs, with soul and funk on Friday and Saturday nights, often with a live band thrown in for good measure, in the club room downstairs. For a more relaxed time of day, the Sunday lunch is highly recommended. Free entry upstairs, with entry to downstairs for club and live acts varying. Doors open 8.30pm.

Gay clubs

Leeds' best gay venues are clustered at the lower end of Call Lane.

Bar Fibre 168 Lower Briggate ⓦ www.barfibre .com. Leeds' finest gay bar comes with plenty of attitude plus outside balcony, DJs most nights and dancing until midnight (2am at weekends).

Queens Court 167 Lower Briggate ⓦ www.queens courtleeds.com. On two floors in the same courtyard as *Bar Fibre* (with which it has wild monthly summer parties), this bar has cool yet comfortable contemporary design, a basic menu, and an upstairs nightclub (*The Loft*).

Viaduct 11 Briggate ⓦ www.viaductleeds.com. Traditional pub converted into a gay venue with live music.

Shopping

When **Harvey Nichols** opened their Leeds store in 1996 (107–11 Briggate; Mon–Wed 10am–6pm, Thurs 10am–8pm, Fri & Sat 10am–7pm, Sun 11am–5pm; ℡0113/204 8888) – their first outside London – it emphasized that the city is one of the very best for shopping outside the capital. In addition to the usual high street chains that you get in all big cities, Leeds also has numerous independent shops, the classy emporia that throng the city's beautifully restored **Victoria Quarter** and other arcades (see p.97), the shopping and entertainment complex of **The Light** (see p.97), the malls that crowd the city centre, such as the **Leeds Shopping Plaza** between Boar Lane and Bond Street, and the **Merrion Centre**, off Merrion Street and the eight hundred traders housed in the Edwardian **Leeds City Markets** in Kirkgate (see p.97).

Listings

Airport Leeds–Bradford ⓦ www.leedsbradford airport.co.uk.
Buses Traveline ℡0871 200 2233.
Car rental Avis ℡08445 446 070, Budget. ℡0113/272 1177, Thrifty ℡0113/245 8111.
Hospital Leeds General Infirmary, Great George St ℡0113/243 2799.
Internet The Internet Café, 64–65 Merrion Indoor Market Centre, off Merrion Way. There's also free access at the Central Library, Calverley St ℡0113/247 8274 (call for hours).
Pharmacy Boots, Leeds Station Concourse ℡0113/242 1713.
Police Millgarth Police Station, Millgarth St ℡0845 606 0606.
Post office New York St and Albion St.

Bradford and around

BRADFORD lies nine miles west of Leeds, in a shallow depression surrounded by hills. Always jealous of its more prosperous neighbour, it has certainly had its ups and downs. A village which mushroomed during the early nineteenth century as it became the world leader in the production of woollen worsted cloth, it was, until the 1850s a byword for filth and squalor. As the untrammelled operation of the free market sparked an unplanned building free-for-all, factories sprang up across the city, their chimneys creating a pall of smoke that hung permanently above it, and dwellings, which quickly became slums, were flung up to house a work-force sucked in from surrounding areas. Little survives from this period.

From around 1850, though, and especially in the 1860s and 1870s, growing prosperity, coupled with the work of the council and the Street Improvement Committee, secured an improvement in housing and public health, and a number of impressive city-centre buildings were commissioned: St George's Hall in 1851–53, the Wool Exchange in the 1860s, the Town Hall in the 1870s, and a host of schools and warehouses of notable splendour. Bradford became a Victorian city with a centre appropriate to its wealth and success.

Although boosted by the need for uniforms during the two world wars, the general trend for the worsted industry in the twentieth century was downward. In the second half particularly, Bradford reeled from the double whammy of the decline of its staple industry and a city-centre redevelopment plan that destroyed great swathes of the nineteenth-century city, replacing dignified factories and warehouses with dull offices, shops, and windswept and bleak residential developments. A further plan dating from 2003 seems to be compounding the damage, with the controversial (and stalled) Westfield development blighting the city, and with a mouldering Odeon cinema next to the Alhambra Theatre growing weeds and water stains.

There is, however, plenty to see in the city centre, and even more in the surrounding area. Some late nineteenth-century buildings are still there to be admired – the **Town Hall**, **Corn Exchange** and **St George's Hall**. "**Little Germany**", an area of warehouses associated with the influx of German–Jewish entrepreneurs, has survived almost intact. The **Alhambra Theatre** has been restored to its previous glory. Interestingly offbeat museums such as the **Peace**

Museum and **Colour Museum** and art galleries – **Impressions Gallery** and **Bradford 1** – abound. Above all, the excellent **National Media Museum**, on the edge of the city centre and overlooking it, is reason enough on its own to visit the city. And being one of the most multi-ethnic cities in the UK gives it some of the best Asian shops and restaurants in the country.

Outside the city, too, there is much to see. **Bolling Hall** is less than a mile from the centre, and the **Moravian** settlement at **Fulneck** is a must-visit. As you'd expect from this area, there are numerous industrial museums: **Bradford Industrial Museum**, **Ingrow Railway Museums** and the **Keighley and Worth Valley Railway** are all worth a look. The **Cliff Castle Museum** in Keighley is a model of its type, and **Shipley Glen**, **Broke Hall Countryside Centre** and the **Cable Railway** offer a delightful countryside day out. Finally, there are the two big tourist beasts of the region: **Saltaire**, for its magnificent mill, containing, among other things, the Hockney gallery and the model village that surrounds it, and **Haworth**, with all its Brontë connections.

Arrival and information

Just two miles from junction 26 of the M1 (and joined to it by motorway spur M606), Bradford is easy to get into and out of by car. There are plenty of **car parks**, but they tend to be just out of the city centre. There are two train stations – **Bradford Forster Square** (off Forster Square) and **Bradford Interchange** (off Bridge St), the latter with a National Express coach station from where **bus** routes link to all parts of the city and the rest of West Yorkshire (Ⓦwww.firstgroup .com), and a 24-hour **taxi rank**. There's a free city bus service linking all parts of the city centre with the two train stations. The **tourist information centre** (Mon 10am–5pm, Tues–Sat 9am–5pm; ℡01274/433 678) is in the Town Hall.

Accommodation

Dubrovnik 3 Oak Ave ℡01274/543 511, Ⓦwww .dubrovnik.co.uk. A mile and a half north of the city centre, on a pleasant suburban street a 2min walk from Lister Park, the *Dubrovnik* is one of the city's larger privately owned hotels. Pleasant public rooms, friendly, helpful staff, well-appointed accommodation, good food, ample free parking. A good alternative to the all-pervasive hotel chains. ❷

Great Victoria Bridge St ℡01274/728 706, Ⓦwww.tomahawkhotels.co.uk. A Victorian station hotel, the work of the architects who designed the Town Hall and St George's Hall, the *Great Victoria* offers solid comfort and individually designed and very smart rooms right in the heart of the city centre. Good restaurant, popular bar, and that Victorian spaciousness you don't get in many modern hotels. And there's free parking, a major plus. It's one of a small chain of three, all palatial, all in Yorkshire. ❹

Holiday Inn Express Vicar Lane ℡0871 423 4878. Standard Holiday Inn accommodation and facilities, within walking distance of the city centre. In a leisure complex, with cinema, casino, bowling and restaurants, yet quiet, with reception and rooms upstairs, above all the noise. Parking £3 per day in Leisure Exchange multistorey. ❸

Midland Foster Square ℡01274/735 735, Ⓦwww.peelhotels.co.uk. Another updated railway hotel combining Victorian spaciousness with modern opulence. One of nine Peel Hotels located across England and Scotland, its city-centre location was rather spoilt at the time of writing by the huge hole across the road that is the stalled Westfield Broadway development. Inside, though, it's a study in old-fashioned elegance and designer chic. Free on-site parking. ❹

New Beehive 171 Westgate ℡01274/721 784, Ⓦwww.newbeehiveinn.co.uk. For a change from the run-of-the-mill, try this terrific CAMRA-rated Edwardian pub, bursting with character and with more accommodation than you'd expect (seventeen rooms, all en suite). It's still essentially a pub, with five gas-lit bars (three with open fires), live music at weekends, and lots of microbrewery real ale, so it can get noisy: ask for a top-floor room, or one of the two across the courtyard. Free car park adjacent. ❷

The city centre

Though largely a hotchpotch of twentieth-century and Victorian styles, the overall impression of Bradford city centre is of yellow stone and brick. Most of Bradford's main streets slope downhill to the level area in and around **Centenary Square**, the best place to start an exploration of the city, and the 1870s-built **Town Hall** (or, since 1897, City Hall), whose clock tower is a useful navigation aid as you walk around the city centre.

Centenary Square

Dotted around central **Centenary Square** are several memorials that together give a fair insight into Bradford's history. The **Bradford City Fire Memorial** remembers the 1985 Valley Parade disaster which killed 56 and injured over 300. In the Memorial Garden, the **Bradford Pals** headstone commemorates the 16th and 18th battalions of the West Yorkshire Regiment, among the many so-called "Pals Battalions" raised across the country during World War I. The idea was to keep volunteers from the same towns and cities together, on the grounds that they would be more likely to sign up if they were among familiar faces. It certainly worked, and towns and cities vied with each other to see who could contribute the most recruits. The **Workers' Memorial Day Plaque** was erected in memory of the 1984 Bhopal disaster, when a chemical leak in that Indian city killed around 20,000 people; another commemorates the help given to **Balkan states** during the Bosnian war; the **Hiroshima and Nagasaki Plaque** does the same for the 100,000-plus people who died as a result of the dropping of the two atom bombs on Japan, and the **Bob Cryer Memorial Tree and Plaque** recalls the Bradford MP and peace campaigner who died in a car crash in 1994. These last memorials indicate the strong links between Bradford and the peace movement – it's no coincidence that Bradford's most famous son, J.B. Priestley, was a staunch anti-racist and CND supporter, that Bradford University is the only one in the country with a Peace Studies Department, nor that Bradford has the only Peace Museum in Britain.

The National Media Museum

On the southern edge of the city centre, and overlooking it, is the best reason for visiting Bradford – the **National Media Museum** (Tues–Sun 10am–6pm, also Mon during bank & school hols; free; ☎0844 856 3797, Ⓦ www.nationalmedia museum.org.uk). Part of the same group as London's Science Museum, it shares with it a terrific, hands-on approach. First pick up the daily *What's On* guide and the seasonal *Family Guide*, then plunge straight in. The first two floors house temporary exhibitions, while the top three have permanent displays. The third floor is about television, and offers you the chance to see how well you can read the news (it's not as easy as it looks), do pratfalls on a sitcom set, or use a blue screen to see yourself against a variety of backgrounds. There are also loads of old tellies on display. The Magic Factory on the fourth floor contains over thirty robustly interactive light-based activities for kids involving lenses, prisms and mirrors. Shake hands with yourself in the convex mirror, or look out across the city centre through the pinhole camera or the TV zoom lens. The fifth floor is devoted to animation, from old phenakistoscopes and zoetropes, invented in the 1830s, to explanations of how modern animation is done and how it has developed from the Wombles or the Mash Martians to Wallace and Gromit.

As well as visiting the galleries, you can fit in a film: there are three **cinemas**, from the small and intimate Cubby Broccoli through the Pictureville Cinema to the giant IMAX (whose projection booth you can see on the sixth floor). There's also a good-sized restaurant (and a picnic area) and an excellent shop. If you want to do the National Media Museum justice, set aside the best part of a day.

Outside the museum, note the large bronze **statue of J.B. Priestley**, bareheaded, pipe in hand and coat tails flying. Unveiled in 1986, it commemorates the famous novelist, playwright and man of letters who was born in Bradford, and wrote very perceptively about it in *English Journey*, an account of a trip taken through England in 1933.

The War Memorial
On returning towards Centenary Square, note the **War Memorial** that stands near the Alhambra Theatre – a cenotaph flanked by two bronze soldiers carrying guns. When it was erected in 1922, peace-loving city that Bradford was, there was a big reaction against what was seen as the overly aggressive stance of the soldiers, in particular the "crude and mistaken symbolism" of the bayonets attached to their guns. In response, the bayonets were removed, only, oddly, to be replaced each year on Remembrance Day.

Bradford's theatres
The **Alhambra Theatre** (see also p.111) is one of the glories of Bradford's city centre. Built on the eve of World War I, its splendidly pillared and domed exterior, echoed in the steel-and-glass extension which was added in the 1980s, is more than matched by a wonderfully plush auditorium with its rich colours, ornate gilded plasterwork, beautifully painted domed ceiling and luxurious boxes. Next to the pristine Alhambra is the sad corpse of the once great twin-domed **Odeon**, originally the New Victoria, built in 1930 as a dual-purpose cinema/variety theatre that could seat three thousand people, whose future has been stuck in controversial limbo – to demolish or renovate – for the past fifteen years.

On the other side of the Centenary Square, at the bottom of Bridge Street, is **St George's Hall**, the first of Bradford's big mid-nineteenth-century public buildings. Designed by Lockwood and Mawson in 1851–53; it's managed jointly with the Alhambra.

Impressions Gallery and Bradford 1
On the western edge of Centenary Square, the modern **Impressions Gallery** (Tues, Wed & Fri 11am–6pm, Thurs 11am–8pm, Sat & Sun noon–5pm; free; ℡0845 051 5882, ⓦwww.impressions-gallery.com) and **Bradford 1** (same hours; free; ℡01274/437 800, ⓦwww.bradfordmuseums.org) are both attractive venues for the display of visual art. Check out the websites for upcoming exhibitions.

The Wool Exchange
Bradford Wool Exchange was the third of the big three city-centre Victorian projects designed by Lockwood and Mawson – St George's Hall for culture, the Town Hall for local government, and the Wool Exchange for Bradford's dominant industry. The Wool Exchange is particularly interesting – almost triangular in shape, as determined by its plot – and in a Venetian Gothic style, with pointed arches on the ground floor and double- and triple-arched windows on the first and second storeys. Its clocktower features statues of Bishop Blaize and Edward III, and around the building, between the ground-floor arches, are medallions portraying figures considered important one way or another to the development of Bradford: Richard Cobden, Sir Titus Salt, Robert Stephenson, James Watt, Richard Arkwright, J.M. Jacquard (inventor of the influential Jacquard loom), William Gladstone and Lord Palmerston, Raleigh, Drake, Columbus, Cook and Anson. And there's a statue of Richard Cobden (1804–65) inside in the main hall.

The side facing Hustlergate has been partly rebuilt in glass, and now houses a group of shops including Waterstones on the ground floor and *Starbucks* – from where there are excellent views of the hammerbeam roof – on the first.

Peace Museum

One of around a hundred museums worldwide dedicated to the twentieth-century peace movement, but the only one in Britain, Bradford's **Peace Museum** (Wed & Fri 11am–3pm; free; ℡01274/434 009, Ⓦwww.peacemuseum.org.uk) is hard to find, tucked away in Piece Hall Yard, immediately opposite Waterstones, hard to get to (the notice on the door says "there are several flights of stairs" and they are emphatically not kidding; there's no lift), and even harder to catch open. But persevere – it's worth it. In three rooms at the top of a fine Victorian bank building, the museum contains over five thousand posters, banners, photographs, letters, films, newspaper cuttings and works of art. They've even got a piece of the Greenham Common fence. But, fascinating though it is, it's not the collection that is the museum's greatest strength, but the activities for which it's the hub. Its outreach projects currently include work with schools, eight travelling exhibitions on such topics as women peacemakers, the Nobel Peace prize, Bradford's many cultures and Hiroshima and Nagasaki, it has helped produce two excellent "peace trails" for Bradford and Leeds, and is promoting the placing of plaques to commemorate important peace activists. If you visit, pick the brains of its enthusiastic and committed development officers – they can tell you a lot more about the museum's work.

Bradford Cathedral

Bradford Cathedral (Mon–Sat 9am–4.30pm; ℡01274/777 720, Ⓦwww.bradford catherdal.co.uk) started life as a lowly parish church before being elevated to cathedral status in 1919, and even with considerable rebuilding between 1951 and 1965 its humble origins are apparent. The resulting design is confused, neither medieval fish nor twentieth-century fowl. However, after climbing up to the churchyard from the remains of Forster Square, the overall impression of the green and the modern houses for the cathedral staff is very pleasant, with what would have been fine views across the city if it weren't for the huge hole of the Westfield development project. A pair of splendid Pre-Raphaelite stained-glass windows is one of the building's great glories, though if visiting specially to see them call ahead, as access is restricted during public recitals on the magnificent organ – the cathedral's other highlight.

Little Germany

Beyond the cathedral is the one area of Bradford that has largely avoided the wrecking ball. **Little Germany**, between the cathedral and the main Leeds road, earned its name from the many German wool exporters who moved into the area in the second half of the nineteenth century. Palatial warehouses were designed (many by Lockwood and Mawson) and built to emphasize the power and success of the woollen companies, and many survive intact, especially along Well Street, Vicar Lane and Currer Street.

Eating and drinking

Bradford is famous for the range and quality of its **Indian restaurants**, and has been called the curry capital of Britain. Most Bradfordians have their own favourites, but among the city's most renowned Indian restaurants, all three on the outskirts of the city centre, are *Akbar's*, *Mumtaz* and *Saffron*. The online curry guide at Ⓦwebsite.lineone.net/~bradfordcurryguide features a lively debate about the delights or otherwise of a range of restaurants.

Though it would seem a shame to visit Bradford and not try its Indian cuisine, there are other types of restaurant in the city.

Indian restaurants

Akbar's 1276 Leeds Rd, Thornbury ☎01274/773 311, ⓦwww.akbars.co.uk. Near the ring road to the east that, is the original of a chain – now has branches across the north of England (and one in Birmingham). It is renowned for the quality of its south Asian cuisine and is hugely popular, so at weekends you may end up waiting, even when you've booked a table.

Anam's Restaurant 211 Great Horton Rd ☎01274/522 626. Newish chrome-and-steel restaurant with buffet and à la carte.

Mumtaz 386–410 Great Horton Rd ☎01274/522 533, ⓦwww.mumtaz.co.uk. Also near the ring road but to the west, *Mumtaz* is probably even more renowned (and there's now another one at Clarence Dock in Leeds). It has earned plaudits from the famous and well-connected – from Dawn French and Amir Khan, through Shilpa Shetty and Frank Bruno, to Queen Elizabeth II herself. With quality Kashmiri food, smart decor and busy atmosphere, the restaurant is heavily used by the local community and visitors from far and wide. Remember, though – no alcohol.

Saffron Desi 1362 Leeds Rd ☎01274/663 999, ⓦwww.saffrondesi.com. Makes much of its modern decor and interesting food, and it too claims royal patronage – Lady Di and Prince William, it claims, have dined there.

Other restaurants and pubs

Chiang Mai Thai Restaurant 198 Keighley Rd ☎01274/499 088. Out beyond Lister Park, and popular for its laid-back atmosphere and fresh tasty food.

Ital Restaurant 626 Bolton Rd ☎0845 201 3165, ⓦwww.italrestaurant.co.uk. A classy, long-established and recently refurbished place, boasting excellent service and a lively atmosphere. With dishes created by head chef Marco D'Adamo, it's amongst the best Italian restaurants in the city. Try the calzone, and his speciality, the filetto Rossini.

New Beehive 171 Westgate. Excellent Victorian CAMRA-rated pub (see p.107).

Titus Salt Morley St ☎01274/732 853. You couldn't ask for cheaper food in better surroundings than the *Titus Salt* just up from the Alhambra, a Wetherspoon's where they have excelled themselves by converting an interesting building (the swimming baths) and choosing to name it after one of the colossi of the city's history.

Entertainment

Bradford's main musical and **theatrical venues** – St George's Hall and the Alhambra (both ☎01274/432 000, ⓦwww.bradford-theatres.co.uk) – are both interesting for their architecture as well as for what goes on inside. **The Alhambra** hosts a wide variety of productions, from the Northern Ballet and Royal Shakespeare Company to pantomime and the *Rocky Horror Show*, while **St George's Hall** seats up to 1500 for orchestral concerts, stand-up comedy, variety and rock concerts. For **cinema**, head to the National Media Museum (see p.108).

Listings

Airport Leeds-Bradford ⓦwww.leedsbradford airport.co.uk.
Buses Traveline ☎0871 200 2233.
Car rental National Car Rental ☎01274/722 155; Bradford Car Rental ☎01274/666 696.
Hospital Bradford Royal Infirmary, Duckworth Lane ☎01274/542 200.

Pharmacy Boots, 23 Bank St ☎01274/723 946.
Post office 52 Sunbridge Rd.
Trains National Rail Enquiries ☎08457 484 950 (local services ☎0113/245 7676).

Around Bradford

The Municipal Borough of Bradford, as opposed to the city itself, has a wealth of odd and interesting things to see, and two attractions of world-class stature: **Salt's**

Mill and the famous home of the Brontës, **Haworth**. For attractions in and around Saltaire there's bus #626; for Keighley bus #662.

Bolling Hall

Only a mile south of the city centre, **Bolling Hall** (bus #624; Wed–Fri 11am–4pm, Sat 10am–5pm, Sun noon–5pm; free; ☎01274/431 814, ⓦwww.bradford museums.org) has been continuously occupied for at least five hundred years. During this time it has been built on and modified, so that it now illustrates changes in architecture and fashion since the end of the fifteenth century. The oldest part of the house is the southwest tower, which dates from the Middle Ages – the southeast tower was built in the seventeenth century to balance it. Each room is furnished in the style of its time (look out for the large bed made for Harewood House by Thomas Chippendale), and there are lots of interesting carvings and some lovely seventeenth-century stained glass. And Bradford's most famous **ghost**. The story goes that when Roundhead Bradford was under siege by Cavalier forces the Royalist commander, the Earl of Newcastle, stayed with Sir Richard Tempest at Bolling Hall. Infuriated by the town's continued resistance, the earl vowed that when the town fell he would put the whole population to the sword. That night he was woken by a ghostly figure who wailed, "Pity poor Bradford", and he was so shaken that, when the town finally succumbed, he spared the civilian population. The museum stands in its own pleasant grounds, and there's a public park and children's playground across the road for picnics and letting off steam.

Moravian Fulneck

FULNECK, on the edge of Pudsey (bus #711, though it's a fair walk from the drop-off point; if you're driving, don't use sat-nav – you're liable to end up in a chicken farm) lies east of Bradford, almost halfway to Leeds. The village, strung out along a single main street on a hillside overlooking pleasant pastoral country-side, has a Grade I listed chapel, a private school, an interesting village museum and a first-class restaurant. Nice, you might say, but nothing special. Notice, however, the signs that you pass as you enter the village from either end – "Moravian Settle-ment Fulneck". This is what makes Fulneck special – it was established by the followers of **Jan Hus** (or John Hus) of Moravia, now part of the Czech Republic, who believed in a simple, rather austere religion free of pomp and ornament. He was martyred in 1415, and his followers left the Roman Catholic church in 1457 to form their own church. The present Moravian church (Unitas Fratrum or Unity of the Brethren, to give it the correct title) started when a group of Moravians settled on land given to them by Count **Nicholas von Zinzendorf** in Saxony. They called the settlement **Herrnhut** (roughly "under the watch of the Lord"). From 1727, missionaries streamed out of Herrnhut to spread the word, especially in the West Indies and America, where there are still considerable Moravian settle-ments. Many of the missionaries stayed in Britain, and there are to this day numerous settlements in Yorkshire and Lancashire, near Bristol and in London.

Moravian Fulneck is a delight. The church is beautifully simple, though when it was built there was much grumbling that the architect hadn't followed the brief and there was too much frippery. **Fulneck Moravian Museum** (Easter–Oct Wed & Sat 2–4pm; free; ☎0113/256 4862) is interesting, though hours are limited. There are plaques in the village to commemorate two of its famous sons – **Benjamine H. La Trobe** (1764–1820), one of the architects of the White House in Washington DC, and **Sir Len Hutton** (1916–90), Yorkshire and England batsman, and one of the country's greatest-ever cricketers. It has even been said that there was a teacher in the local school called Jane Eyre – one wonders if it's where Charlotte Brontë found the name.

Yorkshire's art and literature

Yorkshire has long been fertile ground for the imagination of writers and artists. The Haworth of the Brontës, the Bradford of J.B. Priestly, Ted Hughes's Calderdale – who can doubt the connection between these colossi of nineteenth- and twentieth-century English literature and their little bits of Yorkshire? In art too the inspiration is manifest – the grandeur of the work of Henry Moore and Barbara Hepworth, the light and colour of David Hockney's paintings. Visitors to Yorkshire are blessed indeed to have giants of literature and art to interpret it for them.

A portrait of the Brontë sisters at Haworth ▲

The Brontë Parsonage, Haworth ▲

Carved rabbit, Ripon cathedral ▼

Sylvia Plath's grave, with a pot of pens left by fans ▼

The Brontës

If you read the novels of the three Brontës and bone up on their biographies, there can be few more affecting visits than to **Haworth**. Their story is at once inspiring and tragic. Famously, the Brontë children made up fictions for each other, writing them down in "little books" – tiny, perfectly made volumes, on display at the Parsonage. All four left home to make their way in the world; all four in due course returned. The scene was set for one of the most spectacular literary debuts in history. In 1847 the three sisters had novels published – *Jane Eyre* by Charlotte, *Wuthering Heights* by Emily, and *Agnes Grey* by Anne, under the pseudonyms Currer, Ellis and Acton Bell. A feeding frenzy of interest in the authors soon identified them as women, and Charlotte in particular became the toast of literary England.

Ted Hughes and Sylvia Plath

Surprisingly little is made of the Ted Hughes/Sylvia Plath story in **Calderdale**. *He* was a working-class Yorkshireman who rose to be one of the foremost poets of his generation; *she* was a high-achieving young American poet. They fell in love, married, wrote, had children, became famous. But all was not well in the marriage, and they split up in 1962. Months later, in a flat in London, Plath gassed herself. Since then controversy has raged, with Plath's supporters blaming Hughes for her death. Whatever the truth of the matter, it's hard not to be touched as you look at the humble end-terrace where Ted Hughes was born, or, less than two miles away, the understated grave where Sylvia Plath is buried.

J.B. Priestley

J.B. Priestley's reputation has had its ups and downs since his death in 1984. A prolific novelist, playwright and essayist, he is probably best remembered today for his travel book *English Journey*, in which he considered at length what it meant to be English. His left-wing humanitarianism – he was a founder member of the Campaign for Nuclear Disarmament – makes him a particularly typical Bradfordian. His birthplace (34 Mannheim Road) is blue-plaqued and his statue stands outside the National Media Museum.

Where to find them?

For some of Yorkshire's most interesting literary connections see:

Haworth The Parsonage with its wealth of Brontë memorabilia, and the church containing the family vault (p.116).

The Calder Valley Sylvia Plath's grave in Heptonstall and Ted Hughes's birth-place in Mytholmroyd. (p.126 & p.125).

Hubberholme The churchyard in which J.B. Priestley's ashes are buried. (p.202)

Ripon Ripon Cathedral (p.177) and Beverley Minster (p.286) both claim that their carvings inspired Lewis Carroll in the writing of *Alice in Wonderland*.

Hull Claims two great poets as its own with statues of Andrew Marvell, the seventeenth-century metaphysical poet, in Trinity Square (p.278) and Philip Larkin, the even greater twentieth-century poet, in the Paragon Interchange (p.281).

Coxwold Eighteenth-century novelist Laurence Sterne's house, church and grave in the village of Coxwold (p.230).

Thirsk The house in which vet and writer James Herriot lived and worked is now a museum. (p.227).

Whitby Three chapters of Bram Stoker's *Dracula* are set in Whitby. See the blue plaque on no. 6 Royal Crescent, or listen to a Bram Stoker hologram at Whitby Abbey's visitor centre. (p.250).

▲ Laurence Sterne's house, Shandy Hall

▼ James Herriot's house at Thirsk

▼ Whitby Abbey, atmospheric setting for *Dracula*

Works by Hockney, displayed at Salts Mill ▲

The Hepworth Gallery, Wakefield ▼

David Hockney

Though probably best known for his Californian paintings, much-travelled artist David Hockney has a considerable body of work portraying his native Yorkshire. Having painted scenes from around his home in **Bradford** during the 1950s, from 1997 he made a series of paintings of the Wolds while staying with his elder sister Margaret in Bridlington. Look out for the exhibitions of his work at **Salts Mill**, Bradford (see p.114) – he was a great friend of its visionary developer Jonathan Silver.

Moore and Hepworth

By far Britain's most famous sculptors, Henry Moore and Barbara Hepworth both hailed from Yorkshire – Moore from **Castleford**, Hepworth from **Wakefield**. Both trained at Leeds School of Art, both studied at the Royal College of Art from 1921, and both became internationally famous sculptors, with some of their finest works at **Yorkshire Sculpture Park**.

Yorkshire Sculpture Park ▼

Where to find them?

For wonderful art in Yorkshire, see:
▶▶ **Graves Art Gallery** Sheffield p.54
▶▶ **Cooper Gallery** Barnsley p.73
▶▶ **City Art Gallery & Henry Moore Institute** Leeds p.96
▶▶ **Impressions Gallery & Bradford 1** p.109
▶▶ **Salts Mill** Bradford p.114
▶▶ **Huddersfield Art Gallery** p.128
▶▶ **The Hepworth Gallery** Wakefield p.135
▶▶ **Yorkshire Sculpture Park** p.137
▶▶ **York's City Art Gallery** p.151
▶▶ **Mercer Art Gallery** Harrogate p.168
▶▶ **Ferens Art Gallery** Hull p.275
▶▶ **The Treasure House** Beverley p.288
Also worth seeking out are the many stately homes with their own collections.

Take a look, while you're in the village, at the **Moravian burial ground**, with simple stones laid flat, in line with the Moravian belief that all are equal in the sight of God. The absence of extravagant monuments and obelisks emphasizes rather than diminishing their poignancy – "Harriet Angell, died November 15, 1823. Aged 16 years. No. 1404" says it all. There's a **car park** at either end of the village (bays marked "R" on the main street are for residents), the very pleasant ⅄*Zachary's* **restaurant**, 54 Fulneck (Wed from 6pm, Thurs–Sat noon–2pm & from 6pm, Sun noon–4pm; ☏0113/256 4069, ⓦwww.zacharys.co.uk). In a lovely old Dutch-gabled building enjoying splendid views across the valley behind, the atmosphere in *Zachary's* is friendly and convivial, and the food is out-of-this-world (with main courses around £20), though you can also just drop in for a coffee and a cake. For more traditional **pub** grub try the *Bankhouse Inn* (☏0113/256 4662, ⓦwww .thebankhouseinn.co.uk) just beyond. The village also has a golf club down the road and a signpost to the gentle one-mile walk to village of **Tong**.

Bradford Industrial Museum

In **ECCLESHILL**, three miles northeast of Bradford (10min on the #640 or #641), stands the impressive 1875 Moorside Mills, now the **Bradford Industrial Museum** (Tues–Sat 10am–5pm, Sun noon–5pm; free; ☏01274/435 900, ⓦwww .bradfordmuseums.org). Originally a worsted spinning mill, it was bought by the council in 1970 and developed into the current "Bradford Industrial Museum incorporating Horses At Work". The approach to the mill takes you past the mill-owner's house and the workers' cottages, with interiors from the time, the stables, with examples of horse-drawn vehicles (including a fire engine), and "Horse Power Emporium" full of the paraphernalia associated with working horses. To one side is the paddock, and there are always working horses to be admired (but not fed). Inside the mill are excellent displays on the local woollen industry, from traditional spinning wheels and hand looms to mechanized cloth production, and including biographies of great Bradfordians, including Sir Edward Appleton, winner of the 1947 Nobel Prize for Physics for his work on the ionosphere. Particularly interesting is the huge "Coat of Many Cultures", made of silk, worsted and linen cloth from all over the world, and "From Mirpur to Manningham", about the great influx of people from South Asia and East Africa in the 1950s and 1960s. Elsewhere are collections of steam engines of all types, printing presses, and a wonderful collection of motor vehicles, plus Bradford's last surviving tram and trolley bus. Most afternoons there are also horse-drawn rail tramway rides.

Saltaire

SALTAIRE, five miles northwest of Bradford city centre (bus #626), is an early example of a Victorian mill complex and model village. Built by **Sir Titus Salt** in the 1850s and 1860s, it's still remarkably intact after a century and a half. its name is a combination of its founder's name and the name of the river upon which it stands.

Salt was one of Bradford's great woollen entrepreneurs. Having made a fortune by the age of 40, largely by introducing alpaca and other new fibres into worsted manufacture, he wanted to build a new factory clear of the shambolic mess that Bradford had become during its massive expansion in the first half of the nineteenth century. He chose a green-field site near Shipley which had excellent transport links with the rest of the country – a river (the Aire), a canal (the Leeds and Liverpool) and a railway – with which to bring in raw materials and despatch finished cloth. He also wanted to provide housing and other services for his workers, not just out of necessity but also because he wanted a stable and sober workforce.

Today, both parts of Saltaire – the mill and the village – are worth visiting. **Salts Mill** (Mon–Fri 10am–5pm, Sat & Sun 10am–6pm; free; ⓦwww.saltsmill.org.uk) has developed into a multi-use art and design centre, with art and craft, flower, music, textile, antique, jewellery, clothes, furniture and book shops, a history of the mill, and, in the **1853 Gallery**, one of the biggest displays of the work of **David Hockney** in the world. The famous artist, who was born in Bradford and trained at the Bradford School of Art before transferring to the Royal College of Art in London, was a close friend of the late David Silver, the man responsible for the conversion of Salts Mill into the great art and design complex it is today. There is also a collection of Hockney's opera sets on the top floor (which is open only Wed–Sun). **Parking** is free and plentiful, and refreshment is available in *Salt's Diner and Café*.

A walk around the **model village**, built between 1851 and 1872 to house the mill workers, is fascinating. Designed by Lockwood and Mawson (who were also the architects of Bradford's Wool Exchange and Town Hall) on a grid plan, the size and impressiveness of the houses reflect the status of the people they were built for. However, even the humblest mill hands had two bedrooms, a living room, a kitchen and a cellar pantry, together with a small garden, while overseers and managers had bigger. All houses were supplied with drainage, water and gas. Public buildings included the Congregational Church, almshouses for the elderly, public baths, an imposing Institute, a school and a hospital, plus a park – look out for the statue of Sir Titus Salt in it.

In line with Salt's religious views there were no pubs, though he wasn't a fanatical teetotaller – there was an off-licence, and he had no objections to families having a barrel of beer in their cellars. Apart from Victoria Road and Albert Road, all the streets are named after members of the Salt family – Titus, his wife Caroline, their children, grandchildren and daughter-in-law.

Opinion over Saltaire model village was then, and is now, divided. On the one hand, Salt's workers and their families had far better working and living conditions than other mill workers in West Yorkshire. However, their lives were stiflingly regimented, with a paternalistic employer who frowned upon any dissent towards management. Look around Saltaire, then decide for yourself.

Shipley Glen, Bracken Hall Countryside Centre and the Tramway

Above Saltaire is an area that owed its nineteenth-century popularity to its proximity to the Saltaire mill and to Shipley, Bingley and Keighley. **Shipley Glen** (buses #624 and #627), a beautiful, wooded gash-and-shoulder of moorland, became a local beauty spot, thronged with walkers at weekends and holidays, with farmers often converting barns into temporary tearooms – you can still sometimes see faded signs on walls or roofs. There were also fairground rides. In 1895 a local entrepreneur – Sam Wilson – who'd already built several rides on the Glen, decided to spare visitors from Saltaire the long walk up, and built the Shipley Glen Cable Railway, a tramway with two quarter-mile-long 20-inch tracks with a gradient of 1 in 7 and two opposing trams. Most of the fairground rides have now gone (though sadly dilapidated dodgems still remain next to the upper station), but the **Tramway** (ⓦwww.glentramway.co.uk) survives, owing to the unbelievably dedicated support of local people and the Bradford Trolley Bus Association (though closed for renovation at the time of writing, check the website for news).

In 1989 the **Bracken Hall Countryside Centre** (May–Aug Wed–Sun noon–5pm; April, Sept & Oct Wed, Sat & Sun noon–5pm; Nov–March Wed & Sun noon–5pm; free; ☏01274/584 140, ⓦwww.bradfordmuseums.org) was established in an old farmhouse as an interpretation centre for the Glen, with an excellent children's museum and displays on natural history and local archeology. Look out nearby for the *Old Glen House* pub – good food, nice atmosphere.

Five Rise Locks

Worth a quick visit if you're in the area are the **Five Rise Locks** (buses #622, #623) overlooking Bingley, just beyond Saltaire and six miles northwest of Bradford. Built in 1773–74 and contributing 59ft to the 487ft rise that the Leeds and Liverpool canal has to manage in order to cross the Pennines, they represent one of the great masterpieces of early canal building, and are an excellent example of a "staircase", where the lower gate of each lock is the upper gate of the next lock downhill (not to be confused with a "flight", where the locks are separate, but happen to be in close proximity). There's a café on the quayside at the top, and fine views across Bingley.

Ingrow Railway

A cluster of separate enthusiast-run railway attractions lie on the outskirts of **KEIGHLEY**, around eleven miles northwest of Bradford (take the #500, #696 or #719 from Keighley): the **Museum of Rail Travel** (daily 11am–4.30pm; £2; ⓦwww.ingrowrailwaycentre.co.uk) and the **Ingrow Loco Museum** (Sat, Sun & selected days 11am–4.30pm; £1.50) stand next to the Ingrow West station of the **Keighley and Worth Valley Railway** (all year Sat & Sun, July & Aug daily, check website for timetable; adult fares £4.80–9.40; ⓣ01535/645 214, ⓦwww .kwvr.co.uk). The two museums between them have a wonderful collection of rolling stock and engines, while the railway, run to capture the atmosphere of a 1950s branch line, has such a comprehensive range of features – five miles of track, six stations, including Haworth (see p.116), four signal boxes, two tunnels, two level crossings, a turntable, several bridges and a viaduct – that it is in constant demand for film and television programmes. Its credits include the 1970 film of *The Railway Children*, Victoria Wood's *Housewife 49*, *A Touch of Frost*, *The League of Gentlemen* and a Tetley Bitter television advert, among many others. If you're a railway anorak, you'll be in seventh heaven, with terrific memorabilia shops at Ingrow and at Haworth, but even if you're not, the museums plus the railway provide a pleasant day out.

Cliffe Castle Museum, Keighley

In **KEIGHLEY** itself is yet another of the excellent local authority museums with which Yorkshire is blessed – and this one's an absolute corker. **Cliffe Castle,** Spring Gardens Lane (short walk or bus #903 from Keighley bus station, 15–25 min walk from the train station; Tues–Sat 10am–5pm, Sun noon–5pm; free; ⓣ01535/618 231, ⓦwww.bradfordmuseums.org), was built in the 1830s as the home of a wealthy lawyer, passed through the hands of a millionaire textile manufacturer, and was bought by Keighley Corporation in 1949, who finally developed it into a museum in the 1950s. There's a gallery explaining the geological formation of the Airedale valley, with masses of rock and mineral samples, several Egyptian mummies and the 3000-year-old "black coffin", wonderful displays on local reptiles, amphibians and, especially, birds including a display case of thirteen of the most common species which allows you to test your knowledge of their song. Local agriculture and industry, costume, stained glass and dolls houses are also covered, and, in an octagonal room with a gallery, there are temporary exhibitions and a history of the building. Look out for the "Hen Peck'd Husband's Wife-Taming Cradle", designed, tongue-in-cheek, to rock nagging wives to make them calmer and happier, an animal heart stuck full of pins (a charm against witchcraft), a lamb with two faces on one head, a scrying ball for telling the future (more commonly known as a crystal ball), and glass walking sticks (said to ward off bad luck). An eclectic collection, beautifully displayed.

Haworth and the Brontës

On the moors above the Worth Valley, ten miles west of Bradford, **HAWORTH** is one of Britain's major tourist destinations. An attractive stone village with steep cobbled streets, its pulling power arises solely from its connection with the odd, hugely talented but ultimately tragic Brontës. A visit to the **Brontë Parsonage Museum** (daily: April–Sept 10am–5.30pm; Oct–March 11am–5pm; £6.50; ☏01535/642 323, ⓦwww.bronte.org.uk), at the top of the hill next to the church, is a must. This was where they lived, where their imagination took flight. You can see the toy soldiers that seem to have sparked their earliest attempts at storytelling, the little books that they made for the soldiers to read, the rooms and furniture they used – including the stool Emily used to sit outside on, and the bed she died in.

The church next door (controversially totally remodelled in 1879) is where Patrick Brontë was vicar, where Charlotte was married, and where all but Anne are buried. Out on the moors there's a walk out to the Brontë Falls and Bridge and, beyond it, Top Withens, said by many, wrongly, to be the Wuthering Heights of the novel. Beyond that, Ponden Hall has perhaps a little more of a claim to be Thrushcross Grange.

However crowded Haworth becomes, however sick you get of the Brontë names being used inappropriately for all manner of commercial enterprises, however sternly literary critics tell us that it is the works that are important not the lives, a visit to Haworth – the Parsonage where the Brontës lived, the church where they worshipped, the *Black Bull* where Branwell drank or the chemist where he got his laudanum, the moors where they got their inspiration – is a moving experience for anybody who admires their work or knows about their lives.

Arrival and information

By bus, take the #662 from Bradford Interchange to Keighley (every 10min), and change there for the #663, #664 or #665 (every 20min), which drop at various points in the streets immediately below the cobbled Main Street. On Sundays, only the #663 and #665 operate (every 30min). More fun is the **Keighley and Worth Valley Railway** (see p.115), onto which you can transfer from the main line at Keighley. The two main streets in the village are Main Street and West Lane which are full of cafés, gift shops and guesthouses. The **tourist office** is at the top of Main Street, on the West Street fork (daily: May–Aug 9.30am–5.50pm, Wed from 10am; Sept–April closes 5pm; ☏01535/642 329, ⓦwww.haworth-village .org.uk).

Accommodation and eating

Apothecary 86 Main St ☏01535/643 642, ⓦwww.theapothecaryguesthouse.co.uk. Traditional guesthouse opposite the church, whose rear rooms, breakfast room and attached café have splendid moorland views. ❷

Fleece Inn 67 Main St ☏01535/642 172, ⓦwww .fleece-inn.co.uk. Busy pub/restaurant on the hill, with attractive rooms. Booking advisable, and it's likely to be noisy until closing time. ❸

Haworth YHA Longlands Hall ☏0870 770 5858, ⒺHaworth@yha.org.uk. Former Victorian mill

owner's mansion, refurbished in 2009. It's a mile or so from the centre of Haworth, off the Keighley road. Weekends only Nov to mid-Feb. Dorm beds from £16. Limited number of doubles/twins. ❶

Old Registry 2–4 Main St ☏01535/646 503, ⓦwww.theoldregistryhaworth.co.uk. At the bottom of Main St. Nine rooms, most with four-poster beds and fine views. Two-night minimum stay at weekends. ❸

Rosebud Cottage Guest House 1 Belle Isle Rd ☏01535/640 321. Beautiful stone house on a terrace in the centre of the village, with comfortable rooms and friendly service. ❷

🏃 **Weaver's** 15 West Lane ☎ 01535/643 822, ⓦ www.weaverssmallhotel.co.uk. Popular restaurant-with-rooms in a row of converted cottages. Good, unpretentious food made with locally sourced ingredients available on Tuesday to Saturday evenings, plus Wednesday, Thursday, Friday and Sunday lunch. Most main courses around £16. Booking essential. ❹

The Brontës

The Brontë family moved into Haworth Parsonage when Patrick Brontë became its vicar in 1820. **Patrick Brontë** (originally Brunty), an Irishman from a humble family who'd done well for himself by going to Cambridge University, was, in addition to being a clergyman, himself a published writer, with several collections of poems, short stories and a single novel to his name. Nine months after the move to Haworth his wife Maria died of cancer, leaving him with five daughters and a son to raise with the help of his sister-in-law Elizabeth Branwell who moved up to Yorkshire from Cornwall.

The four older girls were sent away to school, but when the eldest two, **Maria** and **Elizabeth**, were sent home sick and died (in 1825), the surviving two were brought home to join their brother and youngest sister. The four children – **Charlotte**, **Branwell**, **Emily** and **Anne** – started a relatively idyllic six-year period when the three girls and their brother made up stories for each other (many involving a box of toy soldiers given to Branwell by his father). Patrick Brontë, whose own history made him a great believer in the power of education to allow people to rise in the world, encouraged the children to read widely. During this time the children produced the famous "little books" – tiny, perfectly made volumes with minuscule writing, small enough for the toy soldiers to read.

It was clear that, since Patrick Brontë had no private income, the girls would have to be prepared for life as governesses, the only socially acceptable employment for well-brought-up young women. First Charlotte, then Emily and Anne, were sent away to school and, as they grew into young women, became governesses, with varying degrees of success (Emily, in particular, hated teaching, apparently telling her charges in one school that she much preferred the school dog to any of them). Dissatisfied with the role of governess, the girls decided to set up a school of their own at the Parsonage, and Charlotte and Emily went to Brussels for a year (paid for by their aunt) to brush up their foreign languages. Their aunt, however, died in 1842, and Emily returned to Haworth to look after her father, with Charlotte joining her two years later, and Anne the year after that. The reuniting of the three young women and their brother seems to have recreated their idyllic childhood, and they started to write. The scene was set for one of the most spectacular literary debuts in history.

In 1846 the three young women used some of the money left to them by their aunt to publish a selection of their poems, under pseudonyms that were to become famous: **Currer**, **Ellis** and **Acton Bell**. The book (*Poems*) was quite favourably reviewed, but sales were disappointing – two copies. Under the same pen-names, all three sisters had novels published in 1847 – **Jane Eyre** by Charlotte, **Wuthering Heights** by Emily, and **Agnes Grey** by Anne. A feeding frenzy of interest in the authors soon identified them as women, and Charlotte in particular became the toast of literary England.

The family's happiness at their success was short lived. First Branwell, who'd initially been considered the most talented of the siblings, but who'd been laid low by alcohol and laudanum, died in September 1848 at the age of 31. In December of the same year, Emily, aged 30, died of tuberculosis. Anne, also consumptive, travelled to Scarborough to try a sea cure in May 1849 – four days later, she too was dead. She was 29. Charlotte had time to further develop her career as one of the country's foremost authors, to get married to her father's curate, to become pregnant. Then she too died, in 1855. She was not yet 40. All of the Brontës are buried in a family vault in Haworth church except Anne, whose grave is in Scarborough.

Halifax and around

After Leeds, **HALIFAX**, the main town of Calderdale, is the West Yorkshire town that is probably adapting most successfully to the twenty-first century, retaining many of its notable early buildings but still altering to meet the needs of the present. Halifax is the most westerly of West Yorkshire's main towns, and therefore the hilliest – in 1933 J.B. Priestley thought that at night the trams (now alas gone) looked like "luminous beetles swarming up and down a black wall". As you approach the town, downhill from whichever direction you're travelling, you will see before you a forest of perpendiculars – factory chimneys, tower blocks, church spires – interwoven with sinuous roads carried on soaring flyovers and iron bridges, the whole lot cupped by the surrounding hills. It could have been a mess, yet it seems to work.

In town, the **Parish Church**, a Minster since 2009, is well worth a visit, as is the magnificent **Piece Hall**, built while England was involved in trying, and failing, to keep hold of the American colonies. Other notable buildings include the 1855 **train station**, the **Square Chapel**, now a performance venue, the **Town Hall**, the **Victorian covered market** and **Dean Clough Mill**. Look out too for the modern re-creation of the **Halifax Gibbet**, which long predated Dr Guillotine's more famous contraption, and **Eureka!**, Britain's only museum aimed entirely at children.

Arrival and information

Some eight miles southwest of Bradford, Halifax is a ten-minute drive north of junction 24 on the M62. There's ample **parking** in and around the town centre – perhaps the most convenient car park for exploring the town is on the southeast edge, right next to Eureka! (Discovery Rd/Horton St). The **train station** is also here. The **bus station**, notable for its retention of some earlier (nineteenth-century) buildings, is a ten-minute walk away, on the northern edge of the town centre on Winding Road. The **tourist information centre**, also a visitor centre and art gallery (daily 10am–5pm; ☎01422/368 725), is splendidly housed in a series of linked rooms on the middle floor of the downhill side of the Piece Hall, and offers not only a wide range of pamphlets and books on the local area (look out in particular for the *Halifax Town Trail*), but also work by local artists for sale.

Accommodation

Premier Inn Halifax Salterhebble Hill, Huddersfield Rd ☎0870 990 6308, ⓦwww.premierinn.com. Though two miles out of the town centre, the *Premier Inn* is in every other respect a good option – cheap, clean and friendly, and with ample free parking. ❸

Travelodge Dean Clough Industrial Park ☎0871 984 6144, ⓦwww.travelodge.co.uk. In the town centre, cheap, and in a lovely building with all Dean Clough's facilities on the doorstep. Parking is free only overnight. ❷

The White Swan Princess St ☎01422/355 541, ⓦwww.whiteswanhalifax.com. Comfortable, recently refurbished 1858-built traditional hotel in the city centre, within walking distance of all attractions. All rooms have full facilities, yet tariffs are modest. Dining is at *Julio's* restaurant in the basement. ❸

The Wool Merchant Hotel 5 Mulcture Hall Rd ☎01422/368 783, ⓦwww.wool merchanthotel.co.uk. Recently refurbished budget hotel in another fine nineteenth-century building – a wool merchant's warehouse – with dining in *La Taverna* Italian restaurant in the building. Clean and friendly, with a large car park. ❷

The Town

The best place to start any walking tour of Halifax town centre is the Piece Hall – it's famous, central, easy to recognize, and contains the tourist information centre.

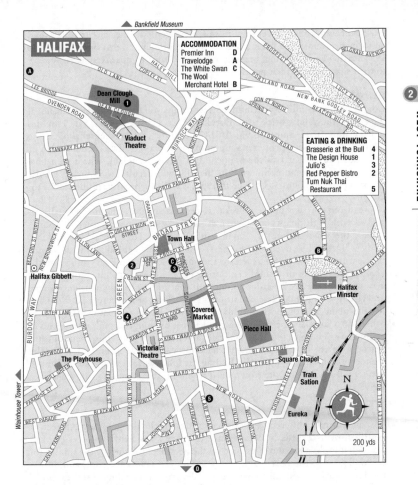

▲ Bankfield Museum

HALIFAX

ACCOMMODATION
Premier Inn **D**
Travelodge **A**
The White Swan **C**
The Wool
Merchant Hotel **B**

EATING & DRINKING
Brasserie at the Bull **4**
The Design House **1**
Julio's **3**
Red Pepper Bistro **2**
Tum Nuk Thai
Restaurant **5**

The Piece Hall and around

The **Piece Hall** (Mon–Fri 9am–5pm, Sat 9.30am–6pm, Sun 11am–5pm; free;
Ⓦwww.thepiecehall.co.uk) was opened in 1779, financed by a group of cloth
manufacturers. It is almost square at 110-by-91 yards, and consists of four colon-
naded sides enclosing a central space. Built on a hillside (there's a 16ft fall), the side at
the top of the site has two storeys, that at the bottom of the site three, and the two
sides that join them go from two to three storeys halfway along. To give access to the
upper storeys there are staircases at each corner (and one next to the Westgate
entrance), and a lift in the southeast corner. There are 315 rooms in which handloom
weavers would display and sell their "pieces" of cloth, consisting of 24-yard by
27-inch strips, each one of which was the result of part-time work for a week – the
rest of the time was devoted to farming. Today, in addition to the tourist office, the
Piece Hall houses a number of small shops and businesses, while the central space
hosts a variety of concerts, community markets and events such as an ice rink during
November and December, and during the summer a "Halifax-on-Sea" beach party.

Downhill from the Piece Hall are the **Square Chapel** (Mon–Fri 9.30am–5pm,
Sat 11am–3pm; Ⓦwww.squarechapel.co.uk) and **Square Church** – the former a

1772 Nonconformist chapel now in our more godless times an art gallery and performance venue, the latter a nineteenth-century church that burned down in 1971 leaving an interesting, brambly ruin. The "square" doesn't apparently refer to their shape, but to their position – in a square.

Eureka!

Continuing downhill across Church Street brings you to the train station and, at the end of the yellow brick road, **Eureka!** (Tues–Fri 10am–4pm, Sat, Sun, hols & bank hols 10am–5pm; £8.95; ☎01422/330 069, Ⓦwww.eureka.org.uk), a modern, purpose-built children's museum for under-11s. The only museum of its kind in Britain, it was the brainchild of Vivien Duffield, who'd seen how popular children's museums were in the US, and decided to launch a similar enterprise in this country. Opened in 1992, it welcomed its five millionth visitor in 2009.

Spread out on two floors, Eureka! is organized into a number of galleries packed with high-quality interactive displays – "Our Global Garden", "Sound-space", the town square of "Living and Working Together", "Me and My Body", "Desert Discovery" and others. The principle behind all the displays is that learning should be fun, even for the youngest visitors. Everything is in the vivid primary hues of a child's colouring book – great for kids, though adults may feel like they've been indulging in illegal mind-altering substances. And everything is in immaculate condition and working order. Perennial favourites are the giant mouth (with wobbly tooth), the cycling skeleton, the Halifax bank, M&S store and petrol station, and a host of things to pull, push, press or manipulate. There's a gift shop and café, and masses of play equipment outside, with one of the largest sandpits in the country. Set aside several hours for this wonderful museum – you'll have to drag the kids away, kicking and screaming. Incidentally, adults on their own need to phone ahead, and sign in when they arrive.

Halifax Minster

For an entirely different experience, walk north along Church Street to **Halifax Minster** (daily 9am–2pm; free; Ⓦwww.halifaxminster.org.uk). Though it looks a bit smoke-grimed on the outside, look out for the sundial (on the wall next to the porch) and the gargoyles just below the roof, and, inside, the intricately carved font cover suspended from the ceiling, the beautifully rich seventeenth-century pews (shortened, alas, by 2ft in the nineteenth century), the figure of Old Tristram, a life-sized carved wooden effigy of a man with a poor-box in front of him ("Pray remember the poor"), and the clear glass windows in the chancel, where the absence of stained glass, enforced by the Puritan church authorities, is subverted by the beautiful intricate patterns of the leading.

The market and Town Hall

Running west from the Piece Hall from the exit opposite the tourist office is **Westgate**, roofed in with a modern arcade and, if you turn right on to Southgate, the entrance to Halifax's large covered **Borough Market** (Mon–Sat 8.30am–5.30pm). Opened in 1896, it has all the usual food and clothes stalls, as well as a wide range of other goods. Raise your eyes from the bargains to examine the intricate iron-and-glass roof, with central dome and clock, beneath which is a circular fruit-and-veg stall.

Further along Southgate and Princess Street stands **Halifax Town Hall**, designed by Houses of Parliament architect Sir Charles Barry. The opening in

1863 by the Prince of Wales (later Edward VII) attracted 70,000 spectators. The town hall clock is over 6ft in diameter, with the largest of its bells weighing over four tons, but it has apparently been silent since 1918, when famous opera singer Dame Nellie Melba, staying in the nearby *White Swan*, complained that the striking of the hours was keeping her awake.

The Halifax Gibbett

A walk from the back of the town hall, west along Broad Street, Cow Green and Lister Lane, brings you to Gibbet Street, and, just across the inner ring road, a reconstruction of the **Halifax Gibbet** – not the usual one of the children's "hangman" game, but a machine for beheading criminals very similar to the French guillotine: an axe head, embedded in a heavy lead-weighted block, descended in a frame onto the neck of the felon, separating the head from the body. It's not easy to find – there are no evident signposts from the town centre, and it's perched on a little park, backing onto a motor repair garage, and with the only plaque giving the names of sponsors (of the reconstructed gibbet, not the executions themselves), rather than an explanation of its historical context. Used especially as a punishment for theft, its severity is explained by the fact that woollen cloth, having been soaked in urine to bleach it, had to be left out on frames to dry, making it particularly easy to steal. It is this horrendous punishment that led to the felon's prayer: "from hell, Hull and Halifax, good lord deliver us". Daniel Defoe, in his *Tour through the Whole Island of Great Britain*, said that he could find no record of such a machine being used in Hull. He also tells of a story where a woman, driving a cart to Halifax market, was passing next to the gibbet while an execution was taking place. The blade descended with such force that the miscreant's head flew off into one of the hampers in the cart, to be discovered later by the horrified country woman when she came to unpack her goods. Defoe noted so many improbabilities, though, "that 'tis reasonable to think the whole tale is a little Yorkshire, which I suppose you will understand well enough!"

Dean Clough Mill

As you enter Halifax from the M1, to the right you will see an enormous mill complex with the words "Dean Clough" mounted on the main building, Hollywood-sign style. This is **Dean Clough Mill** (℡01422/250 250, 🌐www.deanclough.com), built in the mid-nineteenth century to manufacture Crossley's carpets. When the mill closed in 1983, the opportunity to develop the site for community use was seized, and the Grade II listed building was adapted to include several art galleries and display spaces (the Crossley, Upstairs, Mosaic, Community and Education and Photography galleries), the *Viaduct* café/bar (which often hosts stand-up comedy), the *Design House* restaurant, numerous small businesses including an excellent design shop, and the **Viaduct Theatre**, home to Barry Rutter's Northern Broadsides Theatre Company. The latter has made a huge name for itself with an innovative approach to Shakespeare and the classics – its most recent triumph was a version of *Othello* starring comedian Lenny Henry. Dean Clough has plenty of secure parking, even its own hotel (see p.118), and is within walking distance of the town centre. Check the website or by phone for individual venues.

Eating and drinking

Brasserie at the Bull 5 Bull Green ℡01422/330 833, 🌐www.brasserieatthebull.co.uk. Gastropub on the western side of the town centre, with good modern British menu, healthy wine list, smart

unfussy decor and big windows from which to watch the world go by. Not too expensive, and there are fixed-price business lunches and early evening menus. Service can be slow at busy times.
The Design House Dean Clough Mill ☎01422/383 242. Highly regarded restaurant in the Dean Clough Mill complex (see p.121), an ideal place to dine when taking in a play, concert or exhibition. Cool decor verging on the icy. If you'd prefer informal snacks, go for the *Viaduct* café in the same complex instead.
Julio's Princess St ☎01422/349 449, ⊛www .julios.co.uk Popular town centre Italian restaurant. Good, unpretentious food, excellent service and convivial atmosphere.

Red Pepper Bistro 39 Broad St ☎01422/355 694, ⊛redpepperbistro. co.uk. Intimate bistro and bar on what amounts to Halifax's inner ring road. Modern European menu with nods to world cuisine, seasonal ingredients and daily specials board. Good value for money.
Tum Nuk Thai Restaurant 5 Clare Rd ☎01422/352 500. Thai restaurant in stately town centre building (easy to miss – it's on the left as you start to walk up Clare Rd). Good-quality Thai food and decor, though the size of the restaurant tends to bleed it of atmosphere at all but the busiest times.

Nightlife and entertainment

Halifax has a thriving arts scene which makes good use of its stock of nineteenth-century wool-town buildings, including: **Victoria Theatre**, Fountains St (☎01422/351 158, ⊛www.calderdale.gov.uk/victoria); **Viaduct Theatre**, Dean Clough Mill (with the Northern Broadside Company; ☎01422/255 266, ⊛www.deanclough.com); **The Square Chapel**, Square Rd (☎01422/349 422, ⊛www.squarechapel.co.uk); **The Piece Hall**, Blackledge (☎01422/ 321 002, ⊛www.thepiecehall.co.uk); and **The Playhouse**, King Cross St (☎01422/ 365 998).

Around Halifax

Away from the town centre the **Bankfield Museum**, **Shibden Hall** and **Manor Heath Park** are all within a ten-minute car ride, while further afield are the **Wainhouse Tower**, **Ogden Water**, **Hardcastle Crags** and **Gibson Mill**. Above all, Halifax is blessed with the **Calder Valley** (see p.124), which stretches westward to the Lancashire border.

Shibden Hall and estate

On a hill above the main road (A58) from Halifax to the M1 (buses #508, #548, #549 & #681, but all with 15min walk from the drop-off point), well signposted from the town centre and with two adequate car parks, stands **Shibden Hall** (March–Nov Mon–Sat 10am–5pm, Sun noon–5pm; Dec–Feb closes 4pm; £3.50; ☎01422/352 246 or 321 455), a fine house whose earliest parts date to 1420 and whose most famous resident was Anne Lister (see box opposite). The estate includes a wilderness garden, a cascade, a mere and a lodge plus a boating lake, a miniature railway, children's play equipment and a pitch and putt. The house itself illustrates the furniture and styles of different ages in period room settings, and there's a fine folk museum, with a collection of horse-drawn vehicles (in the house's seventeenth-century barn), interiors of craftsmen's workplaces – a blacksmith, a wheelwright, a cooper – and a reconstruction of the *Crispin Inn* (noted for meetings of Luddites). There's a pleasantly intimate café (the cheese toasties are terrific) and a small shop.

Wainhouse Tower

The Wainhouse Tower dominates the skyline southwest of Halifax town centre. Built in the early 1870s by local dye magnate John Edward Wainhouse in response to the 1870 Smoke Abatement Act, it was intended to disperse smoke

Anne Lister (1791–1840)

Famous at the time, and since, for her open lesbianism (she was known in the area as "Gentleman Jack"), Anne Lister inherited **Shibden Hall** from her uncle in 1826. She was a tireless traveller, mountaineer, academic and businesswoman. Her portraits clearly show a woman of masculine dress and demeanour, and her four-million-word diaries contained fascinating accounts of her life and adventures, and (in code) graphic descriptions of her many passionate love affairs with women ("I love and only love the fairer sex and thus beloved by them in turn, my heart revolts from any love but theirs", she wrote on October 29, 1820). When she inherited Shibden Hall, she managed the estate, including farms, a quarry and a coal mine, herself. She travelled widely until, in 1840, she died of a fever in Russia. Her body was brought back to Yorkshire by her companion and lover Ann Walker and buried near Halifax. Anne Lister's life was the subject of a TV programme **The Secret Diaries of Miss Anne Lister**, shown on BBC 2 in spring 2010.

from his factory. However, before the chimney was finished, Wainhouse sold the works, and the new owner refused to take on the expense of completing the chimney. So Wainhouse and his architect transformed it into a tower, which was finished in 1875, with an octagonal shaft on a square base, a height of 275ft, and 403 steps climbing up to a viewing platform set amongst florid decoration. As for Wainhouse's motives in building it, all is conjecture. The world's tallest folly? An astronomical observation tower? A platform from which to spy on his industrial rivals? Who knows. Whatever the truth of the matter, it has achieved iconic status. And you really can't miss it. Following renovation in 2009, the tower is open to the public on most bank holidays (phone ☎01422/368 725 for open days; £2).

Bankfield Museum

A mile or so north of Halifax town centre is **Bankfield Museum** (buses #34 & #576; Tues–Sat 10am–5pm, Sun 1pm–4pm; free; ☎01422/354 823 or 352 334), a curiously old-fashioned museum that is interesting more, perhaps, for its place in the town's history than for what it now contains. The home of Victorian local mill owner Edward Akroyd (1810–87), it started as a relatively modest town house but was increasingly transformed after he inherited money from his father, and as his career progressed from successful businessman, through early supporter of the Yorkshire Penny Bank and Halifax Permanent Building Society, to Lieutenant Colonel of the 4th Yorkshire Halifax Rifle Volunteers to Member of Parliament. By the time of his death Bankfield Mansion was a very substantial Italianate mansion that became, shortly afterwards, the museum it is today.

Edward Akroyd was that typical Victorian mixture of local benefactor and muscular Anglican entrepreneur, with an interest in improving the lot of working people. In particular, he encouraged his employees to progress by their own efforts, saving money, worshipping God and investing in decent housing. He developed Akroyd Park surrounding the mansion, the church of All Souls, and across the Boothtown Road, the model village of Akroydon, designed by George Gilbert Scott, and similar to in date and function, though on a smaller scale than, Saltaire (see p.113), with houses, a square, and a burial ground, much of which remains relatively untouched. There are excellent guides to the area available in the museum, which gives a real feeling for the nineteenth-century development of Halifax.

The museum itself has good collections of furniture, art and costume (on the top floor), and the well-presented **Duke of Wellington's Regimental Museum**, apart from being a historical artefact in its own right. As you approach the museum, by the way, don't drive into the Bankfield Care Home – it's an easy mistake to make.

Manor Heath Park

Manor Heath Park (daily: summer [BST] 10am–4.30pm; winter [GMT] 10am–4pm; free), less than a mile south of the town centre, is what's left of the home of Halifax's great carpet manufacture John Crossley (of Dean Clough Mills). The house was demolished in 1958 after becoming derelict, but the park remains as a leisure area with pleasant views of the surrounding hills, well-tended lawns, a sunken garden, water garden and rather good children's play area. It is in this park that all the plants and saplings needed to decorate the town are grown (any surplus supply is sold off at very reasonable prices), and where the annual Halifax Charity Gala is held. Also here is the **Jungle Experience**, a series of rather shabby greenhouses stuffed with tropical plants, flowers, birds, terrapins, fish and butterflies. Though it's superficially unprepossessing, you should persevere – they've packed a lot of good things into it. And the carnivorous plants will send shivers down your spine.

Calderdale

One of the most picturesque and atmospheric parts of the Metropolitan Borough centred on Halifax is the valley after which it is named – **Calderdale**, which meanders westward towards the Lancashire border. It came to prominence as the local woollen industry left farmhouse, cottage and hill village for water mills along the river Calder. When the mills switched to steam, chimneys sprouted along the riverbank, and transport improved, with the road, canal, and eventually railway forming a multistrand link between Yorkshire and Lancashire.

Today, cleared of smoke and grime since the decline of the woollen industry, the valley of the **Calder** is a beautiful post-industrial landscape, with interesting mills and cottages modernized or put to other uses, canal boats puttering between steep-sided hills, and dry-stone walls, tussocky grass and scribbles of woodland climbing up to heather uplands. The main town is **Hebden Bridge**, and within a couple of miles of it and each other, as reminders of one of the twentieth century's great tragic love stories, there's the birthplace of **Ted Hughes** and the grave of his wife **Sylvia Plath**.

Sowerby Bridge, Mytholmroyd, Hebden Bridge and Todmorden are all on the Halifax-to-Manchester rail line, which is quicker than the bus (#591, #592 & #593).

Sowerby Bridge

Driving west from Halifax, the first town you come to, in about three miles, is **SOWERBY BRIDGE**, though to visit it you need to take a short detour off the main road. Not to be confused with Sowerby itself (a little further south), Sowerby Bridge has many impressive mill buildings, and apart from being an important wool town, also produced stationary steam engines used all over Yorkshire and Lancashire. Sowerby Bridge is where the Rochdale Canal joins the Calder and Hebble Navigation – the resulting eighteenth-century canal basin and its associated buildings are all listed.

Mytholmroyd

A further four miles west from Sowerby Bridge brings you to **MYTHOLM-ROYD**, notable mainly for being the birthplace of Ted Hughes, poet laureate from 1984 to his death in 1998. Little is made of the fact – there don't appear to be any signs to help you find it, and there is certainly no "Ted Hughes" café or "Ted Hughes" guesthouse. Probably the easiest way to find the house he was born is to start at the clog factory just around the corner. **Walkley Clogs** (Mon–Fri 10am–5pm, Sat 10am–4.30pm; ☎01422/885 757, ⓦwww.clogs.co.uk) occupy a unit in Mount Pleasant Mills just off Mytholmroyd's main street (follow the brown sign); you can see the clog-maker at work, browse in the factory shop, or just breathe in the heady aroma of leather and wood. If you don't want to be lumbered with carrying around your purchases for the rest of your holiday, you can order online when you get home, choose a style, then achieve the right fit by sending off paper patterns and measurements of the feet to be clogged. Some of the clogs are very pretty and colourful, but a remarkable number are heavy-duty work clogs, even in this day and age.

From here, walk back down the hill and turn right just before the canal bridge. First right again, and **Ted Hughes's birthplace** is a few yards up, on the left. The small end-terrace house is distinguishable from its neighbours only because of the blue plaque on the wall, and brings home how humble the great poet's origins were.

Hebden Bridge

A couple of miles beyond Mytholmroyd is the Calder Valley's main town, **HEBDEN BRIDGE**, probably the best place to stay if you're exploring this region. A characteristic mill town, it was just a hamlet before the need for water power brought the woollen industry down the hill from Heptonstall (see p.126) which stands high above it. Today it has earned a reputation as a place where dyed-in-the-wool Yorkshire folk live in harmony with faintly left-wing green enthusiasts and gay activists, a place with smart cafés and bars, upmarket independent shops, and lots of nice traditional pubs. It has developed a substantial tourist industry, both for itself and as a centre for walking on the surrounding hills, though many residents still feel that the council doesn't do enough to promote it.

The town is pretty as a picture. The Rochdale Canal arrows straight through the centre, as does the River Calder and its tributary Hebden Water, ensuring lots of bridges and mill buildings which have been converted into hotels, restaurants, shops and lots more. Drop in to the **Visitor and Canal Centre** (Mon–Fri 9.30am–5.30pm, Sat 10.15am–5pm, Sun 10.30am–5pm; ☎01422/843 831) in the Marina (actually a canal wharf and dry dock) on the left as you enter the town, where you can pick up excellent guides (in particular *Discover Hebden Bridge Town Centre Trail*) or consult staff who know the town well.

While wandering around Hebden Bridge there's a lot to look out for. At the heart of the town is pleasantly pedestrianized **St George's Square** (more a triangle), with shops, cafés and pubs dotted around it. Immediately off it is the **Old Packhorse Bridge**, dating from around 1510, but with repairs made (and commemorated in the parapet) in 1602 and 1657. The triangular alcoves were to allow pedestrians to get away from the packhorses if a string was crossing the bridge. One of the three spans now has no water under it, but it used to cross the "tail goit" or mill race that carried water back to the river after it had driven the wheel in Bridge Mill, upstream. Next to the bridge are the recently added "wavy steps", usually host to ducks, geese, pigeons and crows. Beyond the bridge a path rises steeply upwards – the old packhorse route (the "Buttress") to Heptonstall.

Just beyond the town centre, beside the canal, the **Alternative Technology Centre** (Mon–Fri 10am–5pm, Sat noon–5pm, Sun noon–4pm; free, with charges for guided tours and workshops; Ⓦwww.alternativetechnology.org.uk) occupies a series of rooms in Hebble End Mill. Devoted to sustainable technology, it aims to be a source for "inspiration, information and advice", and consists of a small exhibition space, a green shop, an energy room, small-scale organic gardens and various examples of recycling – of books, clothes, coins (made into jewellery) and bikes. Don't expect a slick professional concern – they're either visionary amateurs putting dreams into practice or a bunch of hippies, depending on who you talk to.

Hebden Bridge **train station** is across the canal at the eastern edge of the village, about ten minutes' walk from the centre.

Accommodation and eating

Angeldale Hangingroyd Lane ⓣ01422/847 321, Ⓦwww.angeldale.co.uk. Clean, comfortable and well set-up guesthouse in an imposing Victorian building with nice gardens two minutes from the centre. **❷**

🏃 **Moyles Hotel** New Rd ⓣ01422/845 272, Ⓦwww.moyles.com. On the main road into Hebden Bridge from Halifax, opposite the visitor centre, *Moyles Hotel* is housed in a sedate Victorian terrace, and offers twelve stylish rooms (five designated "signature") and an excellent bar and restaurant. Not many places can combine glowing reviews for its restaurant in the *Manchester Evening News* and the CAMRA pub-of-the-year award (2009). **❸**

🏃 **Organic House** Market St ⓣ01422/843 429. Freshly prepared food including

breakfasts, main meals, cakes and the best coffee for miles. Wood floors, tables and chairs – a ponytails-and-sandals kind of place.

Rim Nam Thai Restaurant Butlers Wharf ⓣ01422/846 888. Next to the visitor centre right on the canal. Meals £10–20, though they do a very good early-bird, four-course menu for £9.95 (Sun–Thurs 6–7pm).

Shoulder of Mutton Bridge Gate. Pretty stone pub in the town centre, with good beer and food, and nice convivial atmosphere.

White Lion Hotel Bridge Gate ⓣ01422/842 197, Ⓦwww.whitelionhotel.net. Mid-seventeenth-century farmhouse next to the town square, and possibly the oldest building in the town. A busy food pub with accommodation. **❸**

Heptonstall

Above Hebden Bridge is the village of **HEPTONSTALL** – you can either take the stiff walk up the trail from the packhorse bridge (about 30min, depending on how fit you are), or drive up (there's a visitors' car park, or, out of season, you can just park on the street). A beautiful stone village on and just below the hill top, it once housed the hand looms that were replaced by Hebden Bridge's water-powered mills in the valley below. There are rows of weavers' cottages – note the rows of windows on the first floor, to give plenty of light to see the fine threads – two rather attractive **pubs**, *The Cross* and the *White Lion*, a tiny post office, and two churches sharing a graveyard. On the right as you walk up into the village, the ruined church, damaged by a gale in 1847, is dedicated to St Thomas Becket, while the newer one on the left is the church of St Thomas the Apostle. The churchyard is paved with flat tombstones.

The grave that most visitors are in search of, however, is not in this churchyard at all. American poet **Sylvia Plath,** who committed suicide in 1963 at the age of 30, is buried in the "New Graveyard" (to find it, turn left at the top out of the old one, and it's just down the lane). Her grave is in the third row back from the lowest tier, about eight graves in from the far edge – there's little to indicate which is hers.

The very presence of Sylvia Plath's body in this graveyard was a cause for controversy – an American, who died in London, she was buried here by her estranged husband Ted Hughes, at whose door many laid the blame for her suicide (it occurred shortly after he left her). Even more controversial was the fact that she is called "Sylvia Plath Hughes" on the gravestone – her supporters felt that this added insult to injury, and it has been chiselled off, and replaced, a number of times.

There are a lot of other interesting things to see in the village, especially the **weavers' square** overlooking the churchyard, the octagonal **Methodist chapel** (built in 1764 after a visit by John Wesley), and the **village stocks** nearby. But it's to pay respects to a wonderful poet, and for the overall feel of a pre-Industrial-Revolution Yorkshire village that Heptonstall is worth visiting – that and the wonderful views down across Hebden Bridge, and west along the meandering Calder Valley.

Huddersfield and around

As you drive into **HUDDERSFIELD** you might at first think that there's little to detain you here. But as with many other such at first unpromising places, persistence brings its own reward. As J.B. Priestley observed in *English Journey* when he visited in 1933: "Huddersfield is not a handsome town", yet he went on to say "but yet is famous in these parts for the intelligence and independence of its citizens". And there are still signs to support this. Though it's not the only town in the Kirklees Metropolitan region – there's also Batley, Dewsbury, Holme Valley and others – Huddersfield is certainly the biggest, yet its residents have persistently refused to apply for city status. And although the town features plenty of undistinguished postwar architecture, there's also a lot of interesting things to see as well, in particular where great efforts have been made to find new uses for beautiful old buildings. Huddersfield's **train station**, for example, a Grade I listed building, is host to two excellent watering holes and overlooks **St George's Square** with its clutch of stately Victorian buildings. One of these is the imposing **George Hotel**, birthplace of **Rugby League** and home to a small museum devoted to the sport. The **Town Hall** is an excellent music venue, **St Paul's** church is part of **Huddersfield University**, the 1819 **Wesleyan chapel** is the **Lawrence Batley Theatre**, and there's a rather nice restaurant in the crypt of the **Parish Church of St Peter**. A plaque on the iron-and-glass **open market** says it all: "Built 1888, restored 1980, repainted 1998, refurbished 2008". The people of Huddersfield believe in looking after what's left of their heritage.

Arrival and information

Huddersfield sits just south of junction 23 of the M62, and the road system around the town – a clearly defined ring road with ample signs telling you where the **car parks** are and how many cars they can take. There's a well-organized **bus station** on the western edge of the town centre, just inside the ring road on Upperhead Row, and the **train station**, though not connected to it, is right beside it across Westgate on St George's Square. The **tourist information centre** (Mon–Wed 9.30am–5pm, Thurs & Fri 9am–5pm, Sat 9am–4pm; ☎01484/223 200) is in the foyer of the Library and Art Gallery.

Accommodation

With Huddersfield not being in itself a hot tourist destination, most of the **accommodation** tends to be within easy reach of the M62.

Titanic Spa Apartments

Billing itself as the country's first eco-spa, **Titanic Spa Apartments** (Low Westwood Lane, Linthwaite; ☎0845 410 3333, ⓦwww.titanicspa.com), occupying a massive old woollen mill, offers a full range of treatments and products, and has become known far and wide, through word-of-mouth and from praise in the national press (including inclusion in *The Independent*'s "Top 50 Spas in the World"). Aiming to be carbon-neutral, it offers guilt-free pampering, and although individual treatments can be pricey, a number of packages bring the cost right down. So, for example, "Fabulous Fridays" or "Sunday Night Stopovers" include overnight luxury accommodation, continental breakfast, light lunch and dinner in the bistro, and a selection of treatments for around £139 per person.

Briar Court Hotel Halifax Rd, Birchencliffe ☎01484/519 902, ⓦwww.briarcourt.co.uk. Modern stone-built hotel on the road from Huddersfield to the M62, and convenient for both. Clean lines, modern, rather severe; decor, cheerful Italian restaurant with wood-burning pizza oven. Good value, and plenty of free parking. ❸

Huddersfield Central Lodge 11/15 Beast Market ☎01484/515 551, ⓦwww.central lodge.com. As you'd expect from the name, *Huddersfield Central Lodge* is centrally located, on the eastern edge of the town centre inside the ring road. Privately run by the Marsden family, hugely popular and boasting a startlingly long list of awards and celebrity past guests. Free overnight parking in high security car park. A real gem in these days of huge hotel conglomerates. ❷

Old Golf House Corus Hotel New Hey Rd, Outlane ☎0844 567 0782, ⓦwww.corushotels.com. Less than four miles out of Huddersfield near the M62, in an impressive "seventeenth-century-style" stone building that was once a golf clubhouse, the hotel has retained splendid grounds and even five holes of pitch-and-putt. There's a variety of different types of room, most of which were renovated in 2009, though some rooms have still to be done. ❸

Pennine Manor Hotel Nettleton Hill Rd, Scapegoat Hill ☎01484/642 368, ⓦwww.thedeckersgroup .com. About five miles out of the town centre, close to the M62, the *Pennine Manor* is owned by the small but select *Decker Group* of hotels, gastropubs and grills. Pleasant medium-sized hotel with all mod cons, fine views, good food and friendly service. ❸

The Town

First stop in Huddersfield has to be at the **Library and Art Gallery** (Mon–Fri 10am–5pm, Sat 10am–4pm; free; ☎01484/221 964), an impressive lump of Art Deco architecture opened in 1937 at the bottom of Ramsden Street, with paintings, drawings and sculptures from the Kirklees Collection, including work by well-known artists such as L.S. Lowry, Francis Bacon and Henry Moore. It also houses a **visitor information** desk in the library foyer.

In this part of town, next to the library, are the **Piazza** and the linked **Queens-gate Market** (Mon–Fri 9am–5.30pm, Sat 8.30am–5.30pm; ☎01484/223 730), which provide between them a wide range of shops and stalls under cover, and an open space which hosts an ice rink over Christmas and a variety of other entertainments during the rest of the year.

A few yards through the passage between them brings you to busy Queensgate, part of the ring road, and what was **St Paul's** church, now a concert hall (ⓦwww .kirklees.gov.uk) which is part of the **University of Huddersfield**, whose buildings loom behind it. The university, which has campuses in Oldham and Barnsley as well, and whose Chancellor is *Star Trek* and *X-Men* actor Patrick Stewart, has done a lot to put Huddersfield on the map, and to enliven its social scene.

Queens Street and around

If you bear left on to **Queens Street**, past the **Lawrence Batley Theatre** (see p.130), and continue north where it becomes Cross Church Street, you come to the **Parish Church of St Peter**, built, it is said, by a Walter de Laci, who when thrown from his horse into a swamp some time around 1100 AD promised God that he would build a church if he could see his way clear to sparing him. He was spared, and the church was built. The current church, however, dates from 1503–06, and a subsequent rebuilding was undertaken in 1830 when a larger, more impressive structure was deemed necessary to reflect the growing wealth of the town. Designed by James Pigott Pritchett of York, the new church was consecrated in 1836, but hasn't, alas, stood the test of time – the external walls of the church have weathered very badly in places. The crypt, created in the 1830 rebuilding, is now leased to the popular *Key's* restaurant (see p.130).

Beyond the church, Byram Street takes you to the quaint **Open Market**, just beyond the gantry that spans the street and bears its name. The market, on the right and brightly painted in blue and red, isn't really completely open, since it boasts an ornate wrought-iron and glass roof over a tiled floor, but it's well worth a visit for the architecture and for the detail (much use is made of the town's coat of arms), if not for the rather limited range of stalls.

St George's Square

A further stroll, this time west along Northumberland Street past the Victorian post office building, brings you to the best-preserved part of Huddersfield town centre – **St George's Square**, dominated by the imposing bulk of **Huddersfield train station**, designed by James Pigott Pritchett, the architect of the rebuilt parish church. Built between 1846 and 1850, and much admired by John Betjeman, the station is a Grade I listed building of great magnificence, which is odd in that Huddersfield's links with the rest of the railway system are not that good – you need to change in Manchester, Leeds or Wakefield if you want access to the main routes. The steps of the station, at the high end of the square, host open-air performances – music, street theatre and so on – and the two single-storey wings on either side of the imposing two-storey classical facade, all with Corinthian columns, are occupied by two excellent real ale **pubs** – the *Head of Steam* and the *King's Head*, accessible from the square or from Platform 1.

On St George's Square, on the left as you face it from the station, stands the **George Hotel**, not only a fine building in its own right (listed Grade II), but also famous as the birthplace of **Rugby League**. The **Gillette Rugby League**

The birth of Rugby League

On August 29, 1895, a group of northern Rugby Union clubs met in the *George Hotel*, and decided to leave the Rugby Football Union, and form the **Rugby Football League**. The cause of the split was simple – the rules of the RFU wouldn't allow the payment of compensation for lost wages when playing, something which wouldn't worry the prosperous public school educated, middle class players that tended to be associated with the game in the south of England, but which was very much a sore point among the more working class players of the north. The RFU reacted ferociously to the split, saying that teams in the RFL had forfeited their amateur status, not only kicking them out of the RFU, but saying that any player who played for or against them would also be banned. As time went on the two codes diverged further, with the original maintaining strict amateurism while the new code became professional. Rules also diverged – for example, the RFL abolished the line-out in 1897, and in 1906 reduced the number of players from 15 to 13. In recent times the differences between the two codes have become blurred, especially by the relaxing of the strict amateurism of the RFU.

Heritage Centre (Feb–Oct Sat & Sun 11am–4pm; free; ☎01484/542 458, ⓦwww.rlheritage.co.uk), in the basement of the hotel, was established in 2005, the brainchild of Sky Sports presenter Mike Stephenson. It consists of a large collection of photographs, shirts, caps, medals, trophies, programmes and other memorabilia of the game, together with video clips on plasma screens.

Eating and drinking

For just a drink, there are also the two traditional **pubs** in the train station (see p.129).

Argento 37 St John's St ☎01484/535 440, ⓦargentosteakhouse.com. Locally owned restaurant just east of the train station specializing in South American food – not only steaks and fish cooked on "hot rocks", but a variety of sausages and *empanadas* (South American-style pasties). Busy and popular, with cheerful, wood-dominated interior.

Bradleys Restaurant 84 Fitzwilliam St ☎01484/516 773, ⓦwww.bradleysrestaurant .co.uk. Big name in Huddersfield eating out. Good value, with prices low for such an attractive split-level dining area. Standards of service can decline during busy periods, and with loads of special offers, tribute nights and so on, there are lots of these. Free parking and, a welcome rule, no mobiles.

Gringo's 8 Viaduct St ☎01484/422 411, ⓦwww .gringos-restaurant.co.uk. Bright no-nonsense Mexican restaurant in earthy colours. Busy, noisy, with two-for-one offers, limited range of enchiladas, burrittos, fajitas and so on, and huge portions.

The Keys Restaurant Byram St ☎01484/516 677, ⓦwww.keysrestaurant.com. A daytime-only restaurant in the crypt of the parish church of St Peter. Big selection of breakfast and lunch meals and snacks in warm surroundings of beautifully lit columns and vaulted ceilings, which were excavated by the YMCA in the 1980s. Don't imagine a soup kitchen – this is a smart, busy restaurant with open-plan kitchens.

Thai Sakon 5 St John's Rd ☎01484/450 159, ⓦwww.thaisakon.co.uk. One of several restaurants in and around the railway arches north of Huddersfield train station, the *Thai Sakon* has earned universally good reviews both from diners and from the local press. Smart surroundings, excellent food, and staff who have the time and inclination to help out less knowledgeable customers.

Nightlife and entertainment

The arts in Huddersfield centre on three magnificent buildings in the town centre – the Art Deco **Library and Art Gallery** (see p.128), the Victorian **Town Hall** on Ramsden Street (☎01484/221 900, ⓦwww.kirklees.gov.uk), built between 1875 and 1881, which seats up to 1200 people for classical and choral music – it has excellent acoustics – and the **Lawrence Batley Theatre** on Queens Street (☎01484/430 528, ⓦwww.thelbt.org), which occupies what was, when it opened in 1819, the biggest Wesleyan chapel in the world, accommodating around two thousand worshippers. The LBT now hosts a variety of plays, dance, music gigs, pantomime and comedy, and has an elegant bar and bistro. Beyond that, having a flourishing university in the town centre means lots of lively pubs and clubs, as well as the world-famous **Contemporary Music Festival** (ⓦwww.hcmf.co.uk) consisting of around fifty events held over ten days every November, including concerts, musical theatre, dance, multimedia, talks and film.

Listings

Buses ☎0113/245 7676.
Car rental Thrifty ☎01484/453 482; Budget ☎01484/427 767.
Hospital Acre St ☎01484/342 000.

Internet access Cybernet, 80 John William St ☎01484/431 010.
Pharmacy Boots, 22 King St ☎01484/421 756.
Post office Northumberland St.

Around Huddersfield

The hilly area around Huddesfield is much disfigured by industry, yet achieves a kind of majesty, with valley floors full of ribbon development, factories, sewage works, railway lines, reservoirs and viaducts, steep hillsides covered in terraced houses, and narrow lanes bounded by dry-stone walls climbing up on to the surrounding empty moors.

In this hinterland there's a good balance of attractions. The most prominent feature, visible for miles around, is **Castle Hill** and the **Victoria Tower**. To the west of the town is the **Bullecourt Museum**, tracing military history from 1815 to the present, to the east the **Tolson Museum**, covering many aspects of Huddersfield's history. Further afield are the **Red House Museum** and **Oakwell Hall** with its country park, while in an arc about six miles south of Huddersfield are three popular attractions: the **Standedge Tunnel and Visitor Centre**, **Kirklees Light Railway** in Clayton West and, of course, **Holmfirth**, whose connection with TV's **Last of the Summer Wine** brings in hordes of visitors.

Victoria Tower

By far the most obvious feature, south of the town, is the **Victoria Tower** on top of **Castle Hill** (bus #341; open only on certain days, phone ☎07968/426 312; £1.30) built to commemorate Queen Victoria's Diamond Jubilee in 1897 and opened in 1899. With a top just short of 1000ft above sea level and despite renovation in 1960 it still isn't in very good condition. It should, however, provide a splendid viewpoint when planned further renovations – renewal of paths, repair of erosion, provision of viewing platform and seating, the construction of a bridge – are carried out.

The Bullecourt Museum

The **Bullecourt Museum** (no convenient bus; Sat, Sun & bank holidays 2–4pm; £2; ☎01484/461 029), west of Huddersfield in the old drill hall of the 7th Battalion, Duke of Wellington Regiment in Milnsbridge, covers military history from 1815 to the present. Named after a World War I battle in which the 7th Battalion were involved, it contains displays, uniforms, weapons and vehicles from all the major campaigns involving the Duke of Wellington's regiment. Look out for the Anderson shelter, the American jeep, a copy of *Mein Kampf* liberated from Hitler's Berlin bunker at the end of the war, and a German map of Huddersfield with all the strategic places marked, ready for the occupation.

The Tolson Museum

The **Tolson Museum** (no convenient bus; Mon–Fri 11am–5pm, Sat & Sun noon–5pm; free; ☎01484/223 830, ⓦ www.kirklees.gov.uk), visible on the right as you travel east on the A629 Wakefield Road about a mile out of the town centre, is a Victorian mansion standing in its own grounds. It covers the history of Huddersfield, and has displays on local history and archeology, textiles, birds, insects and plants, music, weapons, science, toys, dolls and transport. The best-known item in the "Going Places" section is the three-wheeled LSD car, manufactured in Huddersfield between 1919 and 1924 – nothing to do with drugs or money, they were the initials of the designer (Longbottom), manufacturer (Sykes) and accountant (Dyson) responsible for its production. Surely the only time an accountant has been immortalized in such a way. A series of visiting exhibitions and events take place – check out the website for details.

Red House Museum and Oakwell Hall

Seven miles northeast of Huddersfield close to the M62 are the two jewels in the Kirklees crown. In **GOMERSAL** the charming **Red House Museum** (bus #255; Mon–Fri 11am–5pm, Sat & Sun noon–5pm; free; ℡01274/335 100) occupies a cloth-merchant's residence (the family were appropriately called the Taylors), with 1830s period rooms, tableaux showing the family at work and play and formal gardens that complement the house but contrast oddly with the modern properties you glimpse through the trees. An early resident was **Mary Taylor**, one of the many indomitable Yorkshire women that the county seems to produce – feminist writer, businesswoman and leader of women's mountain climbing expeditions. She was a great friend of Charlotte Brontë's, who, in her novel *Shirley*, used both the house ("Briarmains" in the book) and the area (Gomersal) as background.

In nearby **BIRSTALL** is the 1583-built **Oakwell Hall** (bus #255; Mon–Fri 11am–5pm, Sat & Sun noon–5pm; free; ℡01924/326 240), also with period rooms, this time modelled on the 1690s, and also featured in *Shirley* – as the eponymous heroine's home Fieldhead. Rather more splendid than the Red House, it is surrounded by an arboretum, walled gardens and delightful parkland. There's a play area, countryside centre, a café and shop. A fine Elizabethan house with, internally, many late seventeenth-century features (in particular the Great Parlour) and a mixture of original and reproduction furniture, it only just escaped being exported to the USA in the early twentieth century, and is now often used for filming – most recently, the story of Anne Lister (see box, p.123).

Standedge Tunnel and Visitor Centre

To the southwest of Huddersfield is the **Standedge Tunnel and Visitor Centre** (buses #182, #183, #184, #185 from Huddersfield; Tues–Sun: March–Sept 10am–5pm; Oct & Nov 10am–4pm; also Mon bank & school hols; free boat trip £4.50; ⓦwww.standedge.co.uk), near the mill town of **MARSDEN**. The tunnel, which takes the **Huddersfield Narrow Canal** through the Pennines, is, at just over three miles long, the longest tunnel in the country. The superlatives don't end there – it's also the highest above sea level, and the deepest underground. You can take a thirty-minute trip by narrow boat into the tunnel, or you can book a through trip. There isn't, of course, much to see in the dark, and it isn't suitable if you're claustrophobic. The **visitor centre**, which is free, tells the story of the tunnel and the canal, and there's a shop, some excellent information boards and café. A word of warning about parking – the official free **car park**, which is signposted, is next to Marsden train station, and is a good fifteen minutes' walk along the canal to the tunnel entrance. There is some parking across the canal from the visitor centre, but it's limited to blue badge holders. On summer weekends volunteers run a water ferry from the car park to the tunnel (50p).

Holmfirth: Last of the Summer Wine

Due south of Huddersfield is the town of **HOLMFIRTH,** famous now as the setting for popular and long-running TV series *Last of the Summer Wine*. You can see, and take refreshment, in Sid's café, and Nora Batty's house is now the site of the **Last of the Summer Wine Exhibition** (Mon–Sat 10am–4pm, Sun 11am–4pm; Nov–March closed Tues; £2; ⓦwww.wrinkledstocking.co.uk), opened by Bill Owen ("Compo") in 1996, with photos, props, memorabilia, video clips (with out-takes), a time-line and list of episodes, and a great deal more. There's a pleasant tearoom (inevitably *The Wrinkled Stocking*), and a gift shop. The whole package is pretty comprehensive, as you'd expect since the BBC gave its full support to the venture, and if you're a fan of the series a visit is a must. But you may find Holmfirth a bit disorienting, too, since things are not always where you expect them to be – the programme-makers ranged far and wide over the whole area for locations, and by no means all of them are in the town.

Apart from the *Last of the Summer Wine* connection, the town is a mixed bag. Surrounded by the attractive moorland countryside across which the programme's elderly delinquents roam while enjoying their second childhood, the town itself is a mixture of the quaint and the scruffy. There's a lot of nice Pennine architecture with attractive stone cottages, terraces of houses that picturesquely line the banks of the river, nice independent shops, the neat 1912 Picturedrome, the solid *Old Bridge Hotel* and steep flights of stone steps that rise beside the church to the maze of narrow alleys above it. But there's also the large nonentity of the Riverside Shopping Centre, the busy bus station right in the centre of town and ugly concrete walls that guide the turbulent stream through the town centre – either taking the edge off the town's attractiveness, or making it real and unpretentious, depending on how you look at it.

Kirklees Light Railway

To the southeast of Huddersfield, in **CLAYTON WEST**, is the **Kirklees Light Railway** (buses Stagecoach #80 or #81 from Huddersfield; check website for operating days; day rover £9.50; ⓦwww.kirkleeslightrailway.com), a narrow-gauge (15-inch) railway built by enthusiasts on the route of a discontinued branch line that had served local coal mines, and opened in 1991. Four diminutive steam engines (*Hawk*, *Owl*, *Fox* and *Badger*), together with one diesel and one tram, pull passengers along the nearly four miles of track between Clayton West and Shelley, a trip that takes about 25 minutes. All but one of the engines were built by Brian Taylor, the driving force behind the whole enterprise. The **Clayton West** station has a substantial café and shop, an indoor play area and a duck pond around which goes an even smaller miniature railway (7¼-inch gauge 50p), and a large car park. The Shelley station also has a café.

Wakefield and around

An important regional centre that was for centuries the county headquarters of the West Riding of Yorkshire, **WAKEFIELD**, like several other major towns and cities in Yorkshire, is experiencing serious challenges in terms of urban development. Faced with the decline in its traditional industries, especially coal during the Thatcher years, and more recently suffering the effects of global recession, its attempts at urban regeneration have met with mixed success, with the massive Trinity Walk development around the old market hall in particular grinding to a halt as the developers hit the financial buffers. And in truth Wakefield city centre is dominated by uninspired late twentieth-century architecture and an unbeliev-able number of retail parks and shopping malls to the south and west – Ings Road, Trinity, Cathedral, Westgate, Albion Mills and, right in the centre, The Ridings. However, there are still some good things to see, starting with the impressive **Cathedral** right in the centre and the group of grand Victorian civic buildings north of the **Bullring**, plus two small but interesting museums – the **Gissing Centre** and the **Stephen Beaumont Museum of Mental Health** – though the opening hours of both are very restricted. The **Wakefield Bridge** to the south of the centre has a rare **Chantry Chapel**, and beyond it, as plans for south of the river come to fruition, there will be an attractive waterside development, including the eagerly anticipated **Hepworth Gallery**; however the real draws in the district are in the wider area (see p.136). So though Wakefield might see to offer slim pickings to the outside visitor, things are definitely looking up.

Arrival and information

Wakefield's **road connections** are excellent, tucked as it is into the horseshoe formed by the M1, the M62 and the A1. The town is well signposted from all three, and there are numerous **car parks** encircling the city centre – the most convenient is the multistorey in the Ridings Shopping Centre. The town is served by two **train stations**, of which **Westgate**, on the western edge of the city centre, is the most important, being on the main East Coast line with services south to London and north to Scotland. **Kirkgate** to the south of the centre handles local routes. Both stations are within easy walking distance of the town centre. The **bus station** stands on Union Street, at the northern edge of the town centre, just beyond the new market hall (so train-to-bus transfer is not quick). The **tourist information centre** (Mon, Tues, Thurs & Fri 9am–4.30pm, Wed 9am–3.45pm, Sat 10am–3pm; ☎0845 601 8353, ⓦwww.wakefield.gov.uk) stands on the Bullring.

Accommodation

Hotels in the centre of Wakefield are few and far between, and therefore your best bet is to go with one of the big chains.

Holiday Inn Leeds Wakefield Queens Drive, Ossett ☎0870 400 9082, ⓦwww.holidayinn.com. Despite its name, this slightly more upmarket hotel is less than two miles from Wakefield city centre. There's lots of free parking, and a pub serving food nearby. ❸

Wakefield Centre Premier Inn Thornes Park, Denby Dale Rd ☎0870 197 7257, ⓦwww .premierinn.com. Less than a mile from the city centre in quiet parkland setting, this well-run branch of the *Premier Inn* chain is probably the best budget option when visiting the city. ❷

Waterton Park Hotel Walton ☎01924/257 911, ⓦwww.waterton parkhotel.co.uk. If distance from the city centre and cost are no object, then the *Waterton Park Hotel* in Walton Hall is surely worth a look. One of the most beautifully sited hotels in the country (the hotel is modern, but attached to Georgian Walton Hall by a bridge), with swimming pool, gym, and nearby championship golf course, it may at first look expensive but there are often very reasonable offers. ❺

Wakefield Cathedral

At the heart of Wakefield town centre is **Wakefield Cathedral** (Mon–Sat 8am–4pm; ⓦwww.wakefieldcathedral.org.uk) whose 247ft spire is the tallest in Yorkshire. The earliest part of the present building (some of the nave's north arcade) dates from 1150, and bits have been added on ever since – the south arcade in 1220, the western tower and spire between 1409 and 1420, and much else during the rest of the fifteenth century. The seventeenth century saw the addition of the south porch sundial (1635), the quire screen (1636) and the font (1661, to replace one vandalized during the Commonwealth). Major remodelling and rebuilding was undertaken by Sir George Gilbert Scott between 1857 and 1874. Following its promotion to cathedral status in 1888, a new east end was added early in the twentieth century. And throughout the second half of the nineteenth century and up to 1907, stained glass by Charles Eamer Kempe (1837–1907) was added – 23 windows in all. As you go around the cathedral, look out for the many carved animals and green men typical of medieval churches, and for Kempe's emblem – the golden wheatsheaf – on the stained-glass windows. Or better still, do the "Discovery" tour with an electronic guide (for a suggested donation of £3); there are separate versions for adults and children.

The Wakefield Museum

North of the cathedral, on Wood Street, is a cluster of Victorian civic buildings – the **Wakefield Museum**, the **Town Hall**, the **Magistrates Court**, the **Police Station** and **County Hall**. The first you come to, and the only one of interest unless you're a resident or a felon, is the **Wakefield Museum** (Mon–Sat 10.30am–4.30pm; free; Ⓦwww.wakefield.gov.uk) with excellent displays on a variety of topics related to the town – there's a Story of Wakefield gallery, and displays on life in Roman Wakefield, Sandal Castle, the part played by the town in the Civil War, a social history of Victorian Wakefield, the miners' strike and how it affected the town, and particularly interesting, a display on local explorer and eccentric **Charles Waterton**, who travelled widely and wrote *Waterton's Wanderings in South America*, which influenced the young Charles Darwin. He collected animals and plants, many of which are on view in the museum, and his method of preserving animals was unique, leaving them hollow and remarkably lifelike. On his return to his estate – Walton Hall – he built a three-mile-long, 9ft-high wall around it, and turned it into the world's first nature reserve. He also invented the nesting box. His alleged eccentricities included buzz-cutting his hair when longer locks were fashionable, growling like a dog and biting his guests, and creating tableaux with his preserved animals that made fun of people he didn't like.

The Hepworth Gallery

Due to open in 2011, the **Hepworth Gallery** (Ⓦwww.hepworthwakefield.com) will occupy a striking David Chipperfield-designed building in a waterside setting south of the train station. The gallery will display not only a wide range of work by Barbara Hepworth and Henry Moore, but also paintings by British artists like Graham Sutherland, Paul Nash, John Piper, Jacob Epstein, David Bomberg, Walter Sickert, Anthony Caro, L.S. Lowry and David Hockney, as well as a comprehensive collection of images, not only of Wakefield, but of Yorkshire as a whole, and a varied offering of tours, talks and workshops. With a pleasant café/restaurant, the museum promises to be a significant addition to the cultural life of Wakefield, Yorkshire and England.

The Stephen Beaumont Museum and Gissing Centre

The **Stephen Beaumont Museum of Mental Health**, Fieldhead Hospital, Ouchthorpe Lane (Wed 10am–4pm; free; ☎01924/328 654, Ⓦwww.wakefield.gov.uk), offers a salutary lesson in how far we've come in terms of the treatment of mental ill-health. The restraining, medical and surgical equipment, the horrible padded cell, the early ECT equipment (looking like something out of a Frankenstein film) is enough to freeze the marrow.

The **Gissing Centre**, 2–4 Thompson's Yard, just off Westgate (May–Sept Sat 2–4pm; free; ☎01924/372 748, Ⓦwww.wakefield.gov.uk) is a museum dedicated to late nineteenth-century Wakefield writer George Gissing, sometimes mentioned in the same breath as George Meredith, Arnold Bennett and even Thomas Hardy, and author of, among many other novels, *New Grub Street*. A strangely sympathetic man, he loved not wisely but too well – his first wife was a prostitute who became an alcoholic (he separated from her, but continued to maintain her until her death from drink), his second wife was violent and eventually certified insane. He himself died of emphysema in 1903.

Given the limited opening hours, you are recommended to call first at both.

Eating and drinking

Bella Roma 63 Northgate ☎01924/371 059, ⓦwww.bellaromawakefield.co.uk. Something of decor time-warp, but serving good Italian food and robust wines. Plus an ever-changing specials board.

China Wok 24 Teall St ☎01924/370 011. On the opposite side of the Cathedral to the Ridings Centre, the *China Wok* has attracted a committed clientele who swear by the quality and authenticity of its food. A fully licensed and understated restaurant, it offers good value in terms of cost, quantity and quality.

The Cow Shed 53 Northgate ☎01924/291 044, ⓦwww.cowshed.uk.com. A lovely little restaurant and grill housed in an interesting half-timbered, sixteenth-century Grade II listed building just up from the Bull Ring. With many original features and wooden tables it has the feel of banqueting in a medieval hall, but the food is anything but – it's modern European, confined to a limited choice done well, with an emphasis on steak, and an extensive wine list.

Six Chimneys 41–43 Kirkgate ☎01924/239 449. Standard *Wetherspoon* pub, which means low prices, no music and no-nonsense, reasonably priced food. Children are welcome, and there's wi-fi available.

Thai on the Square 3 Cross Square ☎01924/298 555, ⓦwww.thaionthesquare.co.uk. Though the unprepossessing entrance has been likened by some to that of a massage parlour, the first-floor *Thai on the Square* is a pleasant mixture of Thai and English design, the service is discreet but attentive, the food is excellent, and the prices reasonable – main courses come in at between £8 and £12.50.

Nightlife and entertainment

Wakefield seems to be rather short of permanent venues for music and theatre, depending for its several festivals on a variety of temporary venues across the district – usually pubs. The only permanent venue for music, dance, drama and comedy is the **Theatre Royal** on Drury Lane just off Westgate (☎01924/211 311, ⓦwww.theatreroyalwakefield.co.uk). The prestigious **Wakefield Jazz** (ⓦwww.wakefieldjazz.org.uk), for example, uses Wakefield Sports Club for its Friday night sessions. Otherwise, there are one-offs such as occasional concerts or exhibitions at the Yorkshire Sculpture Park, the National Coal Mining Museum or the Wakefield Museum.

Listings

Buses Traveline ☎01709/515 151 or ☎01924/375 521.
Car rental Thrifty ☎01924/378 822, Avis ☎01924/290 280.
Hospital Pinderfields General Hospital, Aberford Rd ☎0844 811 8110.

Internet access *Moccha Café* 63 Kirkgate ☎01924/378 850.
Pharmacy Boots, 26–28 Kirkgate.
Post office Northgate.

Around Wakefield

Outside of town, in the surrounding metropolitan district, Wakefield has three of West Yorkshire's biggest tourist attractions – the **Yorkshire Sculpture Park**, the **National Coal Mining Museum** and **Nostell Priory**. Consequently, the city attracts far more visitors, both domestic and foreign, than you might at first expect.

The National Coal Mining Museum

Whether you're from the UK or abroad, if you want to understand modern Britain, the **National Coal Mining Museum** (daily 10am–5pm; free; ☎01924/848 806, ⓦwww.ncm.org.uk) is an essential stop – it's five minutes from junction 38 on the M1, or get the Yorkshire Traction #128 or the #232 from Wakefield. Coal mining encapsulates everything that made Britain a world power – the entrepreneurial nous of the early coal owners (and, later, it has to be said, their greed), immense engineering ingenuity, the social solidarity of the mining communities, and the brave political intervention of governments stirred by admirably national outrage over conditions to solve hitherto unknown problems.

When you arrive, first book in for the underground tour, then, depending on how long you've got before the tour, look around the rest of the site. First there's the **visitor centre** itself – on its own enough to earn the plaudits, with excellent displays on a whole host of aspects of the history of the coal industry – the lives of the miners and their families, work at the coal face, child labour, mining disasters. But that's just the start. The whole **Caphouse colliery** (it was a working pit until 1985) is one giant museum – the winding engine house, the screening plant and weighbridge, the pit ponies in their stables (two of them called Eric and Ernie), the pithead baths, the medical room. A smaller colliery – the **Hope Pit** – has exciting interactive displays covering the science behind mining: you can walk there (it's about quarter of a mile), or ride on the narrow-gauge railway. In addition, there are nature trails, bird hides, water treatment works and reed beds.

The highlight of any visit to the National Coal Mining Museum has to be, though, the **underground tour**. Having picked up your miner's lamp and hard hat and entered the cage, you plummet 440ft (134m) to the **New Hards Seam**, and a tour which covers methods of extraction from the early hand-hewing days to the big cutter-loaders and modern shearers, the dangers of mine collapse, gas explosion, carbon monoxide poisoning and flooding. Though the big disasters created all the headlines, there was a constant trickle of underground accidents – at the start of the twentieth century, around a thousand men and boys died every year.

The Yorkshire Sculpture Park

The **Yorkshire Sculpture Park** (bus #96, but it involves a walk; daily 10am–5/6pm; free, parking £4; Ⓦwww.ysp.co.uk) is an inspired idea. A stunning estate, designed in the eighteenth and nineteenth centuries around Bretton Hall, has become an outdoor art gallery where lovely parkland is used to display modern sculpture. Over time indoor spaces have been added – **Bretton Chapel**, **Underground Gallery** and **Longside Gallery**, for instance – but the permanent exhibitions change regularly (many of the exhibits are on loan). Pick up one of the excellent free maps as you enter, or fork out for the *Essential Sculpture Guide* (£5 and worth every penny). The park is huge, though some of it's private land, and is divided into eight zones, colour coded both on the map and on the signs, and there's just so much to see – highlights are works by big names like Barbara Hepworth, Henry Moore and Antony Gormley. There's a **visitor centre**, a café/restaurant and a shop. You'll need at least half a day to enjoy the sculpture park.

Nostell Priory

The third of Wakefield's big three attractions is **Nostell Priory** (buses Arriva #496 Wakefield–Doncaster & Arriva #485 from Wakefield; park daily 9am–7pm; house & gardens Wed–Sun essentially 11am–5pm, though check first; closed mid-Nov to Feb; £7.70, gardens only £5.30; ☎01924/863 892; NT) built in the mid-eighteenth century for Sir Rowland Winn – he'd married into money and wanted to celebrate. Notable for the contributions of a number of big names – James Paine, and then Robert Adam, in the design of the house, Thomas Chippendale (himself a Yorkshireman) in its furnishing – the house has been continuously occupied by the same family since. Until World War I it was run as a typical "great house" – after that it went into something of a decline, until it was handed over to the National Trust (who still maintain it) in 1953. The family, however, still use part of the house.

The house contains many treasures, and boasts one of the biggest collections of **Chippendale furniture** in the world, most of it designed specifically for it. Then there's the 1717 **long case clock** made by John Harrison (it's in the billiard room), whose father was probably a Nostell Priory estate carpenter, and who solved the problem of how to work out longitude at sea by inventing the marine chronometer – you can still see it at the Royal Observatory, Greenwich. Probably the most famous of Nostell's treasures, though, is the **dolls' house**, in the south passage. Made at the time that the house was built, it provides a perfect scaled-down version of an eighteenth-century country house.

The Vale of York

CHAPTER 3 # Highlights

＊ **York Minster** Britain's greatest Gothic cathedral. Prepare to be awed, but also amused – the guides will fill you in on lots of interesting and entertaining details. See p.148

＊ **Dig, York** Jorvik's sister attraction takes you through simulated archeological excavations, led by a bona fide archeologist. See p.153

＊ **Jorvik, York** Tenth-century Viking York as seen, heard and smelt from your very own time capsule. Simply the most innovative historical attraction in the country. See p.154

＊ **National Railway Museum, York** The best museum of railway transport in the world, in the country that invented it. See p.157

＊ **Betty's Tearooms** Edwardian splendour, crisp starched linen, cakes to die for. In York, Harrogate and Harlow Carr. See p.160

＊ **Harrogate Turkish Baths** Sweat it out in a Victorian take on a way of relaxing that goes back to Roman times. See p.169

＊ **Fountains Abbey and Studley Royal, Ripon** Spectacularly beautiful ruined medieval abbey set like a jewel in extensive eighteenth-century water gardens. See p.178

▲ National Railway Museum

The Vale of York

T he Vale of York, loosely defined, is the long strip of prime farming land that stretches from the city of York north to the Tees and south to the Humber. Flanked to the west by the Dales and to the east by the North York Moors, the Howardian Hills and the Wolds, it has always been a main north–south route, funnelling road and rail communications from the south of England to the north and Scotland between North Yorkshire's two upland areas. Dotted with villages and market towns, it has some of the county's top tourist destinations, of which by far the most popular is, of course, the **City of York** itself. Walled and historical yet vibrant and modern, it combines a wealth of history with contemporary comfort and convenience. Its museums are unparalleled in the invention of their displays, there's a solid tourist infrastructure of hotels and restaurants, open-topped buses and sightseeing boats, of ghost walks and Viking festivals, yet it is also clearly a real city, with a local life not unduly affected by the tourist hordes.

But it's not only York that merits a visit. **Wetherby** is a peaceful little town that grew up to service Great North Road travellers on their way to and from Scotland. **Harrogate**, large and rather grand, is a spa town that has adapted well to the modern world without sacrificing its Regency and Victorian heritage. **Knaresborough**, with its gorge and its castle and its petrifying well, is just one of the prettiest places in the county. **Ripley**, too, has a castle and a village with idiosyncratic architecture, while **Boroughbridge** is famed for its Roman connections and its Devil's Arrows, and **Ripon** for its hornblower, its cathedral and for nearby **Fountains Abbey** and **Lightwater Valley**. All make for rewarding visits or longer stays. The Vale of York is also the part of the county which can boast the biggest range of annual festivals (see p.30), so there's always something to see or take part in.

The City of York

YORK has a place in the history of England, and in its affections, out of all proportion to its size. Now a world-famous tourist attraction pulling in around four million visitors annually, only 140,000 people actually call it home, putting it in the same bracket as Blackpool, Ipswich or Peterborough. As so much of what makes York a fascinating place to visit originates in the city's past, it's worth knowing something of its history (see box, p.144–145).

The top attractions in York are part of the fabric of the city – individual buildings such as the **Minster**, **Clifford Tower**, the **Fairfax House**, **Barley Hall** and the

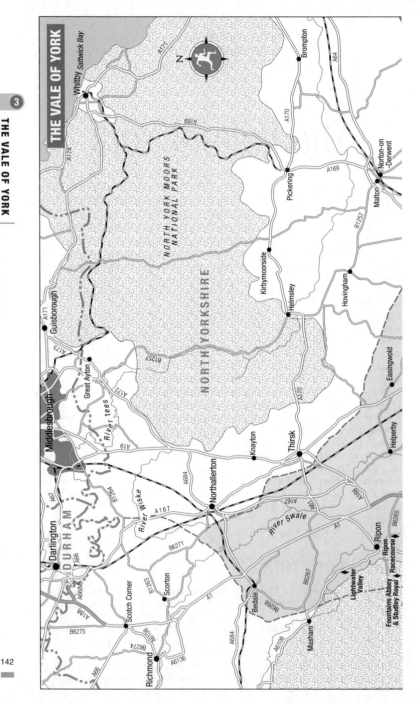

THE VALE OF YORK

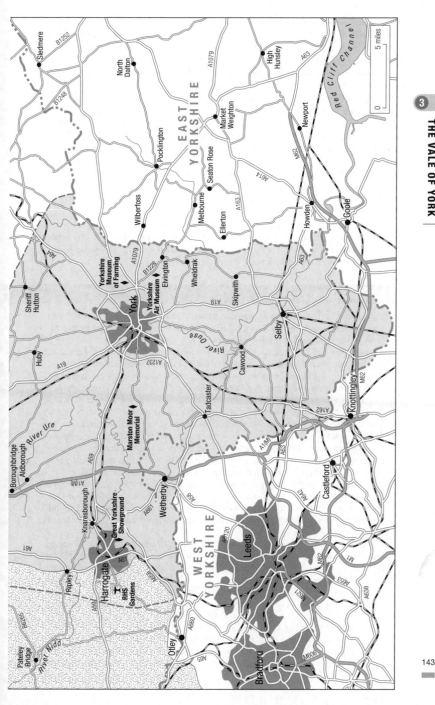

Merchant Adventurers' Hall, but also nearly three miles of thirteenth-century city walls that surround the city centre, and the narrow, cobbled lanes within it such as the picturesque Shambles, overhung by teetering medieval houses.

These are supplemented by a clutch of world-class museums: the Yorkshire Museum in its own beautiful gardens, the York Castle Museum, which occupies what was once the county jail, the mighty National Railway Museum, the innovative Jorvik Viking Museum and its even more hands-on partner Dig, and, representing more recent history, the chilling York Cold War Bunker.

Scattered around the city centre are numerous other attractions – the City Art Gallery, the Grand Opera House, the Theatre Royal and Friargate Theatre, together with a clutch of small museums, from the Bar Convent Museum to two tiny museums lodged in city gatehouses – the Micklegate Bar and Richard III museums. There's even a Quilt Museum, occupying a venerable old guildhall, and the remains of Roman Baths in the basement of a pub of the same name.

All of these are within walking distance of each other, and there are, too, numerous festivals that go on throughout the year (see p.30).

York is one of Britain's major tourist draws. It has developed catering for tourists down to a fine art. It's not a cheap city, and in July and August it can become uncomfortably crowded, but don't let this put you off – York is popular because, quite simply, it's a wonderful place chock-full of treasures.

A potted history of York

York jumped on to the national stage with a bang in Roman times – before then it was a small marshy settlement of the locally dominant Celtic Brigantes tribe at the confluence of the Ouse and the Foss. Then, in 71 AD, the Romans arrived and built a garrison from which to subdue the locals. Around it grew the town of **Erboracum**, which in due course became the capital of the Roman Empire's northern territories. From here Hadrian masterminded the pacifying of the north and the building of his famous wall. Here it was, too, that Constantine was proclaimed Emperor in 306 AD.

When the Romans withdrew their army from Britain in the fifth century AD, York was conquered by the Anglo-Saxons, who made it the capital of the kingdom of Northumbria – **Eoforwic**. Not long afterwards, York added to its undoubted and growing political clout a religious dimension: in 627 AD, bishop Paulinus, pushing the Christian envelope northwards, baptised King Edwin of Northumbria in a specially built wooden chapel. Within six years, that humble church had become the first Minster, and Paulinus the first **Archbishop of York**.

Fast-forward a couple of centuries, and in 867 AD the city of York fell to the Vikings. They renamed it **Jorvik**, and it became the capital of the Viking-dominated Danelaw. Their hundred-year occupation ended in 954 AD when York was regained by the Anglo-Saxon King Eadred of Wessex. This is how things remained until the Annus Horriblis of 1066.

The year kicked off well for the English King Harold, who defeated a combined invasion-cum-insurrection jointly led by Harald Hardrada of Norway and Tostig, King Harold's half brother, at Stamford Bridge just outside York. But then news arrived that William of Normandy had landed in the south. The exhausted English army returned to the south, only to be defeated at the Battle of Hastings.

Norman rule started badly for York – the city was destroyed during William the Conqueror's ferocious "harrying of the north", punishment for having had the temerity to oppose his occupation of the country. As the dust settled, however, York prospered. A new cathedral was built by the Norman Archbishop Thomas, starting in 1080, and this sparked the development of the city as the principal religious centre of the north of England, with the establishment of many religious houses. Economic recovery

Arrival and information

York lies around fifteen miles east of the A1, the main north–south route on the eastern side of the Pennines; the connecting road (the A64) is a fast dual carriageway which becomes the southern part of the York ring road. York has numerous well-signposted **car parks**, and (a very sensible alternative) comprehensive **park and ride** facilities. Arrival by train, too, is perfectly convenient, since the **train station** is right on the edge of the city centre, just outside the walls. The city centre itself (broadly, the part of the city enclosed by the medieval walls) is compact enough to walk, but if you fancy a tour in comfort, choose one of the numerous **open-topped bus tours** (start in Exhibition Square; £9, family ticket £15; ⓦwww.yorkbus.co.uk) or a **boat tour** (daily April–Oct from Kings Staith and Lendel Bridge; £7.50, family £20; ⓦwww.yorkboat.co.uk) on the river. There are several **taxi ranks** in the city, and a regular **road train** links the National Transport Museum with the city centre. The main **tourist information centre** (summer Mon–Sat 9am–6pm, Sun 10am–5pm; winter Mon–Sat 9am–5pm, Sun 10am–4pm; ☏01904/550 099, ⓦwww.visityork.org) is at 1 Museum Street, on the corner with Blake Street, right next to the pub *Thomas's Bar*. There's a small but useful tourist information point in the train station, too. A **Yorkshire Pass**, covering attractions in

followed, with York becoming a major trading hub, importing from, and exporting to, France and the Low Countries. The city's great stock of medieval buildings is the result of this combination of religious growth and economic prosperity during those years.

It didn't last. Tudor times brought economic recession caused by a downturn in the fortunes of the woollen industry, and the effects of the split with the Roman Catholic faith sparked by Henry VIII's desire to divorce Catherine of Aragon and marry Anne Boleyn. The subsequent northern rebellion in support of the Pope and the Catholic faith – the Pilgrimage of Grace – was brutally suppressed. York also suffered from the plundering of the monastic houses during the dissolution of the monasteries which followed (though locals often benefitted from free building stone).

York's regrettable tendency to pick the wrong side continued during Stuart times. First it was involved in the 1605 Catholic plot to blow up the Houses of Parliament – Guy Fawkes was born and brought up in the city – then it strongly supported King Charles I during the English Civil War. In 1644 combined Parliamentary and Scottish forces besieged York. Royalist forces under Prince Rupert came to the rescue, driving the besiegers out. However, not satisfied with that achievement, the prince pursued the superior Parliamentary forces west of the city, then was routed at the Battle of Marston Moor. York was left defenceless, and owes its survival to an accident of birth – one of the Parliamentary commanders, Lord Fairfax, was from York, and stopped his victorious troops setting fire to the city.

During the eighteenth century York's prestige went into something of a decline. The focus of the Yorkshire woollen industry moved west and south as the search for power took it first into the Pennine hills (water power), then into the west and south Yorkshire coal fields (steam). The city remained, however, an important social centre for the middle and upper classes, and their town houses and public buildings remain an important attraction for visitors.

Things looked up with the coming of the railways. York became an important rail centre, and also, through the Rowntree and Terry dynasties, a great manufacturer of confectionery. By the time these two industries went into twentieth-century decline, York's future prosperity was assured by its burgeoning tourist industry.

York and throughout the county (1/2/3/6 days £28/£38/£44/£68, Ⓦwww .yorkshirepass.com), is a good investment since admission prices soon mount up – it's available from the tourist office, gets you into over seventy attractions, and includes numerous discount vouchers for dining, evening entertainment, action activities and shopping.

③ Accommodation

York, being a major year-round tourist attraction, has a good stock of **accommodation**, from its numerous B&Bs and guesthouses to luxurious top-end hotels. It also has two "boutique" hostels and a campsite within ten minutes' walk of the city centre.

Hotels and B&Bs

Alexander House 94 Bishopthorpe Rd ☎01904/625 016, Ⓦwww.alexanderhouseyork.co.uk. Small, friendly B&B in lovely Victorian townhouse renovation, a 10min walk south of the city centre. The owners take a pride in quality of service and comfort and cleanliness of accommodation. Plentiful free parking. ❸

Ashbourne House 139 Fulford Rd ☎01904/639 912, Ⓦwww.ashbournehouseyork.co.uk. Hotel-standard facilities, guesthouse prices, halfway between the city centre and southern bypass (it's a 20min walk or 5min bus ride into the city). Delicious Yorkshire breakfasts and free off-street parking. ❸

🏃 **Bar Convent** 17 Blossom St ☎01904/643 238, Ⓦwww.bar-convent.org.uk. Unique opportunity to stay in a convent. Grand Georgian building housing a museum and café as well as nine single rooms (£33–37 each), three twins, two doubles and a family room, self-catering kitchen and guest lounge. Pay-and-display parking over the road. Continental breakfast included. ❸

Bowman's 33 Grosvenor Terrace ☎01904/622 204, Ⓦwww.bowmansguesthouse.co.uk. Six spotlessly clean rooms in friendly renovated Victorian terrace B&B off Bootham, within easy reach of city centre. They provide a permit for free on-street parking. ❸

🏃 **Cedar Court Grand Hotel** Station Rise ☎0845 409 6430, Ⓦwww.cedarcourt grand.co.uk. York's new (and only) five-star hotel, 10min walk from the train station, housed in what was the 1906 headquarters of the North Eastern Railway. Bags of character, wonderful views of walls and Minster, with luxuriously unique rooms, fine-dining restaurant and relaxing bar. ❼

The Churchill Hotel 65 Bootham ☎01904/644 456, Ⓦwww.churchillhotel.com. Housed in an early nineteenth-century mansion within walking distance of the city centre, the *Churchill* is historic on the outside, smart contemporary within. Piano bar and upmarket restaurant looking out through tall windows on the front garden. Free parking for all guests. ❺

Hedley House Hotel 3 Bootham Terrace ☎01904/637 404, Ⓦwww.headleyhouse.com. Friendly, comfortable small hotel 10min walk from the train station. Best in summer – outdoor area with sauna/aqua spa on garden deck, but rooms can be cold in winter – especially in the (separate) annexe. Free car parking on first come, first served basis. ❹

Hotel du Vin 89 The Mount ☎01904/557 350, Ⓦwww.hotelduvin.com. One of the slick boutique-hotel-and-bistro chain, close to the centre of town. Uniform house style, with alfresco dining in the courtyard. Wide selection of malt whiskies. Limited parking £10 per day. Breakfast not included. ❻

The Judges Lodgings 9 Lendal ☎01904/638 733, Ⓦwww.judgeslodgings.com. Beautifully renovated Grade I listed building in the centre of York, which housed Assize Court Judges for over a century and a half. Luxurious accommodation, attentive but discreet staff. Bar in the basement. Some parking (charge) which you need to pre-book. ❻

Middlethorpe Hall Bishopsthorpe Rd ☎01904/641 241, Ⓦwww.middlethorpe.com. A grand eighteenth-century mansion a couple of miles south of the city, next to the racecourse. Antiques, wood panelling, superb rooms (some set in a private courtyard), gardens, parkland, pool and spa, and fine dining in the formal *Oak Room* restaurant. ❻

Mount Royale The Mount ☎01904/628 856, Ⓦwww.mountroyale.co.uk. Lots of antiques, super garden suites (and cheaper rooms), heated outdoor pool in summer. Hot tub, sauna and steam room, and a well-reckoned restaurant. ❺

Park Inn North St ☎01904/459 988, Ⓦwww .york.parkinn.co.uk. Part of the Residor group, the *Park Inn* is a modern tower block, well placed in the city centre within walking distance of the train station and all attractions. Comfortable, with pleasant, amenable staff, and great views across the city. Excellent packages available. ❻

Hostels

Ace Hotel Micklegate House, 88–90 Micklegate ☎01904/627 720, ⓦwww.acehotelyork.co.uk. Handsome 1752 building, once *York Backpackers*, in the centre of the city, with many impressive features – stone-flagged entrance hall, wide staircase, panelled rooms, vaulted cellar and ornate plaster ceilings. Dorms (sleeping 4 to 14) from £19 per head, more for smaller dorms and weekends, cheaper for multinight stays, plus private rooms at £60 per head. All en suite, and include continental breakfast. ③

🏃 **The Fort** Little Stonegate ☎01904/620 222, ⓦwww.thefortyork.co.uk. An interesting idea – a "boutique hostel" – offering rooms with

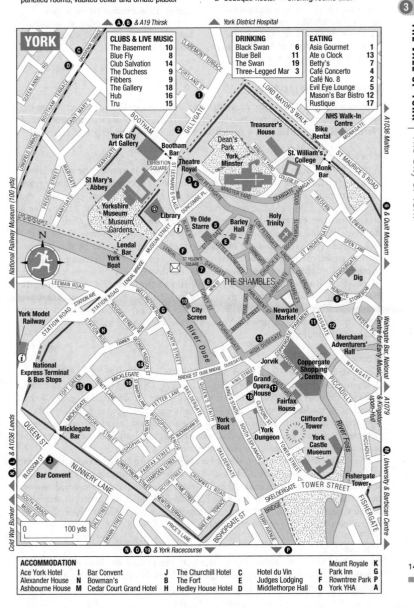

ACCOMMODATION

Ace York Hotel **I**	Bar Convent **J**	The Churchill Hotel **C**	Hotel du Vin **L**	Mount Royale **K**	
Alexander House **N**	Bowman's **B**	The Fort **E**	Judges Lodging **F**	Park Inn **G**	
Ashbourne House **M**	Cedar Court Grand Hotel **H**	Hedley House Hotel **D**	Middlethorpe Hall **O**	Rowntree Park **P**	
				York YHA **A**	

individual decor – with themes such as log cabin or deep sea creatures – in the city centre at a knockdown price (£20 a night). In the words of the owner, "luxury, funky and easy on the pocket". ❸

York YHA Water End, Clifton ☎0845 371 9051, ⒺYork@yha.org.uk. Large Victorian mansion, 20min walk from centre. Mainly dorms, some private rooms that have to be booked well in advance. Licensed café, internet, large garden, parking and discounted tickets for attractions. Buffet breakfast included in price. From £13.95 per person, up to £26.95 at peak times.

Campsite

Rowntree Park Caravan Club Site, Terry Ave ☎01904/658 997, ⓌWww.caravanclub.co.uk. A wonderful site, the best-located in the city, 10min walk from the centre, with a back gate that opens onto a street of takeaways, pubs and shops. Open to non-members. Mainly for caravans and motorhomes, but with a small tent enclosure – those with tents must arrive on foot. Advance booking essential, especially at weekends. £11.80.

The city centre

Although most of York's city centre lies east of the River Ouse, the section on the west bank boasts several attractions that shouldn't be missed – not least the world-class **National Railway Museum** – as well as a long uninterrupted length of **city wall**.

York's walls

A great way of orienting yourself when visiting York is to walk the **walls** (dawn to dusk; free). One of the great glories of the city, York's walls date mainly from the fourteenth century, but contain bits of earlier building, especially the Roman section along Museum Street. The walls are complete, except for a section on the eastern edge where marshland and fish ponds made defence unnecessary, and in the south where the city was already protected by its castle. Where the river prevented the building of walls, chains would be slung across during times of danger. Particularly fine are the several surviving medieval gatehouses – the **Bootham Bar** to the northwest near Exhibition Square, **Micklegate Bar** to the southwest, **Monk Bar** to the northeast, and **Walmgate Bar** (the only one to retain its protective barbican) to the southeast. There are numerous access points to the walls apart from these gates, and walking the walls is one of the great pleasures of York, offering ever-changing views of the city and its surroundings.

York Minster

York Minster (Mon–Sat 9am–5.30pm Nov–March opens 9.30am, Sun noon–3.45pm, though times vary depending on services; £8, free guided tours available; ☎0844 939 0011, ⓌWww.yorkminster.org), one of England's great Gothic churches, is an absolute gem – awe-inspiringly grand but also remarkably easy to comprehend, and with so many human-scale foibles that, on closer acquaintance, it becomes almost endearing. A full tour will take at least half a day, but could spark a love affair that will last you a lifetime.

The **main entrance** to the cathedral leads you into the **south transept**. As you take in the stupendous scale of the building, stand with your back to the entrance, look around and get oriented. Ahead is the crossing below the **central tower**, beyond which is the **north transept** and, in the far right-hand corner, the entrance to the **Chapter House**. Left at the crossing is the **nave**, while to the right is the **quire** and the east end of the cathedral.

The nave

In medieval times the **nave** was the less religious part of the building, a general meeting place thronged with people and animals, stalls selling religious items, even choirboys playing football – a duel was once fought here.

Imagine it without the two aisles on either side – that was the size of the original Norman cathedral. Most of the current nave was built between 1280 and 1350, in the Decorated style. The aisle roofs are made of stone, while that of the nave itself is made of wood, and painted to look like stone, following an 1840 fire. All bar one of the new roof bosses were copies of the originals. The one that was changed showed the Virgin Mary breast-feeding the baby Jesus – in the primmer Victorian version she uses a bottle.

Walk down the **south** (left) **aisle**, past the memorial to anti-slave-trade campaigner William Wilberforce, and examine the lovely medieval stained-glass windows. The most famous is third from the end – the **Jesse window**, showing the claimed descent of Jesus from Jesse (Jesse at the bottom, Jesus at the top). The three dates are of the window's installation and subsequent restorations.

At the west end of the church is the Great West Door, above which is the **Great West Window**. It consists of eight lancets and complicated tracery in which can be seen the shape that gives the window its nickname – the "Heart of Yorkshire". Notice in the range of niches that line up with the middle of the doors an interesting modern addition – twelve figures representing saints. Made of MDF, they are headless (a reference to the effigies defaced during the Reformation), and are using their halos to spell out, in semaphore, "Christ is here". Any feeling that these "semaphore saints" look like people playing with Frisbees must be sternly resisted.

As you return towards the central tower along the **north aisle** of the nave, notice the door that once led to the chapel of St Sepulchre. After the chapel was demolished, the only place that the door led to was an inn, making York probably the only cathedral in the world with its own pub entrance. (The inn, alas, has also been demolished.) Next, up in the roof is a **red and gold dragon**, which swivels on a pivot; it's thought to be a counter-weighted crane for lifting the heavy lid of a long-gone object – either a font or a reliquary containing the head of St William of York. The best-known window along this aisle is the sixth – the **bell-founders window**. It shows scenes of bell-founding and bell-tuning, together with a representation of the miracle of the Ouse Bridge, when the bridge collapsed under the weight of the crowds assembled to welcome St William of York to the city, yet nobody was killed.

The north transept

Turning left at the central tower crossing brings you into the **north transept**, built in 1220 to 1260 in Early English style, and the giant **Five Sisters Window** – the largest lancet window in the world. Made of five lancets of muted grey-silver Grisaille glass, each 57ft high by 5ft wide, it is largely non-representational, except for a colourful circle at the bottom of the central lancet which is glass recycled from the Norman cathedral. The window was rededicated after World War I to the memory of all the women who'd died during that conflict (the ceremony was performed by the Duchess of York, who later became the Queen Mother), and the roll-call of those who died can be seen behind the doors around the **astronomical clock**. The clock itself is a memorial to RAF air and ground crew who served in the area during World War II, and the picture in the centre of the clock represents York as seen from the air – you can see the Minster and the medieval walls. The other clock in the north transept strikes at each quarter hour – the face is eighteenth century, the figures of knights who strike the metal bars are fifteenth century. The clocks have traditionally been wound by members of the same family for the last century and a half.

The Chapter House

Walk through the vestibule – looking out for carvings of green men hidden among the tracery – into the octagonal **Chapter House**, which is the same period and style as the nave, built in 1290 to accommodate meetings of the cathedral's governing body. It's still used today, and you can see the names of the Canons above each of the 44 seats around the walls. Unusually, York's Chapter House doesn't have a central pillar holding up the roof – it's made of wood, and suspended from a complicated system of beams above it (there's a model to show you how this works). Above the seats is a riot of carving where the masons who did the work were given a degree of leeway in what they depicted. So for example, one is of a pig, which were often used by working people to convert food scraps and waste into meat. This leeway has been extended to modern masons doing restoration work – elsewhere in the cathedral, at the east end, there's a man rudely mooning, and two figures from *Star Trek* on the external arch of the Great West Door.

The quire and the east end

Back in the main body of the cathedral, take a look at the **quire**, a wooden room-within-a-room in which day-to-day services are held and choristers sit. The screen through which you enter the quire has effigies of fifteen kings who have reigned during the existence of the cathedral, from William the Conqueror on the left to Henry VI on the right. Within, the choir stalls face each other, and on the right at the far end is the throne (cathedra) of the Archbishop of York. All the woodwork in the quire is Victorian – in 1829 a man called Jonathan Martin, taking exception to the way that services were celebrated, made his displeasure known by coming out of hiding after the cathedral was shut, piling all the medieval choir stalls around the organ, and setting fire to the lot.

Beyond the quire is the **east end** of the cathedral, the newest part, built between 1361 and 1472 in the Perpendicular style. Beyond the quire and the high altar, the **Lady Chapel** is dominated by the gigantic **Great East Window**. Or it will be when the window's restoration, started in 2008, is complete. In the meantime the space is covered by a full-sized replica of the window on a printed banner – at the size of a doubles tennis court, it's the largest high-res graphic in the world.

Returning towards the central crossing along the south aisle, look out for the **Archbishop Lamplugh monument**, carved in 1691 by Grinling Gibbons – in particular at the ends of his legs where he appears to have two right feet. This is thought to be either because left and right shoes weren't differentiated in those days, or, much more fun, that Gibbons went off on a break and told an apprentice to "carve the left foot exactly like the right". So he did.

The central crossing, south transept and tower

Back at the **central crossing** underneath the tower, stand on the lozenge-shaped stone and look upwards. You are now directly below the central boss hundreds of feet above you. To give you an idea of scale, consider that the central boss is the same size as the flagstone you're standing on, and that the tower windows, foreshortened high above you, are in fact the same size as the massive lancets of the Five Sisters Window in the north transept.

The tour ends back in the **south transept**, dominated by the rose window above the cathedral entrance, installed to celebrate the wedding of Henry VII and Elizabeth of York, which finally ended the Wars of the Roses. It remains to climb to the top of the **central tower** (£5), if you've got the lungs for it and suffer from neither claustrophobia or vertigo. The views from the top are spectacular.

The undercroft, treasury and crypts

In the foundations is the **undercroft**, a museum with an excellent exposition of the history of the building as told by the different bits of the foundations that remain. Many of these were discovered when, in 1967, the tower was in danger of collapse. Massive engineering work was carried out to underpin the foundations (you can see the huge concrete blocks, studded with massive bolts, everywhere), and the foundations of the Norman cathedral, and before that the Roman principia, or fortress, that once stood on the site. They even found a Roman culvert along which water was still flowing to empty into the Ouse.

Beyond the undercroft is the **treasury**, full as you'd expect of the cathedral's treasure – ceremonial gold, silver and pewter objects from all over the city, the most famous of which is the Horn of Ulf.

Finally you come to the **crypts**, with their many sarcophagi (including one that holds the remains of St William of York), and the Doomstone of the Norman cathedral.

The Treasurer's House
Just behind the Minster (take the footpath past the Great West Door across Dean's Park) is the National Trust-run **Treasurer's House** (April–Nov Mon–Thurs, Sat & Sun 11am–3/4.30pm; £5.40; cellar £2.40; NT), a fine seventeenth-century mansion. Much restored by its owner from 1897, industrial magnate Frank Green, and organized into period rooms to display his various art and antique collections, it tells far more about the late Victorian and Edwardian taste of the house's reconstruction than of its Jacobean origins. That said, its opulence makes for a diverting visit, as does the famous story of the ghost of Roman legionaries marching through its basement, and anecdotes about its owner's increasingly eccentric and obsessive tidiness – creeping down to the kitchen at the dead of night to check that cutlery was laid out in rows, insisting that the renovation workmen wear slippers, having glass fronts fitted to cupboards so that he could check the organization of their contents. There's a small shop, a licensed tearoom, and for this type of attraction, it's remarkably child-friendly, with baby-changing facilities, infant-carrying paraphernalia, children's guides and quiz-sheets and a small interactive children's room.

Richard III Museum
Beyond the Treasurer's House and past half-timbered **St William's College** in College Street, turn left into Goodramgate to arrive at **Monk Bar**. The tallest of York's medieval gatehouses, it contains the imaginative **Richard III Museum** (daily 9/9.30am–4/5pm; £2.50; ☎01904/634 191, ⓦwww.richardiiimuseum .co.uk). King for only two years (1483–85), and defeated in the Battle of Bosworth by Henry Tudor, there has been much debate as to whether Richard was actually the malformed fiend who murdered his own nephews – the Princes in the Tower – depicted by Shakespeare, or whether this is all propaganda designed to please the Tudor dynasty which succeeded him. The core of the museum is a mock trial in which the evidence for and against Richard is presented, and the jury (ie, visitors to the museum) decides. Other displays include a rather gratuitous "Execution Chamber", the cell in which recusant Alice Bowman was imprisoned during Elizabethan times, and an apparently genuine portcullis.

York City Art Gallery
To the west of the Minster lies Exhibition Square – you can get there from Monk Bar either at street level along Lord Mayor's Walk and Gilleygate, or by taking the scenic route along the city walls to Bootham Bar. The square is dominated on one side by the **York City Art Gallery** (daily 10am–5pm; free; ☎01904/687 687, ⓦwww.yorkartgallery.org.uk), which dates from 1879, as does the square itself. Spread over two floors, its galleries contain samples of decorative arts, painting and pottery from the fourteenth century to the present. The main gallery, facing you as you enter the reception area and shop, hosts a variety of visiting exhibitions, as

does the little gallery on the first floor. The other main room on the ground floor, the south gallery, displays a changing range of paintings, while on the first floor the Burton gallery (to the left) has works organized into three topics – people, places and stories – while the gallery of pots displays, well, pots.

King's Manor

Also overlooking Exhibition Square is the **King's Manor**, a beautiful old building, once the dwelling of the Abbot of St Mary, then, after the dissolution, taken over by Henry VIII, who stayed here, as did James I. The manor housed the court of Charles I during the Civil War (that's his coat of arms over the door), then went through a number of uses (gaming rooms, schools for girls and for the blind), and today it's the home of a number of York University departments, so not open to the public.

Yorkshire Museum and Gardens

Taking the main road along Museum Street brings you to the beautiful **Museum Gardens**, which slope attractively westwards down towards the River Ouse. The Museum Street entrance is flanked by a neat **Victorian gatehouse** and just beyond it, on the right, is the **Multangular Tower**, which is, along with the attached section of wall, the only surviving part of Roman Erboracum – the fortress. Dating from the second or third century AD, the tower has ten sides, and is 30ft high; the bottom two thirds are original – you can see that the stones are much smaller than on the medieval extension above. Uphill from the tower is the majestic Grade I listed building of the **Yorkshire Museum** (daily 10am–5pm; £7; ☎01904/687 687, ⓦwww.yorkshiremuseum.org.uk), reopened in August 2010 after a nine-month, £2million make-over. Not only has the building itself been given a wash and brush up, its collection has been reorganized into five new galleries: "History of York", a multiscreen, audiovisual spectacular; "Extinct", which covers dinosaurs and more recently extinct creatures; "Meet the People of the Empire" (Roman York); the "Power and the Glory" (Medieval York); and "Enquiry" on the upstairs gallery, about how archeology and science can uncover the past. It's an exciting visual and hands-on experience that's now one of York's main visitor attractions.

Looping beyond the museum brings you immediately to ruins of the Benedictine abbey of **St Mary's**, which was established shortly after William the Conqueror's harrying of the north, first in St Olave's, the church next to the western Marygate entrance to the gardens, then in a new monastery built beside it. It rapidly became the greatest monastery in the north of England, a status it retained until its dissolution in 1539.

Barley Hall

A short walk from the Bootham Bar along Blake Street, then left up pretty Stonegate, brings you to medieval townhouse **Barley Hall** (daily 10am–4pm; £4.50; ☎01904/610 275 or 543 400, ⓦwww.barleyhall.org.uk) – it's down an alley on the right, near *Ye Olde Starre*, between a shop called Fudgetastic and a little carved red devil on the corner above no. 33. One of several innovative historical attractions owned and run by the York Archaeological Trust (see box, p.153), and opened after restoration in 1993, entering Barley Hall is like stepping into the Middle Ages. Only floor tiles and some timbers are original, the rest is reconstruction and replica, but it's accurate and doesn't confine itself to the building itself, also providing insights into all sorts of aspects of medieval life – food preparation, drink, sanitation, living conditions, burial practices, heating and lighting, and more than you probably wanted to know about illness, disease and hospitals. The

The York Archaeological Trust

The **York Archaeological Trust** is an independent charity, formed in 1972, which carries out archeological excavation and conservation, runs community projects and encourages archeological education. Calling on a range of expertise, the Trust brings a refreshingly iconoclastic attitude to the preservation and display of historical sites, which, though it may be frowned upon by more traditional archeologists, is a breath of fresh air to the non-specialist. The Trust owns and runs the **Jorvik Viking Centre**, **Dig**, **Barley Hall** and the **Micklegate Museum**, in all of which the watchword is accessibility combined with accuracy – exciting, illuminating and user-friendly.

displays are excellent, and also outline evidence and archeological practices. And in keeping with York Archaeological Trust's philosophy, Barley Hall is delightfully unstuffy – you can sit on the chairs, handle the objects and take as many photographs as you like.

The Shambles and around

Continuing up Stonegate, then right onto Petergate, brings you to **King's Square**. Radiating from it are many of the picturesque streets and lanes for which York is renowned. Most famous among them is **the Shambles**, once a street of butchers, now narrow, pretty and photogenic, the old timber-framed buildings leaning towards each other above a cobbled passage. It was voted Britain's most picturesque street in the first Google Streetview Awards in May 2010. Running parallel to the west of the Shambles is **Newgate Market**, a little street market that the residents of Barnsley or Leeds would scoff at, but nice enough. Just beyond it, in St Sampson's Square, is a pub called the **Roman Bath** which has a small museum in the basement, designed around the remains of the legionary bathhouse which stood just inside the Roman fortress (11am–4pm; £2.50).

Dig

In the church of St Saviour is one of the most remarkable tourist attractions in York – indeed, anywhere in the country. Run by the York Archaeological Trust, **Dig** (daily 10am–5pm, last admission 4pm; £5.50, joint ticket with Jorvik, Barley Hall and Micklegate Bar Museum £13, pre-booking advised; ☎01904/634 436, ⊛www.digyork.co.uk) starts where other museums leave off: most are designed to display historical artefacts, this one shows you how the artefacts are discovered, and how we learn about the past from them. But it's not just what it does that is different – it's how it does it. When you get to the museum, you join a tour run by young and enthusiastic experts. An initial session in the "briefing hut" allows your guide to get a feel for the interests and level of knowledge of the group – you may be asked probing questions or, for example, to put pottery shards into chronological order. Then you grab your trowels, head for the four excavation pits – Roman, Viking, Medieval and Victorian – and start digging. As you reveal bones, masonry, pottery or other artefacts, your guide will ask you questions – what sort of bones are they? Is this the inside or outside of the house? What did these people eat? You might then have a go at sorting finds, just as real archeologists do – into bone, antlers, metal, glass and so on. At the end of the formal tour (it lasts about 45 minutes), you can then use a bank of computers to do more research, or investigate the working methods of archeologists in three areas – the "study zone" deals with historical research, such as using documentary evidence to supplement the archeological finds, "lab works" covers the scientific perspective, while "in the field" takes you through the practicalities of organizing a dig. In each area, your guide is a hologram. Finally, "York Revealed" gives you a holographic and 3D cinematic summing-up. The whole experience is an absolute delight – don't miss it.

Merchant Adventurers' Hall

Best approached through the Tudor arch off Fossgate, just before the bridge over the Foss, the **Merchant Adventurers' Hall** (April–Sept Mon–Thurs 9am–5pm, Fri & Sat 9am–3.30pm, Sun noon–4pm; Oct–March Mon–Sat 9am–3.30pm; £5; Ⓦwww.theyorkcompany.co.uk) is York's biggest and best-preserved half-timbered building. Pictures of the Hall don't prepare you for how beset by other more recent buildings it is, but once inside the medieval atmosphere is palpable. The Merchant Adventurers, investors who risked their capital in overseas trade, were the premier craft guild in York, and controlled imports and exports, especially of wool. The hall was built by them in 1362, and consists of three main rooms, corresponding to the three functions of the guild – business, charity and religion. The upstairs **Great Hall**, dating from the mid-fourteenth century, has a bowed wooden floor and ornate open-beamed roof, and was used for meetings of the guild. On the same floor are three small anterooms leading to the governor's parlour, where you can see some interesting furniture and silverware. This floor was the business-end of the building. Below it stands the **undercroft**, with flagged stone floor, massive wooden posts that support the rest of the building, and a brick fireplace that faces in several directions. This room was used, right up until 1900, as a hospice for the poor and infirm, especially members of the guild who were down on their luck. Finally, off the far end of the undercroft is the **chapel**, which dates largely from the mid-seventeenth century – look out for the "Prayer of the Merchant Adventurers" on the right: perhaps twenty-first-century bankers and hedge-fund managers might pay attention. You can pick up a handset for the excellent audio-tour as you enter the hall – it's included with entry.

Jorvik Viking Centre

In 1976 the remains of a Viking street were found while clearing the site of an old confectionery factory prior to building the Coppergate Shopping Centre. The York Archaeological Trust were called in, who excavated the site, then decided to re-create what they'd found – the houses, shops, markets and workshops – furnish them with the figures, sights, sounds and smells of this part of the Viking city of Jorvik, and open the whole thing to the public. Predictably, many people sneered at the reconstruction, feeling that it was simultaneously sexing-up and dumbing-down an important archeological site. The public didn't agree: during the 25 years after its opening by Prince Charles in April 1984 the **Jorvik Viking Centre** (daily: April–Oct 10am–5pm; Nov–March 10am–4pm; £8.95; ☏01904/543 402, Ⓦwww.vikingjorvik.com) welcomed over fifteen million visitors. Honed and updated over several refurbishments to take account of subsequent research, the latest in 2010, the centre is a superb evocation of life in a York street in 975 AD. As you swoop and swerve across the Viking city in your time-pod, listening to a commentary (choice of languages and age level), you see the sights, hear the sounds and smell the smells of a thousand years ago. And remember, this isn't some brash fairground attraction – everything you experience is historically accurate, even the animatronic people whose bodies (including the faces) are reconstructed from skeletons and skulls found during the excavation. When your trip is finished, you're free to explore a vast array of exhibits that fill you in on the methodology that lies behind the reconstruction of the Viking street, and on the 40,000 Viking objects yielded by the dig. An archeologist will take you through the life of a Viking warrior as reflected in the many injuries you can see on his skeleton, you can work out if you have any Viking blood in your veins, be instructed by holographic Vikings and lots more. The Jorvik Viking Centre really does pull out all the stops in bringing the past back to life, using the most advanced techniques and, if you combine it with a visit to the York Archaeological Trust's other big attraction, Dig, you'll get a vivid picture not only of what we know about Viking York, but also how we know it. A combined ticket will also save you money (combined ticket with Dig £13). During school holidays queuing can become a bind, so pre-booking is advised.

York Dungeon

Five minutes' walk from the Jorvik Viking Centre is the **York Dungeon** (daily: April–Sept 10.30am–5pm; Oct, Feb & March 10.30am–4.30pm; Nov–Jan 11am–4pm; £14.50; ☎01904/632 599, ⓦwww.the-dungeons.co.uk), which might seem superficially similar (bringing the past alive) but is in fact a world away and cross between a ghost train and pantomime, you pass through a series of tableaux (a medieval inn, a Viking battlefield, a torture chamber and so on), are regaled with blood-curdling stories by actors dressed for the part. The special effects are cheesy, the emphasis on pain, gore and horror relentless, but the whole thing is done with great humour and tongue-in-cheek gusto by the young actors, who ad lib merrily in response to customer repartee. For an hour's entertainment, though, it's quite pricey – look out for special deals on the internet.

Fairfax House

Fairfax House on Castlegate (Mon–Thurs & Sat 11am–4.30pm, Sun 1.30–4.30pm; Fri guided tours only 11am & 2pm; closed Jan & early Feb; £6; ⓦwww.fairfax house.co.uk) is one of the most spectacular Georgian townhouses in the country. Its survival is nothing short of a miracle. Built between 1755 and 1762 by John Carr, it had by the 1920s fallen into disrepair, and it was used first as a dance hall, then as the foyer and toilets of the St George's Hall cinema, opened in 1921 (you can still see the facade). With an interior restored to full splendour in the 1980s, and containing the Noel Terry collection of furniture, porcelain and clocks, Fairfax House is an utter delight, a Georgian tour-de-force of English Rococo

York Ghost Tours

No doubt because of its venerable history, York has given birth to a lot of "horrible histories"-type stories of torture and murder, and the resulting unquiet spirits that rise up at the dead of night. You can either enjoy a fixed-site dollop of gore and horror at the York Dungeon (see above), or join one of the **ghost tours** of the city centre. You don't need to book, and they can be great fun, depending on your willingness to suspend disbelief and the narrative powers of your guide, most of whom are Equity card-holders. Pick up leaflets from the tourist information centre (see p.145), or choose one of the following:

ⓦwww.theoriginalghostwalkofyork.co.uk ☎01759 373 090. Starts outside the *King's Arms*, near the Ouse Bridge at 8pm. £4.50

ⓦwww.ghosthunt.co.uk ☎01904/608 700. Starts at the Shambles at 7.30pm. £5

ⓦwww.ghostdetective.com ☎07947 325 239. Starts outside the Jorvik Viking Centre at 7.30pm. £5

ⓦwww.ghosttrail.co.uk ☎01904/633276. Starts at the Minster's west door at 7.30pm. £4

ⓦwww.thehauntedwalkofyork.com ☎01904/621 003. Starts outside the City Art Gallery at 8pm. £4

stucco, classical columns, coved ceilings, palms and swags, busts of Newton and Shakespeare and ornate Georgian decoration. Even the presentation – formal, with hushed attendants keeping an eye on you – seems appropriate.

Clifford's Tower

Clifford's Tower (daily 10am–4/6pm; £3.50; EH), together with the section of wall just south of the Castle Museum and Crown Court buildings, is all that's left of York Castle. Originally a motte and bailey with a wooden keep built by William the Conqueror during the harrying of the north, what you see now was built in the middle of the thirteenth century. It has had a chequered history, including the burning of the old wooden tower in 1190 AD when it was being used as a refuge by hundreds of Jews trying to escape anti-Semitic riots in the city; stays by numerous medieval kings; and the execution, ordered by Henry VIII, of Robert Aske, leader of the Roman Catholic rebellion against the Reformation known as the Pilgrimage of Grace. Of a rare quatrefoil (clove-leaf) design, perhaps an experiment to improve sight lines between the top of the keep and the base of the walls, it once had two floors with a supporting central column. Now just a shell, with subsidence-weakened walls leaning dizzyingly outwards, it has excellent information boards and a model to explain the tower's history. Standing as it does at the top of 55 steps from the car park, the views of the city from the top of the keep are spectacular.

York Castle Museum

Immediately south of Clifford's Tower are three eighteenth-century buildings – the one in the middle built as early a 1705 as a debtors' prison, the ones on either side by John Carr in 1773–77 as a women's prison (on the left as you face them) and Assize Court (on the right). Today the righthand building is the Crown Court, while the other two form the superb **York Castle Museum** (daily 9.30am–5pm; £8; ☎01904/687 687, ⓦwww.yorkcastlemuseum.org.uk). It combines all the solid virtues of the traditional municipal museum with the same openness to innovation characteristic of the York Archaeological Trust sites. At the start, you pass a series of period rooms from the seventeenth century to the 1980s in which every item is genuine, and in which the attention to detail is remarkable – older visitors will be thrust down memory lane by the decor, furniture and hundreds of objects in the twentieth-century rooms. There's a whole large room devoted to Victorian attitudes to birth, marriage and death, followed by a wonderful reconstruction of the sights and sounds of York's Kirkgate during the final years of the nineteenth century, often staffed by people dressed in authentic costume. There are displays, too, of period kitchens – who'd have thought that state-of-the-art equipment from the 1980s could look quite so out-of-date – hygiene, costume through the ages, toys and World War II. There's also a superb re-creation of the fashion, music and news stories of the 1960s. Finally, the cells in the basement of the prison building contain an affecting series of real-life stories, told by video-recordings of actors projected onto cell walls, gleaned from the prison's records. Most notable is celebrity highwayman Dick Turpin (executed 1739; see box opposite), but there's a clutch of others including Mary Burgan (reprieved and released because she became pregnant by the jailer in 1710), William Petyt (a debtor who died of his injuries after being beaten by warders, 1741) and Elizabeth Boardingham (the last woman to be executed in Yorkshire by strangulation and being burned at the stake in 1776).

Quilt Museum

To the east of the centre, a two-minute walk from Dig, is one of York's newest museums, housed in one of its oldest buildings. **The Quilt Museum and**

Dick Turpin (1706–39)

The amazing thing about the myth of **Dick Turpin** is how little of it is true. First the legend – he was a dashing and debonair highwayman, a crack shot, who relieved rich travellers of their money and jewellery, rode from London to Yorkshire in less than 24 hours, and when finally caught and convicted, went to his death on the gallows with great devil-may-care dignity. The truth is somewhat different. An Essex butcher who turned to cattle-rustling, smuggling and robbery with violence in the London area, he operated with a gang which terrorized isolated farmhouses, using torture to discover where their victims had hidden their valuables. He wasn't very good at any of this – at one point he fired at constables who had arrested one of his accomplices and missed, fatally wounding the accomplice – and often had to live rough in Epping Forest until the heat had died down. With his gang dispersed, he turned to highway robbery, and committed several murders. Eventually, when capture seemed a certainty if he stayed in the southeast, he left the capital for Yorkshire. He didn't do it in less than 24 hours (that was another highwayman, John "Swift Nick" Nevison, in the previous century), and he didn't do it under his own name – he took the alias John Palmer. Finally arrested for horse theft, and identified as the notorious southern highwayman Dick Turpin, he was hanged at York racecourse. It wasn't until a century later that the myth of Dick Turpin, highwayman extraordinaire, started to gain ground, largely as a result of fictionalized accounts of his purported exploits by author William Harrison Ainsworth. One thing is true though. Thuggish low-life that he undoubtedly was, he did go to his death bravely, and with great swagger. The condemned cell in which he spent his last night can be seen in the York Castle Museum, and his grave can be tracked down in what was St George's churchyard in Fishergate.

Gallery (April–Sept Mon–Sat 10am–4pm; Oct–March Tues–Sat 10am–4pm; £6; ☎01904/613 242, ⓦ www.quiltmuseum.org.uk) might not seem an obvious crowd pleaser, but the combination of the slightly esoteric nature of its subject matter, the enthusiasm of its staff and the beauty both of its exhibits and of its setting are in fact a winning combination. Grade I listed St Anthony's Hall, a fifteenth-century guildhall in Peasholme Green, is home to the collection of the 1979-formed Quilters' Guild of the British Isles – not only beautiful quilts from the eighteenth century to the present day, but also the templates, tools and equipment associated with the craft. Even non-enthusiasts may be converted by a visit.

National Railway Museum

It can be said that, during its Industrial Revolution, Britain invented modern life. And the most groundbreaking part of this revolution, one that changed first Britain and then the world in a matter of a few decades, was the development of the railway system. The **National Railway Museum** (daily 10am–6pm; free; ☎08448 153 139, ⓦ www.nrm.org.uk) on Leeman Road tells the story of this development, not only through the display of its hundred locomotives and two hundred items of rolling stock, but also through videos, sound recordings, photographs, posters, paintings, station equipment, timepieces and a hundred other things associated with the history of rail travel. The heart of the museum lies in the exhibitions of the steam leviathans of the past and their modern equivalents in the **Great Hall** (through the tunnel on the right of the museum shop) and the rolling stock and associated exhibits in the **Station Hall** (straight ahead). Look out for the stunningly beautiful *Duchess of Hamilton*, which looks as if it has jumped out of an Art Deco poster, the Japanese Bullet Train (the only one outside Japan), the assorted Royal trains, including Queen Victoria's carriage, and the great turntable.

Projected developments at the NRM

Not content with being the best railway museum in the world, the NRM will be undergoing a number of changes in the next few years. The greatest projected development in the near future is a £20million refurbishment of the Great Hall, starting in late 2011 and going on throughout 2012. While the work is being done, some of the exhibits will continue to be on show – under canvas in the car park. Other upcoming developments include a range of events associated with the tenth anniversary of the arrival of the Bullet Train (July 2011), the introduction of a new gallery to show some of the museum's million photos, 11,000 posters and 500 oil paintings (from January 2011), and the reintroduction of steam rides during school holidays.

If you want to see the Mallard, though, you'll have to go to the NRM's other branch, Locomotion, at Shildon in County Durham. Don't miss either the **Warehouse**, with its huge collection of railway memorabilia, the **Works**, where you can see restoration work in progress, or the **South Yard** with its miniature railway, play and picnic areas. There's also a range of talks, activities, demonstrations and events put on each day, plus an excellent shop, a restaurant (in the Station Hall) and a café (in the Great Hall). Entrance to the museum, and even the handy map, are free. It's a truly wonderful day out, even if you're not a railway nerd.

York Model Railway

From the titans to the titches: sandwiched between York train station and a side door of the *Royal York Hotel* is the **York Model Railway** (April–Oct Mon–Sat 8.45am–6pm; Nov–March Mon–Sat 8.45am–5pm, Sun 10am–5pm; £5; ☎01904/630 169). The attractive, Grade II listed building that houses it was, at different times, the station's Victorian tearoom (its postal address is Tea Room Square), and the British Rail staff canteen. It became BR's "Railriders' World" in 1984, and assumed its current reincarnation as York Model Railway, run by a trust, in the mid 1990s. Almost a third of a mile of "00" gauge track (equivalent to 25 miles in the real world) carries up to fourteen trains at any one time through a variety of urban, rural and industrial scenes inhabited by 2500 people, and made up of 600 buildings, 1000 vehicles, 2000 lights and 5000 trees. There are lots of buttons to press, and an immensely well-stocked shop.

Micklegate Bar Museum

The **Micklegate Bar Museum** (daily 10am–3pm; £3; ☎01904/634 436, ⓦwww.micklegatebar.com), located in Micklegate Bar itself, was refurbished and reopened by the York Archaeological Trust to reflect the history of York's city walls. The displays inside introduce some of the people associated with the building – those who lived in it (it was occupied until 1918), and those whose heads were displayed on it – and also take a more general look at warfare and insurrection.

Bar Convent Museum

Just down the road from Micklegate Bar is the **Bar Convent** (daily 10am–3pm; free; ☎01904/643 238, ⓦwww.bar-convent.org.uk), the oldest still-functioning convent in England. Housed in a Grade I listed building, it was established in 1686 by the followers of Mary Ward (1585–1645), the founder of the Institute of the Blessed Virgin Mary (now called the Congregation of Jesus). The museum, on two floors of the convent, tells the story of Mary Ward and the dark days (for Roman Catholics) between the English Reformation under Henry VIII and the repeal of the penal laws in 1777 – a sorry tale of secret worship (there's an altar disguised as a bedstead), heroism and martyrdom. An affecting display deals with Margaret Clitherow (there's a shrine in her memory in the house she lived in on the Shambles), and also on local man Guy Fawkes. Upstairs displays cover the Roman Catholic religion and the convent's history as a school. An introductory video, narrated by York native Dame Judi Dench, covers the history of the convent and the collections in the museum. While you're visiting the museum, you can also admire the beautifully tiled Victorian entrance hall and the chapel. You can even stay the night (see p.146).

Cold War Bunker

Very different from English Heritage's usual type of property, the **Cold War Bunker** (April–Oct Sat & Sun 10am–4pm; Nov–March every 1st & 3rd weekend of the month; tours every 30min till 3pm; £5; EH), about a mile west of the city centre, is one of 29 command centres that were set up across the country in case of nuclear attack. This one was in commission from 1961 (the year before the Cuban Missile crisis) until the signing of the East–West non-aggression treaty in 1991. The bunker was designed to house a sixty-strong No. 20 Group, Royal Observer Corps, working in three shifts to monitor nuclear explosions in the region and the resulting fall-out. You can see the operations room, with all the original communications equipment, decontamination rooms (with air filters and sewage ejection systems), officers' room, telephone exchange and dormitories. There's a ten-minute film about the policy of overwhelming nuclear response to

A weekend in York

Friday night

Get a first view of this beautiful city by **walking the walls** (they're open until dusk), or the less energetic might take an open-top tourist bus. For the rest of the evening, join one of the **ghost tours** – they usually start around 7 or 8pm (see box, p.155) – or take a look at York by night from one of the tour boats that ply their trade on the river.

Saturday

Devote your morning to York's past. Both the Yorkshire and the Castle **museums** are fine examples of the way in which such institutions are bringing themselves bang up to date. Even more user-friendly and innovative are **Jorvik** and **Dig** – at the first you travel in a time capsule across Viking York, experiencing the sight and sounds (and even smells) of the city a thousand years ago; at the second, hard hat on head and trowel in hand, you'll be guided through a simulated archeological dig. For lunch try **Betty's**, a Yorkshire institution, with its staff in starched white aprons and its retro feel. During the afternoon, explore the centre's winding lanes and myriad independent **shops**, which draw people from all over the north of England and beyond. But if shopping fills you with dread, make your way to **York Minster** – you'll have to pay to get in (unless you're just going to worship) but then you can join a free and fascinating guided tour. Finally, spend the evening eating and drinking at one of the many excellent restaurants, bars and pubs in the city centre.

Sunday

Catch the road train the short distance out to the **National Railway Museum** (it opens at 10am), and wander around the biggest collection of bygone locomotives, rolling stock and memorabilia in the world. You can have lunch in the restaurant on one of the platforms. Return to Exhibition Square and grab some culture at the **City Art Gallery**, then stroll out in the nearby Museum Gardens until it's time to go home.

attack (appropriately called Mutual Assured Destruction, or MAD), and you must join a guided tour (no need to book). Bear in mind as you go around that if the bunker had ever been used for its purpose, most of the country's population would have been dead. Chilling for those who remember the Cold War, almost incomprehensible for those who don't.

Eating and drinking

There are plenty of **restaurants** and cafés to suit all tastes in the city centre. As for **pubs**, for a major eighteenth-century coaching town, the number of good options is disappointing: a lot of the old coaching inns have been demolished.

Tearooms, cafés and café-bars, restaurants

Asia Gourmet 61 Gillygate ☎01904/622 728. Small, cheerful restaurant in the city centre with prompt service. Mainly Japanese food (sushi a specialty) though other Asian cuisines available.

Ate o Clock 13a High Ousegate ☎01904/644 080. Dreadful name, but excellent lunches and dinners (last orders 2pm and 9.30pm respectively). Good, largely Mediterranean food, attentive service and relaxed atmosphere. Two-course lunch £8.80, main dishes £13.50–22.

🏃 **Betty's** 6–8 St Helen's Square ☎01904/659 142. Famous across Yorkshire, *Betty's* now has branches in Harrogate, Ilkley, Northallerton and Harlow Carr as well as York. Tea, coffee, cakes and pastries like mother used to make (or not) – try the pikelets or the Yorkshire fat rascals – hot dishes and puddings to die for, and a shop. You can't book, and the queue sometimes snakes out of the door and around the block, so try to visit off-peak. And visit the basement where there's a mirror with the signatures of the hundreds of Allied airmen – mainly Canadians – who used *Betty's* as an unofficial mess during World War II.

Café Concerto 21 High Petergate. Independent bistro with sheet-music-papered-walls, waiting staff in robust aprons and a Belle Epoque feel. Facing the Minster, with papers to browse and a busy relaxed atmosphere. Daily until 10pm.

🏃 **Café No. 8** 8 Gillygate ☎01904/653 074. Limited menu of excellent rustic-ish food in unpretentious surroundings, with main courses around £10 on the daytime menu, between £14 and £17 in the evening. Popular garden with heaters. Closes 10pm, closed Sun.

Evil Eye Lounge 42 Stonegate. Colourful café-bar with Indochinese food – Malaysian, Vietnamese, Thai, Tibetan, Japanese, Indonesian. A relatively cheap night out, with all dishes being £10 or under, and wines by the bottle at £10–25. Shuts Mon–Fri at 9pm, Sat 7pm, Sun 6pm.

Mason's Bar Bistro 13 Fossgate ☎01904/611 919, ⓦmasonsbarbistro.co.uk. An all-day bar/bistro which offers atmosphere and simple breakfast, lunch and dinner menus. The food is good, with generous portions at medium prices – all burgers are under £10, light bites £4–8 and main courses £8.95–13.95.

Rustique 28 Castlegate ☎01904/612 744. French-style bistro serving rustic (of course) food in faintly Belle Epoque surroundings. À la carte and set menus (two courses £11.95, three courses £13.95). Excellent value.

Pubs

Black Swan Peasholme Green. Imposing half-timbered, sixteenth-century pub (York's oldest) across the road from the Quilt Museum. It has wonderful internal detail – flagstones, period staircase, inglenook – and the beer's good. Jazz and folk nights (ⓦwww.blackswanfolkclub.org.uk for details of gigs).

Blue Bell Fossgate. Built in 1798, the *Blue Bell* is a tiny, friendly local with two rooms and a corridor. Oak-panelling, real ales, no mobile phones.

🏃 **The Swan** 16 Bishopgate. Lovely local, a Tetley Heritage Inn, and winner of York District CAMRA's pub of the year title in 2009. Friendly, and with well-kept real ale.

Three-Legged Mare 15 High Petergate. York Brewery's airy outlet for its own quality beer in a converted shop. No kids, no juke box, no video games. It's named after a three-legged gallows – it's there on the pub sign, with a replica in the beer garden.

Nightlife and entertainment

For a city that isn't thought of as a top clubbing or live music centre, York in fact does very well, with relatively intimate **venues** like *Blue Fly* or *The Basement* to the larger *Club Salvation*, *The Gallery* or *Fibbers*.

Clubs

Blue Fly 10 New St ☎01904/621 081, ⓦwww
.blueflyyork.co.uk. A snug establishment offering
high-quality bites and non-alcoholic beverages in
a café-bar environment during the day. These
rapidly turn to shots and cocktails in the evening,
served in the stylish *Lounge* to the accompaniment of current house.

Club Salvation 3 George Hudson St ☎01904/635
144, ⓦwww.clubsalvation.co.uk. A larger club with
two rooms, plus a large heated rooftop smoking
terrace. Indie night "Hang The DJ" on Sundays in
the upstairs room. Thurs & Sun 10pm–3.30am, Fri
& Sat 10pm–4.30am, also Tues till 4.30am for
Student Night during term time.

The Gallery 12 Clifford St ☎ 01904/647 947,
ⓦwww.galleryclub.co.uk/york. York's main
nightclub, boasting two main rooms and a VIP
lounge that cater to a wide variety of musical
tastes. Fridays see house, pop, electro and indie
in room one, with r'n'b in room two and two-for-
one drinks all night. "Pure" runs every Saturday
with dance, r'n'b and indie in room one and a
strong urban flavour in room two, along with
drinks promotions all night long. To round off their
three-day weekend there's "The Sunday Session"
in room one (pop/party classics) and "Vibe" in
room two (r'n'b). Open every day, all year, except
for Christmas Day.

Hub 53–55 Micklegate ☎01904/620 602, ⓦwww
.ziggysnightclub.com. Previously *Ziggy's*, with three
floors of dance-oriented flavours. Fridays feature
techno and electro nights, while most Saturdays
it's house. Student discounts apply all the time and
Wednesdays are designated official Student Night,
when you get in free with ID.

Tru 3–5 Toft Green ☎01904/620 203, ⓦwww
.truyork.co.uk. Previously *Toffs*, prior to an
extensive refurbishment. The club plays a mix of
chart, funky house, indie and r'n'b across its
three rooms. "Double Your Money" runs on Friday
and Saturday nights, where you receive double
your entry fee in drinks vouchers. Thursdays
hosts "Riskie Disco" in room one (pop/electro/old
skool) and "Kinkie Indie" in room two, with 80p
drinks all night. Thurs–Sun
10.30pm–3am/3.30pm.

Live music

The Basement 13–17 Coney St, below City Screen
cinema ☎01904/612 940, ⓦwww.thebasement
york.co.uk. An intimate venue that presents a pleas-
ingly diverse variety of nights – from music to
comedy to arts events. The first Wednesday of every
month is "Café Scientifique" – a free evening of
discussion and debate surrounding current issues in
science. "The Hyena Lounge Comedy Club"
presents stand-up acts every Sunday night. Live
music is smattered through the week, along with
other cabaret, burlesque and discos – full details on
the website. Generally 8–11pm, Sun 7–10pm,
though individual events can differ.

The Duchess 7 Stonebow House ☎01904/641
413, ⓦwww.theduchessyork.co.uk. A spacious,
single-room venue in the centre of town that plays
host to bands every night of the week, varying from
Dreadzone to high-end tribute bands. Fridays and
Saturdays often have club nights such as "Up The
Racket!" and "Popaganda", blasting out indie/electro
and indie/pop respectively. Doors open 7.30pm.

Fibbers 8 The Stonebow ☎01904/651 250,
ⓦwww.fibbers.co.uk. York's primary live music
venue, *Fibbers* regularly puts on bands of both local
and national standing in a lively atmosphere. Club
nights include "Hammertime" (90s) on Fridays and
"Melt" (indie/electro) on Saturdays. Club nights
10.30pm–3am, gigs doors open at 7.30pm.

Theatre and cinema

City Screen 13–17 Coney St ☎0871 704 2054,
ⓦwww.picturehouses.co.uk. The city's
independent cinema – three screens, riverside
café-bar, and *Basement Bar* with regular live music
and a comedy club.

Grand Opera House 4 Cumberland St
☎01904/678 700, ⓦwww.grandoperahouseyork
.org.uk. An unstuffy diet of musicals, ballet, pop
and family entertainment.

The National Centre for Early Music St Margaret's Church, Walmgate ☎01904/658 338,
ⓦwww.ncem.co.uk. Early music, of course, but
also folk, world and jazz recitals.

Theatre Royal St Leonard's Place ☎01904/623
568, ⓦwww.yorktheatreroyal.co.uk. Musicals,
mainstream drama and seasonal panto.

Shopping

York is famous in the North of England for its shops. It has a full range of the usual
high street chains and three main out-of-town **shopping centres** – Clifton Moor
(buses #18 & #18A), Monks Cross (#MX6 from Stonebow) and McArthur Glen
(shuttle from York station or #415). But it's for its range of stylish department
stores and **independent shops** that York is best known. For a more detailed introduction to York's endless shopping possibilities, check out ⓦwww.york-tourism
.co.uk/distinctiveshopping.

Department stores

Browns Davygate ☏ 01904/611 166, ⓦ www
.brownsyork.co.uk.
Fenwicks Coppergate Centre.

Fashion and accessories

The Blue Ballroom 36 Gillygate. Vintage and retro
clothing.
Mulberry Factory Shop 23–25 Swinegate
ⓦ www.mulberry.com. Top-end bags and clothes,
at discounted prices.
Porta Dextra 1 High Petergate. Contemporary
jewellery specialists.
Vivienne Westwood 10 Blake St ⓦ www.hervia
.com. Branch of the famous designer's clothing and
accessories store.

Books

Barbican Bookshop 24 Fossgate ⓦ www
.barbicanbookshop.co.uk. New and secondhand
bookshop.

Minster Gate Bookshop Minster Gates, off High
Petergate ⓦ www.minstergatebooks.co.uk. Five
floors of secondhand and antiquarian books, plus
prints and maps.
York National Book Fair ⓦ www.yorkbookfair
.com. Antiquarian book fair every September.

Food and markets

Continental Market Parliament St. Middle of Feb,
June and Oct.
Farmers Market Parliament St. Usually the last
Friday of the month.
La Via Vecchia 6 Shambles. Italian breads of all
kinds.
Newgate market Mon–Fri 9am–4.30pm, Sat &
Sun 9am–4pm.
Rafi's Spicebox 17 Goodramgate ⓦ www
.spicebox.co.uk. Spices of all kinds, plus their own
curry mixes.

Listings

Bike rental Bob Trotter Cycles in Lord Mayor's
Walk (☏ 01904/622 868, ⓦ www.bobtrottercycles
.com) rents out town bikes at £15 per day.
Buses National Express ☏ 08717 818178; East
Yorkshire ☏ 01482/222 222 (for Hull, Beverley and
Bridlington); Yorkshire Coastliner ☏ 01653/692 556
(for Leeds, Castle Howard, Pickering, Scarborough
and Whitby).
Hospital York District Hospital, Wigginton Rd
(☏ 01904/631 313). The NHS Walk-in Centre, 31

Monkgate (daily 8am–6pm; ☏ 01904/725 401)
offers care, advice and treatment without an
appointment.
Internet City Library, off Museum St (Mon–Thurs
9am–8pm, Fri 9am–6pm, Sat 9am–5pm, Sun
11am–4pm, 1st Thurs of the month 1–8pm).
Taxis Ranks at Rougier St, Duncombe Place,
Exhibition Square, and the train station; or call
Station Taxis ☏ 01904/623 332.

Around York

Though York has more than enough attractions to keep even the most demanding
visitor happy, there are a couple of places on the outskirts that are worth a look.

Yorkshire Air Museum

Clearly signposted off York's southern bypass, about five miles east of the city
centre, the **Yorkshire Air Museum** (bus #195 from Merchantgate; daily
10am–5pm, 3.30pm in winter; £6; ☏ 01904/608 595, ⓦ www.yorkshireair
museum.co.uk) occupies **RAF Elvington**, a World War II bomber station. Its
control tower, hangars, Nissen huts, ops room, radio operators' room, airman's
billet and NAAFI provide an evocative context for the forty-plus aircraft and mass
of equipment such as gun turrets, searchlights and bombs. A series of displays
outline the role of Bomber Command during the war. Uniforms, military vehicles
including jeeps and ambulances are also on show, plus accounts of the pioneers of
aviation and of associated units, such as the Red Berets, the United States Army
Air Force and the Royal Observer Corps. As regards the stars of the show – the
aircraft – as well as the Spitfire, Hurricane, Messerschmit, Halifax, Wellington and
Lancaster, there's also a good selection of less-well-known World War II planes
like the Mosquito and the Dakota, prewar planes that look as if they're made of

string and sealing wax, and postwar planes – the Victor, the English Electric Lightning, the Javelin, the Meteor and the Harrier. The links with Allied countries such as the US, the Commonwealth countries and Poland are evident, but the strongest connection was with the French – their only two heavy bomber squadrons operated from the airfield, and it was the only base operated by French personnel. A Mirage jet, donated by the President of France, is the only one of its kind in Britain, and in the nearby village is a French war memorial.

You can wander about at will, listen to wartime music, eat at the NAAFI where you might be lucky enough to find yourself sitting next to a well-informed volunteer, or buy memorabilia at the shop. For anybody interested in the war in the air, or in aircraft generally, this museum is a must.

The Yorkshire Museum of Farming

In the same area of eastern York as the aircraft museum, and signposted off the same roundabout on the southern bypass, the **Yorkshire Museum of Farming** in Murton Park (bus #10 from Merchantgate; daily 10am–5pm, 4pm in winter; £5.50; ☎01904/489 966, ⓦ www.murtonpark.co.uk) is one of the many British museums that have evolved from the activities of enthusiasts, in this case the Farm Machinery Preservation Society. What's particularly useful is its blend of theory, explanation and hands-on practicality. There's an excellent display on the farming year, and the Livestock Gallery introduces the tools and equipment used by farmers raising sheep, cows, pigs and horses. There's also a small display of celebrity vet James Herriot's personal gear. The highlight of any visit to the museum, though, is its livestock, with many rare or historical breeds of goats, pigs, sheep, poultry and ponies.

The Marston Moor Memorial

Seven and a half miles west of York is the monument to the **Battle of Marston Moor**, one of the pivotal engagements of the English Civil War. In 1644 Royalist York, under siege by Parliamentary forces commanded by Fairfax and Cromwell and Scottish forces under Leven, was relieved by the dashing Prince Rupert. Overconfident after his initial success, the Royalists engaged the much bigger Parliamentary and Scottish forces in a pitched battle at Marsden Moor and were soundly beaten. The Cavaliers lost around four thousand men, plus all their guns and equipment, for the loss of three hundred Roundheads and Scots – they're buried in communal graves on the battlefield. It was the biggest engagement of the war, and effectively ended any pretence of Royalist control of the North of England. At the site of the battle is a memorial obelisk and an information board giving a clear account of the battle.

Wetherby

Though it's just inside West Yorkshire, some fourteen miles north of Leeds and a popular dormitory town for that city, in itself **WETHERBY** feels more at one with Knaresborough, Harrogate and Ripon in North Yorkshire. It's pleasant and pretty without having anything specific to attract the visitor – a good place for an hour's stroll, say, or even a good base for exploring this part of Yorkshire.

The town first grew up to service traffic on the Great North Road fording the River Wharfe, and its prosperity increased when a bridge replaced the ford in 1233 and a market charter was granted in 1240. That this prosperity continued into the Industrial Revolution is reflected in the fact that the bridge was twice widened, once in the eighteenth century, once in the nineteenth, that most of the surviving buildings date from this time, and that the town even today has far more pubs than you'd expect in a settlement of this size. Wetherby was finally bypassed in 1959, and for half a century has settled into a life of quiet prosperity. It still has visitors from the nearby A1(M), it attracts punters to its lovely racecourse, and is home for commuters to not only Leeds but also York and even Bradford and Wakefield, and it has its share of light industry. You could do far worse than use it as a base for exploring the Leeds/Bradford conurbation to the south, York to the east, and Harrogate and Knaresborough to the north.

Arrival and information

Wetherby is eminently accessible by **road**, just off the A1(M), and parking in the town is largely free. The main **car park** is right at the mini-roundabout immediately after crossing the bridge. A left at the same mini-roundabout brings you to the tiny **bus station**. Rail and air are more difficult – the nearest **train stations** are in Knaresborough (8 miles) and York (14 miles), and while the nearest **airport** – Leeds-Bradford – is only twelve miles away, and is therefore an easy drive by car, to bus it you'll have to go into Leeds then back out again. The **tourist information office** (Mon–Fri 9/10am–6/7pm, Sat 9/10am–4pm; ℡01937/582 151) is in Wetherby library, at the top end of the Market Place where it becomes Westgate.

Accommodation

The choice of **accommodation** in Wetherby is straightforward – modern budget hotels or top-end and classy.

Days Inn Junction 46, A1(M), Kirk Deighton ℡01937/547 557, ⓦwww.daysinn.com. On the roundabout at junction 46 of the A1(M). New, but also further out than the *Ramada* – more useful perhaps as a stop-off than for a lengthy stay. ❷
Ramada Hotel Wetherby Rd ℡0844 815 9067, ⓦwww.ramadajarvis.co.uk. Just over the bridge, it has the major advantage of being within walking distance of the town centre, but if you don't want to go out, you can use its own bar and restaurant. Rooms and decor are in line with the Ramada chain. ❸

Wood Hall Hotel and Spa Trip Lane ℡0845 072 7564, ⓦwww.handpicked hotels.co.uk. About three miles from the town at the end of a long drive, the *Wood Hall Hotel* is on another plane entirely – beautiful old building, luxurious rooms, well-appointed spa, magnificent views, fine-dining restaurant and attention to detail (you can borrow wellies and umbrellas if you fancy a walk). Peaceful countryside location, with a long single-lane approach road, which can be a bind if you're back and forth a lot. As is, of course, the tariff – it's not cheap. ❻

The Town

Any tour of Wetherby has to start with its reason for being – the **bridge** across the Wharfe. From the bridge, upriver you can see the weir which used to divert water into the town mill – at different times it milled corn, fulled cloth and pressed rape seed. The mill was demolished in the 1960s, but the weir has been renovated and a salmon leap added. The position of the mill is marked by a cog wheel and a modern sculpture of two fish. Downriver is a small park with a bandstand, the car park and pleasant seats and picnic tables, all linked by a riverside walk which goes under the final town-side arch of the bridge.

Beyond the bridge past the angel-topped war memorial, straight ahead is the **High Street**, and a left turn takes you into the **Market Place**, which climbs up the hill to the imposing 1845 **Town Hall**. There are numerous fine **Georgian buildings**, one of the best being Wetherby House, which was for eighty years up to 1971 a doctor's surgery. Opposite the Town Hall, parallel with and between the

Market Place and the High Street, is the **Shambles**, an eleven-bay covered market erected between 1811 and 1824 – the end facing the Town Hall was smartened up in 1911 to celebrate the coronation of George V.

If, instead of walking down the Shambles, you continue through to the High Street and its continuation North Street, you'll come across a number of Wetherby's old **coaching inns** – particularly splendid are the **Angel**, which could once stable a hundred coach horses, and the **Swan and Talbot**. In North Street, opposite the Horsefair Centre is the **Garden of Rest**, containing the decorative **Huguenot Arch**, built according to tradition by Protestant Huguenots who fled to England during the sixteenth-century French Wars of Religion. And just around the corner in Crossley Street is **Wetherby's Cinema** (☎01937/580 544, ⓦwww.wetherbyfilmtheatre.co.uk), established during World War I to cheer up the local population and reopened after closure in the 1990s. How refreshing in these days of giant multiplexes to sit in a single auditorium seating 150 – a uniplex, perhaps.

For more extensive **walks**, look out for the *Wetherby Town Trail*, the *Wetherby Railway Path* and *Wetherfield is blooming* in the tourist information office, and for the excellent **blue plaques** put up all over the town by the Wetherby Civic Trust.

Eating and drinking

Wetherby abounds in **places to eat**, with some takeaway options on the Market Place and several pubs serving food. If you want to push the boat out try the restaurant at the *Wood Hall Hotel* (see p.164).

Ask Market Place ☎01937/589 831. One of the chain of Italian restaurants, at the bottom end of the Market Place, but with a fair range of food – and it's a good vantage point from which to watch the world go by. It gets busy, though, and can be noisy.

The Gourmet Coffee Shop The Shambles ☎01937/586 031. Good coffee shop in the Shambles with a good reputation.

Jaflong 31 High St ☎01937/587 011. Indian restaurant that offers a wide range of tandoori dishes.

The Swan and Talbot North St ☎01937/582 040. One of the historic coaching inns. Good food with large portions, and a lot of "two-for-one" deals when it can get very busy.

🥾 **Windmill Inn** Main St, Linton ☎01937/582 209. Just outside Wetherby, the gorgeous *Windmill Inn* in Linton is not only a super pub in a lovely village, but does excellent food.

Harrogate

HARROGATE folk have a reputation in the rest of Yorkshire for thinking themselves "a cut above". Its property prices are certainly amongst the highest in the north of England. Yet here is a sizeable modern town – 80,000 people or so – that has successfully reinvented itself as its circumstances have changed. Though still thought of as a spa town, its famous mineral springs now account for very few of its substantial visitor numbers.

Most of those springs were discovered very early on, between 1570 and 1650. Yet Harrogate was slow to capitalize on them, partly because the main landowner, the Duchy of Lancaster, was reluctant for the town to become the new Cheltenham or Leamington, but also because the springs were so scattered. Harrogate started as two separate settlements – **High Harrogate** up on the hill, and **Low Harrogate** in a valley about a mile to the west – with mineral springs dotted around in and between them. In 1778 the horseshoe-shaped open land that looped between them to the south – the **Stray** – was fixed and protected, and remains to this day one of the town's greatest glories and most distinctive features.

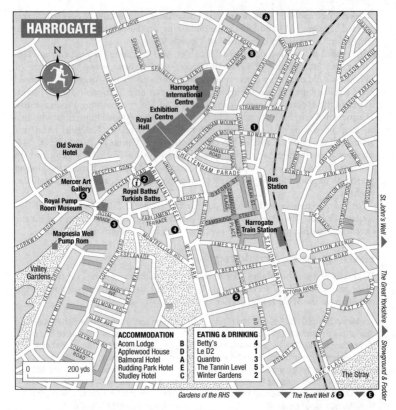

ACCOMMODATION	
Acorn Lodge	B
Applewood House	D
Balmoral Hotel	A
Rudding Park Hotel	E
Studley Hotel	C

EATING & DRINKING	
Betty's	4
Le D2	1
Quantro	3
The Tannin Level	5
Winter Gardens	2

0   200 yds

Gardens of the RHS ▼   ▼ The Tewit Well & D   ▼ E

From the late eighteenth century onwards Harrogate attracted hordes of wealthy visitors, with many of its public buildings being erected during the first half of the nineteenth century. Harrogate's position as one of the UK's great spas rose to another level from about 1860 with the development of an impressive new town centre on the land between High and Low Harrogate, and with the extension of the railway into town. Many of the palatial Victorian hotels date from this period.

During the twentieth century, as belief in the healing powers of spa waters declined, Harrogate seemed in danger of going into serious decline. However, the occupation of many of its hotels by government departments during World War II offered a hint of things to come, and from the 1960s onwards Harrogate became a major player in the corporate conference and exhibition field. Add to this its attractions as a commuter town for the great Leeds/Bradford conurbation, as a top-end shopping destination, as a tourist magnet and as a horticultural centre and you begin to see that the people of Harrogate have every reason to be proud of their town.

Arrival and information

Sitting astride the A61 fourteen miles north of Leeds and nearly seven miles from the A1(M), Harrogate is reasonably accessible by **road** and, being so spread out, there's plenty of on-street and off-street parking. The **bus** and **train stations** are conveniently located next to each other on the eastern edge of the town centre on Station Parade.

The **tourist information centre** (April–Sept Mon–Sat 9am–5.30pm, Sun 10am–1pm; Oct–March Mon–Sat 9am–5pm; ☎01423/537 300, ⓦwww.enjoy harrogate.com) is in the Royal Baths building, facing onto Crescent Gardens.

Accommodation

Because of its history as a popular spa town, and its modern incarnation as a prime conference and exhibition venue, Harrogate has a huge range of **hotels** and **B&Bs**, from the grand to the modest. Some of the great early hotels are perhaps past their prime, waiting patiently for refurbishment. Some are modern, part of the chains you'll find in any big city. Here are some that nod to Harrogate's great past, but ensure that levels of service and comfort are contemporary.

Acorn Lodge Studley Rd ☎01423/525 630, ⓦwww.acornlodgeharrogate.co.uk. A guesthouse with big-hotel ideas (luxury fittings, individual decor, Jacuzzi, massage available in room) but B&B tariffs and friendliness. Well placed for town centre (5min). ❸

Applewood House St George's Rd ☎01423/544 549, ⓦwww.applewoodhouse.co.uk. Imposing Victorian house south of the Stray, five times winner of Visit Britain gold award. Light, airy, spotlessly clean rooms, wonderfully personal service, and with impressive room rates which include breakfast. A gem. ❸

Balmoral Hotel Franklin Mount ☎01423/508 208, ⓦwww.balmoralhotel.co.uk. Recently refurbished boutique hotel occupying a rather grand terrace of three Edwardian houses a few minutes' walk from the town centre. Fixtures and fittings luxurious, rooms spacious and individual, staff pleasant and

helpful. Combines traditional luxury and stylish modern facilities. ❺

Rudding Park Hotel Follifoot ☎01423/872 100, ⓦwww.ruddingpark.co.uk. Top-end hotel in Grade I listed building, in extensive parkland and with its own golf course, three miles southeast of Harrogate. Rooms and facilities are luxurious, service is terrific, the restaurant immaculate – the whole experience is impossible to fault. And though expensive – it's really a special-occasion type of place – check the website for some excellent offers. ❼

Studley Hotel Swan Rd ☎01423/560 425, ⓦwww.studleyhotel.co.uk. Medium-sized independent town centre hotel with attached Thai restaurant. Attractive rooms vary in size and cost, and service is good, though the restaurant can sometimes get very busy. Rates can be surprisingly good if you shop around online. ❹

The Town

The centre of Harrogate falls into four main areas, all within walking distance. Immediately west of the train and bus stations, sandwiched between **Station Parade** and **Parliament Street** lie most of the big shops and chain stores, especially in and around the Victoria Shopping Centre – Oxford Street, Cambridge Street, James Street, Albert Street. On the other side of Parliament Street lies the triangular area known as the **Montpellier Quarter**, all boutiques, cafés, restaurants and pubs. Most of the streets here are Montpellier something – Hill, Parade, Street, Road, Gardens, Mews, Walk. At the bottom of the hill, cutting across the north end of the Montpellier Quarter and the main shopping area are **Valley Gardens**, the **Crescent** and **Kings Road**, along which are most of the public buildings – the **Royal Pump Rooms**, **Mercer Art Gallery**, **Royal Baths**, Exhibition Hall, International Centre and so on. Finally, along the southern edge of this area, on the other side of York Place and Knaresborough Road, is the **Stray**, still open and grassy and un-encroached upon.

Further out from Harrogate town centre lie both the **Gardens of the Royal Horticultural Society** and **the Great Yorkshire Showground**, which between them sum up Harrogate's post-spa nature and are worth visiting.

Montpellier Quarter and Valley Gardens

There's no doubt that Harrogate's main attraction for the visitor is its splendid collection of Victorian and Edwardian buildings, its extensive gardens, and the range of exhibitions and conferences it hosts. A good starting point for an exploration of all three, once you've wandered around the town centre shops and the fashionable **Montpellier Quarter**, is the **Valley Gardens** to the west. In a widening wedge southwest of Royal Parade, the gardens are in every way typically Victorian, with the magnificent **Sun Pavilion** and its attached **Colonnades** on the slope to the right, a pretty babbling brook dropping down through a series of mini-waterfalls to the left, and in between, dotted around among lawns and flower beds, a bandstand (concerts May–Aug Sun pm), children's boating and paddling pools, tennis courts, crazy golf, pitch-and-putt and a recently revamped play area. Take particular note of the wonderful café – it occupies the **Magnesia Well Pump Room**, built in 1895 over one of the celebrated springs.

Royal Pump Room Museum

Directly across the road to the garden entrance is the Royal Pump Room, another exquisite spa building. A stone octagon with a dome built in 1842 over the Old Sulphur Well (the original covering building was moved to the Tewit Well), it has an iron-and-glass annexe added in 1912–13, and it is now the **Royal Pump Room Museum** (Mon–Sat 10am–5pm, Sun 2–5pm, Nov–March closes 4pm; £3.30; ☎01423/556 188) dealing largely with the history of Harrogate, but also with aspects of world history such as the ancient Egyptians. There are visiting exhibitions as well, and, if you've got the stomach for it, you can also taste the foul-smelling waters.

Mercer Art Gallery and around

The Assembly Rooms on Swan Road, yet another example of a Victorian building with a new function, now houses the **Mercer Art Gallery** (Tues–Sat 10am–5pm, Sun 2–5pm; free). The gallery mounts touring exhibitions of paintings, photographs and sculptures as well as selections of the town's own two-thousand-strong collection – appropriately, mainly nineteenth- and twentieth-century works.

Incidentally, at the top of the street, where York Road comes into Swan Road, you can see the **Old Swan Hotel**, established around 1700 and much rebuilt since then, but made forever famous by Agatha Christie's mysterious ten-day stay here in 1926 – perhaps the result of amnesia or depression brought on by her mother's death and her husband's infidelity, but thought at the time by many to be a publicity stunt.

The Royal Baths

On Crescent Road are the Crescent Gardens and the colossal **Royal Baths**, built over two of Harrogate's many mineral springs. Opened in 1897, the baths offered a bewildering array of over ninety treatments for all sorts of ailments. For example, those with skin diseases like eczema, psoriasis and acne would take a saline sulphur bath, those who were bunged-up might opt for a nasal douche and water spray, colitis and constipation might benefit from the Harrogate intestinal lavage treatment, and rheumatism, lumbago and sciatica might be treated with a variety of peat baths. These were based on different combinations of the two main types of water – sulphide and iron waters – together with many other trace elements such as barium, potassium, sodium and magnesium. During the twentieth century, as modern medicine came to grips with such chronic ailments and diseases, faith in such water treatments declined, and visitor numbers dropped. By the late 1960s all such facilities, except the Turkish Baths (see below) had closed. The building has since been colonized by the tourist information centre (on the right), the *Royal Baths Chinese Restaurant* (in the middle), and the *Winter Gardens* pub around the back (there's an entrance on Parliament Street as well), which is worth going in to admire the decor – a riot of columns and staircases, iron and glass.

Beyond the Royal Baths, facing on to Ripon Road and Kings Road, are the impressive **Royal Hall** (on the left, 1903), **Exhibition Centre** (on the corner, 2000) and **Conference Centre** (along Kings Rd, 1982), together with, attached to it, the *Moat House Hotel*. Though as a conference and exhibition space the whole complex is undoubtedly a success, visually it's a bit of a mess.

The Turkish Baths

The far end of the Royal Baths houses the magnificent and still-functioning **Turkish Baths** (entrance on Parliament St; daily, hours vary, call first; £13–19; ☎01423/556 746, ⓦwww.harrogate.gov.uk), seen now as a way of relaxing rather than as a cure for any disease. The most complete example of Victorian Turkish Baths in the country, their Moorish design includes elaborate Islamic arches and screens, lovely glazed brickwork walls and colourful floors and ceilings. You can enjoy the traditional Turkish Bath experience of progressing through the steam room, the plunge pool, the Tepidarium (warm), Calidarium (hot) and Laconium (ferocious), perhaps several times, then cooling off in the Frigidarium, together with more modern facial and body treatments, reflexology, hot stone therapy and massages. For women there's also waxing, eye and nail treatments, and tanning. There's a complicated timetable of mixed and single-sex sessions and a variety of tariffs – standard, off-peak (Tues) and peak (weekends). A minimum of ninety minutes is recommended, under-16s are not allowed in, and towels are provided.

The Stray

Within town, it just remains to explore **the Stray**, the great swathe of rough grass to the south, which is usually dotted with people walking dogs, flying kites and other outdoor activities. In particular, take a look at Tewit Well at the western enjoyig end, and St John's Well to the east, two of Harrogate's earliest discoveries. **The Tewit Well**, the quality of whose water was first recognized, and compared with the water of Spa in Belgium, by Sir William Slingsby in the 1570s, is covered by an open dome with twelve Tuscan columns (it's the one that, until replaced in 1842 by the Royal Pump Room, stood over the Old Sulphur Well); **St John's Well** is marked by a small 1842-built kiosk.

Gardens of the Royal Horticultural Society

A mile and a half west of the town centre are the delightfully informal **Gardens of the Royal Horticultural Society at Harlow Carr**, Crag Lane (daily: March–Oct 9.30am–6pm; Nov–Feb 9.30am–4pm; £7; ⓦwww.rhs.org.uk). A pleasure for anybody, but sheer unadulterated heaven for keen gardeners – not only the 58-acre gardens themselves, but also the new super-environmentally friendly Learning Centre, the glass Alpine Centre, and the shop stuffed with plants, gifts and books related to gardening. And the tearooms are provided by *Betty's* – life doesn't get any better.

The Great Yorkshire Showground

To the southeast of town (take the Wetherby road, and turn right immediately after Sainsbury's), **The Great Yorkshire Showground** is a venue for all sorts of events, in particular the Yorkshire Horticultural Society's spring (April) and autumn (Sept) flower shows and Yorkshire Agricultural Society's Great Yorkshire Show (July). There's also a Caravan Club campsite (see p.148) and **Fodder** (Mon–Sat 9am–5.30pm, Sun 10am-4pm; ☎01423/541 000, ⓦwww.fodderweb.co.uk), opened in July 2008 by Her Majesty the Queen. Championed by the Yorkshire Agricultural Society, Fodder sells top-quality produce from all over the county – meat, bread, cheese and other dairy produce, vegetables, fruit, wine, preserves, pies – in a light, airy, environmentally friendly building. Altogether it stocks over a hundred locally sourced products, and supports sixty-plus family farms in the region. At the far end of the building there's a café/restaurant where you are guaranteed fresh, locally sourced food, and where you can read your complementary newspaper (the *Yorkshire Post*, naturally). Outside, there's ample free parking and a children's playground.

Eating and drinking

Apart from the excellent hotel **restaurants** – *The Orchid* at the *Studley Hotel*, the *Clocktower* at *Rudding Park* (see p.167) – and the café/restaurant at Fodder (see above) there's a huge selection of eating places in Harrogate.

Betty's 1 Parliament St ☎01423/502 746. A Yorkshire institution with branches in several North Yorkshire towns (they've refused to open any outside the county), *Betty's* has a uniquely old-fashioned air, with exterior wrought-iron canopy, large bowed windows, a light airy room, waiting staff in starched linen, and cooking and baking that harks back to more leisured times. Shuts 9pm; they won't take reservations, so you'll sometimes have to wait for a table (often for quite a while), but it's worth it.

🏃 **Le D2** Bower Rd ☎01423/502 700. Quality French food and excellent service in unpretentious surroundings, and at affordable prices – two courses for £9.95 at lunch and £14.95 in the evening. Shut Sun & Mon.

Quantro 3 Royal Parade ☎01423/503 034. Highly rated modern European town-centre restaurant with stylish decor, though the layout is a little regimented. Main courses £14–18, and lunchtime/ early bird "Menu Qu" options at two courses for £10.95, three for £13.95.

The Tannin Level 5 Raglan St ☎01423/560 595. Well-known and popular town-centre brasserie, smartly understated, with a Michelin-trained cook, super locally sourced food and an admirably simple dinner menu – starters and sweets all £5, main courses all £10, with express menu for lunches and early-bird discounts for early evening diners.

Winter Gardens Royal Baths, Parliament St ☎01423/877 010. For rock-bottom prices, you can't beat rough-and-ready *Wetherspoon*'s pubs. A chain renowned for revitalizing interesting buildings, the *Winter Gardens* is one of their best – all wrought iron, glass and ornate staircases.

Knaresborough

At first sight **KNARESBOROUGH** might seem pleasant but unremarkable – a nice little market town clustered around its L-shaped square, worth perhaps a short stop and an aimless wander. Explore more thoroughly, though, and you'll find that it's one of Yorkshire's prettiest, most interesting towns. Perched on an escarpment above a gorge through which the River Nidd flows, the town as viewed from its castle, either of its two bridges or its railway viaduct has what estate agents call "the wow factor" – in spades.

Arrival, information and accommodation

Well signposted from the A1(M) and all other directions, Knaresborough is easy to find by **road**, but is so close to much bigger neighbour Harrogate that you could end up there if you're not careful. There are pay-and-display **car parks** in several places, including one in the centre of town and another on the riverside next to the High Bridge. The **train station** is off Kirkgate, two minutes' walk from the Market Square, and the **bus station** is nearby. The **tourist information centre** (April–Oct Mon–Sat 10am–5pm, Sun 10am–1pm; Nov–March Wed & Sat, 10am–4pm; ℡0845 389 0177) is tucked away in Castle Courtyard, between the Market Square and the Castle.

The only **hotel** in Knaresborough is the *Best Western Dower House Hotel*, Bond End (℡01423/863 302, ⓦwww.dowerhouse-hotel.co.uk; ⑤), just on the edge of the town centre, a few hundred metres from Mother Shipton's Cave. It's a beautiful Grade II listed building with fourteenth-century origins, though most of what you see today is seventeenth-and eighteenth-century. Although blessed with great character, friendly and attentive staff, a pool and a spa (recently upgraded) some parts of the hotel itself are rather tired and in need of refurbishment.

The Town

Knaresborough is a town on two levels: the main part is on top of the hill, clustered around the Market Place and castle. The rest is down along the river, between the High and the Low bridges (it's nothing to do with their height – the first's upriver, the second downriver), with the commanding railway viaduct in between.

The Market Place

In the **Market Place**, L-shaped because of the encroachment of the Town Hall, are two reminders of the town's most famous son – John Metcalfe, or **Blind Jack of Knaresborough** (see box, p.174). The first is a statue of the great eighteenth-century road engineer, slouching on one of the square's benches, his measuring wheel beside him, looking for all the world has if he has just stopped for a breather during his incessant pacing of the surrounding countryside. Immediately beyond is **Blind Jack's**, a lively and historic Georgian brick pub named after the engineer – look out for the trompe l'oeil figure of Jack leaning out of an upstairs window.

Knaresborough Castle

Just off the Market Square, perched high above the Nidd, stands Knareborough's castle. As you approach it, notice the two old **school buildings**, one either side of the street. Set up by the National Society, an Anglican group dedicated to the education of the poor, the one on the left was the boys' school, established in 1814, the one on the right the girls' and infants' school.

Knaresborough Castle (open all year; free) ruins are peaceful and atmospheric, in sharp contrast to their history. Built intermittently over the two hundred years up to 1312, the castle consisted of a keep to the north, where the largest part of the remains, St John's Tower, now stands, an outer ward on the town side, and an inner ward along the cliff top towards the west. Historical celebrities associated with the castle include Hugh de Moreville and his gang, who in the 1170s took refuge in an earlier incarnation of the castle after they'd assassinated Thomas Becket, and John of Gaunt, who took possession of the castle in 1372. The castle came to a spectacular end during the English Civil War when the town sided with King Charles. The Roundheads laid siege, and took the castle in 1644. Finally, as a result of a general Parliamentary order that Royalist castles should be "slighted" (rendered defensively useless), the castle was demolished in 1648, the coupe de grace being delivered by opportunist townsfolk who helped themselves to the masonry. The castle remains – St John's Tower and a few bits of the curtain wall – became a public park in 1897. Also in the environs of the castle is the old courthouse, now the **Knaresborough Museum** (Easter–Oct daily 10.30am–5pm; £2.50).

From the far end of the inner ward (the war memorial end), the upriver views of the town – the houses climbing steeply from a bend in the river, the elegant railway viaduct with the parish church behind it, the surrounding woods – are almost too good to be true. Indeed, when there's a train crossing the viaduct, the whole aspect has the miniature perfection of a model railway layout.

Along the river

Downriver from the castle, a double weir, built to serve the mill buildings, swings the river around a further curve. **Knaresborough Mill** itself, dating from the eighteenth century, has at different times pumped water from the river up into the town, worked as a paper mill, and was involved in a variety of cloth-making processes – cotton and flax spinning, and, right up to its closure in 1972, weaving flax. The buildings are now residential.

Taking the steps that zig-zag down from the castle brings you to the attractive **Waterside**, a road that follows the river upstream under the viaduct. There are several cafés, with *The Marigold Café* renting out boats. On the right are the remains of the **Old Dye House**, built in 1610, where dye was made to supply the local textile factories up to 1840.

After a pleasant riverside terrace, the road passes under the **railway viaduct**. Built by Thomas Grainger of the East and West Yorkshire Junction Railway, it was finally completed in 1851, after an earlier attempt had collapsed. Made up of four arches at a maximum height of nearly 80ft, it is either "a railway crime" (Pevsner) or "in admirable keeping with the style of the ancient castle and town" (Speight).

Beyond the viaduct stands the black-and-white-painted **Old Manor House**, built as a hunting lodge for King John, and believed to be the place where Oliver Cromwell received the formal surrender of the Royalist forces defeated at Marston Moor. Incidentally, you'll see a number of buildings decorated in this garish **black-and-white chequerboard style** – it represents, apparently, an attempt by a Victorian Knaresborough, already aware of the growing tourist industry, to identify places that offered facilities specifically aimed at visitors. Continuing along Waterside brings you to the **High Bridge**, which is medieval in origin though was extensively repaired in 1773.

Mother Shipton's Cave

Over the High Bridge bridge from the centre of town, and on the left, is the entrance to **Mother Shipton's Cave** (Feb Sat & Sun 10am–4.30pm; March Sat & Sun 10am–5.30pm; April–Oct daily 10am–5.30pm; Nov, Dec & Jan closed; £6; ☏01423/864 600, ⊛www.mothershiptonscave.com), which claims to be England's oldest tourist attraction. The site stretches right along the Nidd down to the Low Bridge, offering views of the viaduct, the weir and the town of Knaresborough on the opposite bank, together with walks laid out by Sir Henry Slingsby in 1739. There's an adventure playground, a woodland adventure trail, refreshments and picnic areas. It's a good-quality park stretched along the river bank. The **cave** itself is apparently where sixteenth-century soothsayer Ursula Sontheil (aka Mother Shipton, her married name) was born. The story of Mother Shipton's ability to predict the future is no doubt hokum, but since her death in 1561 the legend of her uncanny prophecies has grown, being added to and embellished over time. The attraction also features a so-called **Petrifying Well** – a spring that deposits minerals on anything immersed in it, petrifying them (ie turning them into stone). As early as the 1720s Daniel Defoe dismissed any claims to its being the only one of its kind in the country, saying that it was "nothing extraordinary" and that he'd come across others in Derbyshire. But the well is certainly great fun, with objects such as the headwear placed there in 1853 by a couple on their way to York races, one of Queen Mary's shoes, and various objects from celebrities like Agatha Christie (handbag), John Wayne (hat) and numerous items from cast members of British soaps. And the well, with its curtains of tufa and travertine, has a strange beauty all of its own.

Henshaw's Arts and Crafts Centre

Back across the bridge and up Bond End on the left, **Henshaw's Arts and Crafts Centre** (Mon–Sat 10am–4pm; ☎01423/541 888, Ⓦwww.henshaws.org.uk) is a project well worth supporting. Henshaw's Society for Blind People is a charity that dates from an 1837 bequest of Manchester hat magnate Thomas Henshaw. The centre has numerous arts and crafts workshops for the visually impaired, including sculpture, textiles, jewellery, pottery, woodwork and paper, with a range of products on sale. There are beautifully crafted handrails and artwork, a café, licensed restaurant and sensory garden, and the centre puts on a variety of events, exhibitions and concerts.

St John's church and around

A right turn further along Bond End brings you to **St John's** parish church, like many churches in Yorkshire, open to the public. One of the first things you'll notice is the sixteenth-century octagonal font which has an ornate lid so heavy that it requires a type of crane to raise and lower it. The Slingsby Chapel to the left of the chancel has monuments to many members of the prominent local family. The oldest, dated 1601, features effigies of Francis and Mary Slingsby, strangely thin and awkward-looking, especially Mary's. Sir William Slingsby (1638) is commemorated by an upright statue in a niche – leaning on his sword, with his legs nonchalantly crossed, looking as if he's waiting for a bus. Sir Henry Slingsby's effigy is headless – he was executed by Oliver Cromwell in 1658. Sir Charles Slingsby (1869) tragically drowned – the very nautical West Window is dedicated to his memory. Before leaving, note the two attractive and typically Pre-Raphaelite stained-glass windows installed by Morris and Co (William Morris's company), designed largely by Ford Madox Brown – one at the west end of the south aisle, the other the right-hand one of two on the south side of the chancel.

Having left the church, notice the blue-plaqued cottage across from the main door – it's where, it is claimed, Blind Jack was born (though some say that the house he was born in was demolished).

Walking back into the town centre along Water Bag Bank and Kirkgate, you may be startled to see a train clattering across the road. Take a quick look at the **train station**, which has the viaduct to the west and a tunnel under the High Street to the east.

South of Knaresborough

Just south of Knaresborough are a couple of things worth looking at. Just beyond the Low Bridge is the **Chapel of Our Lady of the Crag** (open most Sun 2–4pm) an oratory or wayside shrine built by John the Mason in 1408 in thanks for his son being saved from falling rocks. Up a flight of steps that can get very slippery when wet, outside is a small window and doorway, with a knight in armour (added later). The chapel itself, carved into the rock face, is tiny – 13ft by 8ft – and is decorated by masks, also later additions. Above the shrine is a rock dwelling called, variously, **The House in the Rock** and Fort Montague, which was built in the eighteenth century by a local weaver – interesting, but not open to the public.

Blind Jack of Knaresborough

John Metcalfe is one of the great characters of the early Industrial Revolution. Born in Knaresborough in 1717, the son of a horse breeder, he was blinded at the age of 6 by smallpox. He spent his early adult years earning a living by playing the fiddle, dealing in horses, and even acting as a guide to visitors. According to his autobiography, which was written towards the end of his long life (and which, perhaps, needs to be taken with a pinch of salt), he certainly didn't let his lack of sight impede his enjoyment of life, learning to swim, play cards, ride and hunt, as well as going to cock fights. Throughout he capitalized on aristocratic contacts he made while playing in Harrogate, often staying on their country estates or in their fashionable London houses. During the Jacobite Rebellion of 1745 he recruited soldiers in the Knaresborough area, accompanied them to Scotland, and was involved in the engineering problems of moving artillery around on the battlefield. When he returned to Yorkshire he started importing the stockings from Scotland. His love life was equally eventful, getting engaged to a local girl when he was in his early twenties, getting another girl pregnant, and clearing off to the Yorkshire coast to keep his head down. When he heard that his original girlfriend was getting married, he rushed back and married her himself, snatching her from under the prospective groom's nose the night before the wedding. In due course they had four children. So far, then, a picaresque eighteenth-century tale made even more remarkable by his blindness. It is, however, as a **road builder** that Blind Jack made his name. Even before he went to Scotland he'd made a start as a carrier. On his return he started a stone carting business, which grew into a stagecoach company. When the government, in a desperate attempt to improve transport to facilitate the early stirrings of the Industrial Revolution, started to pass Turnpike Acts, devolving road improvements to groups of businessmen who could invest in building a new section of road then charge for its use, there was a shortage of road engineers. Blind Jack stepped in, surveying and building good-quality roads across the north of England. He became a familiar sight, striding across the moors with his measuring wheel and his two sticks – one for feeling his way, the other for poking into the ground to assess its properties. After retirement he moved in with his daughter and her husband in Spofforth, where he eventually died at the age of 92. His grave is in Spofforth Church.

Finally, some four miles south on the Wetherby Road, lies **Spofforth**, a village notable as Blind Jack's burial place, and for **Spofforth Castle** (daily: April–Sept 10am–6pm; Oct–March 10am–4pm; free; EH), actually a fortified manor house most of which dates from the fourteenth and fifteenth centuries, and which once belonged to the Percy family. It's strong on atmosphere, with an undercroft built up against a rock face, but otherwise doesn't offer much of interest.

Eating and drinking

For **places to eat**, again Knaresborough suffers from its proximity to Harrogate.

Blind Jack's Market Place ☏01423/869 148. A good spot for a few drinks, *Blind Jack's* is a lovely traditional pub, named after the famous local character (see above).

Carriages 89 High St ☏01423/867 041. Nice atmospheric little pub/bistro with tapas and à la carte menu.

Mitre Hotel 4 Station Rd ☏01423/868 948. Mediterranean-style brasserie – good range of main courses for around £10.

Verrall's 10 Castle Courtyard ☏01423/868 568. Pretty café which does breakfasts at around £5 and food at lunchtimes and early evenings at weekends. Lunchtime meals average around £8, and there's a children's menu.

Ripley

Three miles north of Harrogate, the attractive model village of **RIPLEY** lies just off the main A61 road to Ripon. It owes its attractiveness to an interesting history tied up with the prominent local **Ingilby** family, who have dominated the village since the early fourteenth century, and have lived in **Ripley Castle** (Easter–Sept daily; March, Oct & Nov Tues, Thurs, Sat & Sun; Dec–Feb Sat & Sun, entrance by guided tour only, on the hour 10am–3pm; ☏01423/770 152, ⓦwww.ripleycastle.co.uk) – actually a house rather than a castle – for 700 years. The incumbent, Sir Thomas Ingilby, is the 26th generation. During the tour of the castle, the oldest part of which is the 1450 gatehouse, you'll hear about how the family won its boar's head crest (an Ingilby saved King Edward III from an injured boar), see the well-hidden priest's hole, hear about their links with most of those involved in the Gunpowder Plot, about "Trooper" Jane Ogilvy who apparently held Oliver Cromwell hostage at gunpoint in the library and about many other tales of their service to the kings and queens of England. There's a pleasant tearoom and shop, and the gardens are beautiful.

All Saints Church, across the road from the castle, has many Ogilvy family monuments, and is open to the public. The **village** itself has a remarkable unity, with all the houses built in gritstone, with hipped roofs and pointed sash windows, the result of it being rebuilt as a piece between 1820 and 1835 by Sir William Amcotts Ingilby. On a European trip he was rather taken with villages he saw in Alsace, so decided to remodel Ripley along similar lines. Look out for the **Ripley Endowed School**, founded in 1707, rebuilt by Sir William in 1830, and still ringing in term time to the shouts and laughter of children, and the **Hotel de Ville** (the name's above the front upstairs bay window), built in 1854 and completed after his death in that year by his widow. The local hotel, formerly the *Star Inn*, was reopened after 71 years in 1990 as the 🍴 **Boar's Head Hotel** (☏01423/771 888, ⓦwww.ripleycastle.co.uk; ❺) in honour of the family crest. Quirky in layout, interesting in decor (cricketing theme, gingham tablecloths), it serves a good choice of beers and wine and excellent food, all with fast, friendly service. In the market place in front of the hotel are the **Market Cross** (probably seventeenth-century) and the village **stocks**.

Across the road, just down the side street, is the **Old Farmyard** (May–Aug Sun & bank hols noon–5pm; £3.50), once Birchwood Farm, a delightful little agricultural museum and petting zoo, with a collection of objects, tools and equipment gathered at the farm over the years, and different breeds of sheep, goats, pigs, cows, rabbits, poultry, and – the stars of the show – the huge and dignified Clydesdale horses. There are demonstrations of sheep-shearing, textile spinning and rug-butter-and rope-making. Altogether a nice, understated attraction. Entry is clearly marked through a little shop.

Boroughbridge/Aldborough

Aldborough and Boroughbridge, about fifteen miles northwest of York, just off the A1, are two sides of the same coin. **Aldborough** ("old borough") was the original Roman town, which had perhaps started as a military camp at a place where Dere Street forded the river Ure, while **Boroughbridge** is the Norman new town established after the bridge across the Ure replaced the ford in the twelfth century. Both are well worth visiting.

ALDBOROUGH is a pretty village centred on a triangular green and maypole. The capital of the Romanized tribe the Brigantes – Isurium Brigantum – during

3

the Roman occupation, and home of the Ninth Legion, it settled into obscurity after the Romans left, and especially after it was overshadowed by nearby Boroughbridge. By the eighteenth century it was a classic "pocket borough", returning two MPs when big cities returned none – Pitt the Elder was one of them. Today the main reason for visiting is the **Aldborough Roman Site and Museum** (April–Sept Sat & Sun 11am–5pm; £3.20; EH) – there are two superb Roman mosaic pavements, part of a Roman house, some of the fort's defences and lots of interesting finds in the museum.

BOROUGHBRIDGE, just down the road from Aldborough, became an important staging post on the Great North Road between London and Edinburgh. Now consisting of three main streets, two squares – St James Square and Hall Square – and the eponymous bridge, there's a small town museum, the **Butter Market Museum** and a **tourist information office** (Easter–Oct Mon–Fri 10am–4pm, Sat 10am–noon; Nov–Easter Sat 10am–noon; ☎01423/322 956), both in Hall Square, and an old coaching inn – the *Crown* – which used to be able to stable a hundred horses. In St James Square is a delightful **Market Well**, put up in 1875 in memory of an Andrew Lawson of Aldborough Manor, and operated by an iron wheel. The **bridge** shows obvious signs of having had a new, wider surface put, in 1949, on top of a much earlier structure – part Tudor, part Georgian. Most of the buildings in the town date from its Georgian coaching heyday, and it's an altogether pleasing townscape. But that's not the main reason for visiting Boroughbridge. Along Roecliffe Lane, on the way to the A1, are three of the most astonishing survivals from prehistory you're likely to encounter anywhere. The **Devil's Arrows** are gritstone monoliths that date from the late New Stone Age or early Bronze Age, and they are gigantic – one is 18ft, one 21ft and one 23ft high, with a further 5ft below the ground. Imagine four average men standing on each other's shoulders. Few of the photographs you'll come across give any hint of their sheer scale. It is thought that there may have originally been four or five stones, but their function, if any, is obscure. The name dates from an eighteenth-century legend that the devil was throwing them at local rivals Aldborough, but they fell short.

Ripon and around

Technically a city, England's fourth-smallest, **RIPON** is in reality a small market town with a population of around 16,000, a long history and a harmoniously agreeable atmosphere. From the twelfth century onwards an important part of England's wool trade, first as a market for raw wool, then for finished cloth, it was also an ecclesiastical centre, based on its cathedral. Hard hit by the Reformation in England, it took advantage of the Tudor fashion for ornately worked spurs, reinventing itself as the spur capital of England. However, the Industrial Revolution largely passed Ripon by, and it became the pleasant little town it is today, attracting visitors to its **cathedral**, its law-and-order **museums**, **Fountains Abbey** and **Studley Water Gardens**, **Newby Hall**, the theme park **Lightwater Valley** and Ripon **racecourse**.

Arrival, information, accommodation and eating

The **bus station** is just off the Market Place, and the **tourist information centre** (April–Oct Mon–Sat 10am–5pm, Sun 10am–1pm; Nov–March Thurs & Sat 10am–4pm; ☎0845 389 0178, ⓦwww.visitripon.org) opposite the cathedral on

Minster Road cathedral. For **accommodation**, try the excellent ☧ *Old Deanery* (☎01765/600 003, ⓦwww.theolddeanery.co.uk; ❺), right across from the cathedral, it's a venerable (1625) building with lots of internal seventeenth-century detail, but the eleven rooms and public areas are bang up to date and very comfortable. The **restaurant's** brasserie menu is very reasonable, with main courses ranging from £12 to £21. The *Royal Oak*, 36 Kirkgate (☎01765/602 284; ❷) is a good alternative since its recent refurbishment – pleasant **pub**, good food and six stylish rooms.

The Town

A knot of narrow lanes clustered around a large **market place**, Ripon is a pleasure to explore, with everything worth seeing within walking distance of this central square. Ripon also offers pleasant walking in the **Spa Gardens** just west of the city centre, and along the rivers and canal just to the south – the **Canal Basin** has several shops and a café, and offers canal tours.

The Market Place

The **Market Place** itself is inevitably a car park except on market days (Thurs with a smaller one on Sat) and farmers' market days (third Sun of the month). Interesting features include a 90ft **obelisk** dating from the 1781 and a quaint little **cabmen's shelter** which was built in 1911, now standing next to four red phone boxes. The square is the scene of a ceremony that tradition claims dates back to 886, when Alfred the Great granted a town charter – at 9pm every evening the **Wakeman** or **Ripon hornblower** blows his horn at each corner of the central obelisk. This ceremony is well worth attending, since he also gives a talk of about half an hour on Ripon's history, peppered with jokes, and hands out little wooden coins to anybody present to bring good luck. Look out for the list of all the hornblowers from 1814 to 2004 attached to the obelisk and, on the south side of the square, the **Georgian Town Hall** (with inscription about the Wakeman) and the half-timbered sixteenth-century **Wakeman's House**. The Ripon Civic Society has done a grand job pointing out all sorts of historical snippets on the numerous green plaques erected around the town.

Ripon Cathedral

Just along curved **Kirkgate** from the Market Place stands the impressive **Ripon Cathedral** (daily 8am–5pm; free) – your first view will be of the splendid early English west front, bare and unadorned compared with many large ecclesiastical buildings. Established by St Wilfrid in 672, most of the cathedral, including the central crossing, north and south transepts, chapter house and vestry, dates from the late twelfth century, early thirteenth century (the west end of the nave), late thirteenth and early fourteenth centuries (the east end of the chancel) and the early sixteenth century (most of the nave). Look out in particular for the only part of St Wilfrid's original church to survive – the crypt, which lies underneath the central crossing. It is said to be modelled on Christ's tomb, and it's certainly tomb-like, with a tiny tunnel-vaulted chamber less than 12ft by 8ft down a sloping passage – not suitable if you're claustrophobic. There's a narrow "eye" through which, it is said, maidens had to crawl to prove their chastity. In the south aisle of the nave is a rough-hewn stone font with a lid which could be locked (to prevent the theft of holy water for curing livestock and such), and in the nave itself, about halfway down, is a wonderful 1913 Art Deco pulpit whose sounding board hanging above it disappeared between the wars and was replaced in 1960 by one which some claim actually started life as a dining table. The most satisfying part of the cathedral, though, is the choir, whose stalls date from the late fifteenth century. There's a wealth of late-medieval detail in the carvings on the misericords, including a man wheeling a woman in a barrow, a pig playing bagpipes, a mermaid brushing her hair as she admires herself in the mirror, and, most famously, a griffon chasing a rabbit down a rabbit hole – said to have inspired Lewis Carroll to write *Alice in Wonderland* – his father was a canon here from 1852. Incidentally, high up in the south transept there's another nod towards this story – representations of the Queen of Hearts and the Cheshire Cat put there by Sir George Gilbert Scott, who renovated the cathedral in the nineteenth century. Before leaving the choir notice the wooden hand that sticks out of the panelling above the entrance to the choir – it could be moved up and down to beat time for the choristers. And finally there's the **Ripon Jewel**, a beautiful Saxon gold and semi-precious stone roundel about an inch across (ask one of the attendants for its location – it seems to move around a lot).

The museums

Elsewhere in the city, three museums offer insights into the lives of Victorian Ripon (all April–Oct daily 1–4pm, longer hours during school hols; combined ticket £7; ☏01765/690 799, ⓦwww.riponmuseums.co.uk). The **Courthouse Museum** (£1.50) directly across the road from the cathedral, was the Quarter Sessions courthouse, where you can see the rooms that housed the jury and the justices, and the courtroom itself with two docks, a witness box, seating for the advocates and so on. A short audiovisual presentation outlines a number of actual cases tried in the court. The **Prison and Police Museum** (£3.50), just north of the cathedral on St Marygate, has, in the courtyard, a pillory, some stocks, a whipping post and a Tardis-like police phone box, while inside you can see the cells, learn about punishment and uniforms, enjoy lots of interactive displays and again watch a short video. Finally, the **Workhouse Museum** (£3.50) on Allhallowgate shows how the poor were treated after the Poor Law Amendment Act of 1832. Those who couldn't support themselves, whether through old age or unemployment, had to enter the workhouse, where families were broken up and housed in spartan accommodation. Men and women were separated, and all able-bodied adults were expected to do hard physical work such as chopping wood or breaking up stones for the roads.

Around Ripon

Though well worth a visit in its own right, Ripon is also an excellent centre for some of Yorkshire's major tourist attractions.

Fountains Abbey and Studley Royal

Four miles or so to the west of Ripon city centre, well signposted from all directions and with plenty of parking, is one of Yorkshire's top visitor attractions – the World Heritage Site of **Fountains Abbey and Studley Royal** (bus #139; daily: April–Sept 10am–5pm; Oct–March 10am–4pm; Jan, Nov & Dec closed Fri; £7.70; ☏01765/608 888; NT). A cluster of complementary delights, at the heart of this National Trust property lie three distinct historic sights – the twelfth-century abbey itself, the ancient Fountains Mill, and the eighteenth-century water gardens that stretch down river, all sitting pretty in the steep-sided and picturesque **Skell Valley**. And the modern **visitor centre** takes nothing away from this historical tranquillity: it offers restaurant, gift- and bookshops, toilets and a children's play area well away from and above the site itself. If you pay the full admission fee and enter via the visitor centre (recommended), there's a fair amount of walking involved – across a sheep-dotted field before you get to the steep paths down to the abbey, then down the valley on either or both sides of the river. However, if you're short of time or money, just enjoy the **Deer Park** (daily dawn–dusk; parking £3), which is free.

Fountains Abbey is a Cistercian monastery established in 1132 when thirteen disaffected monks, expelled from a monastery in York for rioting (muscular Christianity indeed), were granted land in the valley to start their own community. It grew to be one of the richest and largest monasteries in Europe, but was, like all others in England, destroyed by Henry VIII's dissolution of the monasteries in the 1530s for its wealth, and plundered locally for its masonry. It now consists of atmospheric ruins – a large L-shape created by the church and the cellarium and, within the L, cloisters, a refectory, the abbot's house, the chapter house and, across a little bridge, the guesthouse. If you can visit during less busy times, the sound of cawing rooks and running water gives the whole site a pleasantly melancholy feel.

Fountains Mill, across an attractive medieval bridge, is the oldest building on the estate. It's surprising that so little fuss is made of it, but this is probably because renovation, by the National Trust and English Heritage in partnership, started relatively recently. The only twelfth-century Cistercian corn mill in the country, it started just grinding corn and storing flour, but later powered a sawmill, a stone mason's workshop, even an electricity power station. It now has a number of excellent displays about the building's history.

Downriver from the abbey and the mill, and following the contours of the valley, lie **Studley Water Gardens**, a succession of lakes, rills, bridges and little waterfalls, the waters reflecting the beauties of the medieval buildings and the surrounding countryside. A triumph that emerged from disaster, they were the work of John Aislabie, who inherited the estate in 1693, became MP for Ripon in 1695 and Chancellor of the Exchequer in 1718, then was disgraced during the great financial disaster of the South Sea Bubble. Banned from public office for life, he spent the rest of his days on the water gardens, a project which was continued after his death by his son William. As you walk along the numerous paths that weave through the water features, look out for the Temple of Piety overlooking the Moon Pond, the lake below the dam, the Serpentine Tunnel, Octagon Tower, Temple of Fame and Ann Boleyn's Seat.

Apart from the big three attractions, there are two other delights worth having a look at – Jacobean mansion **Fountains Hall**, at the top of the site, and **St Mary's Church** (Easter–Sept daily noon–4pm) in the Deer Park, sister of the Church of the Consoler (see p.180), built for the same reason and by the same architect.

Ripon Racecourse and Newby Hall

On the eastern edge of the city stands **Ripon Racecourse** (buses #142 & #143; ☎01765/602 156, ⓦwww.ripon-races.co.uk) set in pleasantly open countryside and self-billed as the "Garden Racecourse". Beyond it is one of England's great houses, **Newby Hall** (April–Sept Tues–Sun 11am–5pm; July, Aug & bank hols also Mon, house opens noon; 1hr guided tours on the hour; ☎0845 450 4068, ⓦwww.newbyhall.com). Built "under the guidance of Sir Christopher Wren" in the 1690s, its interior was largely designed by John Carr and Robert Adam in the 1760s for its then-owner William Weddell, a wealthy member of the Dilettante Club, to show off his acquisitions after a Grand Tour. Home now of his descendants, Mr and Mrs Richard Compton, both house and gardens are open to the public, who can enjoy the Roman motifs of the blue entrance, the airy drawing room at the end of the red passage, the yellow dining room, the often droll contents of the chamber-pot room, the motto room adorned with French sayings, the almost unchanged tapestry room, designed to show off tapestries obtained from the famous factory in Gobelins, Paris, the Adam library and the Grand Tour statue gallery. The grounds include formal gardens – a series of interlocking rectangles lovingly restored – woodland walks, a sculpture park and an imaginative children's playground. There's also an extensive gift shop, a farm shop, a children's railway shop, a plant centre and a restaurant.

The **Church of Christ the Consoler** within the grounds of the Hall, at Skelton-on-Ure, has a sad provenance. The youngest son of the house, Frederick Grantham Vyner, was captured by Greek brigands in 1870 and, when the demanded ransom was slow in being paid, they murdered him. The money had in fact been collected, and was used instead for the building of the church, designed by William Burges in 1871–76.

Lightwater Valley Theme Park

Northwest of Ripon city centre is an attraction of an entirely different type. A ten-minute drive from the Victorian clock tower that separates North Street and North Road, **Lightwater Valley Theme Park** (bus #159; June–Aug daily, April, May, Sept & Oct Sat & Sun from 10am, closing from 4.30pm, depending on time of year; £19.45, family tickets available; ☎0871 720 0011, ⓦwww.lightwater valley.co.uk) consists of an array of white-knuckle rides including the Eagle's Claw, White River Rapids, Raptor Attack and, what is claimed to be Europe's longest roller coaster, the Ultimate, together with more traditional and gentler fairground rides for all ages. There's also a rather good **Birds of Prey** centre and a **shopping village** with bar, restaurant and coffee shop. The whole park is on a more human scale than many, and is therefore both less expensive and less exhausting.

The Yorkshire Dales

CHAPTER 4

Highlights

✳ **The Settle to Carlisle line** Railway famous for its beauty, but also for the heroic tale of its construction and survival. See p.189

✳ **Malham** A walk from this pretty two-pub village takes in a waterfall, a ravine, a limestone amphitheatre and lake. God's own country indeed. See p.193

✳ **Mart Theatre, Skipton** A heady mix of art and agriculture – the local theatre uses the animal mart for its productions. See p.197

✳ **Bolton Priory** In the village of Bolton Abbey, picturesque ruins in a beautiful setting and mile upon mile of gentle country walking. See p.198

✳ **How Stean Gorge** A chasm that you can either peacefully admire or actively tackle by walking, wading and climbing through. See p.204

✳ **Breweries at Masham** Producers of two of Yorkshire's best-loved beers try to outdo each other with their visitor centres. See the beer made, then drink it, all in a village of outstanding beauty. See p.213

✳ **Swinton Park/Devonshire Arms** Treat yourself to a luxury break at a castle or a country house – *Swinton Park* near Masham, or the *Devonshire Arms Hotel* in Bolton Abbey. See p.214 & p.199

✳ **Richmond Castle** Spectacularly set on cliffs above the Swale, the views of the river, the countryside and the town are unrivalled. See p.217

▲ Richmond Castle

The Yorkshire Dales

There is no doubt that most people are attracted to the Yorkshire Dales for the wonderful countryside: pastoral and idyllic in the river valleys, austere and grand in the limestone uplands. Together the **Yorkshire Dales National Park** and the **Nidderdale Area of Outstanding Natural Beauty** cover a large upland area on the western edge of the county of North Yorkshire, which boasts the county's three highest mountains – Pen-y-Ghent, Ingleborough and Whernside – and is scored by dozens of rivers and streams. Because it is made up largely of carboniferous limestone, and especially where this abuts the much harder millstone grit, there are numerous potholes, caves and waterfalls.

The Dales area can be confusing to the newcomer, with more than twenty valleys apparently scattering in all directions, but it doesn't take long to find your way about. The dales straddle the Pennine watershed, with most of the rivers draining east into the Vale of York and eventually the North Sea, but some draining west into the Irish Sea. Most of the major dales, including **Nidderdale**, **Wharfedale**, **Malhamdale** and **Ribblesdale**, run roughly from north to south, two (**Swaledale** and **Wensleydale**) run west to east, and one (**Dentdale**) runs southeast to northwest. Most of the dales are named after the rivers which run along them, such as Swaledale and Wharfedale, while some take their name from a village (Dentdale, Wensleydale). And very roughly, the southern dales run longitudinally and the northern dales latitudinally.

Those who know the dales well attest to the individual character of each one. However, to visitors they seem to have certain characteristics in common. Lower dales tend to be green and pastoral, with prosperous and picturesque villages, upper dales more austere, with spartan settlements, isolated farms and great tracts of open heathland. Main roads run along the valley bottoms beside main rivers, side roads along tributaries, and valley roads are usually bound on both sides by dry-stone walls. Dales either peter out, or are connected to other nearby dales by narrow roads which climb onto the open land between them. These are normally unfenced, with grazing animals confined to the uplands by cattle grids. Each dale has at least one village, most of which seem to feature a number of things that have died out elsewhere in the country – public conveniences, red telephone boxes, churches which are open to the public.

Many visitors come for the range of outdoor activities offered by this distinctive terrain – walking, cycling, potholing, caving, climbing, hang-gliding, canoeing and other water-based sport. Around nine hundred miles of footpaths, including two major cross-country paths, the **Pennine** and **Dales Ways**, cross the region, as does a new loop of the **Pennine Bridleway** and the **Yorkshire Dales Cycle Way** (see box, p.186).

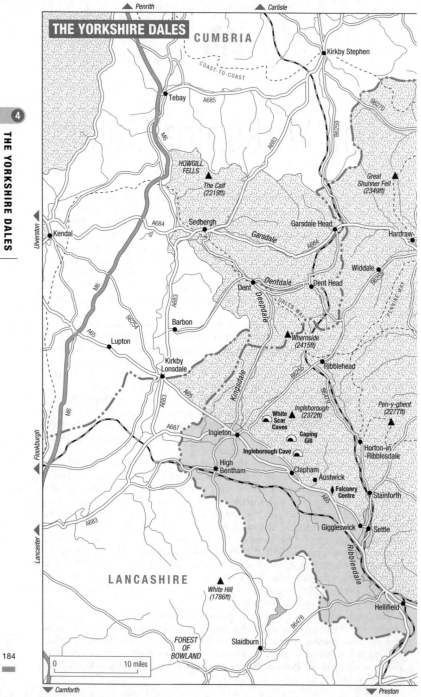

THE YORKSHIRE DALES

CUMBRIA

THE YORKSHIRE DALES

4

▲ Penrith
▲ Carlisle
Kirkby Stephen

COAST-TO-COAST

Tebay

A685

A685

B6259

B6270

M6

HOWGILL FELLS

The Calf (2219ft)

Great Shunner Fell (2349ft)

A684

Sedbergh

Garsdale Head

Garsdale

Hardraw

Kendal

Widdale

PENNINE WAY

Dentdale

Dent

Dent Head

B6255

Ulverston

Deepdale

DALES WAY

A683

Barbon

Whernside (2415ft)

Ribblehead

Lupton

A65

Kirkby Lonsdale

B6254

M6

Kingsdale

Ingleborough (2372ft)

Pen-y-ghent (2277ft)

A687

White Scar Caves

Gaping Gill

A65

A683

A65

Ingleton

Ingleborough Cave

Horton-in-Ribblesdale

Flookburgh

High Bentham

Clapham

Austwick

Falconry Centre

Stainforth

Giggleswick

Settle

A683

Lancaster

Ribblesdale

LANCASHIRE

White Hill (1786ft)

Hellifield

B6478

FOREST OF BOWLAND

Slaidburn

0   10 miles

▼ Camforth
▼ Preston

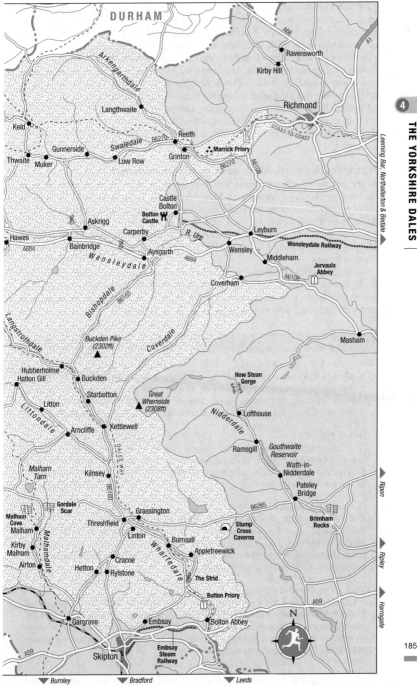

DURHAM

Ravensworth
Kirby Hill
Richmond

Arkengarthdale
Langthwaite
Keld
Swaledale
Reeth
Gunnerside
Low Row
Grinton
Marrick Priory
Thwaite
Muker

Askrigg
Carperby
Castle Bolton
Bolton Castle
Leyburn
Wensley
Wensleydale Railway

Hawes
Bainbridge
Aysgarth
R. Ure
Middleham

Wensleydale
Coverham
Jervaulx Abbey

Bishopdale
B6160
Masham

Buckden Pike
(2302ft)
Coverdale

Langstrothdale
Hubberholme
Halton Gill
Buckden
Starbotton
Great Whernside
(2308ft)
How Stean Gorge
Nidderdale
Lofthouse

Litton
Littondale
Arncliffe
Kettlewell
DALES WAY
Ramsgill
Gouthwaite Reservoir
Wath-in-Nidderdale

Malham Tarn
Kilnsey
B6160
Pateley Bridge

Gordale Scar
Grassington
Stump Cross Caverns
B6265
Brimham Rocks

Malham Cove
Malham
Threshfield
Linton
Burnsall
Appletreewick

Kirby Malham
Airton
Malhamdale
Hetton
Cracoe
Rylstone
Wharfedale
The Strid
Bolton Priory

Gargrave
Embsay
Bolton Abbey
A59

Skipton
Embsay Steam Railway

N

Burnley   Bradford   Leeds

But there's much, too, for the less hearty – attractive villages, exhilarating driving, tearooms, country pubs, museums, castles, fine houses, show caves, waterfalls and numerous village festivals. Notable too are the number of workplaces where you can see things being made, then buy them (cheese, beer, chocolate, rope, teapots) or experience attractions based on what was once part of the ordinary life of the Dales (farm parks, agritourism B&Bs, canal trips, steam train rides). In the Yorkshire Dales you'll find a rural community that is struggling to halt its decline by adapting its traditional life and livelihood to twenty-first-century demands.

Covered below are the most popular and rewarding of the Yorkshire Dales, starting in each case with the main town or village. But don't ignore the minor dales – they are great in number, often little visited and unspoilt. All are worth exploring.

Access, information and getting around

Access to the Dales from outside Yorkshire is via the M6 to the west and the A1 to the east, with major airports at Manchester and Leeds-Bradford. Within the county, the main approaches are from a circle of larger towns – **Skipton**, which styles itself the Gateway to the Dales, **Settle**, **Ingleton**, **Sedbergh** (inside the National Park but actually in Cumbria), **Richmond**, **Ripon** (see p.176) and **Harrogate** (see p.165). Certainly, the most effective way of getting around the Dales is **by car**.

Coverage **by bus** is patchy – within the Dales bus services are better from Easter to September/October and at weekends, less good the rest of the time. Services which give access to the Dales from outside are also more frequent between Easter and mid-October, and include: York, Leeds and Ilkley to Grassington, Upper

---

Long walks and trails

Pennine Way National Trail

A 268-mile, long-distance walk that starts in Derbyshire, finishes in the Cheviot Hills on the Scottish borders, and takes in, on its way, Calderdale in West Yorkshire and Malham, Horton-in-Ribblesdale, Hawes, Thwaite and Keld in the Yorkshire Dales. The whole walk is likely to take from two to three weeks (see Ⓦ www.nationaltrail.co.uk).

Dales Way

At 82 miles much shorter than the Pennine Way, the Dales Way begins at Ilkley, follows Wharfedale right up to its source, crosses the watershed near Ribblehead, then passes down Dentdale to Sedbergh, ending at Windermere in the Lake District (see Ⓦ www.thedalesway.co.uk).

Pennine Bridleway

With 120 miles or so currently open, the Pennine Bridleway is the first purpose-built trail designed for horseriders, mountain-bikers and walkers. As such, therefore, it is notable for not having any stiles to negotiate. The bridleway dips into West Yorkshire along Calderdale, and further north at the Settle Loop which includes Ribblesdale and Malhamdale (see Ⓦ www.nationaltrail.co.uk).

Yorkshire Dales Cycleway

A 130-mile circular route starting and finishing at Skipton (though obviously you can start and finish anywhere you like along the route), the Yorkshire Dales Cycleway falls into six roughly equal sections: Skipton to Malham, Malham to Ingleton, Ingleton to Hawes, Hawes to Grinton, Grinton to Kettlewell and Kettlewell to Skipton via Bolton Abbey (see Ⓦ www.cyclethedales.org.uk).

Dry-stone walls and field barns

Across the Dales you will see **dry-stone walls** – hundreds of miles of them, following roads and swooping up hillsides onto the uplands, representing centuries of hard manual labour. They were built to fulfil several purposes – to mark boundaries between farms, to divide farms into fields so that farmers could separate animals (pregnant ewes from ewes with lambs, for example), and to keep grazing animals off the meadows while the grass was growing. You will also see numerous **field barns** – over six thousand at a conservative estimate – which housed cattle during the winter months, and from which manure could be stored in middens, then spread across the meadows to help to produce the next winter's fodder.

This stock of walls and barns has been built up over centuries, largely between the seventeenth and the end of the nineteenth, and is now an essential part of the character of the Yorkshire Dales. Yet both dry-stone walls and field barns are under threat. If a wall falls down, it is cheaper to replace it with fencing. Field barns are no longer used for their original purpose, and many are now in a dilapidated condition, which is why various concerned bodies – the National Parks Authority, English Heritage, the National Trust, the Yorkshire Dales Society and others – are trying to address the problem by encouraging their renovation and repair.

Wharfedale, Aysgarth and Hawes; Bradford to Ilkley, for connecting buses to Malham and Buckden; Leeds and Otley to Pateley Bridge, Fountains Abbey, Leyburn and Richmond; Harrogate to Brimham Rocks, Pateley Bridge, How Stean Gorge and Middlesmoor; and York to Ripon, Fountains Abbey, Pateley Bridge and Grassington; and Kirkby Stephen to Hawes and Ribblehead (Tuesdays).

Heavy reliance on bus services requires considerable planning – for comprehensive timetables see Ⓦwww.traveldales.org.uk and www.dalesbus.org. "Dales Rover" tickets are available on Sundays and bank holidays, and many bus operators offer rover tickets for their own services for a day or a week.

You can also get into the Dales by **train** – in the west on the **Settle to Carlisle line**, which is part of the national rail network, and in the east and north on heritage lines (the **Embsay and Bolton Abbey Steam Railway** and the **Wensleydale Railway**). Information is available in **National Park Centres** (in Aysgarth Falls, Grassington, Hawes, Malham and Reeth) and in **tourist information centres** across the area.

Ribblesdale

The River Ribble runs south along the western edges of the Yorkshire Dales, starting in the bleak uplands near the Ribblehead Viaduct, flowing between two of Yorkshire's highest mountains, **Ingleborough** and **Pen-y-Ghent**, and through the village of **Horton-in-Ribblesdale** and then on to **Settle**, the upper dale's principal town. Thereafter it meanders south and west across Lancashire, entering the North Sea at Preston. Although the stretch of the A65 between Settle and **Ingleton** is not in Ribblesdale, it is very much a part of the cluster of villages and attractions that mark this western edge of the Dales, including the popular village of **Clapham**. There are **tourist information centres** at Settle and Ingleton.

Settle and around

The main town in Ribblesdale, **SETTLE** sits just off the Skipton to Kendal A65, at the foot of Castleberg, an impressive limestone outcrop from the top of which you can get fine views over the town and the surrounding countryside. To get to it, follow the **Tot Lord Trail** – it takes about ten minutes. Settle is a small market town which owed its existence to a 1249 charter but its continued prosperity first to the Keighley to Kendal turnpike of 1753, then the Settle to Carlisle railway of 1876 (see box, p.189), and is probably still best known as the starting point for this beautiful stretch of railway line. The town also offers access to excellent walking and climbing country to the east.

Settle's central market place contains a first-class **tourist information centre** on the ground floor of the Town Hall (immediately on the right after you enter; daily 9.30am–4.30pm, 4pm in winter, earlier on Sun; ☏01729/825 192), and the rather peculiar **Shambles**. Once a seventeenth- to eighteenth-century market hall, it has late Victorian cottages plonked on top, with a loggia added at the front to give access to them. The whole oddball assemblage now consists of shops and cafés below, private housing above and it really seems, against all reason, to work.

Two minutes' walk to the south of the Market Place is another oddball building, the oldest in Settle. **The Folly** is genuinely old, dating from the 1670s, but earns its name from the strange combination of styles, and the curiously upside-down look created by the fact that there are far more windows on the ground floor than on the first and second – it seems surprising that it hasn't fallen down. The Grade I listed building now houses the **Museum of North Craven Life** (Tues, Sat & Sun 10am–4.30pm; £1.80; ☏01524/251 388), which contains fairly random odds and ends from the history of the town, and that of the building of the Settle to Carlisle railway. In the other direction, along Kirkgate, are the ornate 1853 **Victoria Hall** (now the Victoria Theatre) and, across the road, the beautifully simple 1678 **Friends Meeting House**.

Settle Railway Station, down Station Road off the main street (Duke St), marks the start of the Settle to Carlisle line, a railway enthusiast's dream (see box, p.189). The station in Settle is a good example of the "Derby Gothic" style favoured by the Midland Railway Company, and it is beautifully maintained, looking more like a volunteer-run tourist attraction than a working station.

Finally, to the west of Settle town centre is the village of **GIGGLESWICK**, famous for the venerable **Giggleswick School**, founded in 1507. Old Giggleswickians seem to be notable, surprisingly given their somehow Ken Doddian name, for their rather fusty rectitude, though the roll call is enlivened by the presence of the late Richard Whiteley, television's *Countdown* presenter for many years, and, on the list of ex-teachers, one of the masters who taught him, television chat-show host Russell Harty.

Accommodation and eating

As well as in Settle itself, there are a couple of interesting and individual places to stay in **Austwick**, a couple of miles northwest of Settle, and one in **Hellifield** in the opposite direction.

Austwick Hall Austwick ☏015242/51794, ⓦwww.austwickhall.co.uk. Absolutely solid, old-fashioned but stylish place, in a beautiful stone, ivy-covered and historic manor house. A perfect balance of state-of-the-art comfort and plush traditionalism. ❺

Golden Lion Duke St, Settle ☏01729/822 203. A fine seventeenth-century hotel-pub in the centre of Settle which does good food. ❷

Hellifield Peel Castle Peel Green, Hellifield ☏01729/850 248, ⓦwww.peelcastle.co.uk. Off the A65 about half way between Skipton and Settle, and like *Austwick Hall* originally a Pele tower. The bulk of the current building dates from the fourteenth century. Its renovation was recorded in *Grand Designs* in 2007, and when costs soared its owners decided that the house needed to start paying its way. Hence the opportunity to stay in this wonderfully historic house with lovely rooms and all mod cons. Not cheap, but then many of the good things in life aren't. Booking well in advance is recommended. ❻

The Settle to Carlisle railway

The story of the construction of the **Settle to Carlisle line** in the nineteenth century, and its fight for survival in the twentieth, is truly epic. Opened in 1875 for goods traffic, and 1876 for passengers, the 72-mile line was built by the Midland Railway Company employing an army of navvies and miners. Crossing extremely inhospitable countryside, no fewer than seventeen viaducts had to be built and fourteen tunnels dug – the longest viaduct (Ribblehead) being followed immediately by the longest tunnel (Blea Moor). The irony was that the company only proposed the line as a bargaining ploy in a dispute over access to the west coast line to Scotland, and when the dispute was resolved, wanted to abort it, only to be denied by Parliament. Honourably, the company bit the bullet and built it. More recent attacks on the line occurred in the twentieth century when many stations were closed in 1970 as a result of the Beeching Report, and British Rail planned the closure of the whole line in the early 1980s. This last threat created such a furore, and generated so much interest in the line, that some of the stations had to be re-opened in 1986 to meet growing demand, and the whole plan was shelved in 1989. Today the line is shared by passengers and freight, with six passenger services a day doing the full route from Leeds to Carlisle. The principal stops in the Dales are at **Settle**, **Horton-in-Ribblesdale**, **Ribblehead** and **Dent**, and single fares from Settle to Carlisle are upwards of £16.

Royal Oak Market Place, Settle ☎01729/822 561, ⓦwww.royaloaksettle.co.uk. A pub with rooms, with handsome carved oak panelling in the bar and dining room. Do remember, though, that, like the *Golden Lion*, it's a town centre pub, so it could be noisy during licensing hours. Breakfast not included. ❶

The Traddock Austwick ☎015242/51224, ⓦwww.thetraddock.co.uk. Off the A65, about two miles northwest of Settle, the *Traddock* is a warm and friendly hotel in lovely surroundings, with an excellent restaurant, good but unobtrusive service and comfortable rooms. ❹

🏃 **Ye Olde Naked Man Café** Market Place, Settle ☎01729/823 230. For non-alcoholic beverages and good plain food this café is the best bet. Don't be put off by the twee name – there is a reason for it. The building was once an undertaker's, and the name is a reference to the old Yorkshire saying, "you bring now't into't world and you take now't out".

Yorkshire Dales Falconry and Conservation Centre

First attraction on from Settle towards Ingleton, well signposted and visible from the main road, is the **Yorkshire Dales Falconry and Conservation Centre** (daily 10am–4pm; £6.50; ☎01729/822 832, ⓦwww.hawkexperience.com). Opened in an old farmhouse in 1991 and now housing more than fifty birds, the centre puts on falconry displays, offers half- and full-day falconry courses, breeds birds and has an avian hospital. You can see flying displays of eagles, hawks, falcons, vultures and owls. There's a tearoom, a gift shop and children's play area.

Clapham

Continuing up the A65, about half way between the falconry centre and Ingleton, you come to the village of **CLAPHAM**, just off the main road on the right. Part of the **Ingleborough Estate**, owned since the eighteenth century by the Farrer family, the village is strung out along the Clapham Beck, and is known largely as the gateway to Ingleborough Cave. Indeed, the village's importance is entirely explained by geology and geography. It lies on the Craven Fault, where millstone grit and limestone meet, a guarantee of potholes and caves as the water floods off the impermeable millstone grit and dissolves and erodes the limestone. High above the village, on the slopes of Ingleborough – one of the Dales' famous Three Peaks – the Fell Beck stream disappears into a gigantic hole known as **Gaping Gill**, where it drops over 300ft. Underground, it carved out the impressive ten-and-a-half-mile system that ends in **Ingleborough Cave**. Unknown until 1837, the cave was discovered when limestone formations that had built up at its entrance were washed away by a flood.

Today the cave can be approached via the **Ingleborough Estate Nature Trail** (park in the National Park Centre car park and walk up past the church; daily dawn to dusk; 50p), a walk of just over a mile through old sawmills, electrical installations designed to take advantage of the river's power-generating potential, and through woodland and impressive limestone scars. During this walk, for which you should allow about thirty minutes, you will see many of the plants that Reginald Farrer, the most famous of the Farrers, known as the "patron saint of alpine gardening", collected. He travelled extensively in China, Burma and Tibet gathering plants to bring home to his estate, and the descendants of many of them are still there. **Ingleborough Cave** itself (mid-Feb to Oct daily 10am–5pm, tours on the hour, every 30min when busy; Nov to mid-Feb Sat & Sun 10am–4pm; £6; Ⓦwww.ingleboroughcave.co.uk) is one of Yorkshire's premier show caves, and offers a 250-yard trip into the mountain, with all the calcite flows and stalactites and stalagmites you'd expect, interpreted by an expert guide.

In the village there's the **National Park Centre** (March–Nov daily 10am–5pm; Dec–Feb Sat & Sun 9.30am–4pm; Ⓣ01524/251 419), a **market cross**, a **lake**, and the eighteenth-century **New Inn** (Ⓣ01524/251 203; ❹), with one oak-panelled bar and another decorated with pictures and cartoons about caving.

Ingleton

A further five miles up the A65 is **INGLETON**, famous for its waterfalls, its caves, and as the starting point for the ascent of 2372ft **Ingleborough**. Even more than Clapham, the village owes its character and much of its livelihood to its position on the Craven Fault.

Perched high above the confluence of the Twiss and Doe rivers, with fine views of the Victorian viaduct (and not so fine ones of a static caravan park), Ingleton's winding Main Street has a good selection of small shops and cafés, with a pub at each end. **St Mary's Church**, in the centre of the village, is notable mainly for problems caused by the fact that it was built on compacted river boulders which continued to settle, which has damaged the building – the current church is the result of a rebuild in 1886, and has continued to have problems. The most notable of its contents are the Norman font, rescued from use in the eighteenth century for mixing plaster and whitewash, the British Legion chapel in the south aisle which has wood carving by the Robert Thompson school – the famous "mouseman" (look out for the carving of the mouse on one of the posts) and the 1717 "vinegar bible" which gets its name from the mis-transcription of the "parable of the vineyard" as "the parable of the vinegar". Particularly splendid is the modern carving of the Last Supper (based on Leonardo da Vinci's painting) on the reredos below the east window.

On the edge of the village is the start of the **Waterfalls Trail** (daily 9am, closing times vary; Ⓣ01524/241 930, Ⓦwww.ingletonwaterfallswalk.co.uk) opened up by a Joseph Craven (his memorial is the pump next to the village centre Memorial Gardens) and his Improvement Company in 1885, and now one of the most accessible and most beautiful sets of waterfalls in the country. A well-marked and-surfaced footpath takes you through ancient oak woodland and pretty dales up the river Twiss, across farmland, then down the River Doe. There are fourteen waterfalls and a thousand steps on the trail – so no wheelchairs. The trail is eight miles long – allow two-and-a-half to four hours. There's a gift shop, café and toilets at the Broadwood car park at the start, and at the time of writing a café/kiosk was being planned for the furthest point where the trail turns back. It can get very busy in the summer – to avoid the crowds an early start is recommended.

Another big Ingleton attraction, approximately a mile and a half from the village, is the **White Scar Cave** (Feb–Oct daily 10am–4pm; Nov–Jan Sat & Sun 10am–4pm; £7.95; ☎01524/241 244, ⓦwww.whitescarcave.co.uk), which is guaranteed to take your breath away, even if caves normally leave you cold. Discovered by student Christopher Long in 1923, the cave now has a steel-grid walkway which takes you from the entrance past waterfalls, great sheets of flowstone, cream and red stalactites and stalagmites, through "**the Squeeze**" and the **Bagshaw Tunnel** (not happy experiences if you're claustrophobic) eventually to the colossal **Battlefield Cavern**, at 330ft one of the longest underground caverns in the country. There are the usual fanciful show-cave names for formations – the Witch's Fingers, the Judge's Head, the Sword of Damocles, the Crown of Thorns, the Face – which the guide points out as you work your way through. Hard hats are provided (roofs are low in parts of the cave), and, because of the 97 steps and the steel grid underfoot, high heels are not recommended. The tour of the cave is a mile long (all tours are guided) and takes about eighty minutes. There's a café and shop above the car park – park only when visiting the cave, since staff get very irate with people who park here, then go off for a walk – and wear warm clothing as the cave is at a constant temperature of 8° C.

Ingleton has a **tourist information centre** in the community centre **car park** (Easter–Sept 10am–4.30pm; ☎01524/241 049), and lots of **B&Bs** and **guesthouses**, most of them on Main Street – try *Riverside Lodge*, 24 Main St (☎01524/241 359, ⓦwww.riversideingleton.co.uk; ❷), which is a cut above most. There's a **youth hostel** (☎0845 371 9124; £16) in an old stone house on Sammy Lane, while **Stackstead Farm**, a mile south off the minor road to High Bentham (☎01524/241 386, ⓦwww.stacksteadfarm.co.uk) offers **bunkhouse barn** accommodation (from £11, groups only at weekends) and a touring **caravan site**.

Settle to Ribblehead

To follow the Ribble itself you need to head due north from Settle, on the B6479. The first village you come to is **STAINFORTH** – a bridge and next to it an old-fashioned **pub**, the *Craven Heifer* (☎01729/822 599, ⓦwww.cravenheiferhotel .co.uk; ❷), which offers patterned carpets, brasses and basic but clean accommodation. Just across the river and the railway line from the village is **Stainforth Force,** where the Ribble thunders down a series of limestone steps into a hollow created by the current.

Next is the main village of the valley, **HORTON-IN-RIBBLESDALE**, whose principal industry from time immemorial was stone-quarrying, greatly expanded by the arrival in the mid-nineteenth century of the Settle to Carlisle railway. It's now an important walking and climbing centre (and potholing – Craven Pothole Club has a hut in the village), with the *Pen-y-Ghent Café* being the unofficial headquarters for the Three Peaks Walk (see box, p.192). The village is the most convenient starting point for the ascent of **Pen-y-Ghent**, which glowers off to the east.

In itself the village of Horton-in-Ribblesdale isn't much to write home about. It straggles along for a mile or more, with a **pub** at each end – the *Crown* (☎01729/860 209; ❸), to the north, the *Golden Lion* (☎01729/860 206; ❹) to the south, a train station, post office and church. What should be an attractive river crossing, with two stone bridges and one graceful footbridge next to the Crown, is spoilt by telegraph poles, pipes crossing the stream and general junk cluttering up the river bank.

The Three Peaks

You can't visit the western Dales without becoming aware of Yorkshire's famous **Three Peaks** – in descending order of height above sea level **Whernside** (2415ft), **Ingleborough** (2372ft) and **Pen-y-ghent** (2277ft). While to the people of the Himalayas or the Alps they might not seem very impressive, they dominate this part of Yorkshire completely – even visitors are soon able to identify them by their distinctive shapes. Geographically, they form a triangle around the iconic **Ribblehead Viaduct**, with Whernside near the source of the Ribble on the border with Cumbria, and Ingleborough and Pen-y-ghent on the western and eastern flanks respectively of Ribblesdale itself. Not only are the three mountains an integral part of the landscape, they play an important role in the activities of walkers and cyclists in the region – each is the focus of individual well-trodden walking routes, with walkers setting off for Whernside, usually from **Ribblehead**, Ingleborough from **Clapham** and Pen-y-ghent from **Horton-in-Ribblesdale**.

In addition, the three mountains together form one of the Yorkshire Dales National Park's best-known and most testing long circular walks – the nearly 25-mile **Three Peaks Walk**. Although the mountains can be climbed in any order, and from any starting point on the circular route, most people set off from Horton-in-Ribblesdale, with walkers following an anti-clockwise route to the summits of Pen-y-ghent, Whernside and Ingleborough, in that order. In this respect the ⚲ **Pen-y-ghent Café** (opening hours are complicated, but mainly Feb half-term hols to mid-Oct Mon & Wed–Fri 9am–5.30pm, Sat 8am–6pm, Sun 8.30am–5.30pm, closed mid-Oct to Boxing Day, the rest of the year varies; phone to check ☏01729/860 333) in Horton-in-Ribblesdale has been fulfilling a vital role for over forty years, not only by supplying the much-needed hot drinks, snacks and meals, but also local information and advice – they're a networked **tourist information centre** – and by operating a clocking in/clocking out system. Walkers who complete the route within a twelve-hour period, as evidenced by their clocking in and out times, become eligible to join the **Three Peaks of Yorkshire Club**. The café no longer provides automatic back-up should walkers fail to return, but are happy to do so ad-hoc on request.

As well as the constant stream of individual walkers embarking on the Three Peaks Walk, there are numerous **charity events** at various fixed times. In addition there are two big regular events – the **Three Peaks Race** for fell runners towards the end of April, and the **Three Peaks Cycle Race** at the end of September. Incidentally, don't get the Yorkshire Three Peak route confused with the National Three Peaks Challenge, which is a different thing altogether, involving the highest mountains in England, Wales and Scotland.

From Horton the road climbs upwards through increasingly bleak moorland, and the river peters out. As you approach a T-junction in the middle of nowhere you'll get your first view of the famous, and elegant, **Ribblehead Viaduct**, a triumph of Victorian civil engineering, whose maintenance costs were almost successfully used as an excuse for shutting down one of the UK's most beautiful lines.

Malhamdale

Malhamdale (buses #210 & #211 from Skipton; ⓦwww.malhamdale.com), lying between Wharfedale and Ribblesdale, is the shortest of the most popular dales, but what it lacks in length it more than makes up for in quality. Travel writer Bill Bryson once lived in the valley (in Kirkby Malham), considering it the finest place in the world this side of heaven. And he should know. Prime limestone country, Malhamdale provides some of the best walking in England, and is a top destination for visitors to the National Park. The big attraction is, of course, the wonderful scenery, particularly the spectacular triumvirate of **Malham Cove**, **Malham Tarn** and **Gordale Scar**, together with the lesser known **Janet's Foss**. The starting point for any exploration of the area has to be the dale's main village, **Malham**, which lies in the upper reaches of the valley.

Malham

A stone village fetchingly meandering along the banks of a stream, **MALHAM** has a photogenic bridge, two delightful pubs (see p.194) and a scattering of cafés and shops. It's busy throughout the year and manic in high season, with visitors setting off for or returning from the numerous walks in the area, or just mooching around the village.

Malham Cove is an impressive horseshoe-shaped limestone cliff under a mile north of the village. Soaring 260ft above the surrounding countryside, it can be approached via a broad footpath from which there are fine views of the cliff from below (if there are climbers on the cliff, it gives a sense of the vast scale of the formation), or by bearing left and climbing to the top via rough steps at the western end. The deeply scored limestone pavement that lies across the top of the cliff looks like the skin of some giant pachyderm. The views are spectacular, and well worth the effort of the climb.

From the top of Malham Cove a path strikes north to **Malham Tarn**, a shallow upland lake – England's highest – of glacial origin. It is said to have been the inspiration for Charles Kingsley's *The Water Babies*. The whole area is now owned by the National Trust, and provides excellent walking, cycling and birdwatching.

If, instead of heading north from Malham Cove you strike east, a clearly signposted path leads to **Janet's Foss**, just across Gordale Lane, a pretty waterfall which plunges over a self-created tufa curtain into a tree-fringed pool. Once used for dipping sheep, it's now an ideal place to go for a dip yourself, or at least cool your feet. The name is thought to refer to Jennet, a fairy queen said to live in a cave behind the falls. There is certainly something magical about the Foss and the woodland walk that stretches back to Malham.

A little further along Gordale Lane is a well-marked and surfaced path leading off to the left, signposted **Gordale Scar**. There's an information board explaining how this extraordinary gorge was formed – a million years of glacial scouring followed by deluges of limestone-dissolving meltwater, leaving the tortured chasm with overhanging cliffs and tumultuous waterfalls you see today. It's not far from the main road, but a sign does warn of a "Steep and difficult ascent at Gordale, 1/4 mile".

Malhamdale offers a feast of walking and cycling, and the most heavily used paths are surfaced to almost urban standard. However, some are pretty rough and ready, so proper footwear and clothing are recommended. Look out for a free and widely available pamphlet *Selected Walks in Malhamdale*, which offers detailed instructions for five walks, from just around three miles to just over seven, or sign up for the inaptly named "Malhamdale Meander", a strenuous 23 miles in ten hours, which takes place in May (℡01729/830 588) and takes in most of the main sights. Malhamdale provides some of the most magnificent scenery in the Dales, all within easy walking distance of Malham village and each other – no wonder it's so popular.

Information, accommodation and eating

The main car park is attached to the **National Park Centre**, which also houses a **tourist information centre** (April–Oct daily 10am–5pm; July & Aug opens 9.30am; Nov, Dec, Feb & March Sat & Sun 10am–4pm; ℡01969/652 380), and is where buses pick up and disgorge.

A walk from Malham (seven and a half miles)

This popular circular walk takes in all the main sights of the area, starting and finishing in Malham, and taking in Janet's Fosse, Gordale Scar, Malham Tarn and Malham Cove. It's well signposted, but for most of the year, just follow the crowds.

Turn left out of the **Dales National Park car park**, then cross Malham Tarn by the footbridge on the opposite side of the road from the *Buck Inn*, walk south until you come to a signpost for Janet's Fosse. Follow it along a heavily wooded, National Trust-owned ravine until you come to the **Fosse** itself.

Taking the path up to the left of the Fosse, you'll come to a road. Turn right, walk along it the short distance to a signpost for **Gordale Scar**, off the road to the left. A broad gravel path from the road leads into the Scar itself, a narrow canyon with lofty cliffs either side, with the Gordale Beck tumbling down the rock face. If you're reasonably fit, you can climb up a path (in places rather obscure, in other places stepped) to the left of the waterfall which, after a scramble, levels out at the top. Continuing along the path will bring you to a signpost for Malham Tarn (two miles). Follow it.

If you'd rather not face the scramble up the waterfall, return to the road, turn right then right again off the road, following a signpost for **Malham Cove**. After passing through an ancient settlement and field system, and having rejoined the hardier souls who climbed up through Gordale Scar, you'll arrive at a junction of two paths at Street Gate. Continue straight, and in due course you will be able to see the water of **Malham Tarn** in the distance. Several tracks link Street Gate to the lake. The birdlife around the Tarn is plentiful, though the landscape is a little drab.

From car park on Malham Tarn, first follow the sign "Pennine Way Watersinks ¾ mile", then, having turned right onto the road signed "Malham Cove 1 ½ miles", continue south, following signs for Malham Cove. You will eventually find yourself on the impressive limestone pavement at the top of the natural amphitheatre of Malham Cove. Don't go too close to the edge – it's a 260ft drop. Cross the pavement, then take the steep steps down the western edge of the escarpment. The path back to Malham is clearly defined and well signposted.

Buck Inn ☎01729/830 317, ⊛www .buckinnmalham.com. Pleasant Dales village pub popular with walkers. Good pub and restaurant food, comfortable rooms, relaxed attitude to muddy boots. Ideal base for a walking holiday. ❷
Lister Arms ☎01729/830 330, ⊛www .listerarms-inn.co.uk. The other pub in Malham, just across the bridge from the *Buck Inn*, the *Lister Arms* has a good reputation locally for its food, and has comfortable rooms which are slightly pricier than the *Buck Inn*, but still very reasonable. ❸

YHA ☎0845 371 9529, ⊛www.yha.org.uk. Just past the *Lister Arms*, Malham Youth Hostel is purpose built and good for families with children. At prices that start at £18, a really good choice for serious walkers and for families wanting to enjoy the local walks. Has its own garden in which is the village "pinfold" – an enclosure in which animals that had strayed off the common would be impounded and kept until their owners had paid a fine. ❶

Wharfedale

The River Wharfe runs south from just below Wensleydale through **Bolton Abbey**, **Ilkley** and **Otley**, eventually joining the Ouse south of York. The upper reaches of the river flow through one of the most popular dales in the National Park, with characteristic villages, ruins and waterfalls. There are **tourist information centres** at **Skipton**, the main town for this part of the Dales, and Grassington. Buses from Skipton up the dale towards Hubberholme include #72, #72R and, via Bolton Abbey, #X59.

Skipton

SKIPTON (Anglo Saxon "sheep town") bills itself as the gateway to the Dales, and with good reason. It sits on their southern edge, at the intersection of the two routes that between them cradle the National Park and Area of Outstanding Natural Beauty – the A65 to the western and the A59/61 to the eastern dales. A pleasant market town with a long history, it is defined by its **castle** and **church**, by its long, wide and sloping **High Street**, and by a **water system** that includes the Leeds and Liverpool Canal, its spur the Springs Canal and the Eller Beck. Away from the town centre are two attractions – the innovative **Auction Mart** and theatre and the **Copper Dragon Brewery**.

Information and accommodation

There's a **tourist information centre** at Skipton (Easter–Oct Mon–Sat 10am–5pm, Sun 11am–3pm; Nov–Easter Mon–Sat 10am–4pm; ☏01756/792 809). With several accommodation options, Skipton makes an excellent base for exploring the southern dales – not only Wharfedale, but Ribblesdale, Malhamdale and Nidderdale as well.

Herriot's Hotel Broughton Rd ☏01756/792 781, ⓦwww.herriotsforleisure.co.uk. A short walk along the canal towpath from the centre of Skipton, in a Victorian listed building, the boutique-style hotel and its restaurant, *Rhubarb*, are justly popular. Bright cheerful decor, lots of original features. Not cheap, though there are numerous deals and packages. ❹

Rendezvous at Skipton Keighley Rd ☏01756/700 100, ⓦwww.rendezvous-skipton .co.uk. A modern hotel on the canal side under a mile south of the town centre. With comfortable rooms, contemporary lines, a ballroom and restaurant (*The Baby Swan*), the *Rendezvous* is building up a good reputation. ❸

Skipton Park Guest 'Otel 2 Salisbury St ☏01756/700 640, ⓦwww.skiptonpark .co.uk. Just northwest of the town centre. Rates are eminently reasonable for a warm welcome, comfortable double room and great breakfast. ❷

The Woolly Sheep Inn 38 Sheep St ☏01756/700 966, ⓦwww.woollysheepinn.co.uk. Pleasant town centre Timothy Taylor pub with comfortable and well-furnished rooms, though some are a little tight on space. More rooms (nine) than you'd think looking at the pub from the outside. Ideal for families or friends who want a convivial stopover, or are staying for one of Skipton's festivals, but maybe too noisy for tranquillity-seekers. Free parking at rear. ❸

Skipton Castle

The dominant feature of the town centre is **Skipton Castle** (March–Sept Mon–Sat 10am–6pm, Sun noon–6pm; Oct–Feb till 4pm; £6.20; ☏01756/792 442, ⓦwww.skiptoncastle.co.uk), one of England's best-preserved medieval fortifications. It sits, squat and threatening, at the top of the sloping High Street. Originally Norman, it was granted by the crown to Robert de Clifford in 1310, and remained in the Clifford family for generations. Among the more famous of the clan were John Clifford (1435–61) who fought in the War of the Roses and earned the name "The Butcher", after the battle of Wakefield; George Clifford, 3rd Earl of Cumberland (1558–1605), a famous Elizabethan buccaneer who attacked Spanish shipping

---

Skipton festivals

Skipton is known locally for the number and variety of its festivals – the **Waterways Festival** on the first May bank holiday weekend, with masses of narrow boats, street entertainers, plays and open-air exhibitions; **Sheep Day**, held on the last Sunday in July; **Clogfest** in July; **Yuletide** in December, and, every two years, a wonderful international **Puppet Festival** (the next is Sept 23–25, 2011). For all these events, check ⓦwww.skiptonevents.co.uk.

in the Caribbean using a man o'war which he paid for himself; and, possibly the most renowned, his daughter Lady Anne Clifford (1590–1676), at different times Countess of Dorset, Pembroke and Montgomery. After the Battle of Marston Moor during the Civil War, Skipton Castle was the only remaining Royalist stronghold in the north, eventually falling to Cromwell in 1645. He ordered that it be "slighted" by having the roofs removed. Within ten years Lady Anne Clifford was allowed to replace them, on condition that they were not strong enough to bear cannon. To celebrate, she planted a yew tree in the central courtyard. The castle remained in the hands of her descendants into the twentieth century, and the roofs and yew tree remain to this day.

Entry to the outer bailey of the castle is through the massive gatehouse. Inside, you can visit the Tudor conduit court (where the yew tree stands), the thirteenth-century chapel, and part of the house (the rest is a private residence) – the banqueting hall, the kitchen, the bedchamber, the privy, the dungeon and the watchtower, following a tour sheet that is provided for free. There's a shop, a café and a chapel terrace picnic area.

Right next to the castle is the largely fourteenth-century **Holy Trinity Church**, also repaired by the indefatigable Lady Anne, and worth visiting for its numerous monuments to members of the Clifford family (the earliest is for the 1st Earl of Cumberland who died in 1542), and for the view down Skipton High Street from the churchyard.

The Town

As you follow the High Street downhill from the church and castle, on the right is a statue of Victorian Liberal MP Sir Mathew Wilson, and on the left the Town Hall building which contains the diverting **Craven Museum and Gallery** (April–Sept Mon & Wed–Sat 10am–4pm; Oct–March Mon, Wed & Fri noon–4pm, Sat 10am–4pm; free; ☎01756/706 407), chock-a-block with archeological and social history artefacts – look out for the prehistoric bear skull, the iron age sword, the excellent half-sized reconstruction of a Roman hypocaust (sophisticated under-floor central heating), the hoard of silver medieval coins, the comprehensive costume collection and the domestic bits and pieces (penny farthing bicycle, gas stove) from the Victorian and Edwardian periods. Look out too for the occasional fun days for kids and the interesting information boards in the foyer on the history of Skipton's canals.

The **High Street** itself provides much of the town's character. It is lined on each side with large cobblestones (or setts), upon which, on Mondays, Wednesdays, Fridays and Saturdays, market stalls are erected (the rest of the time they're used for parking). There are the usual shops and, immediately after Otley Street on the left, the nicely done **Craven Court**, a re-creation of a Victorian two-tier arcade, with stone-flagged floor, iron columns, glass roof, hanging lamps, and small shops selling jewellery, clothes, shoes and gifts.

Diverging from the High Street on the right is pedestrianized **Sheep Street** off which, through an archway, lies a cobbled precinct consisting of **Victoria Square**, **Victoria** and **Albert** streets and **Albert Terrace**. In the centre is a columned rotunda housing a souvenir shop, the *Narrow Boat* pub (also columned) and numerous attractive stone cottages.

The canals

To the east of town is the boat-thronged **canal wharf**, at the intersection of the 1770-built trans-Pennine **Leeds and Liverpool Canal** and the **Springs Canal**, a spur added in 1773–74 to move limestone from quarries a quarter of a mile to the north of the town centre down to the main canal. As in many similar towns, the canals have been cleaned up and are now an essential part of Skipton's character. Even in the early days haulage companies sometimes used their boats for excursions, and today the recreational use of the canals is an important part of Skipton's tourist profile. **Pennine Boat Trips** (℡01756/790 829, ⓦwww.canaltrips.co.uk) offer a variety of canal experiences: private charter, public canal trips, theme nights (country and western and swing among others), and on-board food, while **Pennine Cruisers** (℡01756/795 478, ⓦwww.penninecruisers.com), though they do thirty-minute trips, are more of a narrow-boat rental company. The Wharf itself is an attractive waterside area with the odd bar and bistro, while the canal towpaths provide pleasant walking and information boards. Try following the Springs Canal past the High Corn Mill then through the gorge below the castle into Skipton Woods.

Auction Mart

To the west of town, near the A59/A65 bypass roundabout (the one with the *Little Chef*), is Skipton's three-ring **Auction Mart**, erected in 1990 to replace ones originating in 1894. Watching cows, sheep and pigs being paraded, listening to the staccato patter of the auctioneer, mingling with cloth-capped farmers down from the Dales, would be diverting enough, but something of a minority taste. What makes it unique is that, when not in use for the animal mart, the main ring becomes the **Mart Theatre** (℡01756/709 666, ⓦwww.themarttheatre.org.uk), an uncanny echo of Elizabethan players putting on shows in straw-strewn coaching inn yards. On performance nights the tubular steel barriers are removed, the concrete apron scrubbed down, the stage erected, and the show goes on to an audience that sit on the seats vacated by the farmers. The Exhibition Hall becomes the theatre bar. The theatre, led with infectious enthusiasm by Anthea Rathlin-Jones, offers touring productions, workshops, events, comedy, opera, folk music and much else. And we're not talking local amateur talent here – since it opened in 2005, the Mart Theatre has hosted plays by the Hull Truck Theatre Company, *Cosi Fan Tutti* by performers from Opera North, comedy with Jeremy Hardy, Arthur Smith and Mark Steel, and folk with Norma Waterson and Martin Carthy. The only theatre/agriculture collaboration in the country, it's non-profit-making, and is supported by the Arts Council and the cattle marts, as well as by students at the nearby Craven College. And how do arts and agriculture get on, you're probably wondering? Like a house on fire, apparently, with the farmers insisting on using the theatre lights during auctions – they make the animals look their best. An absolute, unmissable gem.

Copper Dragon Brewery

The other edge-of-town attraction lies to the south, along the Keighley Road. A hobby that grew into a successful business, the **Copper Dragon Brewery** (℡01756/702 130, ⓦwww.copperdragonbrewery.squarespace.com), on the modern Snaygill industrial estate, looks anonymous from the outside. But when you've parked around the back, and entered the Visitor Centre, it's a different world. There's a smart bar and bistro, a well-stocked shop selling the company's wide range of beers, branded clothes and bar and brewery paraphernalia. You can't of course, wander off on your own into the business end of the brewery, but there are tours (Mon–Sat noon, £7; evening tours at 6pm with meal, £14).

Bolton Abbey

About five miles east of Skipton, just north of the A59 Harrogate road, lies the **Bolton Abbey estate** (daily: March 22–May, Sept & Oct 9am–7pm; June–Aug

9am–9pm, Nov–March 21 9am–6pm, last admission 1–3hr before closing; £6 per vehicle; ⓦwww.boltonabbey.com), which has been in the Devonshire family since 1753. It incorporates a spectacularly beautiful stretch of Wharfedale, much admired by, among others, Ruskin, who wrote lovingly about it, and Turner, who painted it. A major tourist attraction, the estate consists of 30,000 acres of wonderful countryside – woodland and landscaped grassland – and over eighty miles of footpaths on both sides of the river. **BOLTON ABBEY** is the name of a tiny village, and, by extension, the estate; the famous abbey ruins at the southern end are **Bolton Priory**.

When you turn off the A59, follow the B6160 (signposted Bolton Abbey). The first thing of note you come to is the spectacularly upmarket *Devonshire Arms Country House Hotel and Spa* (see p.199). Beyond it lies the village of **Bolton Abbey** – little more than a cluster of houses, a bookshop, several tearooms, a new-looking village hall and combined post office and village shop, and the first of the estate's three **car parks** – the closest to the priory ruins. **Bolton Priory**, a gentle walk from the car park, is a twelfth-century Augustinian priory, established in 1154 and dissolved in the 1530s, when it met the fate common to all monastic houses in the country. However, the nave of the priory was allowed to continue as a parish church, so this survives in good condition. The rest of the priory, stripped of its roof lead and left open to the elements, began to deteriorate rapidly and was raided for building stone by the inhabitants of the valley, leaving the picturesque ruins you see today. Visitors are welcome to wander among the ruins and enter the church, where there are volunteers available to answer questions, and where you can sign up for a guided tour (downloadable notes are available on the Bolton Abbey website). Opposite the priory are much-photographed **stepping-stones** giving access to the opposite bank of the river.

A mile or so further up Wharfedale is the second car park, stretching along the bank either side of the **Cavendish Pavilion** (turn right at the Victorian ornamental fountain). Being halfway up the estate, this car park gives access by footpath downriver back to Bolton Priory, and upriver to the Strid and Strid Wood. There's a café, restaurant, shop and toilets, and a footbridge across the Wharfe, so you can choose to follow either bank.

Finally, a further drive up Wharfedale brings you to the third car park at **Strid Wood**, where there's a kiosk and a Caravan Club site (see p.199). A path leads through woodland, a Site of Special Scientific Interest because of its acidic oaks, home to many plants, animals and birds, high above the Wharfe, then down to the Strid, where the river's water squeezes with great force through a narrow chasm. The rocks are smooth and pitted with holes created by the rotary motion of small stones driven by the current, and though it's exhilarating to get down close to such elemental power, care needs to be taken – the rocks can sometimes be slippery, and as a notice at the site says "the Strid is dangerous, and has claimed lives in the past". From the car park it's a ten-minute walk down to the river, and a fifteen-minute walk back.

Footpaths continue north as far as **Barden Tower**, the ruins of a hunting lodge which was home to Henry Clifford, 10th Earl of Skipton (nicknamed the Shepherd Lord because of his gentle and pious personality but who, in old age, fought successfully at the Battle of Flodden Field against the Scots). Next to the ruins is the sixteenth-century **Priest's House** built by the Shepherd Lord for his private chaplain, and now a rather swish restaurant (see p.199).

Before leaving the Bolton Abbey area, you might want to visit **Hesketh Farm Park** (April–Sept Tues–Sun 10am–5pm; Sept–Oct Sat & Sun only; £4.50; ⓣ01756/710 444, ⓦwww.heskethfarmpark.co.uk), just up the road from the estate's first car park. A 600-acre family-run farm which raises cattle and sheep, with lots of other animals as well – pigs, goats, hens, donkeys and ponies. There are also tractor and trailer rides, a fine playground, pedal go-karts, a sand pit and a café. Also nearby is the dinky little **Embsay and Bolton Abbey Railway** (ⓦ www.embsayboltonabbeyrailway.org.uk), a forty-minute trip from one terminus to the other and back if you don't get off. Most trains are steam hauled, the scenery is terrific, and there's a shop and café at each station. Check the website for fares and times.

Accommodation and eating

Devonshire Arms Country House Hotel and Spa Bolton Abbey ⓣ 01756/710 441, ⓦ www.thedevonshirearms.co.uk. Top-end luxury hotel with designer rooms, two restaurants – one, the *Burlington*, with a Michelin star – and a spa. Every facility and service you could ask for, and a welcome from the Duke and Duchess of Devonshire themselves, in the brochure if not the flesh. These things don't come cheap, though at certain times you can even get a double room for £69 (you need to eat in the *Burlington* at £65/head to qualify). ⓼

Devonshire Fell Hotel Burnsall ⓣ 01756/729 000, ⓦ www.devonshirefell.co.uk. The sister hotel of the *Devonshire Arms Country House Hotel*, the *Devonshire Fell*, on the very edge of the estate, offers similar luxury, individual rooms designed by the Duchess herself, and wonderful views across the village of Burnsall at considerably less cost. And you still get to use some of the older sister's bells and whistles, like the spa and the chauffeur service. ⓹

Priest's House ⓣ 01756/720 616, ⓦ www .thepriestshouse.co.uk. Beautifully set next to the Barden Tower, with terrific views back down Wharfedale, the *Priest's House* offers fine food in heraldic surroundings. Prices aren't bad either – two courses £21.95, three courses £24.95.

Strid Wood Caravan Club Site ⓣ 01756/710 433. A pretty site set in a woodland glade. Open mid-March to early Jan.

Burnsall

After Barden Tower, the B6160 crosses Barden Moor northwards. In four miles a sweeping hill leads down into the quaint village of **BURNSALL** – the view of the village as you approach, dominated by the elegant 1884-built bridge across the Wharfe, is worth stopping for. On the left as you approach the village is the **Devonshire Fell Hotel** (see above). Just before the bridge is a wide green running down to the river – this is a good place to stop, with the Shop on the Green, the *Wharfe View Tea Rooms* and the *Red Lion Hotel* (ⓣ 01756/720 204, ⓦ www.redlion.co.uk; ⓹). Beyond the hotel is the seventeenth-century village school, established by the "Dick Whittington of the Dales" Sir William Craven (he was Lord Mayor of London between 1610 and 1612), the church of St Wilfrid, probably built in around 1520, but using parts of an earlier church, and the village hall. There's nothing very spectacular to see, but pottering around villages like Burnsall, bathed in the evident civic pride of the people who live there, is one of the pleasures of visiting the Dales.

Linton

Well worth a stop, two and a half miles south of and within walking distance of Grassington, is **LINTON**, a gem of a village. It comes in two parts – the village itself, clustered around a riverside green, and the **church** and **falls**, a ten-minute walk away along a well-signposted footpath.

Linton (or to give it its full title, Linton-in-Craven) is largely a product of the seventeenth and eighteenth centuries. A charming **pub** – the *Fountaine Inn* (ⓦ www.fountaineinnatlinton.co.uk) – sits at the top of the green, which slopes down to the Linton Beck. Beyond the inn is Grade II-listed **Fountaine's Hospital**, almshouses bequeathed to the village in the will of Richard Fountaine,

Tom Lee

The story of **Tom Lee** is one of Grassington's most grisly tales. There seem to be **two versions** of the story. According to one, Tom Lee was Grassington's very own eighteenth-century Dick Turpin. His day job was as the village blacksmith and innkeeper, but at night he pursued his sideline as a burglar and highwayman. In 1766 a **Dr Petty** found out about his nefarious nocturnal activities and threatened to expose him. Big mistake. Tom Lee followed Dr Petty into Grass Wood and did him to death, only to be betrayed by his servant, tried for murder and executed, his body then being hung on a gibbet at the scene of the crime. The second version is that Tom Lee was indeed the local blacksmith, but that he and Dr Petty attended a cock fight in Kettlewell, during which the good doctor won a great deal of money. Returning to Grassington by way of numerous pubs at which they did much celebratory drinking, they got extremely inebriated and, as they crossed Grass Wood, Tom Lee succumbed to temptation and murdered the doctor for the cash. Initially acquitted at York Assizes for lack of evidence, Tom Lee's servant later came forward with more evidence, the miscreant was re-arrested, re-tried, found guilty and executed. Whichever version you favour, there's a plaque up on a building in the village saying that it is the original "Smidy...owned by the notorious Tom Lee".

an undertaker who made his fortune in London during the plague in 1665 and the Great Fire of London the following year. A case of being in the right place at the right time. Built in 1721, the almshouses provided accommodation for six poor men or women of the parish, maintained by the income from lands purchased at the same time for that purpose. In the centre of the building is a chapel (open to the public), at which attendance was compulsory for the occupants. Run by twelve trustees, the charity still operates, though beneficiaries no longer have to attend chapel. The Beck itself is crossed by no fewer than three bridges. The oldest is the flat "clapper" bridge, now the furthest upstream after being moved to make way for the 1892 road bridge. Between them is the elegantly arched "packhorse" bridge, built in the fourteenth century, but with parapets that were raised in the seventeenth century – before that, low parapets were necessary to allow for the panniers slung either side of the packhorses. On sunny days, with the pub terrace packed with drinkers and diners, and the green thronged with people being mugged by marauding gangs of ducks and geese, the village is a picture. But its delights don't stop at the green. The parish church, down by the River Wharfe and said to be the oldest in England still in use, is also a gem. **St Michael's**, a "delightful little church" according to Pevsner, probably dates from the tenth or eleventh century, with further additions in the following three centuries. There's much of interest inside the church – a Norman font, a Lady Chapel partly furnished with pieces by Thompson of Kilburn (the "mouseman"; see p.229), a medieval stone altar. Entrance to the churchyard is through a gate or over a stone-stepped stile.

Finally, if you follow the road from Linton church to Threshfield, on the right a signposted path leads to the moderately impressive **Linton Falls** (which are also accessible from Grassington), and are crossed by a footbridge. The falls are notable for the startlingly white rocks with black patches of weed which the water thunders over and between.

Grassington

Next as you follow the river northwards you come to **GRASSINGTON** itself, the pretty stone capital of Upper Wharfedale. A market town by the end of the thirteenth century, and an eighteenth- and nineteenth-century lead mining community, its twenty-first-century incarnation is as a centre for people, especially walkers, wishing to explore the southern dales. Clustered around a quaint cobbled square and village pump, it has four pubs, a wealth of tearooms, cafés, hotels and B&Bs and shops selling outdoor equipment, furniture, flowers, clothes, paintings, books, wine, food (there's a Spar) – everything in fact that the visitor is likely to need. There's a small **Folk Museum** (Easter–Oct Tues–Sun 2–4.30pm) in a converted lead miner's cottage, an **information centre** (April–Oct daily 10am–5pm; Nov–March Fri–Sun 10am–4pm; ℡01756/751 690) and **National Park Centre** (daily: April–Oct 9.30am–5.15pm; Nov–March check with centre; ℡01756/751 690) with a car park that doubles as the bus station, but, oddly, no parish church of its own. An interesting development at the time of writing was the setting up of the **Grassington Hub** (Manor Hill Barn, 2 Garrs Lane; Mon–Sat 10am–6pm; ℡01756/752 222), a sort of clearing house for local information which, though designed for local residents, might be of use to visitors.

Within easy reach of the village are several places worth visiting: woodland paths at **Grass Wood** to the northwest, the waterfall and church at Linton to the south already mentioned, and the **Grassington Lead Mining Trail** on the moors to the northeast (drive up the village's main street, and keep going for a mile and a half or so), which guides you through the remains of extensive lead workings. This monument to the village's industrial history is particularly well worth visiting – though the mineral agent's house, blacksmith shop, carpenter's shop and counting house are now private residences, there's an excellent general information board, and no fewer than eighteen stop-off points with subsidiary boards giving clear explanations of what exactly you're looking at. Let's hear it for the National Park Authority.

Furthermore, you're now in **Calendar Girls Country** – the area used as the setting from the film of that name. **Cracoe** and **Rylstone**, just south of Grassington, is where the real Calendar Girls came from, while **Burnsall** (see p.199) **Kilnsey**, **Kettlewell** and **Settle** (see p.187) all make appearances in the film.

Accommodation and eating

The Angel Inn Hetton ℡01756/730 263, ⓦwww .angelhetton.co.uk. Ivy-covered walls outside, oak beams and log fires within: a delightful old inn with an upmarket brasserie, just off the Grassington to Skipton road. Top-end accommodation in a barn conversion directly across the road. **⑥**

Ashfield House Hotel ℡01756/752 584, ⓦwww.ashfieldhouse.co.uk. Top-end B&B in attractive converted lead miners' cottages just off the main square. Friendly welcome, lovely decor, excellent food and comfortable, quirky rooms. Guests often meet for drinks before dinner, and the owner Joe has a huge fund of local knowledge upon which guests can draw. **③**

The Black Horse Hotel ℡01756/752 770, ⓦwww.blackhorsehotelgrassington.co.uk. A seventeenth-century coaching inn in the centre of the village, the *Black Horse* has a nice carpeted bar with open fires and settles, and fifteen rooms with barely a right angle between them. Bar and restaurant food with main courses £8–16. **③**

The Devonshire Hotel ℡01756/752 525, ⓦwww.thedevonshirehotel.co.uk. Pretty Dales pub with rooms on Grassington's main square. Good food at reasonable prices (two courses: lunch £7.50, dinner £8.50), clean rooms, convivial atmosphere. This is the village's most popular pub, so it can get a bit noisy during opening hours. **③**

Grassington Lodge 8 Wood Lane ℡01756/752 518, ⓦwww.grassingtonlodge.co.uk. Outstanding service, decor and attention to detail. It has won many awards, and you can see why – it offers that personal touch you just can't get in chain hotels. **④**

Old Hall Threshfield ℡01756/752 441, ⓦwww .oldhallinnandcottages.co.uk. Lovely old pub less than a mile from Grassington, with four bedrooms on site and nearby self-catering cottages. Extensive à la carte menu as well as pub food – main courses from £10.95 to £16.95. **③**

Kilnsey and Kettlewell

Beyond Grassington, Wharfedale is more sparsely settled, with the river narrowing and the field barns proliferating. The first village you come to is **KILNSEY**, a tiny village with a fish farm, a hotel, *The Tennant Arms* (℡01756/752 301, Ⓦwww .tennant-arms.co.uk; ❸), and, just north of the village, **Kilnsey Crag**, a limestone cliff that sweeps down to the village and crouches over the main road, 165ft high with an overhang of 40ft. Mastiles Lane, which heads directly west from the centre of the village and peters out into a footpath, was once a Roman road (it passes through the remains of a Roman camp just south of Malham Tarn), and later became a drovers' route for taking Fountains Abbey sheep to the high summer pastures. There's a trekking and riding centre over the river in Conistone (℡01756/752 861, Ⓦwww.kilnseyriding.com).

A mile or so further on, the road sweeps down into **KETTLEWELL**, where much of *Calendar Girls* was filmed. There are three **pubs** in Kettlewell, all of which do **accommodation**. Two face each other near the bridge – the *Blue Bell Inn* (℡01756/760 230; ❸), a seventeenth-century coaching inn that's still very much a traditional pub, and the more contemporary *Racehorses Hotel* (℡01756/760 233; ❸), in what was once the *Blue Bell Inn*'s stables, while up near the church is another old-school pub, the *King's Head* (℡01756/760 242; ❷). There's little to choose between the three in price, but in terms of comfort the *Racehorses* wins by a nose. There's also an old-fashioned **garage** in the village, and several shops.

Hubberholme

Heading onward through **Starbotton** and left at **Buckden** brings you to the village of **HUBBERHOLME**, which consists of a pub and a church at the highest reaches of Wharfedale and at the entrance to Longstrathdale, small in size but great in renown. It has two main claims to fame. The first is the so-called **Hubberholme Parliament**. The lovely old *George Inn* (℡01756/760 223; ❸), built as a farm in the mid-seventeenth century and all flagstone floors, thick stone walls and mullioned windows, was once the vicarage, and the incumbent developed the habit of putting a lighted candle in the window as a sign of God's grace. A tradition developed that on the first Monday of the year, an auction would be held to decide who would get use of sixteen acres of church pasture land, the proceeds of which would be used to relieve the parish poor. The auction still goes on today. The vicar oversees the auction from the dining room (The House of Lords), the interested farmers make their bids in the bar (The House of Commons), and the highest bid when the candle goes out is the winner. And a good time, be assured, is had by all.

The village's other claim to fame arises from its association with one of Yorkshire's greatest writers, **J.B. Priestley**. Hubberholme was one of his favourite haunts, and he mentions it fondly in *English Journey* ("a tiny hamlet that had a fine little old church and a cosy inn"). The pub is still cosy – with coal fires, no gaming machines or piped music – and the church is still little and old. He liked it so much, indeed, that his ashes are buried here – a plaque inside the church doesn't say where, simply that his ashes are "buried nearby". It quotes Priestley on Hubberholme, too: "one of the smallest and pleasantest places in the world".

Today Hubberholme has a back-of-beyond peacefulness. You can sit on one of the benches facing the Wharfe, with the pub on the other side, and all you'll hear is the sound of the river, the sounds of animals in the farm behind you, and the tinkling of wind chimes in the churchyard trees.

Littondale

If you've time, a detour up **Littondale**, named after the village of Litton, not its river (the Skirfare), is well worth the effort. The road branches west from Wharfedale at Knipe Scar, between Kilnsey and Kettlewell, and is signposted for Arncliffe. As you travel up the dale, you come first to **ARNCLIFFE**, a pretty Dales village with a medieval church next to a medieval bridge, and a long narrow village green over which presides the *Falcon Inn* (℡01756/770 205; ❷), then, if you continue straight, **LITTON**, with an attractive little pub, the *Queens Arms* (℡01756/770 208; ❸), with its own brewery. Both do food and accommodation, and both are popular with hikers. If, instead of going straight at Arncliffe you turn left, you soon climb up into the hills either side of a bleak but beautiful scree-dotted U-shaped valley created by the Cowside Beck, where the views back towards Arncliffe are magnificent. Eventually, having passed several hanging valleys and a waterfall on the left, the single-lane road goes around the top of Malham Tarn and drops down into Malham itself (see p.193).

Nidderdale

The easternmost of the dales, **Nidderdale** (ⓦwww.nidderdale.co.uk) is for some obscure bureaucratic reason not actually in the Dales National Park, but is an Area of Outstanding Natural Beauty instead. The River Nidd, after which the valley is named, rises on Little Whernside, flows south to the dale's main town, **Pateley Bridge**, then wanders off across the Vale of York via Ripley, just outside Harrogate. Peaceful and relatively little-visited, with charming Pateley Bridge as its focus, and **How Stean Gorge** as its main visitor attraction, Nidderdale is sky-high on get-away-from-it-all potential. The **Nidderdale Rambler** bus service goes all the way up the valley, and there's a tourist information centre at Pateley Bridge.

Pateley Bridge

PATELEY BRIDGE, gateway to Nidderdale, is an extraordinarily pleasant little town, though its inhabitants must have strong legs to deal day in, day out with its hills. Sitting astride the B6265 Ripon to Skipton road, it owes its existence to the river crossing that gives it its name. Here the Nidd was forded from time immemorial and bridged in the fourteenth century, the original wooden bridge being replaced with a stone one in the eighteenth century. Today the main road drops steeply to the river via the High Street, crosses the bridge, then climbs steeply up the other side of the valley. A footbridge keeps pedestrians and traffic apart. The main part of the town lies to the north of the Nidd, while south of the bridge lies pleasant **Bewerley Park** and a recreation ground complete with excellent children's playground, bandstand and war memorial.

There's nothing wildly exciting to do in Pateley Bridge, but the town's history is well documented by the maroon plaques of its heritage trail, and in the **Nidderdale Museum** (daily: Easter–July 1.30–4.30pm, Sept & Oct; Aug & bank hols 10.30am–4.30pm; Nov–Easter Sat & Sun 1.30–4.30pm; £2, accompanied children free; ℡01423/711 225, ⓦwww.nidderdalemuseum.com), housed in the Old Workhouse, with eleven rooms of exhibits covering local agriculture, industry, transport, costume and religion. There's a cobbler's shop, a schoolroom, a Victorian parlour and a general store, together with costume exhibits, transport artefacts and much else. If climbing up to the Old Workhouse hasn't been sufficient exercise, find your way to the High Street (it's past the church and the theatre), climb to the top then turn right into the Ripon Road, and look out for the "Panorama Walk" sign that points off to the left – it's a rewarding stroll with uplifting views.

Alternatively, a drive or walk (along the Nidderdale Way) up Nidderdale itself is a delight. Passing a **pub**, *The Bridge Inn*, behind which is an old water mill with a huge wheel, you arrive at the 1899-built dam of **Gouthwaite Reservoir**, a nature reserve and a Site of Special Scientific Interest (SSSI) owned by Yorkshire Water. About halfway along the reservoir there's a car park, and there are three viewing areas set aside for birdwatchers. At the upper end of the reservoir is the village of **Ramsgill**, most famous for the eighteenth-century **Yorke Arms** (see below).

Information, accommodation and eating

There's a **tourist information centre** on the High Street (April–Oct Mon–Sat 10am–5pm, Sun 10am–1pm; Nov–March Fri & Sat 10am–5pm; ☏01423/711 147).

Lyndale Guesthouse King St ☏01423/712 657, Ⓦwww.lyndaleguesthouse.com. Big stone Victorian house just off the High St, with spotless and nicely decorated rooms. ❷

Roslyn House King St ☏01423/711 374, Ⓦwww.roslynhouse.co.uk. Victorian guesthouse with attractive rooms, all en suite. Offers pick up and take out packages for walkers. Free parking and wi-fi. ❸

Sportsmans Arms ☏01423/711 306, Ⓦwww.sportsmans-arms.co.uk. A mile or so out from Pateley Bridge at Wath-in-Nidderdale, the *Sportsmans Arms* is a fine old hotel with unpretentious food, cosy bars, and lovely grounds. ❹

Yorke Arms Ramsgill-in-Nidderdale, Pateley Bridge ☏01423/755 243, Ⓦwww.yorke-arms.co.uk. Something of an institution in Nidderdale, the *Yorke Arms* in Ramsgill, just over four miles up the valley from Pateley Bridge immediately after Gouthwaite Reservoir, is a restaurant-with-rooms. The chef is Frances Atkins, one of only six female Michelin-starred chefs in the country. Accommodation is comfortable and, as might be expected, pricey. Beautiful old ivy-covered building, luxurious decor, and, of course, top-quality food. ❻

Stump Cross Caverns and Brimham Rocks

On either side of the town, not in Nidderdale itself but within Pateley Bridge's orbit, are the Stump Cross Caverns, about five miles to the west, and the Brimham Rocks about half as far to the east. Discovered by lead miners in 1860, and extended several times by further exploration, the four-mile-long **Stump Cross Caverns** (Feb–Nov daily 10am–6pm, last admission 4.45pm; Dec–Feb Sat & Sun only; £6; ☏01756/752 780, Ⓦwww.stumpcrosscaverns.co.uk) have been a show cave now for nearly 170 years. In addition to the usual stalactites and stalagmites, some at least 230,000 years in the making, there are also the bones of reindeer, bison, wolves and wolverine, deposited over 90,000 years ago. The entrance to the caves includes an extensive shop and pleasant tearooms, and you can view an audiovisual presentation about the caves and the area.

While Stump Cross Caverns give a taste of the region's underground delights, **Brimham Rocks** (Ⓦwww.brimhamrocks.co.uk) do the same for the surface. An extensive area (around 20 hectares, or 50 acres) of tortured rock formations created over 300 million years ago by wind, water and ice erosion, the rocks are laced through with footpaths and opportunities for clambering among the nightmarish shapes.

How Stean Gorge

Beyond **Lofthouse** at the northern end of Nidderdale, a road off to the left leads to Nidderdale's main attraction, **How Stean Gorge** (Mon–Fri 10am–5pm, Sat, Sun & school hols 10am–6pm; £5.50; ☏01423/755 666, Ⓦwww.howstean.co.uk), a great ravine gouged out by the rushing waters of a tumultuous stream, which, despite first appearances, is remarkably user-friendly. The path that winds along above the river is manageable for most people, though you need to be relatively able-bodied if you want to take one of the paths or flights of steps down to the water. A short walk upriver brings you to the **How Stean Tunnel** and a statue of Aslan from the Narnia stories, while downstream there's an overhang that forces you to walk in a crouch, two footbridges across the gorge (one, a girder, flexes alarmingly as you cross, the other, made of wood, doesn't), and the entrance to **Tom Taylor's Cave**, a bat- and spider-thronged tunnel which comes out at the top end of the car park (the faint-hearted can skip this bit). At the bottom of the gorge there's access to huge flat rocks from which you can dangle your feet, and everywhere there are excellent information boards to tell you about the geology, history and wildlife that you are experiencing.

You may notice in places fixed ladders, steel cables and beams crisscrossing the gorge. These are for the **Via Ferrata** ("Iron Way") courses that are put on in the gorge – for £45 (book via the website) you can treat yourself to three hours of expert-accompanied wading through waterfalls, rock traversing, abseiling, scrambling up ladders and along beams, with, at the end, your very own DVD of the experience recorded on the guide's head-cam. Invigorating or insane, depending on your point of view. Though How Stean Gorge might not suit those with extreme claustrophobia, arachnophobia or vertigo, it is a lovely way to spend anything from a couple of hours to a whole day. Wear appropriate clothing (especially shoes); hard hats are provided and torches can be rented. The ticket office is in a café with a terrace (the cakes are delicious).

Finally, before leaving Nidderdale do drive up to **Middlesmoor**, the hill village at the head of the valley. A centre for moorland paths and birdwatching, there's nothing much to detain you, but the views down the dale towards Gouthwaite Reservoir are out of this world.

Dentdale

Dentdale, at around ten miles, is one of the shorter of the Yorkshire Dales. It is also one of the most beautiful, named after its only village of any size – Dent – and not after the River Dee which runs through it, rising not far from the sources of the Ribble, but flowing in the opposite direction. The **Dentdale Explorer** bus travels from Dent station, via Dent itself, to Sedbergh, but only on a Saturday. The **tourist information centre** is at Sedbergh.

The valley is a picture of rural peace and quiet, with the road running beside the river with its succession of waterfalls, and crossing bridges to change banks. You're likely to see a lot of walkers, since the Dales Way also runs down the valley bottom. Finally the road crosses the river one more time and enters the delightful village of Dent.

Dent

DENT really is picture-postcard pretty, with cobbled streets, whitewashed stone cottages, two lovely pubs, a few shops and cafés and an interesting church. A good place to start a walk around the village is the car park where context boards include an excellent relief plan of the village, information about its history and suggested walks in the area. Turning left out of the car park opposite the **Memorial Hall** (built as a Church of England elementary school in 1845) you come to a crescent – following it around brings you first to the *Sun Inn*, then to the *George and Dragon* (see below). Opposite the latter is a modernistic fountain, appropriately made of a giant rock, installed in honour of locally born geologist **Adam Sedgwick** (1785–1873), famous for his work on geological classification. The son of the local vicar, he attended Sedbergh School and Cambridge University, and became one of the founders of modern geology. He was an early influence on Charles Darwin, though strongly disagreed with his theory of evolution by natural selection.

Within the centre of the crescent is **St Andrew's** parish church, which offers fascinating glimpses into Dent's past. The first thing you see as you enter is a bicycle-wheeled hand-cart. Next (if walking clockwise), on the wall about halfway down the nave, is the Sill Memorial, dedicated to brothers who made a fortune in the West Indies and returned to Dent with slaves, causing a furore among local people. Along this wall are a double row of the church's seventeenth-century box pews. The final two pillars in the nave are part of the original Norman church. Along the south aisle are a desk from the old village grammar school, what's left of a Jacobean three-decker pulpit, several windows dedicated to the Sedgwick family and a memorial to its most famous son, Adam (see above).

Accommodation

George and Dragon Dent ☎01539/625 256, ⓦ www.thegeorgeanddragondent.co .uk. Opposite the fountain in the centre of the village, the *George and Dragon* is bigger than the *Sun*, with slightly more of a hotel feel to it. Ten comfortable rooms (though some are small) good service and convivial bar. ❸

Sun Inn Dent ☎01539/625 208. Nice old-fashioned little pub in the centre of the village, with three basic rooms at £37 per night. ❶

Sedbergh

From Dent the road continues along Dentdale for four miles to Sedbergh (which, although in Cumbria since 1974, still thinks of itself as part of Yorkshire, and is within the bounds of the Dales National Park). As you enter the town, on the left is probably its greatest claim to fame – the public (ie private) **Sedbergh School** established in 1525 and to this day largely made up of boarders. An interesting archive covering the school's almost five-hundred-year history is open to the public (Mon–Fri 9am–1pm, plus Tues 2–5pm; free; ☎015396/22275), and you can arrange to be shown around the school itself by phoning the archivist – a wonderful opportunity to get an insight into a "public school", one of England's great establishment institutions. Wordsworth's son and grandson were alumni (the latter's name can still be seen carved on a desk), and Coleridge once taught here (and was apparently dismissed for drunkenness). Best-known of more recent pupils are rugby players Will Carling, Will Greenwood and Phil Dowson.

Beyond the school playing fields lies the town of **SEDBERGH**. The narrow Main Street turns right off the tiny town square, where the **tourist office** and **National Park Centre** (daily 10am–5pm; ☎015396/20125) are located on the left, about halfway down – there's a **car park** immediately behind. Sedbergh is a pleasant Dales town with a good choice of shops. In particular, since 2006 it has taken its place alongside Hay-on-Wye (Wales) and Wigtown (Scotland) as England's "book town", boasting so far nine secondhand and antiquarian bookshops, a **Festival of Ideas** each July, and a **Festival of Books and Drama** in September. It's not in the same league as Hay-on-Wye, but it's early days yet.

Other things to look out for are several cannons (at the entrance to Davis Yard, and outside Cannon House on Back Lane), said to have been dumped by Bonnie Prince Charlie's fleeing army during the 1745 Jacobite Rebellion, and a large chimney (in Weaver's Yard) in which the defeated Pretender apparently hid before fleeing in disguise. For further details ask at the tourist office for *A Walk around Sedbergh Town* (free). **St Andrew's Church** is worth a look, too, especially for its late Victorian stained-glass east window, notable in that its depiction of Jesus recruiting Peter and Andrew on the shores of the Sea of Galilee spreads across all five lancets.

The town also boasts a post office with its own pleasant café and, just outside the town, **Farfield Mill Arts and Heritage Centre** (Easter–Sept daily 10.30am–5pm; £3; ☎015396/21958, Ⓦwww.farfieldmill.org), which features art, textile and jewellery exhibitions, displays, workshops and events. There are galleries, working looms and a café, all beautifully housed in a Victorian woollen mill. Finally, two miles southwest of the town is **Holme Open Farm** (March–Sept Mon & Wed–Sun 11am–4pm; £3.50; ☎015396/20654, Ⓦwww.holmeopenfarm .co.uk), a traditional working farm where the animals can be held and fed. There's a nature trail, play and picnic areas, a café and gift shop, and the opportunity to see badgers in the wild.

Wensleydale

The best-known and most populous dale in the National Park is **Wensleydale**, which slashes across the northernmost reaches of the southern dales and is named Wensleydale after the not-very-important village of **Wensley**. Its river, the Ure, heads east, joining the Nidd just northwest of York and becoming the Ouse. Wensleydale has the only main road in the north dales, the A684, which joins Kendal in the Lake District with Northallerton on the edge of the North York Moors. It also has numerous towns and villages, the biggest and busiest being **Hawes**, and therefore is the easiest dale in which to find accommodation, and is the best for even non-enthusiastic walkers to potter around in. Besides, it is the source of one of the world's great cheeses, made even more popular by Wallace and Gromit. There are **tourist information centres** at Hawes and Leyburn. Public transport down Wensleydale from Hawes is fairly good – the #156, the #157 and a postbus travel to Northallerton via Bedale and Layburn, but above Hawes is much more problematic – where it exists, it involves a combination of bus and train, with some walking as well. Travel between Wensleydale and other places involves at least one change.

Hawes

Lying at the head of the valley, **HAWES**, Wensleydale's principal settlement, is accessible from the east and west via the A684, though its most attractive approach is from the south, over the top from the head of Wharfedale via beautiful, empty Langstrothdale and the 20° hill down into the town. As you'd expect of the region's main village, Hawes has a good range of shops, pubs and cafés, plenty of places to stay, and even a number of tourist attractions, including a moderately impressive little waterfall just up from the bridge which crosses it. Thronged with walkers throughout the year, Hawes has an independent life of its own – a fact emphasized by its busy and long-lived (established 1699) Tuesday **market**, ever thronged with farmers as well as visitors, and the livestock mart at the eastern edge of the town (auctions are on Tues, and sometimes Thurs and Sat).

Information, accommodation and eating

An essential first stop when visiting the area is the town's recycled former railway station. It contains the **National Park** and **tourist information** centres (daily 10am–5pm; closed Jan; ☎01969/666 210), plus a museum (see p.208), and is a veritable one-stop-shop: load up with information on what to do and where to go, stock up with maps, walking guides, equipment and outdoor clothes.

As befits a major walking centre, Hawes offers a range of **accommodation** and places to eat, mostly, but not all, in **pubs**.

Bulls Head Market Place ℡01969/667 437, ⓦwww.bullsheadhotel.co.uk. Looks and feels like a pub, but it isn't. Varied rooms, some quite small, all en suite. Right in the centre of Hawes, so the fact that it's not licensed doesn't much matter. ❷

Chaste Market Place ℡01969/667 145. Nice restaurant which offers good, largely sourced food in a relaxed atmosphere.

Crown ℡01969/667 2120. Another walkers' pub with good atmosphere, real ales and fires, outdoor seating and rooms. ❷

The Fountain ℡01969/667 206. Substantial seventeenth-century pub/hotel in the Market Place which offers pub grub and good beer. ❷

The Green Dragon Hardraw ℡01969/667 392. A pretty stone pub with stone flags, open fires, rag rugs, settles, comfortable rooms and suites. Offers access to Hardraw Force (see p.209). ❸

Hawes YHA Lancaster Terrace ℡0870 770 5854, ⓦwww.yha.org.uk. Modern hostel on the edge of town. Some twin and family rooms, otherwise dorm beds from £13.95. Closed Nov–Feb. ❶

Herriotts ℡01969/667 536. Combined B&B and coffee shop which dominates Main St, *Herriotts* offers not only seven comfortable rooms at reasonable rates, but also good food, exhibitions of paintings by local artists and transport for walkers. ❸

Old Board ℡01969/667 223. Pleasantly renovated town centre inn offering a warm atmosphere and hearty food. Much used by walkers. ❷

Old Dairy Farm Widdale ℡01969/667 070, ⓦwww.olddairyfarm.com. Once the home of the original Wensleydale herd, this old farm is now a top-class restaurant and B&B, with contemporary styling and the feel of luxury. In the middle of nowhere, halfway towards the Ribblehead Viaduct. ❺

Stone House Hotel Hawes ℡01969/667 571, ⓦwww.stonehousehotel.co.uk. Country house hotel just north of Hawes in a stunning old building set in magnificent country-side. Old-fashioned decor, traditional food, welcoming bar – all you'd expect from a country house hotel. ❺

The Dales Countryside Museum

In the same building as the tourist information centre is the excellent **Dales Countryside Museum** (hours as National Park Centre, last admission 4pm; closed Jan; £3; ℡01969/666 210), housed in what were once the station's buildings and in three railway carriages attached to a tank engine, looking for all the world as if it has just steamed in. The imaginatively mounted displays cover the geology, wildlife, history, agriculture, industry, transport, domestic life, education and leisure of the region – in fact, of every conceivable aspect of life. You start in the main station building, continue through the railway carriages standing at the platform, and end in the railway shed. Look out for the simulated lead mine, the Roman soldier and milestone, the school room equipment and the evocative children's toys. And don't ask for help from the two walkers consulting a map in the last carriage – they're part of a display.

The Ropemakers of Hawes

At the other side of the station car park, and well worth a look, is the **Ropemakers of Hawes** (Mon–Fri 9am–5.30pm; free; ℡01969/667 487, ⓦwww.ropemakers .co.uk), a working rope manufacturer (Outhwaites Ltd). It's a good example of what the people of Wensleydale seem to excel at – going about their business but adding strings to their bows by opening up for visitors. Most of us give ropes little thought, perhaps even assuming that they largely belong to the past, but a visit to Outhwaites soon puts this right. They make general-purpose rope and string, but also church bell ropes, banister ropes and everything from skipping ropes to carrier bag handles – the list seems endless. Far from being on the edge of extinction, the demand for rope seems incredibly buoyant – sales of bell ropes, for example, doubled in 1999 and 2000 as a result of the bell-ringing that greeted the new millennium. You can see various products being made on a guided, or self-guided,

Walks and waterfalls around Hawes

Beyond Hawes itself, there's excellent walking. Visitors are requested to keep strictly to the paths, though – the revival in grass meadows is very welcome, and leads to wonderful displays of flowers in the spring and summer, but their principal function is to grow grass to be turned into winter fodder for the animals, not to set urban hearts aflutter. A couple of waterfalls make a good target for two short walks from the town:

Aysgill Force (4 miles)

Off the road south towards Langstrothdale, **Aysgill Force** is just upriver from Gayle Bridge and Gayle Mill, and is really impressive only when there's been a lot of rain. From the centre of Hawes take the footpath that starts directly across from the *White Hart* pub. Follow the path uphill behind the Wensleydale Creamery to **Gayle**, walk through the village, then continue along the path with the Gayle Beck to your left to the waterfall. If you want to return by a different route, continue along the Beck until you get to a green lane, then bear right, walking back towards Hawes. When you get to a tarmac road, carry on straight for about 550 yards, then turn right onto a finger-post-marked path which brings you out back at the Wensleydale Creamery.

Hardraw Force (3.5 miles)

Northwest of the town, **Hardraw Force** is much more awe-inspiring than Aysgill Force, at nearly 100ft (30m) being the highest single-drop waterfall in England (above ground at least). From the **Dales Countryside Museum** car park in Hawes follow the Pennine Way north of the old platforms. About 100 yards beyond, follow the paved path off to the left which crosses two fields before rejoining the road. After crossing Haylands Bridge, turn right along a marked public footpath that climbs across a field towards Stone House. Cross the road, and continue up the path to the hamlet of **Sedbusk**. Here you can either cross the village green and follow the signposted path west to **Simonstone**, or if you'd prefer easier walking, take the lane parallel to the path. At Simonstone bear left down the hill to Hardraw, where access to the Falls is through the delightful *Green Dragon Inn* (see p.208). The downside is that there's a charge of £2, payable at the pub, which gets you onto the path to the falls (it's on private land); the waterfall really is worth shelling out for.

Other walks

Apart from these two strolls, there are numerous way-marked walks all around Hawes, and details can be picked up at the tourist information and National Park centres. For the general rambler, Harvey's **Hawes Walks** (£2.50) manages to get eight relatively easy-to-follow walks and a lot of information onto a single sheet. More intrepid walkers might want to follow the seven-mile route through Gayle, up onto the Roman Road (Cam High Road), around Wether Fell then down through Burtersett and back to Hawes, or the ten-mile walk through Gayle, along Gaudy Lane to Tarney Fors, then back via Appersett to Hawes.

tour of the works – the processes of ropemaking are, against all expectations, fascinating.

Wensleydale Creamery

The story of **Wensleydale Creamery** (Mon–Sat 9.30am–5pm, Sun 10am–4.30pm, winter opening times vary; Cheese Experience £2.50; ☎01969/667 664, ⓦwww.wensleydale.co.uk), which makes delicious traditional Wensleydale cheeses using milk from local farms on the southern edge of Hawes, is a heart-warming one. Established in 1150 by Cistercian monks, the creamery made cheese continuously in the dale for over eight hundred years. Having survived the 1930s Great Depression with the support of local people, it finally appeared to have bitten the dust in 1992. But then a miracle happened – a group of ex-managers and a local businessman carried out a successful management buy-out, the creamery was reopened, and a loss of 59 jobs was turned into the creation of more than 200. So successful has the operation been since then that the company has enjoyed a recent triple whammy: a £750,000 expansion programme was announced in 2010; the creamery is bidding to secure Protected Designation of Origin status, whereby non-Yorkshire cheese (more than half the "Wensleydale" sold in the UK) wouldn't be allowed to call itself Wensleydale; and the endorsements of several celebrities have been added to that of Wallace and Gromit (who announced that the Moon was made of Wensleydale) – Radio 2 DJ Chris Evans, cricketer Darren Gough and politician William Hague to name but three. Today you can watch cheese being made, visit the Wensleydale Creamery museum of cheesemaking (there's an excellent ten-minute video), its restaurant and coffee shop – with most of the dishes involving, of course, Wensleydale cheese – its gift shop, and the wonderful specialist cheese shop where you can stock up on all manner of sizes and flavours of cheese.

Gayle Mill

Just up the road from the Wensleydale Creamery is **Gayle Mill** (March–Oct Tues–Sat 1hr tours 11am, 12.30pm, 3pm & 4.30pm, £5; 1st Sun of month 2hr demonstration tour 2pm & 3.30pm; £10; ℡01969/667 320, Ⓦwww.gaylemill .org.uk), a restored mill which started life in 1784 as a textile mill but was converted into a sawmill in 1878, with the waterwheel being replaced by water turbines. In the early twentieth century the turbines were harnessed to generate electricity, and a gas engine installed as back up for when there wasn't enough water to drive the turbines. Abandoned in 1988, Gayle Mill was finally restored by the North of England Civic Trust and is operated by the Gayle Mill Trust as a visitor attraction, an education centre and a commercial sawmill, as well as selling green electricity to the National Grid. Viewing of the mill is by tour only and wooden products made at the mill are on sale.

Askrigg

As you travel down Wensleydale from Hawes, a short diversion off the main road at Bainbridge takes you to **ASKRIGG**, best known as the setting for the TV adaptations of James Herriot's books *All Creatures Great and Small* (though the vet himself lived and worked in Thirsk, see p.227, on the edge of the North York Moors) – the real life *Kings Arms* made many appearances as the *Drover's Arms*. The village's Grade I medieval church, **St Oswald's**, is worth a few minutes. The free information card draws attention to the fine beamed nave ceiling, the very old font mounted on a millstone and the numerous seventeenth- and eighteenth-century memorials. It even invites you to stop by and meet the vicar. The rest of the village is clustered around the curved and climbing Main Street.

Aysgarth

The next village east along the A684 is **AYSGARTH**, which gives its name to **Aysgarth Force**, its triple waterfall. The upper falls can be seen from the road where it crosses Yore Bridge, and there's an attractive eighteenth-century mill complex next to it which contains the *Mill-Race Teashop*, but the middle and lower falls to the east are better value. There's a fine **National Park Centre** and **café** with a large car park just off the A684 between the upper and middle falls, well placed for all three. A pleasantly wooded walk along the bank high above the river gives access to the two lower falls – the middle falls via a flight of steps down to a viewing platform (which keeps you at arm's length), the lower falls down steps to extensive flat rocks beside the cascade. Don't expect the Niagara Falls – they're fairly low key – but the staircase of broken water and the continual roar were impressive enough to be used as a setting for Robin's fight with Little John in Kevin Costner's *Robin Hood, Prince of Thieves*. Warning signs tell you not to stray off the marked paths, and you certainly feel that if you fell into the river here you wouldn't stand much chance.

Castle Bolton

A ten-minute drive (or scenic four-hour way-marked circular walk) from Aysgarth brings you to the village of **CASTLE BOLTON** and its famous castle. Completed in 1399 for Richard le Scrope, **Bolton Castle** (March–Oct Tues–Sun 10am–5pm; £6.50; ☏01969/623 981, ⓦwww.boltoncastle.co.uk) is a splendidly preserved medieval fortress set in sweeping Dales scenery. Oddly, it's not on top of a hill, but halfway down a long slope, which you'd think would give attackers uphill from the castle an advantage. It's certainly of much interest to military architects, representing a time when the demands of defence were becoming balanced by those of domestic comfort. The castle saw Civil War action in 1645, was involved in the Pilgrimage of Grace in 1536 and served as a prison for Mary Queen of Scots in 1569. It was also mentioned in three of Shakespeare's plays – *Henry IV*, *Henry V* and *Richard III*. Visitors get a real feel for what it must have been like to live in medieval times, and much has been done to cater for families with children – there are several family trails to follow, children can dress up in appropriate costume before exploring the castle, there's a medieval nursery with authentic toys for them to play with, and there are special events, such as family fun days, an Armada Weekend and ghost tours, throughout the season. Interestingly, the castle is still owned by the original family – the current Lord Bolton is a direct descendant of le Scrope.

Although the castle is the main attraction, it's well worth popping into the church – another **St Oswald's** – which stands next to it. For a start, it's older than the castle by about seventy years, and its bare simplicity, with small windows, no aisles, and short tower, is pleasing. Note the very old font and the little window on the south side of the chancel, possibly a leper's window designed to allow those afflicted with the disease to participate in services without compromising the rest of the congregation. Local legend has it that Mary Queen of Scots attended a service in the church and expressed some sympathy with the Protestant faith. Hard to believe.

Wensley and Leyburn

From Castle Bolton the road rejoins the A684 just beyond **WENSLEY**. Though it has a fine church in **Holy Trinity**, an interesting, probably fifteenth-century bridge and is the location of **Bolton Hall**, where the owner of Bolton Castle lives (there's a memorial to the Scrope family in the church), there's not much here for the casual visitor. Receiving its charter in 1202, it was once the main village in the dale, but it seems never to have recovered from the plague in the sixteenth century.

Just over a mile beyond Wensley lies the bracing market town of **LEYBURN**, sitting on a hillside astride its three open squares – Market Place, Commercial Square (attached to each other) and, along the short High Street, Grove Square. A handsome town whose prosperity during the great age of coaching has left it with a generous stock of Georgian houses, it's a useful centre for exploring mid-Wensleydale, with a good **tourist information centre** (Easter–Oct daily 9.30am–5.30pm; Nov–Easter Mon–Sat 9.30am–4.30pm; ☏01748/828 747), several banks with ATMs, numerous pubs and hotels, and a range of shops. Leyburn hosts the **Dales Festival of Food and Drink** (Ⓦwww.dalesfestivaloffood.org) early in May each year.

Just west of the centre is Leyburn's crowning glory, the **Shawl**, a limestone escarpment that penetrates right into the centre of the town, which has been used as a recreation area since Victorian times and now offers open grassland, numerous benches and wonderful views across Wensleydale. Take Shawl Terrace which leads from Commercial Square through a kissing gate out on to the grass. The origin of the name "Shawl" is uncertain – it's probably the corruption of a Viking word for huts, or is perhaps derived from "Shaw Hill", meaning wooded hill. However local legend offers a much more romantic explanation. Mary Queen of Scots, the story goes, made an unsuccessful attempt to escape from Bolton Castle along the limestone crag that leads east to Leyburn. During her flight, she dropped her shawl, hence the name.

Other attractions offered by Leyburn all lie along the Harmby Road to the southeast of the town centre. First is the Leyburn station of the scenic **Wensleydale Railway** (up to 5 trains a day, depending on the season; check Ⓦwww.wensleydalerailway.com), a reopened section of the old Northallerton-Garsdale line. The 22-mile stretch from Leeming Bar on the A1 to Redmire is run by a private company, Wensleydale Railway PLC, not only as a visitor attraction, but also as a service to the people of the dale.

Beyond the station, off to the left, and next to each other on Leyburn Business Park, are two fine examples of Wensleydale's propensity for turning workplaces into visitor attractions. They are also great places to buy gifts with a difference. **The Teapottery** (April–Oct daily 9.15am–4.45pm; Nov daily 10am–4pm; Dec–March Mon–Sat 10am–4pm free; Ⓦwww.teapottery.co.uk) calls itself the "home of eccentric teapots", and it's a little gem. A visit to this small, modern factory can include a free tour of the workshops where the teapots are made, with unfussy information boards giving clear explanations of each stage in the production process, and a visit to the factory shop which is packed with teapots of all shapes and sizes, all of them wildly eccentric as promised – policemen's helmets, guitars, old-fashioned radios, wheelbarrows, toasters where the toast has just popped up. Some of the stock was specifically commissioned – Colman's mustard pots, for example, or Aga Rayburn stoves – while the profusion of caravans is explained by the popularity of this type of holiday in the area, and the proximity of a caravan site.

What the teapottery does for teapots, the **Little Chocolate Shop** (Mon–Fri 9am–5pm, Sat 10am–4pm; ☎01969/625 288, Ⓦwww.thelittlechocolateshop.co.uk) does for confectionery, and it's right next door. Displays deal with the geography and history of the confection, different types of chocolate and their production methods, and you can see the processes in action yourself through viewing windows. The shop is a chocoholic's delight, with traditional chocolates (boxes and pick-and-mix), chocolate bars, fudge and, great fun, chocolate shoes that look good enough to wear or eat and novelty figures like farm animals and steam trains.

Middleham

South of Leyburn, across a castellated bridge which was originally a suspension bridge built in 1829, is another fine market town, **MIDDLEHAM**, centred on a sloping market square with good views of the surrounding countryside. The cobbled market place contains a cross which dates back to the town's charter in 1388 and four good pubs (see p.213).

Beyond the market place stands the impressive Norman **Middleham Castle** (April–Sept daily 10am–6pm; Oct–March Sat–Wed 10am–4pm; £4; EH), which replaced an earlier motte and bailey some 550 yards away. Both were designed to protect the main road from Richmond to Skipton. The castle built in the 1170s was militarily functional, but was developed to provide more comfortable living accommodation (à la Bolton Castle, see p.211) in the fourteenth and fifteenth centuries. This was the much-loved fortified palace where Richard III spent much of his childhood – hence the name of the pub in the square. The connection with Richard III is marked, too, by the remains of a second market cross, on Castle Hill, which was erected to commemorate the 1479 granting of a further market charter by Richard when he was still Duke of Gloucester.

Two miles beyond Middleham, across open countryside used by local stables as gallops (Middleham is at the hub of a major horse-training area, with around fifteen stables) is the **Forbidden Corner** (April–Oct Mon–Sat noon–6pm, Sun 10am–6pm; Nov–Dec Sun only; £10; ☎01969/640 638, ⓦwww.theforbidden corner.co.uk), an attraction which is easier to enjoy than to describe. It's a sort of walk-through puzzle, a fantasy labyrinth of spirits, giants, monsters and much else. You walk from area to area via paths and tunnels, coming across follies, surprises and riddles at every turn, egged on by mysterious voices that talk to you in rhyme as you approach. In the garden of Tupgill Park, the Forbidden Corner was put together by owner C.R. Armstrong for his children. It was opened up once for charity, and was such a success that it was further developed and is now a popular and unique Wensleydale attraction. There's a café and gift shop, and across the road to the main entrance, a pleasantly wooded picnic area. Entry is by pre-bought ticket only – you can't just turn up on the day (phone ahead, or go to Leyburn tourist information centre on the day, where a limited number of tickets are available on a first-come-first-served basis).

The pick of the four **pub/hotels** in the market place is the *White Swan* (☎01969/622 093; ❸). The look is contemporary, with stripped pine or stone-flagged floors, nicely turned out bedrooms with cool decor, and a fashionable brasserie-style eating area. There's little to choose between the other three, which are all nice traditional pubs with comfortable bars, flowery bedrooms, and a number of references to the area's connection with the training of horses: *The Black Bull* (☎0845 873 2174; ❷); *The Black Swan* (☎01969/622 221; ❸) and *The Richard III* (☎01969/623 240; ❸).

Jervaulx Abbey

Returning to Middleham, continued progress down Wensleydale along the A6108 will bring you **Jervaulx**, the remains of one of Yorkshire's three great Cistercian abbeys, the others being Fountains (see p.178) and Rievaulx (see p.235). Established in 1156, and a short walk from the main road, Jervaulx Abbey is privately owned, beautifully sited, and atmospheric to a fault. Looking very natural and un-buffed-up, it can seem a little disappointing, and it has no visitor centre, café or gift shop. And yet it's a sort of do-it-yourself attraction. Entry is free, though donations can be made and publications are paid for via an honesty box. There's a tearoom just across the main road. Above all, to serious students of ecclesiastical architecture it's almost a one-stop-shop, with "something of nearly everything monastic" (Pevsner). Try to visit in spring, when the whole site is carpeted in wild flowers.

Masham

The next town of any size as you travel down Wensleydale is **MASHAM**, famous among tipplers for its two highly regarded breweries (the town's name is, alas, pronounced "Mass'm", whereas "Mash'em" would be much more appropriate). The production of industrial quantities of beer would, you'd have thought, dominate the town, but in fact as you park in the large and attractive Market Place you wouldn't know that the two breweries are there – apart, perhaps, from the smell of hops. The square itself is surrounded by mellow cottages, has a market cross surrounded by trees, maps of the town and of local walks, the substantial *Kings Head Hotel*, independent shops selling, for example, old-fashioned sweets ("Bah, Humbug") and ice cream (Joneva), several restaurants and the very good-value *Bordar House Teas*. Try to visit Masham on a Wednesday or Saturday, when the **Market Place** fills with stalls. St **Mary's Church**, also in the Market Place, has monuments to the families who occupied Low Burton Hall (the splendidly named Sir Marmaduke Wyvill) and Swinton Park (the even more splendidly named Sir Abstrupus Danby). The former's tomb has Sir Marmaduke and his wife lying on their sides, heads propped on elbows as if they're lying on the beach. The church's most outstanding monument, though, is the early ninth-century Anglo-Saxon shaft that stands outside, just in front of the porch, which has detailed carvings of animals and legends in four tiers, alas heavily eroded.

As for the breweries: **Theakston's** (tours daily: Jan–June & Sept–Dec 10.30am–4.30pm; July & Aug 10.30am–5.30pm; brewery tours £5.75; ℡01765/680 000, Ⓦwww.theakstons.co.uk), makers of the famous Old Peculier bitter, is the original one built in 1875, and just off the Market Square, well hidden yet well signposted along a narrow lane – look out for the square, iron-strapped chimney; the **Black Sheep Brewery** (Sun–Wed 10.30am–4.30pm, Thurs–Sat 10.30am–11pm; brewery tours £5.95; ℡01765/680 101, Ⓦwww.blacksheepbrewery .com), again not far from the centre on Gun Hill, is the newcomer, set up in 1992 by Paul Theakston, a member of the great brewery family who didn't agree with the takeover of the family firm by big boys Scottish and Newcastle. The name Black Sheep speaks for itself.

Both breweries are overwhelmingly welcoming – both have pub-style bars in excellent visitor centres, offer guided tours, and have shops overflowing with beer and branded goodies. Theakston's gives you, too, a glimpse into a genuine traditional cooper's workshop, while the Black Sheep Brewery has a large bistro with an extensive menu. You can imagine that there's keen competition between the two concerns – Theakston's flagship *White Bear Hotel* stands cheek-by-jowl with the Black Sheep Brewery. But for the visitor competition certainly seems to work – both breweries, and indeed Masham as a whole, make for a wonderful day (or more) out.

Accommodation

The Kings Head Market Place ℡01765/689 295, Ⓦwww.kingsheadmasham.com. A splendid late Georgian building right on the main square, the *Kings Head* has 27 renovated and cheerfully decorated rooms. ❸

🏃 Swinton Park ℡01765/680 900, Ⓦwww .swintonpark.com. The ancestral home of the Cunliffe-Lister family about a mile from Masham, *Swinton Park* styles itself a "luxury castle hotel" and that is precisely what it is. Set in 200 acres of parkland, lakes and gardens it offers fine dining, luxurious individually designed rooms all with lovely views, a spa, and service which is attentive without being intrusive. It must have, too, one of the most innovative managements in the country, offering specialist cookery courses, a host of special events including horse whispering, alfresco dining and even bicycle polo. ❻

The White Bear Hotel Wellgarth ℡01765/689 319, Ⓦwww.thewhitebearhotel.co.uk. Theakston establishment sitting right next to competitor Black Sheep's brewery. Calm, cool decor within walking distance of the town centre. Includes breakfast. ❹

Bedale

Worth a detour north from Masham is **BEDALE**, a handsome town with a long, wide market place in which Tuesday markets have been held since 1251, lots of independent shops, many with Georgian facades and an ancient market cross. On North End First, the extension of the market place beyond the cross, is the church of **St Gregory** and **Bedale Hall**, home to the **tourist information centre** (Easter–Oct Mon–Fri 10am–4pm, Sat 10am–2pm; Oct to mid-Dec & mid-Feb to Easter Tues 10am–4pm, Sat 10am–1pm; ☎01677/424 604, ⓦwww.bedale.org) and the local **museum**, and behind which is a surviving ice house.

To the north of the town centre at Aiskew Mill is **Big Sheep, Little Cow Farm** (playbarn daily 10am–5.30pm, farm tours 12.30pm & 2.30pm; £6.50; ☎01677/422 125, ⓦwww.farmattraction.co.uk), an extensive petting zoo, while near Bedale Beck, which takes water from nearby Swaledale, is the unique Grade II listed **Leech House**, used by an eighteenth- or early nineteenth-century apothecary to house his leeches – it's not open to the public, but can be viewed from outside. Also near the town, in Kirklington, is **Aerial Extreme** (Feb–Nov, days and time vary; £24; ☎0845 652 1736, ⓦwww.aerialextreme.co.uk), a must for adrenalin-junkies who like swinging around on ropes, wobbling across bridges, climbing walls and generally defying gravity. There's also paintballing, quad-biking, archery and clay-pigeon shooting. Finally, to the east of the Masham to Bedale road is **Thorpe Perrow Arboretum Bird of Prey and Mammal Centre** (daily: mid-Feb to mid-Nov 10am–5pm; mid-Nov to mid-Feb 11am–3pm; £7; ☎01677/427 203, ⓦwww.thorpperrow.com), with beautiful gardens, flying displays by hawks, owls and falcons and enclosures of meerkats, wallabies and squirrels.

On the road from Bedale to Leyburn on the A684 is **Constable Burton Hall**, one of England's most perfect, unaltered Georgian houses. Not to be confused with East Yorkshire's Burton Constable Hall, it was designed by John Carr of York, and built in 1762–68 for Sir Marmaduke Asty Wyville. The Wyville family are still in residence, and the grounds (though not the house) are open to the public (mid-March to Sept daily 9am–6pm; £4). A printed sheet is available to help identify the plants, with ten marked stops.

Swaledale

The northernmost of the Yorkshire Dales, running east parallel to Wensleydale, pretty **Swaledale** has a few small villages, a large number of field barns, and, at its eastern end, the impressive town of **Richmond**. The principal **tourist information centres** are in Richmond and Reeth.

Upper Swaledale

As you travel east from the source of the Swale high up on Stonesdale Moor, the first village in the valley is tiny **KELD**, haunt of sheep and hardy walkers, with memories of a lead mining past. There are a few houses, a large United Reformed Church, and a hotel – *Keld Lodge* (☎01748/886 259, ⓦwww.keldlodge.com; ❹), once a shooting lodge, then a youth hostel, now a pleasant hotel "for the active and relaxed" with some singles as well as double rooms – and that's about it. Travelling down-dale, you come to **THWAITE** (a scattering of houses and a red phone box) and then **MUKER**, which is well worth an hour's stop. The first substantial building you come to is the **Old School**, now a craft shop and gallery. You can't miss it – it's got a sheep sitting astride the roof ridge. There are two slate memorials on the outside of the building, to brothers Richard and Cherry Kearton of Thwaite, who went to school here. Richard was a renowned naturalist, Cherry a famous late nineteenth-century wildlife photographer. Other establishments in the village include Swaledale Woollens, *Muker Tea Shop* and the Village Store. Muker exudes a sense of community – apart from St Mary's Church, it has a Literary Institute (1868) which had a stock of over 600 books, a legacy of its nineteenth-century prosperity from lead mining, a Public Hall of 1922 and, of course, a pub – *The Farmers Arms* (℡01748/886 297), which, though it has no accommodation, does own a studio flat across the road (available at £270/week in high season). All in all, Muker appears, both in the past and up to the present, to punch well above its weight.

Continuing east, after about a mile look out just off the road for **Ivelet bridge**, a high single-span crossing that's often described as the most elegant bridge in Swaledale. The flat stones were, it is said, for resting coffins on, since, until the consecration of a graveyard in Muker in 1580, corpses had to be carried all the way to Grinton for burial. About two and a half miles further on, the village of **LOW ROW** boasts one of the best **gastropubs** in the Dales, the *Punch Bowl Inn* (℡01748/886 233, ⓦwww .pbinn.co.uk), which provides delicious, hearty English food in pleasant surroundings at reasonable prices, with main courses around £10 to £20.

Reeth

The main village in the dale is **REETH**, which lies where Arkengarthdale joins Swaledale. On a hillside gathered around a large, sloping, triangular and partially cobbled green, which offers wonderful views of the surrounding hills, Reeth's a village given over largely to walkers and other visitors. It's all stone cottages, Dales pubs, cafés and tearooms, with a newsagent's, an ice-cream parlour, post office/ corner shop, bookshop, gift shop, a small undistinguished church and a large war memorial with a flagpole. The **Swaledale Museum** (Easter–Oct Sun–Fri 10.30am–5.30pm; £3; ℡01748/884 118, ⓦwww.swaledalemuseum.org) beyond the post office, is very good of its kind, with displays, as you'd expect, about geology and prehistory, farming, lead mining and much else. There's a small café and a shop. The two **pubs** on the green – the *Kings Arms* (℡01748/884 259, ⓦwww.thekingsarms.com; ❸) and the *Black Bull* (℡01748/884 213, ⓦwww .theblackbullreeth.co.uk; ❸) – stand next to each other, with the posher *Burgoyne Hotel* (℡01748/884 292, ⓦwww.theburgoyne.co.uk; ❺) maintaining a dignified distance across the green. You'll notice that one of the signs over the door of the *Black Bull* is mounted upside down – a protest by a past landlord, apparently, over a disagreement with Dales National Park officials. The **National Park Centre** (April–Oct daily 10am–5pm; Nov–March Fri & Sat 10am–4pm; ℡01748/884 059) is next door to the pub, and is a wealth of information on the area, with excellent information boards on dry stone walls and barns, heather moorland, meadows, Swaledale sheep, lead mining and much else – half an hour spent reading them is amply repaid by increased understanding of what you're seeing as you explore the dale. Reeth **tourist information centre** is in the same building. And off Silver Street, on the road back to Muker, the **Reeth Dales Centre**, an artist's collective housed in a group of modern buildings, covers sculpture, clocks, furniture, paintings, glass and jewellery (opening hours vary according to the shop).

Richmond

Below Reeth, Swaledale broadens out, with the hills getting lower and flatter, until finally you enter the jewel of the north dales, **RICHMOND**. Built high above a bend in the River Swale, the town centre is easy to get your head around – an imposing **castle** on a crag towering over the north bank of the river, beyond which is a large, tinned-loaf shaped **Market Place** with the main streets radiating from it to the north and west. Further north still are a number of further attractions worth searching out – the Richmondshire Museum, the Theatre Royal, the Greyfriars Tower – and beyond the town limits **Easby Abbey** and the **Cumberland Tower**. But it's the castle and the Market Place that give Richmond its great character – fortunate, you can't help feeling, are the people who live here.

Information, accommodation and eating

At the corner of the Friary gardens is the **tourist information centre** (daily 9.30am–5.30pm; ℡01748/828 742). Bus route #30 links Richmond with the rest of Swaledale.

Frenchgate Hotel 59–61 Frenchgate ℡01748/822 087, ⓦwww.thefrenchgate.co.uk. Boutique hotel in a Georgian townhouse in the centre of Richmond. Superb restaurant (set meal of three courses, £34). Nine individually furnished rooms with lots of period detail and walled gardens. Parking at the rear. ⑥

Millgate House Millgate ℡01748/823 571, ⓦwww.millgatehouse.com. Fine, balconied eighteenth-century town-centre house set in riotously beautiful gardens. Rooms have Georgian proportions with contemporary decor. Breakfast is taken in opulent splendour (they only offer dinner to groups of sixteen or more, but there are lots of restaurants within a 5min walk). ④

Rustique Finkle St ℡01748/821 565, ⓦwww.rustiqueyork.co.uk. Sister of the restaurant of the same name in York. The clue to *Rustique*'s ambience lies in its name – it concentrates on rustic French food and wine in a bistro setting. Though the decor (posters, dancing girls and so on) might be thought a bit passé, the atmosphere is busy and cheerful, and the food's lovely, and very reasonably priced (two courses £11.95, three for £13.95).

Richmond Castle

Richmond Castle (April–Sept daily 10am–6pm; Oct–March Mon & Thurs–Sun 10am–4pm; £4; EH) is not only interesting in itself, but also has the most wonderful views from the top of the keep. Dating from as early as 1071, it is one of the oldest Norman stone fortresses in Britain, though the keep itself is later – between 1150 and 1180. Entry is through a well-stocked shop, there are walls and the cockpit garden to explore, the extensive interior lawns are ideal for kids to let off steam, there are picnic tables available, and the whole castle has well-judged information boards. The star turn is, without doubt, the massive keep, with its stone staircases, spacious main rooms and fine battlements, from which the views down into the town, across the turbulent Swayle, and out across the gentle surrounding countryside are out of this world. It's also well worth taking a stroll along **Castle Walk**, around the outside of the curtain walls: the views again and the roar of the river far below are magical.

Holy Trinity Church/Green Howards Museum

Whichever way around the castle you walk, you end up at the Market Place, sloping, cobbled and with one of the biggest market crosses you'll ever see, erected in 1771. Forming an island in the centre of the square, Holy Trinity Church is now occupied by the excellent **Green Howards Museum** (Feb–Nov daily 10am–4.30pm; £3.50; ℡01748/826 561, ⓦwww.greenhowards.org.uk). Regimental museums these days are often imaginatively organized and presented, none more so than this history of the Green Howards infantry regiment. Originally raised at the time of the Glorious Revolution (1688), the regiment was named, as was the custom, after their new commander, but with the word "green" (referring to the facing on their uniforms) added to distinguish them from an existing Howards regiment. Ranging across three floors, exhibits trace the work of the regiment chronologically, with documents, artefacts and photographs. The Harrison Gallery contains a huge collection of the regiment's medals – including a large haul of Victoria Crosses and two George Crosses – and there's a well-presented gallery of uniforms. As you enter you're greeted by a real jeep, in desert colours, apparently about to crush the reception desk. Much effort has gone into making the museum accessible and child-friendly, and to avoid being too gung-ho.

Richmondshire Museum and Greyfriars Tower

North of the Market Place, on Ryder's Wynd, is the **Richmondshire Museum** (April–Oct daily 10.30am–4pm; £2.50; ☎01748/825 611, ⓦwww.richmondshire museum.org.uk), a museum of local life set up by a branch of the Soroptimist Club (an association of professional and business women, since you ask), which covers lead mining, transport, village life, toys and so on, with reconstructed houses and shops, and even the Herriot set from *All Creatures Great and Small*.

North of Victoria Road lies Friary Gardens, which contain the impressive **Greyfriars Tower**. A new Franciscan monastery was started in 1500 to replace an earlier thirteenth-century one, but the project was overtaken by events when the dissolution of the monasteries took place in the 1530s, so the tower was all that got completed.

The Theatre Royal

Richmond's **Theatre Royal** (☎01748/825 252, ⓦwww.georgiantheatreroyal .co.uk), on the corner of Victoria Road and Friar's Wynd, is not only a present-day venue for music and drama, but also a Grade I listed building dating from 1788 – the oldest unchanged working theatre in the country. It's beautifully restored, and you can either attend a performance there or join one of the guided tours.

Cumberland Tower and Easby Abbey

Finally, on the outskirts of Richmond are a couple of attractions that are worth a visit – you can spot them from the walls of the castle. To the west is the **Cumberland Tower** (sometimes called the Culloden Tower), built to celebrate the defeat of Bonnie Prince Charlie's forces at the end of the 1745 Jacobite Rebellion at Culloden by the Duke of Cumberland (hence the two names it goes under). Having fallen into a sad state of disrepair, it was taken over and renovated by the Landmark Trust, and is therefore now available as holiday accommodation (ⓦwww.landmarktrust.org.uk).

About a mile to the east of the town centre, **Easby Abbey** (daily: April–Sept 10am–6pm; Oct & Nov 10am–5pm; Dec–March 10am–4pm; free; EH) was established in 1152 by Premonstratensian "white canons", a kind of radical splinter group of the Cistercians. Within pleasant walking distance from the centre of Richmond, the ruins are picturesque to a fault. Look out in particular for the thirteenth-century wall paintings in the Church of St Agnes in the grounds, the 1300 gatehouse and the largely full-height refectory. Often subjected to attack by the Scots, the abbey called in the English army for protection in 1346, an act which they were bitterly to regret. The drunken English soldiers in an orgy of unrestrained violence caused more damage than the Scots ever could have done.

The North York Moors

5

THE NORTH YORK MOORS

CHAPTER 5

Highlights

* **Feversham Arms** One of Yorkshire's top hotels containing one of its best restaurants, on the edge of one of its prettiest towns. See p.233

* **Rievaulx Terrace** A walk between two eighteenth-century temples along a broad grassy way, with planned views through the trees of Rievaulx Abbey below. See p.235

* **Castle Howard** An impressive stately home, still lived in by the family who built it. See p.236

* **Kirkham Priory** Ruins of an Augustinian Priory used to prepare soldiers for D-Day. See p.237

* **Eden Camp** A fascinating museum devoted largely to World War II, in a prisoner-of-war camp built by Italians captured in North Africa. See p.241

* **The Esk Valley** Rolling countryside in an unspoilt valley which you can explore on foot, on two wheels or four, or by train. See p.246

* **The 199 steps, Whitby** As the steps climb up onto the headland bearing St Mary's Church and Whitby Abbey, the picturesque town below slowly reveals itself. See p.249

* **Scarborough Castle** Interesting fortification of a commanding headland, with wonderful views out to sea and down across the town's two bays. See p.260

▲ The 199 steps, Whitby

The North York Moors

A swathe of almost unbroken countryside of understated beauty stretches along the eastern side of Yorkshire from the Tees in the north to the Humber in the south. Of this area, the **North York Moors National Park**, the **Hambleton Hills** Area of Outstanding National Beauty and the **Vale of Pickering** are all in North Yorkshire, and are covered in this chapter. The Wolds are largely in East Yorkshire, and appear in the next. Altogether, dotted as they are with towns and villages, stately homes and stone bridges, country churches and isolated farms, they represent one of England's largest and most attractive areas of open countryside. As a bonus, along the eastern edge of the National Park is one of Britain's finest stretches of **coast**. Apart from the joys of driving, cycling or hiking across this landscape, sailing off it, gliding over it or skydiving into it, other pleasures abound.

From just below Middlesbrough, moors and dales stretch south across the Cleveland Hills and Hambleton Hills. A clutch of towns along the Moors' western edge make suitable bases, including **Great Ayton**, **Osmotherley**, **Northallerton**, **Thirsk** – with a broad market place and a James Herriot connection – and **Helmsley**, a delightful town which boasts a castle and stately home and, just to its west, the wonderful medieval/Georgian double-whammy of **Rievaulx Abbey** and **Rievaulx Terrace**. Helmsley is also a good centre for visiting **Sutton Bank**, an escarpment overlooking the Vale of York, **Coxwold**, where Laurence Sterne, author of *Tristram Shandy*, lived, **Kilburn**, with the only "chalk horse" in the north carved into the hillside above it, and **Ampleforth College**, Britain's greatest Roman Catholic school. Further south stretch the **Howardian Hills**, whose principal visitor attraction is one of the greatest of England's great stately homes, **Castle Howard**.

The central North York Moors and the Vale of Pickering are probably best explored from **Pickering** itself, the southern terminus of the **North Yorkshire Moors Railway**. Striking south from Pickering the A169 gives access to theme park and zoo **Flamingo Land**, the terrific **Eden Camp**, an imaginative museum located in an ex-POW camp, and the pleasantly no-nonsense town of **Malton**.

North of Pickering lies a complicated network of country roads that meander hither and yon, through tiny hamlets, across stretches of moor, through woodland and across streams. **Hutton-le-Hole** is a pretty stone village set in a steep-sided valley around a sheep-dotted green, and is home to the **Ryedale Folk Museum**. Further north, the village of **Goathland** attracts the crowds because it is the setting for TV's *Heartbeat*, and also because it's a short walk from waterfall **Mallyan Spout**. To the east the **Dalby Forest** offers invigorating forest driving, walking, cycling and picnicking, whilst, on its edge, **Thornton-le-Dale** is one of the region's best-looking villages.

221

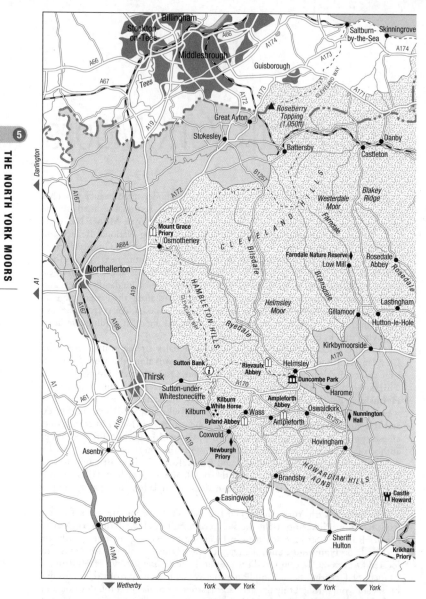

Across the north of the North York Moors lies one of the National Park's most appealing valleys – that of the **River Esk**, which empties into the North Sea at Whitby. Its appeal lies not only in the beauty of its surrounding farmland and moors, but in its lack of main roads – a skein of lanes and minor roads twist and climb between villages on either side of the river. Indeed, one of the best ways of seeing Eskdale isn't by road at all, but via the **Esk Valley Railway**, which links Whitby to Middlesbrough, and passes right along the valley. More generally, you

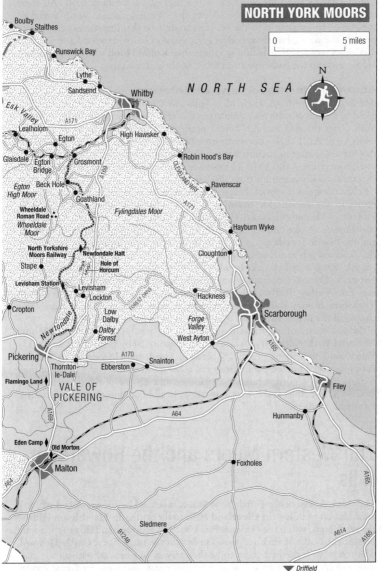

can explore the National Park further by rail if you change onto the North Yorkshire Moors Railway at **Grosmont**.

Finally, along the **North Yorkshire Coast**, three seaside towns with virtually no urban sprawl between them, all very different in character, punctuate a wonderful coastline. **Filey** is genteel, like a breath of early twentieth-century air, **Scarborough** is big enough to be both brash and stately, while **Whitby** seems to have everything – the striking ruins of an abbey overlooking the town, links with

Count Dracula and Captain Cook, and a fleet of busy fishing boats. All three resorts have fine blue-flag beaches. Along the coast in between, North Yorkshire sometimes flings itself in to the sea from a great height, sometimes slips quietly beneath the waves, but always offers great vistas of beach, headland and sea. And don't miss wonderful little fishing villages like **Robin Hood's Bay** and **Staithes**, hidden away in the landscape's odd folds, nooks and crannies.

Access, information and orientation

The North York Moors, Howardian Hills and Vale of Pickering are circumnavigated by a chain of main roads – imagine that they had been lassoed by the City of York. Thus the A19 and A172 head north on the western side up to Middlesbrough, the A171 curves eastwards from Middlesbrough to Scarborough, and the A64 strikes southwest back to York. This roughly kite-shaped area is bisected by one major route – the A170 Thirsk-to-Scarborough road. All the places in this chapter are easily accessible from these roads.

Public transport is remarkably good for a rural area. Several bus companies run routes in the region: for **buses** from Leeds, Tadcaster, York and Malton to Pickering, Thornton-le-Dale, Goathland and Whitby, go to Ⓦwww.yorkshire coastliner.co.uk; for buses in the northern area including Osmotherley, Cleveland and the North Yorkshire Coast, go to Ⓦwww.arrivabus.co.uk; and for buses in the Scarborough area including to Helmsley and throughout East Yorkshire, consult Ⓦwww.eyms.co.uk. In addition, from April to October the Moorsbus Network (Ⓦwww.moors.uk.net/moorsbus) provides an exellent service. Finally, the **Esk Valley Railway** (Ⓦwww.eskvalleyrailway.co.uk) and the **North Yorkshire Moors Railway** (Ⓦwww.nymr.co.uk) allow you to explore large chunks of the northeastern part of the region by train.

The best source of information for most of this area is the **North York Moors National Park Authority**, which has centres in Danby (see p.247) in the Esk Valley and Sutton Bank (see p.228) between Thirsk and Helmsley. The National Park produces a host of publications and other information – have a look at their website (Ⓦwww.northyorkmoors.org.uk) or pick up one of their excellent free guides *Out and About in the North York Moors*. In addition, most towns have tourist information offices.

The Western Moors and the Howardian Hills

The western edge of the North York Moors is defined by and contained within a great bracket of hills – the **Cleveland Hills** to the north, the **Hambleton Hills** to the west (both within the National Park), and the **Howardian Hills** to the south, outside the National Park and most famous for the magnificent **Castle Howard**. The towns with the best claim to be the gateway to this area, with an adequate choice of accommodation and with tourist information centres, are **Great Ayton**, **Northallerton**, **Thirsk** and **Helmsley**, but other places on the western edge of the area are well worth visiting too.

Great Ayton

Almost a suburb of Middlesbrough, which is only about five miles to the north (and was once in Yorkshire), **GREAT AYTON** is an attractive little town that has links to Captain Cook, and which offers access to the Cleveland Hills. The heart of the town is the single, long High Street, strung out along the River Leven from High Green to Low Green. On pleasant High Green stands a statue of the young James Cook, stripped to the waist and looking like a member of a boy band. At the opposite side of High Green is the **tourist information centre** (Mon–Sat 10am–4pm, Sun 10.30am–12.30pm; ☎01642/722 835), at which you can pick up sheets on local walks – to oddly shaped Roseberry Toppin for example (four miles or so), or the Captain Cook Monument (five miles), an impressive obelisk erected on the moors in 1827. Further down the High Street on the right is the **Captain Cook Schoolroom Museum** (daily: April–June, Sept & Oct 1–4pm; July & Aug 11am–4pm; £2; ☎01642/724 296, ⓦwww.captaincookschoolroommuseum.co .uk), occupying the school, opened in 1704, which he attended from 1736 to 1740. The museum includes a reconstruction of an eighteenth-century schoolroom, together with displays, many of them interactive, on his childhood, voyages, navigation methods and much else. On the other side of the road, in **Waterfall Park**, is a bright red Victorian urinal. You don't see one of those every day.

Osmotherley

Southwest of Great Ayton, and eleven miles north of Thirsk, just off the A19, the village of **OSMOTHERLEY** is making a name for itself as a walking centre for the Cleveland and Hambleton hills. It's on the long-distance Cleveland Way (see box below) and is the starting point for the 42-mile **Lyke Wake Walk**, which follows a moorland "burial route" and ends at Ravenscar on the coast. The walk started as a bit of fun in 1955, and completion entitles you to member-ship (free) of the Lyke Wake Club. Multiple completions can lead to the granting of a degree – Master (or Mistress) of Misery, Doctor of Dolefulness and Past Master or Mistress (see ⓦwww.lykewake.org). The walk is also connected to the traditional song *Lyke Wake Dirge*, recorded by, among others, Pentangle and Steeleye Span.

Grouped around Osmotherley's small green are three **pubs**, all of which offer accommodation: the *Three Tuns*, a restaurant-with-rooms and a lovely garden, (☎01609/883 301, ⓦwww.threetunsrestaurant.co.uk; ❹); the *Queen Catherine Hotel*, very much a traditional village pub (☎01609/883 209, ⓦwww.queen catherinehotel.co.uk; ❷); and the *Golden Lion* (☎01609/883 526, ⓦwww .goldenlionosmotherley.co.uk; ❸), a mellow place whose menu is strong on vegetarian and gluten-free options. There's also a hiking shop and a fish-and-chip shop. On the green is an ancient **market cross** and next to it the odd **barter table** made of stone. John Wesley is said to have preached from it during one of his many tours of England. The church, hemmed in by houses and accessible from the green through a narrow alley, is worth a quick look, with a lopsided interior caused by the fact that it has a south but no north aisle.

The Cleveland Way

One of the UK's twelve designated National Trails, the 110-mile-long **Cleveland Way** is distinctive in that it consists in almost equal parts of heather upland and coastal walking. It describes a great semicircle around the western, northern and eastern edges of the North York Moors, following the line of the Hambleton Hills, the Cleveland Hills and the Cleveland and Yorkshire coast. It starts at Helmsley, runs west along Sutton Bank, then swings north and east through Osmotherley and Great Ayton, before turning to follow the coast down through Staithes, Whitby, Robin Hood's Bay and Scarborough. It ends at Filey. For more information, see ⓦwww .nationaltrail.co.uk and ⓦwww.clevelandway.co.uk.

Mount Grace Priory

Two miles north of Osmotherley is fourteenth-century **Mount Grace Priory** (April–Sept Mon & Thurs–Sun 10am–6pm; Oct–March Thurs–Sun 10am–4pm; £4.50; ☎01609/883 494; NT), the best of ten Carthusian charterhouses in the country. Established in 1084 by St Bruno of Cologne, the order set up communities of hermits – an oxymoron if ever there was one – where each monk (or in some cases nun, as it was a mixed order) had their own cell, consisting of several rooms on two floors and a small walled garden. These cells, each with its own door, were located around the outskirts of the abbey grounds. Entrance to the priory is through the guesthouse, which was turned, after the dissolution, into a rather grand manor house. There's a reconstructed cell, an exhibition on the history of the priory, a children's story box and, during school holidays, special children's trails. The **gardens** teem with wildlife, including the famous priory stoats about which David Attenborough made a TV programme in 2005 – apparently they use the priory's drainage system as a way of creeping up undetected on their prey.

Northallerton

NORTHALLERTON is the county town of North Yorkshire, though its residents seem to feel that not enough people realize this. Located in the Vale of York between the two great North Yorkshire national parks, and between the two main north–south routes (the A1 and the A19), and serving as the region's market town, it's an excellent base for exploring the area. Consisting largely of a long and broad High Street, it has a good range of independent shops, including a branch of *Betty's*, the family-owned Barkers department store (🌐www.barkers-north allerton.co.uk) and a famous gourmet deli and café in *Lewis and Cooper* (🌐www .lewisandcooper.co.uk). But in terms of actual tourist attractions, even the town's own published material struggles to identify anything very riveting, though the site of the **Battle of the Standard**, which took place on the August 22, 1138, is worth a look. Marked by an obelisk beside the A167 north of town, and with an explanatory information board, the battle was between the English and the Scots, and was part of the chaotic struggle for supremacy between King Stephen, grandson of William the Conqueror, and his cousin, the Empress Matilda. Although outnumbered, the English won, largely thanks to their bowmen.

Accommodation and eating

Hotels

Allerton Court Hotel Darlington Rd ☎01609/780 525, 🌐www.allertoncourthotel.co.uk. On the outskirts of town, a modern hotel with a good reputation, clean contemporary decor and an attractive restaurant. ❸

Golden Lion Hotel 114 High St ☎01609/777 411, 🌐www.golden-lion-hotel.co.uk. Solid old coaching inn, dating from the 1730s, right in the heart of Northallerton. Old-fashioned, if a little florid, comfort, and efficient, friendly service. Can be noisy if there are functions on. ❹

🏃 **Solberge Hall Hotel** Newby Wiske ☎01609/779 191, 🌐www.solbergehall.co .uk. A handsome country house hotel five miles south of Northallerton. Beautiful setting, fine building, wonderful grounds. ❺

Cafés and restaurants

Betty's 188 High St ☎ 01609/775 154. Another of the top-end chain of Yorkshire tearooms, with delicious meals and cakes.

🏃 **Lewis and Cooper** 92 High St ☎01609/772 880. Famous for its deli and for its hampers, *Lewis and Cooper* also have lovely tearooms on two floors, offering wonderful cakes and lunches.

Tithe Bar and Brasserie 2 Friarage St ☎01609/778 482. Pleasant little brasserie, just off the High St, in what was once the town's tithe barn, where the church's cut of the harvest was stored. Three small bar areas downstairs, main restaurant on the first floor. Closes 11pm during the week, midnight Fri & Sat.

Thirsk

The busy market town of **THIRSK** is forever associated with vet James Herriot whose house (now a museum) is here, but was first mentioned in the Domesday Book. Lying along the Cod Beck river, it pleasantly clusters around a large cobbled square (markets Mon & Sat) many of whose buildings go back to the great days of coaching, when the town was an important stopping place on the way to Scotland. Two main streets run north from the Market Place – Kirkgate and Millgate, from the northwest and northeast corners respectively – while south is the sister village of **Sowerby**. Well north of the Market Place, at the end of Kirkgate, stands **St Mary's**, a product of the fifteenth and sixteenth centuries, which has been called the most spectacular Perpendicular church in North Yorkshire. There was once a castle, just west, but it survives now only in the names of the streets. Being on the edge of the National Park, Thirsk is a convenient centre for visiting not only the North York Moors but also the Yorkshire Dales. And, at the western edge of town is **Thirsk Racecourse** (℡01845/522 276, ⓦwww.thirskracecourse.net), a horseracing venue for over a century and a half.

Information, accommodation and eating

As you walk around the town you'll come across many information boards and blue plaques outlining Thirsk's history – you can pick up maps covering them all in the **tourist information centre**, 49 Market Place (Easter–Nov daily 10am–5pm; Dec–Easter Mon–Sat 10am–4pm; ℡01845 522 755, ⓦwww.visit-thirsk.com).

Charles' Bistro Bakers Alley, 27 Market Place ℡01845/527 444. Bistro food in a relaxed, friendly atmosphere and comfortable surroundings. Around £6–7 a dish, £9.95 for two courses, except Saturday night, when it's more expensive. Known for its steak pie. Closed Sun eve & Mon.

Gallery 18 Kirkgate ℡01845/523 767, ⓦwww.gallerybedandbreakfast.co.uk. An award-winning B&B housed in an eighteenth-century Grade II listed building across the road from the James Herriot Experience. It is on one of Thirsk's main streets, so it can get noisy at closing time, and parking is on-street or in a nearby public car park. Three comfortably furnished and decorated rooms, excellent breakfasts. ❷

Golden Fleece ℡01845/523 108, ⓦwww.goldenfleecehotel.com. Charming old coaching inn nicely located on Thirsk's large cobbled square. Attractive racing-themed *Paddock* bar, restaurant with locally sourced food, comfortable rooms, nice busy atmosphere. ❹

Oswalds Restaurant with rooms Front St ℡01845/523 655. Straightforward English menu with mainly locally sourced food in elegantly old-fashioned surroundings – bar with leather sofas, tables with white linen and candelabras. Look out for music-while-you-eat (jazz, recitals on the grand piano). Open for lunches and early evening dinners, till 9pm, Sat 9.30pm, Sun 8.30pm; closed Mon. More of a boutique hotel than the name would suggest, with individual and relatively luxurious rooms. ❸

The Poplars Carlton Miniott ℡01845/522 712, ⓦwww.thepoplarsthirsk.com. Near the station and the racecourse, *The Poplars* B&B offers both rooms and cottages (actually cabins) which are clean and adequately furnished. All rooms and cottages have own access. Cottages have a three-night minimum. ❷

The museums

Thirsk is now probably best known as James Herriot's Darrowby. Herriot (actual name Alf Wight) was a country vet in the town, and his series of affectionate and highly amusing tales about his life in the area, and his dealings with curmudgeonly and often tightfisted farmers, won a huge following, first from the books published from 1969 onwards, then from two feature films and the TV series *All Creatures Great and Small*. The house on Kirkgate in which he lived and worked is now the popular **World of James Herriot** (daily: April–Oct 10am–5pm; Nov–March 11am–4pm; £6; ℡01845/524 234, ⓦwww.worldofjamesherriot.org), which will delight fans of the books as they match up descriptions of the house with the reality on the ground. It is also a diverting museum of the social history of his time, and the only veterinary science museum in the country. There's an interactive room for kids to learn about veterinary science, displays of props used during filming of the TV series, and a documentary made especially for the museum.

The small **Thirsk Museum** (April–Oct Mon–Wed, Fri & Sat 10am–4pm; £2; ℡01845/527 707, Ⓦwww.thirskmuseum.org), on the same street, has all the things that local museums usually have – penny farthings and wash-day paraphernalia, dolls and butter-churns – located, interestingly enough in the house where **Thomas Lord**, professional cricketer and founder of Lord's Cricket Ground, was born in 1755.

The Ritz cinema

On Westgate you'll find the **Ritz Cinema** (Mon–Sat 9am–6pm; £4; ℡01845/524 751, Ⓦwww.ritzcinema.co.uk), a wonderful survival from the moving picture past. A mechanics institute in the nineteenth century, it became a cinema as early as 1912, and has gone through all the vicissitudes of cinema since then – a heyday from the 1920s to the 1950s, decline in the face of competition from the small screen, successive changes of name and ownership, conversion to a bingo hall, closures and finally, triumphant re-opening in its present form in 1995. It is now run by a volunteer management committee, and combines modern comfort and technology with an engagingly retro feel.

Monk Park Farm

About two and a half miles east of Thirsk, just south of the main A170 to Scarborough, a small children's attraction – **Monk Park Farm** (Feb–Oct daily 10.30am–5.30pm; £5; ℡01845/597 730, Ⓦwww.monkparkfarm.co.uk) makes a useful pit stop. Against the impressive backdrop of Sutton Bank in the distance, it offers children the chance to handle guinea pigs, feed lambs, see unusual breeds, let off steam in several play areas (including a giant sand pit), play on go-karts, and ride ponies (on weekends and holidays only). It also has a tearoom and indoor and outdoor picnic areas. Because of the animals, no dogs are allowed.

Sutton Bank

Approximately five miles east of Thirsk, after passing through the village of **SUTTON-UNDER-WHITESTONECLIFFE** – said to have the longest name in England – the road climbs to the top of **Sutton Bank**, a hill so long and steep (1:3) that cars towing caravans are not allowed to use it. The bank itself is beautifully wooded, and from the top the views back across the Vale of York are inspiring. One of two **North York Moors National Park Centres** (April–Oct daily 10am–5pm; Nov, Dec & mid Feb to March daily 11am–4pm; Jan to mid-Feb Sat & Sun 11am–4pm; ℡01439/770 657, Ⓦwww.northyorkmoors.org.uk) sits right atop the escarpment, and there are two information boards giving details of eight walks and six cycle rides of varying distances and difficulty starting from the centre to points of interest all over the area. The main **viewing point** on Sutton Bank is a two-minute walk away, and even the grounds of the centre have much of interest – you can watch birds feeding just outside the window through binoculars provided, and tick off the ones you see (though the bird-identification board next to the binoculars has at least one bird wrongly named).

On the southern edge of Sutton Bank, the **Yorkshire Gliding Club** (daily 9am–5pm; ℡01845/597 237, Ⓦwww.ygc.co.uk) is well worth a stop, if only for the breakfasts, lunches and teas at its clubhouse. There are splendid views – its location takes advantage of the fact that the escarpment faces west across the Vale of York, into the prevailing wind – and the opportunity to watch, or even take part in, this exhilarating pastime. A test flight costs as little as £88.50, and this entitles you to three months' membership which allows you to take further flights at members' rates. Bear in mind, though, that you have to be under 6' 2" tall and 16 ½ stone in weight. The clubhouse has not only a bar and restaurant, but also has rooms and self-catering kitchens for members. If you're not already an enthusiast, this could be the start of something big.

The Kilburn White Horse

Directly below the Gliding Club, on the face of Sutton Bank's escarpment, is the **Kilburn White Horse**, the only one of its type in the north of England. If you drive down the steep hill off to the right after the Gliding Club, you'll come to a car park. From here a footpath climbs steeply up to the right of the White Horse – if you follow it to the top and along the escarpment, you'll arrive back at Sutton Bank.

The Kilburn White Horse is not some ancient totem whose origins are lost in the mists of time. The horse was cut in 1857 on the initiative of a local man, Thomas Taylor of Kilburn, who had seen similar horses in the south of England and was determined to go one better in regard to size. It had become badly overgrown by 1925, so the *Yorkshire Evening Post* ran a campaign to have it restored. Reader subscriptions paid for its restoration, and the £100 left over was invested to provide for its upkeep. It had to be covered up during World War II, apparently, to prevent it becoming an aid to navigation for German bomber pilots. During protests against the recent hunting ban, a giant rider in full hunting pink suddenly appeared on the horse's back. The horse is made up of whitewashed limestone chippings – visitors are asked not to walk on the horse, as the chippings get moved and the image of the horse degraded. As it is, gravity was causing slippage, so boards have been pegged across the steepest parts to stop the gravel moving downhill. A Kilburn White Horse Association exists to raise money for continued maintenance (the money from the 1925 fundraising is presumably no longer enough) and also to look for a more permanent way of protecting the horse which isn't prohibitively expensive.

Kilburn village

KILBURN village itself, less than two miles south of Sutton Bank, is attractive enough, with its collection of stone cottages gathered around a tiny village square flanked by the *Forresters Arms* (℡0843/208 3374, ⓦwww.forrestersarms.fsnet .co.uk; ④), a traditional **pub** which offers accommodation and is much frequented

---

Robert Thompson, "Mouseman" of Kilburn

Born in Kilburn village in 1876, **Robert Thompson** followed in his father's footsteps as the local joiner and wheelwright. He developed an interest in traditional furniture styles of the seventeenth century, and started to design furniture in a similar mould, using only naturally seasoned English oak. At some point one of the craftsmen he was working with said that they were all "as poor as a church mouse", and this gave him the idea of signing his work with a little carved mouse. From then on, it adorned everything that he made. His business expanded after a commission for the headmaster of nearby **Ampleforth College** led him into ecclesiastical work for churches, convents and monasteries, though he still made domestic furniture as well. Today furniture is still designed and made in the traditional way in Robert Thompson's Craftsmen Ltd in the centre of the village. The factory is run by the mouseman's descendants and sells furniture all over the country and indeed the world. Items range from, say, a fruit bowl at £155 to a refectory table for £5500. Not cheap, but future family heirlooms.

by walkers, and Kilburn Village Stores. However, the person who has put Kilburn on the map is **Robert Thompson**, the famous "mouseman", whose work you'll find in churches all over this part of the country (see box, p.229).

The **visitor centre** (Easter–Sept daily 10am–5pm; Oct Tues–Sun 10am–5pm; Nov & Dec Wed–Sun 11am–4pm; £4; ☏01347/869 102, ⓦwww.robertthompsons.co.uk) is right in the centre of the village on the opposite side of the road to the pub, occupying what was the blacksmith's and joiner's shops. It consists of a café and shop, displays on the history of the village and on the White Horse and an informative video about Robert Thompson, the "mouseman" of Kilburn in the Shoeing Room, introduced by Robert's great-grandson, who you'll see around the place. There's also a fine little museum stuffed with examples of his work and photographs and documents concerning his life. Behind the centre is a garden which climbs up the hillside and offers views over the village towards the White Horse. Across the road is Robert's cottage, which now houses the showroom and offices, and the workrooms themselves with viewing galleries, full of large workbenches and workmen at their craft. Behind, and in the garden of the visitor centre, you'll see lots of oak tree-trunks, sawn into planks and left out to weather naturally.

Coxwold

Continuing south from Kilburn for just over two miles brings you to **COXWOLD**, another attractive village with its own claim to fame. At the top of Coxwold's sloping main street, two buildings associated with a single great man – eighteenth-century writer **Laurence Sterne** – draw your attention. First, on the left, is Shandy Hall, where he lived. A hundred yards beyond it on the right is Coxwold's church, where he was vicar from 1760 until his death in 1768, and where he is buried in the churchyard.

Shandy Hall and Gardens (May–Sept Wed 2–4.30pm, Sun 2.30–4pm; £4.50; ☏01347/868 465, ⓦwww.shandean.org), a beautiful early fifteenth-century house, is where Sterne wrote his most famous works – *Tristram Shandy* and *A Sentimental Journey* – and where he would wander out into the garden between writing sessions "to weed, hack up old roots or wheel away rubbish". The house was rescued from neglect by a group of enthusiasts in the 1960s and is now a museum dedicated to him. It contains the best collection of Sterne's novels in the world, together with displays of prints and paintings illustrating his works. You can see his study, the dining room, kitchen and the lovely gardens. Though the gardens are open every day during the summer (May–Sept), opening hours for the house are limited.

St Michael's Church was where Laurence Sterne worked as vicar, drawing big crowds with his sermons. It is also where he is buried – against the south wall, next to the porch. His internment was the last chapter of a fascinating story. Sterne died in London, and was buried in St George's, Hanover Square. Two days (or rather nights) after his burial, his body was dug up by graverobbers and sold to a surgeon, who used it for an anatomy lesson in Cambridge. Sterne's face was recognized, and his cadaver was returned to its original resting place. Then, in 1969, when the graveyard was due for development, the Laurence Sterne Trust arranged for his body to be exhumed and reburied where it now lies, in the cemetery here.

St Michael's is interesting in its own right. Standing on its hill at the top of the main street, with its octagonal west tower, it's an impressive sight. On entering the church, the first thing you'll notice is the impressive arch that separates the nave from the narrower chancel. Above it are George II's coat of arms, and on either side those of the Fauconberg family, local lords of the manor. Their motto is a pun on Belasyse, the family name: "Bonne et Belle Assez" (good and beautiful is enough). Under the arch on the left is a wooden lectern carved, "to the glory of

God" by Josef Heu, an Austrian sculptor who settled in Coxwold after fleeing from the Nazis in 1941. The box pews and pulpit were built during Laurence Sterne's incumbency, though both have been reduced in height since then. Look out for Mouseman mice in various parts of the church (there's one on the base of the lectern). The roof bosses in the nave are worth getting a stiff neck for – in between the various arms of great families are some wonderfully hideous grotesques. The monuments in the chancel are all worth a look, but the most impressive, to the left of the altar, is that of Sir William and Lady Margaret Belasyse, lying in armour and long robes respectively, hands together in prayer, figures of their five children around the base, ornate canopies and decorations above. The whole edifice would originally have been painted in gold, black and red – the early seventeenth-century equivalent of bling, perhaps.

The churchyard has sweeping views to the south. Note the section, sadly overgrown, enclosed by a yew hedge. This is the private burial ground of the Wombwells, one of whom (Sir George Orby Wombwell) was Lord Cardigan's aide-de-camp during the Crimean War, who took part in and survived the Charge of the Light Brigade.

Further down a main street of beautiful stone cottages, on the left, is the **Fauconberg Arms** (℡01347/868 214, Ⓦwww.fauconbergarms.com; ❹), a superb stone building with a cool contemporary feel inside, and serving good old-fashioned food.

Newburgh Priory

Beyond the pub in Coxwold, about half a mile after the crossroads at the bottom of the hill, and past an artificial lake, is **Newburgh Priory** (April–June Wed & Sun: gardens 2–6pm, £3; house 2.30–4.45pm, £5.50; ℡01347/868 372, Ⓦwww .newburghpriory.co.uk). Built on the site of an 1150 Augustinian priory, it was bought by the Belasyse (or Bellasis) family from Henry VIII at the time of the dissolution of the monasteries (you'll see their coat of arms and motto over the main gate). It has been in the family ever since (the first baron took the name Fauconberg when he got the title in 1627), and is currently the home of Sir George and Lady Wombwell. The most interesting story associated with Newburgh Priory involves the daughter of Oliver Cromwell who married into the family, and who, to prevent her father's body being desecrated after the restoration of the monarchy in 1660, is said to have brought it here and hidden it in the roof. The house, a delightfully mellow melange of many styles, and the gardens are open to the public, though only in the spring and on some bank holidays.

Byland Abbey

If, instead of going straight on, you take a left at the crossroads in Coxwold, within minutes you arrive at the ruins of **Byland Abbey** (April–Sept Wed–Sun 11am–6pm; £4; EH) to which Sterne used to enjoy walking. The third of the Cistercian "shining lights of the north" (the other two are Fountains and Rievaulx), Byland Abbey is not as impressive in either remains or setting, a fact reflected in its entrance – not a handsome visitor centre, but what looks like a garden shed. However, one way in which Byland wins hands down is in the **Abbey Inn** (℡01347/868 204, Ⓦwww.theappletree.org; ❺) immediately across the road, a top gastropub owned by English Heritage. It offers afternoon teas, pub food and an à la carte menu in no fewer than three dining rooms and two comfortable lounge bars, together with three luxuriously appointed bedrooms. In a building which was part of the abbey precinct before being converted first into a farmhouse then into a pub, it has to be the best, possibly the only, hostelry-attached-to-a-monastery in the country. The front door is flanked by large stone dogs chained to the building.

Ampleforth

Most monasteries and convents in Britain are, like Byland, in a ruined state, having been dissolved by Henry VIII in the 1530s, stripped of their wealth by the king, then plundered of land and building stone by local people. Nearby, however, lies an opportunity, rare in England, to visit a working monastery. **Ampleforth Abbey and College** (℡01439/766 000, ⓦwww.ampleforth.org.uk), about two miles beyond Byland Abbey, dates from the return of English monks, forced out of France by the French Revolution, who started a small house here in 1803, now a flourishing and fully functioning Benedictine monastery. It is also the top co-educational Roman Catholic private school in the country, whose ex-pupils include actor Rupert Everett, actor/writer Julian Fellowes, sculptor Antony Gormley, rugby player Lawrence Dallaglio and journalist Hugo Young. The whole impressive complex stands in a beautiful valley, and offers wonderful walking (there's a free booklet of walks of from 3 to 14 ½ miles), a swimming pool and sports centre (Mon–Fri 7am–9pm, Sat 8am–6pm, Sun 9am–8pm), a **tearoom** (Mon–Sat 10am–5.30pm, Sun noon–5.30pm) offering drinks and cakes – try Father Rainer's apple cake or Father Hugh's vanilla and fudge cheesecake – and a **shop** (Mon–Sat 10.30am–12.20pm & 2.30–4.30pm, Sun 11am–noon) with religious gifts and bottles of the monastery's fierce cider and brandy made from the produce of the monastery's orchards. Last but not least is the **abbey** itself, which you can look around or attend services at (matins at 6am, through lauds, mass, vespers and others, to compline at 9pm). There's also a pastoral programme of lengthier retreats and courses; titles for 2010 included "God at the Movies", "A Seaside Saint", "Beach Prayer Walks" and, intriguingly, a series of three called "In Vino Veritas", where Father Jeremy links knowledge of different wines, including tastings, to various aspects of the Bible. In keeping with the Rules of St Benedict, which includes "Let guests be received as Christ Himself", Ampleforth is the most extraordinarily welcoming place, something which it seems determined to expand – a new visitors' car park was being planned at the time of writing.

If you don't eat at the college, try the **White Swan** (℡01439/788 239, ⓦwww.thewhiteswan-ampleforth.co.uk) in the village itself, which serves good-quality, hearty food in a choice of three areas – formal dining room, comfortable wood-floored lounge or bar thronged with locals.

Nunnington Hall

Four miles east of Ampleforth College, **Nunnington Hall** (March–Oct Tues–Sun 11am–5pm; Nov & Dec Sat & Sun 11am–4pm; £6; ℡01439/748 283; NT), on the northern edge of the Howardian Hills, is a Yorkshire country house, owned and run by the National Trust, set in lush countryside in Ryedale. Near an elegant Georgian stone bridge, and with its own brand-new footbridge, its organic gardens throng with peacocks, its period rooms host a variety of exhibitions, and the attic holds a fascinating collection of miniature rooms. The current house dates largely from the sixteenth, seventeenth and eighteenth centuries, and one of its most noteworthy tenants (though he never lived in it) was Dr Huicke, physician to Henry VIII, Edward VI and Elizabeth I. He tried to divorce his wife, a very rare occurrence in those days – perhaps Henry VIII gave him the idea. The house was damaged during the Civil War, and inherited by Richard Graham, 1st Viscount Preston in 1685, Charles II's ambassador to Louis XIV and master of the wardrobe to James II. He, alas, backed the wrong side during the Glorious Revolution in 1688, was put in the tower, and barely escaped execution. He lived the rest of his life quietly at Nunnington Hall, and with time on his hands, did a great deal of the remodelling of the house.

Helmsley

East of Thirsk, about twelve miles along the A170, is the appealing stone town of **HELMSLEY**, clustered around a market place and with a fascinating castle, a large country house, an interesting church, a number of good pubs, hotels and restaurants and a host of small, independent specialist shops which draw in locals and visitors from miles around.

Dominating the **Market Place** is a memorial to the second Baron Feversham (1797–1867), MP for various local constituencies from 1820 until his succession to the title in 1841, when he transferred to the House of Lords. Although he became the President of the Royal Agricultural Society, you still can't help feeling that his Prince Albert-style memorial is perhaps more prominent than his modest achievements deserve.

Just off the northwest corner of the Market Place is **All Saints**, an interesting church which, though dating largely from the 1860s, has the sort of detail that brings it alive to most of us – enough survivals from earlier periods to satisfy the architectural detective, but also colourful paintings that cover the walls and ceilings dating from the early twentieth century (including a 20ft dragon), a wooden yoke from a freed slave, three halberds, and church furniture sporting numerous "mouseman" mice (see p.229).

Information, accommodation and eating

The castle's visitor centre (see below) is also the town's **information centre**.

Black Swan Market Place ☎0870 400 8112, ⓦwww.blackswan-helmsley.co.uk. An interesting Tudor/Georgian ex-coaching inn right on the main square, the *Black Swan* has a lot going for it – comfortable bar, airy restaurant, award-winning tearoom with charming and attentive staff. It also has a beautiful walled garden overlooked by the church. However, rooms are a little tired and in need of a make-over, and the rear extension can be cold in winter. ❹

Feathers Hotel Market Place ☎01439/770 275, ⓦwww.feathershotelhelmsley.co.uk. Pub restaurant food – all the usual staples, from £10.50 to £17.95, and with a surprisingly large choice of rooms from £35per person, with an economy alternative room honestly described as "unmodernized and occasionally noisy" from £30. ❷

Feversham Arms 1 High St, ☎01439/777 0766, ⓦwww.fevershamarmshotel.com. One of Yorkshire's very top hotels, multi-award winning, luxurious yet unpretentious, with a wide range of rooms and suites and service which is attentive without being intrusive. It has a swimming pool, underground car park, Verbena spa and a terrific fine-dining restaurant. Not cheap, but you get your money's worth, and look out for special deals. ❻–❽

Gepetto's ☎01439/770 479, ⓦwww.gepettos -helmsley.co.uk. Busy Italian restaurant just off Market Place. Shuts at 8.30pm.

Royal Oak 15 Market Place ☎01439/770 450, ⓦwww.theoak-helmsley.co.uk. Plentiful bar food at reasonable prices in this sports-orientated Market Place pub with rooms. ❸

Star Inn Harome ☎01439/770 397, ⓦwww.thestaratharome.co.uk. In Harome village, less than three miles southeast of Helmsley. Run by Andrew and Jacquie Pern, the *Star* is not only a spectacularly beautiful thatched inn, but also one of Yorkshire's longest-standing Michelin-starred restaurants. Food is classic British at surprisingly affordable prices (main courses at around £15–24), and the atmosphere is blessedly unpretentious. Rooms available in separate accommodation, and there's even a shop/deli across the road. ❺

Helmsley Castle

Helmsley Castle (April–Sept daily 10am–6pm; March & Oct Mon & Thurs–Sun 10am–5pm; Jan, Feb, Nov & Dec Mon & Thurs–Sun 10am–4pm; £4.70; ☎0870 333 1181; EH) stands to the west of the Market Place – the entrance is through the modern visitor centre which also serves as the town's **tourist information centre**. You can get ample information from the context boards liberally spread around the site or from the audio-guide which is included in the price. Orientation is provided by a scale model of the castle between the entrance and the moat. You enter the castle itself after walking along at the bottom of the moat (never, incidentally, likely to have been filled with water) through the south barbican and south gate.

The castle was started in around 1120 by Walter L'Espec, a man whose large size and loud voice were more impressive, perhaps, than his name, which means "Wally the Woodpecker". Most of the visible medieval fortifications, however, date from the time of crusader Robert de Roos and his descendants. The medieval structures – the barbican and gate, the large west tower and even larger D-shaped east tower – are easily distinguishable from later additions, made in Tudor times to make the castle more comfortable and user-friendly for the Manners family.

The only time the castle saw action was during the English Civil War, when Parliamentary forces under Sir Thomas Fairfax successfully laid siege in 1644, securing the surrender of the Royalists in three months. The castle was subsequently slighted (made useless as a defence by blowing key bits up), the main visible result now being that the east tower, facing the town, had the whole of its outer wall brought down: the rubble from its destruction still lies drunkenly in the moat.

Look inside the twelfth-century west tower, remodelled in the fourteenth and sixteenth centuries, which was used as accommodation – all the floors have gone, but you can see from the quality of the fireplaces and the size of the windows that the basement and top floor were used by servants, the middle two floors by the lord and his family. Beyond is the West Range, remodelled in the sixteenth century to provide greater comfort, and today housing a diverting exhibition telling the castle's story – it includes some impressive cannonballs hurled at it during the 1644 siege. Within the curtain walls and towers, look out for the outlines of the thirteenth-century chapel and the fourteenth-century hall and kitchen.

Duncombe Park

The driveway to **Duncombe Park** (April–Oct Sun–Thurs 11am–5.30pm; £8.25; ☏ 01439/772 625, ⓦ www.duncombepark.com) starts right in Helmsley, and if you proceed directly from the castle to the house here, you'll be doing exactly what the Duncombes themselves did. City banker and Lord Mayor of London **Sir Charles Duncombe** bought the Helmsley and Rievaulx estates, which included the castle and Rievaulx Abbey, in 1689 for £90,000. His nephew Thomas had Duncombe Park built in the early eighteenth century as a more comfortable replacement for the castle. Indeed, the remains of the castle were eventually relegated to being romantic ruins enhancing the views from the house – many eighteenth-century landowners had to resort to building follies, but the Duncombes had their own genuine ruins, ready-made. Most of the house was destroyed by fire in 1879 and later rebuilt, so not a lot of the architecture you'll see on the guided tour is original, but it's still worth an hour of your time. And the house hosts a variety of special events during the year, from dog shows to steam, craft, plant and country fairs – check the website.

Of more general interest are the grounds of Duncombe Park, which have been called "one of the most extensive and boldest landscaping enterprises in England". Particularly fascinating is the **Duncombe Terrace** (completed in 1718) which stretches south and east of the house. A long grassy terrace laid out as a walk or ride from one temple (Ionic) to another (Tuscan), it offers views of a carefully designed landscape through the trees down into the valley. All very expensive you might think, and you'd be right. But in the eighteenth century competition to impress each other between the (often intermarried) wealthy was intense, and similar landscaping can be seen at Castle Howard (see p.236), at Studely Royal (see p.178) and at Roche Abbey (see p.70).

As you return to town down the drive, notice **Helmsley Walled Garden** (April–Oct daily 10.30am–5pm; £4; ☎01439/771 194, ⓦwww.helmsleywall edgarden.org.uk) just behind the castle. It was built as the kitchen garden to the big house when the original one was washed away by a great flood in 1759, and is now open to the public – heaven on earth if you're a keen gardener. Apart from the huge array of plants (many for sale), there's a vegetarian restaurant and an ethical gift shop.

Rievaulx Terrace

Rievaulx Terrace (March–Oct daily 11am–5pm; £4.75; NT), about two miles west of Helmsley, was, like Duncombe Park's terrace (see p.234), built by the Duncombes, though thirty years later – its construction began in 1759 and it took eight years. It's an exact match with Duncombe Terrace – both follow the Rye – and there is some speculation that the ultimate plan was to connect the two, bridging a small valley in between. The plan and purpose of Rievaulx Terrace is simple – it's a broad swathe of grass that drops and curves gently for over half a mile along a ridge above the Rye, from an oblong Ionic temple at one end to a round Tuscan one at the other. The steep slope down from the terrace to the river was planted with trees in such a way that views down to Rievaulx Abbey and across the valley opened up periodically as you passed along the terrace.

The terrace was used to impress visitors. The household would set out from Duncombe House with their carriages, horses and servants, and the visitors would be escorted along the terrace, on foot or horseback, to admire the views and, in due course, dine in the Ionic temple. The modern visitor can still enjoy the views (though you've got to bring your own food), and although you're not allowed into the Tuscan temple, you can see the ornate tiled floor through the windows, and the painted ceiling by means of mirrors set on the window ledges. The Ionic temple, which is open to the public, has a highly decorated upstairs dining room, with what was the kitchen below – it now houses an interesting exhibition on the history of the terrace, and on the plants and animals to be seen on and from it as you promenade.

Rievaulx Abbey

Rievaulx Abbey (April–Sept daily 10am–6pm; Oct Mon & Thurs–Sun 10am–5pm; Nov–March Thurs–Mon 10am–4pm; £5.30; ☎01439/798 228; EH) lies in the valley of the Rye ("Rievaulx" means "the abbey in Ryedale") directly below the terrace – the approach road from the Helmsley side drops down from the B1257 right next to the entrance to Rievaulx Terrace – though there is no direct route between abbey and terrace, which seems odd until you consider that they originated in totally different eras, and had different purposes.

The abbey was established as a colony of Clairvaux in France by twelve Cistercian monks led by Abbot William in 1132 – the first Cistercian monastery in the north of England. As usual with the Cistercians, they chose a site in wild country with a good water supply. When you pay your entrance fee, make sure you pick up the free audio-guide and a copy of the single-sheet pamphlet which gives you a labelled 3D plan of the monastery. From the ticket office and shop, a gravel path leads you up to the right of the monastery ruins, where detailed information boards fill you in on the setting, explaining that the monks eventually diverted the Rye in order to give themselves more room for building, and to pursue the simple life that was part of their order. They established water meadows, fish ponds and a mill for metal working, and used the timber that surrounded them for building and for charcoal-burning. The abbey eventually owned land all over England, and traded with other Cistercian monasteries throughout Britain and Europe. By the middle of the twelfth century Rievaulx had grown to house 140 monks and 500 lay brothers and servants.

Before entering the ruins, have a look at the exhibition "The Work of God and Man", which has fascinating displays on the monks and their lives – farming, raising animals, weaving cloth, tanning leather, working metal, producing tiles, illuminating books – as well as outlining the hierarchy of monks and their functions.

Once in the ruins themselves, it is relatively easy to follow the tour via the nave, south transept, presbytery, cloister, chapter house, refectory, kitchen, scriptorium, infirmary, abbot's house, lay-brothers' range and tannery, with the audio-guide creating a vivid picture of the life of the monastery as you go round.

Kirkbymoorside

East of Helmsley, about three miles along the A170, the village of **KIRKBY-MOORSIDE** (Ⓦwww.kirkbymoorside.com), while lacking the charisma of Helmsley, is still well worth considering as a base. Lining its sloping main street, the Market Place and the High Market Place, are a couple of nice **hotels**: the *Kings Head* (High Market Place; Ⓣ01751/431 340, Ⓦwww.kingsheadkirkbymoorside .co.uk; ❷), all nicely decorated elegance and with a really comfortable guest lounge; and the *George and Dragon* (Ⓣ01751/433 334, Ⓦwww.georgeanddragon .net; ❹), with a formal restaurant, more relaxed bistro and a range of rooms and suites. The town has a good variety of shops, pleasant cafés including *The Penny Bank* and *Tea Time* and a variety of restaurants and take-aways (Chinese, Indian, fish and chips). There are no great tourist attractions, but it's a pleasant place to spend an hour or stay for a few days.

Castle Howard

In the heart of the Howardian Hills, and worth a day to itself, **Castle Howard** (daily: March–Oct & Dec 11am–4pm; house and gardens £12.50, gardens only £8.50; Ⓣ01653/648 333, Ⓦwww.castlehoward.co.uk) is one of England's greatest stately homes, famous for the exuberance of its architecture, the wealth of its interiors and the beauty of its grounds. There has been some dispute as to who designed the house – some claim Hawksmoor – but most experts now agree that it is Sir John Vanburgh's work, despite the fact that he was, until getting the Castle Howard commission, a writer not an architect. And Hawksmoor was his assistant, so that would explain any influences on the style of the house. Conceived in 1699 for Charles Howard, 3rd Earl of Carlisle, and started in 1700, it took over a century to complete, suffered a terrible fire in 1940, has been the subject of continuous restoration since then, and is currently occupied by the Hon. Simon Howard and his family.

Advance warning of the grandeur to come is given by the monument (1869–70) to the 7th earl with its gold-topped column set on a plinth, surrounded by four obelisks, which you pass long before arriving at Castle Howard itself, and by the subsequent five-mile drive along the beech-and lime-lined approach road – the **Avenue**, first laid out in the early eighteenth century.

Access to the house and its grounds is through the handsome former **stables**, gathered around a paved courtyard – there's a café, shops selling farm produce, chocolates, flowers and books, and the ticket office. Once inside the grounds, you can walk or catch the Kelly car – a road train pulled by a tractor. As you approach the house side on, there's a **walled garden** to the right, laid out in the early eighteenth century as a kitchen garden, now planted with roses and ornamental vegetables, and to the left, the **Boar Garden**, with a statue of a powerful looking wild boar at its centre.

At the house, an enormous lawn to the right – the South Parterre – surrounds the famous **Atlas Fountain**, which dates from 1853. Beyond this, in order, lie the South Lake (1720s) with its Prince of Wales fountain (1850s), the Cascade (1860s), the New River Bridge (1740s), the Temple of the Four Winds (1730s) and the mausoleum (1740s). The mausoleum, commissioned by the 3rd earl to be his burial place, continues to be used by the family, and is not open to the public. Beyond the house is Ray Wood, which contains the reservoir that powers the Atlas and Prince of Wales fountains, and to the north, overlooked by the massive north face of the house, the Great Lake (1790s), where there are boat trips, an adventure playground and a pleasant lakeside café. There's also a café on the west side of the house itself.

The entrance to the **house** is in the west wing (the east wing is occupied by the family and isn't open to the public). Visitors are free to explore the rooms at their own speed, and there are knowledgeable guides stationed at intervals throughout. On entering, immediately ahead is the Grand Staircase, which takes you up to the China Landing, then a succession of rooms groaning with priceless antiques, porcelain, furniture, sculpture and paintings. The most important room in the house, the **Great Hall**, soars upwards through two storeys and into the dome which gives the outside of the building its distinctive shape. The Great Hall is wonderfully decorated with wall paintings by Venetian artist Pellegrini (though these must be copies or at least restorations, since the dome was destroyed in the fire). Other rooms of great elegance succeed each other, their functions obvious from their names – the Music Room, the Crimson Dining Room, the Turquoise Drawing Room, the Museum Room, the Chapel and, particularly fine, the Long Gallery. Everywhere you look there are paintings by world-famous artists – Gainsborough, Holbein, Canaletto, Titian, Bellini, Reubens.

As well as its intrinsic beauty and historical interest, Castle Howard also provides a wonderful setting for a range of events – theatrical productions, fairs, polo matches, firework displays, art exhibitions, wine tastings, barbecues, photography and painting courses, jazz afternoons – check out the website. And if you really want to make the best of all these, you can stay at the **Lakeside Holiday Park** or campsite, just across the Great Lake from the house, which offers a touring area (℡01653/648 316; March–Oct; tents from £14, caravan/motorhomes from £18 per night, assuming two adults sharing) as well holiday homes for sale (℡01653/648 576). You can also rent holiday homes on the estate (℡01653/648 605).

Kirkham Priory

Approximately four miles south of Castle Howard, at the very edge of the Howardian Hills, **Kirkham Priory** (April–July & Sept Mon & Thurs–Sun 10am–5pm; Aug daily 10am–5pm; £3.20; ℡0870/333 1181; EH) stands on a river bank next to an attractive bridge, the serenity of the rolling wooded countryside broken only by the occasional train that clatters along on the opposite bank. Kirkham Priory was founded in 1122 by Walter L'Espec, the founder of Helmsley Castle, for the Augustinian order. It had all the usual buildings – a large church, chapter house, dormitory, refectory, kitchen and storehouses – the remains of which are all clearly and fully described by excellent information boards around the site. One of them explains Kirkham Priory's unique history when parts of it were used during World War II for training soldiers in preparation for D-Day. The relatively flat land between the priory and the river was flooded to provide a shallow pool for testing the waterproofing of landing craft and amphibious tanks, while the wall of the western cloister was used to train soldiers in the use of the scrambling nets by which they would transfer from troop transports to landing craft. Churchill visited the priory to inspect the work going on. For refreshment, there's a very good **pub** just past the priory – the *Stone Trough Inn*, in a converted stone-and-tile cottage (℡01653/618 713, ⓦwww.stonetroughinn.co.uk), which offers pub food of a high standard, with main courses from £7.95 to £13.95 and a range of Yorkshire beers.

Pickering and the Vale of Pickering

To the south of **Pickering**, and separating the North York Moors from the Yorkshire Wolds, is the **Vale of Pickering**, a narrow neck of land that stretches from Helmsley in the west to Scarborough on the coast. Though this area isn't in a National Park or an Area of Outstanding Natural Beauty, it is still attractive open country, with a couple of original attractions, notably **Eden Camp** museum.

Pickering

PICKERING is in an enviable position to act as a base for exploration of the surrounding countryside. The A170 Thirsk-to-Scarborough road and the A169 York-to-Whitby road intersect at Pickering, with the town centre lying to the north and west of the intersection, making it very easy to get into and out of, while also allowing through traffic. The main streets of the town form a loop off the A170 – the Ropery, Market Place, Birdgate and Smiddy Hill. However, there's more to Pickering than its convenience as a base – it's a very convivial little town with a number of attractions of its own, notably the **Beck Isle Museum**, the start of the **North Yorkshire Moors Railway** and the **castle**.

Information, accommodation and eating

The **tourist information centre** (℡01751/473 791) is on the Ropery, opposite a substantial Co-Op and a short-stay car park. For **accommodation** and **eating** there's the lovely coaching inn the *White Swan* (℡01751/472 288, ⓦwww.white -swan.co.uk; ⑥), which is highly reckoned for its food, and offers a choice of comfortable "vintage" or "contemporary" rooms. In the town there are also some nice **tearooms**, including: *37 Burgate*, *Russells Café* in the Market Place and *Beckside Gifts, Clothing and Tearoom* on Bridge Street, all of which offer a good range of drinks and snacks. There's also a flourishing **flea market** through an archway off Market Place.

The Beck Isle Museum

Just off the town centre, prettily situated in gardens that slope down to the Pickering Beck next to a stone bridge, the **Beck Isle Museum** (daily 10am–5pm; £5; ℡01751/473 653, ⓦwww.beckislemuseum.co.uk) vividly conjures up a picture of life in Pickering and Ryedale over the centuries. The building itself is historic – its original owner, agricultural pioneer William Marshall, was adapting it into an agricultural college in 1818 when, unfortunately, his death put an end to the project. Today the museum holds a huge collection of artefacts illustrating all aspects of life and work in the area, all in an informal setting. Its rooms overflow with stuff that has drifted down through the centuries, including mock-ups of retail outlets (a chemist, a men's outfitters, the *Station Hotel*) plus displays on traditional occupations, such as cooper, cobbler, blacksmith, lacemaker, grocer, and a host of different topics, all richly endowed with artefacts, photographs and documents. A printer and blacksmith can be seen at work, and periodic special events make good use of the museum's collections. Pickering was blessed with a fine high-street photographer in Sydney Smith, who documented ordinary life and special events, in landscapes, portraits and postcards, from 1914 to 1947, so that the town now has, lodged in the museum, a unique record of life between the start of World War I and the end of World War II.

North Yorkshire Moors Railway

Just around the corner, in Park Street, is the southern terminus of the **North Yorkshire Moors Railway** (July & Aug trains hourly, less frequent at other times; Nov & Dec Sat & Sun only; Jan closed, check website for full timetables; day rover tickets to Grosmont £16, Whitby £21; ℡01751/472 508, Ⓦwww .nymr.co.uk), another exercise in authenticity and aching nostalgia. Everything in the station speaks of the bygone steam age. The suitcases, luggage trolleys, advertising signs and station clock, the signage, porters and station master, the signals and gaslight fittings, and, above all, the great steam engines and carriages, all remind the old how it used to be, and tell the young what it was like before they were born. And the station goes to great lengths to keep everything in period – a sign as you enter explains that, though you can't smoke inside, to maintain authenticity the usually compulsory "No Smoking" signs are not displayed. There's a refreshment room, a ticket office and shop, and from mid-March to late October (and Sat & Sun in Nov & Dec) you can catch trains north through the beautiful countryside of the North York Moors, stopping at Levisham, Goathland and Grosmont. Grosmont is the terminus of the North Yorkshire Moors Railway, but you can transfer there to trains on the Esk Valley line (Ⓦwww.eskvalleyrailway .co.uk) to Whitby. Stations are open only when there are trains running.

Pickering Castle

The third of Pickering's prime visitor attractions takes you even further back in time. At first **Pickering Castle** (April–June & Sept Mon & Thurs–Sun 10am–5pm; July & Aug daily 10am–5pm; £3.70; ℡0870333 1181; EH), a five-minute walk along Castlegate north of the town centre, doesn't look like much, but be patient. Though the castle was founded by William the Conqueror in 1069–70, most of what you see today dates from the thirteenth and fourteenth centuries. As you make your way through the entrance and into the outer then the inner bailey, you can learn all you need to know about early Norman military architecture. Pickering Castle started as a rudimentary motte and bailey, the sort the Normans threw up immediately after the conquest by digging an enormous ditch and piling the earth in the centre to create a "motte", or artificial hill, which they would then top with a wooden fortification. The flat area around it became the "bailey" or enclosure (inner and outer), and the whole thing was surrounded by a wooden

---

Pickering festivals

Pickering realizes that with nostalgia they're onto a good thing, and the town (Ⓦwww .pickering.uk.net) and railway organize a number of special events. So, in August there's a **Medieval Spectacular** with jousting and falconry (organized by the Wilf Ward Family Trust; Ⓦwww.wilfward.org.uk), early in October the whole town puts on a **Wartime Weekend**, based on the life and styles of the 1940s, and in June the 1960s come to life in the **Swinging Sixties Festival** (Ⓦwww.pickering60sfestival .co.uk) with appropriate locomotives, vehicles and live bands at various stations along the line. Other special events include spring and autumn steam galas, vintage vehicle weekends and a diesel gala – for all special events, check the appropriate website.

palisade. These fortifications could be built quickly, but were of course susceptible to attack by fire. So, following the immediate subjugation of the area, the castle was inevitably fortified in stone. Pickering Castle still has its artificial mound, topped now with the ruins of a stone castle, surrounded by a formidable stone curtain wall with towers enclosing the baileys, itself surrounded by a deep ditch. The castle doesn't appear to have figured in any great battles or sieges – its main job was to keep the locals cowed. It was, though, popular with several kings as a base for hunting in the surrounding forests. And, common to most castles (where a good vantage point was essential), the views in all directions are special.

The Church of St Peter and St Paul

Although the castle, the railway and the museum are the main reasons to visit Pickering, the **Church of St Peter and St Paul** (daily 9am–5pm) is also of interest, not only for its position – at the highest point of the town centre, but self-effacingly surrounded by houses and with no access apart from up little stepped lanes – but also because it has some of the best wall paintings of any church in the country. Originating in the mid-fifteenth century, they bring home to modern eyes how colourful places of worship were in the Middle Ages, with their wall paintings and stained-glass windows telling a largely illiterate congregation, in considerable and sometimes gory detail, stories from the Bible and from early Christian history. Look too at the mid-fourteenth century effigy of a knight lying next to the lectern – legs nonchalantly crossed and two little angels poised like vampire bats at his neck – and at the memorial to Robert King in the sanctuary, a local surveyor whose son Nicholas emigrated to America and ended up being appointed by Thomas Jefferson as the first Surveyor of Washington. Nicholas King also did a lot of surveying and map-making of the lands west of the Mississippi, and drew up plans for the defences of the Atlantic seaboard before the War of 1812 between the USA and Britain.

Malton

Due south of Pickering lies **MALTON** (Ⓦ www.malton.co.uk) which, together with sister town **Norton-on-Derwent** and the pretty **Old Malton**, is the principal market town for the Derwent Valley and the Vale of Pickering. It has had a chequered history. The Romans established a fort here – where Orchard Fields in town is today – to command the River Derwent. Later the Saxons settled at Old Malton where, in around 1150, Eustace Fitz John established the Gilbertine Priory of St Mary, and built a castle (now alas gone) next to the old Roman Fort. New Malton, to the west, was also established in the twelfth century. The town prospered, becoming the main market settlement and transport hub for the region. An attractive yet refreshingly un-twee town, it's worth at least an hour's stopover, especially on market days (Sat) or when the animal auctions are on (Tues & Fri). The town is centred on its eccentrically shaped, sloping **Market Place**, which is broken up by an island containing the church and a group of shops and buildings; the Market Place is also used as a **car park** (free).

St Michael's Church stands right in the centre of the Market Place, with no surrounding churchyard. Dating from 1150, the church is one of two new "chapels of ease" granted in that year to the Gilbertine Priory of Old Malton, and has been extensively altered and restored over the centuries. The most obvious survivals from Norman times are the pillars in both aisles, and possibly the font, though this might be Jacobean. The west tower is fifteenth century and, not being strong enough to stand up to the considerable stresses caused by swinging bells, contains ones that are struck rather than swung. Look out for the woodwork in the chancel by Thompson of Kilburn.

The great outdoors

In a county famed for its landscape – from the Dales and the Moors to the dramatic coastline – you can throw yourself around the skies above it, range far and wide on it, venture into the dim dark spaces under it, or enjoy the North Sea off it. And if the usual outdoor adventures don't float your boat, there are one or two oddball activities that you might like to try.

Up in the air

For unparalleled views over the landscape, you can't beat getting up into the Yorkshire skies, and there are several good opportunities to do so. You can ascend in a plane and make the return by parachute at the British Skysports centre, near Bridlington in the Wolds (see p.294), launch yourself off the edge of the North York Moors at Sutton Bank and spiral around above the famous white horse and over the Vale of York in a glider (see p.228), or hang-glide, paraglide or balloon across the Dales (see p.35).

Below the ground

Yorkshire's great potholing and caving region is the Yorkshire Dales, where the area's geology has evolved to produce some dazzling natural phenomena. Where surface millstone grit and carboniferous limestone abut, the water cascading off the impervious former dissolves the soluble latter, creating elaborate formations of caves, gorges and chasms.

Incomprehensible to claustrophobes, unaccompanied clambering about under ground is not recommended for the untrained. However there are numerous show caves, including White Scar Cave (see p.191) at Ingleton near Ribblesdale and Stump Cross Caverns (see p.204) in Nidderdale, where you can enjoy the beauties of stalagmites and stalactites, travertine formations and so on as part of an organized tour.

For more adventurous potholing and caving expeditions, you can arrange instruction from experts and accompanied expeditions through private companies such as Ⓦwww.yorkshiredalesguides.co.uk.

A hot-air balloon high above the Yorkshire Dales ▲

White Scar Cave ▼

The great outdoors

In a county famed for its landscape – from the Dales and the Moors to the dramatic coastline – you can throw yourself around the skies above it, range far and wide on it, venture into the dim dark spaces under it, or enjoy the North Sea off it. And if the usual outdoor adventures don't float your boat, there are one or two oddball activities that you might like to try.

A hot-air balloon high above the Yorkshire Dales ▲

White Scar Cave ▼

Up in the air

For unparalleled views over the landscape, you can't beat getting up into the Yorkshire skies, and there are several good opportunities to do so. You can ascend in a plane and make the return by parachute at the British Skysports centre, near Bridlington in the Wolds (see p.294), launch yourself off the edge of the North York Moors at Sutton Bank and spiral around above the famous white horse and over the Vale of York in a glider (see p.228), or hang-glide, paraglide or balloon across the Dales (see p.35).

Below the ground

Yorkshire's great potholing and caving region is the Yorkshire Dales, where the area's geology has evolved to produce some dazzling natural phenomena. Where surface millstone grit and carboniferous limestone abut, the water cascading off the impervious former dissolves the soluble latter, creating elaborate formations of caves, gorges and chasms.

Incomprehensible to claustrophobes, unaccompanied clambering about under ground is not recommended for the untrained. However there are numerous show caves, including White Scar Cave (see p.191) at Ingleton near Ribblesdale and Stump Cross Caverns (see p.204) in Nidderdale, where you can enjoy the beauties of stalagmites and stalactites, travertine formations and so on as part of an organized tour.

For more adventurous potholing and caving expeditions, you can arrange instruction from experts and accompanied expeditions through private companies such as Ⓦwww.yorkshiredalesguides.co.uk.

On the water

Yorkshire has a long coastline which falls into two sections – the headlands, cliffs and bays of the North Yorkshire coast, and the long gentle beaches of East Yorkshire. Lots of places, then, to swim and snorkel, and not only the famous beaches of Scarborough and Bridlington and Filey, but also lesser known resorts like Runswick Bay, Sandsend, Hornsea or Withernsea. In between are some glorious beaches. Where more facilities are needed – for sailing, water sports and windsurfing, canoeing, sea-kayaking and jet-skiing, there are numerous clubs and water sports centres, not only on the coast but on lakes and reservoirs as well (see p.34).

▲ Canoeing in North Yorkshire

▼ The harbour at Bridlington

On terra firma

Yorkshire has some of the finest walking and cycling in the UK. The best places by far for both are the Dales, the North York Moors and the coast. Some areas – Malham, for example – can get crowded, but it doesn't take much effort to get off the beaten track. Well-marked long-distance routes wend their way through the Dales (see p.186), while the Cleveland Way covers both the Moors and the coast (see p.225). For the more intrepid, bouldering and rock-climbing opportunities abound – and for bad weather, which happens occasionally even in God's Own County, there are indoor facilities (see p.61). Finally, if swinging around in the trees on high wires is your thing, Go Ape at Dalby or Aerial Extreme at Bedale are worth a visit.

If you need the stimulus of hitting a little white ball, be of good cheer – Yorkshire has some of the best golf courses in the country (see p.33).

▼ Mountain-biking in the Yorkshire Dales

▼ Marsden Moor, West Yorkshire

Mountain boarding ▲

Cable waterskiing ▼

Weird and wonderful

Finally, Yorkshire has dozens of places to try out some more unusual sports and activities. Why not give one of these a try:

▶▶ **Husky-trekking** You don't need snow for this husky-trekking – wheels replace it. You can become a "musher" on grass at Pesky Husky (☎01723/870 521, ⊛www.peskyhusky.co.uk) in Staintondale between Scarborough and Whitby.

▶▶ **Mountain boarding** It's like snowboarding but again with wheels instead of snow. Try it at Another World Mountain boarding centre in the hills above Ogden Reservoir north of Halifax (☎01723/870 521, ⊛www.mountain boarding.co.uk).

▶▶ **Bicycle polo** Polo is the toff's sport, but here it's played on bikes instead of horses, though being a team game, it's confined to groups of guests. At Swinton Park (see p.214).

▶▶ **Via Ferrata** Meaning iron road, Via Ferrata at How Stean Gorge is the place for adrenaline junkies. One of only two in England, it offers a lengthy scramble along the chasm using fixed beams, cables and ladders. Invented by the Italians to move troops around the Alps, Via Ferrata centres have now spread across the world. See p.205.

▶▶ **Cable waterskiing** An electric cable instead of a boat drags you around the water at Rother Valley Country Park near Rotherham – there's also fishing, golf and other outdoor activities here. See p.69.

▶▶ **Dry-slope skiing**. Ski or snowboard down the artificial ski-slopes high above the city of Sheffield, one of the largest of its kind in Europe. See p.62.

▶▶ **Petanque** An outdoor activity for the more sedate, you can indulge in the archetypically French boules in the heart of Yorkshire's greatest city, Leeds. And it's absolutely free. See p.95.

Behind the church, in what was the Town Hall, is the well-stocked **tourist information centre** (Mon–Sat 9.30am–5pm; ☎01653/600 048). Ask in particular for the *Malton Heritage Walk* booklet and the *Malton and Norton Town Trails* pamphlet. In the same building is **Malton Museum** (Mon–Sat: March–Oct 10am–4pm; Nov–Dec 10.30am–3pm; £1.50; ☎01653/695 136, Ⓦwww.malton museum.co.uk) which, though it touches on most aspects of the town's history, sensibly concentrates on one period – its Roman legacy. There are useful displays on the fort, army life, Roman artillery and many aspects of Roman life, including a touching case devoted to an infant burial.

The rest of the Market Place is ringed with shops, including the top-class deli **Malton Relish**, pubs, cafés and restaurants; for a drink try *Suddaby's Crown Hotel*, 12 Wheelgate (☎01653/692 038; ❷), an old coaching inn which offers excellent beer, as well as accommodation, and for food *Ambiente Restaurant*, 2–4 Market Place (☎01653/691 992), serving tapas in warm, friendly surroundings. Up the narrow Shambles, lined with small shops, is the **Cattle Market**, with metal-and-wooden pens, the premises of auctioneers Cundals. If you're in Malton on a Tuesday or Friday, it's well worth taking a look, with the market full of farmers and the pens full of animals.

It's also worth visiting **Old Malton**, a mile or so east, for its air of quiet gentility and for Malton Priory. The **Priory Church of St Mary**, to give it its full title, is now the parish church, but you can see traces of its former glory, and imagine its former size from what's left, especially the western part of the nave and one of its two west towers.

Eden Camp

Just north of Old Malton is a unique, award-winning attraction whose own history is almost as interesting as that covered by its exhibits. **Eden Camp** (daily 10am–5pm; £5.50; ☎01653/697 777, Ⓦwww.edencamp.co.uk) started as a Prisoner of War camp set up in 1942, at first made up of barbed wire and tents, then with more permanent accommodation built by its first inmates – Italians captured in North Africa. The Italians stayed until 1944, when they were replaced by Germans. They remained until the last 1200 were repatriated in 1948, and the camp was shut down. Nearly forty years later the derelict site was bought by Stan Johnson who invested £750,000 in renovating the huts and setting up his "modern history theme museum". During the 1990s Eden Camp went from strength to strength, winning a host of awards and attracting the support of numerous ex-servicemen's organizations. It is now one of the most interesting, unstuffy and moving museums you're ever likely to visit.

The scene is set when you enter the museum past full-size replicas of a spitfire and a hurricane, and various big guns and military vehicles. Beyond them are the rows of POW huts, which now house the exhibits. A simple progression takes you through Hut 1 ("The Rise of Hitler") to Hut 2 ("The Home Front"), Hut 3 ("The U-Boat Menace"), and all the way to Hut 22 ("Forces Reunion"). Each hut covers an aspect of the war, often in atmospheric detail. For example, in "The Blitz" in Hut 5 you walk past the mock-up of a bombed house – smoke, smashed furniture, burnt-out windows, ruptured water pipes. Elsewhere you'll see prisoners digging a tunnel to escape from a POW camp, a family listening to Chamberlain's speech announcing the start of the war, land girls at work, staff in a bomber command ops room and so on. Huts 24 to 29 are the "museum within a museum", giving a chronological account of the progress of the war. And though overwhelmingly about World War II, there is a hut dealing with trench warfare in World War I (Hut 11) and post-World War II conflicts (Hut 13). Dotted around the camp are pieces of military hardware, including tanks, artillery and a VI "Doodlebug".

There's a postwar "prefab" with a dig-for-victory garden, several air-raid shelters, sentry towers, a music hall where you can watch a puppet show of the great entertainers of the time, and, to help the kids let off steam, an adventure playground. You can eat in the *Prisoners Canteen* and the *Officers Mess Tearoom* (where meals have appropriate names – Dambusters Stew, for example, or Submariners Feast) or drink Eden Camp bitter in the Garrison Cinema bar.

New exhibits are added all the time, expanding coverage of the "People's War", and Veterans' groups not only donate memorabilia but also increasingly hold their reunions at the camp, and often vouch for the authenticity of the museum displays. This is a gem of a museum, not to be missed.

Flamingo Land

Flamingo Land (March–Oct daily 10am–4/5/6pm; £25; ☏0871 911 8000, Ⓦwww.flamingoland.co.uk), off the A169 Malton-to-Pickering road, is a well-judged combination of theme park and zoo with something for children of all ages – a formidable collection of white-knuckle rides for the older ones, a group of smaller rides and activities for younger children and a rather good zoo for all ages, liberally sprinkled with places to eat and drink. Though it's not cheap, once you've paid your entrance fee only food and drinks aren't included. Rides and activities are roughly grouped together, so with the map provided it's easy to navigate. Most of the big, scary rides are grouped in **Metropolis**, water-based ones in **Splosh**, little kids' attractions in **Muddy Duck Farm** and the zoo in the **Lost Kingdom**, but they're not obsessive about it so there's a fair bit of overlapping and inter-mixing. It's a large park, but tired legs can be rested by using the cross-park **monorail**, the **little train** or the **cable car**.

The **zoo**'s inhabitants generally look healthy, happy and in good condition, living in spacious enclosures. There's a good range of animals, mainly African, including big beasts like giraffes, camels, lions, tigers, white rhinos and zebras; smaller ones such as meerkats, lemurs, chimps, baboons and kangaroos, a variety of birds, including, of course, flamingos; reptiles, and an aquarium and a pool where you can see sealions being fed. The zoo has a partnership with the Centre for Animal Management in Askham Bryan College in York, whose students visit regularly as part of their studies.

You can also **stay** at the *Flamingo Land Resort*, in the campsite (from £44 per night for two people), holiday homes (up to £973 per week) or log cabins (up to £1300 per week). Rates include access to the park and zoo throughout your stay (though if you stay at the campsite there's a one-off charge for admission).

The central and eastern Moors

The main route into the central moors is from Pickering) in the south and Whitby in the north, along the A169 road which joins them. From the A170 either side of Pickering the central North York Moors stretch northward, with turbulent rivers and narrow valleys separated by heather upland. The whole area is a delight to explore, on foot or on two or four wheels. North and east of Pickering, the moors are dominated by Crompton, Langdale, Wykham and Dalby **forests**.

An alternative route into the area is the **North Yorkshire Moors Railway** which, together with the eastern end of the **Esk Valley Railway**, covers roughly the same ground.

Hutton-le-Hole

One of the highlights of the central Moors is **HUTTON-LE-HOLE**, in a steep-sided valley around four miles northeast of Kirkbymoorside. As you approach the village from the south, the road drops steeply down into the valley of the Hutton Beck surrounded by hills, pastures and woods. The village itself lies on either side of an undulating, sheep-dotted common, crisscrossed with footpaths and tidy white fencing, with the river meandering through it, spanned by a little wooden footbridge, all against the backdrop of pretty wooded hills.

However, apart from its own good looks, the village is most visited for the **Ryedale Folk Museum**, right in the centre (mid-Jan to Nov daily 10am–5.30pm; winter closing time can vary; £5.50; ☎01751/417 367, ⊛www.ryedalefolk museum.co.uk), a comprehensive collection of vernacular buildings assembled here from all over the dale. There are domestic houses, such as a crofter's cottage and a manor house, workplaces, including a blacksmith's, cobbler's, tinsmith's, cooper's and wheelwright, farm buildings and shops, as well as reconstructions of an Iron Age settlement and a Victorian classroom. There are plenty of hands-on craft experiences for kids, a trail, a range of special events, music concerts, rallies and displays, all in a stunningly beautiful setting. Also in Hutton-le-Hole, behind the *Forge Tea Room*, is the **Chocolate Factory** (March–Oct Tues–Sun 10.30am–5pm), where you can watch chocolates being made (they've also got a shop in Thornton-le-Dale).

The village has a good **pub**, *The Crown* (☎01751/417 343), a spacious real-ale-and-food pub outside which you can sit with your drink and enjoy the peace of the village, the Shop on the Green which sells food, drink, ice cream and gifts, and several tearooms – try *The Barn Tearooms*, which offers a wide range of home-made cakes, scones, jams, pickles and so on, or the *Forge Tea Room*. Of the small range of **accommodation**, the *Barn Hotel* (☎01751/417 311; ➌) is one of the best, and there's also a central **caravan site** (open only to Caravan Club members). For the village **car park**, drive up through the village, and turn right at the top end – it's immediately on the right.

Lastingham

Less than two miles beyond Hutton-le-Hole, up the same road as the car park, lies **LASTINGHAM**, yet another pretty-as-a-picture village nestling in a steep-sided valley, this time that of the Hole Beck. Its striking church, **St Mary's of Lastingham**, which sits massively on its sloping churchyard overlooking the village, has a fascinating history. As early as 654 AD, a monastery was established here with St Cedd, an important Anglo-Saxon monk written about by the Venerable Bede, as its first abbot. It is said that, after he died of the plague, a group of monks from the south of England came to mourn his death, all but one of whom succumbed to the disease themselves. Nothing now remains of this early building, which was probably destroyed by the Vikings. However, in 1078 a new monastery was begun by Stephen of Whitby, first abbot of St Mary's of York. The building was completed then soon after abandoned. From the outside, the church looks distinctly French, with its squat, square west tower and, at the east end, the apse – a semicircular extension beyond the end of the chancel – giving this end of the church its distinctive round shape. What makes this country church so very interesting is that the Norman crypt from this time is still there, and even still used for worship. The steps down into the crypt start from the middle of the nave. The crypt itself mirrors the structure of the main church above it – nave, chancel, apse; the floor appears to be of compressed earth. Four thick, very short columns hold up the roof in the nave, a further two the chancel, and there's an archway, which starts at the floor level, beyond which is a simple stone altar. There's even a tiny stained-glass window set into the apse, made possible by the fact that the church is built into a steep slope. In the crypt is the remains of an Anglo-Saxon cross which must originally have been over 20ft high, a hog-back gravestone with the carving of a bear and several coffin lids.

The village itself consists of a cluster of lovely stone houses, a small green with benches, and a bridge across the Beck. Beyond the bridge is a drinking fountain dedicated to St Cedd. Opposite the church is the *Blacksmith's Arms* (✆01751/417 247, ⓦwww.blacksmithslastingham.co.uk; ❷), a long **pub** with individually styled rooms, a lovely local atmosphere and standard pub food.

Thornton-le-Dale and Dalby Forest Drive

THORNTON-LE-DALE (ⓦwww.thorntonledale.com), under two miles east of Pickering, stands at the southern end of **Dalby Forest**, and is one of the prettiest villages in Yorkshire, despite the main Scarborough road (the A170) going right through it. Stone cottages line the Thornton Beck, there's a small triangular village green, a pond thronged with ducks, moorhens, dippers and kingfishers, and almost every house has its own little bridge. There are, too, several small independent shops – a couple of bakeries, cafés and tearooms, art and craft shops, the Chocolate Factory shop, a post office and pharmacy.

Due north of Thornton, east of the main road, lies the **Dalby Forest Drive** (visitor centre daily 10am–5pm; car parking £7; ✆01751/460 295), nearly ten miles of footpaths, cycleways and picnic areas. Look out for fun **Go Ape** to the south, with lots of clambering and swinging in the trees (April–Oct daily 9am–5pm, closed Tues in term time; Nov Sat & Sun 9am–2/2.30pm; £30; ✆08456 439 215, ⓦwww.goape.co.uk).

Starting at Low Staindale, just north of the Dalby Forest Drive, is the Bride-stones Trail. The **Bridestones** (open all year dawn to dusk; free, though donations welcome), owned by the National Trust, are huge sandstone formations that have been eroded into wildly tortuous shapes that get bigger the further north you go. Surrounded by heather moorland and ancient woodland, they are much loved by bouldering enthusiasts, though they are also of more general interest.

Lockton and Levisham

North of Thornton-le-Dale, and west of the main road lie two attractive villages – Lockton and Levisham. **LOCKTON** (ⓦ www.locktonlevisham.co.uk) has a tiny church and a **youth hostel** (Old School; open all year; ℡ 0845 371 9128; £18/night), which was renovated recently and is a Green Beacon hostel – that is, one that is designed to be environmentally friendly, while **LEVISHAM**, a mile or so further on, consists of two rows of houses facing each other across the green. At the top end stands the attractive **Horseshoe Inn** (℡ 01751/460 240, ⓦ www.horseshoelevisham.co.uk; ❸), which offers open fires, main courses from £11.50 to £15.95 and comfortable rooms; there are also several B&Bs and the Victorian *Moorlands Country House Hotel* (℡ 01751/460 229, ⓦ www.moorlandslevisham.co.uk; ❻), a multi-award-winning guesthouse with patterned carpets, chintzy designs and nice gardens in a renovated Victorian building on the green. The village offers access to the nearby National Park-owned **Levisham Estate**, over five square miles of beautiful moors, valleys and woods which form a microcosm of the whole National Park. This is absolutely prime walking country, and if you don't want to use the car, you can get to it on the North York Moors Railway – Levisham has its own **station**.

The Hole of Horcum

Continuing north on the A169 brings you to the **Hole of Horcum**, a gargantuan depression in the landscape (3/4 mile long, 400ft deep), which looks as if it might have been caused by a primordial meteor strike. According to legend it was created by the giant Wade scooping out earth to throw at his wife during an argument and missing, creating instead the nearby hill called Blakey Topping. Its actual cause is, alas, considerably more mundane than meteor or giant – it's the result of erosion caused by the Levisham Beck which you can see meandering along its bottom. There's also an ancient earthwork – the **Horcum Dyke** – and you're asked to keep to the footpaths to prevent damaging to it.

Goathland and around

A further five miles north, to the west of the A169, is the unspoilt village of **GOATHLAND** (ⓦ www.goathland.info) which is well worth visiting in its own right. Easily accessible by road or rail, it is strung out on a hillside along a sheep-dotted common (the sheep of the Duchy of Lancaster have long had common grazing rights in the village), with a North York Moors Railway station at the bottom and the ivy-clad stone *Mallyan Spout Hotel* (℡ 01947/896 486, ⓦ www.mallyanspout.co.uk; ❹) at the top. The *Mallyan Spout*, which has an old-fashioned air yet with all modern comforts, manages to cater for both passing walkers in search of drink and pub grub and longer-term guests wanting comfort and good food. Down a footpath to the right of the hotel is one of the National Park's most famous waterfalls – the 80ft-high **Mallyan Spout**. When you get to the beck, turn left, and the waterfall is a couple of hundred yards along the bank; it can be wet underfoot – allow twenty minutes there, thirty on the way back.

However, the reason that Goathland is likely to be thronged with tourists snapping away with their cameras, whatever time of the year, is that the village is the setting for popular TV series **Heartbeat**. As the fictional Aidensfield, it has the village store, police station, garage/undertaker's and the *Aidensfield Arms* (actually the *Goathland Hotel*), though as is the way with TV and film, other familiar buildings, close together in the series, are in reality up to 75 miles away.

West of Goathland is one of the best-preserved stretches of **Roman Road** in Britain, though it's not easy to get to. If you drive west from the *Mallyan Spout Hotel* you'll arrive at a signpost giving you the choice of approaching the Roman Road on foot or by car. Either way, there's not much to see, since although the road was excavated, it is now fairly overgrown, but it does allow you to appreciate the amazing feat achieved by the Romans – the whole of Europe was crisscrossed by hundreds of miles of these wonderfully well-engineered road.

In the middle of nowhere between Goathland and Egton Bridge, and run by the same people as *La Rosa* hotel in Whitby, is the hippyish *La Rosa Campsite*, Murk Esk Cottage (☎07786/072 866, ⓦwww.larosa.co.uk), with vintage and classic caravans, tepee, low-energy lighting and compost loo. Decor and sense of humour are similar in both.

A further five miles along the A169 brings you to the village of **SLEIGHTS**, about three miles short of Whitby. Slung out on the hills either side of the River Esk, its main claim to fame is Flint Jack, a famous nineteenth-century antique furniture faker who lived in the village. Just before the village, a road heads west towards Grosmont, and the beautiful Esk Valley.

The Esk Valley

Cutting right across the northern edge of the North York Moors, from west to east, the **Esk Valley** is an idyllically unspoilt part of Yorkshire which seems as yet undiscovered by many of the holidaymakers who visit the county. This is partly because there are no main roads in the valley itself – just a network of minor roads that meander from village to village through pasture and woodland.

The first village you encounter as you travel west up the valley from the main Pickering-to-Whitby A169, is **GROSMONT**. A farming area which became industrialized in the nineteenth century, first when the railway arrived, then when navvies digging tunnels discovered ironstone, Grosmont enjoyed great prosperity in the mid-nineteenth century by quarrying stone, smelting iron, making bricks and servicing the railway. Its iron industry was, however, destroyed by the wholesale production of steel in Sheffield and elsewhere from about the 1880s, and the village today is pleasantly rural, known largely for being the junction between the **North York Moors Railway** and the **Esk Valley Line** from Whitby to Middlesborough. There's a fine *Grosmont Industrial Past* walk and others, with notes available online from the North York Moors National Park Authority (ⓦwww.northyorkmoors.org.uk).

The next villages west are Egton and Egton Bridge. In **EGTON** it's worth visiting the Roman Catholic St Hedda's Church, famous for its wall paintings and for the shrine to martyr Father Nicholas Postgate, hung, drawn and quartered in York in 1679 for tending to Catholics in the area. Egton also has a station on the Esk Valley Line, and a fine moors **pub** in the *Wheatsheaf* (☎01947/895 271, ⓦwww.wheatsheafegton.co.uk; ❸), with its cosy bar, attractive dining room and accommodation. **EGTON BRIDGE**, just down the road, is a village which climbs from the tree-filled valley on either side of the eponymous bridge and is known for its **stepping stones** (presumably pre-dating the bridge) and **gooseberries** – the Egton Bridge Old Gooseberry Society holds its annual show in St Hedda's Church on the first Tuesday in August. This part of the valley claims the largest gooseberry in the world – it weighed 56g.

Like Egton Bridge, **LEALHOLM** has stepping stones across the river, while **DANBY** is not only a particularly attractive moorland village with an Esk Valley Line station, but is also host to the **Moors National Park Centre** (April–Oct daily 10am–5pm; Nov, Dec & March daily 11am–4pm; Jan & Feb Sat & Sun 11am–4pm; free; Ⓦwww.northyorkmoors.org.uk). One of only two National Park Centres – the other is at Sutton Bank – it's well worth stopping at. From the car park you can take the **Crow Wood Trail**, use the outside children's **play area** and picnic site, follow numerous **walks** or the riverside trail, while in the centre itself, which is housed in a row of stone cottages, there are interactive exhibitions, an audiovisual presentation about the National Park as a whole, an indoor climbing wall for kids, a tourist information centre, a well-stocked tearoom, a gift shop and toilets.

Whitby

WHITBY is the most interesting and atmospheric of Yorkshire's coastal towns. Part fishing port, part seaside resort, it is picture-postcard pretty and rich with geological, historical and literary wealth. Rich in fossils and jet, both of which can be bought in the town, historically, Whitby is important for its medieval abbey where the pivotal Synod of Whitby is thought to have taken place, its long fishing and whaling traditions, and its ship-building, while its literary credentials include connections with medieval poet Cædmon, and with Elizabeth Gaskell, Lewis Carroll and Wilkie Collins. Above all, Whitby is forever associated with Bram Stoker's **Count Dracula**, who made landfall in the British Isles here. The latter explains the popularity of the town with Goths.

It may be that in the past Whitby had its rough edges – what seaport hasn't – but they've been smoothed away of late to create a destination with a little bit of everything you need to make for a good holiday break.

The northernmost of the main North Yorkshire coastal towns, and the only one to face largely north, Whitby occupies the gorge created over millennia by the River Esk, which runs through the town and out between its famous twin piers and breakwaters into the North Sea. The town itself climbs up the gorge on either side. Whitby is thus divided into two clearly defined areas – the **East** and **West Cliffs**, the two joined by a century-old swing bridge.

Arrival and information

Whitby **train station** is right in the centre of town on Station Square, just south of the swing bridge, conveniently just across the road from the **tourist information centre** (daily: May & June 9.30am–5pm; July & Aug 9.30am–7pm; Sept –April 10am–4.30pm; ☎01723/383 637, Ⓦwww.discoveryorkshirecoast.com) and next to the **bus station**. Motorists entering the town are likely to do so along one or other of the banks of the river – either way, there's plenty of **parking** along the riverside, especially around the marina. There's also considerable on-street parking on the hotel-lined streets of West Cliff. Once in town, everywhere is walkable – indeed, walking around Whitby is one of its great pleasures.

Accommodation

Most of Whitby's **accommodation** is up on West Cliff, though a number of pubs and restaurants in the town centre also offer rooms.

Hotels, B&Bs and guesthouses

Dunsley Hall Dunsley ☎01947/893 437, ⓦwww
.dunsleyhall.com. This dignified Victorian country
house hotel (the choice of visiting celebrities) has
spacious, often oak-panelled, rooms, fine gardens,
pool, sauna and leisure club. It's a couple of miles
west of town. ❻

Estbek House Sandsend ☎01947/893 424,
ⓦwww.estbekhouse.co.uk. Georgian house
beside the beck and close to the beach at
Sandsend, two miles from Whitby. Four attractive
rooms (called Alum, Florence, Eva and Nora –
who could resist?), and a restaurant (expensive;
reservations recommended) famed for its fresh
fish and seafood. ❺

La Rosa Hotel 5 East Terrace ☎01947/606
981, ⓦwww.larosa.co.uk. Eccentric B&B with
eight rooms done out in extravagantly individual style
– think French naughty nineties courtesy of auctions,
eBay and car boot sales. Great fun and terrific views
of the harbour and the abbey. Breakfast picnic
delivered in a basket to your door. If you want slick
modern accommodation with comprehensive facilities forget it. But for sheer exuberant fun and faded
glory, try *La Rosa*. Street parking. ❹

Marine Hotel 13 Marine Parade ☎01947/605 022,
ⓦwww.the-marine-hotel.co.uk. Tiny hotel (more a
restaurant-with-rooms) on the quayside which has
done wonders with very little space. Four rooms, two
with balconies, beautiful decor, nice views across the
harbour. The restaurant specializes in fresh, largely
locally sourced seafood. A little gem, and if it's full,
they might get you into sister hotel *Moon and
Sixpence* (see p.253) just along the road. ❺

Number Five 5 Havelock Place ☎01947/606 361.
West Cliff B&B that provides a good breakfast.
Eight rooms with small but smart en-suite showers.
No credit cards. ❷

Shepherd's Purse 95 Church St ☎01947/820
228, ⓦwww.theshepherdspurse.com. Popular
wholefood store combined with clothes and gift
shop and rooms. Its best rooms (with brass
bedsteads and pine furniture) are set around a
galleried courtyard; the two pricier doubles on the
upper level are nicest, and one has its own
balcony. ❷

White Horse and Griffin 87 Church St
☎01947/604 857, ⓦwww.whitehorseandgriffin
.co.uk. In the centre of Whitby's old town, with
wonderful views of the harbour. Nicely renovated
rooms (and several cottages) with many original
features. The restaurant has a good range of fish
and meat dishes, with vegetarian options. If you
like character, this is a good option, but it can be
noisy. ❷

White Linen 24 Bagdale ☎01947/603 635,
ⓦwww.whitelinenguesthouse.co.uk. Superior B&B
in a restored Georgian house. Nine individually
styled rooms with modern feel and good shower
rooms. ❸

Hostels

Harbour Grange Spital Bridge, Church St
☎01947/600 817, ⓦwww.whitbybackpackers
.co.uk. Backpackers' hostel right on the river
(eastern side) with 24 beds in five small
dorms (£17, plus £1 for bedding if required).
Self-catering kitchen and lounge; curfew at
11.30pm. ❶

Whitby YHA Abbey House, East Cliff ☎0845 371
9049, ⓔwhitby@yha.org.uk. Fairly recently opened
flagship hostel, located in a Grade 1 listed building
right next to the Abbey Visitor Centre. Stunning
views, Victorian conservatory, tearoom and restaurant, and every facility. Rates include breakfast and
entry to the abbey. Dorm beds from £19.95, though
more expensive in summer. ❷

The Town

The old town on the East Cliff reeks of history, with the narrow **cobbled streets**
and **tile-roofed houses** of the fishing port, dominated by the church and
graveyard of **St Mary's** and the gaunt ruins of **Whitby Abbey**, high on the
headland above. Here are the **199 steps**, joining the old town to the church and
Abbey, the shops selling **Whitby jet**, the old **Market Place** with its 1788-built
Town Hall, and the **Captain Cook Memorial Museum**.

The West Cliff, mainly Georgian and Victorian, has the modern port and **fish
quay**, a few amusement arcades, gift shops and souvenir stalls, the **Lifeboat
Museum**, the **Whitby Museum** and **Pannett Art Gallery** (they're in the same
building), the **Whitby Pavilion and Theatre** and, on the top of the cliff looking
out across the town towards the Abbey, the **Captain Cook Monument** and the
famous **whalebone arch**.

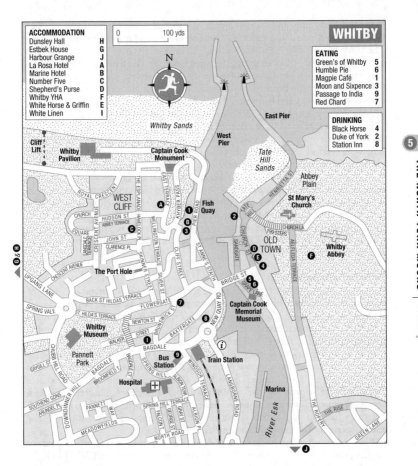

ACCOMMODATION
Dunsley Hall	H
Estbek House	G
Harbour Grange	J
La Rosa Hotel	A
Marine Hotel	B
Number Five	C
Shepherd's Purse	D
Whitby YHA	F
White Horse & Griffin	E
White Linen	I

WHITBY

EATING
Green's of Whitby	5
Humble Pie	6
Magpie Café	1
Moon and Sixpence	3
Passage to India	9
Red Chard	7

DRINKING
Black Horse	4
Duke of York	2
Station Inn	8

The 199 steps

Whether you're staying in Whitby for a few hours or a few weeks, you really must climb up the **199 steps** to St Mary's Church and Whitby Abbey. The 199 steps, or Church Stairs, which curve elegantly up from the end of Church Street onto the headland are now stone-flagged and iron-railed, but once consisted of a wooden staircase constructed to help pallbearers carry coffins up to St Mary's churchyard. It's quite a climb, but there are benches every now and again at which you can take a breather. And if the climb doesn't take your breath away, the views across the roofs of the old town and Whitby harbour to West Cliff certainly will.

If you're pushing a pram or are in any other way restricted, there's a steep cobbled ramp-like street beside the steps (Church Lane) or, if you want to drive, you can go the long way around – the abbey's signposted from the A171 to the southeast of the town.

St Mary's Church

Before visiting the abbey, do make sure you have a good long look at **St Mary's Church**. Though not perhaps one for the architectural purist, it's among the most extraordinary churches in the UK – as Pevsner describes it, from the outside it's "low and spreading and battlemented, a wonderful jumble of medieval and Georgian", and when you enter it's "hard to believe and impossible not to love". The tower is probably Norman, but the windows of the nave don't even pretend to be ecclesiastical – they're straightforward Georgian domestic windows. Inside, the stonework is a jumble of different dates and styles, mainly Norman and Georgian. But it's the furnishings that make this church unique. Everywhere there are wooden galleries and balconies, dating from the seventeenth century onwards, making it look more like a Nonconformist chapel than an Anglican church. Seventeenth-century too is the famous **Cholmley Pew**, one of the galleries which stands on four barley-sugar columns, built in the most conspicuous place right across the chancel arch to celebrate the local lord of the manor's importance, and with its own external wooden covered way to save the great man and his family having to mix with the hoi polloi. Another external covered way gave access to some of the other galleries. Elsewhere in the church, look out for the parish chest, the great candelabra (there's no electric lighting, so the church has to be lit by candles) and the wonderful three-tier pulpit with two "vamping horns" – an early form of public address system. In the **churchyard**, near the top of the steps, you'll see **Cædmon's Cross**, erected at the end of the nineteenth century to celebrate the Anglo-Saxon poet.

Whitby Abbey

Beyond St Mary's Church, crowning the top of the headland, stand the ruins of Benedictine **Whitby Abbey**. Next to it stands a ruined mansion, which is interesting in its own right. After Henry VIII dissolved the monasteries, the land upon which the ruins sit was bought in 1540 from the Crown by the Cholmley family, who moved into the abbot's lodgings. Then, in 1672 Sir Hugh Cholmley II (he of the sacrilegious pew), used stone from the monastery ruins to build himself a new mansion, the shell of which now houses the **Abbey Visitor Centre** (April–Sept daily 10am–6pm; Oct–March Thurs–Mon 10am–4pm; £5.80; EH). The centre introduces the history of the abbey with lots of displays, and touch-screen computers through which Cholmley, for example, or Bram Stoker or a monk will tell you what you need to know and answer your questions. Here, as part of the admission price, you can pick up a useful audio-guide.

Whitby Abbey was established in 657 AD as a double male and female monastery by King Oswy of Northumbria, who appointed a royal princess **Hild** (614–80) as first abbess. A formidable woman, who had previously been the abbess of Hartlepool, she became advisor to kings, and promoter of ordinary men – Cædmon's was a cow-herd until, following a dream and encouraged by Abbess Hild, he became the first English poet. Because of her reputation for wisdom, Whitby Abbey was chosen as the venue for the **Synod of Whitby** in 664, when it was decided that the Roman rather than the Celtic way of calculating the date of Easter should be used.

Nothing of the Anglo-Saxon monastery is now visible. The ruins that you can see are of a monastery built by the Normans in around 1220, and even then only of the monastery church – the rest was plundered by Cholmley. And the church has suffered since then – from the ravages of time, from its position, exposed to the storms that blow in off the North Sea, and from a German naval bombardment in 1914. What it lacks in surviving remains, however, it more than makes up for in atmosphere, hence Bram Stoker's choice of Whitby as the backdrop for Count Dracula's arrival in Britain.

Market Place and around

Back at the bottom of the 199 steps, the cobbled streets and "yards" of the **old town** – narrow Church Street, the Market Place, even narrower Sandgate Street

– are worth exploring for their small independent shops, their cafés and pubs. There are lots of places where you can buy Whitby jet, minerals and fossils, plus an authentic Victorian jet workshop in the **Whitby Jet Heritage Centre** on Church Street (℡01947/821 530, Ⓦwww.whitbyjet.co.uk). Some of the pubs in particular – the **Board Inn** and the **Duke of York** (see p.253) – back on to the harbour with views that look like paintings. The Market Place is dominated by the **Town Hall**, built in 1788 for Nathaniel Cholmley, with an open ground floor of Tuscan columns sheltering a couple of stalls selling clothes, a spiral staircase to the upper floor, Venetian windows and a rather fine clock.

Captain Cook Memorial Museum

Beyond the Market Place both Church Street and Sandgate Street run into Bridge Street. Just before the swing bridge, down pretty flagstoned Grape Lane on the left, is the **Captain Cook Memorial Museum** (daily: April–Oct 9.45am–5pm; March 11am–3pm; £4.50; ℡01947/601 900, Ⓦwww.cook museumwhitby.co.uk), housed in the well-preserved seventeenth-century house that the great man lodged in when he first came to Whitby as a 17-year-old to learn his trade as a seaman. It was the family home of the Quaker ship-owner John Walker, who used to lodge the apprentices from his ships in the attic between voyages. His ships hauled coal to London, and Cook learned everything he needed to know about seamanship and navigation on these colliers between 1746 and 1749. The museum collection includes maps, paintings and documents covering every aspect of Cook's life and times – apprenticeship, navigation, ship-building and cartography. The Green and Blue rooms give a good idea of the austere but attractive decor in-keeping with Walker's Quaker beliefs – simple furniture, no pictures on the walls – while the kitchen features its original seventeenth-century brick floor and a good range of the equipment used at the time. On the first floor is the **Whitby Room**, with a model of the sort of ships Walker owned – note the muster roll of one of them, *Freelove*, from 1747, with Cook's name third from the bottom; the 1772 letter from Cook to Captain Hammond, informing him of the changing of the names of the two Whitby colliers bought from him to *Resolution* and *Adventure*; and John Walker's copy of Cook's *A voyage towards the South Pole and Round the World*. Note too the painting of the Whitby shipyards which built the ships Cook used. The **London Room** covers Cook's early service in the Royal Navy and his subsequent career, when he lived in London; the **Voyages Room** deals with his three great voyages in more detail. On the second floor the **Scientists Room** explores the huge contribution Cook's voyages made to eighteenth-century science – he was elected Fellow of the Royal Society in 1775 – and the **Artists Room** contains a wealth of landscapes, botanical and ornithological studies and a portrait of Captain Bligh (of *Mutiny on the Bounty* fame), who captained the *Resolution* on the third voyage. Finally and most affectingly is the top floor **attic** where Cook slept as a youth, the scene recreated by a pinhole model.

It's not just the contents of the museum that re-create Cook's times. The views from the windows, too, give a great feeling of what it must have been like in the seventeenth century – out across the harbour on one side, into narrow Grape Lane on the other. As you leave, pause on the terrace overlooking the harbour – the boats and the houses may have changed since Cook's time, but the atmosphere of nautical bustle and clutter must surely be the same.

The swing bridge, harbour and piers

Just beyond Grape Lane is the **swing bridge** that links the East and West Cliffs. There's been a bridge here for centuries, but the present steel swing bridge, built by the same company that built Blackpool Tower, was inaugurated in 1908, and after a warning bell, swings open electrically to allow boats to move between the Upper and Lower harbour. Upriver is the **Upper Harbour** with the **Endeavour Wharf** on the west bank and, further up, the **marina**, while on the east bank is the Parkol Marine Engineering works where boats are still built. Downriver on either side of the **Lower Harbour** are fish quays with the Lifeboat Station on the right and the Tate Hill pier. Finally, like jaws at the mouth of the river, stand the **West Pier**, completed in 1831 and with a graceful 65ft-plus lighthouse at its tip, and the **East Pier**, which is shorter, newer (1854), and has a smaller, more functional-looking lighthouse. Look out for the capstans used to haul ships into port when the wind was in the wrong direction. Each pier is extended by concrete-and-wood structures, further protecting the harbour from the elements, their two tiers today often lined with anglers.

The West Cliff

If the East Cliff gives a picture of Whitby's medieval past, the buildings of the West Cliff are more about its Georgian heyday as a fishing and whaling port and its Victorian and Edwardian incarnation as a seaside resort. Right after the bridge, the dockside road (from New Quay Rd to Pier Rd) is lined with cafés, restaurants, pubs, fish-and-chip shops, hot-dog stalls, even a clairvoyant's booth. Goths and gothic novel fans might enjoy the **Dracula Experience** (Easter–Oct daily 9.45am–5pm; Nov–Easter Sat & Sun only; £2.50; ☏01947/601 923, ⓦwww .draculaexperience.co.uk), with tableaux and special effects illustrating the story of Bram Stoker's *Dracula* – you'll either love it or hate it.

A little further down the road is the **Whitby Lifeboat Museum** (Easter–Oct 10am–4pm depending upon the weather; ⓦwww.rnli.org.uk), stuffed with medals, photographs, paintings, models, lifeboat paraphernalia and artefacts from famous rescues. Stories from the archives of individual RNLI crew and survivors rub shoulders with evocative mementos from those involved in wrecks and rescues. Opposite the museum is the western **fish quay**, and beyond it the **bandstand** – a sight for sore eyes on a summer's evening, with the band playing against the backdrop of the East Cliff, its orange-roofed houses overlooked by St Mary's Church, with just the top of the abbey peeping out behind it. From Battery Parade next to it, its gun pointing out to sea, there is access to broad, clean **Whitby Sands**.

A stiff climb to the top of the West Cliff brings you to the main concentration of hotels and B&Bs, centring on the **Royal Crescent**. The whole area owes its existence to George Hudson ("the Railway King") who, determined to develop Whitby as a seaside resort, brought the railway to the town in 1839, and developed this part of the West Cliff as a typical Victorian resort, with handsome buildings and pleasant green areas, all with views across the sea or, in some cases, the town. At the end of the East Terrace is a commanding statue of **Captain Cook**, and the iconic **whalebone arch**, topped with the point of a harpoon. Though there's been a whalebone arch here since the middle of the nineteenth century, the present one (the jawbone of a bowhead whale killed under license by Inuits) was apparently donated to the town by Alaska in 2003.

Beyond the statue and arch, a road leads down the cliff face to the **Spa Pavilion**, opposite but below the Royal Crescent (see p.254). Back at the swing bridge, ahead of it and to the left is the town centre, with its shops, visitor centre, attractively simple 1847 train station and bus station. Look out, between the station and the swing bridge, for the pavement bench in the shape of an ammonite, and the tribute to local sea captain, explorer and minister William Scoresby, inventor of the Crow's Nest.

Whitby Museum and Pannett Art Gallery

Beyond the train station is Pannett Park, recently remodelled, with a state-of-the-art children's playground, fine views over the town and the combined **Whitby Museum** and **Pannett Art Gallery** (Tues–Sun 9.30am–4.30pm; £3; Ⓦwww .whitbymuseum.org.uk), which occupies the fine building of the Whitby Literary and Philosophical Society. Deliberately retaining the atmosphere of an Edwardian museum, with mahogany cases mounted on sets of drawers, it covers local geology, the medieval background to the abbey, Whitby's heyday as a port, including Cook and the Scoresbys, local industry (fishing, shipbuilding, jet, the coming of the railways, tourism), and has rather good collections of ceramics and glass, coins, seals, clocks and watches, weapons, toys and dolls, and, in a new extension, costume. As one might expect, though, the museum's greatest strength is in its **fossil collection**, which includes a wide range of prehistoric life forms, and in particular massive marine reptiles. Indeed, the impetus for the formation of the Literary and Philosophical Society in 1823 came from concern that the large numbers of fossils being found by alum quarrymen in nearby cliffs were being sold to collectors and therefore lost to the Whitby area. The **Art Gallery** has a collection of paintings of the local area, and of the work of local artists.

Eating, drinking and entertainment

Whitby boasts a good range of **pubs** and **restaurants**, most of them gathered around both shores of the harbour. Eating and drinking are, indeed, the principal evening and weekend pastimes – the only large-scale venue for music **gigs** is the Pavilion Complex.

Cafés and restaurants

🚶 **Green's of Whitby** 13 Bridge St ☎01947/600 284, Ⓦwww.greensofwhitby .com. A few yards from the swing bridge, and thought by many to be the best restaurant in Whitby, *Green's* has a lively bistro downstairs and a fine-dining restaurant on the first floor. Ingredients are locally sourced, so lots of fish and meat dishes. Bistro main courses are between £10 and £20, and in the restaurant two courses cost £34.95, three cost £41.95. Great food in friendly, unpretentious surroundings. Very chic boutique apartments available too (minimum stay two nights; ⑤).

🚶 **Humble Pie** 163 Church St ☎07919/074 954, Ⓦwww.humblepiemash.com. Tiny sixteenth-century building serving a range of pies with mash and peas: steak, stout and leek; Romany; Homity; haggis and neep, and many more. 1940s decor and World War II music. Pies cooked fresh to order. Soft drinks only – no license.

🚶 **Magpie Café** 14 Pier Rd ☎01947/602 058. Said by Rick Stein to be one of the best fish-and-chip shops in the country, the *Magpie* has served food from its 1750-built premises since the start of World War II. To call it a fish-and-chip shop is a bit disingenuous – although it provides the normal takeaway service, it also serves lesser-known fish like Woof and John Dory in its restaurant, and has an extensive wine list. 11.30am–9pm.

Moon and Sixpence 5 Marine Parade ☎01947/604 416. Near the quay, with bistro-style ambience, good for fish, meat and game. Also has posh rooms upstairs (sister establishment to the *Marine Hotel;* ⑤), with natty design and top-end fixtures.

Passage to India 30–31 Windsor Terrace ☎01947/606 500, Ⓦwww.passagetoindia.eu. Tandoori restaurant near the station, bright red and black decor, great food, friendly and efficient service, main courses £8–12.

Red Chard 22 Flowergate ☎01947/606 660. Relaxed place for coffee or glass of wine, or dig into dishes ranging from prawn cocktail and bubble-and-squeak to saffron pappardelle. Mains £11–19. Closed Mon, plus Sat lunch.

Pubs

Black Horse 91 Church St. Lovely old pub (parts date from the seventeenth century) in the heart of the old town, with real ale, Yorkshire cheeses and seafood.

🚶 **Duke of York** 124 Church St ☎01947/600 324, Ⓦwww.dukeofyork.co.uk. In a great position at the bottom of the 199 steps, the *Duke of York* is warm and inviting, with black beams, nautical memorabilia (harpoons, propellers, numbers and names of Whitby-based ships, photos), church pews and views across to the harbour and West Cliff. Pub food (no main course above £9), music and

TV, alas. Also has seven rooms, six with harbour views (**②**; breakfast not included).
Station Inn New Quay Rd. A real-ale haunt, with a changing selection of guest beers and live music on Fridays.

Venues
Pavilion Complex (aka the Spa Pavilion) West Cliff ☎ 01947/820 625, ⓦ www.whitby.uk.net.

A glass-and-iron structure built as the *Westcliff Saloon* in 1880, much extended since, and now a complex which hosts pantomimes, comedy, drama and music, as well as hosting events in various music festivals – folk, country, and the famous twice-yearly Gothic Weekend. There's also the pleasant *Crystal Lounge* café, with views over the sea.

The coast northwest of Whitby

Northwest of Whitby the coast becomes increasingly rugged, with headlands, bays, a scattering of small villages and some wonderful views.

Sandsend and Runswick

Two miles beyond Whitby, and accessible from it by road or along the beach, is the village of **SANDSEND**, made up almost entirely of boarding houses and cafés lining the sea wall. The *Wits End Café* has a large car park from which people often fish. Sandsend is great fun when the sea's rough, because the water breaks over the sea wall.

After Sandsend the road bears inland up a winding 25° hill through Lythe. It's worth taking the side road off to the right after Lythe and heading for **Runswick Bay**. When you get to the top of the cliffs (there are two hotels), turn right down yet another steep hill, with wonderful views of the bay. At the bottom is the pretty village of **RUNSWICK**, which has houses stacked steeply up from the sea and one of the few remaining thatched houses on this stretch of coast (it was once the coastguard's cottage). A North Yorkshire smuggling village, Runswick has suffered badly over the years from the ravages of storm and sea, with a whole new village having to be built in the seventeenth century when a landslide destroyed the old one. The village continued to suffer storm damage until a sea wall was built in 1970. Today Runswick is an idyllic little place with café/tearooms (summers only), a pub, the *Royal Hotel* (☎ 01947/840 215, ⓦ www.royalhotelrunswick .com), which does good pub food from £8.25 to £10.50, a chapel and a colossal beach. Look out for the last few remaining "binks" – standing stones outside the front door at which the washing would be done.

The next settlement northwest is **Port Mulgrave**, once a thriving ironstone-mining settlement, now uninhabited and owned by the National Trust. The mine was opened in 1855 and had exhausted the reserves of ironstone by the turn of the century. The port continued to be used for ironstone from another pit, but eventually became disused after World War I, and its facilities succumbed to the weather, to fire, and to the attentions of the Royal Engineers, who didn't want it to be used by the Germans during World War II. There's a steep path down to the remains of the port – a ruined jetty, the entrance to the adit mine – dotted now with corrugated iron sheds, fishing boats and lobster pots.

Staithes

The last village before the industrial sprawl around Middlesbrough is **STAITHES** – just before turning off the A174 for the village, you can see a large cement works in the distance, standing like a Teesside advance guard. When visiting Staithes you have to leave your car in a **car park** at the top of a hill, then walk down into the village. The hill is so steep that there are benches every now and again so that people toiling up it can catch their breath. Most of the village is on the east bank of the Staithes Beck, though some houses on the opposite bank are joined to the rest by a footbridge. The houses are painted in various pastel shades, and there are several independent shops and a couple of **pubs** on the High Street – the *Royal George* (℡01947/841 432) and, on the quayside, the *Cod and Lobster* (℡01947/840 490). There's not much to choose between them for food and drinks, but the *Cod and Lobster* certainly has the edge on location – it's right on the sea wall. There are courts and alleys off the main street, often stepped, and a small, attractive harbour with boat-launching slipway, steps down onto a small beach and a café/sandwich shop. Across the mouth of the Beck stands Cowbar Nab, a sombre, gull-dotted cliff.

At one time one of the biggest fishing ports in England, Staithes depended on the sea for its livelihood – not only fishing, but boat-building, sail-making and even smuggling. Although it would undoubtedly attract visitors for its beauty and quaintness alone, it can also claim a connection to Captain Cook – hard as it is to credit, as a young man he worked in a shop in the village – Sanderson's, which stood near the *Cod and Lobster*, and which was later washed away during a storm. It was no doubt the seafarers' tales and nautical atmosphere in the village that inspired him to move to Whitby to become a seaman. Today, on the right as you enter the village, the **Captain Cook and Staithes Heritage Centre** (daily 10am–5pm, Sat & Sun only in Jan; ℡01947/841 454) offers a tumultuous collection of photographs, paintings, models, books and manuscripts, with a reconstructed street and period rooms, all illustrating the history of the village in general and James Cook's stay here in particular.

From Whitby to Scarborough

The coast between Whitby and Scarborough offers a succession of sea views, headlands and rocky, or in some places sandy, bays. Take any of the minor lanes that strike east from the A171 and you're virtually guaranteed vistas to gladden the heart. Worth a detour in particular are the **Shire Horse Centre** near Staintondale and **Ravenscar**. And **Robin Hood's Bay**, though a little over the top and undoubtedly a little twee, is also very pretty, packed with interest and well worth visiting.

Robin Hood's Bay

North across the bay from Ravenscar (though there's no direct route – you need to return to the main road) is **ROBIN HOOD'S BAY**, one of the prettiest villages in the country. The village, known locally as "Bay Town" or "Bay", is in two parts – the Victorian development at the top of the hill, and the original village at the bottom. The **car park** is at the top of the hill, and you'll need to walk down the steep incline to get to the interesting bit.

Probably originally settled by Saxons and Vikings, it is first mentioned in records from Tudor times. Despite local legend, there's little likelihood that the village was ever visited by, or had anything to do with, Robin Hood of Sherwood Forest. If Dutch trading maps are anything to go by, Robin Hood's Bay was more important than Whitby – the former was identified on the maps, the latter wasn't. The village's great heyday was in the eighteenth century, when it supplemented its earnings from fishing and farming with a well-developed **smuggling industry**. Remote and difficult to get to, the village was ideal for smuggling, with virtually everybody in the village involved – not only the fishermen and their families, but also farmers, the clergy and the gentry, either directly or by providing finance and safe houses. Certainly, all took their share of the profits or of the tea, gin, rum, brandy and tobacco that was being smuggled. Frequent set-tos took place between excise cutters and smugglers' ships, and between excisemen and smugglers on land. It is said that a series of tunnels and passageways ensured that contraband could be moved from the quay to the top of the village without seeing the light of day.

Today you enter the village past a modern (2000) sculpture with the name of the village carved on it among reliefs of – a sea lion? An owl? A flight of steps? Carved by a local sculptor as a millennium project, its interpretation is limited only by the viewer's imagination. On the way into the village down a steep hill, with views across rose-coloured roofs to the sea, you come to a plaque commemorating heroic efforts to save the crew of the brig *Visitor*, which ran aground in the bay in 1881. Local boats couldn't be launched, so the Whitby lifeboat was dragged across the headland by eighteen horses over six miles, rising to 500ft, through 7 snowdrifts, with the way being cleared by hundreds of men. It took a near-miraculous two hours, and all the crew were saved.

The main street drops down between terraced cottages with little lanes off, takes a sharp right at the *Laurel Inn*, and brings you down to sea level at the **Old Coastguard Station** (March–July, Sept & Oct daily 10am–5pm; Aug Tues–Sun 10am–5pm; Nov–March Sat & Sun 10am–4pm; free; ☎01947/885 900; NT) now a visitor centre, with displays explaining how the local landscape was formed, and the slipway. There are little lanes and flights of steps, terraces which allow you to look out across the bay, teashops, pubs, B&Bs and hotels, a post office, and little independent shops selling sweets, books and gifts. The steps to the right of the Old Coastguard Station lead to a cliff top walk across to Boggle Hole and its youth hostel.

Apart from its seafaring traditions, Robin Hood's Bay has other things of interest. When the tide's out the flat rocks that appear (the scaurs), split by a geological fault, are a rich source of rock pool life and fossils. Robin Hood's Bay was also the setting for the **Bramlewick Books** by Leo Walmsley, who lived in the village for most of his childhood – there's a blue plaque marking the house. The **Robin Hood's Bay Museum** (June Wed & Sun 2–4pm; July & Aug Mon–Fri & Sun noon–4pm; also limited other days, check website; free; ☎01947/881 252, ⓦmuseum.rhbay.co.uk) on the south side of the village, and accessible only via one of the village's characteristic cobbled and stepped pathways, has displays on aspects of the village's geology and history.

Finally, **Swell** (☎01947/880 180, ⓦwww.swell.org.uk) is a unique combination of gift shop, café and cinema. It was built as the Wesleyan Chapel in 1779, and John Wesley himself preached (and Leo Walmsley went to school) here. It was superseded in 1936, went through a number of different uses, and in its present incarnation uses the old chapel as a cinema. The box pews can be a little unforgiving, so you're welcome to take a cushion. Check the website for the film listings.

Ravenscar

Next stop south along the coast is the village of **RAVENSCAR**, which boasts spectacular views across Robin Hood's Bay from its access road – there's a line of benches beside the road, and you can quite see why they were put there. The **National Trust Centre** (June–Sept daily 10am–4pm; otherwise Sat & Sun 10am–4pm; ☎01723/870 423), down a short drive on the left just before the village, has displays on the ten miles of this stretch of coast, including its geology, wildlife and the early industrial history – especially the remains of the alum works, which extracted alum from the hillside to be used in dying cloth and tanning leather, and which you can visit on foot from the centre. A few hundred yards further and you'll arrive at an overgrown railway station platform with a long carved sign saying "Peak". This is all that remains of the highest (630ft above sea level) station on the Scarborough-to-Whitby **railway**, opened in 1885, and closed by Beeching in 1965. Because the gradient was so steep, trains had to take a run at it, sometimes several times. And it was called Peak Station because this was the original name of the village. The whole area was bought by the Peak Estate Company in 1890, with plans to develop a new resort to rival Scarborough, and from 1897 the name of the village was changed to Ravenscar. New roads were built, plots of land sold, sewers laid, and works set up to make bricks for the anticipated building boom. The company had, however, misjudged the market, plots didn't sell, and in 1911 the company went bankrupt.

The Shire Horse Centre

The **Shire Horse Centre** (July & Aug Tues, Wed, Fri & bank hol Sun & Mon 10.30am–4.30pm; £5.50; ☎01723/870 458, Ⓦ www.shirehorsefarm.co.uk), which is well signposted off the main road south of Ravenscar, offers not only a chance to get close to these engaging gentle giants but also a variety of live horse and pony shows, stables, forge, a small museum, a café and a variety of walks, together with opportunities for children to stroke Shetland ponies. And the drive to the centre through a wooded glen with waterfalls is in itself a delight.

Scarborough

The undoubted queen of the North Yorkshire coast is **SCARBOROUGH**, which lies halfway between Bridlington in the south and Whitby in the north. Located on a headland with a bay on either side, its significance arose from having a powerful royal fortress overlooking the town. From the thirteenth century onwards Scarborough was also famous for its annual fair, which lasted from mid-August to late September, attracting merchants from all over Britain and abroad (and giving its name to the traditional ballad *Scarborough Fair*). In the seventeenth century, when mineral waters were discovered, Scarborough became popular as a spa town – especially after the 1660 publication of a book about the waters – and in the eighteenth century it increasingly became known as a seaside resort. When the railways arrived in 1845 the trickle of visitors attracted by the sea bathing rose to a flood. All this has led to Scarborough's claim to be the oldest resort in Britain. Today it is a large town which, though still recognizably a seaside resort, is also a player in the corporate events market, a functioning fishing port, the regional capital, and has its share of light industry.

As a destination for holidaymakers Scarborough has something for everybody – a ruined **castle**, two **churches** that are well worth visiting, several good **museums**, the **Sea Life Centre** linked to the town by the miniature **North Bay railway**, a number of beautifully landscaped **public gardens**, an attractive **fishing port**, the world-famous **Stephen Joseph Theatre** and the recently renovated **Open Air Theatre** (the largest in Europe). It also has all the things that go to make up the traditional British seaside resort: harbour cruises and speedboat rides, fairgrounds and amusement arcades, candyfloss stalls and ice cream parlours, donkey rides and cliff lifts, chip shops and tearooms, cafés and restaurants, together with a huge stock of hotels and B&Bs. Above all it has two magnificent **beaches**. Scarborough is also big enough to have a rather good range of shops and a fine collection of Victorian and Edwardian buildings. As you'd expect, a great deal of what goes on in Scarborough is seasonal, though efforts are made to extend the season by encouraging conferences, Christmas specials and so on.

Arrival and information

Those arriving in Scarborough by **car** have a good choice of permanent and seasonal short- and long-stay **car parks** in the town, or they can use one of two park-and-ride facilities, both south of the town centre (one on the A64, the other on the A165). If you're likely to be using the town's car parks a lot, get a copy of the comprehensive *Visitors Guide to Parking in Scarborough* from the tourist information centre. The **train station** is on the southwest edge of the town centre, halfway along Westborough. Buses arrive and depart in the surrounding streets and **National Express** coaches use the car park behind the station. The main **tourist information centre** (Mon–Sat 9/9.30am–5/5.30pm, plus April–Oct Sun 10.30am–4pm; ☎01723/383 637) is in the Brunswick Shopping Centre on Westborough just inside the main ground floor hall, and there's a satellite office on Sandside (April–Oct daily 9.30/10am–5.30pm; Nov–March Sat & Sun 10am–4.30pm). **Open-topped buses** run along the seafront from North Bay to the Spa Complex on South Bay (Easter–Sept daily from 9.30am, March weekends only; £1.60).

Accommodation

As befits one of the UK's great seaside resorts, Scarborough has a wealth of **accommodation**. The largest Victorian and Edwardian hotels are ranged along the cliff tops of both bays, with hundreds of guesthouses and B&Bs in between and back from the front. The advantage of such competition is, of course, competitive prices – shop around.

Alexandra House 21 West St ☎01723/503 205, ⓦwww.scarborough-alexandra.co.uk. One of the traditional guesthouses that Scarborough excels in. Just off the Esplanade, with a selection of twin, double and family rooms. This is a particularly child-friendly hotel, with lots of baby equipment and books/toys/videos/games for older children available – you can even borrow buckets and spades. ❸

Beiderbecke's Hotel 1–3 The Crescent ☎01723/365 766, ⓦwww.beiderbeckes.com. Part of a sedate 1832-built terrace on the South Cliff, *Beiderbecke's Hotel* bills itself as Scarborough's finest boutique hotel. Rooms are comfortable and the bar is old-fashioned in a good way with live jazz on Saturdays. It also features the stylish *Marmalade's Brasserie* with reasonably priced main courses (£12.95–16.95). Free car park for guests. ❹

Crescent Hotel The Crescent ☎01723/360 929, ⓦwww.thecrescenthotel.com. Between the Brunswick shopping centre and the South Shore beach, the *Crescent Hotel* is old-fashioned in atmosphere but contemporary in the facilities it offers. ❺

Crown Spa Hotel Esplanade ☎01723/357 400, ⓦwww.crownspahotel.com. Lovely Victorian building (opened in 1845) in superb position on the cliff above South Shore, with all the facilities you'd expect from a four-star hotel – health club, spa, swimming pool, restaurant and café/bar. Accommodation is not as expensive as you might expect – and prices vary considerably depending on demand. ❸–❻

The Earlsmere 5 Belvedere Rd ☎01723/361 340, ⓦwww.theearlsmere.co.uk. A boutique guest-house, on the cliff above South Shore, housed in an Edwardian terrace building which has retained many original features, in particular the staircase and stained-glass window. The decor of the five guest bedrooms is in keeping with the hotel's origins, but with up-to-date facilities. No children under 12. Free parking. ❹

Raincliffe Hotel 21 Valley Rd ☎01723/373 541, ⓦwww.raincliffehotel.co.uk. Quality traditional hotel/guesthouse in Victorian building back from the South Cliff, with fifteen en-suite rooms, all recently refurbished. Good dinner available. No pets, no children under 8. Street parking. ❷

Scarborough YHA Burniston Rd ☎0845 371 9657. Two miles north of the town, in an early seventeenth-century water mill. A good hostel for families with kids, and 15min walk from the sea. From £12.

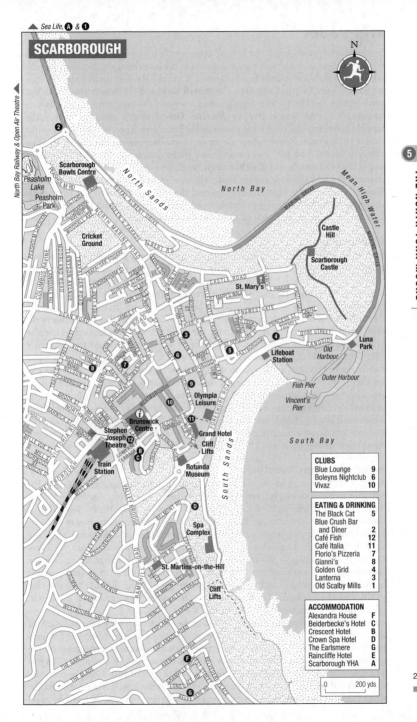

▲ Sea Life, Ⓐ & ❶

SCARBOROUGH

N

North Bay Railway & Open Air Theatre ▲

Peasholm Lake

Peasholm Park

Scarborough Bowls Centre

North Sands

North Bay

Mean High Water

Marine Drive

Cricket Ground

Castle Hill

Scarborough Castle

St. Mary's

Longwestgate

Luna Park

Old Harbour

Lifeboat Station

❸

❺

❹

Fish Pier

Outer Harbour

Vincent's Pier

South Bay

❾

Olympia Leisure

❻

❼

❽

❿

⓫

Grand Hotel

Cliff Lifts

Brunswick Centre

Stephen Joseph Theatre

⓬

Ⓑ

Ⓒ

Train Station

Rotunda Museum

South Sands

CLUBS

Blue Lounge	9
Boleyns Nightclub	6
Vivaz	10

Ⓓ

Ⓔ

Spa Complex

St. Martins-on-the-Hill

Cliff Lifts

EATING & DRINKING

The Black Cat	5
Blue Crush Bar and Diner	2
Café Fish	12
Café Italia	11
Florio's Pizzeria	7
Gianni's	8
Golden Grid	4
Lanterna	3
Old Scalby Mills	1

Ⓕ

Ⓖ

ACCOMMODATION

Alexandra House	F
Beiderbecke's Hotel	C
Crescent Hotel	B
Crown Spa Hotel	D
The Earlsmere	G
Raincliffe Hotel	E
Scarborough YHA	A

0   200 yds

The Town

Scarborough spreads across the base of a promontory which juts out eastward into the North Sea, and is divided by it into three distinct areas: the **headland** itself, which is worth the climb for St Mary's Church, for the castle, and for the wonderful views across both bays, the **North Bay**, and the **South Bay**, with the town centre largely on the high ground between the two bays. North Bay is connected to the South Bay by **Marine Drive**, which circumnavigates the headland, linking the respective promenades Foreshore Road in South Bay (built in the 1870s) with Royal Albert Drive in North Bay (completed in 1890). The centre is bisected by one continuous main thoroughfare, made up of **Westborough**, **Newborough** and **Eastborough**, stretching from the train station right down to the Old Harbour tucked under the southern edge of the headland. Along Westborough are the high-street shops and the main entrance to the Brunswick shopping centre. It is along this partly pedestrianized street and the side streets around it that most of the life of the town centre goes on.

St Mary's

St Mary's (⊛www.scarborough-stmarys.org.uk), up on the headland, Scarborough's parish church, may originally have been part of a twelfth-century monastery, and though it has lost its chancel, north transept and two west towers, what's left has been little altered since it was built. But it's not for the church itself that visitors come to St Mary's, but for the grave of Anne Brontë. Anne was the third of Patrick Brontë's famous children to die within a year – after first Branwell, then Emily had passed away, the clearly very ill Anne was whisked off to breathe Scarborough's sea air by her sister Charlotte in a desperate attempt to avoid their fate. To no avail – four days after leaving Haworth, at the *Grand Hotel* which still stands above the South Bay, Anne died of tuberculosis. To spare her father yet another family funeral, Charlotte decided to "lay the flower where it had fallen" and had her sister buried at St Mary's, the only one of the Brontës not to be interred in Haworth church. Anne's grave – it's in the part of the churchyard that's separated from the church itself by Church Lane – looks out over the town and the sea. Incidentally, the inscription on the gravestone commissioned by Charlotte got Anne's age wrong – she was 29, not 28 years old.

Scarborough Castle

A short walk beyond St Mary's Church is the gatehouse through which is the entrance to **Scarborough Castle** (April–Sept daily 10am–6pm; Oct–March Mon & Thurs–Sun 10am–4pm; £4.70; ☎01723/372 451; EH). Built illegally by a baron during the "anarchy" of King Stephen's reign, it was confiscated in 1154 by his successor Henry II, who carried out many improvements. The ticket office and shop are just inside the gatehouse – be sure to get the audio-guide, since the information boards only give illustrations and the audio-guide number. Once over the barbican bridge, you climb up a steep hill to an exhibition on the history of the headland and the castle, and it's here in the restored Master Gunner's House that you'll find the tearoom. Look out too for the relief map/model of the castle, which provides much-needed orientation.

As you tour the extensive ruins, note that the castle wasn't the first occupant of the headland – with its steep cliffs and narrow point of access, its natural defences had long been recognized. There were at least two prehistoric settlements on the headland: a Roman signal station was built on it towards the end of the Roman occupation, and the Vikings used it not long before the Norman Conquest. But it's the medieval remains that catch the eye – especially the long curtain wall and the ruined keep. The castle has seen a fair amount of action – it was besieged by rebel barons in 1312, and twice by Parliamentarians during the Civil War, after which it was "slighted" to prevent its further use. It was partially restored and strengthened during the Jacobite Rebellion of 1745, and it was bombarded by German naval guns during World War I.

Apart from its historical importance, the castle is also worth visiting for the spectacular views across both the North and South Bays. Though you're not allowed to walk along the walls themselves, there is a viewing platform, and the site is so hilly that you get numerous glimpses across the town and out to sea.

The South Bay

It is on the **South Bay** that Scarborough has the greatest concentration of visitor attractions – the funfair, the harbour with lots of speedboat rides, cruises and fishing trips – together with the main lift up the cliff to the town centre. It has, too, a succession of attractive gardens and open spaces – the Valley Gardens, Belvedere, Italian Gardens and, off to the west, Oliver's Mount Country Park. Access to the South Bay is via several streets at the northern end or, much more fun, via **cliff lifts** – there's one next to Olympia Leisure, another between the Spa complex and the Belvedere Gardens.

Scarborough Harbour is divided into the Old Harbour, full of fishing boats, and, beyond it, the narrow Outer Harbour, with lots of leisure craft and more fishing boats. It's something that the tourist literature on the town doesn't make much of, yet it's a vibrant and thriving place – any doubts that it's a fully functioning fishing harbour will be squashed after seeing the huge mounds of lobster and crab pots piled up on the quaysides, the people working along the Fish Pier and on the fishing boats moored to the quays. Next to the Fish Pier is the **Lifeboat Station** with detailed information boards outside, and at the end of Vincent's Pier, which separates the Old from the Outer Harbour, you can see the *Diving Belle* – a statue of a modern young woman on tiptoes about to dive into the sea next to the lighthouse. Sculpted by Craig Knowles and unveiled in 2007, it has a sister statue – a Victorian lady dipping her toe in the water – which stands on Westborough. There are pubs and restaurants in the harbour area too, and a small tourist information kiosk.

In the angle between the harbour and the headland, **Luna Park** is one of dozens of funfairs named after the original one in Coney Island, USA (see p.264). Along the promenade – Foreshore Road – are numerous amusement arcades, the biggest of which is Olympia Leisure (see p.264). On the cliff top above Olympia Leisure, and dominating the South Bay, is the **Grand Hotel** (T0871/222 0047, Wwww.britanniahotels.com), built in 1867 and once the largest hotel in Europe (and the place where Anne Brontë died) and the old Town Hall, beside which is a small paved garden with a statue of Queen Victoria and wonderful views across South Bay to the castle. Beyond it is the **Rotunda Museum** (Tues–Sun 10am–5pm; £4.50; T01723/353 665, Wwww.rotundamuseum.co.uk), the second oldest purpose-built museum in the country. Constructed to the plans of William Smith, the founder of English geology, it's a fascinating building in its own right and has recently been updated to include in its venerable shell very modern displays on geology and local history. The Dinosaur Coast Gallery is particularly child-friendly.

The Spa Complex

At the southern end of the southern beach is the **Spa Complex** which owes its existence to the original discovery of mineral waters by a Mrs Farrer in the 1620s. By the early eighteenth century a building had been erected to facilitate the "taking of the waters", and other attractions introduced – horseracing on the sands, boating and sea-bathing; Scarborough was one of the first (in 1735) to use bathing machines to preserve modesty. Much of the complex was rebuilt in the nineteenth century as the spa was damaged by fire and storm – the present building dates largely from 1880 (for what's on offer today, see p.264).

St Martins-on-the-Hill

In the streets west of the Spa Complex, in the angle between Craven Street and Albion Road, is **St Martins-on-the-Hill**, a church that it is well worth visiting not particularly for its architecture, but for its Pre-Raphaelite decoration. Look out for the "Mary" window featuring the Virgin Mary by Edward Burne-Jones and Mary Magdalene and Mary of Bethany by William Morris, all three with the strong features and red hair typical of the Pre-Raphaelite artists. Mary of Bethany is said to have been modelled on Elizabeth Siddall Rossetti's mistress and later his wife, and the Virgin Mary on Georgina MacDonald, who married Burne-Jones in 1860. Look out too for the four chancel rose windows by Rossetti and Morris, the west windows by Burne-Jones, and the King David window by Morris. The pulpit is particularly interesting, with designs by Rossetti, Ford Madox Brown and Morris (they designed but didn't paint them). All these were the result of the first commission won by the company William Morris set up in 1861.

Peasholm Park

Dominated by cliffs on which are mounted great ranks of hotels, North Bay has a succession of gardens. Just back from the front is **Peasholm Park** (all day, every day; free; ☎01723/500 954, ⓦ www.peasholmpark.com), a facility which seems distinctly modern yet actually has a long history of mounting events that still go on today. Its Japanese theme goes right back to its inception in 1912, and the naval warfare displays with model boats to 1927. Throughout the interwar and immediate post-World War II period the gardens were the venue for open-air concerts and firework displays, but with visitor numbers falling in the cash-strapped 1970s and 1980s, the gardens became neglected. The early years of the twenty-first century saw a lottery-fuelled renaissance, and the Peasholm Gardens are once again one of Scarborough's main attractions. Three times a week during the season the naval battles take place, with replica ships and aircraft which have been updated as the years passed – at the time of World War I it was all dread-noughts, after World War II British and German battleships and aircraft carriers. Check the website for dates and times. When not in use for the battles, the boating lake has a great choice of boats – swan pedaloes, rowing boats and Canadian canoes. The park also continues to be the venue for a variety of open-air concerts and firework displays.

Between Peasholm Park and the promenade is a skateboard park and the **Scarborough Bowls Centre** (see p.264).

Northstead Manor Gardens: theatre and railway

Immediately north of Peasholm Park, just inside **Northstead Manor Gardens**, stands the **Scarborough Open Air Theatre**. Originally opened in 1932, it was renovated and reopened in 2010, and its 6500 capacity makes it the largest of its kind in Europe (see p.264).

In Northstead Manor Gardens too is the southern terminus of the **North Bay Railway** (April–Oct 10/11am–3/5.30pm; single £2.50, return £3; ⓦ www.nbr .org.uk), a three-quarter of a mile, 20-inch narrow-gauge railway which was opened in 1931. All four of its locomotives and all of its coaches date from the 1930s – some were built specifically for the Scarborough set up, others for railways elsewhere which have since closed. At Peasholm Station there's a new station building, with shop, ticket office and waiting room and bistro/café bar, and there are plans for a new coach shed, café and railway museum at Scalby Mills. The North Bay Railway Company also runs pedaloes on the lake (£3.25/£4.50) and the historic water chute (£1.40/person), one of only two in the country.

Sea Life

At the Scalby Mills end of the miniature railway is **Sea Life** (daily 10am–6pm; £14.50; ☎0871/423 2110, ⓦwww.sealifeeurope.com), the Scarborough Sea Life Centre and marine sanctuary, part of a network of many such centres across the UK, Europe and the US. Under several conical white roofs a series of habitats introduces you to turtles, sharks, seals, jellyfish, otters, penguins, and many more denizens of the deep. It's all done in an accessible way, with demonstrations, feeding times and an ocean tunnel, yet has a serious conservation purpose regarding seals, turtles, whales and dolphins, and for £25 you can adopt a shark, turtle, seal or penguin. There's a soft play area and a gift shop. There's a restaurant, too, but if you want to escape the crowds try the good food and fine beers of the *Old Scalby Mills* pub, just beyond the entrance to the car park.

Eating and drinking

Scarborough has a good mixture of places to eat and drink. As you'd expect there are numerous seaside **pubs** and fish-and-chip shops, but also an above-average number of Italian restaurants.

The Black Cat Eastborough ☎01723/350 653. On Eastborough, just above the harbour, *The Black Cat* is small and friendly, with minimalist decor, beautifully cooked food (try the steaks) and a good wine list.

Blue Crush Bar and Diner Peasholm Gap ☎01723/362 450. Near the beach opposite Peasholm Park, the *Blue Crush* is a music bar in a contemporary glass-and-steel building, which does good food. Open all summer 9am–midnight, with food service to 10pm. Mains £7.50–15.95 – burgers, pasta, salads, sandwiches.

Café Fish 19 York Place, at the intersection with Somerset Terrace ☎01723/500 301. More of a top-end fish restaurant than a fish 'n' chip shop. Dinner only. Main courses from £15, two-course dinner with wine about £28. Gets very busy at weekends.

Café Italia 36 St Nicholas Cliff. Enchanting and tiny Italian coffee bar next to the Grand. Good coffee, ice cream and cakes. Shuts at 4pm; closed Sun. Snacks from £4.

Florio's Pizzeria 35–37 Aberdeen Walk ☎01723/351 124. Highly rated restaurant, popular with locals – noisy, convivial, child-friendly,

with cheerful service and authentic Italian food. Main courses start as low as £5.

Gianni's 13 Victoria Rd ☎01723/507 388. The most immediately welcoming of the town's Italian restaurants, where the good-natured staff bustle up and down stairs, delivering quality pizzas, pastas and quaffable wine by the carafe. Dinner only. Pizzas £8, pasta £8–10, steaks around £15.

Golden Grid 4 Sandside. The harbourside's choicest fish-and-chip establishment, "catering for the promenader since 1883". Offers grilled fish, crab and lobster, a fruits demer platter and a wine list alongside the standard crispy-battered fry-up. Decent portions of fish from £8.95 to £10.95, depending on species.

Lanterna 33 Queen St ☎01723/363 616. Long-established, special-night-out destination, featuring traditional, seasonal Italian cooking in quiet, formal surroundings. Dinner only; closed Sun. Main courses £12.50–37.

Old Scalby Mills Scalby Mills Rd ☎08721 077 077. Next to Sea Life, the *Old Scalby Mills* offers a good range of real ales, pub food, and nice views of the sea.

Nightlife and entertainment

Many of Scarborough's **nightclubs** are in and around St Thomas Street and its extension St Nicholas Street. For **theatre**, as well as the Open Air theatre, there's the excellent Stephen Joseph Theatre.

Theatres and venues

Opera House Casino 56–64 St Thomas St ☎01723/357 940, ⓦwww.operahousecasino.co.uk. Full range of gaming, plus bars and restaurant. Special events such as live football, parties and tribute bands.

Scarborough Open Air Theatre Northstead Manor Gardens ⓦwww.scarboroughopenair theatre.com. Venue for live music, opera, sporting events, family shows and comedy. In addition to the main auditorium it has bars, restaurants, shops and funfair rides, and a programme of large-scale entertainments, plays, concerts and one-off giant-screen TV shows – for example, 2010 World Cup matches could be watched at the theatre free.

Spa Complex ☎01723/376 774, ⓦwww.scarboroughspa.co.uk. A major venue for shows, concerts by the Scarborough Spa Orchestra, comedy, family fun nights and a whole range of music, from opera and ballet to folk and rock'n'roll. The complex includes the Spa Theatre, the Grand Hall, the Ocean Room, the Promenade Lounge, the Suncourt for open-air concerts, and various other performance rooms, cafés and bars. The complex was being refurbished throughout 2010 but managed to remain open.

Stephen Joseph Theatre Westborough ☎01723/370 541, ⓦwww.sjt.uk.com. The world-famous theatre-in-the-round associated with writer and, until he stepped down in 2009, artistic director Alan Ayckbourn, which opened in its current premises (an Odeon cinema) in 1996. Around ten plays a year are put on, mostly first productions of new plays, often including those of Ayckbourn himself.

Clubs

Blue Lounge 4–13 St Nicholas St ☎01723/367 930. Popular bar with comedy, sport and a good range of music – funk, soul, r'n'b and disco classics.

Boleyns Nightclub 17 St Thomas St ☎01723/500 065, ⓦwww.boleynsnightclub.com. Three rooms, five bars – playing mainly pop and house. Thurs–Sun until the small hours, entry £1–5.

Vivaz Huntriss Row ☎ 01723/368 222, ⓦwww.vivaz.co.uk. Just around the corner from St Nicholas St, *Vivaz* has resident DJs and live music – classic rock, blues, contemporary and retro pop, electro, indie, metal and dance.

Activities

Scarborough offers several traditional beachside entertainment complexes and wet-weather **activities**.

Luna Park Sandside ☎01723/361 984. Traditional funfair overlooking the harbour, more suitable for young families than gangs of thrill-seeking teenagers. All the things you'd expect – Ferris wheel, dodgems, helter-skelter, amusement arcades, fairground rides, together with toffee apples, candy floss and ice cream.

Olympia Leisure ☎01723/377 960, ⓦwww.olympiascarborough.co.uk. Bowling alley, pool tables, amusement and video games, a kart track for 4–10 year olds, a soft play area, a snack bar – ideal when the weather's proving uncooperative.

Scarborough Bowls Centre Peasholm Rd ☎01723/353 992, ⓦwww.scarboroughbowls centre.co.uk. Indoor bowling plus two outdoor bowls crown greens, together with a bar, café and a couple of pool tables. Note – this is bowls, using woods, not American ten-pin bowling.

Filey

Of North Yorkshire's three main resorts, **FILEY** is by far the most genteel, offering few specific attractions but a vivid idea of what Victorian and Edwardian seaside resorts would have been like. Its success in attracting visitors after the arrival of the railway in 1846 wasn't simply a confluence of a nice stretch of coast and the means to get there – the worthies of the town set about developing it to meet the needs of visitors, and the result is a classic well-bred British seaside resort of the nineteenth and early twentieth century. Although Filey can't claim any earth-shattering historic importance, it can boast a number of interesting historical anecdotes. Novelist Charlotte Brontë, "Swedish Nightingale" Jenny Lind and composer Frederick Delius all visited the town. It also figures in the country's aviation history, with its broad flat sands being used as an air strip by pioneer Robert Blackburn in 1910 and 1911 as he tested the aircraft he was building for his Leeds company. Above all, Filey was witness to one of the great battles of the American War of Independence, the **Battle of Filey Bay** (sometimes called the Battle of Flamborough Head; see box, p.266). On the evening of September 23, 1779, US and British warships engaged in battle out in Filey Bay, and all evening throngs of people lined the coast from Scarborough to Flamborough Head and watched the moonlit battle, seeing the flashes and hearing the rumble of the guns.

Arrival, information and accommodation

Between Filey and Scarborough the A165 offer a pleasant drive through stone villages and rolling countryside. To the west of the town centre is the **train station** (off Station Avenue), with the **bus station** on Station Avenue just to the east. There are **car parks** behind the bus station, along Church Ravine on the northern edge of the town centre, and there's on-street parking in the town and along the promenade. The **tourist information centre** (Mon–Sat 9am–5pm; ☎01723/383 636) is in the Evron Centre on John Street, which also shows plays, films, art exhibitions and live music and has leisure and sports facilities.

🏃 **5 Leys** 7–10 The Beach ☎01723/513 392, ⓦwww.5leys.co.uk. A mixture of suites and apartments in a terrace of four tall houses overlooking the beach. Well-appointed self-catering accommodation, plus a bar and restaurant – highly reckoned, two courses £25, three courses £30 – with terrific views. Room service to all accommodation. A good, modern way of enjoying a seaside holiday. ❹

All Seasons Guesthouse 11 Rutland St ☎01723/515 321, ⓦwww.allseasonsfiley.co.uk. Two minutes' walk from the beach, this award-winning guesthouse has spotlessly clean and nicely decorated rooms. Lifts seaside B&Bs to a new level. ❸

The Town

Filey's town centre stands on the heights above the sea, with a long **promenade** just above the beach. Along and beyond the promenade are a series of **gardens** – Glen Gardens, Crescent Gardens, Northcliffe Gardens – with their complement of flower beds, a bandstand, boating lake and paddling pool, shelters, cafés and access to the superb beach. Look out too for the contemporary works of the **Sculpture Trail**, by Russ Coleman. At the north end of the promenade is **Coble Landing**, with a slipway that Yorkshire cobles are still winched up. These small wooden fishing boats are said to be descended from Viking longships.

In the compact town centre, the **Filey Museum** on Queen Street (Easter–Oct Sun–Fri 11am–5pm, Sat 2–5pm; £2.50; ⓦwww.fileymuseum.co.uk) traces the history of the town from its early days as a fishing and farming community to its heyday as a seaside resort. It is housed in whitewashed cottages that date from the late seventeenth century, and there are eight rooms on two floors, each with an audio commentary, covering the development of the town, rural and domestic crafts, Victorian times and much else, together with displays on the geology and marine life of the area. One of the rooms deals with the Lifeboat service, and this can be followed up with a visit to the **Lifeboat Station** (ⓦwww.fileylifeboat.co.uk) at the northern end of the promenade next to the Coble Landing, kept busy by the danger to shipping represented by Flamborough Head to the south and the Brigg to the north.

Filey Brigg is the headland immediately north of the town, created by a geological fault whereby the southern edge slipped, bringing the soft clay overlay down to the level of the sea or below, creating today a fascinating succession of flat rocks and rock pools teeming with life. The northern edge of the headland, which didn't slip, is made of steep cliffs deeply etched by the sea. The whole promontory protects the coast to

The Battle of Filey Bay

In 1779, Scottish-born sea-captain **John Paul Jones** became a hero of the American War of Independence when he was despatched to Britain with a squadron of five ships to attack British coastal shipping. Aboard his flagship, the **Bonhomme Richard**, he was heading for Bridlington when he encountered the British warships **HMS Serapis**, captained by Richard Pearson, and the **Countess of Scarborough**, captained by Thomas Piercy, which were escorting a merchant fleet along the east coast. At 7.15 on the evening of September 23, 1779, the American and British ships began one of the most ferocious battles of naval history. Jones, realizing that his gaggle of converted merchantmen were no match for the Royal Navy's purpose-built warships, immediately set about getting to close quarters. To start with he failed, the *Serapis* using her superior speed to circle the *Bonhomme Richard*, firing continuously and causing massive damage. But then the two ships became entangled and collided. Locked together, they drifted, guns still firing at point blank range, with individual hand-to-hand combat taking place all over this floating wooden island. Both ships caught fire. Called on to surrender, John Paul Jones refused (though his famous words "I have not yet begun to fight" have been doubted by some). An American sailor threw a grenade from high in the rigging of the *Bonhomme Richard* through an open hatch on the *Serapis,* its explosion igniting a magazine and killing many men. Finally, with both ships wrecked and the *Bonhomme Richard* sinking, Pearson decided that there was nothing to be gained by further fighting and surrendered. The Americans boarded and took command of the *Serapis*, and the struggle to keep the *Bonhomme Richard* afloat was lost – it sank 36 hours later. John Paul Jones sailed off south, to be showered with praise and honours by Benjamin Franklin, then United States Minister to France, and by Louise XVI. In England, Pearson was cleared of blame by a court martial, and in his own way, for saving the convoy, became a hero. He was declared a freeman of a number of east-coast towns, and received a knighthood from King George III.

The wreck of the *Bonhomme Richard* now lies somewhere off Flamborough Head, and its position is, of course, the subject of intense speculation, not least in the USA, and not least because it might contain the personal effects of John Paul Jones and much else of interest to historians of the War of Independence. The **American Ocean Technology Foundation** runs annual expeditions to search for it, but with hundreds of ships having been wrecked in this stretch of sea over the centuries, it's not going to be easy to identify.

the south from northeasterly gales, which is why the Romans probably had a harbour here, and which is certainly why Filey grew up where it did. Filey Brigg is a Sight of Special Scientific Interest and is now a country park, which provides pleasant walking, benches to sit on, lots of rock-pools to explore and fine views back across the town.

Eating and drinking

Bella Italia 20 Mitford St ☏ 01723/516 001. Small and friendly family-run Italian restaurant (not part of the chain of the same name) with good food at very reasonable prices.

Bonhomme's Bar Royal Crescent Court ☏ 01723/514 054. Just off the Crescent (it's easy to miss – it's on the left as you enter Royal Crescent Court) and named after John Paul Jones' flagship (see box above). Good range of real ales and a recent CAMRA prize-winner.

Filey Tandoori 16 Belle Vue Crescent ☏ 01723/515 992. Good-quality tandoori restaurant which, at time of writing, was unlicensed, so customers are welcome to bring their own beer and wine.

Ingham's Fish Restaurant 40 Belle Vue St ☏ 01723/513 320. Excellent fish-and-chip shop known throughout the region.

East Riding of Yorkshire

CHAPTER 6

Highlights

* **The Humber Bridge** Useful for getting across the Humber estuary, but beautiful in its own right – one of the world's great engineering feats. See p.272

* **The Deep** Fine modern aquarium in what is rapidly becoming an iconic building. Deep underwater viewing tunnel, unique underwater glass lift. See p.280

* **Hull Truck Theatre** One of Britain's best loved theatre companies now has a brand new venue right in the heart of Hull at which to mount its accessible plays, many written by director John Godber. See p.282

* **Beverley Minster** Cathedral-sized church stuffed with the fine and the fascinating. See p.286

* **Nellie's, Beverley** Step back in time – a pub which is heated by open fires, lit by gas, where the local conversation is good and the beer is cheap. See p.286

* **Burton Agnes Hall** Stunning Jacobean mansion bursting with architectural detail and great works of art. See p.293

* **The Rudston Monolith** Britain's tallest standing stone, so old it makes the medieval church in whose churchyard it stands seem positively contemporary. See p.293

* **Spurn Head** A geological phenomenon created by east coast erosion, Spurn Head is home to a nature reserve, a famous lifeboat and the Humber pilots. See p.301

▲ Nellie's, Beverley

East Riding of Yorkshire

Think of Yorkshire and you think of the city of York and its surrounding countryside, the beautiful dales, moors and rugged coast to the north, the hilly nineteenth-century wool towns around Leeds and Bradford to the west, even the coal, iron and steel towns of South Yorkshire. Less well known is the rather remote-seeming **East Riding of Yorkshire**. Yet it has a character all of its own. Its largest settlement is the maritime city of **Kingston–upon–Hull**, quietly making a lie of its rather rough reputation by remodelling its centre into a fine space dotted with references to its history, focused on a busy and colourful marina. Hull offers some of the best nautical and social museums in Yorkshire which, true to the city's left-wing traditions, are free. Many of its old lanes and alleys survive, and it is home to the Deep, a modern aquarium with a strongly conservationist ethos. Beyond Hull the empty and atmospheric **Holderness** peninsula is skirted on one side by the North Sea and the other by the wide Humber estuary, separated by the unique sand-spit **Spurn Head**, lengthening by about 6ft every year. A low-lying land of villages and farms, of old-fashioned seaside towns and impressive churches, Holderness is attractively unobtrusive. North and northeast of Hull are pretty upmarket towns like **Beverley**, which has not one, but two of England's greatest ecclesiastical buildings, and **Driffield**, a busy farming town known, at least to itself, as the capital of the Wolds. The **Yorkshire Wolds** themselves – low, unspoiled chalk hills – lie like an eyebrow across the north of the county, with farms and tiny villages and short steep hills, great houses like **Sledmere** and **Burton Agnes Hall**, the tallest standing stone in the country at **Rudston** and the most famous abandoned medieval village at **Wharram Percy**. East of the Wolds, empty east-coast beaches stretch for miles up to the brash resort of **Bridlington** and the majestic Flamborough Head beyond. East Yorkshire is a land rich in ecclesiastical and domestic architecture, a land that looks outwards to Europe rather than just inwards to the rest of Britain. And it remains relatively undiscovered by modern tourism – at times it seems that the only foreign visitors it sees are the hordes stampeding from Hull docks towards the crowded, and expensive, streets of York.

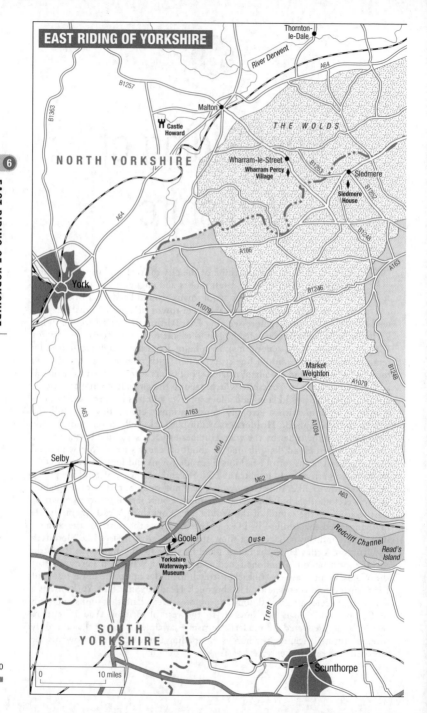

EAST RIDING OF YORKSHIRE

EAST RIDING OF YORKSHIRE

Thornton-le-Dale

River Derwent

A64

B1257

B1363

Malton

THE WOLDS

Castle Howard

NORTH YORKSHIRE

Wharram-le-Street

Wharram Percy Village

Sledmere

B1253

B1252

Sledmere House

B1248

A166

A163

B1246

York

A64

A1079

Market Weighton

B1248

A1079

A63

A163

A1034

A614

Selby

M62

A63

Goole

Ouse

Redcliff Channel

Yorkshire Waterways Museum

Read's Island

Trent

SOUTH YORKSHIRE

0   10 miles

Scunthorpe

6

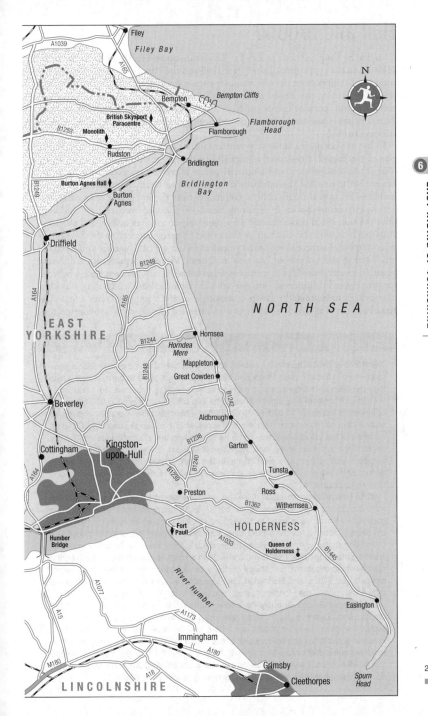

Hull and around

Founded by King Edward I in 1293 as **Kingston-upon-Hull** (still its proper title), **HULL**, on the confluence of the River Hull and the Humber estuary, became the most important port on the east coast. Its stature was reflected by its parish church, the Holy Trinity, the largest by area in the whole country, and by the fact that several of the great religious orders – the Whitefriars, the Greyfriars and the Austin Friars – had houses in the town (though nothing remains of them, except in street names).

Today, as you approach the city centre, Hull doesn't look too promising. It was one of the English cities most vigorously attacked by the Luftwaffe during World War II. As a major port and industrial centre it was always going to be a prime target, but it also had the misfortune to be close to German bomber stations on mainland Europe, and to be easily recognizable from the air because of its two rivers and its city-centre docks. In repairing bomb-damage and erecting new buildings after the war, speed and economy were more important than quality and elegance. And much of what the German air force didn't destroy later fell to the developer's wrecking ball. So there's a lot of unsympathetic postwar tat. But once you reach the city's centre and waterfront, starting at **Queen Victoria Square**, it's a different place. In recent times Hull City Council has turned a city that was once a byword for poverty and urban decay into one with enviable facilities – including a handful of excellent **museums**, the **Deep**, a strikingly modern aquarium, and a first-class **theatre** in the Hull Truck – and sheer unadulterated joie-de-vivre. Hull seems, too,

The Humber Bridge

The **Humber Bridge** across the estuary to the west of Hull is one of the major sights-to-be-seen in the Hull area. Opened in 1981, it took eight years to build, is over a mile long between anchorages, with a main span between the two towers of 1500 yards (1410m). Other gee-whiz statistics abound. The bridge contains 480,000 tonnes of concrete; it contains 44,000 miles (71,000km) of steel wire – almost enough to encircle the earth twice; in high winds the centre of the bridge flexes by 10ft (3m); because of the curvature of the earth, its two towers are 1½ inches (36mm) further apart at the top than at the bottom. When it opened, the Humber Bridge was the longest single-span suspension bridge in the world. Since then it has been super-seded, and now lies fifth in the world rankings, while remaining the longest bridge that you can cross on foot.

At the time of its construction there was much debate as to how useful it would be, with suspicions that it arose out of political expediency than economic necessity – it was sanctioned in 1966 to bolster Labour's chances in the Hull North by-election, when a defeat would have threatened Harold Wilson's slim House of Commons majority. In some ways these doubts have been borne out – numbers crossing the bridge never achieved a level high enough to pay off the building costs. Whatever the argument, the bridge certainly brought together the previously rather isolated East Riding and North and East Lincolnshire, and in doing so provided the region with one of the world's greatest, and most beautiful, bridges.

The **Humber Bridge Country Park** offers nature trails on the Yorkshire side of the bridge, and there's a North Bank Viewing Area with a large car park, clearly signposted from the main road, from where you can walk out along the bridge to examine it and enjoy the spectacular views. There are public toilets, a **tourist infor-mation centre** (daily: May–Sept 9am–5pm; March, April & Sept 9am–4pm; Nov–Feb 10am–3pm), a kiosk selling sweets and drinks, and **Mrs B's Café** (daily 9am–4.30pm, shorter hours in winter). There's a **toll** for driving across (cars £2.70).

a young city; with two large universities and Hull College, its streets are thronged with students, its bars and clubs are vibrant and popular.

Arrival and information

Most visitors to Hull will arrive by train from the west, by car or coach along the A63 (an extension of the cross-Pennine M62) or along the A15 (which branches off the M180), by sea into Hull docks, or by air into Lincolnshire's Humberside Airport, just across the Humber Bridge. The principal bus operators are East Yorkshire Motor Service (ⓦwww.eyms.co.uk) and Stagecoach (ⓦwww.stage coachbus.com). There's an integrated **train**, **bus** and **coach** exchange – **the Paragon Interchange** – in the angle between Anlaby Road and Ferensway, next to the St Stephen's Centre. Those arriving by car can either use the **park and ride** facility or one of the many **car parks** in the city centre – the most convenient is the multistorey in the Princes Quay shopping centre. If you can manage it, though, the best approach to the city is across the spectacular Humber Bridge (see box, p.272).

The city centre is relatively compact, and you can get to most places of interest on foot. The **tourist information centre** is at 1 Paragon St, in the City Hall building (Mon–Sat 10am–5pm, Sun 11am–3pm; ☎01482/223 559).

Accommodation

🏃 **Acorn Guesthouse** 719 Beverley Rd ☎01482/853 248, ⓦwww.acornguest househull.co.uk. Suburban semi on the northwest edge of the city, about 2.5 miles from the centre. Seven comfortably old-fashioned rooms, with big hotel facilities at B&B prices. Friendly attentive service, ample parking at front, nice garden to rear. Regular bus service into town. ❷

🏃 **Earlsmere Hotel** 76–78 Sunny Bank, off Spring Bank West ☎01482/341 977, ⓦwww.earlsmerehotel.co.uk. An old-fashioned guesthouse in a quiet street around a mile from the city centre. Most but not all rooms have en-suite facilities. Friendly service, on-street parking. ❶

Holiday Inn Castle St North ☎0871 942 9043. Standard *Holiday Inn* in an excellent position right in the city centre, overlooking the Marina. Health and fitness centre, pool, parking available. ❸

Innkeepers Lodge Cottingham ☎01482/651 518, ⓦwww.innkeeperslodge.com. In Cottingham, on the main road from the Humber Bridge to Beverley (it's across the road from the *Ketch* pub), the *Innkeepers Lodge* is a really good budget alternative for visits to both Hull and Beverley. Big, clean rooms, cheap food at the *Toby Carvery* next door, and plenty of free parking at prices that barely make a dent in the budget. ❷

🏃 **Kingston Theatre Hotel** 1–2 Kingston Square ☎01482/225 828, ⓦwww .kingstontheatrehotel.com. Nicely furnished rooms with all the usual facilities. Highly rated *Clapham* restaurant on the premises. Five minutes from the city centre, yet quiet. On-street parking, and public car park nearby. ❸

Little Weghill Farm Preston ☎01482/897 650, ⓦwww.littleweghillfarm.co.uk. About five miles east of the Deep, *Little Weghill Farm* is a beautiful eighteenth-century farmhouse that has kept many original features. Quiet location, barn-conversion rooms that are all en suite, and many local walks in the area. ❸

Premier Inn, Hull City Centre 99 Citadel Way ☎0871 527 8534. Modern building in perfect position for the Deep and all city-centre attractions. Cheap rooms and food, and plenty of parking. The surroundings aren't brilliant, but the hotel starts on the seventh floor so the views from the bar, and from rooms, are great. ❸

Royal Hotel 170 Ferensway ☎01482/325 087, ⓦwww.hotels-hull.co.uk. Large Victorian hotel near the station. Fully refurbished, comfortable rooms, with leisure centre and pool. Many offers available. ❺

The City

A good place to start exploration is **Queen Victoria Square**, south of which stretches the water of the **Prince's Dock**, with twin fountains spouting out of its

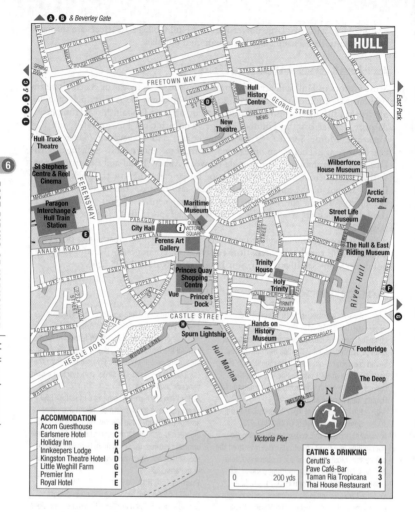

surface, and to the left cobbled and brick-paved quaysides and fashionable pavement cafés bustling with people. To the right is the imaginatively designed **Princes Quay Shopping Centre**, sitting on stilts over the water, looking like some latter-day Crystal Palace, the clouds reflected in its acres of glass, the flags on its roof snapping in the breeze blowing in off the North Sea. Beyond the dock, across Castle Street, the **marina** is crowded with boats of all types, including a **Spurn Head lightship**. East of the Prince's Dock are the main shopping streets, most of them branching off **Whitefriargate**.

Dotted around the city centre are Hull's excellent **museums** – a couple on Queen Victoria Square, and a handful more in the **Museum Quarter** on and near the **High Street**. Narrow, cobbled and lined with many old buildings, this is one of the most attractive streets in the city, and is joined to the River Hull by several "staithes" – narrow cobbled lanes that allowed the ships in the river to be unloaded directly into wagons. Look out for the remains of the merchants' grand houses and offices, the lowly courts in which ordinary workpeople lived, the pubs and the warehouses, all of which started to decline when the port activities moved elsewhere in the city, and which have been restored and reinvigorated since the 1980s. Finally, by the Humber the city is blessed with a fine **river** frontage along which to wander.

Queen Victoria Square and around

Dominated by a statue of Queen Victoria mounted on a stepped island (and it's not just decorative – there are public toilets underneath it), **Queen Victoria Square** is a handsome triangular open area surrounded by fine buildings – the **City Hall**, the Nautical Museum in what was once the Dock offices, the classical Ferens Art Gallery, the ornate *Punch Hotel*, the Yorkshire Penny Bank building (now a *Caffè Nero*), and a couple of modern entrances to the Princes Quay.

Between Queen Victoria Square and Whitefriargate is the end of the **Prince's Dock** and a paved excavation, liberally dotted with (slightly forlorn-looking) information boards, which was the site of the old Beverley Gate and the Monument Bridge. The **Beverley Gate** was the main entrance to the walled city, and was where the governor, Sir John Hotham, famously refused entry to King Charles I in 1642, thus sparking off the English Civil War. The **Monument Bridge** was built in 1829 to span the access to the Queen's Dock from the Prince's Dock, with a bigger replacement erected in 1905 to accommodate trams. Both consisted of two halves that could be raised to allow ships to come and go. The name "Monument Bridge" refers to a statue of William Wilberforce on top of a tall column which was erected here in 1835. This second bridge was demolished in 1932 when the Queen's Dock was filled in, turning it into **Queen's Gardens**. The statue of Wilberforce was moved, and now stands outside Hull College, at the other end of the Gardens.

Ferens Art Gallery

The **Ferens Art Gallery**, just across Carr Lane from City Hall on Queen Victoria Square, houses Hull's collection of paintings and sculptures from the Middle Ages onwards. There's a children's area with lots of hands-on activities, imaginatively placed in the centre of an upstairs gallery featuring images of Hull through the ages. Ask for the three pamphlets put together by the Gallery's "Art Ambassadors" – a group of 18–25 year olds who have picked some of their favourite works of art and compiled themed trails to include them: *The Battle of the Sexes*, *The Energy Collection* and *The Contemplative Collection*. There are also six free family activity boxes that can be borrowed with suggestions for things to do, as well as regular guided tours and numerous one-off events and exhibitions.

The Seven Seas Fish Trail

It's impossible to escape the seafaring and fishing theme as you walk around the city. For example, you will come across the witty **Seven Seas Fish Trail**, with life-size metal fish embedded in appropriate positions in the pavement – an electric eel outside an electricity sub-station, a plaice in the Market Place, a shark outside a bank. There are 41 pieces in total, created by artist Gordon Young in 1992 – an ideal way of getting kids to explore the city's streets. The tourist information centre will provide a leaflet identifying where they all are, and they will also issue a certificate if you complete the trail. They'll even get you going by pointing out the first fish on the trail – a shoal of 36 chromed bronze anchovies set into the pavement outside the City Hall ticket office in Queen Victoria Square.

Hull Maritime Museum

On the other side of the square the triangular former Dock Offices now house the **Hull Maritime Museum**, one of the best such museums as you're likely to encounter anywhere. To the right as you enter is the **whaling gallery**, with whale skeletons, fearsome exploding harpoons, the sort of flimsy boats in which whalers of old used to chase the leviathans of the deep a crow's nest made of a barrel, and oddities such as a whalebone seat, a blubber cauldron and a group of narwhal tusks. As you move through the gallery, you are surrounded by the eerie, ululating, unearthly song of the whale. To the left as you enter the museum (or you can continue through from the whaling gallery), a series of displays explain the different types of fishing and the specialist ships they used – North Sea herring drifters, Flamborough long lines, Paull shrimpers, trawlers – and outline the most common breeds of fish that are caught.

Upstairs are displays on sailing in general: the figurehead (a carved dog) of groundbreaking transatlantic paddle steamer *Sirius*, magnificent ship models, a ship's wheel and binnacle, carved whalebone (or scrimshaw), the work of whalers of the past and exhibits to do with the city's famous Wilson shipping line. There is, too, a stuffed polar bear, illustrating the practice of some whalers of capturing them to sell on when they got home. The whole museum is a record of centuries of skill and expertise, not to mention courage and fortitude, now slowly fading into the past. An exhilarating and humbling experience.

The Hull and East Riding Museum

The first of four museums clustered closely together on the High Street, the **Hull and East Riding Museum**, lodged in the old Corn Exchange building of 1856, emphasizes the archeology of the region. It gets off to a flying start with an impressive full-size model of a woolly mammoth (he's called Mortimer by museum staff), accompanied by information and dioramas covering early mankind. This is followed by superb displays on the Iron Age Celts who inhabited East Yorkshire before and during the Roman occupation, with a succession of realistic tableaux, complete with sound effects (in ancient Welsh; pick up a leaflet for translations).

Next is a fascinating display of information about and photographs of the Ferriby Boats, three Bronze Age boats discovered between the 1930s and the 1960s on the shore of the Humber at North Ferriby, which were made of planks of wood sewn together with yew withies. The amazing thing about them is their great age – they have been carbon-dated as 4000 years old – and their impressive size. A later, Iron Age boat, discovered at Hasholme in 1984, is preserved in a long glass case, constantly showered with water and wax, and as you walk beside it you can pace out the length – 41ft. These boats could negotiate estuaries and even go out to sea. Beyond this, a series of mosaics introduces the Romans, with further tableaux, mock-ups of rooms (a bathhouse, a paymaster's office) and information boards. Finally, smaller displays cover the Middle Ages (wooden coffin lids, a huge tub for keeping live fish in) and the Civil War.

The Street Life Museum

Across the courtyard next to the Hull and East Riding Museum is the **Street Life Museum**, which outlines the history of transport. The very first exhibit will bring a smile to most, especially to anybody who lived through the 1950s and '60s – a bubble car or, to give this one its proper title, the BMW Isetta 300. Similarly the Morris 8 of 1939 – there were plenty around right into the 1960s – and the Morris Minor 1000 van dating from 1969, pretty in its Hull City Council blue-and-yellow livery (though it's not an actual car, but one made up of bits of others). A balance of explanation and exhibit, and a succession of even older cars, do full justice to motoring history. A collection of trams (the Kitson steam tram is particularly impressive) and buses, a mock-up of a level crossing complete with signal box, a low-flying biplane, shops, penny arcade machines – the whole museum is stuffed with interest.

The Wilberforce House Museum

The **Wilberforce House Museum**, in its own gardens next to the Street Life Museum, occupies the house in which William Wilberforce was born. It has a dual focus: the life and times of Wilberforce himself, and details of the horrible trade in slaves that he successfully devoted his life to abolishing. So there are a number of his possessions – his journals and personal effects, including his court suit, a tea service he gave his sister as a wedding present in 1790, his collection of books, his inkwell and candlestick – the display of which might be thought risible, yet which builds up a remarkably human picture of the great man. There's even his waxwork likeness made originally for Madam Tussauds. The story of the campaign to outlaw slavery is then told, with information on the many who played a creditable part in the struggle – the great Staffordshire potter Josiah Wedgwood, for example, who created a ceramic medallion of a kneeling slave with the slogan "Am I not a man and a brother?", and Thomas Clarkson, whose travelling chest of visual aids used in anti-slavery meetings is on show. The fight against the slave trade was a long one – while it gathered pace in the 1780s, the slave trade wasn't abolished in the British Empire until 1807, and even then the Act only got rid of the trade – slavery itself didn't become illegal until 1833. Further displays on the culture of West Africa, source of most of the slaves sold in the Americas, on the processes of enslavement and human trafficking and on the inhuman treatment meted out to the slaves make for harrowing viewing – neck shackles, the famous plan of the Brooks slave ship showing the barbarous overcrowding, and all the other obscene paraphernalia of control and punishment. An unflinching view of a brutal part of our history, and an uplifting homage to those who successfully fought it.

The Arctic Corsair

The last of the museums in this area, and perhaps the most vivid, is the **Arctic Corsair**, a Hull sidewinder trawler moored in the Hull river directly behind the other three museums. Built in 1960, she has had a chequered career – holed in a collision off the Scottish coast in 1967, hauling a world-record amount of cod and herring in the White Sea in 1973, rammed by an Icelandic gunboat during the Third Cod War of 1976, retired, brought out of retirement in the 1980s, and finally sold to Hull City Council in 1993, who moored her in the Hull river as a museum ship. Supported by the council and run by volunteers who also provide guides, visiting the ship is an unforgettable experience. Whenever again you hear the shipping forecast on the radio, or hear of maritime disasters, you'll be reminded of this visit.

The Hull History Centre

A new institution – not quiet a museum yet concerned with studying the city's past – is the **Hull History Centre** (Mon & Wed 9.30am–7.45pm, Tues, Thurs & Fri 9.30am–5.30pm, Sat 9am–4pm; free; ☎01482/317 500, ⊛www.hullhistory centre.org.uk), in the angle between George Street and Worship Street, directly across the road from the Hull Fire Station. A stylish modern building with similarities with Sheffield's Winter Garden, the centre was set up by the city and the university to rationalize and make more accessible Hull's documentary archive. While designed principally for local people interested in the city's past, visitors to Hull might usefully check out the events, behind-the-scene tours and temporary exhibitions offered by the centre.

Trinity Square and the Holy Trinity Church

West of the High Street, between the River Hull and Princes Quay, lies another attractive square, with an ensemble of church, historic buildings and statues. **Trinity Square** is flanked on one side by **Holy Trinity Church**, the largest parish church in the country. When you're inside, it's difficult to believe that it's not a cathedral. The order of its building is pleasantly straightforward – the transepts (1300–20) came first, then the chancel (1320–60) and the nave (1389–1418), with the crossing tower being built last (around 1500). The transepts, the chancel and the lower parts of the tower are built of brick, the earliest use of brick on this scale in the country, giving it an odd, rather attractive two-tone look.

In the square stands a statue of **Andrew Marvell** (1621–78), the Metaphysical poet associated with George Herbert and John Donne, and friend of John Milton. Born in the Holderness village of Winestead just north of Patrington, he attended Hull Grammar School and, at the remarkably young age of 12, Trinity College, Cambridge. His most famous poem is *To His Coy Mistress*, though during his lifetime he was better known for his political pamphlets than for his poetry. Although with distinctly Parliamentary leanings and Puritan sympathies (though not himself one), he seems to have sat out the English Civil War on a tour of Europe. After the war for nearly twenty years until his death he served as a conscientious local MP for the area.

Behind the statue is the old **Grammar School** building which Marvell attended as a boy, and that now, together with the Fish Street Day Schools building added in 1871, houses the **Hands on History Museum**. Slightly oddly, it combines an interesting series of displays on Hull's social history with one on the Egyptians, the latter presumably because the city happens to have a rather good Egyptian mummy. A large display area contains some of the most famous of King Tutankhamun's grave goods, though don't get too excited – they're replicas. Completely genuine, however, are the 2600-year-old mummy and its elaborately carved catafalque, which occupy a very dimly lit room off the main one.

Hull's telephones

You may notice as you walk around Hull that the city's **phone boxes** are different from those you'll see in the rest of the country. They're similar in design to the old style that has largely disappeared in the rest of Britain, but are cream coloured rather than red and have no royal crown above the door. They were part of Hull's independent phone system, established in 1902 and owned by the city. Although now privatized, the unique cream phone kiosks have been retained.

Elsewhere in (or just off) Trinity Square, don't miss the unspoilt **Prince Street**, through an arch on the opposite side of the square to the church, nor the lovely old building of **Trinity House** ("rebuilt 1753" it says over the door), with its carved pediment (a coat of arms and figures of Britannia and Neptune) over a doorway with Tuscan columns. Trinity House started as a fourteenth-century religious guild, became a mariners' guild by the fifteenth century, and in the seventeenth and eighteenth centuries took increasing responsibility for shipping and navigation in the Humber, as well as becoming a charity for seamen. It retains its charity functions to this day, though it isn't part of the larger Trinity House organization which is nowadays responsible for light-houses and navigation buoys.

Further down Trinity House Lane on the right as you walk away from the square is the entrance to the Trinity House **indoor market**.

Hull Marina and the riverside

From Trinity Square any of the attractive streets heading west will bring you to Prince's Wharf. Just across the busy dual-carriageway Castle Street, in **Hull Marina**, is moored the **Spurn Lightship**. Though when riding mountainous seas it must have looked rather insignificant, close up it appears impressively big. It was, at the time of writing, being renovated, but when finished will take its place as another maritime museum.

Beyond the *Spurn Lightship*, at the southern end of Hull Marina, a couple of heavy-duty lock gates with a swing bridge between them allow boats to move in and out of the marina. A businesslike naval gun on one side of the gates and a "Welcome to Hull Marina" sign on the other convey amusingly mixed messages. Beyond the gates the whole area has been redeveloped and landscaped, providing modern office space and a pleasant riverfront along which the city's residents and local office workers can promenade. Alongside the naval gun, there's a **statue** of a man, woman and child, erected to commemorate European immigrants who entered Britain via Hull, and an identification guide to the birds you're likely to see on the Humber estuary – ringed plover, redshank, curlew, dunlin, black-headed gull and turnstone.

East across the swing bridge, the riverfront continues past an old muzzle-loading cannon to the Humber Ferry Terminal and the **Victoria Pier**. The site of a port since medieval times, a new dock was built here at the start of the nineteenth century, and a ferry service to New Holland across the river started in 1825, with a booking office added in 1880 – it's still there, though now converted into flats. The pier itself has largely disappeared, but there's a wide wooden deck (beyond the *Café Gelato*) with lots of benches facing south, east and west, with good views of the river, the Deep (see p.280) and the North Sea ferries coming and going.

Beyond the Victoria Pier a couple more statues commemorate aspects of Hull's history. One is of Hull's first mayor – **Sir William De-la-Pole**. Nothing very startling about that, except how long ago it was – he served from 1332 till 1335. The next statue, directly across the mouth of the River Hull from the Deep, is **Voyage** – the figure of a man atop a tall column. It was erected to celebrate the links between Hull and Iceland – there's a corresponding statue at Vik, Iceland's southernmost village. Though it refers to a thousand years of sea trading between the two lands, it's actually a lot more to do with the Cod Wars of the 1950s to the 1970s, when Icelandic and British fishing boats and naval vessels were involved in a series of confrontations over territorial waters and fishing rights. The two statues represent a sort of burying of the hatchet between the two countries.

The riverside footpath now heads north up the west bank of the River Hull. The large structure spanning the river is the **Hull Tidal Barrier**, opened in 1980 to prevent a recurrence of the flooding suffered by the city in 1969. In front of it is a modern **footbridge** which crosses the river to the Deep.

The Deep

A fitting attraction for a great seaport like Hull, the **Deep** (daily 10am–6pm; £9.50; ☎01482/381 091, ⓦwww.thedeep.co.uk) calls itself, somewhat obscurely, "the world's only submarium", but the rest of us will recognize it as a varied, interesting and very hands-on aquarium. Sitting on the eastern bank of the River Hull where it flows into the Humber, it looks for all the world like your first view of the Great White Shark in *Jaws*, thrusting obliquely out of the water.

The best approach is to take the lift to the top of the building, then make your way down the sloping ramp which winds around the main tank through a series of areas dealing with different aspects of the world's oceans. Though everybody seems to head for the **sharks** and **rays**, don't be rushed – there are hundreds of wonders to see: "Spud", the potato grouper which was rescued from an Australian mall fish tank, the Pacific hagfish which tunnels into its prey then eats its way out, the horribly poisonous arrow frog, the giant African land snail which grows to 10 inches long, the beautiful moon jellyfish, the curious, friendly, but frightening giant octopus, the nightmarish fangtooth with teeth so huge it can't shut its mouth. At the very least a visit to the Deep will fill you with wonder at the multiplicity of life forms to be found in the world's oceans. At most, you'll learn a huge amount about the dynamics of our seas and oceans, of the dangers that threaten them and the work being done to protect them. The aquarium has one of the world's deepest underwater tunnels along the bottom of one of the world's deepest tanks, together with a magical glass lift in which you can ascend or descend surrounded by the denizens of the deep. You'll need at least three hours for the visit, but to make the most of it, go for the day. There's a restaurant, *Two Rivers*, a café, the *Observatory*, and parking is £3, though that includes a voucher for £2 worth of goods from the shop or café.

East Park

For families who are footsore after touring Hull's wonderful museums or following the Seven Seas Fish Trail or the Philip Larkin Trail, it's worth taking

---

Immigration through Hull

Between 1836 and 1914 more than 2.2 million people from Scandinavia, Germany and Russia landed at Hull and the other Humber ports, travelled by train across Britain to Glasgow, Liverpool, London and Southampton and there took ship for America, Canada, South Africa and Australia. The biggest shipping line involved in this mass migration was Hull's famous **Wilson Line**, which began steamship services from Norway and Sweden in 1843. By 1914 the flow of Northern European immigrants was so great that a special Wilson Line landing station, called Island Wharf, was built near where the statue of the man, woman and child stands today, with the Wilson Line becoming the largest privately owned shipping line in the world (there's much more information about it in the **Maritime Museum**). The era of mass Victorian and Edwardian migration ended suddenly in 1914 with the start of World War I, and the introduction of immigration controls in a number of destination countries.

Philip Larkin

Philip Larkin (1922–85), who was chief librarian at Hull University, was one of the twentieth century's greatest poets, though it is only recently that the powers-that-be in Hull have realized that his wide popularity might be something that could be turned to the city's advantage. **Larkin25** in 2010 marked the 25th anniversary of his death with theatrical, musical and literary events, the launching of a permanent **Larkin Trail** of around 35 places of significance in his life and work, and the raising of money for a statue of him to be erected in the Paragon Interchange. A "Larkin with Toads" project, involving the placing of 74 one-metre-high, artist-designed multicoloured toad statues around the city, took place during the summer; local businesses sponsored the statues, which were auctioned off at the end. A reference to his poems "Toads" and "Toad Revisited", one can only speculate what the famously acid-tongued poet would have made of this – despite his name and his mordant sense of humour, he wasn't the jolliest of men. While the toads were auctioned off in 2010, the trail and the statue should remain – enquire at the tourist information centre.

a short drive or bus ride east along the A165 to **East Park** (daily: April–Oct 9.30am–4pm; Nov–March 9.30am–3.30pm; free; ☏01482/300 300, ⓦwww .hullcc.gov.uk). Following the trajectory of many parks across the country, East Park was established to celebrate Queen Victoria's Golden Jubilee in 1887, became a Grade II listed park, saw reduced numbers of visitors during the twentieth century, became dowdy and run down, then enjoyed a new lease of life as Heritage Lottery money was pumped into it. It's now a little (or at 130 acres, not so little) gem. There's an "outdoor gym", a "youth zone" with skateboarding and climbing facilities, a pavilion with café, the Khyber Pass (a rock folly with waterfall, built from stones rescued during demotion work in the city), an excellent waterplay area and a more general playground, the prewar (1929) Wicksteed Splash Boat or waterchute – one of only three in the country – together with everything you'd expect in a public park: model yacht pond, boating lake, flower beds and bowling greens. Throughout the year a variety of activities for kids are organized.

Eating and drinking

Cerutti's 10 Nelson St ☏01482/328 501, ⓦwww.ceruttis.co.uk. Facing the site of the Victoria Pier overlooking the river – perfect for a restaurant known for its fish. It has been so successful since it opened in 1974 that another (*Cerutti 2*) was opened in Beverley train station. Main courses £14–20, but look out for special two- and three-course deals. Mon–Fri lunches, Mon–Sat eve, closes at 9.30pm.

Pave Café-Bar 16–20 Princes Ave ☏01482/333 181, ⓦwww.pavebar.co.uk. Nice laid-back atmosphere with lots going on. Live jazz/blues and comedy club Sundays. Readings by the likes of Alexei Sayle, Will Self,

Simon Armitage. Food till 7pm. Most main courses well under £10.

Taman Ria Tropicana 45–47 Princes Ave ☏01482/345 640, ⓦwww.tropicana-hull.co.uk. Specifically Malay (rather than the more generic Malaysian) cuisine. If you're not particularly well up on Malay food, go for the "pick three dishes for £10.50" option – it's a good way to try things out. Otherwise main courses up to £12.50. Closed Mon.

Thai House Restaurant 51 Princes Ave ☏01482/473 473. Fairly Authentic Thai food, good service (though drink refills can be infuriatingly slow), slightly eccentric decor with lots of potted plants.

Theatre and entertainment

The jewel in Hull's entertainment crown is the **Hull Truck Theatre Company** (☎01482/323 638, ⓦwww.hulltruck.co.uk), which recently moved into brand-new, purpose-built premises in the St Stephen's development on Ferensway. With a main auditorium and a small Studio Theatre, bars and cafés, it's a long way from its 1971 origins operating out of the back of a lorry, and even from their previous Spring Street premises where certain seats couldn't be used whenever it rained. The Hull Truck company has a national and international reputation, yet has deep regional roots and loyalties, and its productions go out into theatres, school and church halls, sports centres and any other space in which a play can be mounted, not only in East Yorkshire but all over the country. The formidable driving force behind all this hyper-activity is award-winning writer, director and national treasure John Godber, whose credits include *Bouncers*, *Up 'n' Under*, *Lucky Sods* and *Teechers*.

Other venues in the city include the sumptuous Grade II listed **Hull New Theatre** in Kingston Square and the **City Hall** in Queen Victoria Street (both on ☎01482/226 655). There are several cinemas in the city centre – the **Odeon** Kingston Park (☎01482/586 421), the **Reel Cinema** in the St Stephen's complex in Ferensway (☎0870 801 0870, ⓦwww.reelcinemas.co.uk), and **Vue** in the Princes Quay development (☎0871/224 0240).

Shopping

The two best shopping malls in Hull are the **Princes Quay** (ⓦwww.princes -quay.co.uk) and **St Stephen's** (ⓦwww.ststephens-hull.com). The former has the best setting – built out over the water of the Prince's Dock – the latter is the most up-to-date. And although not in the same league as Leeds for arcades, Hull does have a couple – **Hepworth's Arcade** off Trinity Square, and **Paragon Arcade**, off Paragon Street. Otherwise, the main high-street shops are in White-friargate, while there are two retail parks, one to the west off the A63, the other to the east off the A165.

Listings

Buses Traveline ☎01709/515 151.
Car rental Avis ☎01482/228 871; Hertz ☎01482/323 906; National Car Rental ☎01482/343 223.
Hospital Hull Royal Infirmary, Anlaby Rd ☎01482/875 875.

Internet access Central Library, Albion St ☎01482/210 000.
Pharmacy Boots, Prospect Centre ☎01482/223 334.
Post office Lowgate ☎01482/221 754.

Around Hull: Fort Paull

Less than five miles east of Hull, on the Humber shore, lies the village of **PAULL**. Here you'll find **Fort Paull** (March–Oct daily 10am–6pm; £5; ☎01482/896 236, ⓦwww.fortpaull.com), built in 1864 as one of the Palmerston Forts (named after the Prime Minister at the time), a series of fortifications built around the coast of Britain in the 1860s. Sitting on the banks of the Humber, it is pentagonal in outline, had been shut down by the Ministry of Defence in 1960, and became a place of crumbling brickwork and weeds in which children played. Then a local group was formed – the Friends of Fort Paull – to renovate it as a military museum. It finally opened in 2000.

Today Fort Paull is an odd ragbag of guns, tank turrets, planes, wartime memorabilia and information about the Women's Land Army, POWs, carrier pigeons and the days when the fort was used for supplying ammunition to naval ships anchored in the river. There are several fascinating planes – a 1916 bi-plane, a Hawker Hunter and the colossal Blackburn Beverley troop transport which itself contains displays – and lots of cannons and field guns. There are numerous tableaux, including a rather tasteless one of a man hanging in a cell (a miscreant, imprisoned for petty theft who, apparently, terrified by the fort's alleged ghosts, took his own life), child evacuees and Winston Churchill. Some of the exhibits are really interesting – a 3D viewer with which you can look at reconnaissance photos of German ground installations, the "corgi" motorbike used by paratroopers which folded into its own container for the drop – and some are bizarre. You can let the kids have the run of the play area, have a picnic on the walls overlooking the estuary, or eat a snack in the *Berliner Tea Rooms* (a troop restaurant car) or the *Dukes of York Bar and Café* (whose counter is made of sandbags).

While there seems to be no clear narrative thread or rationale behind Fort Paull's collection, it's still great fun – a bit like rummaging through an elderly relative's loft.

Yorkshire Waterways Museum, Goole

Not known for its good looks, **GOOLE** is a determinedly workaday inland port in the area where the Ouse, the Don and the Trent come together to become the Humber, around thirty miles west of Hull. Though it's not near anywhere that tourists and holidaymakers are likely to fetch up, it is easy to get to, being in the angle formed by the M62 and the M18. There's only one reason for visitors who do not have business there to visit Goole, and that's to take in the **Yorkshire Waterways Museum** (Mon–Fri 9am–4pm; Sat & Sun 10am–4pm; free; ☏01405/768 730, Ⓦwww.waterwaysmuseum.org.uk) – for anybody interested in British inland waterways, it's a delight. Covering the Aire and Calder Navigation and the creation of the Port of Goole, the museum has displays on the life of barge families, the import/export trade, the carrying of coal through the Port of Goole, shipbuilding and much else, with interactive and audiovisual displays and a photographic archive. Above all, the museum has boats, including the 1910-built Humber keel *Sobriety* and the *City of Hull*, built in 1995, both of which are available for trips, and a former grain barge which is now an art gallery (Room 58).

Beverley

The town of **BEVERLEY** lies about eight miles north of Hull – when you allow for Hull's urban sprawl, that means that there's barely three miles between the edges of the two settlements. Daniel Defoe remarked of Beverley in the 1720s: "One is surprised to find so large and handsome a town within six miles of Hull". Still true today. Being so close to a large city, you might expect Beverley to be a dormitory town with few shops and little character of its own, but this couldn't be further from the truth. Indeed, the people of Beverley seem to regard its sprawling neighbour with considerable suspicion – historically, whenever there's been a choice, Beverley has chosen the other side. So, during the English Civil War where Hull supported Parliament, Beverley was Royalist, and today where Hull tends to be Labour or Liberal Democrat, Beverley is Tory.

Beverley owes its birth to the building of a **Minster** here by St John of Beverley at the end of the seventh century, with a settlement developing to support pilgrims to the Minster (John, and his tomb, had a reputation for miraculous cures). During the Middle Ages Beverley continued to prosper as an important regional capital, with a busy market, healthy woollen industry and flourishing trade guilds. Its religious credentials were further enhanced with the coming of Knights Hospitallers and Dominican and Franciscan establishments, and the town became a renowned place of pilgrimage across Roman Catholic Europe. While many much bigger towns don't have any notable churches, Beverley has two, the second being the parish church of **St Mary's**, established in the twelfth century to serve people frequenting the town's market and the members of its many guilds. It's a beautiful church, best known today for its "minstrels capital", a colourful carving of a group of five musicians on top of one of the church's columns.

So when Henry VIII ended the pope's authority in Britain in order to get his hands on Anne Boleyn, then dissolved the monasteries in order to get his hands on their wealth, it's no surprise that Beverley was involved in the backlash – it contributed five hundred men to the Pilgrimage of Grace, the pro-Catholic rebellion against the King. One of the most prominent Roman Catholic martyrs executed by Henry VIII for his opposition to the break with Rome – St John Fisher – was from Beverley. The closing of the religious houses in Beverley, and the substantial reduction in the number of pilgrims, hit the town hard, and it became something of a backwater during the seventeenth century. A modest revival of its fortunes in the eighteenth century, when it became not only the main commercial centre for this part of Yorkshire but also the East Riding's county town, is reflected in the large number of Georgian buildings you see today. The nineteenth and twentieth centuries saw continued prosperity, with the coming of the railway in 1846 and the establishment of a number of large factories serviced by the **Beverley Beck** to the east of the town, though this area has now been cleared pending redevelopment. The Beck itself is now lined with desirable twenty-first-century housing, and the town's prosperity has continued to rise, supported by a large **Saturday market**, a succession of **festivals** (see p.30) and a burgeoning tourist industry, attracted by the **Minster**, the **racecourse** and the charming ambience of the **town centre**. Though light on obvious stand-alone attractions (except the two churches), Beverley is certainly worth at least a day's visit, might well repay a longer stay, and indeed makes an excellent centre for exploring the whole of East Yorkshire.

Arrival and information

Beverley is easy to get to by road from the south and west, either via the M62/ A63 into Hull, or the M180 across the Humber Bridge, both of which routes are linked to Beverley by the A164. From the north and east it's a bit more difficult, in that roads from York and Bridlington are not dual carriageway. The town centre is kept free of through traffic by an efficient bypass. There's ample **parking** in town, mostly to the northeast of the town centre. Beverley's direct transport links are otherwise more regional than national, with rail links to the rest of the Yorkshire coast via the Yorkshire Coast Line, and bus services to Hull, Bridlington, York and Scarborough, and to surrounding towns and villages. The **train station** lies to the east of the town centre, the bus station to the north, so it's a bit of a walk between them. There's a taxi rank in the Saturday Market. The friendly and helpful **tourist information centre** (Mon–Fri 9.30am–5.15pm, Sat 10am–4.45pm; July & Aug also Sun 11am–3pm; ℡01482/391 672, ⓦwww .realyorkshire.co.uk) is on Butcher Row, just up from the Wednesday Market. You can pick up here a **Beverley Town Trail** leaflet. Dotted around the town are a number of public art works on the theme of Beverley's medieval guilds and

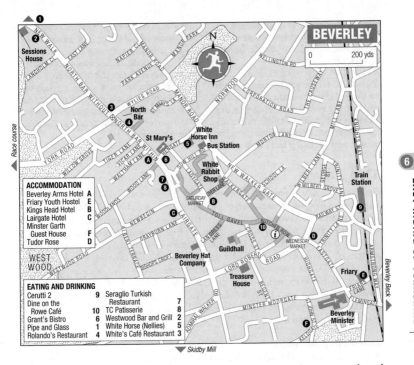

BEVERLEY

0   200 yds

ACCOMMODATION

Beverley Arms Hotel	A
Friary Youth Hostel	E
Kings Head Hotel	B
Lairgate Hotel	C
Minster Garth Guest House	F
Tudor Rose	D

EATING AND DRINKING

Cerutti 2	9	Seraglio Turkish Restaurant	7
Dine on the Rowe Café	10	TC Patisserie	8
Grant's Bistro	6	Westwood Bar and Grill	2
Pipe and Glass	1	White Horse (Nellies)	5
Rolando's Restaurant	4	White's Café Restaurant	3

Skidby Mill

the crafts they represented. Thus, slung high up between the *Beaver* pub and Barclay's Bank in North Bar Within is a jerkin, representing the Jerkin Makers' Guild; on top of the signpost where Lairgate comes into North Bar Within is a jester's hat (Hatters' Guild); there's a cut-out ox carcass next to the *Angel* pub in Butcher Row (Butchers' Guild), and a flight of arrows on the gable of HSBC bank in Old Waste, between the Saturday Market and Lairgate (Fletchers' Guild). The trail leaflet includes all the pieces that have so far been installed, with addendum sheets as others are added – there should be a total of 39 when the project is complete. Another option is a **guided tour** by Paul Schofield. There's a choice of three – Ghost and History Tour, Town Trail, and Pub Walk ("an intoxicating tour"); book through the tourist information centre.

Accommodation

Beverley Arms Hotel North Bar Within ☏01482/870 907, ⓦwww.brook-hotels.co.uk. A 1794 coach-house (it appears in one of Anthony Trollope's novels) in a brilliant position directly opposite St Mary's. Nice ambience, stone-flagged bar and brick patio. Rooms a little tired but refurbishment imminent. Jazz on Friday nights. ❸

Friary Youth Hostel Friar's Lane ☏0845 371 9004, ⓦwww.yha.org.uk. Beautiful medieval monastic house (see p.290) in the shadow of the Minster. What it lacks in luxury it makes up for in atmosphere, location and of course economy. £14 per adult. ❶

King's Head Hotel 38 Saturday Market ☏01482/868 103, ⓦwww.kingsheadpubbeverley .co.uk. Tucked into a corner of busy Saturday Market, with contemporary bar and room decor in a period building. Can be noisy, especially at weekends – it's a popular pub in the heart of the town centre – but you can always ask for one of the rear rooms, and ear plugs are provided. It's bustling, friendly and unpretentious. A Marston's pub, it has an eclectic, if standard, menu. ❸

Lairgate Hotel 30–32 Lairgate ☏01482/882 141, ⓦwww.thelairgateinbeverley.co.uk. Attractive listed Georgian building right in the town centre. Many

period details (staircase, windows), pleasant courtyard, good food, friendly staff. Signposted parking down Grayburn Lane immediately before the hotel. ❹
Minster Garth Guest House 2 Keldgate ☏01482/882 402. Perfectly located right next to the Minster, facing the meadow from which it is usually photographed, this elegant Georgian guesthouse bills itself, for what it's worth, as Beveley's first boutique guesthouse. It has rooms which are varied in decor and level of luxury, starting at £80.

DIY in-room breakfasts. Quiet location except for the Minster bells, which ring every quarter hour. ❸

🏃 **Tudor Rose** Wednesday Market ☏01482/882 028, ⓦ www.thetudorrose hotelbeveley.co.uk. Nice little hotel/restaurant in the town centre. Rooms, all en suite, are pleasantly old-fashioned. Main courses £10–15, meat and fish with much use of sauces. Also Polish food on offer. The 1pm check-in is useful for getting a first quick look at the town. ❷

The Town

Beverley is a fine town with a wonderfully quirky medieval layout, a stock of impressive Georgian houses, two truly magnificent churches – the **Minster** on the southern and **St Mary's** on the northern edge of the town centre – a good selection of shops, restaurants and pubs, a large open-air Saturday market and a reputation as a venue for musical events. To the west of the town centre is the large stretch of common land called the **Westwood** and Beverley's **race course** (☏01482/867 488, ⓦ www.beverley-racecourse.co.uk) – wide open spaces for walking, flying kites and, on race days, having a flutter. To the east is **Beverley Beck**, a canal that leads from the River Hull to within a mile of the town centre, and that once served a substantial industrial area, which has recently been cleared ready for development.

Beverley Minster

A tour of Beverley should start with the undoubted jewel in its crown: **Beverley Minster** (May–Aug Mon–Sat 9am–5.30pm, Sun noon–4.30pm; April, Sept & Oct Mon–Sat 9am–5pm, Sun noon–4pm; March Mon–Sat 9am–5pm, Sun noon–4pm; Nov–Feb Mon–Sat noon–4pm, Sun noon–4pm; free but donations welcomed; ⓦ www.beverleyminster.org). Widely considered to be the best non-cathedral church in the country, the Minster has a long and complicated (and in many cases disputed) history. It starts with a monastery established by John, the Archbishop of Hexham (and later York), in around 690/700 AD as a sort of retirement home. St John of Beverley – he was canonized in 1037 – was reputed to have performed a number of miracles both during his lifetime and after his death and burial in the church in 721. Pilgrims flocked to his tomb from all over the country, and a town grew up to provide for their needs. St John's church was destroyed by the Vikings, and was rebuilt as part of a monastery by King Athelstan in 935 AD, reputedly in thanks for a vision of victory he experienced here before the Battle of Brunanburh. He also granted the church the right of sanctuary, and the people of Beverley a number of tax concessions which helped, it is said, to explain their subsequent prosperity. After the Norman invasion a new Minster replaced the Saxon one, and finally, after a fire in 1188, the present building was begun. Most of the current Minster dates from the thirteenth to the fifteenth centuries.

Despite its complicated ancestry, Beverley Minster is architecturally straight-forward – if you start from the **west doors** and walk the length of the building, you travel backwards in time from the Perpendicular west end (1380–1420) through the Decorated nave from the entrance onwards (1308–49) to the Early English chancel (1220–60). Starting from the **Highgate Porch** through which you enter, turn left and notice the wealth of carvings down the north aisle of people playing musical instruments – a lute, a lyre, drums, bagpipes, zither, fiddle, accordion, hunting horn, tambourine, guitar and many others. You'll see angels playing instruments high up in the nave as well. Beyond the crossing with the north and south transepts (where there was once a tower, but it collapsed) is a double flight of steps meeting at what was once a doorway halfway up the wall – this was the entrance to the Chapter House, pulled down following the Reformation. To the right of these steps is the choir, which has nice carved **misericords** (brackets placed on the underside of hinged choir seats, so that priests could take the weight off their feet whilst still seeming to stand). Though not medieval (they date from the sixteenth century), they follow the tradition that no two are alike, and that they illustrate a succession of everyday activities, animals or strange events – people dealing with a domestic fire, hare riding a fox, woodcarvers quarrelling, fox preaching to geese, geese hanging fox, man wheeling woman in a wheelbarrow and so on. There are 68 of them – hours of fun.

Towards the end of the Minster, on the right along the north side of the building, is one of its star attractions – the ornately Gothic fourteenth-century **Percy tomb** and canopy. The Percys were the foremost Roman Catholic family in the North of England – virtually every Catholic uprising after the Reformation had its Percy supporter – though it's not certain whose tomb this is (it's thought to be that of Eleanor Percy, who died around 1340). Here too is the **Frith Stool**, a stone chair in which a minster official would sit while dealing with people who had claimed sanctuary. The final area before the east window is the retro-choir, where pilgrims would pray. This was where St John of Beverley's tomb was located (though his body has since been moved, and is buried under the floor at the east end of the nave). It now contains memorials to several members of the Warton family. The **East Window** itself is the only one that contains medieval stained glass – all the Minster's windows were blown out in a storm in 1608, the surviving glass eventually being incorporated in the East Window in 1725.

The Minster's **south transept** has three chapels dedicated to the East Yorkshire regiment, the first of which contains the wooden **Menin Cross** erected on the Menin Hill on the Western Front in April 1917, where men of the 64th infantry brigade fell in battle. It was replaced by a stone memorial in 1931, and the original one brought to Beverley Minster.

On the south side of the nave are **statues** of King Athelstan and St John of Beverley. Though painted to look like stone, they are actually made of lead, and were cast in nearby Driffield in 1781. Beyond the statues is the Norman **font** (about 1170 AD), with an ornate eighteenth-century canopy. It and the figures of the four Evangelists, Matthew, Mark, Luke and John, on the west doors were designed, it is thought, by Nicholas Hawksmoor, the great eighteenth-century architect and pupil of Sir Christopher Wren.

Despite its importance as an architectural and historical artefact, Beverley Minster comes across as delightfully unstuffy. The verve of its carved musicians and misericords, the big box of toys to keep children occupied while their parents worship or sightsee, the welcoming friends of the Minster who are happy to show you round, all speak of an establishment that is warm and welcoming. If you've only time to do one thing while you're in Beverley, visit the Minster.

The markets and around

Walking north along either Highgate or Eastgate from the Minster will bring you to the first of Beverley's public squares – the small, triangular **Wednesday Market**, with several restaurants, shops and pubs. A handful of stalls sell fruit and vegetables, watches, rugs, mats and clothes. From here, turn up pedestrianized **Butcher Row** into the town centre, and left up **Toll Gavel** – both streets are crammed with shops – and make a quick diversion to the **Guildhall** (Fri 10am–4pm; free), the palatial seat of government for the town. Parts of the building date back to a fourteenth-century merchant's house, but after it was acquired by the town in 1501 it was remodelled several times, especially in 1762 and the 1830s, and was refurbished recently. The splendid architecture and interesting historical contents – minstrels' chains from the fifteenth century, a seventeenth-century mayor's bench, even eighteenth-century graffiti left by boys from the school next door, and a collection of silver and pewter used by a succession of mayors, together with paintings by Fred Elwell, make for an interesting half-hour. The only downside is that the Guildhall is only open on Fridays.

From the Guildhall, continuing up Toll Gavel brings you to the **Saturday Market**. Much bigger than the Wednesday Market, it would be square if it weren't for a large pub (the *Push*) and the red-brick-fronted **Corn Exchange** (1886, being converted into a branch of Browns department store at the time of writing). It is, nevertheless a handsome open space, cluttered, alas, with cars and taxis during the week, but vibrant with market stalls on Saturdays. There's a fine **Market Cross** with eight Tuscan columns, coats of arms, urns and an ornate roof, erected in 1714. Notice the two cream phone boxes outside the *Push* and the Corn Exchange – Beverley's phones were part of the Hull municipal system (see box, p.278).

The Treasure House

From the Wednesday Market, a short walk westwards along either Lord Roberts Road or Well Lane will bring you to the **Treasure House** (Mon, Wed & Fri 9.30am–5pm, Tues & Thurs 9.30am–8pm, Sat 9am–4pm; free; ☏01482/392 750, ⓦwww.eastriding.gov.uk) on Champney Road – a distinctive modern building with circular tower and two wings, the right-hand one attached to the old public library. The name says it all – this building contains much that the town treasures. The ground floor offers access to the library and a research centre, the next floor consists of four galleries containing the **East Riding Museums Collections** (Gallery 1), part of the town's art collection (Gallery 3) and two temporary exhibition spaces (Galleries 2 and 4), and the top floor consists of a circular viewing platform from which you can see the town's other treasures – the Minster, St Mary's, and the jumbled rooftops of the town centre. Gallery 2 has a café in the middle which does good coffee, excellent sandwiches and snacks, and delicious Yorkshire-produced crisps. The **museum** is small but very well organized, with displays on the South Cave Iron Age weapons cache, geology, shipbuilding, religious history, archeology and much more, some of it very hands on and with questionnaires for kids. The permanent art collection (Gallery 3) has a number of works by prominent local artist Fred Elwell, and an ostrich made of leather on a metal frame by Karen Trower – it's 10ft high, so you can hardly miss it.

St Mary's Church

Continuing beyond the Saturday Market brings you to **St Mary's Church** (April–Sept Mon–Fri 9.30am–4.30pm, Sat 10am–4pm, Sun 2–4pm; Oct–March Mon–Fri 9.30am–noon & 1–4pm, Sun before and after services only free; ⓦwww.stmarys beverley.org.uk), founded in the twelfth century though now mostly Georgian. "One of the most beautiful parish churches of England" according to architectural historian Nikolaus Pevsner, St Mary's is if anything more satisfyingly proportionate externally than the Minster. If you're taking photos of it, though, be careful – the best viewpoint is from opposite the entrance, where one-way traffic sweeps into Hengate.

After entering the church through the south porch, look first beyond the west door and large fifteenth-century west window to the intricately carved **font** made of solid Derbyshire stone dating from 1530. Look too down the length of the nave towards the chancel – the arch between them is truly colossal. At the eastern end of the nave, high on the pillar nearest the pulpit, is the "famous, funny and loveable" (Pevsner) group of five carved minstrels, colourfully painted, indicating that it was they who had donated the money for that pillar to be built. Other pillars have donor inscriptions, but no carvings. Incidentally, there are 33 other musical carvings in the church – a recurring theme in Beverley.

Proceeding beneath the tower (which collapsed in 1520 and had to be rebuilt), you come to the north transept organ with the vestry next to it (the vestry ceiling, with its sun and stars is worth a look), and beyond that St Michael's Chapel. Look out for the wonderfully vaulted roof and, on the right of the doorway, a carving of a hare or rabbit, dating from around 1330, with pilgrim's staff and scrip (a shoulder bag). It is said to have given Lewis Carroll the idea for the white rabbit in *Alice in Wonderland*, but then Ripon Cathedral makes the same claim for one of its wood carvings. In the choir, notice the chancel ceiling, with its colourful paintings of forty English kings up to Henry VI, dating from 1445 (George VI was added during its 1939 restoration). In the choir is an excellent set of 28 misericords with, as in the Minster, elaborate and sometimes satirical carvings – for example, one depicts an ape dressed as a doctor. Others include foxes, eagles, dogs, monkeys and much else, as well as numerous green men.

Outside, look up at the octagonal turrets above the western end of the church. They were rebuilt in the mid-nineteenth century by famous Victorian architect A.W.N. Pugin. In particular, look at the weathervane on the nearest turret – it was the very last thing he ever designed – he sketched it on the back of an envelope shortly before his death from a stroke.

Now turn left along Hengate, and you'll spot an oval memorial plaque attached to the side of the church, just beyond the south transept. It tells the story of two Danish soldiers, part of a mercenary force that William of Orange was sending to Ireland to engage with the Roman Catholic supporters of James II, which landed at Hull. The two men quarrelled and fought a duel, during which one was killed. The other was tried by court martial and executed. The poem puts it succinctly:

Here two young Danish soldiers lie
The one in quarrel chanc'd to die;
The other's head, by their own law
With sword was sever'd at one blow.
December 23, 1689

Just opposite here, also on Hengate, is the **White Horse Inn,** known locally as *Nellies*, an essential stop on any visit to Beverley (see p.291).

North Bar and around

Beyond St Mary's lies the intriguingly named **North Bar Within**, lined with stately Georgian houses. At the end you will see the **North Bar** itself, a crenellated brick building with a pointed archway through which alternate streams of traffic have to squeeze. Built in 1409 this is the only surviving town gate (the position of the others is indicated by several street names – Keldgate, Highgate, Hengate, Eastgate, Lairgate). Beyond it lies **North Bar Without** lined with trees and very large houses. Just after it becomes New Walk is the **Sessions House**, with four unfluted Ionic columns holding up a pediment above which is a figure of justice holding up her scales. Once the court building, it now houses a health and beauty spa in the centre, *Westwood* restaurant (see p.291) in the lefthand wing, and the police station on the right.

The Friary and Beverley Beck

Just east of the Minster, across Eastgate and on Friars Lane, on the left just before the railway line, is the **Friary**, what's left of the Blackfriars (Dominican) monastery, now a youth hostel (see p.285). Established in 1240, the building is wonderfully mellow, showing its age with leaning walls, a hotchpotch of building materials (some brick, some stone), the carving of a woman that dates back to the early fourteenth century, and attractive brick-walled gardens impressively overlooked by the Minster. The venerable old building leans heavily on the shoulders of a small modern annexe. Notice, incidentally, the "tumble-gabling" – a herringbone pattern of bricks where the roof meets the end of the building, used to add strength as well as decoration. You'll see it on many buildings in Beverley.

From here, take the footbridge over the railway line, from where you will see the chaotic results of the clearance of industrial land to the south – it looks like the aftermath of wartime bombing. This was once Beverley's industrial heartland, clustered around the navigation called **Beverley Beck**. To get to the Beck turn right along Armstrong Way after the footbridge, then left along Flemingate. A ten-minute walk (past the Leisure Centre on the right) brings you to the **Beck End**.

Originally, as the name suggests, a stream, the Beck was made navigable in medieval times, and a lock gate installed where it runs out into the River Hull in 1802, after which it became an important means of getting raw materials to and finished products from within half a mile of the centre of Beverley. Tiles, pottery, cloth, leather, flour, ships and later motor-vehicle parts were manufactured here, with the Beck becoming a major thoroughfare until the development of road and rail transport made it redundant. Heavily polluted for a time, it has since been cleaned up, and today desirable housing lines its banks, wildlife flourishes, anglers trail their lines in the water, and narrow boats and the Humber keel *Comrade* are often moored to its quays.

Skidby Mill and the Museum of East Riding Rural Life

A four-mile drive to the south of Beverley brings you to **Skidby Mill** (daily 10am–5pm; £1.50; ℡01482/848 405), a pristine four-sail working tower-mill. Built in 1821, it has been grinding grain ever since, and still does from Wednesdays to Sundays, weather permitting. The whole mill creaks and groans as the four huge sails (1.25 tonnes each) drive the three pairs of millstones and all the ancillary machinery like hoists and hoppers. In the warehouses that are part of the complex is the **Museum of East Riding Rural Life**, which has displays and interactive materials covering the history of the Wolds. There's a blacksmith's shop and café in the courtyard, a picnic area, wildlife garden and pond, and next to the mill a field is being developed as a wildlife area – you can borrow a children's "Explorasack" (£5 returnable deposit) which contains materials to help in the exploration. Parking is in the lane about 100 yards from the mill, or in the cul-de-sac opposite.

Eating and drinking

Beverley has a wonderful selection of **restaurants**, several of them outstanding, with, as you'd expect in an agricultural area, many making use of locally sourced food. Later on in the in the evening, the pubs get packed out, with Saturday Market at weekends being, according to taste and age, rowdy or lively. See also accommodation, p.285, for a couple of pub and restaurant recommendations.

Cerutti 2 Station Square ℡01482/866 700, ⓦwww.ceruttis.co.uk. Occupying what had been the station waiting rooms, *Cerutti 2*, run by the same family as *Cerutti's* in Hull, specializes in fish, though there are meat and vegetarian options too. Popular with locals, so it's as well to book, especially at weekends. Main course prices range from £10.95 to £20.95. Tues–Sat noon–2pm & 6.45–9.30pm.

Dine on the Rowe Café 12–14 Butcher's Row ℡01482/502 269, ⓦwww.dineontherowe.com. On one of the main shopping streets, just up from the Wednesday Market, named for its address and the name of its owner – Jason Rowe. Brasserie-type food, breakfast, lunch and dinner menus, lots of specials offering, for example, Yorkshire tapas and venison saddle, and offers such as two dine for £25 or choose five dishes from sharing board for £25. Open daily, and late Wed–Sat. Reservation recommended.

Grant's Bistro 22 North Bar Within ℡01482/887 624, ⓦwww.grantsbistro.co.uk. In an eighteenth-century building on the corner between North Bar Within and Hengate, opposite St Mary's, *Grant's Bistro* offers a good range of grills, fish and meat dishes, in one of three small rooms. Strong on steaks, and offers rarer meats like buffalo and wild boar. Booking advised, especially for its "candlelit dinners" – a five-course meal for two for £47, including a bottle of wine.

Pipe and Glass 8 West End, Dalton ℡01430/810 246, ⓦwww.pipeandglass .co.uk. A fifteenth-century inn idyllically set in a pretty village about five miles northwest of Beverley, and with nice views across open countryside, the *Pipe and Glass* has been transformed by owners James and Kate Mackenzie into an outstanding restaurant without losing its pub feel. East Yorkshire's only Michelin-starred restaurant, it uses top-quality ingredients to provide a range of delicious meals at amazingly reasonable prices – the most expensive main courses on the evening menu come in at well under £20. The *Pipe and Glass* keeps normal pub hours, but food service stops at 9.30pm (11pm Sat, 4pm Sun). Closed Mon.

Rolando's Restaurant 28 North Bar Within ℡01482/861 590. *Rolando's* has made a name for itself for its rustic, good-value Italian food. It has a café menu during the day and a restaurant menu at night. Mon 9am–5pm, Tues–Sat 9am–9.30pm.

Seraglio Turkish Restaurant 5 North Bar Within ℡01482/887 878. Atmospheric restaurant tucked away down an alley off North Bar Within (there is a sign above Hawley's Auctioneers, but it's easy to miss). Nicely understated decor, and delightful alfresco dining if the weather's good – flagged area with potted plants. Lots of grilled meats, but with fair choice of vegetarian options, friendly staff, reasonable prices (most main courses are under £10). Lunch noon–2.30pm, dinner 5–10pm.

TC Patisserie 101 Lairgate ℡01482/863 781, ⓦwww.tcpatisserie.co.uk. Unpretentious little patisserie, serving wonderful breakfasts, together with a mouthwatering range of tartlets and pastries.

Westwood Bar and Grill 4 New Walk ℡01482/881 999, ⓦwww.thewestwood.co.uk. Five minutes from the town centre along North Bar Without, in one wing of the lovely old Courthouse building (the other's the police station). High-quality, locally sourced food in cool and elegant surroundings – or try the chef's table, overlooking the kitchen. Outdoor seating available if the weather's good. Set menus (two courses for £17.95; three for £19.95) or á la carte, with main courses £16.95–21.95.

White Horse (Nellies) 22 Hengate ℡01482/861 973, ⓦwww.nellies.co.uk (not an official website, but useful). Opposite St Mary's and an institution in Beverley, *Nellies* is a wonderful old pub, a coaching inn since the seventeenth century. Dingy with exhaust fumes and with bulging walls, it doesn't look much, but entering it you enter another world. A warren of small rooms surrounding a central bar, it has stone-slabbed, quarry-tiled and wooden floors, gas lighting, coal fires, smoke-blackened ceilings, embossed wallpaper and brass coal scuttles. It's like going back to Victorian times and, being a Sam Smith's pub, even the prices hark back to the past – a pint of bitter will cost you £1 less than anywhere else. Good selection of lunchtime pub grub as well.

White's Café Restaurant 12a North Bar Without ℡01482/866 121, ⓦwww .whitesrestaurant.co.uk. Overlooking the cross-roads immediately outside the North Bar. Highly regarded chef John Robinson is widely expected to earn a Michelin star in the near future, and has earned rave reviews from top critics like Jay Rayner. Clean simple decor, delicious food, interesting creative menu, good use of fish like wild sea bass and monkfish, and prices that are not unreasonable for such a restaurant – main courses on the á la carte menu from around £17–20; set menus are two courses for £13.50, three for £15.95 (lunchtime) and £16.00/£20.00 (dinner). Closed Sun & Mon.

Shopping

The prosperity of Beverley is reflected in the large number of specialist, shoe, jewellery, antique and clothes shops, with lots of well-known names – Barbour, Laura Ashley, Monsoon. There are also some interesting one-off shops – the **White Rabbit Shop** (a reference to Lewis Carroll) on Dyer Lane (Ⓦwww.white -rabbit-chocolate.co.uk) which makes its own delicious and extensive range of chocolates on the premises, and which runs a number of tastings, and the **Beverley Hat Company** (Ⓦwww.thebeverleyhatcompany.co.uk) at 46 Lairgate – unadulterated bliss for anybody who likes hats. **The Treasure House** has paintings for sale, and there's always, of course, the **Saturday market** (held on the Saturday Market), which brings in visitors from miles around.

Driffield and the Wolds

The swathe of countryside that stretches east from the city of York to the coast between Bridlington and Filey is known as the **Yorkshire Wolds** – rolling hills and broad farmland interspersed with hedgerows and stands of trees. It's pretty countryside, though with few specific attractions to detain the visitor. However, it provides pleasant driving, and also walking along the two long-distance paths that cross it – the **Wolds Way** that curves for nearly eighty miles from Hessle just outside Hull through the Wolds to Filey, and the fifty-mile-long **Minster Way**, connecting Beverley and York minsters. There are also several sites of historical interest – the Rudston **monolith**, **Wharram Percy Medieval village**, **Sledmere House**, **Burton Agnes Hall** – to provide a focus for days out. For anyone more action-oriented, the **British Skysports Paracentre** just outside Bridlington offers the opportunity of seeing the Wolds from above – far above. There's little in the way of tourist infrastructure – **Driffield** is the nearest thing to a capital of the Wolds, and makes a good centre for their exploration, though it's difficult to recommend accommodation in the town – the best places to stay are in surrounding villages. Otherwise, you could probably experience a lot of what the Wolds has to offer in a day out from elsewhere in the county.

Driffield

Much smaller than Beverley, **DRIFFIELD** is very much a working market town, though it is also significant because of its perceived role as the gateway to the Wolds. A bustling if low-key place, the town is easy to find your way around because the street names are unashamedly geographical – the single main street is called Middle Street (north and south, separated by the Market Place), which stretches from the train station in the south to and beyond imposing **All Saints Church**. Its parallel streets are Eastgate and Westgate, and all are crossed at the top by North Street. There are numerous cafés, restaurants, pubs and shops along Middle Street, and during term time the whole town centre is thronged with pupils from the nearby comprehensive.

There's not a lot to see in Driffield. A small stream – intriguingly called Water Forlorns – meanders through the centre, but the most attractive part of the town is **Riverhead**, behind the station, where converted canalside warehouses and cottages are reflected in the calm waters of the Driffield navigation. The canals and becks of the town offer pleasant walks and wildlife-spotting – try to get a copy of *Town Walks Guide* from the **tourist information centre** in the Town

Council offices, 2–4 Market Walk (Mon–Fri 9am–12.30pm & 1–4pm; ☎01377/254 160) which is just west of the Market Place. Driffield is better known for its two weekly **market**s (Thurs & Sat), a monthly farmers' market (first Sat of the month) and the biggest one-day Agricultural Show in the country (July), together with a trucking spectacular (May) and an annual traction rally (Aug).

Driving west or north from Driffield brings you immediately into the fine rolling countryside of the Wolds.

Burton Agnes Hall

A six-mile drive northeast from Driffield along the A614 Bridlington road is one of the finest early Jacobean houses in the country. **Burton Agnes Hall** (April–Oct daily 11am–5pm; £7, gardens only £4; ☎01262/490 324, ⓦwww.burtonagnes .com). Begun in 1601 by Sir Henry Griffith and held by his family line – Griffiths, Boyntons and Cunliffe-Listers – ever since, it is now owned by a trust and is open to the public. Just off the A614 (you can see it from the road) it's entered through a pink brick, turreted gatehouse of 1610 directly from the village.

The view of the front of the house through the gatehouse arch is out of this world, with a small central statue, clipped lawns and dark topiary yews against the beautiful red-brick, multi-windowed, perfectly symmetrical facade of the house itself. Inside, enjoy the magnificent **Great Hall** with its incredibly ornate screen and chimneypiece, the complicated plaster decoration containing biblical references and celebrations of the family who owned the house. The Hall also contains works of art commissioned by the family over four centuries. It is also home to a famous resident ghost – that of Katherine Griffith, who was mugged in 1620 and died of her injuries. On her deathbed, the story goes, she asked that her head be kept in the house, and when it wasn't, played merry hell until it was brought in from the churchyard. Several subsequent attempts to get rid of the gruesome object were met with further furious spectral manifestations. The skull is now, apparently, incorporated in one of the walls, but nobody seems sure where.

The **Drawing Room** beyond the Great Hall and the bedrooms above are equally sumptuous, the staircase joining them shallow and stately, the rest of the house a little more Georgian and restrained. The **Long Gallery** which runs along the top floor, and which was restored in the 1950s and 1970s is covered in priceless works of art by artists such as Cézanne, Corot, Gauguin, Matisse, Renoir and Pissarro. Indeed, the artistic theme is repeated elsewhere in the house – a series of artists in residence occupy the summer house, and there's an interesting gallery for local artists to display their work in a red double-decker bus in the courtyard. Also in the courtyard are several shops, a café, a good children's play area and toilets. The house puts on a host of talks, tours, re-enactments, rallies and festivals – check out the website for details.

The **Blue Bell Hotel** (☎01262/490 050, ⓦwww.bluebellhotel.net; ❷), opposite the Hall, is a good place to eat or spend the night. Traditional English food, with main courses in the £10.95 to £17.50 range.

The Rudston Monolith

About three miles north of Burton Agnes is the village of **RUDSTON**, worth visiting for its spectacular **monolith**. Standing in the churchyard of All Saints, on a hill above the village, it is 25ft high and nearly 6ft wide at the base. It dates from about 1600 BC, and the nearest source of gritstone from which it could have come is ten miles north – given the technology available at the time, moving its forty tonnes must have been quite a feat. Since All Saints dates from Norman times, when the church was built the stone must have already been standing there for two millennia, prompting the speculation that its site may have been chosen because it was already considered sacred. Eighteenth-century excavation turned up a number of human skulls, prompting further speculation that the stone might have been associated with human sacrifice. On the other hand, it is a churchyard, and church-yards are full of bones.

British Skysports Centre

A different perspective on the Wolds can be attained from high above it. The **British Skysports Centre** at East Leys Farm in Grindale, just outside Bridlington (℡01262/677 367) is a one-stop shop for all those who want to hurtle through the skies above the Wolds. The centre has a small clubhouse and its own grass landing strip – it was shut for two years following a fire, and is only now getting back on its feet. Anybody over the age of 16 can arrange a jump, though under-18s need permission from their parents, and over-40s need a note from their doctor. Flying takes place at weekends – phone to arrange a jump.

Sledmere and Sledmere House

The village of **SLEDMERE**, seven miles northwest of Driffield and right in the centre of the northern part of the Wolds, is a wonderful example of a village that is dominated by one great family – the Sykes family – and its stately home – Sledmere House. Apart from a handful of cottages, the whole estate and village is currently owned by Sir Tatton Sykes (8th baronet).

Sledmere House (April–Sept Sun & Tues–Fri 10am–5pm, house 11am–4pm; £7.50, park only £5; ℡01377/236 637, ⓦwww.sledmerehouse.com) was built by Richard Sykes, starting in 1751, with parts added by Sir Christopher Sykes in the late 1770s and 1780s, when the park was laid out, partly from designs by Capability Brown. Much of the current village was built by Sir Tatton Sykes II in the half-century before World War I.

Despite a major fire in 1911, the house is still well worth visiting, for its unfussy, almost austere design, its beautiful parkland dotted with grazing deer, its kitchen garden, and the converted stable block which houses the *Terrace Café*, a shop, and displays on Sledmere and on the history of the Waggoners Special Reserve, which was raised locally by Sir Mark Sykes at the outbreak of World War I and was one of the first units to enter the war, driving horse-drawn wagons to supply soldiers at the front. There's a pleasantly shaded car park under the trees.

Inside, the house still has the feel of the eighteenth century, even though much of it is restored. The library is very impressive, and the Sledmere Grand Organ, built in the 1920s, is one of the finest pipe organs in the country. The house puts on a programme of events and organ recitals – look out for them on the website.

Although the great house is likely to be the principal reason for a visit to Sledmere, it's worth looking around the rest of the **village**. The church which lies in the grounds of the house is rather dull, but on the main road is a collec-tion of monuments – a stone bench dedicated to Sir Richard Sykes, who died in 1978, a copy of an Eleanor Cross (one of those built by King Edward I in honour of his wife Eleanor) which was erected as a village cross in 1896/8, then modified to act as a war memorial after World War I, and next to it a Waggoners Memorial, a cylinder with four columns with battle stories in relief, again in memory of those lost in the war. Opposite the entrance to the house, occupying what was formerly a model farm, is **Triton House**, a venue for local artists to show their work. Beyond this, in the centre of the village, you can see that all the houses are part of the estate, from the rather grand estate office and clerk's house, to the post office and villa, the Triton Cottage, the school and workers' cottages.

It's fortuitous that such an interesting village has an excellent inn, making it a really good centre for exploring the Wolds: the **Triton Inn** (℡01377/236 078, Ⓦwww.thetritoninn.co.uk; ❸) does hearty English food and has en-suite rooms.

Wharram Percy Medieval Village

Just off the Beverley to Malton Road (the B1248), to the right about a mile south of the village of Wharram-le-Street, is **Wharram Percy Medieval Village** (open all year, any reasonable time; free; EH). It's clearly signposted, and has its own car park, from where it's a pleasant half-mile walk, steep in places, to the village itself.

Wharram Percy is the best known and most thoroughly excavated of England's thousands of deserted medieval villages. After it was discovered in 1948, a team of archeologists and historians worked on the village every summer for forty years under the leadership of Maurice Beresford and John Hurst. Their conclusions were that Wharram Percy was established some time in the tenth to the twelfth centuries, suffered from the effects of the Black Death in 1348–49, was flourishing in the fourteenth and fifteenth centuries, and finally died in around 1500, probably because the local landowners, spurred on by high wool prices, evicted families in order to end cultivation and turn the whole area over to sheep-rearing. What can be seen today are the remains of St Martin's church, one or two cottages, the floor plans of several more outlined by footings, ditches or banks, and the village pond. Information boards around the site tell you exactly what you're looking at.

Bridlington and around

In character **BRIDLINGTON** has more in common with North Yorkshire's Scarborough than with any of the rest of the East Yorkshire coast. It has two magnificent **beaches** – the reason for its growth as a resort in the first place – and where they collide an extensive fishing port/harbour/marina which is busy, workaday yet exhilarating. Apart from the harbour, the whole of the seafront area is dominated by traditional English seaside things – amusement arcades, fish-and-chip shops, candyfloss stalls, ice-cream parlours, bingo halls, fun-fair rides. Behind the harbour and the seafront sits the town itself, somehow small and lacking in TLC, but with much renovation going on. Under a mile to the north is the historic **Old Town**, unexpectedly quaint and full of character.

Arrival and information

Bridlington's **road links** with the rest of Yorkshire and England are fair but not brilliant, with the A165 striking south to Beverley and Hull and north to Filey and Scarborough, the A614 west to Driffield, the A64 to York. These are not fast roads, and you'd have to drive a long way to get to the nearest dual carriageway, even to the nearest motorway. The town has a **train station** on Station Road just north of the town centre, with links to Scarborough and Hull. The town centre and seafront are well supplied with **car parks** (typical rates £1.30/hr or £3.50/day). The **tourist information centre** (April–Sept Mon–Sat

9.30am–5.30pm, Sun 9.30am–5pm; Oct–March Mon–Sat 9.30am–5pm, Sun noon–4pm; ☎01262/673 474) is on Prince Street, just above the harbour.

Accommodation and eating

For a big seaside resort, Bridlington isn't well supplied with quality hotels. However, it does have a good choice of **guesthouses**.

Accommodation

Bluebell Guest House 3 St Anne's Rd ☎01262/675 163, ⓦwww.thebluebell guesthouse.co.uk. A minute's walk from the North Promenade, five minutes from the centre of town, the *Bluebell* offers a warm welcome, clean accommodation and a good range of breakfasts. ➋

Expanse Hotel North Marine Drive ☎01262/675 347, ⓦwww.expanse.co.uk. Big family-owned seaside hotel which looks like an ocean liner, with comfortable, if tired, rooms, large bar and restaurant, many rooms with sea views, and a fine location on the seafront. ➌

Oakwell Guest House 84 Windsor Crescent ☎01262/674 238, ⓦwww.oakwell-guesthouse -bridlington.co.uk. Off South Cliff Road, two minutes' walk from the town centre, *Oakwell Guest House* is small and family run. Rooms are all en suite, spotlessly clean and well supplied with all the usual hot-drink making facilities, satellite TV and so on. A good-value traditional seaside B&B. ➋

Sewerby Grange 441 Sewerby Rd ☎01262/673 439, ⓦwww.sewerbygrange.co.uk. Comfortable mid-Victorian vicarage converted into privately owned hotel and restaurant located in Sewerby just east of Bridlington. Modern decor, friendly service. Two-course lunches £10.95, three courses £11.95, Table d'hote £18.95. Look out for room deals. ➍

South Cliff Caravan Park Wilsthorpe ☎01262/671 051, ⓦwww.southcliff.co.uk. Pleasant camping and caravan park with bar, shop, chip shop, small leisure complex, amusement arcade, launderette. Five minutes' walk to a magnificent beach, from where there's a road train into town during the summer.

Café

Seasalt and Passion 22 West St ☎01262/671 117, ⓦwww.seasalt-passion .moonfruit.com Something of a surprise in the heart of burger and fish-and-chip territory, this deli-type vegetarian café mixes food and art, ideal for getting both the gastric and creative juices flowing. The menu has a good choice of pies, flans, breads, cakes and cheesecakes. You can also buy much of this to take away.

The beaches

Bridlington exists because of its beaches. The broad and sandy beach of **South Bay** is the best, accessible via the South Promenade on foot, by car or on the land train service to the Belvedere jetty which runs approximately every twenty minutes. Wide and clean, with fine sand, the beach stretches off into the distance, and is far too big ever to become really crowded, even at the height of summer. Added to the pleasures of bathing and building sandcastles, there are usually donkey rides on the beach, there's a **Children's Corner** of small rides for younger kids (1 token 50p, 45 tokens £20; each ride 2–7 tokens), and the **Spa, Bridlington** (☎01262/678 258, ⓦwww.thespabridlington.com) has a full programme of film, comedy, music, dance, sport and variety, together with a series of summer shows and winter pantomimes. It also has a café/bar (Mon–Sat 10am–6pm, Sun 10am–4pm). The whole area around the Spa was being renovated at the time of writing, part of ongoing work being done in many parts of the town, and it should be pristine when it's finished. Pity about the colour – the building is a hideous (though admittedly hard-to-miss) bright orange. Incidentally, as you wander around the Spa, look out for the **Royal Yorkshire Yacht Club** just off South Cliff Road. This is where T.E. Lawrence (the future Lawrence of Arabia) stayed when it was the *Ozone Hotel* off and on between November 1934 and February 1935, while he was working on the boats of the RAF Marine Craft Unit based in the town. There's a memorial sundial dedicated to him in nearby Southcliff Gardens, in front of the block of flats (known to locals, apparently, as "The Carbuncle").

The beach to the north of the harbour, the **North Bay**, which is accessed from the North Promenade, also has its own land train which runs from just outside **Leisure World** (leisure, training and learner pools; ⓣ01262/606 715, ⓦwww.bridlingtonleisureworld.co.uk) out to Sewerby Hall.

Sewerby Hall (daily 10am–5pm, some parts close at 4.30pm; £4.30; ⓣ01262/673 769, ⓦwww.sewerby-hall.co.uk) is a pleasant small country house, with pretty gardens, a pitch-and-putt golf course, a small children's zoo, craft units and a tearoom. There's a decent pub nearby – *The Ship* (ⓣ01262/672 374), which does food – and also **Bondville Miniature Village** (Easter–June & Sept 11am–4pm, July–Aug 10am–5pm; £3.25; ⓣ01262/401 736), which modestly claims to be a masterpiece, and is certainly diverting for kids.

Whie the South Bay simply disappears over the horizon into the haze, North Bay has as its backdrop the escalating white cliffs that lead out to Flamborough Head (see p.298). Both beaches have cafés, beach huts, gardens, and both have pleasant walks – North Bay in particular, beyond the prom, has lots of rock pools on the beach and a pleasant cliff-top walk.

The Town

The town of Bridlington lies back from the harbour, and is a mixture of normal town-centre shops, cafés and pubs. There's a single shopping mall – the Promenades Shopping Centre – and a large amusement arcade which also contains a multiplex cinema and a bowling alley (the Forum). Despite being quite small, it also boasts no fewer than three museums – the Beside the Seaside museum, the Harbour Museum and Old Penny Memories (the last is currently closed but hopes to re-open in new premises in 2011, phone ⓣ0774/265 8059 for details).

Beside the Seaside – the Bridlington Experience (Easter–Sept daily 10am–4pm; £1; ⓣ01262/608 890) on Queen Street explores Bridlington's past in a lighthearted way. You can sit in a railway carriage and eavesdrop on a Victorian group talking about their imminent visit to Brid, look at a 1950s boarding house and its landlady and guests, take in a Punch and Judy show (or even take part) and listen to the voices of stars who have appeared at the Spa Theatre. Great fun at very little cost. **Bridlington Harbour Heritage Museum** (Easter–Oct daily 10am–4pm; 30p; ⓣ01262/609 598), on the harbour side, is devoted to the history of the harbour, and contains many models of ships, nautical paintings, a ship's bell and a figurehead and other memorabilia. The museum is run by the Bridlington Sailing Coble Preservation Society, and the prize exhibit isn't in the museum at all, but floating in the harbour – it's the sailing coble *Three Brothers'* built in 1912.

Bridlington Old Town

About a mile inland from the current town centre is the original market town, now called **Old Town**. With its narrow lanes, many Georgian houses, Priory Church and Priory Green, the Old Town comes as a complete surprise to visitors to Bridlington who expected only a brash holiday resort. It has bags of character, with lots of pubs, many independent shops, and an ancient pillory and stocks.

The **Priory** was founded by Augustinian canons in the twelfth century, though nothing remains from earlier than the thirteenth. When the last prior, William Wood, was convicted of treason after supporting the Pilgrimage of Grace, and executed in 1537, the Priory was taken over by the Crown and much of it demolished. All the monastic buildings (apart from the Bayle) were pulled down, and what was left – the nave, aisles and towers of the priory church – became the parish church of **St Mary the Virgin**. Much restored by Sir Gilbert G. Scott in the 1870s, it looks odd, with its mismatched towers, yet is somehow in keeping with the surrounding streets.

The only part of the original Priory to survive apart from the church is the Grade I listed **Bayle**, or gatehouse. With a lower stone storey, and upper brick one, and with a large coach and small pedestrian entry, it now houses the **Bayle Museum** (June–Aug Mon–Fri 10am–4pm; £1; ☎01262/674 353), which offers an eclectic, if a little hit-and-miss, collection of life-size figures – a monk sitting on a garderobe (a toilet), a female prisoner sitting in her cell, a farmer sitting at his table – scale models, interactive games and information points outlining some aspects of Bridlington's social history. You can also see, up a spiral staircase on the first floor, the courtroom in which local miscreants were tried. There's a fine collection of dolls, a display about the history of the Green Howards, a glove belonging to Henrietta Maria (wife of Charles I) a breech-loading swivel gun dating from 1600 and a number of documents important in the town's history.

Flamborough Head

North of Bridlington the cliffs of **Flamborough Head** sweep eastwards into the North Sea. These lofty chalk cliffs and the headland in general offer good cliff-top walks, birdwatching (see below), fossil hunting, fishing, diving, and lots of sea views. Pick up a copy of the voluntary "Codes of Conduct" for the area from tourist information points. The best place to park for the general visitor is at the lighthouse beyond the village of Flamborough on the B1259. **Flamborough Head Lighthouse**, still operational, is open to the public (opening hours are complicated, phone in advance; £3; ☎01255/245 011, ⊛www.trinityhouse .co.uk). A visit involves a short introductory talk from one of the lighthouse keepers there for the purpose – the light is now fully automatic – then the steep climb up the spiral staircase to the top of the tower and up a ladder into the light itself. Not advised for the infirm or for vertigo sufferers – unlike off-shore light-houses, Flamborough has no intermediate floors. Although the first lighthouse was built here in 1669, the current one dates from 1806, when a light giving two white flashes followed by a red one, designed by George Robinson, was installed. This was the first time alternating white and red flashes had been used, an innovation that was quickly copied elsewhere.

The lighthouse sits on the cliff top above formidable chalk cliffs, and there are way-marked paths to take you down to the sea. Along the northern edge of Flamborough Head are two nature reserves – first the Yorkshire Wildlife Trust's Flamborough Cliffs nature reserve, then the Royal Society for the Protection of Birds reserve at Bempton Cliffs. Each has its own car park and access points (see Wildlife in Yorkshire, p.323).

The Holderness peninsula

South of Bridlington lies the **Holderness peninsula**, the large hook of land that curls around from the Hull/Beverley/Bridlington axis to the mouth of the Humber, bounded on one side by the North Sea and on the other by the Humber estuary, with, between them, the spit of land called **Spurn Point** or **Spurn Head**. Compared to the North Yorkshire coast, this East Yorkshire seaboard is undra-matic and understated. Holderness consists of slightly undulating and relatively empty countryside dotted with villages, but as with many peninsulas the area is defined more by its coasts than its interior. It sweeps in a gentle curve all the way south to Spurn Head, with miles of beaches, low bluffs and sea defences dotted with small seaside towns and isolated villages.

The eastern coast of Holderness suffers badly from erosion, with the tides scouring the sand off the beaches and depositing it on the eerie and ever-lengthening (about 2 yards a year) Spurn Head. Consequently, although there are numerous little seaside towns and villages along the North Sea coast, they tend to be disfigured by necessary, but ugly, concrete sea defences.

Hornsea

Fifteen miles south of Bridlington is **HORNSEA**, a typical small English seaside town, with a promenade, lots of amusement arcades and fish-and-chip shops, the Freeport Shopping Complex just south of the town, and a beach which is suffering particularly badly from erosion, despite all sorts of measures taken to combat it.

If you approach Hornsea from the south, the views of the town and its church reflected in its large **Mere** are delightful. Said to be Yorkshire's largest natural freshwater lake, the Mere is a nice place to eat your sandwiches, potter around in a rowing boat (£3/person/hour) or have a round on the putting green (£1.20). Visitors who picnic by the Mere may feel that it's the human beings, not the birds, who need sanctuary – from the gangs of swans and geese who aggressively demand feeding. Incidentally, follow the signs for the Mere carefully – the road down to it is easy to miss.

Despite, indeed perhaps because of, the fight that the town has had with erosion in the past, the resulting **sea front** is extremely pleasant, with the old promenade below a substantial sea wall, built in 1985 following serious flooding, topped with a second, modern promenade. There are numerous places to sit, and a kiosk/shop in what was a public shelter. The beach makes an excellent fossil-hunting-ground, especially after the storms that sometimes lash the east coast, and there are invigorating beach walks both north and south of the town (though be careful – even experienced walkers have found themselves cut off by the tide). Look out for the start of the **Trans Pennine Trail** (Ⓦ www .transpenninetrail.org.uk), Britain's first long-distance multi-user trail. It links Hornsea on the east coast with Southport on the west. There's an impressive marker and an information board.

Hornsea's main non-seaside claim to fame is for its **pottery**, though its production ceased in 2000. The most comprehensive collection in the world of the colourful, stylish ware can be seen in the **Hornsea Museum** (Mon–Fri 11am–5pm, Sat 11am–5pm, Tues 2–5pm; £2.50; Ⓣ01964/533 443, Ⓦwww.hornseamuseum .com). Housed in a row of cottages along the main street, Newbegin, the museum has, in addition, extensive displays on the social history of the area, including a series of residential and workplace rooms.

Just outside the town centre, on the road to Withernsea, the **Freeport Outlet Shopping Village** (Mon–Sat 9.30am–6pm, Sun 11am–5pm; Ⓦwww.horn seafreeport.com), claims to be the country's first, and is certainly one of the most pleasant, discount retail villages. On a sloping, landscaped site, the retail units are in single low-rise buildings – you could almost be on an upmarket housing estate. At the top of the site is Potters Square, with a small food court, ATMs and toilets – given the choice, park in Car Park 3, which is next to the square.

South of Hornsea the coast is quietly attractive, with crumbling bluffs and wide empty beaches. A succession of small villages dot the coast – Mappleton, Great Cowden, Aldbrough, Garton and Tunstall. Just inland, the village of **Roos** has a nice Grade I listed church, and a notable ex-resident in J.R.R. Tolkien.

Withernsea

Another of Holderness's windblown minor resorts, **WITHERNSEA** has more about it than most. In particular, you can't miss the stately 124ft-high tall **lighthouse** which stands just back from the beach. No longer functioning, it is now the **Withernsea Lighthouse Museum** (Easter–June & mid-Sept to Oct Sat 1–5pm, Sun noon–4pm; June to mid–Sept Mon–Fri 11am–5pm, Sat & Sun 1–5pm; £2.50; Ⓦwww.withernsealighthouse.co.uk), with sections dealing with the RNLI, HM Coastguards and the history of the town, and, more intriguingly, with the town's most famous daughter – Kay Kendall, the glamorous 1950s film star. Containing tableaux, memorabilia, stills from her pictures and movie posters, it is not only unexpected but oddly moving. The lighthouse itself is of course the central exhibit – built in 1892, it seems odd that it is a quarter of a mile from the coast, with the town between it and the sea. This is because, when it was built, there was only sand and a mere where the town now stands. You can mount the 144 steps that spiral up to the lamp room, from which there are terrific views across the town and the coast. But the same warnings as for Flamborough lighthouse apply here too – there are no intermediate floors and the steps are steep, so if you suffer from vertigo or ill health, stay at the bottom – you can see the views on CCTV. There's a tourist information point and a small café.

Another thing to look out for in Withensea is the pair of crenellated structures – the **Pier Towers** – on the promenade. They were once the entrance to a splendid 1150ft Victorian pier, built in 1877, which got shorter and shorter as boats kept crashing into it, until what was left was finally dismantled during the building of sea defences in the 1930s. The towers remain, like fingers pointing into the past towards the town's vanished heyday. Next to the towers are the **Valley Gardens**, venue for free entertainment on Sundays and some Saturdays during the summer.

RAF Holmpton

Just outside Withernsea, a short detour off to the left from the A1033 Hull Road leads to **RAF Holmpton** – it's signposted **Underground Bunker**. RAF Holmpton (March to early July, Sept & Oct Tues–Thurs, Sat & Sun 2pm; July daily 2pm; Aug daily 11am & 2pm; Nov Sat & Sun 2pm; in all cases the guided tour starts 30min after the gates open; £6; Ⓣ01964/630 208, Ⓦwww.raf holmpton.com) is the site of a huge RAF and Military Command Bunker 80ft underground, built in 1951–52 as part of the Cold War Early Warning System. It consists of not only the military installation (a message centre, coding and encryption centre, computer and radar rooms, Command HQ offices, Royal Observer Corps operations room and more) but also all the backup services that turn it into an underground village – hospital, cinema, canteen, dormitories – together with the life-support systems that would make the bunker self-sufficient in the event of an attack. Look out particularly for a chilling Weapons of Mass Destruction room. The bunker is accessible only on formal tours which take about 90 minutes.

The Queen of Holderness

From Withernsea a four-mile detour inland along the Withernsea to Hull A1033 road brings you to **PATRINGTON**. Patrington is famous for one thing – the magnificent **St Patrick's Church**, widely known as the **Queen of Holderness**, which earns plaudits from far and wide. Pevsner loved its "calm perfection", saying that "for sheer architectural beauty, few parish churches in England can vie with Patrington". The village's pride in St Patrick's is obvious – a notice inside says simply "this is England's finest village church". These rave reviews arise from its consistency − it was built quickly and was then little added to, so it represents a single style − early fourteenth-century Decorated − rather than the more usual extended muddle. It is built of pale grey limestone, its exterior and interior are of a piece, its spire is pretty and in proportion, its interior is consistent throughout, and uncluttered by too many monuments and memorials. Even the approach to it has a lot to commend it − you can see it for miles across the rolling cornfields of Holderness in any direction, but when you get to the village, because of its position, it seems to disappear until you're right on it when suddenly there it is in all its beauty. Incidentally, poet Ted Hughes was once stationed at RAF Patrington (now Holmpton), and there are several references to the area in his work.

From Patrington, the road to the end of the peninsula − the B1445 − strikes south through a succession of villages − Welwick, Weeton, Skeffling (look out for its wind turbine), Easington (notable as the landfall for the mighty North Sea gas pipeline) and **Kilnsea**, which has a Grade II listed acoustic mirror dating from World War II, used to listen out for approaching enemy aircraft, and a rather nice **pub**, the *Crown and Anchor*, outside which you can enjoy a drink and fine views of the estuary and the ships coming and going.

Spurn Head

Beyond Kilnsea it's edge-of-the-world stuff. You can either park at the Blue Bell, once a pub, now the Heritage Coast **visitor centre**, and catch the Spurn Ranger bus to the end of the point (it takes just under 20min), or pay a toll (£3 per car) to drive there yourself. If there's nobody at the rather ramshackle **Yorkshire Wildlife Trust Information Centre**, carry on − somebody will leap out of the marram grass to take your money. By now you'll be rumbling along a single-lane road that was built during World War II to supply the Spurn Head defences − before that, the only link was a railway, stretches of which can still be seen. Finally, after about three and a half miles of sand dunes, marram grass and water (at times you can see the North Sea to your left, the Humber estuary to your right), you'll pass the most recent of the point's several **lighthouses** (it was decommissioned in 1985) and turn into the **car park** above its predecessor which stands on the shore.

Although Spurn Point is a nature reserve run by the Yorkshire Wildlife Trust (so dogs are not allowed), it is also strategically important, dominating the Humber estuary and this part of the North Sea. As a result, it is littered with wartime defences, and is currently the home of the Humber lifeboat and pilot stations. Apart from the two lighthouses, there's a small **café** in a static caravan, the homes of the lifeboatmen, and the radio-and radar-festooned Humber Pilots' Control Tower. After parking it's well worth climbing up past this huddle of buildings to a vantage point on top of the ridge. From here to your left you can see the ships riding at anchor in the North Sea waiting their turn to enter the straits, whilst to the right the Humber Pilots' Jetty stretches out into the estuary, with, beyond it, the bright orange-and-black Humber lifeboat. The waters around Spurn Head are so dangerous that this RNLI station is the only one in England with a permanent professional crew.

Every few minutes one of the pilot cutters peels away from the jetty and ploughs out towards one of the anchored ships. Then, with the pilot on board, the ship will get under way and thrum through the gap between Spurn Head and Bull Fort (one of two built on sandbanks in the estuary), heading upriver towards Grimsby, Immingham, Hull, or the Trent and Ouse river ports. When the British economy is booming, the straits get very busy, but during recession you might have to wait hours to see a ship − there's a summary of shipping movements on Ⓦwww .humber.com.

Contexts

Contexts

A history of Yorkshire

To get full value from a holiday in Yorkshire it's well worth knowing something about its past. Yorkshire has played an important part in the history of Britain as a whole, especially during the struggles between Celts, Anglo-Saxons and Vikings, successive rebellions against the invading Normans after the Battle of Hastings, the medieval period of great religious houses and the Reformation that brought their fall, the English Civil War when the county was mainly Royalist but with important Parliamentary enclaves, the seventeenth- and eighteenth-century growth of great houses and estates, and, perhaps most importantly of all, the period from the mid-eighteenth century onwards when the Agricultural and Industrial revolutions changed the world. The region's attempt to find a response to the post-industrial decay that followed is shared by many of the other parts of Britain, with Yorkshire often taking a lead during that great upheaval.

As you holiday in Yorkshire you'll come across names and places that are very familiar – York and Sheffield, Whitby and Wakefield, Halifax and Huddersfield and Harrogate. You'll also come across evidence of the cultural diversity caused by Yorkshire's tumultuous past. You can best appreciate it if you have a broad historical framework in which to fit what you see. But first, a couple of health warnings:

Because of its size, the historical experience of different parts of Yorkshire varies enormously – the Dales sheep-farmer had little in common with the South Yorkshire coal miner, the Whitby whaler with the Halifax clothier, the occupant of the stately home with that of the back-to-back. So bear in mind that the experiences of individual parts of Yorkshire, and individual Yorkshire men and women can be very different.

Secondly, far from being a succession of accepted facts, Yorkshire history abounds with the unknown and the disputed. So what appears below is inevitably a simplification, and focuses on the events that are most significant to the sights covered in the guide.

Prehistoric times

There are, of course, no written records of prehistoric times, so we have to rely on archeological evidence and its (often difficult) interpretation. Evidence from the early eras – the Old and New Stone Ages especially – is sparse, though many local museums across Yorkshire have displays of what there is. For the Bronze and Iron Ages, probably the best museum to visit is the **Hull and East Yorkshire Museum** in Hull.

The Stone Ages (up to 2200 BC)

Remains from the **Old Stone Age** (up to 4500 BC), the period when people used roughly shaped flint tools, deer antlers, animal bones and wood, and survived by hunting wild animals and gathering wild fruit and seeds, have been found in many parts of Yorkshire. Antler points, mammoth, rhino and hippo bones, worked flints and wood and bone implements from the early Old Stone Age have been found in the Dales and in South Yorkshire, from the later Old Stone Age in the Dales, the Pennines, the Vales of York and Pickering, the Wolds and on the Holderness peninsula.

The big change from the Old to the **New Stone Age** (4500–2200 BC) was the development of agriculture. Instead of leading a nomadic life following the herds, people settled down, domesticating animals and sowing crops, rather than relying on the bounty of nature. From this period the evidence in Yorkshire includes grooved pottery, flint tools and weapons (axe heads, arrow heads), which were infinitely better quality than those from the Old Stone Age, stone circles and the barrows which are marked as tumuli on OS maps. Finds have been particularly rich in the Yorkshire Wolds and the Vale of York. Specific artefacts dating from the New Stone Age include the **Rudston Monolith** and the **Devil's Arrows** (see p.293 & p.176), the three circular henges in Thornborough near Ripon, which have a slight kink in their alignment corresponding exactly to that of the stars in Orion's Belt, and rock art that has been found above Wharfedale near Ilkley.

The Bronze Age (2200–700 BC)

The introduction of things made of bronze – an alloy of copper and tin – led to a new age not only of sophisticated tools and weapons, but also of earthworks, tombs and presumed ceremonial centres. Numerous finds near Driffield and Thwing, axes, tools and prestige ceremonial weapons, together with a few earthworks in Holderness, the famous **North Ferriby boats** (see p.276), crop marks in the Vales of Pickering and York, burial mounds on the North York Moors, low cairns, stone circles and walls in the Pennines, several lengthy boundary dikes, all date from this period.

The Iron Age (700 BC – coming of the Romans)

When the much harder iron started to replace bronze as a material for making tools and weapons, serious clearing of woodland using iron axes and ploughing of land using iron ploughshares started to transform the Yorkshire landscape. The two Iron Age tribes to dominate the area were the **Brigantes**, who settled what is today South, East and West Yorkshire, and the **Parisii**, who dominated East Yorkshire. Although as you'd expect with farming people the greatest population density was in the fertile lowlands, most of the surviving remains have been found in the uplands – lowland remains have been largely ploughed under by subsequent generations. So there are lots of Iron Age remains in the Dales (the settlement platforms of Wharfedale and Swaledale, for example) and also in the North York Moors. The Wolds, too, have their fair share, including the spectacular "carriage burials" where skeletons have been found accompanied by two-wheeled carriages or chariots. One of the most important finds was made in **Hasholme**, where a third-century BC 45ft-long log boat was unearthed (see p.276). There are, too, lots of iron-smelting sites and evidence of coppicing. Hill forts have been discovered, many of them being reinforced Bronze Age fortifications. The biggest is the enormous one that covers the summit of **Ingleborough**, but many others have been identified as a result of air surveys.

The Romans (43–410 AD)

Despite Julius Caesar's punishment/exploratory raids in 55 BC and 54 BC, the actual invasion of Britain didn't begin until almost a hundred years later. From 43 AD the invading Roman armies worked their way inexorably northwards, probably reaching the Don, the southern edge of the Brigantes' homeland, around 45/46 AD. To start with, the Brigantes, under their **Queen Cartimandua**, became a Roman client state, with the queen gaining favour by handing over Celtic rebel Caradoc to the conquerors. When Cartimandua divorced her husband Venutius and he responded with armed rebellion, the Romans sent powerful forces to support her. The second time this happened, however, they didn't have the soldiers to spare and sent only auxiliaries. They rescued her, leaving Venutius in charge. Losing patience in 69 AD, the Romans conquered the Brigantes and incorporated them into the Roman Empire.

During Rome's almost four-hundred-year rule, Roman roads spread across Yorkshire and forts were established in various places, with different ones becoming prominent at different times. In due course, **York (Eboracum)** became the undisputed Roman capital of the North, but other Roman sites were important at different times – Aldborough, Malton, Doncaster, Castleford, Tadcaster, Catterick and Brough. In each case a fort would be built to protect a river crossing or an important road intersection, then a "vicus" or civilian settlement would grow up nearby. There are numerous Roman remains to be seen in Yorkshire, not only in towns like York and Malton, but also out in the country – the piece of Roman road called Wade's Causeway, for example, or the Military Camps at Cawthorne. York has a statue of Emperor Constantine the Great near the Minster – Constantine was in York when he was proclaimed Emperor. Towards the end of the Roman period, attacks from the sea along the east coat led to the building of signal towers, for example, at Scarborough, Filey, Flamborough and Holderness, though much of the evidence has since been washed away by the sea.

The Anglo-Saxons

The traditional story of what happened after the Roman legions left Britain around 410 AD is that hordes of Germanic **Angles**, **Saxons** and **Jutes** flooded across the North Sea and drove the native **Celts** out of England into what is today Wales, Scotland, Cornwall and Brittany. The story involved British chief Vortigern inviting Anglo-Saxon mercenaries to help him against rival Celtic chieftains, only for the mercenaries to rebel and seize the territory for themselves. It is, however, very difficult in reality to know what went on, since so little evidence has survived – the account of what happened taught in most schools until recently was based almost exclusively on the Venerable Bede's *The Ecclesiastical History of the English People*.

Modern research, however, indicates that the process was a great deal more gradual and more confused than this, with Angles coming in and settling down alongside the native Celts. Any warfare, it's now believed, was limited to a small number of warriors, with most of the population unaffected. If there was a major change during the fifth to the seventh centuries, it was that a Celtic aristocracy was probably replaced by an Anglo-Saxon one. In Yorkshire the infiltration of the **Angles** started on the western edges of the Wolds, then spread through the Vale of York and across to the coast. In around 600 AD Aethelfrith formed the new kingdom of Northumbria and, although he was killed at the Battle of the Idle near Bawtry in 616 AD, the English conquest of the region continued under Edwin, with struggles between Northumbria and Mercia. The new kingdom's capital was set up in **Eoforwic**, or **York**. Roman fortifications were renewed and strengthened. Internecine troubles continued, with kings being killed in battle, assassinated or exiled until the beginning of the Viking invasion in 867 AD.

The story of the **growth of Christianity** is, of course, dealt with in great detail by Bede – he was, after all, a monk. The Roman Empire had become Christian under Constantine, and remnants of Christianity remained among the Celts after the Roman evacuation. The stronghold of this **Celtic church** was across the sea in Ireland, from which Columba had set up a monastery on Iona off the Scottish coast in 563 AD, with the Celtic church making inroads in the north of England. Then, Augustine landed in Kent in 597 AD and began a campaign to convert the English to the **Roman** version of Christianity as it had survived in Rome itself. As this was going on, King Oswald of Northumbria invited Aidan to set up a Celtic monastery on Lindisfarne and, shortly afterwards, established an abbey at Whitby (see p.250). The spread of Christianity of both types continued apace: the Celtic church from the north, the Roman church from the south. Eventually, in 663 at the **Synod of Whitby**, King Oswy of Northumberland heard the arguments of both sides regarding the differences between the two churches – specifically, the date of Easter – and ruled that the Roman Church should prevail.

In the eighth century, **York** became the major Christian religious centre for the region. New monasteries were established by members the Northumbrian royal family, and Christianity was imposed top-down. Great efforts were made to suppress surviving pagan beliefs among ordinary people, and where they stubbornly persisted, they were incorporated into the Christian church – the **Rudston Monolith** almost certainly has pagan religious significance, so the church for the village was built right next to it, and it was incorporated into the churchyard. If you can't beat them, join them (see p.293). Survivals from the Anglo-Saxon period are uncommon, but you can visit **Ripon Cathedral crypt**, look at the carved column in the churchyard at **Masham**, or go down into the crypt of **Lastingham church** – actually the remains of the monastery of St Cedd established there in 659 AD (see p.244). Look out too for the many **place names** in the area that end in …ton, … ley, …burgh and …field.

The Vikings

The first sign of the imminent **Viking** storm came in 793 AD, when Lindisfarne was attacked. Subsequent raids became increasingly frequent. Finally, waves of Viking attacks started in 866. York was taken in 867, East Anglia was conquered in 870, Mercia in 874. Monasteries were sacked, their monks killed or dispersed, their lands confiscated, though minsters seem to have survived. In due course, though, Viking leaders started to adopt Christianity. Warfare continued between the Vikings and the Anglo-Saxons until, in 886, Alfred the Great of the Saxons and Guthrum of the Vikings signed a treaty fixing the borders between Wessex and the Danelaw. Towards the end of the Viking period Christianity flourished and many parish churches were built, sometimes incorporating elements of their Saxon predecessors (take a look, for example, at **St Peter's Church** in Kirkgate, Leeds). The three Ridings had a definite flavour of the Scandinavian, and the term **Yorkshire** itself was first used in 1065, the year before the Battle of Hastings.

The main evidence for the Viking occupation of the region was until fairly recently the spread of Viking **place names** – ones ending in …by, …thorpe and …thwaite. And the famous three "**Ridings**" of Yorkshire are derived from the Danish "thrithing" or third. There are also Viking carvings in parts of Yorkshire, like the crosses at St Andrew's Church, Middleton (just outside Pickering) with warriors and scenes from Scandinavian mythology carved on it.

In the 1970s, however, our knowledge of the Vikings in Yorkshire took a big leap forward when the Coppergate excavations in York revealed evidence of a large Viking city. Imaginatively developed by the York Archaeological Trust into the **Jorvik** attraction (see p.154), and with complementary **Dig** (see p.153) dealing with the processes and methods of archeology, we now have a remarkably vivid idea of what Viking life was like shortly before the Norman Conquest.

The Normans

Yorkshire played a crucial part both in the events preceding the Norman Conquest, and in what happened during the years following it. While **King Harold of England** was waiting for the expected invasion by William of Normandy in the south of England, news arrived that a force under his disaffected brother Tostig, supported by Harald Hardrada of Norway, had attacked Scarborough, then sailed up the Humber, and started on their way to York. King Harold sped northwards, and destroyed the invaders at **Stamford Bridge** east of the city, on September 25, 1066. Three days later, William and his invading Normans landed on the south coast. So King Harold and his exhausted soldiers had to rush back south, only to be beaten at the **Battle of Hastings** on October 14, 1066. King Harold, as every schoolchild knows, was killed, William seized the throne, and his Norman commanders and supporters were granted extensive estates in return for their support, going on to replace the top level of Anglo-Saxon aristocracy as the country's ruling class.

From the start, Yorkshire was at the heart of resistance to William the Conqueror, and it was to pay dearly for it. The ruling class in the area was largely Danish in origin, the language spoken a combination of Anglo-Saxon and Danish which the southern English couldn't understand (no change there then), and indeed the hold of the Anglo-Saxon kings of England over the area was at best tentative. It might even have seemed to the people of Yorkshire themselves that the area could, with the help of Scottish and Scandinavian allies, remain independent of Norman England. William the Conqueror, of course, didn't see it this way. A series of northern rebellions caused him increasing frustration, until in 1069–70 he undertook a series of ferocious attacks on the area which has since gone down in history as the "Harrying of the North". Whole populations were ruthlessly cut down, villages destroyed and survivors deprived of food by a scorched earth policy. His soldiers even salted the land to make it barren. It has been estimated that up to 100,000 people died directly or indirectly as a result of this pitiless campaign. The action was followed by the wholesale division of Yorkshire into "honours" ruled over by William's most trusted, competent and ruthless lieutenants. Castles sprang up across Yorkshire, with pressed labour building first the quickly erected earthen motte and bailey castles, then, when the county was secure, more permanent and less easily attacked stone castles with powerful keeps, gatehouses and curtain walls (Richmond Castle, for example). Castles of increasing power and sophistication were built during the following centuries, at first for purely military reasons, but becoming more comfortable and residential as the threat of rebellion receded. Today, castles, or what's left of them, can be seen in Conisbrough, Pontefract, Tickhill, Richmond, Middleham, Skipton, Skipsea, Scarborough, Pickering and Helmsley – most are covered in this guidebook.

In addition to the castles, the new Norman overlords also built or restored numerous monasteries, with the different orders going in and out of fashion (see box, p.310).

From the thirteenth century onwards many monasteries, especially those of the Cistercians, expanded their wealth, power and influence both in Yorkshire and elsewhere. They were known for their entrepreneurial spirit – Fountains Abbey, for example, became a major sheep owner with huge flocks in the Dales, while

The Norman monastery-building boom

Yorkshire is renowned for the number and beauty of its monasteries and convents. Most of these were established between the Norman Conquest and the mid-twelfth century, in phases when the different main orders seemed to be favoured in turn. A word of warning – the dates when religious houses were established are often unclear – they are sometimes only rough approximations, or several dates could be given depending on when the original monastery was established, when it changed orders, or when it was restored.

The Benedictines
Selby (1069)
Whitby (1078)
Lastingham (1078)
York: St Mary's (1088)
Holy Trinity, Micklegate (1089)

Augustinian
Nostell Priory (1114)
Bridlington (1114)
Kirkham (1122)
Bolton Priory (1154/5)

Gilbertines
Old Malton (1150)

Cistercian
Rievaulx Abbey (1132)
Fountains Abbey (1135)
Roche Abbey (1138)
Byland Abbey (1143)
Kirkstall Abbey (1152)
Jervaulx (1138)

Premonstratensians
Easby (1151)

Cluniac
Pontefract (1154)
Monk Bretton Priory (1154)

Rievaulx, Kirkstead and Byland Abbeys undertook a lot of mineral extraction. Another feature of the time was the growth of friars who preached, lived off charity and owned no property beyond their churches and monastery buildings. Thus the Dominicans (Blackfriars) had houses in York, Beverley, Scarborough and Pontefract, the Franciscans (Greyfriars) in York, Beverley, Doncaster, Hull, Richmond and Scarborough, the Carmelites (Whitefriars) in York, Hull, Scarborough, Doncaster and Northallerton, and the Augustinians (Austin Friars) in York, Tickhill and Hull.

It wasn't just the big monastic houses that made their first appearance at this time – many **parish churches** were built which survive today with recognizably Norman features – St Mary's in Armthorpe, St Helen's in Austerfield and many more.

Many new **market towns** were also founded at this time. Virtually every one in Yorkshire can trace its origins to the early Norman period, even some, like Bradford, Halifax, Rotherham and Barnsley that came to prominence much later as Victorian industrial centres. In the countryside royal forests and deer parks were established, and many field patterns and town layouts that were to last for centuries can trace their origin to the Normans.

The Wars of the Roses

A series of dynastic struggles fought between 1455 and 1485, the **Wars of the Roses** are often mistakenly thought of as a simple battle between Yorkshire and Lancashire. They were in fact a struggle between two branches of the **Plantagenet** royal house, the descendants of two of the younger sons of Edward III in the previous century. A tangled web of plots, rebellions and battles, the struggle was between the **House of York** (emblem, the White Rose) and the **House of Lancaster** (the Red Rose). Geographically, support for the two houses was by no means cleanly divided between Yorkshire and Lancashire – most of the great families in the East and West Ridings of Yorkshire supported Lancaster, and in the North Riding allegiance was divided. Two of the major battles of the Wars of the Roses were fought in Yorkshire. On December 30, 1460, in the **Battle of Wakefield**, Richard Duke of York was killed, beheaded, and his head displayed on Micklegate Bar in York. Three months later, on March 29, 1461, the bloodiest battle ever to have been fought on British soil took place at **Towton**, south of Tadcaster. Although they outnumbered the Yorkists, the Lancastrians lost the battle. Estimates of the size of the armies and the number of casualties varies – somewhere between 60,000 and 80,000 soldiers took part, with perhaps 28,000 losing their lives. Lancastrian heads replaced the Yorkist ones on Micklegate Bar. **Edward IV** of York, who had been crowned shortly before the battle, emerged as undisputed king.

However, the Wars of the Roses continued, ending only on August 22, 1485, at the **Battle of Bosworth** when the Lancastrian Henry Tudor, Duke of Richmond, defeated King Richard III, who had succeeded his brother Edward IV two years earlier. **Henry VII** was crowned on the battlefield. This might well have been just the latest battle in the Wars of the Roses had it not been for Henry's exceptional ability as king. He cut through the York/Lancaster tit-for-tat of the preceding thirty years by being merciful during subsequent rebellions, by using taxation and legislation to bring the overmighty barons to their knees, and by marrying Elizabeth of York, uniting the red and white roses into the new two-colour Tudor Rose – as seen in the rose window in the south transept of York Minster. In so doing, he laid the foundations for a Tudor dynasty which ruled England for more than a century.

The dissolution of the monasteries

Henry VII built up a fortune during his 24-year reign, making the monarch by far the richest and most powerful man in England. His son **Henry VIII** had spent all the money within two years of his 1509 succession. This set the scene for years of financial problems for the crown. An issue of succession also emerged as Henry's wife, Catherine of Aragon, failed to provide a son and heir. Famously, the two problems were solved during the 1530s by related events – Henry pressed for a divorce from Catherine so that he could marry Anne Boleyn, and when the pope refused to grant it (he had problems of his own), the train of events was set in motion that led to England's break with Rome, the establishment up of the Church of England, and the start of the English Reformation. Once the pope's authority in England had been denied, it gave Henry the excuse to dissolve the monasteries, whose money, lands and treasure went some way towards stopping up the hole in the royal finances.

All these events had important consequences for Yorkshire. Being one of the regions with the most monasteries and convents, it was most affected by their dissolution between 1536 and 1540. Commissioners had earlier been sent around the religious houses to gather evidence of their wrongdoing (the excuse) and taking an inventory of their wealth (the real reason), and now the monasteries were closed, their abbots, monks and nuns expelled, their gold and silver carted off to London, their lands rented out or sold to local people, their buildings partially dismantled to become sources of free dressed stone for construction. At a stroke, Henry's financial problems were eased and a whole class of people had been created with a vested interest in the continuation of the break with Rome.

However, though the dissolution was supported in Yorkshire by those who benefited from it, it was deeply unpopular with others in what was largely a conservative, Catholic area, and in October 1536 a rebellion against the changes and in favour of the Roman Catholic church started in Lincolnshire and spread to Beverley, the Wolds, Holderness and York. This was the **Pilgrimage of Grace**, led by lawyer Robert Aske. Tenants who had newly taken over monastic lands were expelled, dispersed monks and nuns were returned to their monasteries and the Roman Catholicism restored. Further rebellions occurred around Ripon and Richmond, and these fresh rebels joined the pilgrimage. By the end of October, almost the whole of Yorkshire was up in arms. Though with hindsight it seems likely that the rebellion had little chance of success, at the time it was perceived as a serious challenge to the king's authority. Henry at first played it softly, promising to consider the rebels' grievances and demands. Aske naively accepted the king's word and stood his forces down. Early in 1537 Henry had Aske arrested and executed, and his body displayed on the walls of York Castle. His leading noble supporters, together with numerous abbots, monks and priests, were also executed – 216 in all died.

The English Reformation

The break with Rome was political and financial. But despite Henry's innate religious conservatism, he couldn't prevent the arguments which were raging on the continent between Protestants and Roman Catholics, which started with Martin Luther in 1517, spreading to England. The disagreements – over the power of priests, the authority of the pope, corrupt practices like nepotism, simony and the selling of indulgences, the disapproval of "idolatry" and pomp in churches and services – started to lead to piecemeal change in the English church.

Conservative Yorkshire had little enthusiasm for the new ways. It is significant that no Protestant martyrdoms occurred here during Roman Catholic Bloody Mary's reign but twenty Roman Catholics were martyred, in the 1580s alone, during Protestant Elizabeth I's – including Margaret Clitherow of York, pressed to death at the age of 30 for harbouring priests.

Many of the county's upper-class families, like the **Nevilles** and the **Percys**, were famously Roman Catholic – it is said that there wasn't a Catholic rebellion that didn't involve at least one member of the Percy family. The Wakefield Plot (1541), the Seamer Rising (1549), and in particular the Rebellion of the Northern Earls (1569–70), all involved members of the great Catholic families. The Rebellion of the Northern Earls was by far the most serious, but it failed: one of its leaders, Neville; fled into exile, another, a Percy, ended up with his head on a spike at Micklegate Bar in York. The focus of many Catholic rebellions was, of course, **Mary Queen of Scots**, and she spent a considerable proportion of her long imprisonment in England under the control of the Earl of Shrewsbury in Sheffield (see p.55). Yorkshire disaffection with the growing Protestantism continued into the reign of James I – Guy Fawkes, one of the leaders of the Roman Catholic Gunpowder Plot to blow up king and parliament, was from York.

Economically Yorkshire flourished during the Tudor years. In the countryside the early harbingers of the Agricultural Revolution can be detected, with considerable enclosure of open fields in Holderness to help with the growing of grain and cattle, and in the Wolds to facilitate the change-over to more profitable sheep. In industry, too, the early shoots of industries that were to flourish during the later Industrial Revolution can be seen – cutlery in Sheffield, woollen cloth in Wakefield and Halifax, even liquorice in Pontefract.

The English Civil War

During the English Civil War Yorkshire as a whole remained true to the county's conservative traditions by staying firmly **Royalist**, though Hull supported **Parliament** throughout – indeed, it can be claimed that it was the refusal of the burghers of Hull to allow Charles I into their city that sparked off the war in the first place. There was much fighting between the forces of both sides across the county, with sieges of York, Hull, Pontefract, Skipton and Bradford. Parliamentarians from Hull captured Bridlington and Whitby for a time, and the biggest battle of the Civil War was fought at **Marston Moor**, just west of York, in 1644. References to Civil War battles and sieges can be found throughout this guide. When the war ended with a Parliamentary victory, many of Yorkshire's castles were destroyed, such as Sheffield and Pontefract, or "slighted" – made unusable by partial destruction – including Helmsley and Scarborough.

The eighteenth century: population explosion

Up to the eighteenth century, population, both in Yorkshire and in England as a whole, generally remained fairly static. Good times would be reflected in moderate increase, bad times in moderate (or in the case of the Black Death, catastrophic) decline. From the restoration of the Monarchy in 1660 after the Commonwealth period under Cromwell until the beginning of the eighteenth century, there was little change. But throughout the eighteenth century population grew, at first slowly but then more and more quickly. Bearing in mind that until the coming of the census in 1801 population estimates are little more than informed guesswork, the population of England seems to have risen slightly from 5 million in 1700 to 5.8 million in 1750 and then to 9 million in 1800. From then on it doubled to 18 million by 1850 and doubled again to 36 million by 1911.

This increase was not consistent across the country. Rural areas stagnated or even became less populous, towns and cities grew disproportionately. The industrial north grew in comparison with the rural south, except for London. It was long thought that this implied a mass migration of people from the countryside to the towns, from the farm to the factory, from the south to the north. This didn't happen – people seemed, rather, to move in concentric circles, with those near the towns moving into them, those a bit further away moving in to replace the migrants, and so on. And a great deal of the population increase in the industrial cities and towns of the north appears to have been self-generated, with families having more children.

This population increase was the single most important fact of the period. It created an expanding market for food and finished goods, and at the same time provided a rapidly increasing workforce. The needs of the growing population were met by the improved agrarian and industrial methods that were being introduced – that is, by the Agricultural and Industrial revolutions.

The Agricultural Revolution

Small-scale changes in the way the land was managed can be detected in Yorkshire as early as Tudor times. These changes gathered pace during the seventeenth and eighteenth centuries, whereby villages would move from the open-field system where each family held strips on open fields, and also had grazing and fuel gathering rights on the common, to the consolidation of land-holding into separate farms. This was not only more efficient but also reduced the spread of animal diseases. Enclosure could only be done with the agreement of everybody in the village, though, and as the eighteenth century progressed, the need for a unanimous decision to enclose in each village became increasingly onerous. Parliament started to intervene, a process that culminated in the 1845 **General Enclosure Act**, which implemented procedures for any village to enclose with the minimum of fuss. Though there was a great deal of opposition to the enclosure movement, it is hard to see what alternative there was if the growing population was to be fed.

The other development in farming, very noticeable in Yorkshire, was the introduction of new methods and new machinery. Crops such as turnips and clover were introduced (in Hatfield, for example), the practice of spreading lime on acid soils was more widely adopted, potatoes were introduced in the Dales, rape was cultivated to feed sheep and produce oil. New machines, too, became popular – the Rotherham plough, for example, patented in 1730, became the precursor of many future metal ploughs. As the century wore on, Yorkshire farming became an enthusiastic adopter of the new ways and the new machines (though the enthusiasm wasn't universal). Symptomatic of this enthusiasm is the story of William Marshall (1745–1818), an enlightened agricultural reformer and writer who was instrumental in setting up the British Board of Agriculture, and who established an agricultural college in Pickering (see p.238).

The Industrial Revolution

In industry, too, small changes detectable in Tudor times gathered pace during the seventeenth and eighteenth centuries. Coal mining, iron smelting, glass manufacture, pottery production were all under way by the end of the seventeenth century and while woollen manufacture had been long established in West Yorkshire. Road and river transport was being improved piecemeal – new packhorse bridges were built, rivers were made more navigable. With hindsight, one can almost imagine that Yorkshire was waiting for the Industrial Revolution with bated breath.

From the middle of the eighteenth century, in common with other industrial areas like Lancashire, the West Midlands and the Northeast, Yorkshire towns and cities grew, and improvements in transport, extraction and manufacturing processes accelerated, at such an unprecedented rate that what was happening was not just an industrial revolution – it was a revolution in human life that was to sweep the planet.

Textiles

At the forefront of this revolution was West Yorkshire's textile industry. Organized loosely in a domestic system, it was uniquely suited to fast and widespread change. Across the hills of **West Yorkshire**, families lived on smallholdings where they grew food part-time, the rest of their year being spent making woollen cloth. The head of the household would weave cloth on a loom in the house, the other processes – preparing the wool, spinning and finishing – being done by the women and children. Each household financed and produced its own cloth and sold it in the town wool markets. Here then was a great stock of small entrepreneurs ready to innovate when the chance came, and with time available – when necessary, they could simply spend less time farming and more time spinning and weaving. Furthermore, a wide variety of types of cloth was produced – worsteds, kerseys, woollens, broad cloths and narrow cloths – so that production could be switched easily from one to the other as prices and fashions changed.

From being just one of the UK's wool producing regions (the others were East Anglia and the West Country), West Yorkshire shot ahead to become supreme, the area, with Lancashire, that clothed the world. Indeed, mechanical innovation occurred earlier in Lancashire than Yorkshire, and a number of places on the western edge of West Yorkshire followed Lancashire's lead and started to produce cotton cloth.

Towards the end of the eighteenth century, large woollen mills started to be built, first powered by water and then by steam. Machines, too, took over – Hargreaves's spinning jenny, Arkwright's water frame and Crompton's mule on the spinning side, bracketed by Kay's flying shuttle and Cartwright's power loom in weaving. Giant factories, the chimneys of their engine rooms belching smoke, the back-to-back housing that snaked along the valley floors and up onto the hills, the horrendous overcrowding and lack of sanitation in living conditions, the severe workplace in discipline, child labour, long hours and dangerous conditions, presented a problem that nobody in the world had ever faced before.

Coal

As steam replaced water power and increasing amounts of iron and steel were needed for making machinery and building factories, the demand for coal grew rapidly. The existing coal mines in South and West Yorkshire had to expand – old-fashioned bell-pits and adit mines were not enough, and deep mining had to go progressively deeper to produce the necessary coal. Although there were innovations – such as the use of underground tramways, steam winding and ventilation and the use of safety lamps–rock falls, the build-up of poisonous gas, flooding and methane explosions began to make coal mining one of the most dangerous jobs in the country. Thirty men died in Barnsley in 1803, 73 at the Oaks colliery in 1847 and 75 at Darley Main in 1849. Children as young as 7 or 8 were employed as "trappers", though the practice of using young girls to pull trucks of coal like tethered animals was not common in the Yorkshire pits. Output did rise quickly, and some coal owners developed reputations for being good employers, but others were grasping and incompetent and in general conditions remained appalling, safety standards poor, hours long, wages low and relations between management and workers dreadful.

Iron and steel

South Yorkshire was the region's great iron-and steel-producing area. The building material of the early Industrial Revolution was iron; that of the late

Industrial Revolution steel. There were, broadly, three types of iron, each with its own properties and uses. **Cast iron**, as it emerged from the furnace in which it was extracted from the ore, had a high carbon content and was very hard but relatively brittle. It was cast into moulds in foundries to make such things as kitchen ranges, gutters, downpipes and manhole covers – anything where it wouldn't be put under lateral stress. **Wrought iron**, made by heating cast iron and beating out the carbon and other impurities, was softer, more malleable and less brittle than cast iron. Able to stand up to stress without shattering, wrought iron was widely used during the early Industrial Revolution for such things as bridges and machinery, as well as in ornamental ironwork. **Steel**, with a higher carbon content than wrought iron but lower than cast iron, was tough and malleable, with excellent edge-retaining properties. It was initially very difficult to make – cast iron was turned into wrought iron, and then the carbon content had to be raised to a precisely calculated level: too much and it reverted to cast iron, too little and it remained as wrought iron. This long and tedious process ensured that steel was prohibitively expensive, and was only used for things like clock springs, surgical instruments, cutlery, weapons and razors. However, with the invention of the Bessemer process in the 1850s and the open-hearth process in the 1870s, steel could be mass produced, and it replaced wrought iron as the engineering material of choice during the later Industrial Revolution, produced in vast quantities in Sheffield in particular (see box, p.56).

Transport

The rapid development in the production of textiles, coal, iron and steel made massive demands on the region's transport system. In the eighteenth century each parish was responsible for the repair and maintenance of its own roads, a system which resulted in many roads that were impassably muddy in winter and dusty and rock-hard in summer. Wherever possible, heavy goods were moved on navigable rivers.

Attempts were made to improve things during the early eighteenth century – stone packhorse bridges replaced wooden ones, way-markers were set up to guide travellers across moorland (on the North York Moors for example) and attempts were made to improve existing rivers by means of "navigations" – straightening and deepening hitherto non-navigable stretches. However, as the Industrial Revolution really took off from the 1740s onwards, the need for better transport became critical. A series of Turnpike Trusts were set up whereby local businessmen could raise capital, improve an existing road or build a new one, then cover the costs, and possibly make a profit, by charging for its use. Many roads were turnpiked – especially those across the Pennines to Lancashire, where five routes were opened between 1751 and 1772. Yorkshire's greatest native road builder was **John Metcalf** – Blind Jack of Knaresborough – who built roads across Yorkshire, Lancashire and elsewhere (see p.174). His first road, between Minskip and Ferrensby, was opened in 1752. The new turnpike roads were not popular with local people who had to use them often, but they did improve transport between industrial areas, though carrying heavy goods by road was still slow and expensive. The new roads did have an impact, however, in speeding up long-distance coach travel and also in carrying mail. The growth of (relatively) fast passenger and mail transport was certainly important to the new class of entrepreneur that was developing in Yorkshire.

The search for a cheap way of carrying heavy raw materials and finished goods was still on. When, in Lancashire in 1761, the opening of the Bridgewater Canal from the coal mines of Worsley to the city of Manchester led to an immediate drop in the price of coal in the latter, it was not lost on businessmen elsewhere in

England. Canals started to be built in many parts of the country, a process which became known as "canal mania" from the 1790s onwards. In Yorkshire the most ambitious canal scheme was to link Leeds with the industrial centres of Lancashire – ambitious because of the technical problems presented by the intervening Pennines. Though started in the mid 1770s, the **Leeds and Liverpool canal** wasn't completed until 1816.

When the Stockton to Darlington **railway** was opened in 1825, and even more so when the Liverpool to Manchester railway was opened in 1830, it was immediately obvious that the holy grail of the Industrial Revolution had been found. Rail transport with steam locomotives pulling wagons or coaches could provide industry with a fast way of moving heavy goods around, passengers could get anywhere in the country in a day, mail trains sped up communications to an unbelievable extent – the impact was similar to that of computers in the late twentieth century. A frantic "railway mania" was sparked with schemes to build railways starting up all over the country, the economy got a huge injection of capital, whole towns grew up to service the new wonder of the age. Even the previous rather slapdash approach to time had to be standardized as, in 1840, the Great Western Railway introduced "railway time" along its length. It was such a good idea that within a couple of years all companies had done the same, and time throughout the country was standardized to "London time" controlled from Greenwich. And the influence of the railways wasn't confined to the UK – they spread all over the world.

1850–World War I

The rapid expansion of Yorkshire's industry that occurred between about 1780 and 1850 was largely unplanned, and it left a terrible mess. Cities like Leeds, Bradford and Sheffield existed under a pall of smoke, untreated sewage and uncollected refuse built up in the streets and people lived in overcrowded hovels with poor sanitation, their lives threatened by epidemic diseases like cholera. Conditions at work were no better – instead of working in their own homes, in small workshops, or in relatively safe bell-pits, they now had to cope with colossal factories or dangerous deep mines. Things that had gone unnoticed in small pre-industrial towns and villages, or were considered at least acceptable, now became not only unpleasant but life-threatening. The Victorians have got a bad press ever since, attacked by social commentators, authors like Charles Dickens and left-wing activists alike. Yet it must be remembered that Britain invented the Industrial Revolution, and was faced with problems that nobody had ever faced before. What is perhaps remarkable is not how little was done to solve the problems, but how much and how quickly. Despite the continued population explosion and ongoing industrial development, attempts to address the problems began almost immediately.

Across Yorkshire the clean up progressed – patchy and piecemeal, certainly, but increasingly effective. Cities set up improvement societies and commissions (in Sheffield, for example, in 1818) which started the work, Parliament set up properly constituted local councils with the Municipal Reform Act of 1835 and the County Councils Act of 1888. Fresh water supplies were created, sewers built, roads paved, refuse collected, streets lit, trams laid out, building regulations drawn up and enforced, police and fire services instituted. Great outbursts of civic pride led to the building of magnificent town halls, libraries, museums, baths, art galleries, indoor markets, colleges and public parks. Schools, hospitals, churches and chapels sprang up across Yorkshire. Architects like Broderick Crawford in Leeds, and Lockwood and Mawson in Bradford, vied with each other in the magnificence of their designs. Other developments arose because of the improvement in transport and travel caused by the railways. Towns became entertainment centres, with concert halls, theatres, music halls, racecourses and sports grounds attracting people from miles around. And coastal resorts like Bridlington, Filey and Scarborough flourished as trippers flooded in from the rest of Yorkshire. So it's no wonder that the county's towns and cities have such an enormous stock of Victorian buildings, and that the resorts have retained a great deal from their Victorian heyday.

Despite attempts by Parliament to insist on improvements in working conditions, life for many in Yorkshire continued to be hard. Working in the West Yorkshire textile mills or Sheffield's steel works was still no picnic, but it was in the **coal mines** that the worst conditions were to be found. The coal owners were renowned for their obduracy, the miners for their militancy. And as the mines went deeper and deeper, the death toll climbed. 189 miners died in a disaster at Lundhill in 1857, 59 died in Edmunds Main in 1864, and a staggering 361 died in the Oaks colliery in 1866, 27 of them rescue worker killed by a second explosion. This last horrific disaster is symptomatic of the way things were in the Yorkshire mining industry. Seventy-three miners had died in the Oaks Colliery in 1847 and the subsequent enquiry had made recommendations regarding ventilation at the mine. They were ignored, resulting in devastation seventeen years later. The country was horrified, but the deaths continued – 140 at Swaithe Main in 1875, 90 in Cadeby in 1912. Coal miners responded by uniting. In 1889 the **Miners Federation of Great Britain** was founded, and a series of strikes and lockouts took place right up to, and indeed after, World War I.

The two World Wars: 1914–45

Thousands of Yorkshiremen volunteered for service when **World War I** broke out in 1914, especially though not exclusively in the York and Lancaster, West Yorkshire, East Yorkshire, Yorkshire and Duke of Wellington's regiments, and the King's Own Yorkshire Light Infantry. As with recruits from elsewhere in the country, they were fed into the mincing machine that was the Western Front.

Despite the attack on Scarborough and Whitby by German naval vessels at the end of 1914, Yorkshire in general had a good war. The South Yorkshire iron and steel industry worked at full blast making steel and armaments and tools, the West Yorkshire textile industry fulfilled orders for uniforms and blankets, factories all over the county turned their hands to armaments and ammunition, and gaps in the labour force created by recruitment for the armed forces were filled by women, for the first time taking on work that had always been done by men. Farming and coal mining too flourished as a result of wartime demand.

The good times continued to 1921, but then a severe postwar depression hit, and unemployment soared. Hard times came to the textile workers and the steel workers. The depression hit the coal industry particularly hard, and the bitter struggle between owners and unions resumed, with a strike in 1921 followed by the **General Strike** in 1926. Although West Yorkshire was also hard hit, seeds were sown in Leeds that would grow into household names – Burton, John Collier and Hepworth's in clothing, Arnold in school equipment and notebooks, Waddington in board games and playing cards. And the Town Planning Act, together with the growth of the Labour Party in Leeds and Sheffield led to further advances in road-and house-building.

During the years running up to **World War II**, and during the war itself, Yorkshire's ailing industry was given a new lease of life as it responded to wartime demand. Civilian life was, however, affected much more than during World War I. Everybody experienced rationing, the blackout, and all the other effects of wartime legislation. Numerous fighter and bomber airfields appeared around the county – have a look at the signatures of allied aircrew on the mirror in the basement of *Betty's* in York. Hull and Sheffield were particularly hard hit by the Luftwaffe.

1945–the present

After the war the decline of the county's traditional industries resumed, and during the 1960s and 1970s many old firms ceased trading. The Hull fishing industry went into decline, Sheffield cutlery suffered from fierce competition from the Far East, as did West Yorkshire's textile industry. Above all, two of Yorkshire's great staple heavy industries, steel and coal, went into a free fall. Although there were real underlying economic reasons for their problems (especially competition from elsewhere in the world), these two industries also became an ideological battleground between the recently elected (1979) Conservative prime minister **Margaret Thatcher** and organized labour. Intent on reorganizing British industry and breaking the power of the trade unions, Thatcher put in Scottish-American hard man Ian MacGregor to take on the unions, first in the steel industry, where he was appointed Chairman of the British Steel Corporation in 1980, then in the coal industry, where he became leader of the National Coal Board in 1983. In both, MacGregor's uncompromising restructuring, with minimal consultation, swingeing plant closures and mass redundancies provoked the expected national strikes, led respectively by Bill Sirs of the Iron and Steel Trades Federation in 1980 and firebrand **Arthur Scargill** of the National Union of Mineworkers in 1984–85. Convinced that it was the unions who had cost the Conservatives the election in 1974, Thatcher had prepared carefully before deliberately provoking the strikes. Both were defeated, with much bitterness and hardship, especially in traditionally militant South and West Yorkshire. Thatcher's furious reaction to the miners' strike of 1984–85 in particular, in confrontations between police and pickets such as that at the **Orgreave Colliery** (the "Battle of Orgreave") just outside Rotherham, led to a loathing towards her and hostility and suspicion towards the police which has survived in many areas to this day. Employment in the South Yorkshire steel industry fell from 60,000 in 1971 to 16,000 in 1987 and less than 10,000 by the mid-1990s, whilst the Yorkshire coal mining industry virtually disappeared, surviving in only a handful of privatized pits. The industrial changes in Yorkshire might best be represented by the Meadowhall Shopping complex – once the site of a great steelworks, it is now one of the country's largest shopping malls.

Just as the industrial profile of Yorkshire has changed beyond all recognition since World War II, so too the urban environment in many of Yorkshire's towns and cities has been transformed. The Town and Country Planning Act of 1947 gave local councils the power to clear away urban slums and bomb-damaged buildings, increase the housing stock and refashion town and city centres, not always with fortunate results. Understandably, there was more emphasis during the rebuilding on speed and economy than on heritage and aesthetics, but a lot of damage was done – in Leeds and Bradford, for example, a large number of fine

Victorian buildings were lost, replaced by unimaginative, anodyne and flimsy modern construction, and huge council estates were built that later became crime-infested and down-at-heel.

Since the 1990s the situation has to some degree been retrieved, with the attractive development of canal basins (Leeds and Sheffield), the adapting of old buildings to new uses (Leeds Corn Exchange, Salt's Mill, Halifax's Dean Clough Mill, for example), and the cleaning up and remodelling of city centres, particularly in Sheffield, Leeds and Hull. Sterling work has been done, too, by local councils in attracting new industries and inward investment, including EU funds.

Yorkshire approaches the immediate future under the Conservative/Liberal Democrat coalition with some trepidation. Almost half of Ed Miliband's shadow cabinet, and more than half of the senior posts, are filled by MPs representing Yorkshire constituencies, prompting many press references to the "Yorkshire Mafia", while the coalition cabinet itself features a high number of notable Yorkshire men and women – William Hague, Baroness Warsi and Eric Pickles, while deputy prime minister Nick Clegg represents the constituency of Sheffield Hallam. Whether this dominance of Yorkshire MPs proves to be an advantage to the region or not remains to be seen.

The geology of Yorkshire

As you enjoy the majestic Mallyan Spout or wooded Janet's Foss, as you look through the whalebone arch at Whitby's red-tiled roofs below or go underground at the National Coal Mining Museum in Wakefield or admire magnificent Castle Howard or thrill to the exciting Big Melt in Rotherham's Magna or follow the Fish Trail in Hull or…enjoy a hundred other unique experiences during a visit to Yorkshire, bear in mind that all of this – absolutely everything – depends on what lies, sometimes at great depths, beneath your feet.

Just as the features of a face depend on its underlying bone structure, so Yorkshire's geographical make-up and topography are determined by its underlying geology. The rocks and the way in which they are weathered decide the surface features, the types of soil and the flora and fauna above them, with wildly varying results from one part of the county to another. Moreover, it also decides which materials the people use to build their cottages, castles and cathedrals, how they earn their living, some would say their very nature and character built up by generations of living in, and wresting a living from, the landscape.

The biggest deciding factor in the way Yorkshire looks is the distinction between impervious **millstone grit** and **soluble limestone**. The dark millstone grit of South and West Yorkshire, with its associated **coal** and **ironstone** deposits, creates a landscape of steep-sided alluvial valleys separated by bleak moorland and sandstone escarpments, dotted with wool towns like Halifax and Huddersfield, pit villages like Maltby and Rossington, industrial cities like Sheffield and Leeds and Bradford, canals like the Leeds and Liverpool, and railways like the Leeds and Selby, with dour, dark buildings and walls further blackened by centuries of industrial smoke.

To the north, where the millstone grit is overlaid with **carboniferous limestone**, the landscape becomes a network of dales gouged out of the rock by water and ice. Where surface millstone grit and carboniferous limestone abut, the water cascading off the impervious former dissolves the soluble latter, creating elaborate formations of **caves**, **gorges** and **chasms**, **waterfalls**, **fells** and **crazed limestone pavement**. This is the land of the Yorkshire Dales National Park, of beautiful glacial U-shaped valleys, pretty limestone villages, field barns and dry-stone walls, of spring-flowered meadows, grazing sheep and cattle, a land in which to walk and climb and cave and pothole.

East of the Dales lies the broad Vale of York, largely **Triassic sandstone** and **mudstone** overlaid with deposits created by the receding ice sheets and glacial lakes, now prosperous farmland as far as the eye can see. As this is the only continuous flat land between the Dales and Pennines to the west and the North York Moors and Howardian Hills to the east, most of the north–south traffic between England and Scotland passed (and still passes) this way, particularly the Great North Road/A1 and the East Coast Line. The result – of the fertile soil and the transport links being funnelled through – has been a land of farming villages, historic market towns, places that grew up to service coaches and trains (Wetherby, Knaresborough, Boroughbridge, Ripon) and the great religious, economic and cultural city of York. Geology, too, explains the growth of Harrogate, built to facilitate the taking of the waters from its numerous **mineral springs**.

East of the Vale of York rise the North York Moors and their little sisters the Howardian Hills, lying on a confused mixture of **shale**, **sandstone** and **coral limestone** laid down by Jurassic tropical seas. Consisting largely of heather-clad uplands slashed by deep and verdant valleys, with substantial areas of forest, they support farming in the valleys and managed grouse-moors on the hills. Despite seeming to be an area of natural beauty, this is in fact a man-made and carefully managed landscape. At their eastern edge, the North York Moors plunge into or slide under the North Sea, allowing its people to harvest the deep as well as the land – hence the pretty fishing and whaling ports like Staithes, Whitby, Robin Hood's Bay, Scarborough and Filey. To the north the moors fade into the Teeside conurbation and Middlesbrough, and to the south into the Vale of Pickering.

Further south still, the rolling **cretaceous chalk** swells of the Wolds provide countryside that is a pretty patchwork of fields, farms and villages, of prosperous, unspectacular agricultural land with deceptively deep valleys. Beyond this, the land becomes one of river and estuary – above all, of the Humber, with the great industrial port of Hull and the once marshy, now drained Holderness peninsula. Here the North Sea scours its eastern edge and deposits its gains on the ever-lengthening spit of Spurn Head.

So as you travel around this largest of England's counties, enjoy the varied landscape, but give a thought too to the rock strata that underlie it. This is "God's Own County", and he spent eons of geological time and considerable ingenuity making it the place that it is.

Wildlife in Yorkshire

There are plenty of chances to see wildlife in Yorkshire. Whether you're a knowledgeable dyed-in-the-wool amateur naturalist, or simply somebody who would like to see some of the birds, insects and plants of the county, perhaps with a bit of help with identification, wherever you find yourself in Yorkshire you won't be far from a nature reserve, run either by the **Yorkshire Wildlife Trust** or by the **RSPB**. In addition, both Yorkshire's **National Parks** offer a great deal of information and help.

For all 66 YWT nature reserves, send for their excellent *Your Guide: Yorkshire Wildlife Trust Nature Reserves* and/or check out their website – it has printable guides to each reserve.

The Yorkshire Wildlife Trust

The best way to see the maximum wildlife in the minimum of time is to go to a Yorkshire Wildlife Trust (℡01904/659 570, ⓦwww.ywt.org.uk) nature reserve. The YWT has 66 spread across Yorkshire with, unsurprisingly, almost half of them (32) in North Yorkshire. East Yorkshire has 14, South Yorkshire 11 and West Yorkshire 9. Some have no facilities, others are well endowed with hides, toilets, cafés and information boards, and have free parking and access for wheelchairs and pushchairs. They cover a range of habitats – grassland, heathland, wetland, woodland and coast. Unless stated, reserves are free and are open all hours every day throughout the year.

North Yorkshire

Askham Bog Lying just southwest of the city of York, Askham Bog was the reserve which started it all off – the Yorkshire Wildlife Trust was set up in 1946 specifically to protect it. A circular boardwalk with a spur off to a pond makes negotiating the bog a doddle, and there are interpretation boards to tell you what to look out for. The amazing thing about this site is the breadth of plant life that's found here – great fen sedge more commonly seen in East Anglia near bog myrtle which is usually found on the west coast, marsh orchids, yellow flag irises and water violets, yellow loosestrife which attracts dentated pug moths, alder buckthorn which is fed on by brimstone butterflies. Birds commonly seen on the site include redpoll, siskin, woodcock and lesser spotted woodpeckers, while mammals include roe deer and water voles. There's free parking, and access for wheelchairs and buggies is good, courtesy of the boardwalk.

Grass Wood Just outside Grassington, Grass Wood consists of an ancient ash wood and later beech plantation with lovely views of Wharfedale. Under its woodland canopy you'll find lily-of-the-valley, wood sorrel, bloody cranes-bill, rock-rose, melancholy thistle and the rare bird's nest orchid, and see willow warblers, nuthatches, tree creepers, a variety of tits, and green and spotted woodpeckers. Best visited in late spring, or for a wealth of fungi, in autumn. There are interpretation boards and parking. Visitors should keep to the paths (which are not really suitable for wheelchairs) and dogs must be kept on a lead.

East Yorkshire

Spurn Head (see p.301) A long finger of sand that has been drawn out by erosion between the North Sea and the Humber estuary, the Spurn Head reserve is a wonderfully windswept three miles of sand dunes, marram grass, sea buckthorn, lyme-grass, sea-holly, cord grass and sea rocket, with a variety too of butterflies and moths. But it is for its birds that Spurn Head is famous – the thousands of migrating swallows and house martins that pass through in spring and autumn, the great flocks of wintering wildfowl and waders, the rare visitor blown in by storms. With luck you might, too, see grey seal or minkie whales out at sea. Ample parking, toilets, a refreshment caravan, hides and information boards, but dogs not allowed. And there's a £3 charge.

North Cave Just off the M62 between Hull and Goole, this fairly recent acquisition is a former gravel quarry and an excellent example of what can be achieved by careful management – in this case by controlling the water levels to create a variety of habitats. The result is that in this one reserve you can see 170 species of birds, 200 plant species and 24 species of butterfly. There can't be many places in the country that you might see, at different times of the year, reed warblers, reed buntings, ringed plover, little ringed plover, oystercatchers, redshank and avocet, goldeneye, pochard and smew, sand martins and kingfishers, skylarks, meadow pipits and redshank, goldfinch, redpoll and siskin, buntings and tree sparrows, hobby, merlin and peregrine falcons. Insect life includes common blue, small skipper and wall brown butterflies, and hawker and four-spotted chaser dragonflies. The reserve has parking, toilets, a mobile café and interpretation boards, and is wheelchair-friendly. No dogs allowed.

South Yorkshire

Potteric Carr Only two miles south of Doncaster, Potteric Carr (daily 9am–5pm; £3) is one of the largest urban nature reserves in the country, and has a mixture of habitats – woodland, grassland, marsh and open water – which ensures a wide range of birds, insects and plants. Over 158 species of bird have been recorded, including bittern, kingfisher, reed and sedge warblers, all three woodpeckers and woodcock, 28 species of butterfly, including comma, gatekeeper, whiteletter hairstreak, purple hairstreak and brown argus, and twenty species of dragonfly, including black-tailed skimmer, banded demoiselle, hairy dragonfly, broad-bodied chaser and ruddy darter. Plants include orchids, great spearwort, lesser water-plantain, lesser reedmace, greater tussock sedge, purple small reed, great water dock, yellow-wort and traveller's-joy, and there are five species of bats. The full range of services are on offer, including fifteen hides and a splendid café that serves hot meals. No dogs.

West Yorkshire

Adel Dam East of Leeds-Bradford airport next to Golden Acre Park, Adel Dam is based on a lake created by the damming of a beck to create a mill pond about 250 years ago. Good for bluebells in the spring and fungi in the autumn, it has seen over 100 species of bird since its establishment in 1968, though it is the more common woodland and lake birds that dominate – kingfishers, herons and all three species of woodpecker. Car parking, toilet and refreshment facilities in Golden Acre Park can be used, the site is wheelchair friendly, and there are two hides, but dogs are not allowed.

The Royal Society for the Protection of Birds (RSPB)

The Royal Society for the Protection of Birds has four reserves in Yorkshire – two in East Yorkshire and one each in West and South Yorkshire (none, surprisingly, in North Yorkshire). Check the website (@www.rspb.org.uk) for details and maps, and also for the numerous special events that most reserves put on.

Bempton Cliffs East Yorkshire. The top site in England for watching seabirds, Bempton Cliffs (open all year; visitor centre daily: March–Oct 10am–5pm; Nov–Feb 10am–4pm; £3.50/car) is on the north coast of Flamborough Head, just outside Bridlington. The most northerly chalk cliffs in the UK, this is seabird watching heaven – so much so that not only does the RSPB have a reserve here, but so does the Yorkshire Wildlife Trust, just along the headland. From April to August the towering cliffs are home to 200,000 birds: gannets, guillemots, razorbills, kittiwakes, fulmars and puffins, which set up a deafening roar – you can hear the colony long before you see it. There are five cliff-top viewing platforms (one is wheelchair accessible), and it's easy for even total beginners to learn to identify the main species. In spring the birds are nesting, in summer you'll see fledglings taking to the air for the first time, in the autumn large flocks of birds get ready to migrate, and in winter the remaining birds mass to feed and roost.

Blacktoft Sands East Yorkshire. On the largest tidal reed beds in England at the confluence of the Ouse and the Trent, Blacktoft Sands (reserve 9am–9pm, or dusk if earlier; reception hide April–Oct daily 9am–5pm; Nov–March Sat & Sun 9am–4pm; £3) boasts no fewer than 270 different species of birds, including avocet, bearded tit, bittern, hen harriers and marsh harriers. There are seven hides all but one of which are easily accessible.

Dearne Valley Old Moor South Yorkshire. In the heart of the Dearne Valley not far from Doncaster, the Old Moor reserve (visitor centre daily: Feb–Oct 9.30am–5pm; Nov–Jan 9.30am–4pm; April–Sept reserve open until 8pm; £3) has kingfisher, little owl, lapwing, golden plover and tree sparrows, together with lots of ducks, geese and swans. But it's not just birds you need to look out for – there's a wide variety of butterflies, dragonflies and orchids. Accessibility is easy, and there's a café.

Fairburn Ings West Yorkshire. Along three trails through a variety of habitats near Castleford, at Fairburn Ings (daily: March–Oct 9am–5.30pm; Nov–Feb 9am–4.30pm; free, but parking costs £2) you can see chiffchaff, green sandpiper, kingfisher, little ringed plover, reed warbler, tree sparrows and willow tits. There's a visitor centre and four hides.

Books

Many books have been written about Yorkshire, by Yorkshire men and women, or set in Yorkshire. Included below is a very select selection – only those books that have been used during the writing of the *Rough Guide to Yorkshire*. Read them all, and you'll get a good feeling for Yorkshire, though you may not have time to actually visit.

Simon Armitage *All Points North*. From his home in the Pennines, close to the border with Lancashire, Yorkshire poet Simon Armitage dissects the characteristics of his home county (and other parts of the north) in a collection that is part travel journalism, part autobiography and part diary. It's acute, observant and witty.

Kate Atkinson *Behind the Scenes at the Museum* (set in York) and *Started Early, Took My Dog* (set in Yorkshire from Leeds to Whitby). Born in York, Kate Atkinson writes novels that are a fusion of whodunit and mainstream fiction. They are clever, exciting and very funny. The former won the Whitbread Book of the Year prize in 1995, the latter is the latest of a series featuring ex-police inspector Jackson Brody.

Catherine Bailey *Black Diamonds – the Rise and Fall of a Great English Dynasty*. An absolutely riveting account of the social history of one small part of South Yorkshire, of the paternalistic relationship between the Fitzwilliams of Wentworth and the farm workers and miners who lived on their estate, and of the vicious manoeuvring among family members in the nineteenth and twentieth centuries, the effect of which can still be seen today. Read it, and you'll never look at a coal-mining area through the same eyes again.

Beryl Bainbridge *English Journey*. To mark the fiftieth anniversary of J.B. Priestley's *English Journey* (see below) Beryl Bainbridge, with a team from BBC Bristol, set out to follow in his footsteps. Only part of the journey was through Yorkshire, but this book of the series captures a snapshot of the county in the 1980s which is vivid and amusing. She visits a number of places described in *The Rough Guide to Yorkshire*, and stays in one of the hotels reviewed (the hotel is directly across the road from the train station, a fact which her fed-up taxi driver points out with some disgust after he's loaded her numerous suitcases into the boot).

Alan Bennett *Writing Home* and *Untold Stories*. In these collections of Alan Bennett's prose, there are many autobiographical pieces which build up a picture of his childhood in Leeds. Hilarious, sad, touching – Alan Bennett is incapable of writing a dull sentence.

Dickie Bird *My Autobiography*. Not really an autobiography, more like sitting with the great cricket umpire as he reminisces over a pint of Barnsley Bitter. And absolutely none the worse for that.

Brontës – Charlotte (*Jane Eyre*), **Emily** (*Wuthering Heights*) and **Anne** (*Agnes Grey*). The writing of the three world-famous sisters was strongly influenced by the landscape (both natural and human) they saw around their Haworth home. Their novels in turn influenced the way in which Yorkshire is perceived in the rest of the world. Read the books, visit Haworth – it's an unforgettable and deeply moving experience, despite the crowds.

Daniel Defoe *A Tour through the Whole Island of Great Britain*. Based on a tour of Britain that he made between 1724 and 1726, here Defoe describes Yorkshire's towns, villages and countryside in great and fascinating detail, over 54 pages (in the Penguin Classics edition), from "hence we entered the great country of York" to "I must now leave Yorkshire". Dip in and enjoy.

John Godber *Bouncers, Up 'n' Under, Teechers* and many more. Founder and director of the Hull Truck Theatre Company, John Godber's own plays, in performance or on the page (they're published singly and in collections), are a wonderfully entertaining way of getting into the hearts and minds of Yorkshire.

Harry Gration *Yorkshire Sporting Heroes.* By sports commentator and much-loved co-host of BBC's regional news programme *Look North*, Harry Gration, this account of his thirty top Yorkshire sportsmen, written with a journalist's flair, is a good introduction to Yorkshire's obsession with sport. He doesn't limit himself to Yorkshire men and women either – his top player is John Charles, the great Welsh centre forward who played for Leeds United. Including his favourite sports grounds, traditions and quotes, it's like eavesdropping on a discussion between knowledgeable locals in a Yorkshire pub. Imagine Dickie Bird, Michael Parkinson and Harry Gration wagging the chin and bending the elbow, and you'll get the flavour.

Tony Harrison *Collected Poems.* A poet born and educated in Leeds, Tony Harrison's has wide-ranging interests. However, it is for the wonderful poems describing his working-class childhood, parents, family and ancestors that he's included here.

James Herriot *All Creatures Great and Small.* A Scottish vet who settled in Thirsk in North Yorkshire, James Alfred Wight, writing under the pen name James Herriot, wrote a series of books about his experiences (for example *If Only They Could Talk*, or *It Shouldn't Happen to a Vet*) which have collectively come to be known as *All Creatures Great and Small*. A huge success, his books were turned into much-loved films and a television series, and offer pictures of Yorkshire folk which, while stereotypical, are nevertheless sympathetic and amusing.

David Hey *A History of Yorkshire.* Detailed, well-written and with lots of excellent photographs, this book does exactly what it says on the tin. Probably on the heavy side for casual visitors to the county, but residents shouldn't be without it.

Ted Hughes *Birthday Letters.* Widely felt to be one of the best poets of the twentieth century, poet laureate for the last fourteen years of his life, and controversial because of his relationship with his wife Sylvia Plath, Ted Hughes is often seen as a typical Heathcliff-like Yorkshireman. He developed a love and healthy respect for nature during his upbringing in the Calder Valley, and his poems about animals and birds (in his *Collected Poems*) can be read as a way of developing an insight into the area's natural world. *Birthday Letters*, on the other hand, is more about his relationship with his wife, and includes several poems set in Yorkshire – *Wuthering Heights* and *Stubbing Wharfe* for example. Sad and poignant, especially if combined with a visit to his birthplace and Plath's grave.

Simon Jenkins *England's Thousand Best Churches* and *England's Thousand Best Houses.* Many of Yorkshire's houses and churches are included in these accessible architectural guides.

Arnold Kellet *Blind Jack of Knaresborough.* A short and readable biography of the very long and eventful life of John Metcalf (1717–1810) – road builder, musician, drinker, gambler, smuggler, horse trader, tourist guide, and blind from the age of 6. If you're staying anywhere near Harrogate or Knaresborough, try to read this book.

Philip Larkin *Collected Poems*. Though not of course a Yorkshireman, Larkin was the librarian for Hull University for the last thirty years of his life. Many of the poems in the collected work are set in East Yorkshire and although they are not overtly about the area, and there's little detail, between them they create a picture of Hull and East Yorkshire. Try *Arrivals, Departures* ("Tame water lanes, tall sheds"), *Friday Night at the Royal Station Hotel*, *Whitsun Weddings*, *Show Saturday* and many more.

Anne Lister *The Secret Diaries of Anne Lister 1791–1840*. Fascinating and astonishingly candid ("I love and only love the fairer sex") diary of the famous early nineteenth-century lesbian, who lived at Shibden Hall in Calderdale.

Ian McMillan *The Best of Ian McMillan* and others. The bard of Barnsley's poetry is local, graphic and very funny, though you only get the full flavour when you hear it read by the poet himself.

Stuart Maconie *Pies and Prejudice*. Subtitled *In search of the North*, this is a brilliant laugh-out-loud book about the north of England. Although covering the whole of the north, and although written by a Lancastrian, the sections about Yorkshire give an excellent picture of the parts of the county he visited. The prejudice of the title isn't that of Lancashire against Yorkshire or vice versa – it's more a common cause book aimed at southern views of the north, his attempt, as he puts it, to "discover both the north itself and my own inner northerner". Fans of his work on radio will love it.

Michael Parkinson *Parky*. The autobiography of one of Yorkshire's many national treasures. Michael Parkinson, TV superstar, journalist, film critic, chat show host, cricket enthusiast and all-round good egg was born in Barnsley and never lost his accent (though he did tone it down, otherwise viewers wouldn't have understood a word he said).

Nikolaus Pevsner *The Buildings of England*. Yorkshire is well served in this remarkable series, with three volumes covering "The North Riding", "York and the East Riding" and "The West Riding", together with two *Pevsner Architectural Guides* to Sheffield and Leeds. Virtually every building of note in the county is covered in detail. Providing probably more than the casual visitor needs to know, these books would be invaluable to anybody interested in architecture, and to any long-term resident of the county.

J.B. Priestley *English Journey*. The full title says it all – "English Journey, being a rambling but truthful account of what one man saw and heard and felt and thought during a journey through England during the Autumn of the Year 1933". Being one of Yorkshire's most famous writers and journalists, Priestley devotes a considerable chunk of the book to his home city of Bradford in the chapter "To the West Riding".

Bram Stoker *Dracula*. So overlaid by more recent books and films has the famous vampire story become that many people may not have read the book that started it all. This is a shame – it's a beautifully written and wonderfully readable story, with accounts of places (the Carpathians, and particularly relevant here, Whitby) that would put the attempts of specialist travel writers to shame. The long section set in Whitby is extraordinarily graphic – although it was written well over a century ago, you can still see everywhere mentioned in the book, and follow the action on the ground.

Alex Turner, Arctic Monkeys *Whatever People Say I Am, That's What I'm Not*. Though not a book or a poetry collection, there's no better evocation of the life of young clubbers in Sheffield than this album of Arctic Monkeys songs. Non-tykes, though, may struggle with the accent.

Small print and
Index

A Rough Guide to Rough Guides

Published in 1982, the first Rough Guide – to Greece – was a student scheme that became a publishing phenomenon. Mark Ellingham, a recent graduate in English from Bristol University, had been travelling in Greece the previous summer and couldn't find the right guidebook. With a small group of friends he wrote his own guide, combining a highly contemporary, journalistic style with a thoroughly practical approach to travellers' needs.

The immediate success of the book spawned a series that rapidly covered dozens of destinations. And, in addition to impecunious backpackers, Rough Guides soon acquired a much broader and older readership that relished the guides' wit and inquisitiveness as much as their enthusiastic, critical approach and value-for-money ethos.

These days, Rough Guides include recommendations from shoestring to luxury and cover more than 200 destinations around the globe, including almost every country in the Americas and Europe, more than half of Africa and most of Asia and Australasia. Our ever-growing team of authors and photographers is spread all over the world, particularly in Europe, the US and Australia.

In the early 1990s, Rough Guides branched out of travel, with the publication of Rough Guides to World Music, Classical Music and the Internet. All three have become benchmark titles in their fields, spearheading the publication of a wide range of books under the Rough Guide name.

Including the travel series, Rough Guides now number more than 350 titles, covering: phrasebooks, waterproof maps, music guides from Opera to Heavy Metal, reference works as diverse as Conspiracy Theories and Shakespeare, and popular culture books from iPods to Poker. Rough Guides also produce a series of more than 120 World Music CDs in partnership with World Music Network.

Visit www.roughguides.com to see our latest publications.

Rough Guide credits

Text editor: Alice Park
Layout: Sachin Tanwar
Cartography: Lokamata Sahu
Picture editor: Nicole Newman
Production: Louise Daly
Proofreader: Samantha Cook
Cover design: Nicole Newman, Dan May
Photographer: Diana Jarvis
Editorial: **London** Andy Turner, Keith Drew, Edward Aves, Lucy White, Jo Kirby, James Smart, Natasha Foges, James Rice, Emma Beatson, Emma Gibbs, Kathryn Lane, Monica Woods, Mani Ramaswamy, Harry Wilson, Lucy Cowie, Alison Roberts, Lara Kavanagh, Eleanor Aldridge, Ian Blenkinsop, Joe Staines, Matthew Milton, Tracy Hopkins; **Delhi** Madhavi Singh, Jalpreen Kaur Chhatwal, Jubbi Francis
Design & Pictures: **London** Scott Stickland, Dan May, Diana Jarvis, Mark Thomas, Sarah Cummins, Emily Taylor; **Delhi** Umesh Aggarwal, Ajay Verma, Jessica Subramanian, Ankur Guha, Pradeep Thapliyal, Anita Singh, Nikhil Agarwal, Sachin Gupta
Production: Rebecca Short, Liz Cherry, Erika Pepe
Cartography: **London** Ed Wright, Katie Lloyd-Jones; **Delhi** Rajesh Chhibber, Ashutosh Bharti, Rajesh Mishra, Animesh Pathak, Jasbir Sandhu, Swati Handoo, Deshpal Dabas
Marketing, Publicity & roughguides.com: Liz Statham
Digital Travel Publisher: Peter Buckley
Reference Director: Andrew Lockett
Operations Coordinator: Becky Doyle
Publishing Director (Travel): Clare Currie
Commercial Manager: Gino Magnotta
Managing Director: John Duhigg

Publishing information

This first edition published April 2011 by
Rough Guides Ltd,
80 Strand, London WC2R 0RL
11, Community Centre, Panchsheel Park, New Delhi 110017, India

Distributed by the Penguin Group

Penguin Books Ltd,
80 Strand, London WC2R 0RL

Penguin Group (USA)
375 Hudson Street, NY 10014, USA

Penguin Group (Australia)
250 Camberwell Road, Camberwell, Victoria 3124, Australia

Penguin Group (NZ)
67 Apollo Drive, Mairangi Bay, Auckland 1310, New Zealand

Rough Guides is represented in Canada by Tourmaline Editions Inc. 662 King Street West, Suite 304, Toronto, Ontario M5V 1M7

Cover concept by Peter Dyer.

Typeset in Bembo and Helvetica to an original design by Henry Iles.

Printed in Singapore
© Jos Simon, 2011
Maps © Rough Guides
No part of this book may be reproduced in any form without permission from the publisher except for the quotation of brief passages in reviews.
344pp includes index
A catalogue record for this book is available from the British Library
ISBN: 978-1-84836-603-9

The publishers and authors have done their best to ensure the accuracy and currency of all the information in **The Rough Guide to Yorkshire**, however, they can accept no responsibility for any loss, injury, or inconvenience sustained by any traveller as a result of information or advice contained in the guide.

1   3   5   7   9   8   6   4   2

Help us update

We've gone to a lot of effort to ensure that the first edition of **The Rough Guide to Yorkshire** is accurate and up-to-date. However, things change – places get "discovered", opening hours are notoriously fickle, restaurants and rooms raise prices or lower standards. If you feel we've got it wrong or left something out, we'd like to know, and if you can remember the address, the price, the hours, the phone number, so much the better.

Please send your comments with the subject line "**Rough Guide Yorkshire Update**" to ©mail @uk.roughguides.com. We'll credit all contributions and send a copy of the next edition (or any other Rough Guide if you prefer) for the very best emails.

Find more travel information, connect with fellow travellers and book your trip on ⓦwww .roughguides.com

Acknowledgements

Jos Simon Heartfelt thanks to the following for helping me to plan, research and write this book: at Rough Guides, to Jo Kirby for the commission and Alice Park for sympathetic editing and enthusiastic encouragement throughout; to English Heritage and the National Trust for access to their many wonderful properties, and to Welcome to Yorkshire and all its partners for advice, materials and inspiration, in particular, to press officer Andrew Denton for unflagging practical support; to holiday and tourism professionals – in hotels, restaurants, Tourist Information Centres and a wide range of attractions – across Yorkshire, for information and access; to my wife Doulla for support and encouragement, to son Daniel for information about Sheffield and brother Chris for help with Yorkshire's gay scene, to grandchildren Lazaros, Eliza and Arianwen, test pilots for numerous children's attractions, and in particular to my daughter Catherine and her partner Matt for detailed research and priceless help with map research; to John and Jenny Deans for guidance during visits to some of their favourite places in Yorkshire, and to their daughter Sarah Jones for insights into family attractions; and to Nigel Khan for computer support.

This book is dedicated to mother Olive Simon, who left us, and granddaughter Arianwen, who joined us, whilst this book was being written.

Photo credits

All photos © Rough Guides except the following:

Introduction
York Minster © Paul Harris/AWL-images
Staithes Beck, Staithes © Photolibrary
Scarborough © Photolibrary
Victoria Quarter shopping centre, Leeds
  © Vicki Couchman/Axiom
Twisleton Erratic, the Dales © Daryl Benson/Getty

Things not to miss
01 Hutton-le-Hole © Superstock
02 The remains of conisbrough Castle © Martin
  Priestley/Alamy
06 Bradford curry houses © s E White/Alamy
07 Flamborough Head © Photolibrary
09 Tilting © Royal Armouries, Leeds
11 Landmark flight © Mike Smith /Yorkshire
  Gliding Club
13 Whitby Harbour © Panoramic Images/Getty
14 Black Sheep Brewery © Black Sheep Brewery
15 Jorvik tour group © Jorvik Viking Centre
16 Yorkshire Dales, Swaledale, © Superstock
19 Terraced houses, Saltaire © Ian Dagnall/Alamy
20 The Deep © PCL/Alamy

Yorkshire's art and literature colour section
Hepworth Gallery exterior © Hepworth Gallery,
  Wakefield

The great outdoors colour section
Moorland scenery with walkers © Photolibrary
Hot-air balloon flight, Kettlewell, Yorkshire Dales
  © Photolocate/Alamy
Straw stalactites, White Scare Caves © Robbie
  Shone/The White Scare Caves
Pleasure boats in the harbour at Scarborough
  © Robert Francis/Corbis
Female mountain biker, Yorkshire Dales © Wig
  Worland/Corbis
Canoeing in North Yorkshire © Peter Denton/
  Getty
Wessenden Valley, Marsden Moor © Naki
  Kouyioumtzis/Axiom
Cable waterski, Rother Valley Country Park
  © Daniel Morgan/Alamy

Black and whites
p.182 Richmond Castle © Superstock

ROUGH GUIDES

SMALL PRINT

Index

Map entries are in colour.

INDEX

INDEX

O

INDEX

Map symbols

maps are listed in the full index using coloured text

— — ···	County boundary		⊠	Gate
▬▬▬	Motorway		♦	Point of interest
═══	Main road		⬩	Church (regional maps)
──	Minor road		❀	Country Park
▬▬	Pedestrianized road		⊞	Hospital
▬●▬	Railway		⍑	Gardens
──	Waterway		ⓘ	Information office
------	Footpath		@	Internet access
⌣	Bridge		⊠	Post office
◠	Cave		♯	Castle
〰	Gorge		⊙	Statue
▲	Mountain peak		🏛	Stately home/palace
⍭	Lighthouse		∴	Ruins
▤	Cove/rocks		▬	Building
⚡	Waterfall		✚	Church (town maps)
✈	International airport		▨	Park
⌂	Abbey		⌐⊦⌐	Cemetery
⚲	Boat		▦	Beach

Ordnance Survey data © Crown copyright and database rights 2011

So now we've told you about the things not to miss, the best places to stay, the top restaurants, the liveliest bars and the most spectacular sights, it only seems fair to tell you about the best travel insurance around

WorldNomads.com
keep travelling safely

Recommended by Rough Guides